Inspection and
Inspection Management

ALSO AVAILABLE FROM QUALITY PRESS

Design of Inspection Systems—Selected Readings
Tvzi Raz and Marlin U. Thomas, editors

To request a complimentary catalog of publications,
call 800-248-1946.

Inspection and Inspection Management

CHARLES SUNTAG

Sponsored by the
ASQC Inspection Division

ASQC Quality Press
Milwaukee, Wisconsin

Inspection and Inspection Management
Charles Suntag

Library of Congress Cataloging-in-Publication Data

Suntag, Charles
    Inspection and inspection management / Charles Suntag.
        p.   cm.
    "Sponsored by the ASQC Inspection Division."
    Includes bibliographical references and index.
    ISBN 0–87389–174–0
    1. Engineering inspection—Management.   2. Engineering inspection.
    I. Title.
    TS156.2.S86   1993
    658.5′68—dc20   92–27248
                                                                CIP

10 9 8 7 6 5 4 3 2 1

ISBN 0–87389–174–0

Acquisitions Assistant: Deborah Dunlap
Production Editor: Mary Beth Nilles
Marketing Administrator: Susan Westergard
Set in New Baskerville by A-R Editions, Inc.
Cover design by Barbara Adams.
Printed and bound by BookCrafters.

For a free copy of the ASQC Quality Press Publications Catalog,
including ASQC membership information, call 800-248-1946.

Printed in the United States of America

 Printed on acid-free recycled paper

ASQC
Quality Press
611 East Wisconsin Avenue
Milwaukee, Wisconsin 53202

C O N T E N T S

Throughout my 40 years in the quality profession, I have been searching for a text or manual which could serve as an introductory and training document for inspectors and their supervisors. I have found few books which are specifically directed to the inspection function, and its role within the quality control department. Those that do exist, generally address a specific operation or a distinct industry.

The absence of inspection publications was made painfully evident during the preparation for my inspection management seminars. To prepare background information, I had to extract applicable portions from company inspection manuals and quality control publications. Due to the diverse nature of the organizations represented by seminar attendees, I had to prepare these lectures around generic inspection operations, applicable to any manufacturing or service industry. Then, case histories, illustrating the application of these concepts, were presented and discussed.

This book, resulting, in part, from these seminars, presents the fundamental principles of the inspection function, illustrates the application of these principles to actual operations, and describes inspection's contribution to the enhancement of the company's competitive position in the marketplace.

The book is structured for use as both an introductory text and as a guide to inspectors and their supervisors. The text is designed for use in formal classroom applications and home study courses. In-house training programs, vocational schools, and community and junior colleges can incorporate this book into their curricula to prepare students entering manufacturing and service industries.

Elements applicable to the development of an effective and economical inspection operation are incorporated into the text. These will be useful to the inspection and quality manager who must create and implement a new department or evaluate an existing one.

Other department supervisors will benefit from the sections of this book which discuss inspection's role in the day-to-day operations of other departments. Valuable information is also provided to the production supervisor, whose personnel may be required, at times, to perform inspection operations.

Currently, American industry finds itself at a disadvantage against foreign competitors. Many writers of newspaper articles and business publications express concern over the effect that the unfavorable trade balance has on U.S. industries. Numerous suggestions for the correction of this problem have been made. Included in these recommendations, is the necessity to develop programs, within each company, to provide greatly improved products at consistent quality levels and competitive prices. Many discussions in this book recognize the importance of individual workers and their supervisors in their pursuit of this mission.

A vital aspect of employee motivation that is often overlooked, is the adversarial attitude between personnel from one department and those of another. This attitude is most evident in the relationship between inspection and other company departments, especially production. This attitude is an impediment to the successful economical production of quality products and services. I have attempted to address this problem, and have presented a number of suggested methods for its resolution. Case histories are provided, illustrating the methods used by some companies to promote a closer, more cooperative relationship among various personnel. These cases also illustrate the success of recognizing that each worker and supervisor provides a unique contribution to the company's welfare.

In order to perform their assigned functions intelligently, inspectors and their supervisors must be fully aware of the quality control/assurance functions associated with their operations. This is particularly important in small and medium-sized companies. In many instances, they incorporate many of the quality control functions into the inspection operation.

Accordingly, a considerable part of this book describes the related quality control and assurance functions. Thus, an intelligent and comprehensive understanding of the total quality function is provided which will enable inspectors and their supervisors to fully understand the contribution of their operations to the success and well-being of the whole quality function, whether performed by their personnel or by those of other departments.

Subsequently, this knowledge should provide motivation to inspectors because they will understand their relation to other quality control operations and their contribution to the company's overall success. In addition, this knowledge may show inspectors the path to promotion within the quality control department.

This book has attempted to address the problems of many small and medium-sized organizations, as well as those of large multiplant companies. To this end, some suggestions are specifically directed to the quality improvement of these small organizations who have, at the present, little or no sophisticated, well-structured quality control and quality assurance departments.

ACKNOWLEDGMENTS

To my wife, Henrietta, whose patience, encouragement, and support enabled me to prepare this manuscript.

To my friend and critic, Stanley Abramson, former IBM manager, whose many hours of editing and critiquing the text helped to make it more readable and applicable for its intended purpose.

To my colleagues and co-workers through the years of my professional experience, whose activities provided much of the details and examples noted in this book.

CHAPTER ONE

Historical Background[1]

INTRODUCTION

This chapter provides a brief description of the development of the quality control organization from primitive times to the present.

PREHISTORIC PERIOD

In prehistoric times, primitive people hunted for their raw materials, such as animals and rocks, which they converted into food, clothes, and weapons. They were both producers and users of the products, and coordinated all their actions to the satisfaction of their perceived needs.

EARLY CIVILIZATION

As communities developed, producers met their customers in the marketplace, where the quality of the product and its suitability was determined on a face-to-face basis. There was no need for specifications in these transactions, since buyers could determine product acceptability and negotiate, when needed, any correction at the point of sale. Of course, once the transaction was completed, buyers had to live with any subsequent problems, since *caveat emptor* (let the buyer beware) was the rule of the day.

Large construction projects were generally performed by highly skilled specialists and thousands of workers. Since safety of the structure was a prime factor, rigid construction specifications were developed and enforced. Elementary inspection devices, such as squares, levels, and plumb bobs, were employed and found to be adequate. One of the earliest indications of an inspection operation is portrayed on a wall painting at the tomb of ancient Thebes, traceable to about 1500 B.C. This painting depicts an inspector measuring the quality of a stone cutter's work by means of a simple scale and plumb bob.

PRE-INDUSTRIAL REVOLUTION

As communities grew and the number of shops proliferated, material produced in one town was often shipped for use in another town. Since face-to-face meetings between producers and users were not possible, the necessity for developing specifications, standards, and warranties became essential. To insure that products met buyers' requirements, it became necessary to provide inspection agencies at the source. These agencies had to be acceptable to the buyers.

The introduction of craft guilds for each trade provided the means to cope with this problem. Apprentices at each guild served under the direction of master craftsmen before being admitted as acceptable artisans and full-fledged members of the guild. To keep the standards of quality and workmanship high, the guild masters maintained strict control over the production and inspection of their products. As a result, the guilds enjoyed the reputation for excellent product quality. And buyers in the different towns readily accepted these products.

In small shops, owners were able to personally supervise their workers and insure that acceptable products were produced. Owners trained workers individually, and maintained close surveillance over their work, inspecting each item fabricated, until workers exhibited the ability to provide consistently acceptable products.

As shops became larger, owners could no longer maintain close controls over their workers. This necessitated the delegation of a portion of the management to a supervisor who was responsible for the training and directing of a number of workers, and for inspecting their products. As the amount of work increased, supervisors could no longer adequately perform their functions. Accordingly, they assigned the inspection function, on a part-time basis, to reliable workers, who in the course of time became full-time inspectors reporting to the supervisors.

INDUSTRIAL REVOLUTION

Mass production was made possible as a result of the concept of interchangeability which was developed by Eli Whitney. This concept allowed product components made at one plant, to be shipped to another plant for assembly without the need for selective fitting or modification. This was due to the fabrication of the component to rigid specifications and tight tolerances. As a result, stricter inspections were needed, and more sophisticated measuring equipment and inspection techniques were developed.

EARLY TWENTIETH CENTURY

At the start of the twentieth century, a change of major significance resulted from the work of Frederick Taylor. He established that the method for doing each job or operation was to be based on scientific studies, and not on the judgment of supervisors or workers. Payment for this work was to be based upon scientific measurements. This led to one operator performing a single operation. This concept subsequently led to the use of conveyer lines for production and assembly. And that led to the separation of inspection from the production operations.

As problems arose because inspectors reported to production supervisors, the need for further separation became apparent. Since supervisors were each obligated to oversee the work of 20–30 operators as well as that of a few inspectors, inevitably more attention was paid to the many production workers with less attention given to the few inspectors. Further, as inspection operations became complex and used more sophisticated measuring equipment, supervisors found themselves unable to keep up to date with new technology. In addition, there was always the temptation for supervisors to overrule the inspectors' decisions to meet production schedules. Unfortunately, this temptation has not been completely eliminated.

Thus separate inspection departments were created. They were under the supervision of a chief inspector who reported to the official in charge of manufacturing.

The chief inspector's functions expanded by developing a number of support services. These included developing workmanship and quality standards, implementing inspection training programs, selecting measuring equipment and controlling their accuracy, refining the inspection record system, and the like.

WORLD WAR II

As a result of World War II, the importance of the inspection operation was recognized. Because of the tremendous quantities of increasingly complex production material needed for the war effort and the requirement for tight production schedules, delays encountered by 100 percent inspection, subsequent rejection, rework, and reinspection could no longer be tolerated. Accordingly, a new concept of prevention arose, largely through the efforts of such scientists as Shewhart, Dodge, Romig, Edwards, and others. They developed the concept and application of statistical quality control. This enabled the determination of the capability and stability of the process to produce conforming products. Also, statistically valid sampling plans took the place of 100 percent inspection.

Through the efforts of the War Production Boards, thousands of defense workers, inspectors, and production supervisors and managers were subjected to short courses in statistical quality control. Unfortunately, more emphasis was placed on the preparation of control charts, than the need for corrective actions when out-of-control conditions were perceived. In addition, these workers and managers received only a bare understanding of the statistical concepts underlying these control charts. Accordingly, they were unable to provide satisfactory explanations to the "Doubting Thomases" in the shop. Many, through their enthusiasm, promised utopian results. When the program failed to produce the promised effects, a loss of confidence resulted. Those personnel in the production operations, as well as members of management who from the start did not understand or believe in, the concepts which were being implemented, turned away from the use of the statistical control charts and refused to cooperate in their implementation.

Thus, a considerable delay in the use of statistical control charts in most companies resulted. It was only when Drs. E. Deming and J. Juran showed the positive effects of this concept in Japanese production, that interest was revitalized in the use of statistical control techniques.

POST WORLD WAR

As a result of the technology created during the war, new products with increased quality and reliability were developed. Thus the position of reliability engineer was born. This new position caused some jurisdictional problems. Where did the function of reliability engineering belong? A number of options existed within the Engineering and the Quality Engineering departments. Some companies developed a Quality Assurance department, consisting of Quality Control, Quality Engineering, and Reliability Engineering, all reporting to a vice president of the company.

The growth of consumerism and the increase of product liability litigations lent greater emphasis to the quality function. The concept of considering the effects of the product in service, and the anticipation, during the design phases, of the possibility of misuse, gave greater emphasis to customers' needs. At the same time, formal quality assurance functions were being incorporated into other industries, such as nuclear and non-nuclear construction, biomedical and chemical processes, food production, and others. This required the development of quality controls tailored to the specific needs of these industries.

Currently, the large trade deficit, resulting from extensive competition from foreign companies, has caused a shift in emphasis from inspection of the product after the fact, to, in the words of Phil Crosby, "making it right the first time." In addition, the term *world class quality* began to appear. This concept changed the emphasis from providing products which will meet the perceived needs of *current* customers to a program which will insure continuous improvement of quality levels, capable of satisfying the anticipated needs of *potential* customers.

To provide competitively priced products and services meeting or exceeding the quality levels of foreign products, the development of programs with new emphasis on personnel motivation and training of all organization members was needed. Everyone, from the corporate head, through all levels of upper and middle management, to the first level of supervision and their personnel in the production and supporting service groups, needed training.

Lessons learned from the Japanese quality programs, such as the use of quality circles, just-in-time production, Taguchi methods, and others, are being applied to American industry. Unfortunately, there are problems. Many organizations adopted and used the terms of these techniques as buzz words. These companies apparently did not understand that the concepts were merely additional tools, supplementing the traditional elements of existing quality control programs. These companies quickly became disillusioned and dropped the programs after a short time. Others, who utilized and understood the concepts, are reporting excellent results.

Recently, this country has experienced a great expansion in the service industries, providing employment for more workers. This has created a challenge to the quality profession to develop and implement more sophisticated quality programs for these industries. Chapters 37–39 of this book provide additional information about service quality programs.

In order to focus attention on the need for continuous improvement of products and services, leaders of corporate America have joined the American Society for Quality Control (ASQC) in advocating programs of quality excellence. Together they are implementing Quality Month campaigns to alert American industries of the importance of striving for constant quality improvement. These CEOs describe in quality seminars, trade magazines, and business journals the programs developed in their companies to accomplish the objectives of quality excellence.

In addition, national quality awards are being given to those organizations who have shown the ability to consistently provide outstanding quality levels in their products and services. The Malcolm Baldrige National Quality Award, named for a former Secretary of Commerce, was created by public law. This program is managed by the National Institute of Standards and Technology (NIST), (formerly the National Bureau of Standards—NBS), and administered by the Malcolm Baldrige National Quality Award Consortium in conjunction with the ASQC and the American Productivity Center. Awards are presented each year, by the President of the United

States, to those companies who have demonstrated their proven ability to meet the quality challenges of the world market. See Chapter 4 for additional details about this award program.

A number of states are considering providing similar awards. Connecticut was the first state to implement such a program.

REFERENCES

1. Juran, J. M. and Frank M. Gryna, Jr. *Quality Planning and Analysis*. New York: McGraw Hill, 1970. Chapter 3.

CHAPTER TWO

Terminology

INTRODUCTION

In today's complex and competitive environment, the concept of quality, as perceived by individual organizations, must be specifically identified within the company, with its suppliers and customers, and, when applicable, with regulatory agencies. This need includes a definition of the customer requirements and, in many instances, the means of determining and assuring that these requirements have been attained. To meet these needs, companies, industrial and technical associations, and regulatory bodies have, in the past, developed a hodgepodge of definitions relating to quality. This has led to considerable confusion as to the meanings of the various terms used.

One has only to review quality journals and texts of the past several decades, as well as discuss "quality" with different industry members, to realize that the terminology is loosely defined. Terms such as *inspection, testing, quality, quality control,* and *quality assurance* often mean different things to different people. In many instances, it appears that the terms are established, not so much as to provide an operating definition within the company, but to meet some perceived requirement of the marketplace. It was not so long ago, and perhaps continues to this date, that, to satisfy a potential customer, an Inspection Department became a Quality Control Department, and a Chief Inspector became a Quality Manager, without any significant change in the functions and duties of the department or its personnel.

QUALITY SYSTEM STANDARDS

To try to bring some order out of this chaos, the American Society for Quality Control (ASQC), in coordination with the American National Standards Institute (ANSI), developed a set of standard definitions and terminology applicable to the quality profession. ANSI/ASQC A.3 *Quality System-Terminology* identifies most of the principal terms customarily encountered in the quality operations of the American industrial environment.

In addition, a glossary of terms used in quality control, ISO-8402 *Quality Vocabulary,* was developed by the European Organization of Quality Control (EOQC). This glossary defines, in English, as well as in 14 other languages, approximately 400 terms. Also, the North Atlantic Treaty Organizations (NATO) developed a series of quality system standards, called *NATO Applied Quality Assurance Publications,* or AQAPs, for use by the NATO companies.

Recently, the International Community developed a series of International Quality Assurance System Standards, ISO-9000–9004 for use in international trade. The United States, in order to provide compatible standards, developed the ANSI/ASQC Quality System Standards ANSI/ASQC (90–94). These standards are technically equivalent to the ISO–9000–9004 International Standards.

See Chapter 34 for additional information concerning the International Standards.

EXTRACTS FROM ANSI/ASQC A.3–1978[1]

QUALITY: The totality of features and characteristics of a product or service that bears on its ability to satisfy given needs.

This standard necessitates the identification of those characteristics of the product or service which bear upon the ability to satisfy Dr. J. M. Juran's terms of "fitness for use" or "given needs." Since a product or service is frequently provided in an economical environment, consideration of the given needs should also include the price and delivery schedule of the product or service. Most of today's quality organizations have encountered problems using this standard.

The concept of delivery and price as attributes of quality is a shocker to the average inspector or quality control practitioner. Traditionally, these requirements were often considered in conflict with the ability of meeting the physical quality requirements of the product or service. In addition, meeting the delivery schedule and the concern with the cost of production have normally been considered the responsibility of other departments within the company. We are all familiar with the cry of "holding up production" as a technique used by production personnel when requesting the use of nonconforming products. Now, the standard infers that, in evaluating the acceptability of the product, the elements of cost and delivery must also be considered.

It is becoming increasingly apparent, however, that for a company to stay in business in today's competitive market, it must provide products which not only consistently meet the customers' requirements of fitness for use, but must also be economically produced and delivered at a specified time.

Chapter 3 details the functions of the inspection/quality department in helping to accomplish these objectives.

Another problem arises in utilizing the standard's definition of quality. Most companies consider that it is merely necessary to meet the product or service requirements as stated in the contract and the referenced specifications. However, in many instances, the contract does not specify the total needs of the customer relative to the use of the product or service under consideration. In fact, many customers may not be aware of all the parameters of use to which the product or service may be subjected in actual operation. The following is an illustration of the problem as experienced by one organization.

EXAMPLE

This company produced standby generators which were used to provide power in the event of a failure or temporary shutdown of the conventional power source. At one time, there had been a large scale power blackout over a three-state area, which lasted for many hours. When an attempt was made to utilize these generators to provide the power needed during the emergency, a significant number of units could not be started. One can visualize the "hue and cry" which was raised, and the vilifications heaped upon the equipment supplier. After all, the prime purpose of these generators was their availability for use during just such an emergency, and when the need actually arose, they failed to perform.

The generator supplier stated that it had fulfilled its contractual responsibility by delivering units which operated at the time, and in accordance with contractual requirements. Hence, the supplier should not be responsible for the lack of performance many years after delivery.

Subsequent investigation into the causes of the problem found that the equipment's inability to operate was due to a number of conditions, none of which represented contractual nonconformance. Many of the generators had been in the user's possession for a lengthy period of time without operation. During the emergency, when the attempt was made to start the generators, it was found that the drive belts had exceeded their shelf lives and had deteriorated. No replacement was immediately available at the user's site. Also, the user's personnel did not know how to start and operate the equipment.

It was apparent that, notwithstanding the conformance of the generators to the contractual requirements at the time of shipment, the ability to satisfy the given needs of the customer had definitely not been met. In spite of the contractual logic provided by the supplier, many of its customers remained highly dissatisfied.

In retrospect, it became apparent that, in addition to the contract requirements, the supplier had a responsibility to advise its customers, at the time of sale, of the need for periodic maintenance and operation of the equipment, adequate training of its personnel in starting and operating the equipment, and the availability of a buffer stock of replacement parts, with a periodic review and replacement of those parts whose shelf life had expired. At the least, the supplier should have arranged to provide, with each generator, an operating and maintenance handbook.

In today's market, suppliers must determine the full needs of customers, and make them aware of these needs. This may present some problems. Chief among them would be the customers' suspicion that the supplier was attempting to sell products and services over and above perceived needs. However, buyers must be made to realize the possible effects of using products or services, and of the absence of the additional suggested elements.

QUALITY, RELATIVE: Degree of excellence of a product or service.

It is important that, when a comparison between two or more grades of a product or service is made, the term *relative quality* be used. For example, it is generally understood that when the quality of a $50,000 house is compared with that of a $250,000 house, one does not expect the features of the more expensive house for the price of the less expensive one. However, occasions may arise when the comparison is not that evident; for example, in the quality of a sand casting relative to that of a permanent metal mold casting.

QUALITY SYSTEM: The collective plans, activities, and events that are provided to ensure that a product, process, or service will satisfy given needs.

This term encompasses all the traditional elements of quality control and quality assurance, including inspection, quality engineering, data collection, analysis and reports, audits, and corrective actions. It should be understood that some plans and activities may be in addition to those functions normally performed by an inspection/quality department. The total quality system involves the coordinated activities and plans of all departments in the company directed to economically satisfying customer needs.

Many companies do not fully understand this concept which often leads to major gaps in the definition and implementation of the total quality system. It should be the responsibility of a member of management, preferably the head of the inspection/quality department, to assure that this concept is fully understood by the heads of all the company's departments. In this way each element of the quality system is identified, together with specific departmental responsibilities.

QUALITY PROGRAM: The documented plans for implementing the quality system

This program includes the recorded planning of all inspection, quality engineering, auditing, reporting, and corrective actions. It assures that the design is adequate for the intended purposes and that the product is produced in accordance with the design. The recorded evidence should be utilized to provide the required assurance that the product or service meets given needs.

Here too, in the past, many companies considered that all the plans and procedures of the quality program were to be documented in the company's quality manual. Considering the scope of the quality system as defined in the standard, the quality manual would need to incorporate the plans and procedures of the entire company. To avoid this problem, companies should implement a plan similar to the following.

The inspection/quality manual should identify all the elements and their controlling features of the entire quality system. The manual should designate the departmental responsibilities for the planning, implementation, and control of each element under their designated jurisdictions. Each named department should prepare and control its procedures and instructions for this implementation. The quality/inspection manual should also identify the independent company agency which will perform periodic audits on each department to assure that full implementation of each function occurs. The policy statement, signed by the head of the company, would designate the authority for these assignments and specify the responsibility for each department.

QUALITY CONTROL: The operational techniques and the activities which sustain a quality of product or service that will satisfy given needs; also the use of such techniques and activities.

QUALITY ASSURANCE: All those planned or systematic actions necessary to provide adequate confidence that a product or service will satisfy given needs.

The overall system integrates several related steps including: the proper specification of what is wanted; the design to meet these requirements; production to meet the full intent of the specification requirements; and inspection to determine conformance to the specification. Generally, the term *Quality Control* refers to the planning, implementation, evaluation, and corrective actions utilized during the production phase of the product or service. The term *quality assurance* identifies the programs supplementing the quality control functions, which by audits and evaluations, assures that the design parameters comply with the specific contractual requirements, and that the performance of the product and service, in actual use, complies with users' needs. This program also provides for the issuance of periodic reports to management, describing the adequacy of the quality program, as well as the corrective measures taken or recommended when any activities are found wanting.

INSPECTION: The process of measuring, examining, testing, gaging, or otherwise comparing the unit with the applicable requirements.

TESTING: A means of determining the capability of an item to meet specified requirements by subjecting the item to a set of physical, chemical, environmental, or operating actions and conditions.

In the past, the term *examination* often reflected the complete method of comparing the product with its stated requirements. The term *inspection* denoted the evaluation by the unaided eye. *Gaging* referred to the performance of the evaluation with the aid of mechanical, electrical, and electronic gages and instruments. *Testing* was designated when the product was subjected to a set of physical, chemical, environmental, or operating conditions.

To perform an inspection operation, it is necessary to have well-defined criteria of acceptability. The inspection operation would then consist of comparing the product or service with the acceptance criteria, and accepting or rejecting the item as a result.

At times, the concept of inspection, as defined in this standard, is not fully satisfied. There have been occasions when an inspector was required to evaluate a product and no acceptance criteria were provided. For example, an inspector may be asked to perform a measurement operation, record the findings, and submit the data for consideration and acceptability by other personnel. This is not a true inspection operation, since there are no specific criteria of acceptability to compare with the inspection results. When such a criteria of acceptability is not provided, a condition could result when the acceptance of the item would be performed on a purely subjective basis. This approach would often provide a lack of consistency regarding the acceptability of the product. This too may provide inadequate criteria for the production personnel to manufacture the product, thus hampering the implementation of corrective measures when the product is rejected. The following examples are illustrative of the conditions noted here.

An electronic assembly was tested for the shape and range of its output, as depicted on an oscilloscope display. Testers took a photograph of the display reading for each unit tested, and submitted it to an engineer who determined if the unit was acceptable. Upon comparing the results of the individual analyses of several engineers, no pattern of acceptability could be found. Accordingly, the project engineer was requested to prepare a set of curves, outlining the extreme ranges of the oscilloscope patterns which were deemed acceptable. An overlay, representing these limits of acceptability, was then provided to the testers, and used by them as the criteria of acceptability.

Another example where no criteria of acceptability are provided is in the inspection of raw castings. In many companies, the engineering department does not provide separate drawings for the procurement of raw castings. Instead, they utilize the drawing of the finished piece, to be machined from the casting, as a source of reference of the requirements of the casting. Although the finished part drawing includes some requirements for the maximum and minimum wall thickness, and the draft angle of the castings, no complete information is provided for the determination of the acceptability of the cast dimensions. Accordingly, the inspector is required to record measurements of each casting dimension on a qualification inspection record, and submit the final results to the manufacturing engineer. The engineer then evaluates the recorded dimensions against the ability to machine the casting to the finished part drawing using the available manufacturing processes and tooling.

Since the foundry could not truly determine whether the raw casting, as poured, could be machined to the required finished part drawing, and was not aware of the machining process and tooling to be used by the manufacturer, there were many occasions when the foundry disputed the rejection by the manufacturing engineer. After a number of costly and time-consuming discussions and arguments, the engineering personnel were convinced of the necessity of creating a set of casting drawings for each item. This resolved the problem and enabled the inspectors to properly evaluate the raw casting upon receipt. Chapter 8 describes, in greater detail, the problems encountered in meeting the inspection requirements, when a full definition of the product or service acceptance criteria is lacking. It also provides some suggested solutions to this problem.

REFERENCES

1. *ANSI/ASQC A3–1978. Quality System Terminology.* Milwaukee, WI: ASQC Quality Press, 1978.

Role of the Inspection Organization

INTRODUCTION

This chapter describes the part that the inspection function plays in the efforts toward the enhancement of the company's competitiveness in the world market.

Inspectors often perceive their function as one of the most frustrating operations in the manufacturing and service industries. People in other operations can see the product of their efforts. Bricklayers see the building slowly rising before them. Machine shop operators touch the product they fabricated. Beauticians participate in the client's admiration of the new coiffure. All workers except inspectors have the opportunity to enjoy the results of their labor visually or by tactile contact.

The inspection function has traditionally another troublesome aspect. The better the inspection operations are performed, the more effective the data feedback and subsequent corrective action; and the better the control of the product by the process and operator, the greater the ability to implement a program which will make the inspection operation unnecessary. Therefore, if everyone did his or her job correctly, a conforming product or service would result every time. Thus customers would receive defect-free products or services which had no need for prior inspection.

However, in the modern organization, the inspection operation performs a continuing and vital function towards the maintenance and enhancement of the profitability and competitiveness of the company.

ENHANCEMENT OF THE INSPECTION FUNCTION

In practice, no process is inherently stable. All are subject to variation. Hence, very few processes provide products which are inherently defect-free.

The true mission of the inspection operation is to implement, or contribute to, a program which will identify these variations and provide appropriate and rapid feedback for an adjustment of the process. During the establishment of the process controls, some product inspection must be performed to insure that no deviant shipments are made pending the establishment of a final controlled process.

As more knowledge of the process is obtained, it may eventually be possible to establish suitable process controls in advance of production. This would then enable the variability of the process to remain within the product tolerance limits, thereby insuring the fabrication of all conforming products. Here too, however, it would still be necessary to monitor the process, by some degree of inspection, to insure that it does not stray from the controlled path.

Obviously the inspection function is more than one of sorting out the bad products from the good. It is the additional areas of the inspection operation, which if recognized, provide to the inspectors a greater sense of satisfaction.

The ability to study, control, and correct the process depends to a great extent upon the inspection and test records provided by operators and inspectors. These records are, for the most part, the prime source of data which can be used to determine the variability of the process, as well as the quality of the resulting product or service. This data also assists in the establishment of statistical quality and statistical process control programs.

Unfortunately, many organizations fail to recognize the importance of the inspection data as a means of review and correction of the process. Often these records are filed away without any further consideration, and forgotten until it is time to have them destroyed.

EFFECT ON PRODUCTIVITY

An additional aspect of the inspection function which is often overlooked, is its positive effect on the productivity of the operating personnel.

The traditional concept of inspectors as snoops, delighting in ferreting out a nonconformance in the product, and zapping the operator with a rejection, is fast fading away. Instead, today's inspectors have a credible knowledge of the process and the product. This knowledge enables inspectors to advise operators when the process appears to be getting out of control. This information, when provided in a timely manner, and followed up by the operator or the production supervisor, often prevents the fabrication of additional nonconforming product. The inspector is thus recognized by the operator and the production supervisor as an ally. This provides the motivation for manufacturing personnel to call the inspector's attention to any problem areas in their products, and to request assistance in seeking a remedy.

In addition, the inspectors, through knowledge of the processes and the product quality levels, as well as the difficulties encountered during the production phases, are often called upon to support the manufacturing personnel in their efforts to have the process or tooling revised to increase the productivity and quality level of the operation. At times, the inspectors' support becomes a valuable asset to the operational personnel: for example, when the design engineer is being approached by manufacturing for a review of a drawing tolerance, which would better reflect the process capability.

This relationship with other company personnel cannot but help to provide a message to the inspectors that they are not merely perceived as getting "kicks" out of product rejections, but are considered as valuable assets to the entire organization.

EFFECT ON COMPANY COMPETITIVENESS

The inspection function provides a valuable contribution to the profitability and competitiveness of the company. In these days of high competition and potential loss of business, not only to the traditional competitors, but to foreign companies as well, it becomes essential that the company, to stay in business, utilize the talents of all its personnel.

During my seminars on inspection management, it was quite revealing to note the initial attitudes of many of the participants. During our discussions, inspectors and their supervisors revealed an adversarial attitude toward personnel in other operations of the company. They visualized their prime function as "holding the fort" against the onslaughts of operating and production personnel, whose main interest appeared to be meeting production schedules without regard to product quality. The inspectors thought that others perceived them as obstacles to meeting their schedules. The inspectors, at times, believed that even the engineer, whose specification was being safeguarded, was constantly watching them, waiting for an error to be made. In particular, this attitude would be exhibited, when the engineer was asked to provide a waiver for the use of a nonconforming product. The question frequently asked by the engineer was not "How did it happen?" but "How do I know that the inspection results are correct?"

In the area of purchased supplies, there had been an ongoing battle with the buyers, who are seen by the inspectors as obtaining the cheapest products without regard to quality. This attitude was also directed at the supplier, whose prime mission, in the inspectors' minds, was to get junk past the inspectors.

During the latter part of the seminar, discussions with attendees reflected their admission that the prime mission of the company to make a profit was perfectly valid, and in fact essential, if the company were to stay in business and the inspectors' jobs to be retained. In short, *profit* is not a dirty word.

Further, it had become apparent to them that, in order for a company to make a profit, it was essential that it have satisfied customers. It then followed that, to keep customers satisfied, it was necessary, not only to ship consistently conforming products, but to make these shipments on time and at the specified price.

We then discussed the inspectors' role in enabling the company to meet these objectives. It became obvious that the inspection organization needs to exercise a greater role in the company's operation than just sorting out the bad products from the good.

This led to the realization, that the elements of inspection/test, data preparation, collection, evaluation, and analysis, and rapid feedback to correct any problems in the process, are integral parts of the inspection operation. The ability to form a partnership with the other functions of the company, was then seen as vital to the enhancement of the company's profitability. This concept also embraced the need for a cooperative approach with the company's suppliers as well as with its customers.

As a result of these discussions, it became more apparent to the seminar participants that the inspectors' role included support for the scheduling and cost aspects of the company operation, in addition to the inspection and testing of the product.

This enhancement of the inspection function opens up areas of considerable opportunity and greater satisfaction to the inspectors and their supervisors. Once it is recognized by manufacturing that inspectors are, in fact, team players, the need for the production operators to hide an occasional nonconforming product no longer makes any sense.

This concept further mandates that the other company departments include a consideration of the inspection department in their previously considered sacrosanct operations. Thus, it makes sense that the company's planning, scheduling, and budgeting operations take into consideration the time and cost needed to inspect the product. Selection of manufacturing processes and tooling, as well as the establishment of production stations, need to be coordinated with the inspection operation. This can take advantage of the inspectors' knowledge of the process capability on previous products. It also coordinates inspection and production operations at a given manufacturing station. When manufacturing tooling is discussed with the inspection personnel prior to its design and procurement, it becomes possible to consider the utilization of this tooling as a medium of inspection. It can also be determined if in-process monitoring of the manufacturing operation is possible, thereby reducing the need for duplicate inspection equipment and operations.

In addition, the selection of sources of supply becomes a cooperative endeavor with the inspection function. Inspection personnel can provide a suppliers' quality history. Inspectors can also review the potential capability of a new supplier to consistently meet any purchase order quality requirements.

Further, the input of inspection information during the design, development, and issuance of engineering and manufacturing drawings, can provide information about the capability of the manufacturing process to meet the drawing tolerances, and the ability to inspect the drawing characteristics on an economical basis. Also, engineers can be advised of previous problems encountered during the manufacture of same or similar products. This can have a significant impact on minimizing the number of drawing changes subsequent to the start of production, thereby reducing production delays and the costs of scrap and rework, as well as field retrofit of parts made obsolete by these drawing changes.

INSPECTION IN THE QUALITY ORGANIZATION

In the above discussions, many elements of traditional quality control/assurance operations which are not generally associated with the inspection function, were included.

Many companies, particularly small and medium-sized organizations and service operations, have only an inspection department. For marketing purposes, this is generally referred to as a quality department. In reviewing the elements of this department, it is evident that they include functions generally associated with traditional inspection operations.

In larger companies, the inspection function is often incorporated as one section of the company's quality department. At times, the inspection operation is part of the production operation. More about this later.

In these larger organizations, the lines of demarcation are often based on the various functions of the quality department. The inspection section's primary functions are inspection, product testing, and recordkeeping. A planning section of the quality department provides to the inspectors the drawings of proper issue, the specifications suitably digested, the inspection/test instructions and procedures, and the criteria of product acceptability. Another quality department section selects, maintains, and calibrates the measuring equipment, analyzes the inspection and test records, and includes the results of these analyses in management reports. Other sections initiate and implement corrective actions and maintain liaison with other company departments as well as supplier and customer personnel. An evaluating section of the quality department might participate in the review and disposition of nonconforming material.

Many companies, however, include a number of these elements in the inspection section function, reserving the auditing and evaluating functions for other quality department sections.

Whether these functions are performed under the auspices of the inspection department, or by other sections of the quality department, it is important that the inspectors and their supervisors have an understanding of all elements of the company's quality program, and the inspectors' functions in its implementation. This is necessary so that they may be aware of their degree of participation as members of the company's team engaged in the implementation and maintenance of the program for the enhancement of the profitability and competitiveness of the company.

Accordingly, the following chapters of this book address many elements of the quality program which are traditionally not considered as part of the normal inspection function.

INSPECTION BY THE PRODUCTION DEPARTMENT

In a number of companies, production personnel perform some, or all, of the inspection and testing of their products. Normally, these inspections are utilized as an interim measure of the in-process quality of the item being fabricated. One example might be checking the measurements of a rough machining operation prior to subjecting the part to final machining.

When the results of the production operators' inspections are to be used for product acceptance purposes, it is generally desirable that they be evaluated by someone else. Samples of the items inspected by production operators are selected by inspectors and reexamined to validate the initial inspection results. The degree of reinspection can be diminished, or altogether eliminated, as confidence is established in the production inspectors' capabilities.

EXAMPLE

Here is an example of one method of evaluating the production inspector's results.

Parts, after being inspected by the production operator, are placed into bins adjacent to the machining areas. Conforming and nonconforming parts are placed into separate bins. Patrol, or roving inspectors, select conforming samples from the appropriate bin and perform a reinspection for the specified characteristics. The results of this inspection are recorded on the inspectors' audit forms.

Determining product acceptability is made in accordance with the sampling inspection rules. Failure to meet the rules is cause for the contents of the bin to be rejected and returned to the operator for screening (or 100 percent inspection) of parts for nonconforming characteristics. The reinspected lot is then resubmitted to the patrol inspectors for verification of the production operator's results. Similarly, nonconforming parts are also sample inspected for confirmation of the rejection status.

Records of the inspector's sample reinspection are subsequently analyzed. When an out-of-control condition, based on predetermined criteria, occurs, the applicable operator is subjected to an inspection retraining program prior to being permitted to perform any further acceptance inspection.

EXAMPLE

A production lot of electromechanical equipment is subjected to acceptance testing by production operators. At a given period, there may be 20–30 production units of the same model under test. Each unit is subjected to a three-hour test of approximately 40 characteristics each, in accordance with a procedure prepared by the company's engineering department.

Before the new program was initiated, each unit had been tested by members of the inspection department. Since the contract with the customer merely specified that each unit was to be tested by the company, without identifying the test agency, it was determined that the performance of the test by the production department would not be in conflict with the terms of the contract. Since management decided that the test by production personnel was desirable, the procedure for production testing was implemented. However, to insure the integrity of the quality of the equipment shipped to the customer, it was decided to have these test results verified by the inspection department. To avoid the necessity of performing a retest of each unit of equipment, the following procedure was implemented.

Each characteristic of the test procedure was recorded on the inspectors' audit sheet. During testing, the inspection department's auditors would visit each test position and request a retest of one or more characteristics. The inspectors would record, on the audit sheet, whether the reinspection results reflected the same data as noted on the production test record. Those characteristics found nonconforming during the audit, were corrected and retested. The test characteristic(s) audited by the inspectors could vary for each production operator, and for each unit of equipment. The only condition of the audit was the assurance that all 40 characteristics were retested during a specified audit period. All the test characteristics were not audited on any one unit of equipment, but rather over the entire number of units being tested during the specified period. At the conclusion of the audit period, the results of the retests for each production operator were evaluated. Those operators whose scores fell below a predetermined value would be subjected to a retraining program prior to being permitted to perform any additional acceptance testing.

The audit program was not designed to determine product acceptability, since that determination had been made by the production operators. The audit program was for the purposes of determining the reliability of the production operators' data and to validate its use for product acceptance.

Increasingly, acceptance inspections and tests are being performed by production personnel. To utilize these test results, audit programs, similar to the above, need to be implemented to assure the validity of the production test data. Subsequent chapters of this book provide additional discussion about the use of production inspection/test personnel for acceptance purposes.

CHAPTER FOUR

Inspection Organization

INTRODUCTION

An organization is the arrangement of people's responsibilities and authorities to accomplish a common objective. This arrangement is generally represented in a company organization chart, which delineates the paths along which orders and company information flow. Clear-cut organization lines prevent overlapping of responsibilities and duplication of authority.

The president of one company did not believe in publicizing his organizational structure. He believed that by doing so, some functions would be missed, thus having them "fall between the cracks." His understanding was that a good management team should police itself and implement any functions within the organization, when they were needed, without any specifically defined areas of responsibilities.

For this theory to work, it was necessary that the management team be highly motivated, and more concerned with the good of the company than with the furtherance of their individual departments. As experience subsequently revealed, some functions were actually missed, because the individual managers did not have a full understanding of the company's total requirements and needs.

INSPECTION ORGANIZATION DEVELOPMENT[1]

While there are many guidelines as to what constitutes an acceptable inspection/quality function, there is generally considerable latitude as to how this function is to be organized and implemented.

In any company, the requirement for the development of the inspection/quality organization, and for assuring compliance with the company's quality requirements, should be the responsibility of top management. Many companies lack this initial effort. This often results in the inspection/quality organization being developed, by default, by middle management or even lower level supervision, with unpleasant consequences, since these personnel are not always privy to the policies and objectives of the company.

However, middle management should not wait to be directed by top management in the development of their organization. They should instead seek to provide input and assistance to top management for this effort. The supervisors and managers, in turn, should seek advice and guidance from their subordinates. This approach insures that the personnel in their department will feel that they have a proprietary interest in the organization that they helped to develop. This feeling of ownership would provide a great motivation in its implementation, and in the correction of any areas found lacking.

THE UNOFFICIAL ORGANIZATION

Every company has an unofficial function which, while not depicted on any company organization chart, is, at times, an important element for providing information, and occasionally misinformation, about the company. These companies have employees who are looked upon by their colleagues as unofficial leaders in the company organization. These leaders often spread information they have obtained prior to its official release. At times, this information may contain rumors which are only partially correct. An alert supervisor should be aware of the presence of these individuals and take measures to control the information provided by them. At times, management can utilize these leaders as pacesetters or sparks, motivating the other personnel in the performance of their assigned duties.

IMPLEMENTING THE INSPECTION/QUALITY PROGRAM

Since the control of quality is affected by many departments, it is not necessary, or even desirable, that it be under the direction of a single department. This is emphasized, for defense contractors, by a clause in the military quality specification Quality Program-Mil-Q-9858 A, which states "the term 'Quality Program' identifies the collective requirements of this specification. It does not mean that the fulfillment of these requirements is the responsibility of any single contractor's organization, function, or person."

It is the custom of some companies to assign to the inspection/quality department the responsibility for defining all elements of quality which are to be controlled, and to identify, in a company inspection/quality control manual, the departmental responsibilities for the implementation of each element. The manual is then reviewed by all department heads, including the members of top management, for their comments and approvals. Final approval is evidenced by the signature of the company CEO, thereby making the implementation by each department a mandatory requirement.

DETERMINING THE ELEMENTS OF THE ORGANIZATION

An understanding is needed of all the functions required to implement and control the company quality requirements. Since the functions of an inspection/quality organization must go beyond those of mere product inspection and testing, consideration must be given to all the elements necessary to support and supplement these functions.

Table 6-1 in Chapter 6 lists a number of supporting elements for a typical inspection/quality operation. See Chapter 6 for a description of each of the elements.

It should be understood that during the development of the inspection/ quality organization, consideration of all elements affecting the quality requirements must be made. This applies for those elements which are under the cognizance of company organizations other than the inspection/ quality departments. This consideration is necessary to ensure that no function is omitted from the company's quality program.

WORKING WITHIN AN EXISTING INSPECTION DEPARTMENT

In most cases, inspectors, supervisors, or managers come into companies with existing inspection/quality organizations. Accordingly, there will be little opportunity to provide input and recommendations for the formation of a new department. In other instances, new supervisors may not have a complete understanding of the departmental functions, authorities, and responsibilities, and its relations to the other departments in the company. Chapter 5 of this text illustrates a number of examples of this situation, and provides several recommendations for coping with the resultant conditions. However, the importance of the inspection supervisors' need for total awareness of their functions and responsibilities, whether identified by upper management, or developed by them and presented to their superiors for approval, must be repeatedly stressed.

TAILORING THE INSPECTION ORGANIZATION

There is no single type of inspection/quality organization which is applicable to every company. Each organization should be tailored to the company in question. This tailoring depends upon many elements, such as the type of industry or service organization, the size of the company, its products or services mix, its customers and their requirements, the phase of the product or service (Research and Development, Production, and so on), as well as the quality policy of the company management.

ORGANIZATION FORMS IN THE PROCESS INDUSTRIES[1]

The center of product acceptance activities for the process industry, as well as much of its process controls, is lodged in the laboratory (chemical, metallurgical, physical, etc.)

The laboratory generally makes product acceptance across the board, that is, on purchased material, on goods in process, and on finished goods. Often the visual examination and sorting of products are performed by inspectors responsible to production, but subject to an independent check by the laboratory.

In the process industries, the functions of setting quality standards and issuing specifications are often the responsibility of the quality manager, who assigns these duties to a standards section. This section may be part of the laboratory or a separate unit reporting directly to the quality manager.

MECHANICAL AND ELECTRONIC INDUSTRIES

In the mechanical and electronic industries, the inspection of purchased parts, in-process inspection, and the acceptance of the final product are generally the responsibility of the chief inspector or quality manager. Alternatively, many companies have the functional testing conducted under the responsibility of the technical manager. The more critical the product for human safety, the more likely for the functional testing to report to top management through some channel other than manufacturing.

MULTIPLE-FACTORY COMPANIES

In multiple-factory companies, there is usually a quality manager at each plant, generally reporting to the plant manager. The functions of this organization include inspection, testing, and related inspection support services. A quality engineering staff, at headquarters, develops quality policies and objectives; publishes, distributes, and controls quality and inspection manuals; and issues inspection/quality and workmanship standards.

This group also provides, when applicable, reliability engineering services, and performs other services relative to the quality of product design and marketing quality requirements. This staff also publishes executive reports on quality performance and represents the company in its relations with industry and government on quality matters. See Figures 4-1 and 4-2 for examples of typical multiplant organization charts.

In the company represented by Figures 4-1 and 4-2, the Quality Assurance Director is located at the company headquarters, with all the company department heads and the members of the Executive Committee. The Director of Quality Assurance, through the Quality Engineering Section, develops all the company quality policies and standards, acts as consultant to the company management on all quality matters, and serves on industrial organization and government committees in the development of product standards and specifications. The Quality Engineering Section, which is also located at the company headquarters, prepares the company inspection/quality assurance manual, and all inspection and quality control procedures and instructions which affect more than one plant. This section is also responsible for maintaining liaison with external customer personnel, as well as with the company's suppliers. Included in its functions is the responsibility for the development and implementation of all training and motivation programs for the members of the Quality Assurance Department and, in conjunction with the Personnel Department, for personnel in other departments of the company. This section also performs periodic audits at each plant to assure that the company's quality assurance policies are being implemented by the plant Quality Managers. An additional function performed by the Quality Engineering Section is the review of the inspection/quality assurance elements of all contract proposals and new contracts, and the dissemination of the applicable contractual requirements affecting their quality elements to the plant Quality Control Managers.

At each plant, there is a Quality Control Manager, reporting to the Quality Assurance Director. These managers are responsible for all plant-wide inspection/quality control activities.

MULTIPLE DIVISION COMPANIES[1]

Each division is a company in itself (e.g., the Buick Division of General Motors), and is responsible for meeting budget and profit goals, procuring equipment for its factories, product design, manufacture, marketing, and so on. A high degree of autonomy of the quality function is given to each division, including self-sufficient inspection and inspection services, quality engineering, and reliability engineering. In many companies, there are corporate quality control managers who develop quality control policies, provide consulting services to the divisions of the company, publish executive reports on quality, serve on industrial and governmental committees, study and report on quality effectiveness of each division and of the whole company, and provide many other related consulting functions.

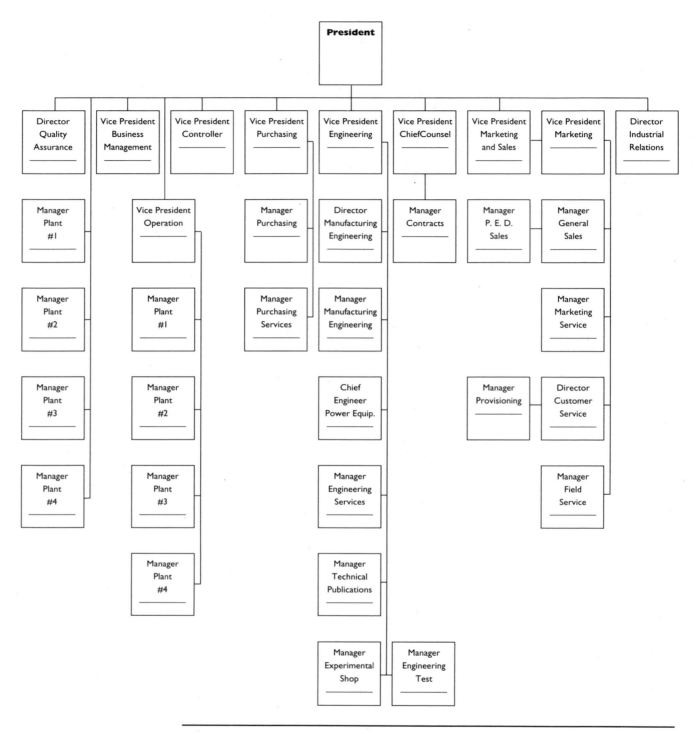

FIGURE 4-1   Multiplant Organization

During the late 1980s, a considerable rash of company takeovers provided a special problem for the establishment and implementation of companywide quality controls. Many companies that were taken over bore little

FIGURE 4-2 Quality Assurance Functional Organization

or no relationship to the product or service mix of the original organizations. Other cases of corporate takeovers were performed with almost no interest on the part of the new corporation in standardization or development of product quality controls. This condition made it difficult, if not impossible, for a company quality executive to manage an effective operation.

INTERNATIONAL COMPANIES[1]

These companies provide to their divisions wide delegation of authority due to unique cultural differences. There are some restraints on technology, especially if subsidiaries sell in overlapping markets. In those cases, imposition of common and uniform product specifications and uniform controls to ensure adherence are found necessary. This requires technical staff at company headquarters to issue these specifications and establish the uniform controls, as well as conduct performance audits.

JAPANESE QUALITY PROGRAM ORGANIZATION[1,2]

Organization

The Japanese quality organization differs considerably from that of most western world industries. As a result of intensive quality training programs to all Japanese employees, it is possible to have line managers plan and control quality in the company. Accordingly, these companies do not include a quality control department, as such, within their organizational structure.

Japanese companies have only a small number of staff specialists who do not participate directly in the operation or control of the quality functions. They primarily provide consultant and advisory services, and assist in the company quality training programs.

Top management participates in the quality planning function, developing both long range and annual quality programs. This effort is highlighted by the annual president's audit, which is conducted by the chief executive officer and members of upper management. These audits evaluate the progress of the quality program, and set the guidelines for the forthcoming annual program. This visible involvement by top management emphasizes the intense interest and ownership by upper management in the company's quality program.

Middle management carries out the interdepartmental planning and coordination of the company's quality program. Lower level supervision, by virtue of their training in quality techniques and feedback from such activities as quality circles, statistical quality control and similar programs, are able to fulfill the responsibility for the quality of the products produced in their organizations. They also play a significant role in the planning, control, and improvement of the company's quality efforts.

The operating personnel participate in the solution of quality problems through their involvement in the quality circle activities. This results in providing strong incentives and motivation for the development and fabrication of quality products.

Self Control

Japanese industries have adopted the concept of self-control in their production operations, based on Dr. Deming's elements of Plan-Do-Check-Act. See Chapter 6 for a detailed discussion of the elements of this concept as illustrated by one company's quality program.

It is interesting to note that the above concepts of quality improvement have been adopted by a number of companies in the United States during the late 1980s. See the discussion below of the Malcolm Baldrige Quality Improvement Award Program.

Supplier Relationship

In contrast to western industries, Japanese companies do not perform extensive inspection of purchased supplies upon receipt at their facilities. In order to produce products with a high degree of reliability, Japanese purchased components must consistently meet high quality levels. These levels cannot be easily determined by the buyers upon receipt at their facilities. Components which must meet quality levels of parts per million cannot be examined with the use of an AQL sampling plan, or even by 100 percent inspection.

Accordingly, a considerable degree of confidence must be placed upon the suppliers' control over the quality of components provided. Buyers screen their potential suppliers carefully. They evaluate them on the basis of their financial status, facilities, policies, and the degree of enthusiasm about product improvement as conveyed by top management, as well as the amount of education and training in quality techniques of all their employees. The relations developed between customers and suppliers are ones of mutual trust and confidence. This degree of trust often takes a number of years to develop.

Suppliers are required, by contract, to provide documented evidence of their quality efforts, including the results of the qualification and acceptance testing of their components. This data is utilized by customers during the design and production of their products. Audits are conducted by the buyer's organization at the supplier's facilities. These audits are frequently observed by the supplier's top management.

Purchase orders contain the requirements for mutual assistance and for the assurance that the quality of the supplier's components will provide full satisfaction to the consumer and user of the end product.

THE MALCOLM BALDRIGE QUALITY IMPROVEMENT
AWARD PROGRAM[3]

One of the most significant quality programs was the establishment of the Malcolm Baldrige National Quality Improvement Award. This award was created by public law and is implemented by U.S. industry and government. The program was developed to promote quality excellence and greater quality awareness among businesses and industries.

In the 1980s, as a result of lost business to foreign competition, partially due to superior products, an intensive program was inaugurated to re-evaluate the quality levels of products and services in the United States, with a view to their improvement. Accordingly, the term *world class quality* became the standard for quality improvement programs.

The program, administered by the Malcolm Baldrige National Quality Award Consortium Inc., in conjunction with the American Society for Quality Control and the American Productivity Center, is managed by the U.S. Department of Commerce and the National Institute of Standards and Technology. The award is given to qualifying companies on an annual basis and presented to them by the President of the United States.

Applicants are examined and evaluated against seven criteria, including Leadership, Information and Analysis, Strategic Quality Planning, Human Resource Development and Management, Management of Process Quality, Quality and Operational Results, and Customer Focus and Satisfaction. See Chapter 6 for additional details of this program.

Companies in the United States, in order to qualify for the award, as well as meet and exceed the quality levels of their foreign competitors, found it necessary to reevaluate their organizational structure vis-à-vis improvement of the quality levels of their products and services. This has led to the incorporation of structural elements into the quality organizations which promote leadership of company management, involvement of all levels of personnel in quality control and improvement, improvement of production and quality in equipment and human resources, and customer and supplier involvement with the design, production, evaluation, and improvement of their products and services.

QUESTION OF REPORTING

In the past, it was considered poor policy for inspectors to report to their production supervisors. This concept was based upon the understanding that it was not desirable for production operators to inspect their own work, since they would be motivated to overlook their mistakes in order to meet their production schedules. Further, an inspection operation, under the jurisdiction of the production supervisor, was considered undesirable, since the prime mission of the supervisor was to meet production schedules, thereby leaving the determination of product quality as a secondary responsibility.

More recent developments in industry have, to some extent, departed from this concept. This new determination is based on the idea that quality is the responsibility of the producer. Making a determination of conformance to quality requirements a responsibility of another department, such as inspection or quality control, would appear to shift the responsibility away from production personnel. This can be seen in many organizations. When a product line is held up by the inspectors due to their rejection of a nonconforming lot, it is often necessary for the inspectors to defend themselves for the obstruction, instead of blaming the operator for producing the nonconformance. An example of how this attitude prevailed is illustrated below.

In a plant producing electromechanical equipment, inspection department personnel were responsible for product testing upon assembly completion. When a unit failed to pass any of the characteristics of the test procedure, it was necessary for the tester to troubleshoot the equipment to identify the characteristic which was responsible for the failure, and then have the product repaired by the production personnel. Since, at times, the amount of time needed for the troubleshooting operation was lengthy, the test personnel were frequently criticized by management for the subsequent delay to the production schedule. At times, it was suspected that the assembly operators, in an effort to meet their schedules, particularly at the end of the month, were less than thorough in assuring that the assembled unit was capable of passing the test requirements.

To correct this condition, a new procedure was adopted. This required that equipment which failed to meet a test parameter be returned to the production department for their determination of the cause of the test failure, and to make the necessary repairs, before resubmitting the product to the inspection personnel for retest. While this required the production department to include a tester on its staff, the improvement in the quality level of equipment submitted for testing to the inspection department appeared to merit this additional cost. Further, making the assemblers responsible for this additional operation provided the motivation for a more careful assembly of a conforming unit.

Another method of correcting this problem was the performance of the required test by the production department, but under the surveillance of the inspection department. This example was described in detail in Chapter 3.

One major problem associated with inspection by personnel other than those from the production department, is evidenced by the pressures put upon the inspectors who perform their functions at stations on the production line. The production supervisor may, at times, hover over inspectors, impatiently waiting for them to finish their job. The production line could not move until the inspectors had completed their operation. When it was necessary for the inspectors to reject a product, the production supervisor would be at their sides, questioning their rejection and asking them to reevaluate their decisions. These pressures upon the inspectors could, and at times, did, react upon the inspectors. This reaction could take the form of inspectors passing products of questionable quality, or at the other extreme, rejecting products which may be acceptable, just to get even with the production supervisor. See Chapter 31 of this book for a description of the methods of correcting improper inspection.

There are a number of reasons why inspection, under the jurisdiction of the production department, may be considered acceptable. The production department's prime mission is for the manufacture of a product within a specified time period. Its secondary function is to produce an acceptable product. When the production operation is in trouble, and it appears that the schedule will not be met, there is a strong incentive for the supervisor to pay less attention to product quality than to meeting the schedule. However, when it is in the supervisor's interests to produce a quality product, as well as meet the production schedule, the motivation is provided to use equal consideration for accomplishing both missions—schedule and quality. This occurs when the ability to meet production schedules is adversely affected by the production of a nonconforming product. For example, the production supervisor may be responsible for both the machining and assembly operations. If a nonconforming machined part is produced, it would probably result in a difficulty in the assembly of the part in the final product. Thus the production schedule would be adversely affected at the assembly operation. Accordingly, the production supervisor would have a strong incentive to produce a conforming machined part. In this instance, it would not seem unreasonable for the production supervisor to be responsible for both the production and inspection of the machined part.

The more recent procedure for having production departments assume inspection responsibilities is being increasingly advanced. However, to make this work, another element needs to be added. To ensure that product quality is not compromised, it has become the policy in many companies that inspection activities are audited by quality departments. See Chapter 3 for detailed illustrations of the operation of this policy.

In addition, methods are being employed in more modern companies, to include the control of quality of the manufactured products by the production equipment and tooling. See Chapter 26 for additional information about these methods.

Inspection of the product by production personnel has been in effect in a number of industries, such as the chemical process and the construction industries.[1]

In the chemical process industry, the manufacturing department is generally responsible for the in-process quality, since that department is also accountable for the yield of the product. The final product, of course, is tested by the quality control or laboratory departments, which report to a department other than the manufacturing department.

In the construction industry, the functional departments are responsible for the quality of their operations, with an overview by the construction engineer or designee.

See Chapter 35–36 for additional details about these and other nonmanufacturing industries.

REFERENCES

1. Juran, J. M. and Frank M. Gryna, Jr. *Quality Planning and Analysis.* New York: McGraw Hill, 1970. Chapter 7.

2. *Kondo Yoshio: Quality in Japan: Juran's Quality Control Handbook* (4th ed.) New York: McGraw Hill, 1988. Chapter 35F.

3. *Malcolm Baldrige National Quality Award Criteria.* Gathersburg, MD: NIST, 1992.

CHAPTER FIVE

Inspection Supervision

RESPONSIBILITIES OF THE INSPECTION SUPERVISOR

The inspection supervisor, as any supervisor, is the leader of the group. Upper management transfers responsibilities for the inspection function to the supervisor, who in turn delegates the actual operations to the members of the inspection organization. However, it must be understood that, notwithstanding this delegation, the inspection supervisor is totally responsible for all the actions of the group.

To be effective supervisors, it is necessary to develop a group of subordinates who will perform their duties willingly and efficiently. Good supervisors will get the best efforts from the personnel by working with them and showing them how to be productive. A good leader will plan the functions of the group, including the details of operation of all personnel. The supervisors must be able to maintain discipline and be fair, firm, compassionate, and impartial in dealing with group members. The more enlightened company solicits advice and suggestions from all its supervisory and management personnel relative to the development and implementation of its programs of quality control and improvement. The inspection supervisors should do the same with their personnel. The past authoritative role of the supervisors is currently being replaced by the concept of supervisors as group leaders, motivating and guiding the group in the performance of its duties.

Further, sloppiness should not be tolerated by the supervisors in the performance of the group's duties or in the personal appearance of its members. The inspection process is one of critical analysis of another person's work. Neatly appearing individuals carry within them an aura of integrity as well as competence. Thus, they are more readily believed and trusted. To encourage excellence in the work of the group, it is important that supervisors set an example by the quality of their work, as well as by their appearance.

THE INSPECTION ORGANIZATION

In any well-run company, the outline of responsibilities of each group emanates from top management down, starting with the corporate policy, through the complete echelon of the organization, to the first-level supervisor, and finally to all personnel under the supervisors' jurisdiction. The inspection supervisors should utilize a similar method within the applicable section of the inspection organization.

In order to properly fulfill the responsibilities of the group, supervisors must be totally aware of those functions which are under the section's jurisdiction, and how they fit into the overall structure of the quality department, as well as within the complete company organization, relative to the achievement of the corporate quality policies. This is at times easier said than done. More often than not, these relationships are not completely defined.

Whether the supervisors are provided with detailed descriptions of their responsibilities or not, in order to perform these functions properly and completely, all responsibilities and authorities must be clearly defined and understood by the inspection supervisors and agreed to by their superiors. To this end, in the absence of formal definitions of their responsibilities, it would be highly desirable that supervisors prepare an outline of what they believe their functions to be. The outline could then be submitted to their superiors for review, comments, and/or approvals. Once this outline is approved, it could then serve as a basis of the supervisory duties. This does not infer that, from time to time, additional functions could not be imposed. When that occurs, the supervisors should determine whether these changes are of a temporary or permanent nature.

Occasions may arise wherein the supervisors or their personnel receive conflicting orders from various levels of management, as well as from personnel outside of the quality department. Several examples of these conditions are discussed below.

While it is often assumed that inspectors should be aware of the duties of their job, there are a number of occasions wherein these duties are not so clearly understood. For example, the inspector performs an operation in accordance with the specified procedure. Product acceptance is based upon a defined criterion. The results are recorded on an inspection report. If the product is rejected, a rejection report is made out in accordance with the departmental procedure. The product is identified with a rejection tag, and moved for transportation to a holding area. (See Chapter 16 for further details of this operation.) All the above functions are fairly standard, only the details of the documentation may differ in each company. In many companies, the product is examined by a materials review committee, consisting, as a minimum, of members of the quality and engineering departments. This committee determines the possibility of using the nonconforming product "as is," or of requesting that it be reworked to enable its use in accordance with the materials review procedure.

During the evaluation of the rejection, the engineering department's representative on the committee may, at times, express impatience with the inspector's presumed lack of using judgment, instead of rejecting the product. This criticism, when it is directed to the inspector, may be enough for the inspector, during examination of the next lot of the product involved, to disregard the criterion of acceptability and, using judgment, accept the variant material. The inspection supervisor must emphasize to the inspector that, unless the concept of inspection for conformance to the specified acceptance criterion is rigidly enforced, the inspector may repeatedly accept nonconforming product, which could at times go beyond the level which even the complainant would consider acceptable.

Frequently, problems may arise over the priority of the inspection of a product. This generally occurs when there is a backlog of material awaiting inspection. Production or production control personnel may at times attempt to have the inspector inspect a lot which, to the production personnel's understanding, is urgently needed before the processing of lots next in line for inspection. In those instances, the production personnel replace the inspection supervisors' orders for the routing of the inspector's work. If this becomes a frequent occurrence, it will usurp the inspection supervisors' responsibility and serve as a precedent for the substitution of the supervisors' authority in other, more important issues. It therefore becomes important that the inspection supervisors take measures to initially establish their authority. Instructions should be issued stating that any prioritizing of the inspectors' work must come only from the supervisors or their designated personnel. Another way would be to set up a special procedure, whereby a list of priorities would be prepared by the production supervisor, on a daily or periodic basis. After review and approval by the inspection supervisor, this list could be posted in the inspection area, and used by the inspector in establishing the work schedule.

In all instances, the supervisors must impress on the inspectors and other personnel in the section that they are to perform their operations in accordance with the inspection supervisors' or their designee's instructions only. When, for any reason, a temporary departure from the documented procedure is necessary, an interim instruction should be provided, identifying the period of time that this procedure is to be in effect.

In the same way, the supervisors must follow the practice of not assigning an individual to perform work previously delegated to another member of the organization, without first advising that individual of the change along with the reason for the reassignment. It is understood that, in the hustle and bustle of the daily activities, strict adherence to this principle may be difficult. However, to insure orderly operation of the section, supervisors must be constantly alert to their responsibilities in the management of the group's activities.

A more serious problem arises when the supervisor's superior, or another member of higher level management, requests some action of the section personnel, without first discussing it with the section's supervisor. What should be done? The inspection supervisor cannot tell the personnel to disregard the orders of higher level management. The most effective procedure may be to discuss the matter with the responsible manager calmly, and note that it would be appreciated if the request were first discussed with the supervisor so as to enable an arrangement for the request to be carried out in an effective manner. It should also be emphasized that, in order to maintain credibility in the eyes of the subordinates, it is important that all orders come from the designated inspection supervisor.

Another problem may arise when a customer's resident representative requests some action from the section personnel, which is beyond their normal functions. Here too, good customer relations dictate that this matter be handled in a diplomatic fashion. Chapter 32 provides more details about the methods of dealing with customers' representatives.

It is important that all such discussions among supervisors and their inspectors, higher level management, or customers' representatives be conducted away from the production or inspection areas. It is also recommended that these discussions be held in such a manner and location so that they are not overheard by personnel who are not a part of the conversations. This is to insure that no embarrassment is experienced by the participants, and that any information concerning the actions under discussion is not circulated. This is essential so that, if there is a subsequent need for retraction by either party, no confusion is developed in the minds of the observers.

CORRECTIVE ACTION

Due to the nature of the function, the inspector is probably one of the most severely criticized employees in the company's organization. The production supervisor, when a product has been rejected, will, at times, seek out the inspection supervisors, and protest the inspector's decision. To support the arguments, the production supervisor may introduce a whole litany of complaints about the inspector's operation. It is important that the supervisors promise to look into the complaint. Of equal importance is the need to avoid expressing any agreement with the complainant about the accusations until the complaint has been reviewed. The supervisors should then insure that any charges about the inspector are brought to the inspector's attention, thus providing the accused with the opportunity of responding to these allegations. It should not be necessary that the name of the complainant be divulged, pending the completion of the investigation. In addition, the supervisors must take care that any investigations made be kept in the strictest confidence, and that the names of the participants remain confidential.

The supervisors should ensure that any subsequent corrective actions are taken away from the eyes and ears of other members of the organization, so that undue embarrassment of the employee is avoided.

SELECTION OF INSPECTION DEPARTMENT PERSONNEL

An important element of the functions of the inspection supervisors, is the authority to hire and fire the members of the department. However, in the normal operation of most companies, this function has, to a great extent, been taken over by the company's personnel department. The reason generally given for this transfer of responsibility, is that many elements associated with this function are not under the control of and understanding by the inspection supervisors. In addition, it is generally considered important that one agency of the company control the hiring and firing of all employees so as to provide a centralized method of implementation of this important function. This is particularly evident in companies operating under a union contract, where hiring and firing, as well as the assignment of personnel and their functions, are controlled by the contract terms.

Be that as it may, for supervisors to have any control over the operations of the personnel in their departments as they affect the ability to operate efficiently, they must have some say in the hiring, firing, and deployment of the department members. In most companies, this retention is provided by having the supervisors interview prospective employees and provide their recommendations to the personnel department about hiring these personnel, or terminating, for cause, current employees. (See Chapter 23 for additional details of the means of the selection of employees.)

ASSIGNMENT OF INSPECTION PERSONNEL

Inspection supervisors generally have the authority to temporarily or permanently reassign their personnel to other jobs under their jurisdiction. When this is done, care must be exercised to insure that the new assignment is within the capabilities and job description of the employee, and, in a union shop, within the provisions of the union contract. When a temporary assignment calls for the exercise of employee's capabilities which are greater than those of the previous assignment, it is important that any subsequent merit reviews of the employees be based upon the skills of the former job, so as not to unfairly evaluate the worker. If the reassignment is on a permanent basis, the employee could then be subjected to the evaluation criteria of the new job, after a reasonable length of time, sufficient to allow the employee to gain experience on the new assignment.

DELEGATION

Inspection supervisors normally have the authority of delegating some of the department's functions to their subordinates. These functions may include inspection, testing, qualification, auditing, record preparation, retention and analysis, and so on. The inspection supervisors, however, should not delegate any part of the management elements, such as disciplining employees or their reassignment. It is possible, with the approval of the responsible management personnel, to create the position of a group leader. The group leader could then be delegated the authority of assigning work to the designated group personnel, within the specified area of the inspection operation. Here, too, the terms of the union contract, when applicable, should contain the provisions for a group leader position.

In some companies, the position of group leader is a part of the organizational structure of the inspection department, with a specific job description and wage scale. This category provides the inspection supervisors with the ability of delegating some part of the management functions. However, it is important to understand that in most companies, a group leader is not usually considered a member of management and therefore not subject to the advantages or disadvantages of management. For example, when it is the company policy to pay overtime to all nonmanagement personnel, and not to management, the group leader will be paid overtime. This distinction, at times, is important. In an organization where the nature of the work load requires extensive overtime, a good inspector who merits promotion to a supervisory position will often refuse this promotion, since it may cause a reduction in pay, even though the basic pay scale for the new job may be higher than for the previous position. By creating the group leader category, the inspection supervisor is then able to delegate a portion of the management responsibilities to the individual, while allowing the retention of earnings from the overtime payments. Of course, the use of overtime on a long-range basis is never recommended, since the inspectors begin to consider the extra pay as an integral part of their earnings, and when it is eliminated or severely reduced, feel as if there had been a wage reduction.

MOTIVATION

The need for motivation of inspection personnel is, to some extent, uniquely essential to the profession. As discussed in Chapter 3, the inspector frequently sees the inspection function in a most frustrating light, and is, at times, criticized by co-workers in other departments as an impediment to the progress of the production operation. It therefore becomes a matter of the greatest importance to convey to inspectors the valuable contributions of their operation and that of each individual to the company's operations.

While adequate pay is important to inspectors, an equally significant factor in their motivation is the knowledge that their supervisors care about them as individuals, and not just as ones who fill specific functions in the organization. They want a boss who is fair, honest, and truthful; someone they can trust. Inspectors like to feel that what they do is important, and that they are a vital part of the company's operation. Many inspectors would like to have challenging assignments that provide increased measures of responsibility. They also appreciate having a say in their operations.

Inspection supervisors and quality managers play essential roles in providing to inspectors the information which will present a favorable aspect of the function in which they are involved. It would be most desirable if a company-sponsored training program, including an emphasis on the positive aspects of the inspection operation, were developed and implemented. In the absence of such a program, inspection supervisors must perform the necessary task of sponsoring and implementing the motivational activities for the personnel under their jurisdiction.

Initially, supervisors should describe and illustrate the important role of inspectors in the implementation of the company's quality assurance program, as well as the part that the total quality department plays in enhancing the profitability and competitiveness of the company. Inspectors involved in the examination of components of an end product frequently have no concept of the final product or how it is used. To correct this problem, one company has a policy of routinely taking a group of inspectors to the plant where the end product is assembled and tested. They point out the location, in the product, of the part on which each inspector had been working, and describe its function in the equipment. A description of the effect that a deficiency in the part could have, is pointed out. Other companies provide audiovisual presentations of the actual operation of the end item equipment in the field. In still other companies, inspectors are taken to the actual site of the equipment operation, where they are able to question the user and maintenance personnel about the application and importance of specific equipment details.

A motivational program should also include demonstrations of those elements of the inspection/quality operation beyond the mere inspection/ test of the equipment. Examples of the use of the inspection/test records for analysis, corrective action, and subsequent improvement of the manufacturing process should be given.

The effectiveness of the inspection motivational program is enhanced when it is combined with similar programs for the company's manufacturing and service elements. One company developed a competitive approach to the program. A chart of the quality levels of each manufacturing section was posted in a prominent position at each manufacturing or inspection site. The inspection results were posted on these charts by the area inspector. At a specified interval, a determination was made of the department which had shown the greatest improvement in their quality level over that of the previous period. That department was then given a banner, which proclaimed its leadership for the period, and was posted in the department during the subsequent rating period. The inspectors of the section were also considered as part of the winning team.

Some companies include the inspectors, or their representatives, as members of the company's quality circles, quality improvement committees, or corrective action teams. Their contributions are recognized by management at periodic meetings. When statistical quality control or statistical process control programs are utilized, the inclusion of inspection personnel in the development and implementation of these programs provides an increased awareness of the elements and benefits of the quality improvement programs. All of the above programs serve to recognize inspectors' contributions to quality improvement programs.

Many motivational programs, such as zero defects, quality circles, and others have considerable merit and have resulted in a fair degree of product improvement and positive effects on employees' attitudes. However, the failure of these programs in many companies resulted in a large part, from the lack of continuous effort on the part of management to keep the programs going. For many companies, these programs were used as buzz words, and when management's interest lagged, they often fizzled out and were eventually dropped. Another problem with these programs was the expectation by management that implementation of the programs would itself, solve all the quality problems. However, when used as supplements to existing effective quality programs, and sustained by management, these programs often prove to be viable assets in the motivation of personnel, and in the improvement of quality levels.

COMPENSATION

The question of inspector's compensation is discussed in Chapter 23. However, there are many nonfinancial incentives which can be utilized in motivating the inspector. A number of them are described in other sections of this book.

Since inspectors are in close contact with production operators, they frequently have the opportunity to compare earnings. Accordingly, inspectors will become aware of any discrepancy in their earnings as compared to those of the operators. If the discrepancies are broached, alert inspection supervisors can point out that there are many advantages that inspectors enjoy over production operators. These advantages include the fact that the inspectors have a wider range of contacts in their day-to-day activities. It could also be noted that inspectors often develop their own procedures, while operators must abide by a set of standard work instructions. In addition, inspectors are in the position of evaluating the operators' work. It should also be pointed out that the inspection function is often a stepping stone to a higher position. Examples where this has been effected could be pointed out. The enhancement of the inspector's career path described in Chapter 23 should also be emphasized.

Chapter 23 of this book also discusses the subject of inspection compensation as an element of employee motivation.

UNION SHOPS

When an inspection department operates under a union contract, the inspection supervisors have a special problem in managing the organization, since the interrelationship of the inspectors and their management is defined by the contract. It is therefore vital that the supervisors are highly knowledgeable of the elements of the contract as they apply to inspection personnel. The personnel or industrial relations departments should provide guidance under which the elements of performance of the union employees are to operate.

The supervisors should document all instances of improper behavior, or poor performance, of the union inspectors. This documentation may be utilized when corrective action is taken. The supervisors should also be aware of the grievance steps which are described in the union contract, and the part to play at each step.

Salary increments and promotions are subject to the rules of the union contract, and the supervisors usually do not have too much say in the granting or denying of these increases when they are due. Some companies, however, have included in the union contract, employee merit reviews, as a basis for salary increases.

When specific skills and qualifications of the inspectors are applicable, it is important that the right to transfer an inspector to a lesser skilled operation, as when the inspector's proficiency is found below the required level, are included in the contract. For example, welding or soldering inspectors or nondestructive testers must, in general, pass qualification tests to be certified for their jobs. The contract should contain provisions allowing transfer of an inspector to a lower skilled job pending retraining and requalification, if the inspector fails to pass the qualification tests, or if it is found that the inspector's work is not up to the required standards. However, most union contracts, while allowing this reassignment, insist that the inspector be paid at the wage grade of the original position.

Supervisors must exercise caution during conversations with union officials. Since the inspection supervisor is a member of management, any casual comments about the job may be considered, by the union, as official management statements, and the union could hold the company responsible for any commitments made during these conversations.

One major problem in dealing with union employees is the restriction of job assignment to the terms of the union contract. This impinges, at times, quite adversely on the flexibility of the organization, unless special provisions are included in the contract. One company tried to avoid this problem by making the job descriptions in the union contract so broad that they could be applied to almost any job in the inspection department. This subsequently had a highly undesirable effect, when it was found necessary to reduce manpower in the department. The provisions of the contract, which called for laying off the newest employee first, resulted in the bumping of personnel with a higher degree of skill in a particular inspection discipline, to make a place for a more senior inspector, whose previous position did not require the specialized skills of the new job. For example, a welding inspector was scheduled to be laid off. The job that the inspector was bumped into was that of an instrument calibrator. The inspector had absolutely no knowledge or skill in the new job. It therefore became necessary to lay off several additional members of the inspection department through a series of bumps to insure that the reassigned inspector was able to meet the more extensive qualifications.

The inspector's function, at times, includes an element of requiring a production management member to implement corrective action. The exercise of this function could then result in a dilemma, since this would result in a condition where a union employee directs the actions of a member of company management. To ensure that this does not provide an organizational problem, the function of corrective action requests should be removed from the job description of the union inspector and transferred to a nonunion member in the inspection or quality department.

The above discussions relate to the normal management-union relations that generally existed in the past. Currently, more enlightened relationships exist in many companies. Union officials are often part of management decisions relating to the development of new processes, subcontracting of work to outside companies, and the like. Some companies have union representatives participate in quality circles, quality improvement, and corrective action programs. When a program of professional development or quality improvement is contemplated, the assistance of the union officials are solicited, and they are made a part of the quality improvement team. Major companies are beginning to utilize this concept in the introduction of new products and new concepts of production. To encourage this support, the supervisors must insure that union officials do not interpret the new programs as a threat to the welfare of the inspectors under the union contact.

The inspection supervisors must keep in mind that all inspectors in the department, whether they are union or not, are part of the inspection organization, and that the effectiveness of their work impinges upon the success of the entire group. Accordingly, the discussions noted above about the application of motivational programs and concerns over the welfare of employees should apply to union and nonunion personnel alike.

THE SUPERVISOR AS A MEMBER OF MANAGEMENT

Inspection supervisors must be constantly aware that they represent company management to their inspectors. Frequently, supervisors, in order to ingratiate themselves with their inspectors, will take the position that the problems of the company are the fault of upper management. This often occurs when an inspector has not received an anticipated increase or promotion. The supervisors may blame upper management for the inability of the inspector to get the raise or promotion, saying that the recommendation for the change had been turned down by upper management. This type of action violates the basic premise of good management, and does not result in the desired effect. Instead of being accepted as a friend by the inspector, the supervisors in question are often looked upon as untrustworthy, and the employee wonders about any stories that the supervisors may be spreading.

Inspection supervisors must nevertheless try to understand the position and constraints upon upper management. Supervisors must be aware that they may not be cognizant of all these restraints. Unfortunately, there are many companies whose management's position is based upon a close-to-the-vest attitude. They believe that the knowledge about company problems should be kept secret from lower echelons of management and supervision. Thus, when a problem arises affecting employees' welfare, the supervisors, who have not been privy to the company problems, feel the necessity to blame upper management. However, supervisors must understand that when employees are dissatisfied with the degree of attention paid by the company to their problems, it does not matter who is responsible, since the effect on their performance results in a reduction in the efficiency of the entire group.

THE SUPERVISOR AS A REPRESENTATIVE OF THE EMPLOYEE

On the other hand, inspection supervisors must also recognize that they are the employees' representatives to upper management. No other member of the company will generally intercede with the company hierarchy in the defense of employees. Unfortunately, this concept is often not practiced by many supervisors and managers.

I have sat in executive meetings and heard top executives malign their employees for some seeming infraction of the duties of their position. This approach is as destructive to the operation of the company as the condition where supervisors blame upper management for inadequate consideration of the employees.

Inspection supervisors are responsible for the actions of all their employees. They cannot be absolved of a poor performance of the group by blaming, in absentia, the efforts of any of their employees. It is the supervisors' responsibility to correct any problems in their organization. If they fail to do so, then it is their fault. The supervisors cannot cover up their own inadequacies by blaming some member of the group.

Another element to be considered is that, in time, the statements of the supervisors may eventually leak out to the maligned employees and probably include some embellishments to the actual statements made by supervisors.

CHAPTER SIX

Inspection/Quality Program Elements

INTRODUCTION

The elements of the inspection/quality program are based upon the kinds of products and services marketed, customer needs, phase of production, size of the company, and many other things. The prime consideration of each element must emanate from the company policy as directed by the chief executive officer. This policy must be more than a motherhood statement. The company head must be aware of the need for a sincere belief and support of the objectives of the company's quality policy.

"SELLING" THE INSPECTION/QUALITY PROGRAM

Unfortunately, many top executives are unaware or unsupportive of many elements required in inspection/quality programs. What should an inspection or quality manager do in view of this lack of concern? All the texts and articles about program implementation stress the necessity for the whole-hearted support and cooperation from top management. While this support is highly desirable, its absence does not necessarily prevent the development and implementation of a successful program.

Initially, the individual responsible for the development of the inspection/quality efforts, if fully committed to the desirable objectives, should attempt to provide management with the type of information which would insure its motivation to support the program. Merely citing the motherhood statement of good quality will rarely provide the necessary degree of motivation needed. Management has traditionally believed, and at times, not without good cause, that providing good quality will cost. They, at times, firmly believe that they have been able to stay in business, and provide their products and services at reasonable costs, without the incorporation of new inspection/quality programs, which may not work, but will certainly detract from their profits. Most of them have not read Phil Crosby's book *Quality is Free,* or if they read it, did not believe that it applied to their operations.

The quality salesperson must be thoroughly cognizant of, and have a strong belief in, the benefits of the inspection/quality program he or she is trying to develop. The proper sales approach should provide for the accumulation of evidence of the effects of a viable inspection/quality program on the company's profitability and competitiveness. This should be done before approaching top management. The cost effectiveness of the program, in dollars and cents, should also be demonstrated in the proposal.

To help in these efforts, it is desirable to implement a part of the program in an area of the company which provides a reasonably good chance of success. According to Dr. Juran's gold-in-the-mine concept, every company has several such areas. Once the section of the company is selected, the actual benefits in dollars of the incorporation of that element of the program should be accumulated and illustrated to management. It is also helpful to try to enlist the support of a member of management, preferably in the area which is utilized for the trial program.

EXAMPLE

A company making machined parts showed a high cost of scrap and rework due to product rejection. Weekly, the inspection manager had met with section supervisors involved and reviewed with them the rejected parts with the highest quality failure costs. On one occasion, the reviews reflected that the most costly failure rates resulted from the operations of one manufacturing section. An audit of that section was conducted. It was found that the supervisor was spending an inordinately high percentage of time obtaining tools and fixtures for the section's workers, and thus was unavailable to provide adequate personnel surveillance.

Upon further review, it was established that the section operators were on an incentive system based on the quantity of products each fabricated in a given time period. It was also discovered that the union contract did not permit the workers to perform any nonproductive operations, such as obtaining the necessary tools, which would detract from their earnings, or premium pay. When the section supervisor was questioned as to why a lower paid employee had not been hired to obtain this material, he stated that management would not allocate the necessary funds for this additional position.

The inspection manager then accumulated the quality failure costs resulting from the scrap and rework and presented the data to the applicable management personnel. This data demonstrated the gain in dollars which would result from a significant reduction of these quality failure costs brought through use of an additional employee in the section. Subsequent to the hiring of this employee, the inspection manager continued to accumulate the quality failure costs in this section. A reduction in these costs represented the cost effectiveness of the move and its contribution to the resulting improvement in product quality, as well as a significant increase in the section's productivity. The production supervisor was highly pleased with these results and supported the inspection manager when other quality improvement efforts in this, as well as in other sections of the manufacturing departments, were proposed.

EXAMPLE

In one company, a considerable number of drawing changes needed to be issued immediately after the release of these drawings to the manufacturing department. The quality engineer researched the causes for these revisions, and found that most of them were due to the manufacturing processes' inability to consistently meet drawing tolerances. The quality engineer had earlier advocated a manufacturing capability review of the drawings prior to their release, but the engineering department turned this request down, citing the anticipated delay in the issuance of the drawings. The quality engineer then estimated the costs for the preparation and distribution of each drawing change, and estimated the cost effect on the manufacture of the product due to the necessity for reworking and scrapping products which failed to meet the drawing tolerances. This analysis was then shown to the engineering manager, who agreed to a trial review of the drawings for manufacturing capability prior to release of the next project's drawings. Subsequently, the quality engineer estimated the cost savings due to the decreased number of drawing changes and lower quality failure costs on the manufactured product. The significant reduction in these costs was recognized and acclaimed by the departments involved, with their enthusiastic support of other inspection/quality improvement programs. Word of the success of these efforts circulated among other departments and upper levels of management, making it easier to obtain support for additional quality improvement efforts.

While this piecemeal approach may appear time consuming, its success will often lead to management recognition of the potential effectiveness of the quality improvement programs on the company's profitability. However, care must be taken to insure that the initial programs are directed to those areas where success is most likely to result. By demonstrating the cost effectiveness of these programs in one area, it will not be long before the supervisors of other areas will request assistance in their sections. Subsequently, word will reach the upper levels of management. At that point, an approach to top management for the incorporation of a full program of quality control and improvement will probably be sympathetically viewed and supported.

An important element in reporting quality improvement program results, is for the proponent of the proposal to make sure that these efforts do not appear to cast any criticism on the work of the department head, and that credit for program success is shared with the department's supervisory personnel.

INSPECTION/QUALITY POLICY

The company quality program should take into account, among other elements, the degree of leadership the company wishes to display in the marketplace, and in its relationship with its personnel, customers, suppliers, stockholders, and community. Further, a strong component of today's corporate policy is the degree of ethics that the company will pursue in its day-to-day operations.

In many companies, the quality policy is not often well defined. Many times, the policy is provided not so much to dictate the actual, or desirable operations of the company, but to meet some prescribed or anticipated requirements of the company's customers. Phrases such as "conformance to the customer's specifications" are evidenced in many companies policy statements. Companies working under the quality specifications of its customers (government or commercial) will frequently develop policy and quality elements around the customers' quality specifications such as Mil-Q-9858-A "Quality Program Requirements" or Mil-I-45208-A "Inspection System Requirements." In these instances, the company, in order to be responsive to the customers' requirements will often deal with only the elements of these specifications.

As noted in earlier chapters, many companies consider the inspection/quality program as consisting only of those elements that are implemented by inspection/quality personnel. However, in order to accomplish the objectives of assuring the economical and consistent attainment of a quality product or service, the company CEO should be aware that upper management, as well as personnel from all departments of the company, must be involved in the quality efforts. An example of one company's policy statement follows:

> It is the policy of the company to so operate, that its products and services shall be provided at those levels of quality, performance, and reliability which will ensure full customer satisfaction, as well as compliance with all contractual terms, conditions, and specifications.
>
> The implementation of all elements of the quality program shall be accomplished through the coordinated efforts of all groups within the company, for the economical attainment of the company's quality assurance objectives.

INSPECTION/QUALITY ELEMENTS

Once the quality policy has been defined and disseminated to all personnel, the elements of the program should be identified along with the departmental responsibilities for its implementation.

Guides for the selection of these elements are available in the military inspection and quality program specifications noted earlier. In addition ASQC and ANSI have developed standards for an acceptable inspection or quality program: They are ASQC Standard C-1–1985 "Specification of

PLANNING

Company policy

Organization

Procedures

Measuring Equipment

Drawing and Design Control

Training and Motivation

Proposal/Contract Review

Program Control

Selection of Inspection/Quality
Personnel

IMPLEMENTATION

Supplier Control

Manufacturing Control

Special Process Control

Nonconformance Control

Stores/Handling

Status Identification

Assembly/Test Control

Shipping Control

Installation Control

EVALUATION

Statistical Control

Audits

Records

Quality Related Costs

Data Analysis

Reports

Budget Control

CORRECTIVE ACTION

QUALITY IMPROVEMENT

TABLE 6-1 Suggested inspection/quality program elements.

General Requirements for a Quality Program" and ANSI/ASQC E-2–1984, "American National Standard—Guide to Inspection Planning." Recently, a set of quality system guidelines Q90-Q94 have been issued to reflect the requirements of the international standards ISO-9000 series. See Chapter 34 for additional information about these standards. Table 6-1 provides a listing of suggested elements of an inspection/quality program.

An example of one company's development of an inspection/quality program is provided below. In order to clarify these elements they were categorized in the company's quality manual in accordance with the principles of good management. These categories were identified by the acronym PIEC, as follows:

P—Planning
I—Implementation
E—Evaluation
C—Corrective action

Planning

Policy

Clearly outlines the company's quality policy.

Organization

Contains the company's organization charts, as well as the functional chart of the inspection/quality department. A brief discussion of the functions of each department, relative to the quality function, is included. Additional details of an inspection/quality organization are provided in Chapter 4.

Procedures

Describes the preparation and control of the company's quality manual, the implementing of inspection/quality procedures, and the company's engineering, quality, and inspection standards. See Chapter 8.

Measuring equipment

Describes the methods and responsibilities for the selection, design, procurement, manufacture, calibration, and maintenance of all measuring equipment utilized by the company in the implementation of its inspection/ quality program. A description is included of the control of measuring equipment utilized by suppliers for products and services provided to the company. See Chapter 25.

Drawing and design control

Delineates implementation methods of various elements of the design and development phases of products and services. Presents the controls utilized in the issuance of drawing and company-developed specifications and their subsequent changes. The implementation method of these changes at the specified points of effectivity is described. In addition, the company's configuration control, reliability, and product liability prevention programs are described. See Chapter 10.

Proposal/contract review

Outlines the role played by the inspection/quality control department in the evaluation of new work proposals, and of the resultant contracts received by the company. See Chapter 11.

Program control

Describes the development of inspection/quality programs for each new product and service, and the definition of the inspection/quality elements for each new contract received by the company. See Chapter 11.

Selection of inspection/quality personnel

Details the methods used in the selection and qualification of personnel who implement the inspection/quality program functions. See Chapter 23.

Training and motivation

Examines the programs used by the company in the training of all its employees who are involved in the design, procurement, inspection and test, and service of the company's products and services. A portion of the section elaborates upon the selection and utilization of employee motivation programs. See Chapter 23.

Implementation

Supplier control

Outlines the procedures in the control of company suppliers. Includes the selection, qualification, monitoring, and rating of the company's suppliers. This section also includes the controls exercised to insure that supplier purchase orders contain the appropriate contractual requirements, as well as the applicable inspection/quality elements. See Chapter 12.

Manufacturing control

Describes the control of all elements of manufacture, including the preparation and implementation of manufacturing procedures and inspection/quality instructions. Also included are the identification and descriptions of each inspection and test station. See Chapter 14.

Special process control

Details the control over all special processes, such as the application of organic finishes, welding, soldering, plating, nondestructive testing, and the like. See Chapter 15.

Nonconforming material and process control

Defines the methods of control over nonconformances detected during the manufacturing process. Describes the identification, segregation, review, and disposition of nonconforming products and processes. Also defines the actions of the company's materials review committee, including the follow-up actions to correct the causes of nonconformances. See Chapter 16.

Stores/handling

Describes product handling controls throughout the manufacturing process and in the company's stores areas, to insure material identification retention and to provide protection against handling and environmental damage. See Chapter 17.

Status identification

Outlines the methods used to identify the manufacturing and inspection status of the products throughout the manufacturing process and while in the stores areas. See Chapter 17.

Assembly/test control

Identifies the controls used during product assembly and testing. This includes the performance of the engineering, prototype, and qualification testing, and the feedback of the test results to the engineering and manufacturing agencies for corrective action. See Chapter 18.

Shipping control

Defines the controls used in the preparation of the product for shipment. Describes the processing, packaging, marking, packing, and loading of the product upon carriers. See Chapter 19.

Installation

Describes the controls over the installation of the product in the field, including inspection and testing. See Chapter 19.

Evaluation

Statistical controls

Examines the development and implementation of various statistical techniques used during the design, development, manufacture, and examination of the product. Included is a description of the use of statistical sampling plans, statistical quality control and process control methods, process capability studies, analysis, and other statistical disciplines. See Chapter 24.

Audits

Delineates the procedures for the performance of in-house and supplier facility audits to determine the degree of conformance to company and inspection/quality procedures and instructions. See Chapter 21.

Records

Describes the development and use of inspection, test, and audit records prepared during the processing, manufacture, and use of the product.

Includes a discussion of the company's record retention policy, including the needs of the company's product liability prevention program. See Chapter 20.

Quality related costs

Details the company's quality-related cost program and its use as a management tool in the evaluation and improvement of the company's product quality levels. Discusses the use of the quality-related cost data in the implementation of the applicable corrective action and the enhancement of the quality improvement program. See Chapter 28.

Data analysis

Describes the methods used in the analysis of inspection, test, and audit records. See Chapter 20.

Reports

Discusses the preparation of various management quality reports. It presents the pyramid reporting methods and the use of these reports in product correction and improvement. These reports include a description of the effectiveness of earlier corrective actions and identify the quality levels of each area of the company operations, including the need for additional management attention, if required. See Chapter 20.

Budget control

Discusses the procedures used in the preparation of the inspection/quality departmental budgets. Describes the methods of justifying each budgetary item as well as the procedures of accounting for any variances from the established budget. See Chapter 28.

Corrective Action

This section describes the initiation and implementation of corrective actions resulting from adverse conditions and trends revealed in the analyses of the inspection, test, and audit records. These analyses include the report of field failures and customer complaints. These actions are implemented within the company and suppliers' facilities. See Chapter 22.

Quality improvement program

Outlines the methods utilized by the company in its program of continuous quality improvement. See Chapter 31.

MALCOLM BALDRIGE NATIONAL QUALITY AWARD PROGRAM[1]

Companies competing for this prestigious award are evaluated in seven categories, described in the following sections. See Table 6-2.

Leadership

This element measures the effectiveness of all levels of company management in providing leadership for the quality improvement process. This category reviews the involvement of senior corporate personnel, the establishment of corporate ownership of this policy by senior management personnel, and the method and degree of its dissemination to all employees.

The leadership category reviews the management system and quality improvement process, and its integration into the company's organizational structure. Also evaluated are those elements of the quality improvement process which facilitate coordination among company functions, and the routine management of that process.

Included are reviews of the allocation of the company's resources for quality improvement efforts, such as funds, facilities, staff, and equipment. Review is also made of the methods for external communication concerning the quality improvement program, and the extent of the company's public responsibility in publicizing this program for the motivation of other companies.

Information and Analysis

This category determines the effectiveness of the company's efforts in collecting and analyzing information for quality control and improvement. It provides for the review of the statistical techniques used for the evaluation of quality levels and improvement throughout all phases of the company operations. Included are methods of processing, analyzing, and evaluating data accumulated from both within and outside the company.

Methods include those utilized in the collection of customers' data concerning the quality improvement process, as well as that of suppliers, distributors, and dealers. This category also evaluates the type of data and implementation methods concerning the extent of employees' involvement, and their attitudes concerning the improvement process. A review is made of the methods of evaluating employee performance, and the degree of consideration given, in the employees' merit reviews, to their contributions to the quality improvement program.

Strategic Quality Planning

This category evaluates the effectiveness of the company's planning process when considering quality factors. This includes an evaluation of the corporate strategic and operational goals, and the planning function relative to

Leadership

Information and Analysis

Strategic Quality Planning

Human Resource Development and Management

Management of Process Quality

Quality and Operational Results

Customer Focus and Satisfaction

TABLE 6-2 Elements of Malcolm Baldrige Award program

the quality improvement program. A review is also made of the corporate plans for quality improvement and their relationship to the general business plan.

Human Resource Development and Analysis

This category reviews the effectiveness and thoroughness of human resource utilization in the quality improvement process. The review of the corporate plans and methods of operation is included, as well as the methods used to inform employees of the company's quality goals and its progress in the attainment of these goals.

A review is made of the means used by the employees to communicate their ideas and concerns to top management, including their involvement in the identification and resolution of quality problems. The method and extent of corporate involvement in the implementation of these recommendations are also evaluated.

This category includes review of the company's programs for employee training and education. It includes the methods used for the determination of the strengths and knowledge of quality improvement technology of its personnel, as well as the means for corporate evaluation of its quality training programs. Evaluation is made of the methods used to provide incentives to, and recognition of, employees for their contributions to the quality improvement program plans and implementation strategies.

Management of Process Quality

This category evaluates the effectiveness of the process for ensuring defect-free and error-free products and services. This review includes the method of encouraging the receipt of customer input about its products and services, the means for evaluating this input, and the method by which it is used.

Elements of the methods used by the company in planning for new and improved products and services are reviewed, including the methods in which the customer requirements are incorporated into the plans. Evaluation is also made of the extent to which customer requirements and their degree of satisfaction are considered in the planning process for product and process improvement.

The method of incorporating quality objectives in the design of new and improved products and services is reviewed. Consideration is also given to the method of disseminating quality objectives and customer requirements to new product or service development staff. A review of the use of analytical methods in new product development and how the quality design requirements are functionally integrated into the product or service systems is made.

A review is also conducted of the measurements, standards, and data systems used in product development. This includes the evaluation of the analytical and physical methods used to establish the capabilities of the processes and the monitoring of their control. Consideration is also given to the methods of measuring the precision and accuracy of the physical/chemical methods and the validity of their data.

The specific technologies used for quality improvement are evaluated in this category. Included is a review of the auditing methods used to monitor and evaluate the effectiveness of the quality management system, as well as the documentation developed to support the quality improvement program.

Included in this category are the corporate goals and requirements for protecting the safety, health, and environment of the company's employees, its customers, and the community. A determination is also made of the company's degree of compliance with the mandated health and safety standards.

A review is also made of the procedures utilized to inspect and validate the quality of finished products and services, and the methods of validation through all phases of operation. The degree of subsequent improvement as a result of these evaluations is also reviewed.

Quality and Operational Results

This category deals with the results of the quality improvement process in terms of measurable and verifiable factors. This includes an assessment of the types of data used and the results of system maintenance after installation in the field.

Methods used for scrap and rework reduction are reviewed. This includes the evaluation of the company's measurements of the reject levels and trends of in-house evaluations, as well as the failure levels of products and services in use. A review is also made of the reduction in warranty claim and field support costs, as well as the reductions in claims, litigations, and customer quality complaints.

Customer Focus and Satisfaction

This category evaluates the degree of customer satisfaction. The method used by the company in determining customers' views, and the methods for measuring these opinions are evaluated. Included are the methods used and evaluation results of the quality efforts against those of competitors.

How customer complaints are handled and the success of customer service operations are reviewed. Consideration is given to the use of this data to improve the quality of products, customer service, and other services. Customers' opinions about product and service guarantees and warranties, and how the company utilizes this data in the improvement of the products and services, are analyzed.

It is interesting to note that the inspection/quality program illustrated earlier in this chapter bears a strong resemblance to the plan-do-check-act elements of the Japanese quality programs described in Chapter 3. This merely serves to emphasize the point that many U.S. companies had adopted Dr. Deming's teachings long before they became popular as a result of their use in Japanese industries.

REFERENCES

1. *Malcolm Baldrige National Quality Award Criteria.* Gathersburg, MD: NIST, 1992.

CHAPTER SEVEN

Planning the Inspection/Quality Program

INTRODUCTION[1]

The essential function of the planning program is the assurance of an orderly attainment of the corporate quality goals. The major purpose of planning is to identify and schedule the functional elements of each department as they relate to the inspection/quality program. The resulting schedules not only provide guidance in daily operations, but also serve as the basis for comparing results and establishing variances for review and control.

An additional element of the planning process is the development of the manpower and budgetary schedules for each department. These are prepared in detail for each function, activity, project, or program in the operating plan. See Chapter 28 for a detailed discussion about the inspection/quality budgetary process.

PLANNING THE INSPECTION/QUALITY FUNCTION[2]

As described in Chapters 4 and 6, the elements and functions of the inspection/quality organization are largely dependent upon the type and size of company, and its product mix. The quality policy of the company also plays an important part in the manner and degree of implementation of the inspection/quality operation.

Once the quality policy has been delineated, the organization defined, and the functional responsibilities assigned, the details of the planning operation can be developed by designated departments and their personnel.

Inspection planning includes designating the inspection stations and providing inspectors with the facilities, equipment, and instructions needed to perform their duties. This planning may be performed by inspectors, inspection supervisors, or special planners, depending upon the nature and size of the organization, and the complexity of the products and services involved.

ELEMENTS OF THE PLANNING FUNCTION

Chapter 6 divided the inspection/quality operation into four basic management steps: planning, implementation, evaluation, and corrective action. This chapter is devoted to examining the elements of the planning function. Chapters 12–19 discuss plan implementation. Evaluation is covered in Chapters 20 and 21, and corrective action is detailed in Chapter 22.

Several elements of the inspection/quality planning missions are further discussed in the following chapters.

- Chapter 8—Preparation and use of company standards, standard procedures, and inspection/test instructions

- Chapter 9—Amount of inspection and inspection stations

- Chapter 10—Engineering design, drawing/specification preparation, and control

- Chapter 11—Customer requirements review, and project program control

LONG RANGE PLANNING

Both short and long range plans are required for the inspection/quality function. Initially, a long range plan of three to five years should be prepared to allow for the anticipated needs of the organization. At times, sufficient detailed information concerning the type and quantity of products anticipated may not be completely available. Nevertheless, some estimates can be made.

Attention should be focused on any potential new product which the company may consider producing in the future. Some determination should be made for the possibility of improving existing processes for current production, as well as developing new processes for new products.

Long range planning generally utilizes the forecast provided by the marketing department. This forecast may include a factor of probability for each element of new business, based on the anticipated chance of obtaining this business. When available, this probability factor could be utilized by all departments when considering their anticipated needs to develop and process new products.

PERSONNEL
  EQUIPMENT
    PROCESSES
      CONFIGURATION
        OUTSIDE SUPPLIES
        COSTS
          STANDARDS
            PRODUCT LIABILITY

FIGURE 7-1 Quality Assurance Challenges

Figure 7-1 shows elements that should be considered in the long range plan. Each element is briefly discussed in the following sections.

Personnel

The amount and type of personnel required to inspect and control the quality of anticipated products and processes should be considered. Production and inspection/quality department heads should review, with the personnel department, the potential in-house availability of needed personnel. They must also consider if the company is located in an area with a significant shortage of skilled labor of the type needed. Alternate programs, such as out-of-state recruitment or employee training, may need to be considered.

Training

Training programs, addressing the specific disciplines, should be developed. These would be directed to all suitable personnel as well as the current inspection/quality departments. Here is one example of a training program developed by an electronics company.

It had been decided to start utilizing designs containing semiconductor componentry, for which the manufacturing capability had not yet been developed. At that time, the use of this discipline was in the process of development by the company's research department.

The inspection manager was given the responsibility for staffing the department with personnel capable of setting up the necessary process controls and inspections for the new products. Since there was no one in the department who had any prior microcircuitry experience, an inspection engineer was selected from the company's chemical engineering department, and transferred to the inspection operation. Initially, this individual helped to develop the necessary inspection and process control procedures and inspection instructions for the current processes. He was subsequently assigned to the task of visiting companies who were currently engaged in the manufacture and assembly of microcircuits. Then the engineer worked with his company's training personnel to develop orientation programs for production and inspection personnel. These included the establishment of controls over production and inspection of the components and processes to be utilized for the microcircuit assemblies.

During the initial prototype production, the inspection engineer worked with the manufacturing engineering and inspection supervisory personnel in the development and qualification of the necessary processes. The applicable instructions and checklists, which were to be utilized during the production and control of the new assemblies, were also developed. The engineer continued his training of the inspection personnel and the development of the inspection and test instructions throughout the preproduction and production phases of the new microcircuit-designed product.

Equipment

In order to provide the necessary capabilities for new product inspection, the use of more sophisticated measuring equipment should be considered. This would enable lower skilled inspection personnel to perform the required measurements.

One company used this method by procuring a coordinate measuring machine for the layout inspection of complex raw and machined castings and forgings. This equipment allowed low-skilled personnel the capability of performing this inspection to the degree of accuracy and speed necessary to meet department needs.

Measuring equipment

A review of future measuring equipment needs should be assigned to inspection/quality engineers who have gaging design experience. They should inventory the existing equipment and evaluate its capabilities for future product inspection needs. If the required discipline is not available in-house, experts versed in gage design should be consulted.

These personnel should survey the market to see if suitable equipment is available. They should conduct a literature review and attend exhibits and conferences where equipment is displayed. After narrowing down the equipment choices to those which appear most suitable for use, the quality engineers should contact the equipment's distributors and sales personnel, and request demonstrations. These should be performed on sample components and assemblies representative of the products the company makes. The equipment sales personnel should then assist the department manager in developinig a preliminary budget for the equipment purchase.

At times, suitable equipment may not be readily available in the current measuring equipment market. Then it would be necessary to develop some special designs. This would be done in conjunction with manufacturing engineering personnel.

During the design and development of tooling and fixturing equipment, the incorporation of product inspection capabilities should be considered. These features would result in savings, because the need for special measuring equipment would be reduced; the production equipment would be utilized as media of inspection for specific characteristics.

Processes

Working with design and manufacturing engineering, the inspection/quality department should review the anticipated manufacturing processes. Joint studies should be conducted and preliminary controls developed for their introduction into the anticipated manufacturing processes. Here too, efforts should be made to incorporate, into the manufacturing processes, inspection and quality control elements.

Configuration Control

Studies should be conducted and procedures developed for the configuration control of new equipment. The critical, major, and safety-related components and assemblies should be identified and controls established for the traceability of these components and assemblies in each end item of equipment. Tentative procedures should be prepared to serialize these components and assemblies for this identification. A fuller description of the configuration control program is provided as part of Chapter 10.

Outside Supplies

Since a considerable portion of components utilized by most companies are obtained from external sources, it is desirable to identify and qualify potential suppliers for new products. Working with the design and development engineers, the inspection/quality engineers should identify the components and services which will be obtained from outside suppliers.

These components and services should then be classified into the applicable commodities. After the purchasing department has identified the potential sources for each commodity, the inspection/quality engineering personnel should visit these suppliers and conduct in-depth surveys of the production and quality capabilities of their facilities. Vendor survey checklists, applicable to the product or service, should be utilized. These survey results should be catalogued by vendor commodity code and production/quality capabilities, and utilized by the purchasing department when the suppliers are selected. See Chapter 12 for more details about the control of subcontracted supplies and services.

Quality Costs

The existing quality-related cost program, if available, should be reviewed and amplified to include any additional elements which would be introduced by new products and processes. See Chapter 28 for details.

Standards

Current engineering, workmanship, and quality standards should be evaluated for the incorporation of those elements applicable to new products and processes. New elements should be reviewed and additional or improved standards developed, as needed, for incorporation into the production and quality programs. See Chapter 10 for additional information about this program.

Product Liability Prevention Program

In view of increased consumerism, a company-wide product liability prevention program should be developed (see Chapter 10). If a program is available, it should be reviewed in light of any changes to the product liability laws. It should also be examined when new products and customers are developed.

World Class Quality

To attain current standards of world class quality, a program should be developed to insure the continuous improvement of products and processes. Consideration should be given to establishing quality improvement objectives through the development of quality councils, at the highest management levels; utilizing cross-functional teams to pursue the company's quality improvement objectives; and establishing benchmarks to provide goals for quality improvement in products and services. See Chapter 6 for a discussion of the Malcolm Baldrige Quality Award program which includes the elements of the world class quality program.

REFERENCES

1. Stiles, Edward M. *Handbook for Total Quality Assurance.* Waterford, CT: Prentice-Hall Inc., 1969, pp. 33–36.

2. Juran, J. M., & Frank M. Gryna, Jr. *Quality Planning and Analysis.* New York: McGraw Hill, 1970, pp. 310–315.

Company Standards and Procedures

STANDARDS

The use of company standards is essential to insure that information is consistently provided to all personnel for the performance of their duties.

Standard Procedures

Using standard procedures keeps the number of detailed operating procedures low. For example, a standard procedure for the inspection of a general commodity, such as simple electronic components, will eliminate the need for the preparation of separate inspection instructions for each individual component. See Figure 8-1.

In addition, standards provide guidelines for the preparation of detailed procedures. For example, a standard, detailing the elements of inspection procedures, describes their formats and the general contents of the procedure. See Figure 8-2.

Engineering Standards

Engineering standards are provided as supplements to drawings and specifications especially when certain characteristics are omitted or vague. All characteristics cannot be adequately identified on engineering drawings. For example, the engineer may assume that the depiction of a rectangular object would be interpreted as one which has all the sides perpendicular to each other. However, when it becomes necessary to fabricate and inspect the product, the question will arise as to the degree of perpendicularity. A

| | Date: _____ |
| | Originator: _____ |

This form is to used at Purchased Material Inspection - for Standard Commodities per QCI 0600.8

AQL	CHARACTERISTIC TO BE INSPECTED (Orginator to Underline Applicable Characteristics)	METHOD
	1. <u>Documentation:</u> Government Source Inspection Release, Cert. of Compliance Clause 4 Data.	Visual/Cert.
6.5	2. <u>General:</u> Appearance, Good Workmanship, Finish, Burrs, Rough Edges, Sharp Corners, Damage	Visual
6.5	3. <u>Processes:</u> Plating, Anodizing, Heat Treating, Annealing, Carbonizing, Welding, Magnaflux, etc.	C of C Visual
6.5	4. <u>Identification:</u> Part No., Stock No., Elec. value coding, Marking, etc.	Visual
6.5	5. <u>Completeness:</u> Missing Parts, Hardware, Machining, Operations, etc.	Visual
	6. <u>Testing:</u> Functional, Hardness Chemical Physical Test, Ultrasonic, Mag Particle, Penetrant.	C of C Review of test data if applic.

FIGURE 8-1   Standard Commodity Inspection Instruction

quantitative tolerance should be specified, such as $90° + / -2°$. Another example would be the interpretation for spacing holes, when the drawing specifies "six holes equally spaced."

Figure 8-3 illustrates characteristics defined in a quantitative manner. Without these standards, considerable disagreement could result between the manufacturing and inspection personnel in determining product conformance to drawing requirements.

Specification Standards

Here is an example of the problem resulting from specifications.

A vehicle specification noted that there was to be no evidence of fluid leakage from any component. Leaks could come from a variety of sources such as radiator hoses, transmissions, rear axles, crankcases, and fuel lines.

AQL	CHARACTERISTIC TO BE INSPECTED (Orginator to Underline Applicable Characteristics)	METHOD
	7. Unfinished Parts: Castings, Forgings, Coupons for test analysis, Associated Xrays.	Coupons verified periodically for Phys. & Chem. x-ray reviewed.
4.0	8. Dimensional: Outline Dimensions, Diameter Length, Width, Thickness, Taper, Concentricity, Hole Location, Threads Hole Diameter, Grip Length, Thread Length, Head Configuration, Inside Diameter, Mounting Dimensions, etc.	Standard Measuring Equipment Threads-Thread gage, Three wire method or thread Micrometer.
4.0	9. Additional Instructions:	

Date: _____
Originator: _____

This form is to used at Purchased Material Inspection - for Standard Commodities per QCI 0600.8

FIGURE 8-1 Continued

Since no statement was made, in the specification, concerning the amount of leakage from each area, any vehicle which exhibited the slightest sign of a leak, was subject to rejection. This posed a major problem to the vehicle manufacturer. Many of the leaks came from seals which, normally, would release a small amount of fluid before becoming seated in their final position. Since the inspection was conducted on new vehicles after a short trial run, the appearance of fluid outside the seal location would almost always occur, resulting in the rejection of nearly all the vehicles.

To correct this problem, the company's inspection engineer, after consulting with the vehicle using agency, prepared a standard which provided a quantitative criterion for each category of leaks, while meeting the customer's criterion of fitness for use (see Figure 8-4).

This standard, after customer approval, served as an acceptability criterion for each category of leaks during current and subsequent contracts. This criterion provided the necessary positive determination of acceptabil-

3. **Preparation**

   3.1 All QCIs and IIs shall be prepared in accordance with a format, subject to the disapproval of Quality Engineering.

   3.2 Quality Assurance Policies (QAPs) shall define the objective of each element of the quality program, the controls necessary to assure the attainment of these objectives and the organization(s) responsible for their implementation.

   3.3 Inspection/Test Instructions and Inspection Check Lists shall be prepared to the extent necessary to supplement the applicable drawings and/or specifications. These shall define, as applicable, and to the extent necessary, the following elements:

   (a) Characteristics to be checked.
   (b) Inspection criteria (drawing, specification, and issue, etc.).
   (c) Quantity to be checked (sample plan/frequency of check).
   (d) Special inspection/test equipment and environmental conditions.
   (e) Criteria for acceptance/rejection (inspection/test limits, etc.).

   3.4 Work Instructions shall be issued to the extent necessary to provide the criteria for the performance of the work function. These instructions shall be compatible with acceptance criteria for workmanship and shall, as applicable, define the following elements:

   (a) Operations to be performed.
   (b) Special equipment/environmental requirements.
   (c) Acceptance/rejection criteria.

   3.5 Maximum consideration shall be given to the incorporation of all or any combinations of production control, manufacturing, inspection, and test instructions in a single coordinated document.

FIGURE 8-2 Preparation of Inspection Procedures

ity for use by manufacturing, inspection, and customer personnel, resulting in a sharp reduction of the rejection rate.

Process Standards

These standards define the classifications, material, and general controls over special processes, such as plating, painting, welding, and the like. See Figure 8-5.

Workmanship Standards

Definitions of quality should be provided to the same degree of explicitness that will avoid any confusion by the producer, inspector, and customer. All participants should "read from the same book" and use the same acceptability criteria. To this end, it may, at times, be necessary to describe the quality characteristics of a product or service by means other than the written word.

There are standards which provide a description of the required workmanship characteristics of a product, which are generally not elaborated in

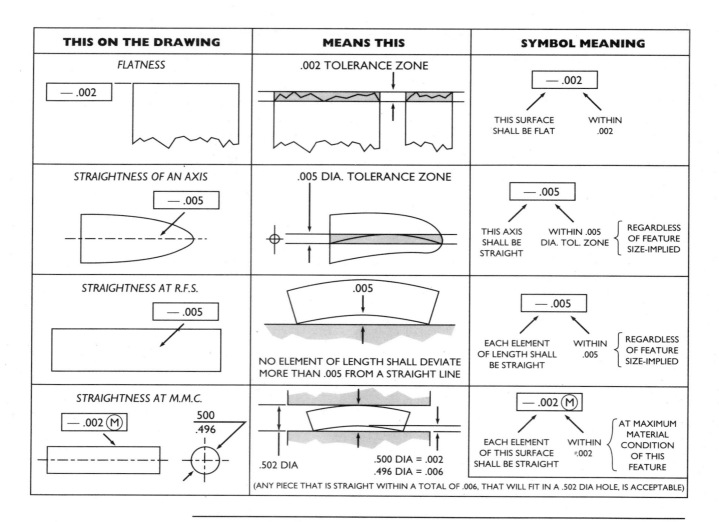

THIS ON THE DRAWING	MEANS THIS	SYMBOL MEANING

FLATNESS

— .002

.002 TOLERANCE ZONE

— .002

THIS SURFACE SHALL BE FLAT — WITHIN .002

STRAIGHTNESS OF AN AXIS

— .005

.005 DIA. TOLERANCE ZONE

— .005

THIS AXIS SHALL BE STRAIGHT — WITHIN .005 DIA. TOL. ZONE — REGARDLESS OF FEATURE SIZE-IMPLIED

STRAIGHTNESS AT R.F.S.

— .005

.005

NO ELEMENT OF LENGTH SHALL DEVIATE MORE THAN .005 FROM A STRAIGHT LINE

— .005

EACH ELEMENT OF LENGTH SHALL BE STRAIGHT — WITHIN .005 — REGARDLESS OF FEATURE SIZE-IMPLIED

STRAIGHTNESS AT M.M.C.

— .002 Ⓜ

500
.496

.502 DIA

.500 DIA = .002
.496 DIA = .006

— .002 Ⓜ

EACH ELEMENT OF THIS SURFACE SHALL BE STRAIGHT — WITHIN .002 — AT MAXIMUM MATERIAL CONDITION OF THIS FEATURE

(ANY PIECE THAT IS STRAIGHT WITHIN A TOTAL OF .006, THAT WILL FIT IN A .502 DIA HOLE, IS ACCEPTABLE)

FIGURE 8-3 Engineering Standard

drawings or specifications. These standards often include several means of describing acceptability. Examples of such standards include illustrations of acceptable solder connections, welded joints, and casting surfaces.

One method which is often found useful, is the development of visual aids to describe quality characteristics. For example, in electronic manufacture, color pictorial representations of solder connections are available. These photos usually present three degrees of configuration—acceptable, preferred, and unacceptable. References to these presentations are included in the bibliography.

EXAMPLE

A company, procuring raw castings from a foundry, found itself in trouble in obtaining the desired surface finish of the product as delivered. The normal method of expressing surface finish by means of specifying the root

OBJECTIVE: To provide a means for classifying defects, relative to leakage of fluid.

SCOPE: This instruction is to be utilized in the inspection of equipment/assemblies (as applicable) described herein unless otherwise specified.

1. **Controlling Elements**

    1.1   This instruction shall be implemented through the control of the following elements:

    (a) Definitions
    (b) Method of Inspection
    (c) Criteria of Acceptability

2. **Definitions**

    2.1   The following definitions describe the various conditions which classify a leak.

    (a) *Weep*—Any evidence of fluid beyond the seal.
    (b) *Seep*—Any evidence of fluid beyond the seal that does not result in the formation of a droplet.
    (c) *Droplet*—Any evidence of fluid beyond the seal that results in the formation of a droplet.
    (d) *Drip*—Any evidence of fluid beyond the seal where a droplet forms and falls.

3. **Method of Inspection**

    3.1   The following method of inspection shall be used.

    (a) Assure that tanks, lines, components, etc. contain a sufficient amount of fluid to enable the detection of a leak if existent.
    (b) Visually check all suspect surfaces for dryness. Wipe dry.
    (c) Functionally exercise vehicle or assembly as applicable.
    (d) Check for leak.

4. **Criteria of Acceptability**

    4.1   Indications of leaks shall be evaluated using the following criteria of acceptance.

    4.1.1   *Fuel System*

    Any indication of a leak defined in paragraph 2.1 (a) appearing within a 30-minute period shall be cause for rejection.

    4.1.2   *Cooling System*

    Any indication of a leak defined in paragraph 2.1 (b) appearing within a 30-minute period shall be cause for rejection.

    4.1.3   *Brake System*

    Any indication of a leak defined in paragraph 2.1 (c) appearing within a 30-minute period shall be cause for rejection.

    (a) If any indication of a leakage occurs upon initial inspection of brake system, the brake should be activated for a period of 30 seconds and suspect area re-inspected.

    4.1.4   *Power Train and Steering Unit*

    Any indication of a leak defined in paragraph 2.1 (d) appearing within a 30-minute period shall be cause for rejection.

    4.1.5   *Engine and Hydraulic Systems*

    Any indication of a leak defined in paragraph 2.1 (c) appearing within a 30-minute period shall be cause for rejection.

FIGURE 8-4   Inspection Standard

PROCESS SPECIFICATION

1. **PURPOSE**

   1.1 To provide a method for adhesive bonding of rubber products to aluminum surfaces.

2. **APPLICABLE SPECIFICATIONS and/or STANDARDS:**

   2.1 None.

3. **MATERIALS:**

   3.1 EC 847 Adhesive, Minnesota Mining & Mfg. Co., St. Paul, Minnesota.

   3.2 METHYL ETHYL KETONE—Commercial grade

   3.3 ACETONE—Commercial grade

4. **PROCEDURE:**

   4.1 Aluminum surface to which adhesive is to be applied must be free of oil, grease, dust and other foreign substances. Clean with suitable degreasing solvent.

   4.2 Rubber product should be free of soil, dust, and grease. Talcum should be removed with acetone.

   4.3 Apply EC-847 by brush or flow gun to both the rubber surface and metal surface to be joined.

   4.4 Allow to dry until tacky, but no longer transfers to the finger when lightly touched.

   NOTE: Parts which cannot be conveniently assembled when tacky may be joined immediately after application of the adhesive.

   4.6 Equipment or excess adhesive may be cleaned with *METHYL ETHYL KETONE* or *ACETONE.*

   4.7 For 90% of ultimate bond strength allow to dry, undisturbed, for a minimum of 48 hours.

   4.8 Coverage—approximately 200–250 sq. ft/gallon for medium brush coat of adhesive.

5. **LIMITATIONS:**

   5.1 Before using EC847: Extinguish all flames and pilot lights. During application and until vapors are gone, keep product and its vapors away from heat, sparks and flame. Avoid using spark producing electrical equipment such as switches, appliances, etc. Keep container closed when not in use.

6. **DRAWING NOTES:**

   6.1 "Bond per PSN 54".

FIGURE 8-5   Special Process Standard

mean square (RMS), as measured by a profilometer, is generally not applicable for use on raw casting surfaces. The final resolution was to select three samples with the desirable surface finish from the pilot casting run. The samples were marked. One was returned to the foundry and two maintained in the company's receiving inspection areas, to be used as acceptability criteria.

The glass-box model is another method of visually ensuring product quality. Two product samples, such as electronic modules, are enclosed in transparent containers. These are located at the production and inspection stations and used as examples of the desired product configuration. Both the production and inspection personnel have a common basis for acceptability using this method.

A similar procedure is frequently utilized by service industries, such as the post office. Completed examples of forms used in postal service, such as those for registered mail, are prominently displayed as guides for customers.

There are many workmanship standards provided in written procedures. One specifies weld quality characteristics and nondestructive test criteria. This standard is supplemented by visual samples of acceptable weld quality.

There are many other examples of the use of visual and written standards in all types of industries. The important consideration is to describe quality characteristics without vagueness or ambiguity. Standards must be easily understood and accepted by all personnel: producers, inspectors, and customers.

PROCEDURES AND INSTRUCTIONS

Inspection/Quality Manual

Documentation of the inspection/quality program is essential to assure a complete understanding by all company personnel of the authorities and responsibilities of their organizations. Most companies define their inspection/quality program in a compilation of documented policy statements, procedures, and instructions. This information is generally incorporated or referenced in a company manual. A well-written inspection/quality manual can also be utilized as a source of instruction and indoctrination of new employees.

Manual Contents

Many company inspection/quality manuals include all or most of the following information.

Policy statement

This is a positive statement, by top management, of the company's inspection/quality policy. See Chapter 6 for an example. All subsequent procedures and instructions are based upon this statement.

Organization

The manual shows the company's organization. It presents inspection/quality organizational charts and functional charts of the other departments involved in implementing the inspection/quality program. See Chapter 4 for an example.

Standard procedures

These are references to the standard procedures utilized to implement policy requirements. As noted in Chapter 4, at one time, the inspection/quality manual of most companies merely reflected the perceived requirements of their customers as they affected the quality personnel's functions. However, it is now understood that the implementation of an effective inspection/quality program requires ongoing efforts of personnel from all departments.

Therefore, the inspection/quality manual should include, or reference, the operating procedures of all the company departments as they relate to the inspection/quality program. To avoid duplication of procedures, it is advisable to define the inspection/quality functions performed by each department, and denote where their operating procedures are located. For example, in discussing engineering drawing control, the manual's standard procedure may specify the engineering department's responsibilities in implementing its portion of the procedure. The manual would also refer to the engineering standards manual, located in the engineering library, for the details of that department's program for the preparation and control of drawings.

In many large or multiplant organizations, it is the common practice for the manual to contain policies and standard procedures which define the elements of the quality program, and denote the implementation responsibilities and authorities of the department(s). The detailed procedures and instructions are developed by the operating sections of the department(s). This provides flexibility for the operating departments. However, it must be understood that the departmental procedures must conform to the standards noted in the inspection/quality manual. For example, a standard procedure may define the elements and format of inspection records. The department responsible for the development of the inspection records prepares them in accordance with the manual's guidelines, and includes copies of the actual documents in its operating procedure.

Coordination and Approvals

Once the manual has been prepared, and all the standard procedures incorporated, it should be distributed to affected departments' representatives and members of upper management for their comments and/or approvals. All comments should be resolved before the manual is issued.

This review and approval may often be time consuming and quite troublesome. This is evidenced, in particular, when there is an objection to some portion of the manual. However, it is important that these approvals are obtained and that the concerns of all affected departments are attended to. In order to hasten manual approval, affected departmental representatives should be consulted during manual development. This encourages these personnel to develop a feeling of ownership in the procedure, and provides the motivation for them to consider themselves participants in the development of the inspection/quality program. Therefore, their enthusi-

A. *Purpose:*
   To define the company's Quality Assurance Policy

B. *Policy/Objective:*
   It is the policy of the company to so operate, that its products and services shall be provided at those levels of quality, performance, and reliability which will ensure full customer satisfaction, as well as compliance with all contractual terms, conditions, and specifications.

C. The elements of the "Quality Program" of the company are defined in a set of Quality Assurance Policies (QAPs) contained in the company's Quality Assurance Policy Manual.

Responsibility	*Action*
Director of Quality Assurance	1. Formulates and maintains a "Quality Program" which will enable, through the coordinated efforts of all departments within the company, the economical and consistent attainment of the quality assurance objective as stated above.
All company department heads	2. Implement the applicable portions of the policies and procedures as described in the company QAP manual.
	Signed
	Company President

FIGURE 8-6   Quality Assurance Policy

astic support in the implementation of their facets of the program can be expected.

Upon receipt of all required approvals, the manual should be signed by the head of the company. This provides the required authorization for program implementation. Some companies issue a special directive which specifies the responsibility of the inspection/quality department to prepare the manual, and the requirement, after their concurrence, for the referenced departments to implement their designated functions. See Figure 8-6.

Inspection/Quality Procedures

It is important that the procedures and instructions are prepared so that they can be fully understood by manual users. Both the language and technical content should be addressed to the users' level of understanding.

EXAMPLE

The maintenance department experienced considerable difficulty training its personnel to apply the proper lubricants during scheduled machine tool servicing. The principal cause of the problem was that most employees had difficulty understanding the lubrication instructions, since many could not speak or read English. The solution to the problem was to put different colored marks on the lubricant dispensing equipment. Each color was duplicated on the applicable lubrication point of the machine. Accordingly, the only instruction necessary was to apply the lubricant, from the dispenser of a specific color, to the lubrication point marked with the same color. Since none of the maintenance employees were color blind, the problem was simply resolved.

The responsible inspection/quality control personnel prepared the instructions necessary to implement the standard procedures. These instructions addressed the questions of Who? What? Where? and When? and were prepared in accordance with the format and guidelines defined in the manual.

Inspection/Test Instructions

Inspection/test instructions implement procedures by telling users how to accomplish tasks. There are various types of instructions that are customarily developed by or for inspectors. These may be classified into the following categories.

General inspection instructions

Inspection instructions may be prepared for a general type of product or service, such as for simple components or standard hardware. The use of general instructions eliminates the need for detailed part or assembly instructions. General instructions are customarily utilized when a category of parts has related characteristics. For example, general inspection instruction for a category of resistors specifies the size, width, color code, value, tolerance, finish, and other visible characteristics. The specific values for each characteristic may be listed in a matrix in the instruction sheet or referenced to the individual resistor drawing.

Detailed parts instructions

These inspection instructions are prepared for individual parts or assemblies. They identify the characteristics and quantity of each element to be inspected, the method of inspection, the acceptance criteria, the measuring equipment to be used, and any special environmental conditions, as applicable. See Figure 8-7.

Qualification instruction

This type of instruction is utilized when a product is being inspected on the first shipment, or at the start of production. In most instances, the instruction calls for the inspection of 100 percent of the characteristics of one product item. The instruction may specify the actual characteristics, or refer to the product drawing. When the characteristic is listed on the instruction it is generally the policy to specify its location, on the drawing, using zone number/letter. This saves time by quickly locating the characteristic in question.

When the product is being qualified to a specification, it is standard practice to identify the essential element(s) of each paragraph of the specification and, when necessary, the method of inspection.

CLASS	CHARACTERISTIC	PER DWG AND/OR SPEC	INSPECTION METHOD
MAJOR		**A.Q.L. 1.0% DEFECTIVE**	
101	.034/.026 LOCATION OF 1.00 DIA PIN BORES	D3XXXXX00	INDICATOR GAGE F3XXXX522 REV B 7–12–68
102	SQUARENESS OF 1.000 DIA PIN BORES TO PISTON AXIS WITHIN .0005 PER INCH OF SKIRT LENGTH	D3XXXXX00	SQUARENESS FIXTURE F3XXXX523 REV E 6–28–68
103	1.0000/1.0005 DIA (2 PLACES)	D3XXXXX00	DIAL BORE GAGE
104	MICROFINISH (32 RMS)	D3XXXXX00	SURFACE ANALYZER
MINOR	**A.Q.L. 2.5% DEFECTIVE**		
201	.250/.260 DIMENSION	D3XXXXX00	WIDTH GAGE
202	MICROFINISH (125 RMS)	D3XXXXX00	COMPARATOR BLOCKS
203	IDENTIFICATION MARKING	D3XXXXX00	VISUAL

TABLE II—SPECIAL SAMPLING INSPECTION

1. *INITIAL PRODUCTION APPROVAL:* FIVE (5) OF THE FIRST ITEMS PRODUCED UNDER MANUFACTURING METHODS USED IN PRODUCTION, SHALL BE SUBJECTED TO INSPECTION BY THE CONTRACTOR. THIS INSPECTION SHALL DETERMINE CONFORMITY TO ALL REQUIREMENTS OF DRAWING D3XXXXX00 and SPECIFICATION MIL-X-XXXXX.

1.1 *FAILURE:* FAILURE OF ANY ONE OF THE FIRST FIVE (5) ITEMS PRODUCED SHALL BE CAUSE FOR REJECTION AND PARAGRAPH 1 SHALL APPLY UNTIL ACCEPTABLE ITEMS ARE PRODUCED.

FIGURE 8-7   Detailed Parts Instruction

In a qualification inspection operation, it is advisable to record, when practicable, the variables measurement obtained during the inspection.

Special process instructions

This type of instruction is utilized when process element implementation is verified, in addition to product characteristic inspection. This is performed when the quality cannot be completely determined by the inspection of the product alone, but requires a review of the fabrication process. For example, when a welded part or assembly is inspected, recourse is made to determine if manufacturing conformed to the applicable weld procedure. See Figure 8-8.

Objective:	To provide an effective method of process control for welding operations.
Scope:	To implement the applicable portions of QAP710/QAP1010 and will be used for auditing the welding processes on Job 2280/81/82.
General:	The Welding Process shall be audited utilizing the Audit Check List (A). Results shall be recorded on the Audit Record Sheet (B) and processed in accordance with QAP1010. The audits shall be performed initially every month and the frequency may be adjusted as dictated by Quality History.

Requirements:

1. <u>Welder Qualification</u>
   All welder operators shall be qualified for the joints and processes in accordance with P.S.N. 2270-0200 and P.S.N. 2271-0108 respectively as required by job assignment.
   Quality Control shall monitor the result of this qualification and maintain a list of currently qualified personnel.

2. <u>Weld Procedures</u>
   All weldments shall be manufactured in accordance with the approved welding procedures.

3. <u>Protection of Electrodes</u>
   Electrodes shall be stored adequately to prevent contamination that would effect quality of weld deposited. Steel electrodes to be protected in accordance with P.S.N. 02270-20.

4. <u>Visual Inspection of Welds</u>
   All weldments shall be examined visually in accordance with Q.C.I. 2281-101s.

5. <u>Radiographic Inspection of Weldments</u>
   Radiographic Inspection when required shall be performed in accordance with Q.C.O. 2280-103s.

6. <u>Control of Critical Weld Notch Break Testing</u>
   Notch Break Testing will be required for Weld Operators in accordance with Q.C.I. 2281-102s.

FIGURE 8-8 Special Process Inspection

Assembly inspection instructions

This type of instruction is utilized when the product is examined at a sequence of inspection or assembly stations. To better establish the points of inspection, it is customary to prepare a flowchart, identifying the stations.

QAP AUDIT EVALUATION RECORD SHEET

II NO._____ QAP NO._____ TITLE OF QAP_____

ISSUE DATE _____ EFF. DATE _____ _____

AUDITOR_____ AUDIT DATE _____ NEXT AUDIT DATE _____

ELEMENT	1	2	3	4	5	6	7	8	9	10	11	12	13	14	15	16	17	18	19	20	TOTAL
OBSERVATIONS																					
DEFECTIVES																					

COMMENTS AND/OR DEFECTIVES	PROPOSED CORRECTIVE ACTION

FIGURE 8-8 Continued

The inspection points are noted on the chart, including the characteristics to be examined, as well as the methods of inspection, when applicable. When the listing is lengthy, a special inspection method sheet may be prepared for the characteristic. Reference to the method sheet is made at the inspection point on the flowchart. See Figures 8-9, 8-10 and 8-11.

AUDIT CHECK LIST		
Element	Verification Method	Reference
1. Weld operators are to be Qualified for the Joints and Processed in accordance with P.S.N. 2270-0220 and P.S.N. 2271-0108. Q.C. shall monitor qualification and maintain a list of Qualified Personnel.	1.1 Review record of operator qualified since last audit for completeness.	Q.C.I. 2280-100[S] Para. 1
	1.2 Verify list of Qualified Welders by comparing record review (1.1 above) against list.	Q.C.I 2280-100[S] Para. 1
	1.3 Randomly select welders on job and ascertain that they are on Qualification List for Joint and Process they are currently welding.	Q.C.I. 2280-100[S] Para. 1
	1.4 Randomly select weldments and review for presence of Welder Identification.	
2. Weldments shall be manufactured utlilizing approved Weld Procedures.	2.1 Randomly select areas of the Weld. Dept. and verify that the applicable Weld Procedures are present and available to operator.	Q.C.I. 2280-100[S] Para. 2
	2.2 In areas selected for 2.1 above, verify that material being welded has been properly cleaned prior to welding.	Q.C.I. 2280-100[S] Para. 2

FIGURE 8-8 Continued

Test instructions

Test instructions or procedures list the characteristics to be tested, the acceptability criteria, the test equipment to be used, and the methods of test to be applied.

In many companies, the test instructions are prepared by the test engineering department. In those instances, it is advisable for the procedures to be reviewed by inspection/quality engineers, who verify that all operational characteristics of the contractual specification, and all functional elements, are considered.

AUDIT CHECK LIST		
Element	Verification Method	Reference
	2.3 Using applicable Weld Procedure, verify visually that correct filler metal is being utlized.	Q.C.I. 2280-100[S] Para. 2
	2.4 Using applicable Weld Procedure, verify that actual welding is being conducted with-in the range of values specified on Weld Procedure.	Q.C.I. 2280-100[S] Para. 2
3. Electrodes shall be adequately stored to prevent contamination that will effect weld quality, Steel electrodes to be protected in accordance with P.S.N. 02270-20.	3.1 Review storage of weld filler metal to ascertain that material is maintained in manufacturer's container prior to use and that containers are not in an area susceptable to water damage.	Q.C.I. 2280-100[S] Para. 3
4. All weldment are visually examined in accordance with Q.C.I. 2280-101[S] and Q.C.I. 2281/2282-101[S].	4.1 Verify that applicable Q.C.I. is being utilized for the Visual Weld Inspection Process.	Q.C.I. 2280-100[S] Para. 4
	4.2 Verify that the approved workmanship specimens are available for use as directed by the applicable Q.C.I.	
5. Radiographic Inspection as required shall be performed in accordance with Q.C.I. 2280-103[S].	5.1 Randomly select reports of Radiographic Inspection performed since last audit. Review report for completeness and evidence that proper quantity of x-rays were taken in accordance with Q.C.I. 2280-103[S].	Q.C.I. 2280-100[S] Para. 5
6. Notch Break Test Required for welders assigned to Job 2281/2282.	6.1 Randomly select "Weldment Operators Assignment/Test Record" since last audit to assure completeness and conformance of data.	Q.C.I. 2281/22 100[S] Para. 5.1

FIGURE 8-8 Continued

CHAPTER EIGHT Company Standards and Procedures 79

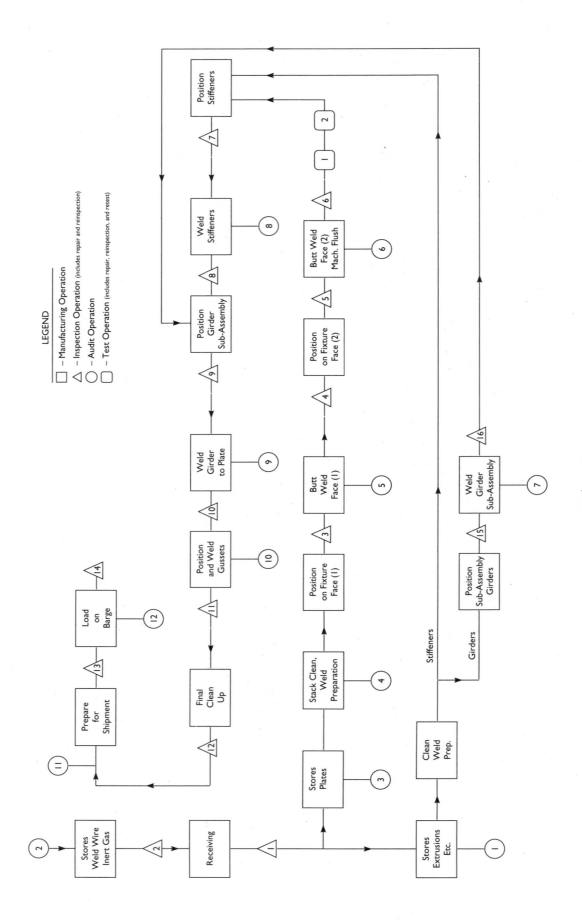

FIGURE 8-9 Assembly Flowchart

SUBJECT:	CODE FOR FLOW CHART—	APPENDIX B
	TANK WELDMENT ASSEMBLIES	QCOP NO: 2283-13
	(Appendix A)	ISSUE NO: 2

APPROVED BY: **EFFECTIVE DATE:**

NO. ON Appendix A	OPERATION	QCOP NO 2283-	QCI NO 2283-
	A. *INSPECTION OPERATION—CODE*		
1.	Receiving Inspection—Customer Supplied Material. Check for count, condition, identification, and material identification code.	4	
2.	Receiving Inspection—Company Supplied material.	7	4
3.	In-Process Inspection—Plates fixturing—Face (1). Check for: a) Condition of weld preparation area b) Cleanliness c) Use of correct parts d) Alignment and fit up in fixture	13	
4.	In-Process Inspection—Plate Butt Weld Face (1). a) Visual inspection of weld quality b) Dimensional inspection of weldment c) For sheet bottom plate panels only, measure the surface flatness in the weld zone.	13 & 9	6
5.	In-Process Inspection—Plate Fixturing Side (2). a) Condition of weld preparation area b) Cleanliness c) Position of fixture d) Identification marking (lot, code, and configuration identifier)	13	
6.	In-Process Inspection—Plate Butt Weld Face (2). a) Visual inspection of weld quality b) Dimensional inspection of weldment c) Inspection of flush operation d) Condition of plate identification marking	13 & 9	
	B. *Test Operation—Code*		
1.	Plate Butt Welds. a) Radiographically inspect butt welds for conformance to specified requirements. b) Reinspect rejected welds after repair (visual and radiographic).	9 9	
2.	Plate Butt Welds. a) Leak test welds after repair or when a start and stop weld has occurred.	9 10	
	C. *Audit Operation*		
1.	Stores—Customer Supplied Material a) Audit stores area material for segregation from company material b) Protection against damage and environmental conditions c) Proper maintenance of material control log d) Identification by part number, material lot, code, etc.	11 & 17	
2.	Stores—Weld Wire and Inert Gas. a) Audit stores area for storage under specified environmental conditions b) Identification coding	11 17	
3.	Stores—Plates Same as C-1 above	11 & 17	

FIGURE 8-10 Flowchart Codes

For example, an instruction listed all the test characteristics which the engineer deemed necessary to meet the performance requirements of the contract. The inspection engineer noted that these test characteristics did not demonstrate the quality of several electrical circuits in the equipment. After consultation with the project engineer, it was agreed that some additional testing was necessary to demonstrate, during the process of assembly, the quality of the characteristics which would not be evaluated during the final equipment test.

Required information

The following information, as applicable, should be incorporated in the inspection/test instructions.

- Name and drawing/part number of the item or commodity to be inspected.

- Configuration level/revision letter of the drawing or specification utilized in the inspection.

- Characteristic(s) to be checked. Reference to the characteristic(s) on the drawing by zone designation or paragraph number of the specification may be utilized in lieu of spelling out the entire characteristic on the inspection instruction.

- Inspection method and/or special measuring equipment to be used. Standard inspection methods or measuring equipment are not usually specified. When the method of inspection is complex, it may be advisable to develop a special inspection method sheet, which would then be referenced at the appropriate location. See Figure 8-11.

- Number of product units to be checked for each characteristic or group of characteristics. When sampling inspection is to be used, reference to the acceptable quality level (AQL) number of the sampling plan should be specified. See Chapter 9.

- Special environmental conditions during the inspection/test, when applicable.

- Inspection results. These are recorded when the inspection record sheet is part of the instructions. When a separate sheet is utilized, reference to the results is noted at the applicable location of the record sheet. Some companies denote, on the record sheet, only the nonconforming characteristics. This implies that all other characteristics have been found conforming. This procedure is not considered satisfactory.

- Disposition of the inspected lot, and processing of nonconforming lots and parts. Most companies utilize a special procedure to process nonconforming products.

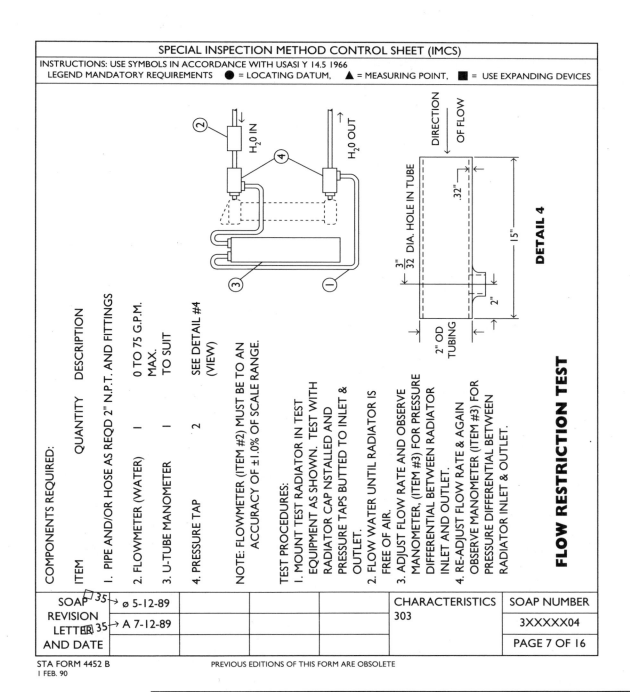

FIGURE 8-11   Special Inspection Method Sheet

Preparation of Inspection Instructions

In a small company, instructions may be prepared by inspectors or supervisors. As the company grows or the products become more complex, the development of these procedures is usually performed by a separate section of the inspection/quality department.

Certain requirements must be considered before the preparer assignment is made. These individuals should be aware of the organization structure, especially the production and inspection stations. When the inspection instruction is to be used for the acceptance of the item, the preparers should be knowledgeable of the product's function. This is essential in order to determine the importance to the user of each characteristic. When the preparers are not fully informed about the product use, the project engineers should be consulted. When the inspection instruction is for the in-process inspection of the product, it is essential that the preparers be knowledgeable of the subsequent production and assembly operations. Accordingly, coordination with manufacturing engineering personnel is needed to provide the necessary background information.

It may be advantageous for the preparers to develop a chart depicting the flow of the product through production and inspection areas. Inspection and production points are identified on the charts, including reference to any production tooling which may be utilized as a medium of inspection.

It is desirable that inspection instructions are prepared well in advance of the start of production, so that the appropriate measuring devices and inspection facilities are available and so that the necessary efforts of production and manufacturing engineering personnel can be coordinated.

Inspection instruction preparers must be aware of the basic purposes of the instruction. This knowledge includes the realization that, in order for inspectors to properly perform their functions, they must be provided with the necessary product characteristics, acceptance criteria, and facilities. It must be understood that general instructions are inadequate in defining the operation to be performed. Thus, the preparers must break down the drawing or specification requirements into specific identifiable characteristics, each containing a precise criterion of acceptability.

It is recommended that the inspection/quality engineers, prior to the start of the production program, review each drawing and specification with the project and the manufacturing engineers, to establish the order of importance, the production location, and the method of manufacture for each characteristic. Based upon the results of the review, the inspection/quality engineers should classify each element to be inspected, by assigning to the characteristic an AQL number on the inspection instruction. See Chapter 9 for more detailed information concerning this classification.

When the item to be inspected is relatively large, such as a major assembly, the selected characteristics to be examined at a specific station should be listed in a sequential manner in accordance with the location of the characteristic on the item.

COORDINATION OF INSPECTION INSTRUCTION DOCUMENTS

Whenever possible, coordinate the inspection instruction with other documents in use at the production facility. Frequently, documents such as production control travelers and manufacturing operation sheets, provide space for the incorporation of inspection information. A problem with using coordinated documents is the necessity of reviewing all subsequent changes with the applicable personnel of the other departments.

Another method in use by some companies is to combine the inspection record for the item with the applicable inspection instruction. See Figure 8-12.

REVIEW OF INSTRUCTIONS BY USING PERSONNEL

Before the release of the instructions, the inspection/quality engineers should discuss any unique details with the applicable inspection and production personnel. This is particularly important when the inspection instruction contains characteristics that are not defined on the drawing or specification.

EXAMPLE

The inspection instruction for an electronic assembly required a visual examination of the orientation of each component installed into the assembly. The acceptability criterion required all components to be assembled in a parallel manner and their tolerance code markings to be easily visible.

Shortly after the instruction was released, and the initial assemblies examined, the manufacturing engineer stormed into the inspection engineer's office and voiced strong objections to the orientation requirements. It appeared that the manufacturing engineer had designed a special component insertion machine at considerable cost, and that, since there was no specification or drawing requirement for special component orientation, the machine designer had not considered this characteristic. The manufacturing engineer noted that the standard was probably desirable, and could have been easily introduced into the machine, had he been consulted in a timely manner. At present, changing the equipment to meet the new requirement would necessitate an expensive and time-consuming redesign. As a result, the inspection engineer found it necessary to postpone the implementation of the desirable workmanship attribute to a later period.

Distribution and Control

When the procedures and instructions have been completed and approved, they are distributed to the applicable project and area personnel for information and use. The distributing agency should maintain a record of the recipients so that they can be provided with any subsequent revisions.

Periodic Reviews

The preparing personnel are generally provided with information concerning the quality history of the product during subsequent fabrication, as-

INSPECTION INSTRUCTION AND QUALITY RECORD SHEET

P/N REV. OR ENC		VENDOR/MFG. DEPT.			DISPOSITION/DATE	
NOMENCLATURE		PO/LOT NO.	DATE	QPL NO.	SUBJECT	
JOB NO.	QUANTITY	PO NOTES			SUBJECT	
SAMPLE SIZE	MAJOR	MINOR A.	MINOR B.	CONTROL	DR NO.	

SEC NO.	CHARACTERISTIC	AQL	ZONE	INSPECTION/METHOD	ACC	REJECT

SQAP REQUIREMENT
FORM 0700.1   CUSTOMER IDENT. _____ DATE _____

FIGURE 8-12 Combined Inspection Instructions and Record

sembly, and test, and its performance in the field. This information is used to enable the inspection/quality engineers to adjust the degree of inspection.

Procedures are developed which require a periodic review to ensure that the procedures and instructions are current and applicable. In many companies, the procedures of the inspection/quality manual are reviewed, at a minimum, on an annual basis.

Audit

While the procedures and instructions are provided to users, there is no assurance that they are being implemented, or even understood. By performing periodic audits, a determination can be made as to their degree of implementation. These audits may, at times, reveal that the recipients are not cognizant of the specific requirements relative to their functions, or that they do not entirely agree with the contents. The audit information can be utilized to make the necessary adjustments to the procedures to reflect operating conditions, or to initiate the corrective actions necessary to insure implementation. See Chapter 21 for additional details concerning the audit program.

CHAPTER NINE

Points of Inspection

IN-PROCESS INSPECTION STATIONS

The points of in-process inspections are usually determined by inspection planners. This is accomplished prior to instruction preparation, and after coordination with manufacturing engineering. Providing information about the locations and sequences of production stations, the methods of manufacture, and the tools and fixtures to be used is the responsibility of manufacturing engineering.

Some companies, in the interests of economy, have an established procedure for in-process inspections. They are performed at the last production point at which the characteristics are available for proper examination. Other companies believe that it is more effective if inspections are done at the station closest to the production stage. This provides early opportunities to detect nonconformances, and sets the stage for early corrective actions. Both concepts, if utilized judiciously, have merit.

Some companies have their in-process inspections, at the outset, conducted at the earliest inspection station, and subsequently, at later stages of the production cycle. This approach is usually implemented when a new product is initially fabricated, or when no prior quality history is available. When the production process has reached a level of stability and little or no nonconformances have been detected, the point of inspection is generally moved to a later station in the production cycle. Companies utilizing statistical controls, can easily determine the stability of the process and make any necessary adjustments with confidence.

Under usual conditions, inspection stations are normally located in the following areas, as applicable. See Figure 9-1 for a typical inspection station chart.

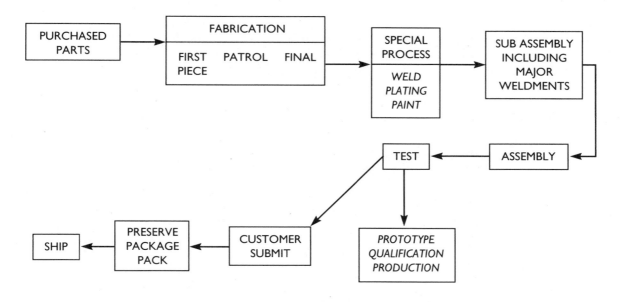

FIGURE 9-1 Inspection Stations

- Receiving inspection
- First piece inspection
- Patrol (roving) inspection
- Toll gate piece parts inspection
- Assembly inspection
- Special process inspection
- Nondestructive testing
- Final testing
- Final inspection
- Preparation for shipment inspection

Receiving Inspection

Stations for the inspection of purchased supplies are at or near receiving areas. This insures that all material is routed through the receiving inspection areas before being moved into manufacturing or stores locations.

In some companies, the receiving inspection procedure is not followed for certain nonproduction items, such as furniture, office supplies, maintenance equipment, tools and fixtures, sundries, and the like. This may lead to some problems. The material handlers often become confused over material identification which is not to be routed to inspection. Consequently, supplies which require inspection may, at times, be transported to the production or stores areas without examination. To overcome this potential problem, some companies require that all materials, regardless of their nature, be routed through the receiving inspection station.

Another reason for this position, is based upon the realization that all supplier material is of value and cost to the company. Consequently, it is not remiss for some determination to be made relative to their compliance to the purchase order requirements. The degree of inspection of this material is generally minimal, often restricted to identification, count, several visual characteristics, and a determination of the presence of handling or environmental damage.

In multiplant companies, where one plant produces supplies for use by another plant of the same company, a procedure which eliminates duplicated inspection efforts of the sending plant may be used. In these companies, the material is routed through the receiving inspection station at the receiving plant. The inspection is usually restricted to the identification of the material against the shipping document, count, presence of in-transit damage, and evidence of prior inspection by appropriate personnel of the sending plant. The latter determination is made by assuring that a move tag, bearing the acceptance stamp of a sending plant's inspector, is present with the shipment. At times, a problem may arise due to the inadvertent removal of the tag during transit. This can be overcome by the prior receipt, by mail, of a duplicate copy of the inspection tag.

At times, it may be necessary for material to be routed to a location other than the receiving inspection station. This applies to heavy or bulky products, such as castings, bar stock, and sheet metal. This material is often received at a loading station close to the applicable material stores location. When a receiving inspector is not available at that location, a procedure is used which authorizes the receiving personnel, after identifying the material, to attach a hold tag to the lot, which is then moved into the stores areas. This tag indicates that the material had not yet been inspected. The receiving personnel or stores clerk subsequently presents the shipping documents to the inspectors at the receiving inspection station, who then visit the pertinent stores area and perform the required inspections. The hold tag is removed and the inspection move tag attached. In some companies, a patrol inspector visits the pertinent stores areas at periodic intervals to perform the required inspections.

In a number of companies, some inspection is performed, by the receiving personnel, upon the receipt of the purchased supplies. This inspection is generally restricted to a visual review for material identification against the shipping documents, or as specified on the purchase order, count, condition of the shipping containers or boxes, and the presence of the shipping documents as noted on the purchase order, such as certificates of compliance, test data, evidence of customer inspection at source and so on. Then the shipping documents are suitably noted with the results of the inspection, and transported, with the material, to the receiving inspection station. Any nonconformances detected by the receiving personnel are processed in accordance with company procedures.

At times, the receiving inspection station does not have the required capabilities to perform all of the specified inspections. In those instances, the required sample of the product is selected and transported to the applicable in-house inspection areas. The balance of the lot is held in the receiving inspection station pending the completion of this inspection. The results of the in-house inspections are then combined with those performed by the receiving inspection personnel, and the material routed to the appropriate area.

Upon completion of all the required inspections, records are prepared, and the material, with the pertinent inspection move tags, are routed to the designated production, assembly, or stores areas. Nonconforming material is suitably identified and located in a hold area, apart from the other material, for routing to the designated materials review area for disposition. See Chapter 16 for a discussion of nonconforming material processing.

First Piece Inspection

Many companies perform a first piece or setup inspection when each manufacturing operation is completed. In some companies, after the operation has been set up, and the first piece inspected by the setup personnel, a number of additional pieces are then produced, which are checked by the inspection personnel. This first piece inspection is performed to assure that the setup has been properly performed, and that the operator has not disturbed the original setup position. Frequently, subsequent parts production is delayed until the first piece inspection has been successfully performed.

This holdup often presents a problem by causing delays in the production operation. This is particularly evident when the inspection takes longer than the actual production operation. For example, an operation may require that holes be punched in a piece of sheet metal. The production operation for each part usually takes a few seconds. However, the determination, by the inspector, of the size and location of each punched hole could take several minutes. In the interim, the operator must wait.

This problem may be alleviated in a number of ways. The operator could be assigned several machines, allowing production on a second machine while awaiting the inspection results from the first. Production could also be allowed to continue until the first piece inspection has been completed. Then appropriate action could be taken on the balance of the lot if a nonconformance is detected.

But most importantly, the need for a first piece inspection should be evaluated. Tooling as a medium of inspection should be considered. If it can be determined that tooling control of the product dimensions are adequate, periodic qualification of the tooling in lieu of actual inspection may suffice. Thus, the tool in the dye punch example is inspected before the start of production. Then a frequency of reinspection is assigned, based upon the number of pieces to be produced with the tool. At the end of the production of a specified quantity of parts, the tool, or the parts produced from the tool, can be reinspected for controlling characteristics. This method not only eliminates the need for the first piece inspection, but also negates the requirement for subsequent lot by lot inspection.

The same consideration can be given to a set of drilled holes, where the location of each hole is controlled by a rigid drill fixture. The hole location remains constant during the fabrication of an appreciable number of parts. The fixture, after its initial qualification, can be requalified at scheduled intervals based upon a predetermined number of pieces produced.

In this situation, first piece inspection is restricted to the assurance that the proper qualified fixture is being used, and that there are no machine chips or other material underneath the fixture which could prevent the proper seating of the part. At times, it may be necessary to inspect several control holes to verify the proper product seating.

Production operators can perform the inspection of the first piece as well as a sample of the subsequently produced parts. These pieces are kept separated from the balance of the lot, and the production continued. Subsequently, the patrol inspector reviews sample characteristics of the inspected pieces. If the inspector's results indicate nonconformance, all pieces produced subsequent to the first piece production inspection are returned to the production operator for a 100 percent inspection of the nonconforming characteristics. If the inspector's results indicate conformance, the lot is permitted to continue through the production cycle.

This method is particularly important in overcoming accusations directed at the patrol inspector, when nonconforming parts are found. This method emphasizes the operator's responsibility to produce a conforming part.

It must be emphasized that first piece inspection is rarely valid in predicting the conformance of the balance of the lot. Conformity can only be assured when the production variables are consistent and known, and the operator's actions do not materially affect the quality of the produced characteristics. This generally occurs when the operation depends almost entirely upon the tool or fixture or is essentially computer controlled. Here too, the location of the part on the machine and the configuration of the part before the machining operation can affect the outcome, unless the design of the fixture or the computer program has taken these features into consideration.

However, first piece inspection does have some merit, provided the limitations of its results are considered. This inspection establishes that the setup is correct, and that the machine and operator can produce a conforming part, at least once. If the first piece inspection proves otherwise, corrective action can be taken before nonconforming products are made in quantity.

It is for this reason that some companies utilize a qualification or first article procedure, which provides for the inspection of a completed first part produced or procured at the start of production of each project or contract. The inspector performs a complete inspection of all the product characteristics. It must be emphasized that the results of this inspection do not provide assurance of the continued production of conforming parts. However, failure to provide conforming product highlights not only a possible problem in the production operation, but also some inadequacies in the drawing which may prevent production to the specified tolerances.

Patrol (Roving) Inspection

Patrol inspection is conducted by quality assurance personnel roaming around a production area and performing inspections of manufacturing operations. As noted, this patrol inspector may perform first piece inspections. Another function is the inspection, at the machine, before the entire lot has been completed, of a sample of the parts, for the characteristic(s) which have been fabricated at that operation. By this inspection, the presence of nonconforming product can be detected before the lot has been completed, thus minimizing additional nonconforming part production. Another operation of the patrol inspector has been discussed before; that is, the verification of the adequacy of the production operator's inspection. At other times, patrol inspection may be needed when the product is too bulky or too large to permit its movement to the inspection station. The patrol inspector may work at the machine or have an inspection bench in the production area.

When a process is found to be fairly stable, the sample inspection results may be counted into that of the final inspection. The results of the in-process inspections are recorded on the production traveler, a document which accompanies the lot through the production cycle, and shows the progress of the parts fabrication. When the completed lot is submitted for the final piece parts inspection, the number of pieces examined for that characteristic at the final station may be reduced by the number of pieces examined in-process.

At times, the results of the in-process inspection can not be used in reducing the sample size at the final inspection operation. This occurs when the lot is split into a number of sublots during the production run. This split lot occurs when a portion of the lot is manufactured at the next production sequence prior to the completion of the entire lot at the previous operation. However, this problem can be alleviated through the preparation of a split lot traveler, which denotes the quantity split off from the initial lot. At that time, the travelers for the initial and the split lots are brought, by the production personnel, to the inspector. The inspector notes the number of pieces examined on the original lot. Thus the final inspector can use this information to reduce the number of pieces sampled at the final lot inspection.

Another function of the patrol inspector, is determining the stability of in-process quality. The inspection results are posted on control charts in the production areas, providing indication, in a timely manner, when the process is approaching an out-of-control point. This will permit the adjustment of the process before nonconforming parts are produced. These charts are sometimes posted by the production operators when they perform the in-process inspection of their products.

<table>
<tr><td>

EXAMPLE
</td><td>

To avoid duplicating inspection performed by production personnel and still provide an independent determination of the reliability of their inspection results, one company undertook the following program.
</td></tr>
</table>

Initially, this company had production operators perform in-process inspections in the machining areas. Final piece part inspection was performed on each lot by members of the inspection department. This final inspection often caused major delays, since, at the final inspection station, all the piece part characteristics were inspected in accordance with the specified sampling plans. Since many of the parts inspected were complex and contained a large number of characteristics, the inspection, at times, took a considerable length of time. This delay caused the final inspectors to be constantly harassed by production and production control personnel.

The revised procedure called for the patrol inspector to select samples of parts previously inspected by production operators. Results of patrol inspection were recorded on the production traveler, at the applicable operation location. At the final piece parts station, the inspectors did not reexamine the items in the lot, but merely reviewed the traveler to verify that the entries reflecting the completion of the production and inspection of each characteristic were present.

The results of these verifications were analyzed by the inspection engineer, and rated in accordance with a predetermined plan. When the analysis reflected an out-of-control condition, the production operators were required to perform subsequent in-process inspections to a tightened sampling plan. When analyses of subsequent production-inspected lots continued to reveal inadequate results, the production operator was subjected to a retraining program before being permitted to continue the performance of in-process inspections. This procedure emphasized the responsibility of the production department to assure the fabrication of conforming products.

To insure adequate outgoing quality levels of the products in question, the quality inspectors at the final inspection station performed a sampling of those nonconforming characteristics revealed by the patrol inspection verification records. Before the new procedure was incorporated, the quality level, as determined by the inspection department's earlier inspection records, had to have attained an acceptable level.

Toll Gate Inspection

Toll gate inspection requires that production material is not to be moved to the next operation, production station, or stores area, until it has been subjected to the specified inspections/tests.

This inspection is usually performed on a lot-by-lot basis and is conducted at a designated inspection area within the production facilities. The lot, unless the material is too heavy or bulky, is transported to the inspection station. At times, the lot may be moved to a specifically designated location within the production area. At that point, the inspector selects the specified number of sample pieces from the lot, and performs the required inspections.

In the chemical process industries, product samples are selected from the production batch and brought to the analytical laboratory for analysis prior to disposition of the batch.

Toll gate inspections are generally conducted at the following points of production.

- Upon completion of all fabrication operations

- Before completion of irreversible, expensive operations

- Before completion of characteristics which cannot be easily inspected at a subsequent station

- When the previous inspections reveal an out-of-control condition

- Before movement to another manufacturing department, assembly, or stores area

- Before packaging and shipment to another plant or to the customer

- Before submission to a customer's representative, or to the company's inspection/quality personnel, for acceptance inspection

- After rework or repair of a previously rejected part or lot

- In an assembly station at selected inspection points or at other production stations which are conveyorized

The results of the inspections are recorded on the record sheet, and the lot is identified with an acceptance move tag (see Figure 9-2). Some companies utilize colored move tags to designate the nature of the inspected lots, such as semifinished, raw material, and finished parts.

Upon inspection completion, the accepted lot is moved to a designated area in, or adjacent to, the inspection station, for transportation to the next manufacturing, assembly, shipping, or stores area. If the lot is rejected, it is identified by a special tag, and moved to a segregated area for transportation to the designated materials review area, for the evaluation of the discrepancy and disposition by the members of the materials review board (see Chapter 16).

The disadvantage of toll gate inspection is largely due to the fact that the production lot must be held up pending the completion of the inspection operation. This may also result in congestion at the inspection station with material awaiting examination. Accordingly, provisions should be made to provide for temporary storage. See Chapter 25 for additional information about planning inspection facilities. In addition, the production planning phase should take into consideration the inspection time as it affects the production cycle.

MOVE TICKET			
JOB NO.	PURCHASE ORDER NO.	PART NO.	REV.
LOT QUANTITY	MOVE FROM	MOVE TO	
INSPECTOR	DATE	CUSTOMER	DATE

FIGURE 9-2 Acceptance Move Tag

Assembly Inspection

In assembly or progressive manufacture using conveyor lines, toll gate inspection is generally performed at the completion of each operation and before the equipment is moved to the next production station. To insure that material is presented at the appropriate points of inspection, procedures are developed for the applicable production, assembly, and inspection personnel. The most effective method of information dissemination is through assembly or production flowcharts. These portray the flow of material through the production and inspection processes. This is done by indicating, at the appropriate location of the chart, each production and inspection/test station. A notation may be made on the chart to specify the inspection procedure or refer to the procedure by its number.

At each inspection station, special provisions must be made for the inspection, subsequent rework, and reinspection operations to be performed without the assembly or conveyor lines being delayed. This is done by allocating space on the line, equivalent to several stations. Where adequate space cannot be provided, arrangements should be made for the rework and reinspection operations to be performed at off-line stations, located parallel, or adjacent to the production line. After rework and reinspection, the material is returned to the production line at the appropriate station. Production planning should take into consideration the time and space requirements for these operations.

At some companies, procedures are available permitting the continuation of the assembly or conveyor line prior to rework and reinspection. This requires the concurrence of the inspection supervisor. The records and product should be suitably identified to assure that rework and reinspection are subsequently performed. It is important that the affected characteristics are easily available at the later stations for those operations.

To minimize the delay caused by toll gate inspection, it is important that, during the inspection planning operation, special emphasis is given by the planner, to substitute, whenever possible, audit inspection for the lot-by-lot production toll gate inspections. This audit inspection provides for the examination of product or process at random time intervals without holding up the production operation.

Special Process Stations

These are used to inspect special product characteristics such as painted surfaces, weldments, and plated parts. These characteristics require a review of the operation, in addition to the examination of the product, to determine the quality of the characteristics. At these stations, a sample from the processed lot is submitted for the specified examination. In addition, the patrol inspector audits the special process areas. The special process stations generally maintain the inspection and audit records and the workmanship and test specimens.

E X A M P L E

At periodic intervals, the examination of the painting process may include a review of the cleaning and rinsing tanks for proper temperature, evidence of the scheduled solution analyses, and use of the specified immersion times. In addition, reviews are made, on the paint lines, for the implementation of the proper sequence of operations, types of pretreatment and prime coats, surface preparation, the number and layers of prime and final coats, and the application of the proper drying times between layers. Samples of the various layers are generally evaluated by the processing of a sample test plate through the paint line and subsequently submitting this plate to adhesion, thickness and, at times, salt spray tests. The painted surfaces are also examined for their appearance in accordance with a paint inspection checklist.

E X A M P L E

During weld inspection, the patrol inspector examines the use of the proper welding rods, specified feeds, and speeds of the welding machines, and the use of the required amperage and voltage. The audit includes a review of the implementation of the proper sequence of the welding operations in accordance with the appropriate, approved procedures. Evidence of the qualification of the welder and the machine, and performance of the scheduled preparation and testing of the weld specimens, are also determined on a periodic basis. The weld surfaces are also examined against a weld inspection checklist and workmanship sample for the various visual attributes.

Nondestructive Examination Stations

Tests performed at these specially equipped stations include such examinations as radiographic, liquid penetrant, ultrasonic, and similar nondestructive tests. Here too, samples of the lot to be inspected are subjected to the appropriate examinations. Large items are routed to the test equipment.

Certain tests, such as radiography, must be conducted in enclosed or isolated areas, to prevent the exposure of personnel to the effects of the x-rays. In one company, where such an enclosed area was not available, radiographic inspection had to be conducted during shifts where the number of personnel in the area was at a minimum. In those cases, the test area was cordoned off, and special signal horns and flashing lights were utilized to warn the personnel to stay away from the test site while it was being operated.

Records of the inspection, including x-ray film as well as the appropriate nondestructive test standards, are kept at these stations.

Test Stations

These stations are utilized for in-process and final product testing. The final test stations are usually located away from the fabrication areas, in specially designated test bays or test tracks. Prototype and qualification tests are usually performed under the cognizance of the engineering department. The inspection/quality personnel often monitor these tests. Since they are often quite lengthy, the use of production test facilities would be uneconomical. Consequently they are performed at engineering or customer test sites.

Final Inspection Stations

These stations are utilized for the final inspection of the parts and equipment prior to presentation to the customer's representative or the company's inspection/quality control personnel. At these stations, the inspection records and/or production travelers are reviewed to insure the completion of all production, inspection/test, rework, and reinspection operations. Some visual inspection of the equipment is conducted for evidence of handling or environmental damage. When a company has a configuration control program, the verification of the as-built configuration of the equipment is performed at the final inspection station. See Chapter 10.

When required, the parts and equipment are submitted to the customer's representative after the company's final inspection. Any necessary rework is performed on site, whenever possible. Otherwise the equipment is moved to the appropriate manufacturing station for the necessary rework. Reinspection is usually performed at the rework station. Evidence of the rework and reinspection is recorded on the appropriate documentation and transmitted to the final inspector. Records of the company's and customer's final inspection are maintained at the final inspection station.

Preparation For Shipping Inspection Station

Usually there is at least one station in the shipping area where preparation for shipment inspections are done. These inspections include a review of the cleaning, sealing, labeling, and packaging of the parts and equipment; audits of the packaging, packing, and crating operations; and parts processing through the various prepackaging steps.

At the final packing stations, the shipping inspector usually reviews the shipping documents for the incorporation of the appropriate information.

This includes the contents of the boxes listing and the shipping destination. The inspector verifies the availability of specified operating and maintenance manuals and peripheral equipment such as spare parts and tools, as noted on the shipping documents. A review is also made for the appropriate marking on the boxes and crates. On carload shipments, the inspector reviews the loading and blocking operations on the carrier.

When the material is to be transported to another plant of the company's organization, the shipping inspector attaches an acceptance tag to the material. This identifies the material and contains the inspector's acceptance stamp.

Prior to the preparation for shipment inspection, the examiner insures that the documentation accompanying the equipment and parts contains evidence of the company's final technical inspection and that all rework and reinspection operations have been performed.

When a customer's representative is resident at the plant, the shipping inspector may be required to present the packaged or crated parts and equipment for the customer's inspection. At that point the shipping inspector may also present the required documentation for indication of customer acceptance. Whether the shipping documents require evidence of customer's acceptance or not, it is important that an indication of the acceptance by the company's inspection/quality department is included with the shipment.

Many companies experience considerable problems when it is necessary to return rejected subcontracted material to the supplier for repair or replacement. These companies often spend little time or effort preparing those products for shipment. This often results in damaged material arriving at the supplier's facilities. At times, the shipping damage incurred far exceeds the cost to repair the original deficiency. Accordingly, some companies protect material to insure that it arrives at its destination undamaged. In those companies the shipping inspector assures the adequacy of the packaging and packing of the subcontractor's supplies.

AMOUNT OF INSPECTION

Introduction

After the inspection planner has identified the characteristics to be examined (see Chapter 8), the amount of inspection of each characteristic must be determined. If time and cost were not involved, or the production process included self-inspection capabilities, consideration of the degree of inspection would not be needed, since each characteristic of every part could be inspected. At times, when the quality level of the parts must be so that no nonconformances can be tolerated, or the level is expressed in parts per million, determining the degree of inspection for acceptance purposes is also moot, since assurance of attainment of the quality level cannot depend upon the inspection operation, but is based almost entirely on the capability of the manufacturing process. Since inspection does not, in general, add to the quality of the product, the amount of inspection is only second in importance to the capability of the process to consistently provide conforming parts.

However, most products and services do require some degree of inspection to determine their quality level. Hopefully, the process capability at all organizations may some day reach the level of quality to abrogate the need of product inspection for acceptance purposes.

How Much Inspection

During the inspection planner's review, it may be determined that some characteristics do not need lot-by-lot inspection. These are characteristics which are almost completely controlled by the manufacturing process or tooling. For example, once the pattern of a raw casting has been qualified, it can be expected to provide a predetermined number of parts at identical levels of quality. The same is true of characteristics controlled by jigs and fixtures as well as in computer-controlled manufacturing operations.

When using the tool or computer program as a medium of inspection, care must be taken to separate out those characteristics which are not controlled by tool or tape, but which are affected by operator performance or other variables. For example, when using a jig or fixture to determine the location of one drilled hole from another, there is a possibility that the individual unmachined part may vary in configuration to an extent that it will not be properly seated at the appropriate location in the fixture. Similarly, the presence of machining chips under the fixture may also introduce a variable.

This may be partially overcome by the operator or patrol inspector, during the in-process audit of the manufacturing area, checking for the cleanliness of the surface under the fixture, or by the inspection of certain control dimensions on the part, to assure the perpendicularity of the applicable surfaces.

In determining the degree of inspection of the other characteristics, the inspection planner ordinarily confers with the project engineers to determine the importance of the product characteristics on its function or, as noted by Dr. Juran, on its "fitness for use."[1]

The inspection planner also reviews, with the manufacturing engineers, the method of manufacture of the characteristics, including the use of any tools with built-in process controls. The planner also determines, from the manufacturing engineers, the importance of the characteristics to subsequent manufacturing or assembly operations. For example, the squareness of a part may be of little importance in product use, but could have a significant relation to locating the part in the fixture at a subsequent operation.

Attention is initially paid to the contractual requirements. The customer's specification, at times, identifies the characteristics to be inspected or tested.

Most of the time, however, the amount of the product to be inspected is not defined. When it is, the inspection/test instruction must specify these requirements. The instructions for the other characteristics should denote the amount of inspection based upon their degrees of importance. The more important the characteristic, the more inspection is to be performed.

Classification of Characteristics

Once the order of importance has been established, the planner can then prepare the inspection instructions. Characteristics are listed by their order of importance to the product. This listing is frequently referred to as the part's classification of characteristics or C/D.

Selection of the Sampling Plans

There are an infinite number of sampling plans available for purposes of acceptance inspection. However, the administrative costs and problems involved in the implementation of a large number of such plans would not prove cost effective.

Many companies utilize three or four sampling plans corresponding to the three or four groups of characteristics in the standard sampling guides. These companies generally utilize the government specification for sampling, MIL-STD-105 D *Sampling Procedures and Tables For Inspection By Attributes*[2] or ANSI/ASQC Z1.4–1981,[3] as guides. These publications provide three classifications of defects: Critical, Major, and Minor. At times, the Minor classification may be broken down into Minor A and Minor B.

The MIL-STD-105 plan defines the classifications as follows:

CRITICAL DEFECT: A defect which is likely to result in hazardous or unsafe conditions for personnel, or is likely to prevent performance of the tactical function of the major end item of the product.

Characteristics classified as Critical generally require 100 percent inspection.

MAJOR DEFECT: A defect, other than critical, which is likely to result in failure, or reduce materially the useability of the unit of the product for its intended purpose.

MINOR DEFECT: A defect that is not likely to reduce materially the useability of the unit of product for this intended purpose, or is a departure from established standards having little bearing on the effective use or operation of the product.

Minor A and Minor B, when used, may further break down the levels of importance. Thus Minor A defects may have a slight departure from an insignificant dimension. Minor B defects may represent a failure to meet a minor workmanship characteristic.

Some companies use this subclassification as an interim measure when enhancing the workmanship quality of a product. For example, when a visual characteristic is initially incorporated into the inspection criteria, the procedure may stipulate that the first failure to meet the requirement will be classified as a control defect and will not result in product rejection, but emphasize to the manufacturing personnel the presence of the characteristic. Subsequent evidence of nonconformance will, however, result in rejection and the necessity for rework. This procedure is utilized when the workmanship standard has been recently applied and it is considered desirable to allow some time for the manufacturing operation to adjust.

When reviewing the drawing or specification to determine the order of importance of the characteristic, keep in mind that many drawings contain both engineering and manufacturing information. The planner, with the aid of the project engineers, should distinguish between both needs of the characteristics. The engineering requirements affect the useability or fitness for purpose of the product, while the production information is utilized to assist in the fabrication of the product, and may not directly affect the useability of the item.

Some companies do not spend much time reviewing drawings and specifications. They often use a ballpark determination which is based upon the assumption that the tighter the tolerance on the drawing, the more important the characteristic. Accordingly, the classification of characteristics for these companies is often based upon the parts' tolerances. For example, the practice may specify that when a dimension has a tolerance below 0.001 inch, the characteristic is to be classified as a major. When the tolerance is above 0.001 inch, the characteristic is to be classified as a minor. Obviously, this method of analysis for the determination of the level of importance of the characteristic is not very precise, but as an initial estimate, it is often acceptable.

The following is a recommended procedure for the establishment of a classification of characteristics.

The inspection planner assembles all the drawings and specifications applicable to the product before the start of production. After review with the project and manufacturing engineers, the contractually specified characteristics and those judged as critical and major in importance to the function of the product, are first established. All other characteristics are then considered as secondary in importance, resulting in the assignment of a lower degree of inspection.

Then, based upon the knowledge of the manufacturing process, the planners determine the effect of the characteristics on the capability of manufacture and fit in the assembly. Once that is completed, each part characteristic is incorporated into the proper group for sampling purposes. Each group of characteristics is assigned to a sampling plan in accordance with the sampling system, such as MIL-STD-105, and the corresponding amount of inspection per group is established.

See Chapter 24 for additional information concerning sampling inspection.

Adjusting the Degree of Inspection

Once the initial amount of inspection is determined, and the production operation is in effect, a procedure for inspectors to obtain quality information should be outlined. Feedback concerning the product during subsequent fabrication, assembly, testing, and field operations should be obtained. This information is then utilized to adjust the degree of inspection during subsequent examinations.

MIL-STD-105, in addition to providing a set of sampling plans, presents methods for adjusting the amount of sampling inspection. These methods are based on the switching rules utilized as a result of the quality history during subsequent product inspections. More about this in Chapter 24.

Some companies, at the start of production, perform an initial qualification inspection of all characteristics of one part whether produced or procured. This inspection demonstrates, at the outset, that there are no drawing errors affecting the ability to fabricate and assemble the product, as well as the capability of the characteristic to be produced by the specified tooling. Any characteristic found nonconforming is subject to investigation of its process and the implementation of the necessary corrective actions.

The degree of subsequent lot inspection is often affected by the results of this inspection. Thus any characteristic found nonconforming during the qualification inspection may be assigned a tighter degree of inspection for several subsequent lots, until it has been demonstrated that adequate controls have been established during the manufacture of the characteristic.

Companies utilizing a statistical quality control program in their manufacturing operations often utilize the control charts, in lieu of the standard lot-by-lot sampling plans, for acceptance purposes after attainment of statistical process control.

Chapter 24 includes descriptions of the uses of the various other sampling plans, such as variables, multiple and zero acceptance, and the use of control charts for acceptance inspection.

REFERENCES

1. Juran, J. M., & Frank M. Gryna Jr. *Quality Planning and Analysis.* New York: McGraw Hill, 1970, pp. 1–3.

2. *MIL-STD-105D. Sampling Inspection and Tables for Attributes Inspection.* Washington DC: US Government Printing Office, Superintendent of Documents.

3. *ANSI/ASQC Z1.4–1981. Sampling Procedures and Tables for Inspection by Attributes.* Milwaukee, WI: ASQC Quality Press, 1981.

CHAPTER TEN

Engineering Design, Drawings, and Specifications: Preparation and Control

INTRODUCTION

In order to assure appropriate control over the processing of engineering designs, preparation of drawings and specifications, and implementation of their subsequent changes, each company must develop a documented set of procedures identifying the elements of control and methods of implementation. This program depends, to a significant extent, on the size of the company, its product mix, and whether it is engaged in design and development operations, or merely in providing its products and services to customers' drawings and specifications.

Each company should develop its own procedures for the preparation and control of engineering drawings and specifications. However, to assure adequate control, the following elements should be considered.

- Drawing preparation
  —Review and coordination, with the affected departments, and, when applicable, customers and suppliers
- Distribution
  —Controlled distribution
  —Conversion of drawing information to manufacturing and procurement documentation
  —Implementation of drawing requirements

- Drawing changes
  —Controlled distribution
  —Implementation of changes at specified effectivity
  —Interim change control

- Special requirements (when applicable)
  —Configuration control program
  —Product liability prevention program
  —Reliability/maintainability program

The following discussion presents an example of a typical program many equipment design and fabrication companies use. The terminology and exhibits are examples of those used by several different companies. They are provided to illustrate the various elements under discussion.

PREPARATION

Early in a program requiring the preparation or modification of drawings, the project engineer or program manager should analyze the contractual and product technical requirements, and the need for any special drawing format. This information should be shared with design and drafting personnel. The technical information may be provided in a set of drawings and draft specifications or black boxes for each major assembly. These specifications denote each assembly's inputs and outputs and exterior configuration requirements. Internal design constraints, such as the use of special hardware, parts interchangeability, and other similar requirements, may also be included in these specifications.

The drafting personnel should then prepare the required drawings, specifications, and drawing formats based on the project engineers' instructions, the company's drafting standards, and the appropriate contractual requirements.

DRAWING REVIEW

The completed drawings should be reviewed by drafting supervisors for conformance to the engineering and drafting standards and the project engineers' instructions. The project engineers should also examine the drawings for technical adequacy and conformance to contractual or company standard technical requirements. In some companies, inspectors or inspection engineers are assigned to review the drawings for conformance, in format, to the drafting and engineering standards. See Figure 10-1 for an example of a checklist for this inspection.

Contract No. _____
Applicable Specifications: _____
_____
_____
_____
_____

Authorized _____ Date _____ Date Effective _____ Document
Approved _____ Date _____ Page___of___

COMPREHENSIVE CHECKLIST AND GUIDE FOR ENGINEERING DATA
Prepared in accordance with MIL-STD-100A

Description

1. <u>Drawing Practices</u>

   a.   Third angle orthographic projection shall be standard for engineering drawings.
        Isometric and perspective may be used where particular advantage exists.

   b.   One view drawings are permissible for objects that are cylindrical, spherical, hexagonal,
        square, rctangular, etc., or objects where one view and such features as thickness or
        length, stated as a note or dimension can completely define the object.

   c.   Partial views of symmetrical objects are permissible and may be represented by half
        views. Half views shall extend slightly beyond line of symmetry and terminate with a
        break line.

   d.   Auxiliary views not projected directly shall be clearly marked to indicate the location
        and direction from which viewed.

   e.   Detail views to show a part of the drawing in the same plane and in the same
        arrangement, but in greater detail and larger scale if necessary. Detail shall be suitably
        identified.

   f.   Avoid crowding of views. Provide ample space between views for dimensions and
        notes.

   g.   Intentionally exaggerate features too small to be drawn to scale.

   h.   Drawings need show only the information necessary to clearly delineate the part.
        Excessive illustration of superfluous details shall be avoided, such as rows of bolts, long
        constant section lines, repetition of holes, features in a bolt circle, repetition of slots,
        splines, gears, screws, or any other details of repetitious nature.

FIGURE 10-1   Checklist and Guide for Engineering Data

SIZE	DRAWING NO.		SHEETS	TITLE		
NEXT ASSY	INITIAL RELASE NO.	DATE	DRAWN	DATE	CHECKED	DATE
	APROVED PER ETCLOI		DATE	CORRECTIVE ACTION — CA—		
	REVISION	ECN	DATE-OUT	DATE-IN	WITHDRAWN	ECN APPROVED

DRAWING INSPECTION RECORD ETCLO2

ITEM	CA	ITEM	CA	ITEM	CA	ITEM	CA	ITEM	CA	ITEM	CA	ITEM	CA	ITEM	CA	ITEM	CA	ITEM	CA
1a		4c		6g		6w		8b		11c		16a		18g		20b			
1b		4d		6h		6x		9a		12		16b		18h		20c			
1c		4e		6j		6y		9b		13a		16c		18j		21			
1d		4f		6k		7a		9c		13b		17a		19a		22			
1e		4g		6l		7b		9d		13c		17b		19b		23			
1f		5a		6m		7c		9e		14a		17c		19c		24			
1g		5b		6n		7d		9f		14b		17d		19d		25			
1k		6a		6p		7e		9g		14c		18a		19e		26			
1l		6b		6r		7f		10a		14d		18b		19f		27			
2		6c		6s		7g		10b		14e		18c		19g		28a			
3		6d		6t		7h		10c		14f		18d		19h		28b			
4a		6e		6u		7j		11a		14g		18e		19j		29			
4b		6f		6v		8a		11b		15		18f		20a					

FIGURE 10-1   Continued

For companies that have a reliability engineering program, it is at this time that the drawings should be reviewed for the incorporation of the company's standard or derated components and other factors pertinent to system reliability.

Some companies conduct a system of design and drawing reviews at the various stages of design and development.

EXAMPLE

Upon receipt of the completed drawings from the drafting department, the project engineer or program manager may call for a drawing review meeting. Attendees, as applicable, include personnel from engineering, purchasing, manufacturing engineering, manufacturing, customer service, inspection/quality engineering, and other related departments.

Manufacturing engineering reviews the drawings for manufacturing capability, special tooling, and process control needs. Consideration is also given to past problem areas encountered during the manufacture of the same or similar items.

Purchasing reviews the drawings for unique or unduly restrictive requirements which may impact upon the cost or delivery of the procured items.

Inspection/quality engineering reviews the drawings for special inspection, gaging, and process control requirements, conformance to contractual and company workmanship standards, and unique or costly inspection/quality assurance provisions. Consideration is usually given to those characteristics which had resulted in high defect rates, encountered in this or similar components in the past. Personnel from the other departments review the drawings for elements pertinent to their operations.

The reviewing personnel, generally, note their findings on a drawing review form provided to the project engineer. Any changes or recommendations which are not subsequently incorporated in the drawings are resolved between the project engineer and the reviewing personnel.

Upon completion of the review, the project engineer indicates approval in the designated location of the drawings, and authorizes their distribution by the drafting department in accordance with the company's standard practices.

In some companies, the review and approval of the drawings is part of the company's configuration control program, and is usually performed by the configuration control board. More information concerning this operation is detailed later in this chapter.

When drawings require a format in accordance with contractual requirements, the project engineer, or designated drawing inspector, usually insures compliance with these requirements.

DISTRIBUTION

Prior to the release of the drawings, the project engineer prepares a list of recipients. This is maintained in the issuing agency's file, in order to insure that subsequent drawing changes are provided to all recipients.

On occasion, a copy of a drawing may be requested by personnel other than those on the official distribution list. Unless provisions are made to have these drawings returned upon completion of their use, they are stamped UNCONTROLLED COPY. Drawings bearing this notation cannot be utilized for manufacturing, procurement, or inspection purposes, since no provisions are made to provide subsequent updates.

Normally, an engineering release form (ER) is issued with the drawings (see Figure 10-2). This ER usually contains a list of the attached drawings, their configuration level (revision number or letter), the job number, and other pertinent information. Generally, the entire package of drawings for the program is released at one time. However, at times, in order to meet production schedules, it may be necessary to release, in advance of the rest of the package, certain drawings for the long lead time operations, such as those for castings, forgings, and raw materials.

Drawing recipients should be required to review the package for the presence of all the drawings at the appropriate configuration level, as listed on the ER. Some companies require that personnel sign a form certifying the receipt of all the drawings listed on the ER. All recipients are responsible for maintaining the drawings at the latest configuration, at the appropriate location in their areas. They then take the following actions.

1. Manufacturing engineering initiates the development and preparation of the appropriate instructions, tooling, and special processes required for product manufacture.

    In some companies, production control retains the drawings until the receipt of the appropriate manufacturing instructions, and the preparation of the manufacturing shop orders or travelers. Then they release everything at the appropriate time in the production schedule. Other companies have the drawings and manufacturing instructions transmitted directly to manufacturing supervisors.

2. Production control, in many companies, prepares the appropriate purchase order requisitions for outside materials or services. These requisitions, after review by project and quality/inspection engineering personnel, are submitted to the purchasing department for action.

3. Purchasing then selects the appropriate source(s) and prepares the purchase orders which are transmitted, with the referenced technical documents, to the designated suppliers.

4. Inspection/quality engineering assures the availability of all special and standard measuring equipment, as well as the standards for use in subsequent calibration of this equipment. In addition, the appropriate inspection instructions are prepared and, together with the applicable drawings, provided to the pertinent inspection stations.

    Some companies maintain a central crib where the inspection instructions, drawings, and measuring equipment are maintained and issued, upon request, to the pertinent personnel.

5. Test engineering prepares the appropriate procedures and provides them to the applicable test station or to the central test crib.

DWG. SIZE	PART NUMBER	REV LET.	NO. PCS. PER UNIT	TITLE	PURCHASE REQ. NO.	REQ'ND BY ENG.	B	M

ENGINEERING RELEASE   **NUMBER:**

☐ EXPERIMENTAL   ☐ PRODUCTION

PROJECT:	GOV. CONT. NO.	NO. OF UNITS AFFECTED:

REMARKS:

— PRINT DISTRIBUTION —

PROD. C.	3	FILE	I
QUAL. C.	2	ACCT. (IBM)	
PUB.	I	PURCHASING	
CUST. SERV.	3	EXP. SHOP	
PROD. C.	3		
QUAL. C.	2	MAT'L CONTROL	B/M BUY
QUAL. C.	I	ENGINEERING	

DEPT.	APPROVED BY	DATE	DEPT.	APPROVED BY	DATE
DRAFTING			ENGINEERING		
MANUFACTURING			U.S. D.O.D. QUAL. CONT.		

DISTRIBUTION DATE:

FIGURE 10-2   Engineering Release Form

When contractually required, the test procedures are transmitted to customer personnel for review or approval. In some companies, the test procedures are controlled and distributed as part of the engineering drawing control program.

Preparation and Release

Requests for drawing changes may be made by engineering, manufacturing, manufacturing engineering, inspection/quality engineering, field service, or customer personnel.

Some companies require that all change requests are prepared on a company engineering change request form (ECR). This identifies the drawing being changed and its current as well as new configuration level. In addition, the name of the requesting department and the details of the change requested are included in the ECR. This request should specifically show which characteristics should be revised and how the changes should be made. The reason for the change is generally included on the ECR, as well as the degree of urgency for implementation of the change(s).

On government contracts, this urgency is expressed by one of two classes of change, as defined in DOD-STD 480.[1]

CLASS I CHANGES: Those which affect the interchangeability, performance, or reliability of the equipment, or logistically supported components or assemblies.

Class I changes generally result in a revision to the drawing number of the affected item(s).

For companies having a product liability prevention program, changes to designated critical or safety-related items are also classified as Class I.

When a company has a configuration control program, all Class I change requests are reviewed by the configuration control board (CCB). After CCB approval, the request is reviewed by the project engineer, or designee, for verification of the need for the change and for any prior customer approval requirement.

CLASS II CHANGES: Those changes which do not affect any of the above parameters.

When a decision to initiate a change has been approved, the project engineer prepares an engineering change notice (ECN) (see Figure 10-3). The ECN notes the following: drawing number; its current and new configuration levels; the affected drawing characteristics; and the actual change to be incorporated. The ECN may also reference all other drawings affected by the change, as well as whether the item is an in-house manufactured part, or one that is procured from an outside source.

One important item that must be noted on the ECN is the required effectivity of the change (serial number, date, or production order number). This determination involves coordination with the appropriate manufacturing engineering, production control, and procurement personnel, relative to the ability to meet the specified point of effectivity. In addition, products which had been manufactured to the former configuration level

DESCRIPTIVE CHANGE – CARD CODE NO.4   NO.

☐ EXPERIMENTAL	☐ CHANGE	☐ DEVIATION
☐ PRODUCTION	☐ VARIATION	☐ CANCELLATION

PROJECT:	GOV. CONT. NUMBER	INCORPORATE W/UNIT NO.

① RFC	② DISP	PART NUMBER	REV LTR	DWG SIZE	PART NAME	BUY	MAKE

(1)

① REASON FOR CHANGE:		REMARKS:
A DRAFTING ERROR	G MANUFACTURING REQUEST	*ALL CHANGES WILL BE CONSIDERED "CLASS II" CHANGES UNLESS INDICATED OTHERWISE IN CHANGE BLOCK ABOVE.
B TYPOGRAPHICAL ERROR	H CUSTOMER REQUEST	
C ENGINEERING ERROR	J FACILITATE ASSEMBLEY	
D MANUFACTURING ERROR	K TO SUIT AVAILABLE TOOLING	
E VENDOR ERROR	L CANCELLATION	
F VENDOR REQUEST	M SPECIFICATION CHANGE	
	N SEE REMARKS	

② DISPOSITION OF MATERIAL: 2 NOT AFFECTED...   4 SCRAP..............
     1 USE UP AS IS..................   3 REWORK............   5 SALVAGE........

PRINT DISTRIBUTION	PROD. C.		FILE		PROD. C.	
	QUAL. C.		ACCOUNTING		QUAL. C.	
	PUBLICATIONS		PURCHASING		PROD. C.	
	CUST. SERVICES		EXPERIMENTAL SHOP		QUAL. C.	
	PROD. C.		MATERIAL CONTROL			
	QUAL. C.		ENGINEERING			

DEPT	APPROVED BY	DATE	DEPT	APPROVED BY	DATE
DRAFTING			MANUFACTURING		
ENGINEERING			U.S. D.O.D. QUALITY CONTROL		
DISTRIBUTION DATE:			SPECIAL DISTRIBUTION:	FORM 2189 REV. "B" - 4/88	

FIGURE 10-3 Engineering Change Notice

may need to be removed from the stores, production, or finished equipment areas or from the field. This must be determined and specified on the ECN.

The revised drawings and ECN are distributed to the personnel on the official distribution list.

All recipients should review the availability of the drawings listed on the ECN, and remove the obsoleted issues from current files and points of use. When the revised drawings are not immediately incorporated, it may be necessary to retain the original drawing issue for use until the specified effectivity point. It is then necessary to note on the superseded drawing that it has been replaced and should be removed at the appropriate time.

Some companies require that the obsoleted drawings be returned to the distributing agency before the receipt of revisions. This, at times, proves to be a problem. Occasionally, the superseded drawings may have been temporarily misplaced and are not immediately available. However, in order to implement the change, the revised drawings must be provided even if the superseded drawing is not available for return. However, if this is done, it is possible that the old drawing may surface at a later date, and be utilized in lieu of the new issue.

To overcome this problem, some companies which do not require the return of old drawings rely upon periodic audits of the affected files or areas of operation.

Implementation of the Change

Manufacturing engineering, upon receipt of the revised drawings, prepares new work instructions, when necessary, and provides copies of these instructions, together with reference to any revised tooling, to production control.

Production control, depending upon the change effectivity and the ECN instructions, reviews the stores areas, and work in process for the obsoleted material. In addition, the availability of any assembled equipment, which may require the replacement of the superseded parts, is also determined. Production control also reviews the equipment records containing the superseded parts which had been shipped and, when necessary, prepares instructions for their modification in the field in accordance with the methods provided by project engineers. Following these actions, production control prepares shop orders providing for the production of the revised parts and, when required, rework or scrap of the superseded parts. The revised drawings, shop orders, and manufacturing instructions are forwarded to the applicable manufacturing stations at the indicated points of effectivity.

Manufacturing implements the changes in accordance with the revised production control shop order, manufacturing instructions, and revised drawings.

Inspection/quality engineering revises the inspection/test instructions and forwards these instructions, and the revised drawings, to the inspection crib or to the applicable inspection station.

When the drawing change is to be implemented at a later date, a problem often arises relative to the processing of the superseded parts through the inspection operation. In some companies, the product is always inspected to the latest revision, regardless of its point of effectivity. When it is not in compliance with the latest drawing, the product is rejected. When the rejected material is subsequently analyzed by the materials review board, the determination is then made relative to the ability to use the part fabricated to the earlier issue (see Chapter 16).

Another approach is for the periodic issuance, by the drafting department, of a computer run of the latest drawing issues and their points of effectivity. Inspectors then refer to this list for a determination of the acceptability of the parts produced in accordance with earlier issues.

Some companies provide an additional control over the implementation of drawing changes. This provides for the inspection/quality engineers to prepare a key characteristic inspection form (KCI) (see Figure 10-4). This form notes the pertinent drawing issue and its point of effectivity, by equipment serial number, when so specified in the ECN. The KCIs are inserted into the final inspection folders of several initial units for which the change is to be implemented. When those units are examined at the final assembly station, the assembly inspector verifies the incorporation of these changes. This inspection is continued for a specified number of units, as noted on the KCI, following the designated serial number effectivity. In addition, some companies have the inspection/quality personnel perform audits immediately prior to the time of effectivity specified on the KCI. These audits of the stores and assembly areas determine the presence of any obsoleted parts. When they are found, actions are taken to remove these parts from all points of current use.

Production control provides the latest drawings to the purchasing department for transmission to the applicable suppliers. The purchase orders are revised to reflect the new drawing issue, and the specified points of effectivity.

DRAWING CHANGE BLOCK

In most companies, the standard practice dictates that each drawing contain provisions for the incorporation, in a drawing change block, of the drawing change information (see Figure 10-5). This section is utilized to denote all the revision levels of the drawing since its initial release, the nature of the change, and the ECN number for each revision. Some companies do not denote the nature of each change, but merely reference the ECN number. The problem with this concept is that, when it is desired to determine the nature of the change, it is necessary to have available the copy of the applicable ECN. In addition, since the drawing does not note the point of effectivity, recourse to the ECN is needed.

ADVANCE/INTERIM CHANGES

At times, it is necessary to make some emergency changes to the drawings on the production floor. The urgency may not allow sufficient time for the standard full review and approval cycle. This need, at times, occurs when a problem develops in the manufacturing area, relative to a drawing error,

KEY CHARACTERISTIC INSTRUCTION

PREPARED BY: _____   KCI NO: _____

DATE: _____   UNIT S/N _____

INSTRUCTION: INSPECT EACH KEY CHARACTERISTIC WHILE IN EFFECT AS INDICATED
BELOW. RECORD NONCONFORMANCE ON VARIANCE SHEET. WHEN
THE AREA OF VERIFICATION IS OTHER THAN ASSEMBLY, E.G. PMI, FAB,
ETC. IT SHALL BE IDENTIFIED IN THE REFERENCE COLUMN FOR EACH
CHARACTERISTIC AS APPLICABLE.

INSPECTION INTERVAL	CHARACTERISTIC	REFERENCE	INSP	DISP

FIGURE 10-4   Key Characteristic Inspection Form

affecting the ability to manufacture a specific characteristic of an item. The project engineer is generally called to the production area, and marks up the change information on the drawing. This provides authorization for the item to be fabricated according to the revised marked-up requirements. Subsequently, the engineer is required to prepare the necessary official

REVISIONS					
NOTICE	ZONE	SYM	DESCRIPTION	DATE	APPROVAL

RELEASE			
NOTICE	DESCRIPTION	DATE	APPROVAL
	RELEASE FOR JOB EXPERIMENTAL		
	RELEASE FOR JOB PRODUCTION		

FIGURE 10-5 Drawing Change Block

change on the drawing's master copy, and, after the receipt of the required approvals, the engineer has the ECN and the revised drawing distributed in accordance with standard procedures.

This procedure has a number of inherent problems. First, it is considered poor practice to have any marked-up, handwritten notations on a drawing, since the tendency would be for others, not authorized individuals, to mark up drawings for whatever reason they may consider necessary. Second, this procedure detracts from the concept of the legality of the official drawing, that is, once issued, it is not to be tampered with. Third, the drawing, marked up by the engineer, may suffice for the manufacturing personnel to proceed with its operation in accordance with the revised requirements; however, when the subsequent inspection is to be performed, the inspector may not be aware of the authorization for the revised requirements. Consequently, the product will be rejected, with the resultant delay. Finally, and most important, the engineer may subsequently forget to make the official drawing change and to release the required ECN. This can cause havoc, particularly when it is found necessary to make another revision to the same drawing affecting another characteristic. To overcome this problem, recourse to the following advance engineering change procedure is recommended.

After the engineer has marked up the drawing with the revised requirements, signed and dated the entry, an advance engineering change notice (AECN) is prepared (see Figure 10-6). The AECN number is then noted on the drawing adjacent to the marked-up change. The AECN shows the applicable drawing number, its current revision level, and the detailed

ADVANCE ENGINEERING CHANGE NOTICE   No. 01407

DWG.No. _____   **REV.** _____   **JOB No.** _____

THE FOLLOWING CHANGE IS REQUESTED ON DWG. INDICATED ABOVE
<u>CHANGE:</u>

DELETE ITEM 15 FROM
F/D AND L/M (ALSO B/M
GROUP 12, SHT 6, LINE 14)

CHANGE NOTE 2 TO PAINT
PER PSN 35-2093

$\frac{1}{4}$ .62
(WAS .69)

ADD NOTE 3:
    3. BREAK ALL SHARP EDEGES .020 MAX.

REASON: *REMARKS:*

[X] DRAFTING ERROR   [ ] CUSTOMER REQUEST
[ ] ENGINEERING ERROR   [X] FACILITATE ASSEMBLY
[ ] MANUFACTURING ERROR   [ ] TO SUIT AVAILABLE TOOLING   FIGURE 9
[ ] MANUFACTURING REQUEST   [ ] SPECIFICATIONS CHANGE
[ ] VENDOR REQUEST   [ ] OTHER (EXPLAIN)

DISPOSITION OF MATERIALS

[ ] USE UP AS IS   [ ] NOT AFFECTED   [X] REWORK   [ ] SCRAP   [ ] SALVAGE

PIECE COST	*TOOLING COST*	*EFFECTIVITY*
[X] NO CHANGE	[X] NO CHANGE	[X] ALL UNITS
[ ] INCREASE	[ ] INCREASE	[ ] UNIT No. ___
[ ] DECREASE	[ ] DECREASE	[ ] EFFECTIVE DAY

APPROX. $ _____ PER UNIT   APPROX. $ _____ PER UNIT
(INCLUDING SCRAP COST OR SALVAGE VALUE)

REQ. BY _____ DEPT. _____ DATE _____   PRINT DIST.

ACTION TAKEN

[ ] APPROVED   PROJ. ENG.: _____ DATE: _____
[ ] DISAPPROVED CH. ENG.: _____ DATE: _____
          AFQCR: _____ DATE: _____

METH.	3	FILE	I
QUAL C.	2	ACCT.	
PUBLICATIONS	I	PURCHASING	BUY/BM
CUST. SERVICES	3	EXPER. SHOP	
METH		PROD. CONTROL	SEPIA B/M
QUAL C.		MATERIAL CONTROL	
QUAL C.		ENGINEERING	

**IMPORTANT: THIS NOTICE IS AUTHORITY FOR ACTION AND MUST BE
ATTACHED TO THE DRAWING OR OTHER SPECIFICATION**

FIGURE 10-6 Advance Engineering Change Notice

change information. Copies of the AECN are distributed to all recipients of the original drawing. The notation ON CHANGE is entered on the drawing's master copy in the drafting file.

When the official change is prepared, the AECN number is referenced in the change block of the drawing adjacent to the subsequent revision number, and the normal distribution is made. Pending the issuance of the revised drawing, no other changes are permitted to be made until the AECN information has been recorded on the drawing.

Until the receipt of the revised drawing and the official ECN, inspection of the part is performed to the original issue of the drawing and the AECN requirements. The inspection record and the subsequent move tag note both the original drawing revision level and the AECN number. To insure that the engineer subsequently processes the official change, the assembly inspector should maintain copies of all AECNs at the final assembly inspection station. When the assembled unit, containing the initial advance change, is given its final inspection, the examiner verifies that the official ECN, and the revised drawing, reflecting the AECN, have been issued. In some companies, the use of the KCI may be incorporated in the procedure.

CONFIGURATION CONTROL

There is frequently a degree of confusion concerning the distinction between an engineering change control and a configuration control program.

An engineering change control program applies to the preparation, distribution, and control of *all* changes to engineering drawings and specifications utilized in the manufacture and procurement of the company-supplied equipment and spares.

A configuration control program applies to the engineering drawing and specification changes relating to *specific* parts and assemblies. This program generally applies to all Class I changes, that is, those changes which affect safety, reliability, performance, or interchangeability of the part or assembly and its logistically supported components and assemblies.

The level at which the configuration is to be controlled is generally specified by the company's program manager or the project engineer. One way in which this configuration level is denoted is by the preparation and distribution of a configuration control log (CCL) (see Figure 10-7). This log is a listing of all the major assemblies, subassemblies, and designated critical or safety-related components, with their drawing numbers and revision levels at the noted configuration level. This CCL is distributed and controlled in accordance with the company's standard engineering drawing control program.

The program manager or project engineer usually organizes a configuration control board for each product for which configuration control is to be implemented, and appoints a configuration control manager, who acts as the CCB chairperson. Some companies, who implement a configuration control program for all their products, generally provide a single company CCB.

CONTRACT: DAAA09-78-C-2006				CONFIGURATION CHANGE LOG
M 39 CARRIAGE ASSEMBLY - SERIAL NO: REV:				
PART NUMBER	REV. LEVEL	AS BUILT REV. LEVEL	SERIAL NUMBER	REMARKS
F12007700				ELEVATING SCREWS
F12009054				ELEVATING GEARBOX ASSY
F12008010				ACTUATOR ASSY
F12009040				EQUILIBRATOR
F12008099				CLUTCH ASSY
K12008100				TOP CARRIAGE ASSY
F12008200				CRADLE ASSY
F12008230				GEAR BOX ASSY
F12008250				RING GEAR BEARING
K12008300				BOTTOM CARRIAGE ASSY
F12008302				AXLE
K12008450				TRAVEL LOCK ASSY
D12008453				CYLINDER
F12009030				SPEED SHIFT
K12008600				TRAIL RIGHT
K12008601				TRAIL LEFT
		VERIFIED BY:		DATE:

FIGURE 10-7 Configuration Change Log

As applicable, the other members of the CCB usually include the program manager or project engineer of the configured product; inspection/quality engineer; material control manager; service manager; contract administrator; and representatives from manufacturing, manufacturing engineering, and the purchasing departments. Each member designates an alternate for his or her representation. The CCB manager convenes regularly scheduled meetings and special meetings, as needed. Most CCB members attend every meeting except those from manufacturing, manufacturing engineering, and purchasing. They only attend those meetings where the proposed changes may affect their operations, as determined by the CCB chairperson.

The CCB evaluates and provides appropriate disposition for all Class I change requests prior to the issuance of the ECN. A revised CCL is also prepared and issued for all Class I changes approved by the CCB. This revised CCL denotes the change information and its effectivity at the applicable part or assembly number location on the list.

A copy of the CCL, and its subsequent revisions, are incorporated in that equipment unit history inspection folder for each end item of equipment. As part of the final assembly inspection, the as-built configuration level, as noted on the CCL, is validated by the final inspector. The results are entered on the applicable CCL for each component and assembly. When the inspection reveals a difference in the configuration level between the as-built equipment and the level specified on the CCL, the equipment is held and the matter referred to the configuration manager, who presents the discrepancy to the CCB for disposition. This may include the replacement of the applicable component or assembly with the item of the proper configuration level, or the revision of the effectivity of the indicated change.

The results of the disposition are then forwarded to the engineering, material control, and inspection personnel, who take the necessary steps to implement the CCB's disposition.

When the assembly inspection of the end item is completed, the executed CCL copy, signed by the assembly inspector, is filed in the equipment inspection history file. A second copy is forwarded to the configuration control manager.

The configuration control manager maintains a copy of the CCL. It includes information about parts accepted by the materials review board. It also includes any subsequent Class I changes to these parts, either performed in house or in the field. The configuration control manager maintains copies of the CCLs for all equipment, in a control file. This is utilized as a history of the configuration level for each end item of equipment shipped. The manager also maintains records of all CCB meetings and the results of the configuration control program's periodic audits.

PRODUCT LIABILITY PREVENTION PROGRAM

As a result of the continuing emphasis on consumerism, and the large number of product liability suits which resulted in tremendous awards to the claimants, many companies have found it necessary, and desirable, to develop in-house product liability prevention programs (PLP).[2]

Initially, the company should review its current procedures against a checklist provided by their loss insurance company. This will determine the degree of change needed in the existing procedures in order to develop an effective program. Any company which has been operating under a viable and effective quality assurance program will find that the number of changes needed are, in fact, minimal.

The company CEO should appoint a product liability coordinator, who will form a PLP steering committee. This committee consists of all the company's department heads and their alternates. A safety engineer is also included.

The PLP steering committee then develops and issues a PLP manual of procedures and instructions. See Figure 10-8 for a suggested table of contents. This manual, after approval by the CEO, is then distributed to all affected personnel.

The PLP steering committee should meet regularly and when requested by the coordinator. At these meetings, in-house and field failure reports, as well as any potential claims actions, are evaluated. In addition, in-house product nonconformances which affect safety-related components and assemblies are discussed.

The committee members should follow up all corrective actions resulting from these reviews, as well as the results of systems and procedural audits pertinent to their operations, and implement the PLP program within their areas of responsibility.

Design and engineering standards should be updated to reflect the latest engineering practices of the industry relative to the products involved.

Safety analysis check lists should be developed by the safety engineers for use, by the engineering personnel, during the various phases of the design/development cycle (see Figures 10-9, 10-10, and 10-11).

The company engineering department should hold reviews at the preliminary concept phase, the intermediate or development phase, and prior to final drawing release. All the meetings should be attended by representatives of the inspection/quality engineering department, the program manager, and project and safety engineers. Manufacturing, manufacturing engineering, purchasing, and customer service personnel should attend the final meeting.

At these meetings, attendees may comment on and must approve the results of the engineering reviews. The safety engineer should list the critical and safety-related components, assemblies, and end item characteristics. These should be subsequently identified on the applicable drawings and specifications.

Publications department personnel should review the safety-related characteristics in the user's technical manuals and against the publications safety checklists. Information relative to any product changes affecting these items or, as defined by the safety engineer, should be provided to the manual users in the field.

Copies of all design information, product specifications, inspection and test results, field failure reports and the corresponding corrective actions, and all other data relative to the safety-related characteristics, should be retained in a secure, fireproof, temperature and humidity controlled library under the cognizance of the engineering department head. Access to these records should be limited to the members of the PLP steering committee and to any other personnel designated by the PLP coordinator.

PLP checklists should also be developed for activities of the other departments, including marketing and sales, administration and training, purchasing, manufacturing, manufacturing engineering, inspection, and quality assurance.

Special procedures and inspection instructions should be developed by the quality engineering department for the designated safety-related components, assemblies, and end item characteristics. When these items are

PLANNING			ISSUE	AMEND.
	100	Policy	I	
	110	Objectives and Scope	I	
	120	Organization	I	
	130	Procedures/Instructions	I	
	140	Design/Development	I	
	150	Marketing/Sales	I	
	160	Contracts	I	
IMPLEMENTATION				
	200	Administration/Training	I	
	210	Purchasing	I	
	220	Manufacturing, Assembly, Storage	I	
	230	Quality Assurance	I	
	240	Product/Program Engineering	I	
	250	Engineering Change/Configuration Control	I	
	260	Preparation for Shipment/Shortage	I	
EVALUATION				
	310	Records/Data Analysis	I	
	320	Audits/Reports	I	
CORRECTIVE ACTION				
	400	Product/Process Deficiencies	I	
	410	Product Recall	I	
	420	Claims Action	I	

FIGURE 10-8   Product Liability Prevention Program Table of Contents

referred to the MRB for nonconformance disposition actions, all decisions regarding accepted material should be submitted to the safety engineer for concurrence. A copy of the executed report should also be forwarded to the configuration manager for incorporation into the CCL.

SAFETY CHECKLIST

Product _____ File Code _____ Work Order/ Job No. _____

Checklist for Hazards associated with various Hazard Sources:

	REVIEWED		COMMENT
	Applicable	Not Applicable	
Mechanical			
Rotating, reciprocating, and transverse motions			
Cam action			
In-running nip points			
Cutting actions—motion			
Cutting exposure—sharpener			
Punching, shearing, and bending actions			
Rate of speed			
Unstable			
Entrapment			
Lack of clearance			
Misleading appearance of quality			
Stored energy			
Improper rigidity			
Impact			
Electrical			
Shock			
Short circuit			
Fire			
Insulation			
Ventilation			
Insultation failure			
Radiation—X–ray			
Sparks			
Arcing			
Explosion			

FIGURE 10-9 Safety Checklist

The quality engineering personnel should coordinate the investigation of all customer product complaints, and follow through the implementation and investigation of all corrective actions (see Chapter 22).

During the manufacturing process, the inspection/quality and manufacturing engineers should report to the safety engineer any operations of safety-designated items which appear difficult to manufacture at a consistent quality level. The safety engineer should then coordinate a review of

	REVIEWED		COMMENT
Radiant Energy (Electromagnetic or Nonionizing)	Applicable	Not Applicable	

Ultra violet emission
Visible light emission
Infrared emission
Microwave emission
Radio wave emmision

Identifying Potential:

Failure or Malfunction

"Failure or malfunction" are
situations where breakdown of
a product or component occurs,
or a product operates in a
nonstandard or unintended
manner, and injury or loss
may result.

Physical stress
Wear
Overload
Temperature-variation, extremes
Aging
Moisture
Inadequate or improper maintenance
Improper use
Work defects
Design defects
Stored energy
Electrical leakage or short
Air-pockets in a closed system
Maladjustment
Unrealistic service requirements
Loss of power

FIGURE 10-9 Continued

the process and drawing tolerances, with the design and manufacturing engineering personnel, to correct the problem.

The PLP manual should also include elements relative to the processing of customer product complaints, field failure reports, and potential claims actions. In addition, the manual should provide procedures outlining the degree of participation by the applicable company personnel during all liability litigation procedures.

	REVIEWED		COMMENT
	Applicable	Not Applicable	

Noise (Pressure)

High intensity
High frequency
Impulsive
Vibration

Fire and explosion-related

Fuel source
Rate of flammability
Ignition source
  Heat (chemical)
  Heat (spontaneous)
  Heat (mechanical)
  Spark (mechanical)
  Spark (electrical-static)
  Open flame

Chemical

1. Corrosive

        to animals
        to plants
        to materials

2. Toxicity

        by inhalation
        by skin absorption
        by ingestion

Radiation

Alpha emitter
Beta emitter
X-ray emitter
Gamma emitter
Neutron emitter

FIGURE 10-9 Continued

PRODUCT_____

         (Name)   (Type)   (Model No.)   (File Code No.)   (Work Order No.)

1. List all critical components* on the critical components form. List the method used to determine critical parts, and the safety standards applicable to them. *(Critical parts or components are those whose failure could cause serious bodily injury property damage, business interruption, or serious degradation of product performance.)

2. List here any critical parts not covered by adequate safety standards.

   A. _____
   _____

   B. Has adequate testing and research been done to establish the safety and reliability of these critical parts? ☐ Yes ☐ No   If No, what do you recommend?
   _____
   _____

   C. Have minimum quality control standards been specified for critical parts? ☐ Yes ☐ No
   For noncritical parts? ☐ Yes ☐ No

3. Have adequate guards been provided for all danger points (transmission points, nip points, and all locations where hazard through contact exists)? ☐ Yes ☐ No If No, what do you recommend? _____
   _____

4. Have warnings been reviewed with legal department?

   A. On product or container? ☐ Yes ☐ No
   B. In instruction manual? ☐ Yes ☐ No
   C. Recommendations: _____
   _____

5. Have sales and advertising material been reviewed by the design department? ☐ Yes ☐ No
   Recommendations: _____
   _____

6. List the types of accident which could occur during

   A. Normal operation _____
   _____

   B. Maintenance or adjustment _____
   _____

   C. Product failure or malfunction _____
   _____

   D. Misuse _____
   _____

   E. Unintended foreseeable uses _____
   _____

7. How can the product be modified to reduce accident hazards, improve reliability, or reduce maintenance problems? _____
   _____

Evaluated by _____ Date _____ Checked by _____ Date _____

FIGURE 10-10 Critical Component Checklist

CRITICAL COMPONENT ANALYSIS									
PRODUCT			FILE				WORK ORDER/JOB NO.		
CRITICAL COMPONENTS	SYSTEM SAFETY ANALYSIS	RELIABILITY STUDIES	FAILURE STUDIES	FIELD TESTING	OUTSIDE LABORATORY	TYPE OF ACCIDENT OR DEGRADATION OF PRODUCT PERFORMANCE POSSIBLE AS RESULT OF PART FAILURE	SAFETY STANDARDS APPLICABLE TO CRITICAL COMPONENTS	DOES THE DESIGN MEET MINIMUM STANDARDS	
								YES	NO
EVALUATED BY			DATE			CHECKED BY		DATE	

FIGURE 10-11 Critical Component Analysis

REFERENCES

1. *DOD-STD-480A. Configuration Control: Engineering Changes, Deviations and Waivers.* Washington, DC: Government Printing Office, Superintendent of Documents.

2. Suntag, Charles. *Product Liability Prevention Program.* (37th Annual Quality Conference). Milwaukee, WI: ASQC, 1983, p. 396.

CHAPTER ELEVEN

Customer Requirements Review and Project Control

CUSTOMER REQUIREMENTS REVIEW

Introduction

One of the major elements of the inspection/quality function is to provide the assurance that the company's supplied products and services are in accordance with customers' requirements. Accordingly, it is important that the inspection/quality department personnel be cognizant of all contractual technical and quality requirements.

Most companies require the contracts department to review all customers' contracts and disseminate the applicable requirements to all affected departments, including inspection/quality. These provisions, with the technical requirements issued by the engineering department, are reviewed and disseminated throughout the department in the form of an inspection/quality control program plan.

Some companies find that, at times, all information pertinent to the inspection/quality operation is not completely disseminated. Accordingly, those companies judge it beneficial for the inspection/quality personnel to conduct their own review of the contract and associated technical specifications. This then provides assurance that they are made cognizant of all of the customers' inspection/quality requirements.

This chapter outlines a procedure used by inspection/quality engineering personnel for the review of proposals and contracts.

Bid/Proposal

The inspection/quality engineering department should review a customer's bid or proposal for its quality requirements, anticipated costs, and applicable departmental functions. It may be advantageous to prepare, in advance of the review, a set of pages, each titled with the procedure incorporated into the anticipated quality program. During the review, the inspection/quality engineer should record the proposal elements which relate to that procedure. A section should be reserved for each element of the proposal which may require a special inspection/quality procedure. Another section should be reserved for recording any ambiguities or inconsistencies in the inspection/quality requirements. Finally, manpower and cost breakdowns for the various elements of inspection/quality provisions should be prepared.

Many companies do not normally require this cost information for incorporation into the proposal, since they consider the inspection/quality function as part of indirect labor costs. However, the determination of these costs is of value to inspection/quality management to enable them to determine their in-house budgeting and manpower needs. See Chapter 28 for further details.

Upon the completion of the review, the quality engineer should prepare a report, identifying the inspection/quality elements of the proposal and any ambiguities or discrepancies among the specifications, technical documents, and the body of the proposal which may require clarification. This information should be forwarded to the proposal manager, and incorporated with questions from the other members of the company for discussion with the customer's buyer.

Contract Review

The inspection/quality engineer should perform a review of the pertinent sections of the contract, its specifications, and referenced technical documents for the same elements that were reviewed during the proposal stage. As before, any questions, ambiguities, or inconsistencies should be recorded and forwarded to the company's contract manager.

Contract Planning Meeting

In many companies, it is customary for the pertinent members of the company's management to participate in a contract planning conference. At this meeting, the specific requirements of the contract are discussed, and the preliminary elements of contract implementation developed. These elements usually include the establishment of schedules and the assignment of departmental responsibilities.

The following inspection/quality program elements, as applicable, are generally included in the agenda of this meeting.

1. Special controls or processes
2. Unique inspection and quality requirements
3. Special design/engineering/reliability requirements and techniques
4. Special manufacturing processes and controls
5. Special inspection/test procedures and measuring equipment needs
6. Special manufacturing equipment and tooling
7. Documentation requirements
8. Processing contractual changes, waivers, and deviations
9. Contractually required submissions and approvals
10. Unusual skill requirements
11. Acceptance/test criteria
12. Unique technical or specification requirements
13. Configuration/drawing control requirements
14. Schedules and budgets
15. Specific or implied quality levels
16. Any unresolved questions about the ambiguities and contract discrepancies noted during the proposal and contract review

Contract Post Award Meeting

It is extremely desirable that arrangements are made for a post award contract meeting to be held as soon as possible after the receipt of the award. This meeting should be attended by the company personnel who participated in the preplanning conference, and the customer's personnel, including representatives from the customer's purchasing, contracts, engineering, and quality departments.

In order to avoid subsequent problems during the contract implementation, it is important that any questionable items be clarified at this time. All items resolved at this meeting are generally incorporated into a supplementary contractual document.

Based on the results of meetings and the contract review, the inspection/quality engineer should be able to prepare the quality program for the new contract.

PROJECT CONTROL

As noted, some companies develop special inspection/quality control programs for each individual product line or contract. It is desirable that these procedures parallel those of the company quality assurance policies manual

Objective:

Scope:

Controlling Elements:

1. Organization

    1.1 The inspection/quality program organization shall be as prescribed in the standard inspection/ quality assurance policy (QAP 110), as modified for project 1026.

2. Procedures and Instructions

    2.1 The project inspection/quality program operating procedures (QCOPs) and quality control instructions (QCIs) shall be prepared, maintained, and controlled in accordance with the applicable provisions of QAP 200.

    2.2 copies of the QCOPs, QCIs, and subsequent revisions shall be transmitted to the customer's quality assurance representative via the contract department. These documents shall be subject to their disapproval, when they do not meet the objectives of the contractual quality requirements.

3. Control of Measuring Equipment

    3.1 The selection, maintenance, calibration, and control of measuring equipment, utilized for the determination of supplies and services to contractual requirements, shall be performed in accordance with the applicable requirements of QAP 300.

    3.1.1 Measuring equipment provided by the customer shall be maintained and controlled in accordance with the provisions of QAP 310.

    3.1.2 Upon completion of the contract, the customer-supplied measuring equipment shall be submitted to the customer's personnel for inspection of their condition and evidence of excess wear. Upon approval by the customer's representative, the equipment shall be prepared for shipment in accordance with contractual instructions, and shipped to the customer's designated destinations.

4. Engineering Drawing and Change Control

    4.1 The maintenance, distribution, and control of drawings and other technical data prepared by the company, shall be performed in accordance with QAP 400.

    4.2 The configuration status of the equipment shall be controlled in accordance with the provisions of QCOP 1026–1.

    .

    .

    .

22. Corrective Action

    22.1 Corrective action, when required by a discrepant condition or customer's complaint, shall be implemented in accordance with the applicable provisions of QAP 1100.

    22.2 Failure of an end item to meet a specific test requirement during in-house and field testing shall initiate the following actions:

    22.2.1 The company project and inspection/quality engineering personnel shall perform a detailed examination and analysis of the applicable components to determine the cause of the failure.

    22.2.2 Upon completion of the evaluation, a corrective action request shall be prepared by the inspection/quality engineer in accordance with QAP 1100, and forwarded to the responsible personnel for review and correction of the process which was responsible for the nonconformance.

FIGURE 11-1   Inspection/Quality Program for Job 1026

(QAP). Thus, each company inspection/quality control standard procedure should be included, as applicable. However, instead of duplicating the contents of the QAP, the applicable project procedure should merely make reference to the company procedure and delineate those elements of the program which depart from the standard. See Figure 11-1 for an example of an inspection/quality program, utilizing procedures from the company's quality assurance policies manual.

Inspection/Quality Program Operating Procedures (QCOP)
(Prepared by the company inspection/quality engineer)

QCOP 1026–0—Inspection/Quality Program

QCOP 1026–1—Configuration Control

QCOP 1026–2—Quality Conformance Inspection

QCOP 1026–3—First Article Inspection

QCOP 1026–4—Initial Production and Comparison Tests

QCOP 1026–5—Quality Conformance Testing

Inspection/Quality Program Instructions (QCI)
(Prepared by the project inspection/quality engineer)

QCI-1026–1—General Examination

QCI-1026–2—Definition of Inspection Methods

QCI-1026–3—Inspection of P/N 1026–413

QCI-1026–4—Inspection of Assembly# 146678A

.

.

.

QCI-1026–15—Inspection of Preparation For Shipment

FIGURE 11-2   Table of Contents for Project 1026

Any contractual inspection/quality element not provided for in the company's quality assurance manual will necessitate incorporation, as a special procedure, into the project program. The inspection/quality engineer should then prepare the special procedures in accordance with the company's standard guidelines. The draft program would then be distributed to the applicable personnel for their review, comments, and approvals.

During the preparation of these project procedures, the inspection/quality engineer should refer to the comments that had been made during the proposal and contract review, as well as to the pertinent information obtained during the post award and planning conferences.

Upon receipt of the approvals from the reviewing personnel, the inspection/quality program should be distributed to all applicable personnel engaged in the contract implementation. The procedures are distributed and controlled in the same manner as described in Chapter 8.

Upon receipt of the project procedures, the quality engineer should then develop the necessary inspection instructions which would be combined with the inspection/quality program procedures, and distributed to all affected personnel.

Figure 11-2 presents a table of contents of a typical inspection/quality program.

When contractually specified, the project quality program would be submitted to the customer for review and approval.

CHAPTER TWELVE

Implementation: Control of Purchased Supplies and Services

IMPLEMENTATION

The inspection/quality program shall implement the program plan developed in Chapters 7–11. This portion of the text is discussed in Chapters 12 through 19.

INTRODUCTION

Control of Purchased Supplies and Services

In most companies, purchased supplies and services comprise approximately 60 percent of the cost of the entire product or service. Accordingly, the control of the quality of these supplies is important to maintain and improve product and service quality.

The objective is to create relationships with suppliers that assure the consistent receipt of products which will meet the requirement for the fitness for purpose, with a minimum of inspection or corrective action.

Further, companies wishing to apply the principles of just-in-time production to their operations, must be assured that supplies of the proper quality and quantity are provided to meet the needs of the first production run. The quality level must be assured by the suppliers, at their facilities, without recourse to the buyer's receiving inspection operation.

In the past, many companies treated their suppliers in an adversarial manner, often with a cautious and negative attitude. Frequently, price was the prime consideration in supplier selection.

Currently, a more realistic attitude prevails in these relationships. Some companies have followed the lessons of Japanese organizations in considering their suppliers as important parts in their efforts to provide and maintain quality products.

An important consideration of supplier relationships is the understanding that suppliers are not only contracted to provide products or services on order, but are also responsible for the maintenance of acceptable technical and quality programs to ensure consistent quality levels. This requirement is frequently incorporated as an element of the purchase order.

At times it may be necessary to show skeptical purchasing department personnel the high cost of buying from the lowest bidder without regard to product quality. To convey this information, the method described in Chapter 13 is recommended.

THE SUPPLIER AS A TEAM MEMBER

To provide products and services which merit the title world class quality, suppliers are considered members of the company team. Accordingly, buyers provide the technical, training, inspection/quality techniques, and administrative assistance, as needed, to their suppliers. The buyers also receive the necessary technical information from their suppliers relative to their product designs.

During the design and development phases, the supplier's information is solicited so that the final design will reflect the ability of the supplier to provide the necessary components. This is particularly important when the product is one of the supplier's own design.

Some companies select their sources of supply with an eye to minimizing the supplier base, following the recommendation of Dr. Deming in his Fourteen Points. This results in long-term commitments with the selected supplier(s) and provides the motivation for the chosen vendors to fulfill the purchase order requirements in an enthusiastic and effective manner. In addition, the supplier, aware of being considered as a team member, has no fear of revealing, in a timely manner, any problems in meeting the quality and shipping schedule requirements of the purchase orders.

CONTROLLING ELEMENTS

In the development of a program for the effective control of purchased supplies and services, the following elements are recommended for consideration.

- Selection of suppliers
  —Vendor survey

- Purchase order review

- First piece qualification

- Receiving inspection

- Inspection at source

- Vendor rating

- Corrective action

- Use of vendor data
  —Use of raw material data
  —Certificates of conformance

SELECTION OF SUPPLIERS

Buyers must use great care in selecting suppliers who have the qualifications and motivation to consistently provide products and services at ever-improving quality levels. Several departments are involved in the preliminary considerations.

- Purchasing, which has the prime selection responsibility

- Project and production engineering, which assess the supplier's technical capability and understanding of the required product or service elements

- Finance, which evaluates the financial structure of the potential supplier to assure its capability of maintaining the necessary cash flow throughout the production period, and meeting unanticipated cash problems during production

- Inspection/quality, which determine the adequacy of the supplier's quality system to consistently provide quality products

VENDOR SURVEY

The need for an on-site review of the vendor's facilities is usually established on the basis of the complexity of the product, the supplier's past quality history, if available, and the importance of the supplied item to the function of the end product. Prior to performing the survey, participants should assemble information of any prior supplier experience, if available. At times, a pre-survey questionnaire may be sent to the supplier. Then the survey team can be organized, and the supplier notified of the time and date of the review.

The survey is conducted primarily by the members of the inspection/ quality department. At times, personnel from other departments of the company may participate to determine the supplier's capability to meet the needs applicable to their functions.

As noted, the prime objective of the inspection/quality survey is to evaluate the supplier's process capability to consistently provide products or services at the required quality level. Another objective is to determine how well the supplier understands the terms and conditions of the purchase order as it relates to quality requirements. This is important since, at times, a supplier may not be entirely cognizant of, or concerned with, all the quality requirements.

In the past, some buyers considered their only responsibility was to obtain supplies at the lowest possible price. When the supplier expressed doubts about its ability to meet a specified quality requirement, the buyer would often state that there was not a problem, and any question would be resolved by the purchasing department.

Performing the Survey

In the past, the supplier's only contact had been with the buyer who issued the purchase order. When a technical or quality problem arose, the buyer was often unable to provide the necessary information and often was reluctant, or did not have sufficient time, to refer the matter to the responsible company personnel. Face-to-face discussion between the supplier and the buyer's inspection/quality personnel, during the survey, establish points of contact in the event of any subsequent technical or quality/inspection problems.

Occasionally, the quality auditor, while in the process of reviewing with the supplier the terms of the purchase order, is advised of some problem with the technical or administrative requirements. While still at the supplier's facility, the auditor can call the appropriate personnel in the buying company to review the matter. Very often the problem can be resolved at that time. If additional time is needed, the commitments can be made for the resolution of the problem within a specified time frame.

Thus, the auditor not only reduces the potential of a problem at a later date, but also demonstrates to the supplier that there is a means of resolving any future problems in a timely manner. This often encourages the supplier to notify the buyer's inspection/quality personnel of any problem in advance of the production or shipment of nonconforming product, with the expectation that the nonconformance will be overlooked by the buyer's inspection personnel.

Generally the survey is performed against a vendor survey checklist (see Figure 12-1). Vendor survey forms are tailored to the type and complexity of the product or service. For example, special checklists are used for foundries or simple off-the-shelf items.

At the outset, the auditor should meet with the supplier's top personnel to explain the intent and objectives of the survey. The auditor describes the methods used, and requests that the supplier personnel responsible for

VENDOR QUALITY SURVEY CHECKLIST

Originating Group	Requested by	Date
Surveyed by	Group	Date
Approved	Disapproved	Conditionally Approved to
Vendor	Address	Phone
Type of Business, Principle products	Yrs. in business	Area	No. of Employees

CONTACTS	TITLE
1.	
2.	
3.	

1. Q.C. ORGANIZATION   Yes   No

- 1.1 To whom does Q.C. report ☐ ☐
- 1.2 Is Insp. a part of Q.C. ☐ ☐
- 1.3 How many Q.C. ☐ ☐
- 1.4 How many Mfg. ☐ ☐
- *1.5 Does manual meet MIL-Q-9858 ☐ ☐
- *1.6 Is there a requirement for vendor selection ☐ ☐
- *1.7 Is there a requirement for vendoring monitoring ☐ ☐
- *1.8 Is there a transferring of Q.C. requirements ☐ ☐
- *1.9 Are documented work instructions available & used for all operations which affect quality ☐ ☐

* Asterisked items to be answered when MIL-Q-9858A is invoked

2. INCOMING INSPECTION   Yes   No

- 2.1 Are P.O.'s, Drawings available ☐ ☐
- 2.2 Are certifications, etc. filed ☐ ☐
- 2.3 Are Insp. instructions available ☐ ☐
- 2.4 Equipment adequate ☐ ☐
- 2.5 Are records maintained ☐ ☐
- 2.6 Is rejected material identified ☐ ☐

3. STOCK CONTROL

- 3.1 Is material clearly identified ☐ ☐
- 3.2 Stored properly ☐ ☐

FIGURE 12-1 Vendor Quality Survey Checklist

each area to be visited be available to respond to any questions that may arise. The auditor then should review the company's inspection/quality manual against the survey checklist to determine whether the applicable elements are covered adequately. While examining the supplier's pertinent

4. INSPECTION TEST EQUIPEMENT	Yes	No
4.1 Are recalibrations made	☐	☐
4.2 Traceable to N.B.S.	☐	☐
4.3 Records maintained	☐	☐
4.4 Due dates on instruments	☐	☐
4.5 Due dates observed	☐	☐
4.6 Is equipment handled well	☐	☐
4.7 Is equipment adequate	☐	☐

5. IN-PROCESS OPERATIONS	Yes	No
5.1 Are travelers, etc. used	☐	☐
5.2 Does Mfg have latest change information	☐	☐
5.3 In-Process Insp. a Q.C. task	☐	☐
5.4 Are Insp. records made	☐	☐
5.5 Used for corrective action	☐	☐
5.6 Are Insp. instructions available	☐	☐
5.7 Is OK material identified	☐	☐
5.8 Is rejected material identified	☐	☐
5.9 Is rework controlled	☐	☐

6. NONCONFORMING SUPPLIES	Yes	No
6.1 Are vendors notified of rejects	☐	☐
6.2 Is defective material segregated	☐	☐
6.3 Is there a M.R.B.	☐	☐
6.4 Properly staffed	☐	☐
6.5 Are M.R.B. records maintained	☐	☐
6.6 Used for corrective action	☐	☐
*6.7 Is defective material identified	☐	☐
*6.8 Is defective material dispositioned	☐	☐

7. DRAWING/CHANGE CONTROL	Yes	No
7.1 Is latest engineering information available to Q.C.	☐	☐
7.2 Does Q.C. verify incorporation of changes at effectivity point	☐	☐
7.3 Do records show changes	☐	☐
7.4 Is superseded information controlled	☐	☐
7.5 Does a central file exist	☐	☐

8. FINAL INSPECTION	Yes	No
8.1 Final Insp. a Q.C. task	☐	☐
8.2 Final Insp. a 100% inspection	☐	☐
8.3 Does Q.C. sample after 100% inspection	☐	☐
8.4 Are inspection procedures used	☐	☐
8.5 Are inspection records kept	☐	☐
8.6 Used for corrective action	☐	☐
8.7 Is OK material identified	☐	☐
8.8 Is rejected material identified	☐	☐
8.9 Is rework controlled	☐	☐

9. PACKAGING	Yes	No
9.1 Do controls exist to prevent packaging of uninspected material	☐	☐
9.2 Do controls exist to assure inclusion of C and C, etc.	☐	☐
*9.3 Are inspection instructions utilized	☐	☐

*Asterisked items to be answered when MIL-Q-9858A is invoked

FIGURE 12-1 Continued

areas of production, engineering, purchasing, and inspection/testing, the auditor should review random samples of documents and events to determine the extent and the degree of the inspection/quality program implementation as described in the supplier's manual. Since the product to be

10. GENERAL	Yes	No
10.1 Are facilities adequate	☐	☐
10.2 Are they properly maintained	☐	☐
10.3 Is housekeeping adequate	☐	☐
10.4 Is lighting adequate	☐	☐
10.5 Are MIL-STD-105 plans used	☐	☐
10.6 Are AQLs adequate	☐	☐

*Asterisked item to be answered when MIL-Q-9858A is invoked

11. COSTS RELATED TO QUALITY	Yes	No
11.1 Has vendor determined specific quality cost data that is needed	☐	☐
11.2 Is the data in (11.1) being collected	☐	☐
* 11.3 Does data identify cost of prevention or correction of defects or both	☐	☐
* 11.4 Are the cost data used in managing quality	☐	☐

INSTRUCTIONS:

1. Complete all spaces with the information called for. If not applicable, indicate by N/A.
2. Explain briefly in space below reason for checking "No" block. Key the comments to the checklist number.

FIGURE 12-1   Continued

supplied on the purchase order is not normally in process at the time, samples of documents reflecting products or services similar to those ordered, should be selected. Care must be taken to insure that the selection of the samples is unbiased and random. With prior permission from the supplier's management personnel, the auditor may discuss various aspects of the program with the section supervisors and operating personnel to determine their understanding of their role in the inspection/quality program. Review results are annotated by the auditor on the survey form. Any questionable areas should be pointed out to the accompanying supplier personnel for comments and to provide them with the opportunity of responding to these areas.

Postsurvey Meeting

After the survey, the auditor generally meets with the supplier management personnel to discuss the survey findings. Particular attention should be paid to any areas found questionable, not conforming to the supplier's inspection/quality manual, or which could result in a possibly negative effect on the purchase order's inspection/quality requirements. At this point, the accompanying personnel from the buyer's other departments may provide their comments relative to the areas under their jurisdiction. Comments relative to the questionable elements should have been solicited from the supplier's representatives, including any promised actions and anticipated times for correction. The results of these discussions, including any areas under dispute, should be noted on the survey form.

Survey Report

The auditor usually prepares the survey report. Based upon the results of the visit, the auditor can recommend the capability of the supplier to meet the terms of the purchase order. A supplier can be approved, conditionally approved, or disapproved. Conditional approvals can be revised if the supplier subsequently implements corrective actions for the negative items noted on the report and discussed at the postsurvey meeting. When the buyer's other departmental personnel participate in the survey, their findings should be included in the survey report, and their comments relative to the auditor's disposition are included. Copies of the final report are distributed to the managers of the inspection/quality control, purchasing, and other participation departments, for their comments and/or concurrence.

At times, mitigating circumstances may require that the disapproval action be waived and the supplier utilized. For example, these circumstances may arise when the supplier is a sole product source or other potential sources are unable to meet the quality or schedule requirements of the purchase order.

These waivers should be approved by the heads of the company's purchasing and inspection/quality control departments. The quantity of product ordered should be at the minimum level possible. Further, the purchasing department should commit itself to finding an alternate source as soon as possible. The engineering department should be requested to review the specifications of the item in question with the view toward revising the requirements, if possible, to enable the use of another supplier. If the sole source designee had been requested by the company's customer, the problem can be presented to them by the engineering and contracts department, with a request that the sole source designation be waived and the use of an alternate source, when available, be permitted.

When all actions fail, and the purchase order must be placed with the disapproved supplier, the inspection/quality engineer should prepare a plan for substituting, to the extent possible, company efforts for those of the supplier, to offset negative elements. These efforts may include closer surveillance at the supplier's facilities or a greater degree of product inspection upon receipt. Technical assistance may be provided by the buyer's engineering, production engineering, or inspection/quality control personnel, if requested. The costs of these extraordinary efforts to overcome the supplier's deficiencies should be included, for internal use, in the price of the supplied product.

In the case of conditionally approved suppliers, the company's quality auditor should visit the supplier's facilities to determine the effectiveness of their committed corrective action. These reviews should also be performed at subsequent intervals during the production period.

PURCHASE ORDER REVIEW

In most companies, purchase order requirements are incorporated in the body of the document, in its general provisions, and in the referenced and attached drawings, exhibits, and special clauses. The purchase order[1] should include, among other elements, conditions which provide for mutual cooperation, agreed methods of evaluation of the product or service, methods to settle disputes, requirements for exchange of essential information, adequate performance in related functions, responsibility to provide good products and supporting data, and the provision that the user's interests are to predominate.

Since supplier conformance is vital to the quality of the products delivered by the company, it is necessary to assure that the purchase order includes all the contractual or company technical, inspection/quality, and workmanship requirements relative to these supplies. To insure that this is totally accomplished, some companies arrange, prior to purchase order issuance, for an independent review by members of the inspection/quality department, of the purchase order requisition. The following procedure for this review is recommended.

All purchase requisitions should be reviewed by the inspection/quality planner before being transmitted to the purchasing department for processing. This review is made to insure that the purchase orders include or reference, all applicable drawings and specifications, at the effective configuration level as well as any other technical, administrative, and inspection/quality requirements (see Figure 12-2).

1. Controlling Elements

1.1   This instruction shall be implemented through the control of the following elements:

(a) Receipt of Requisition
(b) Requisition Review
(c) Purchase Order Review

2. Receipt of Requisition

2.1   Requisitions submitted for review must be accompanied by the engineering data (drawings, gauge, detail and assembly, and SQAP's) and referenced documents. These shall be provided by Drafting who shall, on requisitions for assemblies, list each document and its revision letter on the requisition or supplementary documentation.

3. Requistion Review

3.1   Quality Engineering Planners shall;

(a) Check requisition package for completeness and accuracy (Ref. Para 2.1). Incomplete packages shall be returned for completion unless immediate correction is possible.

(b) Coordinate with the cognizant government representative at the facility for "PQAP": requirement at source.

(c) Using Table I, incorporate the necessary applicable Purchase Order Clause requirements on the requisition and attach QC Form 2227 and Certificate of Compliance Form (attached) as applicable to the requisition package. Initial requisition in appropriate block.

(d) Retain a copy of the purchase requisition or record on the Requisition/Purchase Order Review, Log all requisition munbers and invoked Quality Clauses except those for MS-AN hardware, raw materials or commercial items requiring only a Certificate of Conformance (Clause I).

4. Purchase Order Review

4.1   The Quality Engineering Planner shall:

(a) Audit subsequent Purchase Orders upon receipt for completeness as to quality requirements invoked as a result of his requisition review. Corrections as required will be noted and corrective action requested.

4.2   (b) Four (4) copies of each purchase order requiring "Government Inspection at Source" (Clause 5) shall be forwarded to DCAS-QAR.

FIGURE 12-2   Purchase Order Review

In addition, a set of quality clauses should be developed, which, when referenced in the purchase order, incorporate specific quality requirements. See Figure 12-3 for an example of one of these clauses. The inspection/ quality planner should note on the requisition this requirement. After

TABLE I

ITEM CATEGORY	A. –See Note Below Purchase Order Clauses		
	#1 (C of C) ExhG	#4 (QC 2227c)	#5 (GSI)*
Assemblies	X	X(A-1) (Exh A) X(B&D) (Exh's B&D)	
Major Components	X	X (B)	
QPL Items	X		
Source Control Items (Not included above)	X	(Exh C) X (B) Comm	
Spec Control Items (Not included above)	X	X (B) Comm	
Castings (Aluminum)	X	** (Exh E&F) X (E) & (C)	
Castings and Forgings (Other)	X	X (C)	
Raw Materials	X		
Minor Components and Commercial Items	X		
Hardware and Minor Detail Parts	X		

* CLAUSE #5 SHALL BE IMPOSED AS REQUIRED BY THE RESPONSIBLE GOVERNMENT REPRESENTATIVE.

** WHEN DRAWINGS OR OTHER P.O. RELATED DOCUMENTATION IMPOSES SOUNDNESS REQUIREMENT ONLY THE FORM 227C SHALL BE IMPOSED.

A.-2227A-1 shall be involved on complex assemblies, as applicable, when used on contracts with MIL-Q-9858A requirements. -2227B or D shall be invoked on major components or assemblies, as applicable, when used on contracts with MIL-I-45208A requirements.

FIGURE 12-2 Continued

completing the requisition review, the inspection planner should forward it, and the attachments, to the purchasing department.

On a periodic basis, the inspection planner reviews a sample of purchase orders processed to assure the incorporation of the appropriate quality notes.

The following quality requirements shall be applicable to the purchase order and shall supplement those requirements specified on the purchase order and its attachments and referenced documents, drawings and specifications with no increase in purchase price.

A-1 The supplier shall maintain a procedure for performing inspection/test to the extent required to assure delivery of product which conforms to the requirements of the purchase order and drawings, specifications and/or other document referenced therein. A written description of this procedure shall be available to authorized company and or government personnel for review within 30 days after receipt of this order.

A-2 The supplier shall invoke the applicable portions of the purchase order on his suppliers and conduct such inspections, tests and surveillance as necessary to assure compliance with these requirements.

B-1 During performance of this order, your inspection system is subject to review, verification and analysis by authorized company and/or government representative. Company and/or government inspection or release of product prior to shipment is not required unless you are otherwise notified.

B-2 When so notified, you shall promptly notify the government representative who normally services your plant and provide a copy of the order upon his request, so that appropriate planning for government inspection can be accomplished. The shipping document for each shipment shall include evidence of government quality assurance action.

C-1 The supplier shall maintain records of inspection/test data as required to assure conformance to paragraph A-1 above.

C-2 These records shall be kept complete and available for delivery upon request to company and/or government for a period of three (3) years following completion of the order.

D-1 Except as otherwise provided under the order, the supplier is responsible for the supply and maintenance of all inspection and test equipment necessary to assure that supplies conform to purchase order requirements. This equipment shall be controlled in accordance with an established calibration procedure which is traceable to NBS.

FIGURE 12-3   Quality Clause

FIRST PIECE QUALIFICATION

Upon the receipt of the initial shipment from each supplier, some companies perform a qualification which usually consists of the examination of one piece of the product for conformance to each characteristic or note on the drawing. When the supplier has been requested to provide a first piece

E-1   When any of the items to be supplied on this order are of themselves or contain one or more components which are required by the applicable specifications to be qualified products, such components shall have been tested and qualified for inclusion in the Qualified Product List.

E-2   An Inspection Report, detailing the inspection/test results of each characteristic of the drawing(s) specified on the order shall be prepared for the initial production lot shipped on this order.

        (a)   When the item(s) are procured to a company or government specification, this qualification report shall include data attesting to the conformance of each paragraph of the specification.

        (b)   The report shall be identified as a Qualification Sample Report. When Government Source Inspection has been applied to this order, the report shall bear evidence of government concurrence to the specified results.

        (c)   One copy of this report must be included with the initial shipment and another copy mailed to the company, Attn: Purchasing Department.

F-1   All items on this order shall be identified as specified on the applicable drawing and/or specification.

F-2   In addition, each shipment shall be identified by the applicable drawing number and revision letter. This identification may be applied by label, stamp or tag. All inspection records maintained at the supplier's facilities shall be identified with the appropriate drawing number and revision letter. This information shall be noted on the shipping documents, test data and/or certifications provided with the shipment.

FIGURE 12-3   Continued

qualification report, the receiving inspector may use this in lieu of inspection. In that case, the qualification review can be made by the inspection of a sample of the drawing characteristics for verification against the supplier's qualification report.

As noted in an earlier chapter, when the external surface condition of a raw casting is important, the receiving inspector may select three samples of castings which represent the acceptable surface finish condition. These castings are marked SAMPLE, one returned to the supplier, and the other two retained in the receiving inspection area to be used as criteria of acceptability on subsequent casting lots.

When the supplied product is produced in accordance with a specification, the supplier should be required to provide in the qualification report a paragraph-by-paragraph demonstration of the conformance of the first piece to the specification. This action is necessary in order to provide assurance, to the buyer, that the supplier is cognizant of, and has considered, every specification requirement. At times, some of the specification characteristics may require meeting requirements which were previously demonstrated by the supplier through costly and time-consuming tests. Accordingly, the supplier's report need not include the inspection or test data of those characteristics, but only provide evidence of an earlier compliance determination.

At times, the first piece qualification samples are required in advance of the shipment of production quantities. For example, items such as raw castings or forgings are qualified before the supplier is permitted to start production. The supplier's inspection results and the initial qualification pieces are shipped to the buyer for approval in advance of the start of production.

Qualification Report

The results of the first piece qualification inspection are usually recorded on a qualification report (see Figure 12-4). When the item being inspected is a raw casting or forging, the inspector often records the actual measurement results of each finished part characteristic unless there is a special casting drawing. A copy of the final report is supplied to the project and production engineers for their review. They must also determine whether the item can be fabricated using the planned production tooling and equipment, and whether it meets the applicable characteristics of the finished part drawing.

The qualification report for the submitted sample can then be classified as approved, disapproved, or conditionally approved, and provided to the purchasing department for transmission to the supplier.

The following actions are then taken:

- An approved disposition authorizes the production and shipment of the production quantities on the order.

- A conditionally approved disposition authorizes the shipment of production quantities after correction of the indicated nonconformances. The supplier is also requested to provide corrective action evidence. Subsequent production shipments are inspected for the applicable characteristics.

QUALIFICATION INSPECTION RECORD

PAGE   OF

SUPPLIER/DEPT.	P.O.#	JOB NO.	INSP.STAMP
DWG. NO. REV.	NOMENCLATURE		DATE

DR NO.	CHARACTERISTIC	ZONE	INSP. RESULTS	ACC	COMMENTS

FIGURE 12-4 Qualification Report

- A disapproved disposition requires a resubmission, before the start of production, of corrected samples for the requalification inspection/ testing. Corrective action evidence is also required.

QUALIFICATION REPORT (continued)

PAGE NO.

SUPPLIER/DEPT.	P.O.#		JOB NO.	
DWG. NO. REV.	NOMENCLATURE			

DISPOSITION

☐ ACCEPTED

☐ REJECTED

☐ CONDITIONAL APPROVAL

* EXPLANATION AT BOTTOM OF PAGE

SUPPLEMENTAL INFORMATION	REQD	RECD	REMARKS
AFFIDAVIT OF CONFORMANCE			
QC FORM 2227 REQUIREMENTS			
GOV. INSP. AT SOURCE			
INSP. AT SOURCE			

PROJECT ENGINEER RECOMMENDATION:

SIGNATURE:

MANUFACTURING ENGINEER RECOMMENDATION:

SIGNATURE:

QUALITY ENGINEER RECOMMENDATION:

SIGNATURE:

* ACCEPTED – PRODUCTION MAY BE INITIATED.
  REJECTED – NEW SAMPLE REQUIRED WITH NOTED DISCREPANCIES CORRECTED
  CONDITIONAL ACCEPTANCE – PRODUCTION MAY BE INITIATED WITH CORRECTION AS NOTED

DR NO. _____

FIGURE 12-4 Qualification Report

RECEIVING INSPECTION

Introduction

It is important to realize that inspection can rarely determine the quality levels of all the important product characteristics.

EXAMPLE

One company had a highly sophisticated receiving inspection and qualification laboratory at its facilities. The laboratory contained many types of test equipment, including environmental chambers, vibration tables, altitude chambers, and the like. In addition, a large array of precision mechanical and electronic measuring equipment was available. The laboratory was housed in a humidity, temperature-controlled, and dustfree chamber. Its personnel were highly skilled technicians and inspectors.

Qualification inspection was conducted on samples selected from the first shipment of each product provided by outside sources. Unless a qualification sample was provided in advance, the production lots were held in abeyance pending the completion of testing. This often took a considerable length of time, and held up the release of the production quantities. When some discrepancy was noted, the production lot was held up still further, pending the receipt and the inspection of other samples.

The company assigned a quality engineer to review the laboratory activities with the objective of determining means to speed up the qualification program and subsequent release of materials to the manufacturing facilities.

Initially, the quality engineer reviewed the specifications and drawings of the items being qualified against the characteristics being tested by the laboratory. This revealed that a number of characteristics were not being tested. These characteristics were discussed with the project engineer, who noted that several untested characteristics were important for the intended use, performance, or reliability of the components. Subsequently, the quality engineer discussed the situation with the laboratory director. It was revealed that the laboratory was incapable of testing these characteristics. When questioned as to what the director did relative to the untested characteristics, the response was that the supplier was requested to certify the product conformance. It was also revealed that, generally, no further action was taken concerning these characteristics. Also of note, after additional investigation, some of the tests performed by the laboratory used equipment which did not have the required accuracy levels for the specified tolerance.

The quality engineer concluded that the characteristics subjected to the time-consuming and expensive tests were selected, not on the basis of the importance to the end product, but primarily upon the availability of the laboratory equipment. It was further established that as a result of the extensive testing used in the qualification, no program had been considered necessary for any subsequent review of the important missing characteristics. Apparently, the assumption was made that, since a highly sophisticated laboratory had performed qualification inspection/tests of most component characteristics, the item was considered as having met all the drawing and specification requirements.

It was also determined that, in view of the operation of the qualification laboratory, no action had been taken to determine which methods were used by the component manufacturer to establish product conformance.

The quality engineer's report provided the following summary, conclusions, and recommendations.

1. The responsibility of the supplier includes the availability of an inspection/quality program to ensure conformance of its products to the specified purchase order requirements.

2. In order to assure this compliance as well as provide objective evidence of conformance, upon buyer request, the component manufacturer is required to have available at its facilities the appropriate measuring and testing equipment of the proper accuracy.

3. Suppliers will inspect or test products in advance of shipment to the buying company. Hence any deficiencies noted during this testing are capable of being corrected before shipment.

4. It is the responsibility of the supplier to provide conforming components to the buyer and to have objective evidence of the conformance available for the buying company to review.

5. The component purchase orders should be revised to include the supplier's responsibility for actions 1–4.

6. The project and inspection/quality engineers, for each program, should develop a list of important component characteristics which require qualification. This should be performed by the supplier, and the inspection/test data should be provided with the first shipment on the purchase order of each product.

7. The company qualification laboratory personnel should review the supplier's data and subject a sample of the product characteristics to verification inspection/test at the company's facilities. These tests should not be designed as a means of determining the component quality, but purely to establish the reliability of the supplier's inspection/test data.

8. A pre-award survey and periodic visit should be made, by the inspection/quality personnel, to the supplier's facilities, to determine its production capability and its inspection/quality program reliability.

As a result of this review and follow-up action, the amount of qualification testing, at the company's facilities, was significantly reduced, the delay in processing purchased lots virtually eliminated, and the principle of supplier responsibility for providing quality products emphasized.

In addition, the number of personnel in the qualification laboratory was reduced, reassigned to participate in an enhanced vendor source inspection operation. This action also resulted in minimizing the receipt of nonconforming products from the supplier.

Performance of Incoming Inspection

The evaluation of supplies upon delivery can be performed in a number of ways. These include one or more of the following:

- 100 percent inspection
- Sampling inspection
- Identification and transportation damage check
- Evidence of prior inspection by the supplier or other plant of the company check
- Supplier data use
- Vendor certifications use
- No inspection; material sent directly to stores or to the processing departments

The degree of incoming inspection is based upon the following:

- Prior quality history of the supplier
- Criticality of the part in the end item
- Effect of the part on subsequent manufacturing operations
- Warranty or use history
- Supplier process capability information
- Availability of required inspection skills and equipment
- Necessity of partial or total disassembly of the product
- Use of supplier data
- Cost of inspection versus possible consequences of no inspection

As noted in earlier chapters, the characteristics examined and the degree of incoming inspection should be performed in accordance with the inspection/test instructions. This may also include additional characteristics resulting from the qualification inspection operation. The instructions, inspection copies of the purchase orders, and measuring equipment are usually obtained from a central inspection crib, when it is available.

When the inspection supervisor determines that some characteristics cannot be examined in the receiving areas, arrangements should be made to move a lot sample to the designated in-house area. The receiving documents and the balance of the lot should be retained in the receiving inspection area pending inspection results.

Inspection results are usually annotated on an inspection record (see Figure 12-5). An acceptance move tag is prepared, and the material and documents are then moved to an area for transportation to the applicable stores, fabrication, or assembly areas. Rejected lots should be identified by a rejection tag, and moved to the appropriate location, apart from the production material, for transportation to the materials review area. See Chapter 16 for information concerning the processing of nonconforming material.

At periodic intervals, the inspection/quality engineer should review the records for each vendor/part, to determine the applicability of incorporating the sampling switching rules (see Chapter 24). Suitable revisions should then be made on the inspection instruction sheet for the applicable parts.

INSPECTION AT SOURCE[2]

During the inspection planning stage, and subsequent to the performance of the vendor facilities survey, the inspection/quality engineer should determine if inspections should be performed at the supplier's facilities. This should be based upon the following elements.

- Supplier's past quality history

- Possible effect of the purchased part on the performance, safety, and reliability of the end product

- Product complexity

- The ability to determine the product quality upon receipt at the buying plant

- Availability of special measuring equipment at the buyer's plant necessary to perform the required inspection/tests

- Nature of the product and its quality characteristics: Does it need to be disassembled to inspect?

It may be found desirable to retain a resident company inspector at the supplier's premises for a sufficient period of time to assure adequate product control. Some companies use independent external inspection services at the supplier's plant.

Some buyers select an individual from the supplier's organization to act as the buyer's representative. This delegation is awarded to the suppliers who have demonstrated consistently high product quality. Periodic audits at

STAMPED ON REAR OF PURCHASE ORDER (INSPECTION COPY)			
JOB NO.	PURCHASE ORDER NO.		LOT DISPOSITION ☐ ACC. ☐ REJ. DEF. REP.
	REQUIRED	AVAIL.	COMMENTS
CERT. CONF.			
INSP. DATA TEST			
SOURCE INSP.			
APPROVALS			
CHARACTERISTICS			
INSPECTED			
(PLEASE LIST)			
	SAMPLE SIZE	ACC.	REJ.	COMMENTS
IDENTIFICATION			
QUANTITY			
CONDITION			
OTHERS			

INSPECTOR   DATE

FIGURE 12-5 Inspection Record

the supplier's facility are performed to insure that the designated representative's actions are correct and unbiased.

VENDOR RATING

Vendor ratings are used for many reasons.

- Provide quantitative measures of supplier conformance
- Determine relative quality levels for each supplier

- Initiate any required corrective actions, by pinpointing a supplier's weak areas

- Determine supplier retention if it is intended to reduce their number for each commodity

Some companies have rather sophisticated programs of rating their suppliers. They use factors which measure product quality and how well suppliers meet their committed schedules. Some companies use inspection results on receipt, which are based on the number of pieces inspected, the number of pieces rejected, the classification of the rejects (major, minor, or critical), the degree of out-of-tolerance of the discrepancy, and many others. Chapter 24 further discusses the various methods of vendor rating.

Other companies develop ratings based upon their complete relationships with the suppliers. This includes the results of surveys and visitations; the vendor's quality program, and how well it is implemented; the results of their product quality at receiving inspection, and during assembly, test, and field performance; and the vendor's demonstration of the adequacy of its in-house efforts to maintain acceptable process control, rapid and effective corrective actions, and the application of continuing quality improvement programs.

In establishing the vendor rating system, the actual amount of receiving inspection should be considered. If only a few characteristics are inspected, then a vendor rating based upon these results is not very accurate. Thus the use of a sophisticated rating system may be an overkill.

In view of the limited data on which many vendor ratings are based, a simple rating method is suggested.

This rating is based on the following: the position that a vendor's failure to meet any purchase order quality requirements reveals a shortcoming in its inspection/quality program; and the number of discrepancy reports generated for the vendor's products. For the purposes of the rating, all nonconformances are treated equally. For example, missing documents specified on the purchase order, such as certificates of conformance or supplier's inspection/test data, is treated as significant as the failure to meet a major product characteristic. Discrepancy reports include any rejects on receipt, problems encountered during assembly, and problems reported from the field. The rating system also includes the results of the buyer's visit to the supplier's facilities, the adequacy and rapidity of the supplier's corrective actions, and the relative standing of the supplier against the other suppliers providing the same commodity.

In this program, the inspection engineer accumulates all discrepancy reports and corrective action requests for each supplier who had shipped at least ten lots during the reporting period. The number of lots less than ten are included in the next reporting period. A vendor which has shipped over 95 percent of its lots with no nonconformances, is considered as an *A* vendor, and one who had shipped less than 75 percent acceptable lots is considered as a *C* vendor. A similar type of rating is given for on-time shipments. A supplier who is classified as *A* in three successive reporting periods for both categories, is given preference in the ordering of subsequent supplies. A vendor who is given a C rating is subjected to corrective action. The inspection/quality control and purchasing department heads are required to give approval for the use of a C vendor in future procurements. When these C suppliers are used, a tighter sampling plan is employed for receiving inspection.

CORRECTIVE ACTION

Some companies follow a vendor corrective action program directed to the philosophy of not eliminating vendors, but making poor vendors into acceptable ones. Thus their corrective actions are predicated upon efforts used to help the vendors overcome their quality and delivery problems.

Some companies do not notify their suppliers of nonconforming shipments unless they are returned for repair or replacement or on occurrence of a major problem. Thus the suppliers, when accused of the problems with their supplies, rightfully display ignorance of the deviant shipments.

Other companies, however, notify their suppliers as soon as possible, in order for them to take the necessary corrective actions. When a product is found nonconforming upon receipt or use, a copy of the rejection report is immediately forwarded to the vendor with a request that appropriate corrective measures are taken. In addition, when the supplier appears on the vendor rating list as a C vendor, a corrective action request is sent, advising the vendor of the poor rating, and asking for a response within a specified time period. It may be necessary to have the vendor's facilities visited by an inspection/quality engineer to discuss the problem and offer support in overcoming the variant condition. The corrective action request sent to the vendor includes a Pareto analysis of the deficiencies discovered. See Figure 12-6 for an example of a vendor corrective action request. See Chapter 22 for further discussion of the corrective action program.

In some companies, the A suppliers are notified that as long as they retain this rating, it will not be necessary for them to await the results of the company's inspection of the lot before receiving payment. It is provided immediately upon receipt of the shipment. This provides additional incentive for the supplier to continue to ship conforming material. This procedure also overcomes the problem of delayed payment which is often detrimental to the supplier/customer relationship.

USE OF VENDOR DATA

Vendor data is reviewed by the receiving inspection personnel upon receipt of the shipment. The supervisor may designate the use of some character-

Vendor Discrepancy Report (VDR)

Subject: P.O. No.: _____   Discrepancy Report No: _____   Qty: _____

Part No: _____   Part Name: _____   Debit Memo: _____

Attention: Q.C. Manager

Parts have been rejected by our facility as specified within the discrepancy report attached.
AN ACCEPTABLE RESPONSE IS REQUIRED PRIOR TO FUTURE SHIPMENTS DETAILING:
Cause of Discrepancy, Correction of Defect and Corrective Action Taken to Preclude Future
Recurrence. Direct all correspondence or questions to my attention.

Cause of Discrepancy: _____
_____
_____

Correction of Defect: _____
_____
_____

Corrective Action: _____
_____
_____

Name/Title/Signature/Date: _____

Upon completion of form, mail to above mentioned address.

_____

PMRB Coordinator
Quality Assurance Group

cc: Prior to Vendor Completion: After Vendor Completion:
        PMRB DR file - White   PMRB DR file
        Vendor - Yellow   Manager, Purchasing
        Manager, Purchasing - Pink   Manager, Quality Engineering
        Receiving Inspection file - Orange

114-036

FIGURE 12-6   Vendor Discrepancy Report

istics of the data in lieu of performing inspections. This is permitted only
when the supplier had shown evidence of the implementation, at its facilities, of an acceptable inspection/quality program, thereby providing confidence that the supplier's data is reliable.

USE OF RAW MATERIAL DATA

Many companies do not have the capability of performing physical and chemical tests required by raw material specifications. These tests must be performed by an outside laboratory at considerable cost and delay. Consequently, the material supplier is usually requested to provide, with each shipment of raw material, castings, or forgings, copies of the specified chemical and physical test data. The receiving inspector verifies this data against the material specifications to assure that it meets the requirements.

In some companies, the project engineer, at the beginning of a program, classifies the raw material of the product as to its degree of criticality to the function of the end product. Also, the production engineer identifies which material's physical or chemical characteristics are significant to the manufacturing operations. The inspector subsequently uses these classifications, on a lot-by-lot basis, in deciding which material is to be subjected to the physical or chemical tests. When this material is received, samples are cut from it and shipped to an outside laboratory for testing. The balance of the shipment is held, with a hold tag pending the test results. On a periodic basis, confirmation of the suppliers' raw material data is made for the other classes of raw material.

CERTIFICATES OF CONFORMANCE (C/C)

These certificates are generally required for each shipment from a supplier. The C/C shows that the product conforms to the purchase order requirements. It is often believed that the request for a C/C is redundant, since the shipment of the material is, by itself, a statement by the supplier that its products meet the purchase order requirements. However, a C/C, properly designed, should do more than state that the supplies conform. It should also certify that the material has been inspected by the supplier, and that this data is available for a buyer's review (see Figure 12-7). This information is only of value to the buyer if the following action is taken.

Periodically, the buyer's inspection/quality engineer should request a copy of the supplier's inspection/test data for a particular shipment. This data is then subjected to verification by testing the product for a sample of relevant characteristics. At other times, the inspection/quality engineer may visit the supplier's facilities and request a copy of the data for a shipment previously made, to verify that, in fact, the data is available and complete.

Certificates of conformance are sometimes utilized by the customer as a means of accepting material upon receipt, without inspection. This is done when the supplier has been found to be reliable, has sent previous shipments with no nonconformances, and has shown that its inspection/quality programs are capable of maintaining the required quality for an extensive time.

For additional information on purchased material control, see ASQC's *Procurement Quality Control.*[2]

The following information is required relative to the quality of material being furnished against this purchase order. The signature required is that of an authorized agent of your company. Enclose one copy with the shipment and mail one copy to:

XYZ Corporation

ATTN: Quality Engineering.
This is to certify that all required inspection/test has been performed and that the item (s) delivered on the reference purchase order complies with the requirements of said order. Data attesting to the inspection/test shall be available to XYZ Corp. and/or designated government personnel upon request. Similar information to that listed below shall be available for all subsequent shipments on this purchase order.

Part Number ———————— Nomenclature ———————————— PO ————

1. Lot number, production date, or item serial number   ——————————

2. Specification, or drawing number, revision and date   ——————————

3. *Grade, type, or value for which product was inspected/tested ——————————

4. Number of specimens inspected/tested   ——————————

5. Nature of inspection i.e. "go/no go" or variables   ——————————

6. Location and date of inspection/test   ——————————

7. Location of available inspection/test records   ——————————

*   Applicable only when grade, type, or value are characteristics specified by drawing or specification.

Authorized Agent: ———————————————————————————————————————
                        Signature   Job Title   Date

Company: ——

FIGURE 12-7 Supplier's Certificate of Conformance

REFERENCES

1. Gryna, Frank M. *Supplier Relations: Juran's Quality Control Handbook* (4th ed.). New York: McGraw Hill, 1988. Chapter 15.

2. American Society for Quality Control. *Procurement Quality Control* (4th ed.). Milwaukee, WI: ASQC Quality Press.

CHAPTER THIRTEEN

Liaison with Company, Supplier, and Customer Personnel

INTRODUCTION

It is vitally important that inspectors maintain close relationships with all the departments, both inside and outside the company. The positive contribution of the inspectors' expertise and knowledge of the product and process can be of inestimable value. In addition, the effect of these contacts upon the inspectors will provide a sense of job satisfaction.

Where in the past, the inspection function was considered by the production personnel as a necessary evil, today, there is a continuing awareness of the need for close coordination of all personnel to maintain the ability to meet the ever-increasing competition from the world markets.

Inspection personnel, in order to overcome the past prejudices, must adopt an attitude that their operation is primarily a service to the rest of the company. They must demonstrate that their operation is more comprehensive than the mere acceptance or rejection of the product. In current manufacturing and services organizations, management has recognized that, to be competitive in both domestic and foreign markets, all employees of the company must participate in producing goods and services at an ever higher quality level. The attainment of this goal requires more activity for the inspection/quality personnel than acting as a traffic cop. Most managers now realize that quality must be built, and not inspected, into products.

This chapter discusses the role that the inspection/quality organization plays with each function of the company, as well as with its suppliers and customers. The following areas of operation are discussed.

Within the Company

- Marketing
- Contracts
- Engineering
- Production Engineering
- Manufacturing
- Manufacturing Services
- Purchasing
- Field Service
- Personnel
- Inspection/Quality Control

Outside the Company

- Suppliers
- Customers

MARKETING

Progressive companies take considerable pains to insure that the marketing organization does not attempt to sell any products or services which are beyond the capability of the company to provide, economically and consistently. Inspectors, who are intimately aware of the manufacturing operations' capabilities, as well as past problems experienced on product components, can provide considerable information to the marketing department.

In addition, since the marketing personnel are in constant contact with the company's customers during, and subsequent to, product shipments, good working relationships should insure rapid feedback to the inspection/quality organization of any problems the customers are experiencing or any new customer requirements. The inspection/quality organization will thus be able to provide rapid feedback to the company about any problems encountered in the field, and initiate the needed corrective actions.

In return, this relationship will provide to the marketing personnel, information to determine the validity of any customer's complaints, and enable them to refute any complaint which is not within the company's responsibility. The role of the inspection/quality organization in reviewing and commenting on proposals and new contracts is described in Chapter 11.

CONTRACTS

In many companies, the contracts department maintains liaison with the customer throughout the entire contract period. Contractual changes are generally received by the contracts department, who disseminates the change information to the applicable company personnel, including the inspection/quality organization. Also, by virtue of their daily relationship with the customer, the contracts personnel are aware of any complaints that the customer may have. The inspection/quality organization frequently maintains close liaison with the contracts personnel, and is thus aware, in an expeditious manner, of these complaints, and, as noted above under Marketing, can thus initiate the appropriate corrective actions. Further, investigation, corrective actions, and responses to the customer's complaints are usually coordinated by the inspection/quality organization and routed to the customer via the contracts department.

ENGINEERING

Modern companies recognize the importance of designing quality into the product. To this end, the role of the inspection/quality organization is vital to the success of this policy. Engineering departments conduct periodic reviews during the product's design phases. Inspection/quality engineering personnel usually attend these reviews and provide information about the capability of the company to meet the specified requirements. They also provide information about past production problems encountered on the same, or similar, products. In some companies, the inspection/quality engineering department reviews the drawings before issuance to the procurement or production functions. These reviews determine the drawing's conformance to format requirements and to the contractual and company's quality and workmanship standards.

A number of companies include the reliability engineering functions as part of the quality organization. The designs and drawings are reviewed by the inspection/quality personnel for their compliance with the product's reliability requirements. Engineering, reliability, and preproduction testing, performed on the products during the various phases of design, are conducted by the engineering department. However, most companies have these tests monitored by members of the inspection/quality organization.

In some companies, the inspection/quality engineering organization is part of a committee which reviews the early phases of design to assure its adequacy to meet the performance and reliability standards of the company and the contract, when applicable. During these reviews, attention is also paid to simplifying the design and evaluating user needs.

The inspection/quality personnel usually maintain close liaison with the project engineers during the production phase of the program. Problems encountered during, and subsequent to, the production operations are discussed by both organizations and joint plans of corrective actions are developed.

During production testing conducted by, or under the surveillance of, the inspection/quality department, rapid feedback can be provided to the engineering department about any operational problems. Corrective actions can then be monitored by the inspection/quality personnel.

Close coordination is maintained between the inspection/quality personnel and the engineering members of the materials review board, as discussed in Chapter 16. Also, engineering personnel are advised, by the inspection/quality engineers, of any drawing problems encountered during the performance of vendor surveys.

Implementation of engineering changes is, in many companies, performed by, or under the surveillance of, the inspection/quality personnel. They also play an important role in the implementation of the company's configuration control program, when it exists. See Chapter 10 for details.

PRODUCTION ENGINEERING

In most companies, the inspection/quality personnel maintain close liaison with the production engineering department. This is of particular importance during the early manufacturing planning phases when machine tools, processes, and equipment are selected and designed. Frequently, production equipment can be used as the media of inspection. This reduces the amount of special inspection equipment required to measure the characteristics controlled by production processes.

Also, in well-run organizations, any development of new or revised elements of plant layouts is coordinated with the inspection/quality personnel. This is beneficial as it will insure that sufficient facilities, space, and time are made available for the inspection, test, subsequent rework, and reinspection/retest operations.

As noted, the inspection/quality department often performs capability analyses of the machine tools, equipment, and processes. The results are usually maintained by production engineering and utilized by them to designate machine tools and processes. This information is also included in the work instructions and operating sheets. Similarly, the production engineering personnel often coordinate with the inspection/quality personnel in qualifying the personnel, equipment, and processes used for special operations such as welding, plating, organic finishing, and soldering.

In many companies, inspection/quality and production engineering personnel join other departments to form teams to troubleshoot problem areas and implement applicable corrective actions.

MANUFACTURING

Traditionally, the inspection organization has the greater degree of contact with manufacturing personnel, than with any other personnel in the company. This relationship varies from one of high antagonism to one of mutual respect and understanding. Customarily the inspector is in the position of allowing, or barring, the movement of the fabricated product to the next operation. This exerts a tremendous influence on the operators and their supervisors, whose efficiency ratings and production schedules could be adversely affected by the inspector's actions. So, it is no small wonder that frequently, the inspector is looked upon by the production personnel as an impediment to meeting the production schedule, and as a personal affront to the individual operator.

To overcome this attitude, it is important that the inspector's decisions are rendered in a scrupulously fair and just manner. It is also vital that the operators and production supervisors are made aware that the inspectors' decisions are not arbitrary, and that the responsibility for meeting the required specifications is that of the operators, and not of the inspector. This concept is, at times, difficult to apply, particularly when the criteria of acceptability to the specifications or drawing requirements are not fully and clearly identified. Thus it is always highly important that the specifications have precise definitions of acceptability, and that determination of conformance does not depend upon the inspector's arbitrary judgment. When an occasion does arise for some degree of judgment to be exercised, it is essential that the criterion of acceptability is first discussed with the production supervisor and that agreement is reached, before it is implemented. For example, when a visual characteristic, such as the appearance of a painted surface, is to be inspected, a positive agreed-upon criterion of acceptability or unacceptability, such as a painted sample, is available to both the production and inspection personnel.

Most important to the relationship between the production and inspection personnel, is the attitude of the inspector. As noted earlier, it is important to understand that the inspection function is not primarily that of a traffic cop, but instead one of service. It is essential that the inspector truly understands that the acceptance or rejection of the product is to be used as a service to the company rather than to satisfy a whim.

To truly implement this concept, the inspector should be ready to assist the operator in providing a conforming product. The success of this concept is most evident when the operator consults with the inspector, during the production process. When an operator is not entirely sure that the operation would result in a conforming product, discussion with the inspector can often lead to receiving this assurance before any additional operations are performed. In addition, the operator should contact the inspector before commencing an operation on a nonconforming part so received from the previous operation, thereby possibly impacting upon the operator's ability to perform in a satisfactory manner. The inspector, fulfilling the duty of serving the operator, should review the problem with the inspector of the earlier operation, and implement any necessary corrective action.

A number of companies develop corrective action committees or quality circles, consisting of members of the production and inspection organizations. These committees review current or potential problem areas and recommend actions to correct nonconformances. Committees are often utilized to investigate and recommend better methods of performing the production operation, resulting in a more efficient and competitive company. These committees not only serve to provide motivation to its members by giving them a voice in the performance of their operations, but also provide a means of joint action between production operators and inspectors which frequently results in a sense of camaraderie between the two groups.

More important, if, during the performance of a lot-by-lot or in-process inspection, the inspector finds nonconforming product, this information should be expeditiously transmitted to the production supervisor to preclude the fabrication of additional discrepant items.

Analysis of the data generated by the inspection operation may, at times, reveal adverse quality trends. The results, when called to the production supervisor's attention, often provide the necessary information for the correction of the condition leading to the nonconforming products. This too serves to demonstrate to production operators and supervisors the value of the inspection vis-à-vis the production process.

When the inspection/quality operation includes the use of control charts, posting these charts in production areas frequently alerts operators and production supervisors to the quality of the products being produced, thereby enabling operational adjustments of out-of-control situations.

Another service rendered by the quality/inspection operation is its performance of capability studies on the various machine tools and production processes. These studies demonstrate what the operators probably already suspect, the inability of some tools to meet the specified drawing tolerances. These studies often aid the production efforts to obtain equipment with a higher degree of capability.

The use of the inspection data and its analysis can also provide the necessary factual information to assist production supervisors in convincing the project or production engineer of the existence of a problem, or potential problem, and hence result in a revision of the process, or relaxation, when feasible, of the specification requirement.

When a customer representative is resident at the production facility, the inspection/quality organization often acts as a barrier between the representative and the production personnel. In many companies, a program is established which requires the customer to refrain from complaining to the operator about any perceived problems in the product or process. These companies provide a program requiring that all such complaints are referred to designated inspection/quality personnel. This has the effect of preventing any undue interference with the manufacturing operation. In addition, the assigned inspection/quality personnel, being cognizant of the contractual requirements, can, at times, negate the customer's complaint and prevent uncalled for rejection or rework of the disputed characteristics.

To insure that the production personnel are aware of all of the aids and assistance available, and to correct any interdepartmental problems or misunderstandings, it is recommended that regularly scheduled meetings be held with the members of both organizations. These should be conducted in each manufacturing center, and production operators should be encouraged to voice any perceived problems or disagreements between the two organizations. The inspectors involved should have the opportunity to respond to the complaints. If the problem cannot be resolved at that time, it should be referred to the department supervisors, who should be committed to an expeditious investigation and resolution of the problem. At the following meeting, the progress of the action should be presented.

MANUFACTURING SERVICES—PRODUCTION CONTROL

The inspection/quality organization has contact with personnel from all manufacturing services, especially production control. Since inspection results have a strong impact upon the production schedule, the two organizations are interdependent.

In most cases, the expediting function of the production control organization makes it necessary for them to insure that purchased and fabricated products are processed and inspected expeditiously. This often causes conflict. Generally, inspection is conducted on a first-in, first-out basis. However, at times, the schedule requires that some material move into the production flow in advance of others. This is particularly evident when there is a slip in the production schedule either at the supplier's or the company's facility. When the members of the production control organization try to have the items in short supply inspected in advance of the order provided by the inspection supervisor, a conflict arises, at times resulting in angry confrontations between the affected personnel.

In some companies, the production control personnel consider that the material is ready for movement to the next manufacturing operation as soon as it has been received from the supplier or has completed the previous production operation. Accordingly, all too often, the production planners fail to allow sufficient time for the inspection, rework, and reinspection, when required.

Therefore, it is imperative that inspection/quality supervision insist that they be present during the production planning phase and incorporate into the schedule the time needed for inspections, rework, and reinspection or replacement, as required.

Inspection personnel should be aware of production control's responsibility to move the product through the production cycle expeditiously. As a service organization, inspection should provide assistance, whenever possible. Taking a hard-nosed attitude toward production control personnel, as is often the case, only serves to antagonize them, and does nothing to enhance the company's profitability.

To accommodate production control needs, some inspection/quality organizations have developed special procedures which are used under temporary conditions. For example, the inspection schedule can accommodate any variations in the production control schedule, when the first-in, first-out concept cannot be used. This is done by production control posting a list of the order in which the material is needed. The inspection supervisor can then authorize personnel to work on the lots in the order designated. When material is urgently required, and there is a backlog in the inspection area, inspectors from other areas can be used.

When requested by the production supervisor, and authorized by the inspection supervisor, part of a lot can be moved to the fabrication or assembly area, before the entire lot is inspected. Precautions should be taken to insure that material is adequately identified, in the event the lot is subsequently rejected. Then the material may be recovered and included with the rejected sample. To minimize the possible effect of recalling material, only lots from suppliers or manufacturing areas which have an acceptable quality history should be so treated. Similarly, equipment in the assembly area can be allowed to move down the production line prior to the completion of rework operations, provided that the nonconformances are properly noted on the equipment traveler, and the subsequent reinspection can be readily performed.

To insure fairness, the requesting production supervisor must accept the responsibility of identifying the uninspected material in the manufacturing areas and returning this material to the inspection area, if the sample has been rejected. The supervisor should also accept responsibility for any cost or delay occasioned by this return or by removal of the deficient material from the assembled equipment.

Frequently, production control personnel may request that a lot whose sample has been rejected, be 100 percent inspected instead of returning the complete lot to the supplier. The inspection supervisor should, whenever possible, honor this request. However, the requesting supervisor should agree, for in-house products, to accept the cost of this additional inspection, or, for purchased parts, arrange for the purchasing department to have the supplier accept these costs.

On a temporary basis, other departmental personnel can help reduce the inspection backlog. For obvious reasons, personnel from the production area which originally fabricated the products should not be utilized. In addition, pending the determination of the competence of these personnel to perform the inspections, a sample of their results should be reinspected by quality personnel.

To meet an unexpected backlog in an inspection area, inspectors from outside job shops are sometimes used. The inspection budget should provide for this extra expense. Based upon the potential need for job shoppers, the inspection supervisor should, early in the production period, review the shops' availability and determine the acceptability of their work.

Since the amount of unplanned inspection and the resultant delay due to rejection of the supplies is of considerable concern to the production control personnel, the inspection/quality supervisors can enlist their support in the implementation of corrective action, both at the supplier's and at manufacturing's areas. Thus team approach can help to improve the quality of the purchased and fabricated supplies. This effort is essential when a company decides to utilize the just-in-time concept. In that type of operation, since no inventory is accumulated to take the place of rejected items, the material must be of acceptable quality upon receipt.

MANUFACTURING SERVICES: STORES, RECEIVING, SHIPPING, AND MAINTENANCE

The inspection/quality organization has regular contact with the personnel from these organizations. In all instances, the product quality is affected by the method of handling them. It is important that the personnel in these support areas are made cognizant of their responsibilities in not detracting from the product quality. Periodic audits of these service areas should provide indications as to how well they perform and how they relate to product quality.

Similarly, inspection/quality department personnel should make themselves available to provide any information and assistance to these departments to implement their quality-related functions. For example, when notified by the stores personnel that damaged material has reached the area, the inspection/quality personnel should expeditiously investigate the condition and initiate suitable corrective actions. When the investigation of the causes of deviant material reveals that the nonconformances were caused by worn-out machine tools, inspection/quality personnel should take prompt measures to inform the maintenance personnel of this condition and assist them in obtaining authorization for the repair or replacement of the deficient tool.

It is important that the progress of any corrective actions taken by the inspection/quality personnel is transmitted to the other affected departments.

PURCHASING

In the past, there has been an adversarial attitude among personnel from the inspection/quality organization and those of the purchasing department. The quality personnel, at times, thought the purchasing department's goal was to buy from the supplier with the lowest price and let the product quality take care of itself. The purchasing personnel felt that inspectors were impediments to the receipt of material and, by their "unjust" demands and "nit-picking" inspections, caused the price of the supplies to escalate, or worse still, result in many suppliers refusing to deal with the company.

There may be some merit to both arguments. Frequently, the buyer, who after diligent search finds a supplier who can provide the product at the required schedule, does not wish to place a stumbling block in the path of obtaining the supply by questioning the potential supplier's ability to meet the specified quality requirements. On the other hand, there are occasions when an inspector's rejection of the product for nonconformance appears, to the purchasing personnel, based on an arbitrary judgment.

To insure that products are received on time and at acceptable quality levels, both organizations must work together. The purchasing department must be convinced that the criteria used by the inspection personnel are not arbitrary, but reflect the engineering requirements and company standards of workmanship. The inspection personnel must understand the buyers' position and take steps to alleviate their concerns. One way is for the inspectors to work with the buyers in explaining to the suppliers before shipment what criteria of acceptability will be used when products are received. This may resolve any problems beforehand.

When the purchasing department appears adamant about the seeming infringement of the inspection/quality organization upon their supplier selection, the following procedure is recommended. It is based on the importance of good quality and the most effective language purchasing personnel understand, dollars.

A number of suppliers whose past quality history reflect high rejection rates should be selected for review. The costs of processing the rejected lots should be added to the purchase price of these supplies. These additional costs include the following:

- Preparation of the rejection reports

- Processing of the rejected lots through the materials review board

- Applying tightened inspection as a result of the high rejection rate

- Screening (100 percent inspection), or reworking nonconforming items, when necessary, to meet the production schedule

- Inspection of the replacement parts

- Packaging and shipment of rejected lots returned to the supplier

The assistance of the production control and material handling personnel can be solicited to help accumulate costs figures. These may include the costs of the additional movement of the rejected products, and the costs of revising the production schedule to accommodate substitute parts.

All costs should be totaled, added to the contracted price of the supplies, and presented to the purchasing department head as the true cost of the low-quality supplies.

Unquestionably, this total cost will prove to be many times the original purchase price. The results of this study would surprise and impress the purchasing manager, and result in a purchasing department more sympathetic to supplier selection with higher quality products.

Having won the support of the purchasing department, inspection/quality personnel should provide assistance in the selection of acceptable suppliers. Initially they should hold seminars with all the buyers and their supervisors, and acquaint them with the quality operation requirements as they relate to purchased supplies. As discussed before, inspection/quality personnel, together with the purchasing department, should conduct surveys at the potential suppliers' facilities. They should also make available, to the purchasing department, the quality ratings, by commodity, of the current suppliers and provide explanations concerning the development of these ratings. When subsequent supplier quality problems arise, they should work with the buyers to resolve these problems. When the suppliers have questions regarding some of the quality and technical requirements of the purchase orders, they should assist the buyers in explaining these requirements, so as to convince the suppliers of the lack of arbitrariness, by the inspectors, during their product examination. In short, the inspection/quality personnel should assist the purchasing department in making acceptable suppliers out of marginal ones, instead of eliminating them.

Inspection/quality personnel should also assist the purchasing department in discussing with the engineers the possibility of relaxing requirements, when feasible, when the purchasing department is unable to find suitable suppliers. When items can only be procured from a single source, inspection/quality personnel should attempt to qualify an alternate source.

In today's climate of World Class Quality and just-in-time operations, greater cooperation between the purchasing and inspection/quality departments is essential. In attempting to implement Dr. Deming's philosophy of using a single qualified supply source for each commodity, it is necessary to weed out the marginal suppliers who cannot be improved, and use only the few suppliers that prove capable of consistently providing quality supplies while maintaining the specified shipping schedule.

FIELD SERVICE

Liaison with field service by inspection/quality personnel is highly important to enable rapid feedback of the product's quality perception by its users. Field service personnel, by immediately notifying inspection/quality of any problem with the equipment in the field, allow immediate corrective action to be taken at the production facilities, thus precluding the shipment of additional nonconforming product.

While the members of field service must address their efforts to rectify all problems, as a result of any company or supplier shortcomings, there are occasions when solution to the problems are not within the company's jurisdiction.

Some customers provide their own components for installation into the company's equipment. On other occasions, the company may produce products designed by the customer. This knowledge is frequently not available to users, who generally consider any problem the fault of the company providing the end product.

Since field service members are in close touch with users it is necessary to insure that they are well informed of the extent of the company's obligation towards its delivered product. During their indoctrination, field service should be advised of those components in the equipment which are supplied by the customer. When users' complaints are not applicable to the supplier's contractual responsibilities, the members of the service department should advise the users, and notify the inspection/quality engineering personnel. While the solution of the problem is not within the company's responsibility, the inspection/quality personnel should promptly notify the customers of the condition and assist them in rectifying the problem. In addition, the procedure described in Chapter 22, relative to the processing of field complaints, should be implemented. This requires that a review of the reported problem components or equipment in production, stores, or assembly be performed, to determine whether the problem exists at the company's facility, and to take the appropriate action as needed.

When an item is to be returned from the field for repair or replacement, the inspection/quality organization works with field service to determine the validity of the complaint.

Many companies have amplified field service operations to include monitoring services of the initial installation and operation of the equipment. These services may include the performance, with the engineering personnel, of the initial qualification testing at the customer's facilities. Frequently, when this is done, members of the inspection/quality organization are also present. At times, the company may require that only representatives of either the field service or the inspection/quality department participate in the monitoring of tests or installations. When the field service personnel are delegated to monitor testing, the inspection/quality organization must insure that any data reflecting an equipment failure, plus the engineering analysis of the cause for this failure, are quickly made available to them. This way they may take appropriate actions to insure that the problem does not appear in the production equipment. On the other hand, when the inspection/quality personnel monitor the test, they should insure that the appropriate information is provided to the field service department.

PERSONNEL

The inspection/quality organization maintains constant communication with the personnel department. This organization usually processes requisitions for additional personnel and is involved when workers are removed from the inspection/quality organization. Both departments coordinate their efforts to develop and upgrade job descriptions in inspection/quality organization. Many companies have the personnel department periodically review the wage scales of the various jobs in the company against those of similar local companies, and make suitable adjustments, when applicable. The inspection/quality supervisors usually participate in these reviews.

When employees in the inspection/quality organization are members of a union, close coordination with the personnel department is needed. It usually provides guidance to the inspection/quality department relative to the processing of complaints and grievances by the union against the department.

In many companies, motivation and training programs are developed under the jurisdiction of the personnel department. The inspection/quality supervisors help develop and implement these programs when they affect their departments. In some companies, the inspection/quality personnel participate in those programs which affect the quality elements of the operation even when they are directed to other personnel. More about this in Chapter 23.

Currently, companies have developed programs of quality review and improvement throughout the organization. This includes joint committee actions, which review proposals and recommendations for quality improvement. They meet regularly, during working hours, to investigate suggestions and make recommendations for their implementation. Generally, the members of the joint committees participate voluntarily. The personnel department, acknowledges the committees' success.

INSPECTION/QUALITY DEPARTMENT

Occasionally, inspection/quality personnel are not fully aware of the organization and functions of their department, and how their job assignments fit into the structure of the department and of the company. This condition is rectified in a number of ways. For example, new members of the department, as part of the indoctrination program, are made aware of the organization and responsibilities of the total department as well as their respective functions within it. The inspection/quality managers hold periodic sessions and review their respective functions and relationships to the other members of the organization, as well as their contributions to the profitability of the company. Recommendations, relative to their functions, are solicited from the inspectors and discussed at these meetings. These sessions serve to emphasize to the inspection/quality personnel that they are essential parts of the organization and the company.

Personnel interaction should manifest itself throughout the daily work period. For example, when a problem with the quality of items inspected in one section becomes evident during a subsequent operation, the inspection personnel of the second department should notify the original inspection agency, and lend assistance in the definition and correction of the problem. This coordination may be conducted on an inspector-to-inspector basis, or the problem may become the subject of a joint corrective action committee.

Notification of problems with products received at the plant or at the next production operation, including requests for corrective actions, should be addressed to the supervisors of the responsible departments. Information copies of the notifications should also be provided to the area inspection/quality personnel, enabling them to follow up on the corrective actions taken by the area production supervisors or suppliers. The effect of not addressing these problems is demonstrated in the following example.

EXAMPLE

In one company, inspection/quality or production supervisors notified inspection personnel from previous production sections of all product quality variances detected subsequent to the inspection operation. Thus, it became the inspector's responsibility to initiate corrective actions and provide suitable responses to the complainant. This practice led to production's impression that the delivery of conforming products was the responsibility of the inspection/quality department. Often production personnel condemned the initial inspectors and sometimes tried to charge the inspection account for the costs incurred by the receipt of the nonconforming part. Thus, production shrugged off its responsibility for the nonconformances, and, when corrective action was requested, responded that it was the obligation of the inspection department to perform additional inspection to insure that any deviant material was not released from the manufacturing center.

To overcome this problem, meetings were held with members of the inspection/quality, production, and purchasing departments. At these meetings, the vice president of operations, supported by the director of quality assurance, presented an overview of the relative responsibilities of each department concerning the delivery of conforming products. It was emphasized that, for a company to stay competitive and provide products of world class quality, it was essential that the products be made correctly the first time. It was also stressed that quality cannot be inspected into the product. The function of the inspection/quality organization was explained as one which, through its audits, surveillances, and inspections, maintained a review over the manufacturing and procurement processes to insure that they were in control. It was further pointed out that, through the data and analyses of these reviews, the inspection/quality personnel were able to pinpoint the problem, and identify to the production supervisors, those areas which failed to provide consistently conforming product. The role of the inspection/quality organization was described as one of assisting the responsible organizations to initiate and implement the necessary corrective actions, and to review the effectiveness of these actions. It was emphasized that it would be highly uneconomical and ineffective to depend upon the inspectors to detect, after the fact, all product nonconformances, especially with many products at a quality level of parts per million.

SUPPLIERS

Liaison of the inspection/quality organization with the company's suppliers is a vital part of its functions. See Chapter 12 for the discussion of the control of purchased supplies.

The initial contact with the suppliers is usually made during the facilities survey when the inspection/quality auditors review the capabilities of the supplier's equipment, organization, and procedures to verify that they will be able to consistently provide products which conform to the necessary technical and quality requirements. At this survey, the auditors also review the purchase orders' quality and technical requirements to assure that the supplier has a total understanding of all the elements.

During this initial contact, the inspection/quality engineers should try to impress upon the supplier the importance of complying with all the technical and quality requirements of the purchase orders. The supplier should be advised that having a good quality rating is important to a continuing relationship with the company. If the supplier has a problem in meeting the requirements, or has inadvertently produced some nonconforming products, it would be advisable to notify the company prior to the shipment of these products. If applicable, the auditors should explain their company's program for processing vendor's requests for waivers or deviations from purchase order requirements (see Chapter 16).

Throughout the production, supplier contact should be maintained by the inspection/quality personnel. Some companies require purchasing department personnel be present during these contacts. When a shipment is rejected at the company's facilities, the supplier should be immediately notified, usually through the company's buyer. At times, the supplier may question the validity of the rejection. In those instances, the supplier should be invited to visit the company's facilities to discuss the rejection with the applicable inspection personnel. At that time, and in the supplier's presence, the rejected product may be reinspected. It is important that this demonstration is performed without prejudice and with an open mind. It is also imperative that the validity of the inspection process is impressed upon the supplier's representative. At times, an inspector's error may be detected by the supplier. The company's inspector should acknowledge the error and take measures to prevent future occurrences. Occasionally, the problem is due to the different methods of inspection used by the supplier and the company. This must be corrected to the satisfaction of both participants.

EXAMPLE

On one occasion, a supplier used a measurement method which did not have the required accuracy. At another time, both the supplier and the company used fixed gages during their respective product inspections. The company had used a new gage and the supplier used an older one. In those instances, it was apparent that, while both were using gages of the proper degree of accuracy, as a result of the gage's wear allowance and gage tolerance built in the new gage, a product whose measurement was close to the tolerance could be considered acceptable to one but not to the other. See Chapter 25 for additional information about this condition. When this occurs, the use of a variables means of inspection would demonstrate the actual measurement of the product, and serve to rectify the problem.

During production, inspection/quality personnel may need to meet with the supplier. This occurs if the supplier requests assistance from the company in evaluating or improving its quality program, such as personnel training in special techniques being used by the company. At other times, when some problem arises with the use of the supplied product in the field, it may be necessary to confer with the supplier about the causes of the nonconformance. This may also require that the inspection/quality engineer visit the supplier's facility to review its quality controls to assure that some deficiency did not contribute to the problem.

EXAMPLE

A purchased component failed during field operations and was returned to the company. There, part of the component was sent to an independent laboratory for failure analysis.

The company inspection/quality engineer visited the supplier, who was also given part of the failed component for analysis. The engineer reviewed the undelivered components in process at the supplier; witnessed the supplier's retest of these components; and re-audited the supplier's quality and manufacturing systems.

The results of the audit revealed a heat treat processing change, which could have caused the component failure. This was confirmed by the independent laboratory's analysis. Thus, all subsequent components subjected to the new heat treat process were retested using more stringent procedures. Those components which failed to pass the test were rejected and scrapped. The supplier expressed appreciation for the rapid notification of the field failure, and of the support of the company's inspection and engineering personnel to resolve the problem expeditiously.

Progressive companies generally invite their suppliers to periodic meetings wherein they discuss new development and products. This helps suppliers anticipate new requirements which may, subsequently, be placed upon them. In addition, suppliers' recommendations are solicited concerning the components they may be expected to provide for the new products.

At other times, meetings are arranged with those suppliers whose vendor ratings reflect some problem. At these meetings, ratings analyses are presented by the company's inspection/quality personnel, and the possible corrective actions, as outlined by the suppliers, are critiqued. Subsequently, inspection/quality personnel may visit the supplier's facilities to determine the effectiveness of the corrective actions.

Periodically, the company's inspection/quality personnel may visit suppliers to verify the accuracy of inspection/test data which has been submitted to the company in accordance with the purchase order requirements.

All these actions are used for the primary purpose of assisting the supplier in providing quality products to the company. Through these efforts the supplier senses a partnership relation with the company.

CUSTOMERS

The inspection/quality department usually confers with the in-house customer representative and often with the customer's external personnel.

In the past, a few companies used the inspection/quality department to appease an angry customer. We are all familiar with the cartoon depicting a Casper Milquetoast-type of character* in the customer service department, being berated by the supervisor in front of an irate customer. After the customer departs, the supervisor informs the inspector to forget the matter and take no further action to rectify the complaint. The inspector has no immediate recourse. There is no question that this procedure is not conducive to good customer relationships. It is also quite detrimental to company morale. The affected personnel lose credibility in the eyes of the

*Milquetoast—a much timid person; comic strip character created by H. T. Webster (1885–1952).

customer, further damaging relationships. Fortunately, most companies consider inspection/quality personnel as valuable assets for attaining acceptable quality levels, and maintaining good customer relationships. They, therefore, see no need to engage in this questionable activity.

In well-run companies, the inspection/quality organization acts as an ombudsman, protecting the customers' rights. This is often easier said than done. Protecting these rights may necessitate stopping shipments of products which do not meet customer requirements. When the monthly billing is at stake, management, at times, may take a different view of the situation.

The successful inspection/quality organization, however, makes every effort to insure that it rarely withholds a shipment. Through planning, audits, and surveillances, most product problems may be detected, and corrected, well in advance of the shipping date. However, there may come a time when it is necessary to stop a shipment of a product regardless of the effect to the company's billing.

EXAMPLE

A major electronic equipment producer was severely behind in its initial shipping schedule of a product. At long last, the product was ready. Before the shipping date, an in-process inspection of component parts found them to be defective. Their use could have a deleterious effect on the equipment's function. The inspection manager notified the project engineer that, in all good faith, the equipment should not be shipped until the suspect component was removed and replaced. This would be time-consuming, and necessitate some retesting of the end item, and impact the delivery data. The project engineer was adamant that the equipment be shipped and that correction be made at the customer's facilities at a later date. The inspection manager refused to accept this condition, but noted that it may be acceptable to ship the equipment provided the customer was first made aware of the deficiency, and approved of its shipment. The project engineer was concerned that the customer would not approve. The matter was brought to the attention of the company's vice president of operations.

After hearing both sides of the argument, the vice president ruled that the shipment should not be made unless the suspect component was removed, or the customer agreed to accept suspect shipment. He stated that the customer was already upset with previous delays, and he would no doubt be furious, if after this new delay, equipment failed. The matter was finally resolved by the inspection manager notifying the customer of the problem, and obtaining agreement to have the equipment shipped as is with the provision for correction at the customer's site. The customer was truly appreciative of the inspection manager's actions, which enhanced the company's credibility in the eyes of the customer.

USER

To maintain customer confidence, inspection/quality personnel must take pains to insure that no nonconforming product is knowingly shipped or submitted unless the deficiency is made known to the customer. In some companies, it is policy for inspection/quality personnel to contact major equipment users just prior to the initial shipment and elicit their comments of the equipment's performance and quality. This serves to establish a point of contact to be used by the customer in the event of any problems at the customer's site. This action also provides an indication, to the user, of the company's interest in insuring full customer satisfaction.

When the product is transported to a distributor for subsequent shipment to the user, this procedure cannot usually be followed. However, the inspection/quality personnel, can make certain that the distributing agency immediately notifies them when there is a customer complaint, so that rapid corrective action can be implemented and the user advised accordingly.

This ombudsman function of the inspection/quality organization extends beyond assurance that products shipped conform to contractual requirements. That department should also insure that attention is paid to customer needs beyond these requirements. Close liaison between inspection/quality and engineering personnel, during the product development stage, goes a long way to satisfying these needs.

When the company has resident customer representatives the inspection/quality department should submit the product to them, when required, for acceptance prior to shipment. Of course, the inspectors should insure that the product meets all the contractual requirements prior to this submission. If, for some reason, it is necessary to submit a product with an uncorrected variance, this should be brought to the customer's attention before submission. The inspection/quality personnel should also make sure that any rework resulting from the customer's inspection, is satisfactorily performed prior to resubmission. When there is no customer's representative at the plant, the inspection/quality personnel should act for the customer, and insure that the product is in full compliance before shipment. This is done by affixing an acceptance stamp to the shipping documents.

Another function of the inspection/quality organization is to insure that the customer makes no demands upon the company that are in excess of the contractual requirements. Based upon a factor of judgment independent of contract requirements, the customer's representative may decide that a product is not in full compliance. This must be refuted diplomatically. To insure that these unauthorized demands are not made to production personnel, a procedure must be used so that the customer only contacts an authorized member of the inspection/quality department. To insure that no event embarrasses the customer's representative, procedures must ensure that any conflicts are discussed away from the production area. One company has developed a program which provides for weekly meetings with the resident customer's representatives. Here, any unresolved problems are discussed, and assignments made to the attendees, both customer and company, to follow up for the resolution of these problems. Minutes of these meetings are issued, and at subsequent meetings, the status of the open items are discussed. To insure that the local representatives do not persist in making uncalled for demands, efforts are usually made to include their supervisors in these meetings.

CHAPTER FOURTEEN

Manufacturing Control

INTRODUCTION

This chapter continues the presentation of the implementation of the inspection/quality program during manufacturing operations. It discusses the elements of control during the following fabrication stages.

- Preliminary planning
- Capability analysis
- Qualification of processes and tooling
- Preparation of work and inspection instructions
- Inspection of work in process
- Surveillance during manufacturing operations
- Final parts inspection, acceptance, and in-house movement
- Records
- Corrective action
- Just-in-time manufacture

PRELIMINARY PLANNING

The control of the inspection/quality operation is based on two concepts: (1) the process should not relieve the manufacturing supervisor from the responsibility of producing and releasing quality products; and (2) the inspection/quality control process should assure the production of quality products at acceptable and reasonable costs.[1]

Here is how a company's manufacturing planning operation should be conducted.

Based on engineering drawings and specifications, production engineering prepares charts delineating the flow of material during the fabrication and assembly processes.

Inspection/quality engineering reviews the charts and incorporates the anticipated positions for in-process and final inspections and tests.

Production engineering reviews the characteristics to be manufactured and determines the availability of the necessary equipment, such as machine tools, fixtures, and other facilities. Prior to assigning the appropriate machine tools for the manufacturing processes, a capability analysis, as discussed in the next section, should be done.

When a product feature is beyond the capability of the available machine tools, production engineering should consider whether to fabricate the product at an outside facility, or whether the machine tool can or should be updated or replaced to increase the plant's capability. When necessary, the department prepares designs for new or altered tooling. The inspection/quality engineering personnel participate in the tooling and fixturing review. This is done to establish the possibility of using the tooling as a medium of inspection. When feasible, recommendations are made to incorporate, in the tool design, the features of accuracy needed.

CAPABILITY ANALYSIS

The inspection/quality engineering personnel perform a capability analysis for each machine tool and process to be used in the manufacture and assembly of the product. This is done by inspecting a series of parts for the specified tolerances. This is done at periodic production intervals, after it has first been determined that the machine tools or processes are operating in a state of statistical control. See Chapter 24 for detailed techniques of determining capability and statistical control of production equipment and processes.

The results of these analyses should be maintained by the production engineering department for each machine tool and process, and utilized in their assignment for the fabrication of assembly or each manufactured product. After a major overhaul or maintenance action, or upon the receipt of a new machine tool or fixture, a similar capability analysis, and the determination of the statistical control for the tool, should be performed.

QUALIFICATION

After fabrication or procurement of each machine or assembly tool, a sample part, should be submitted to the tool room inspector for qualification inspection. This is done by comparing the tool to the tool drawing, if available, and by comparing the first produced part, to the piece part or assembly drawing. This qualification should be performed prior to release of the tool to the production area. When the tool is procured from an outside supplier, the purchase order should contain the provision that the supplier ship, with the tool, a piece part or assembly. The qualification inspection can then be performed.

When it is not feasible to perform this qualification before the start of production, the inspection should be conducted on one of the first pieces of the lot. Continued fabrication should be held in abeyance until the tool qualification has been successfully performed.

When a machine tool is tape or computer controlled, the accuracy of the program should be qualified before it is allowed to be put to use. Similarly, all jigs and fixtures to be utilized, should be submitted to a qualification inspection prior to release. Subsequent revisions of the computer programs or fixtures require a requalification for the revised characteristics.

Notations on the qualification record should explain the frequency of subsequent requalifications. These tools and programs are thus treated as media of inspection and controlled in the same manner as that of measuring equipment (see Chapter 25). All characteristics controlled by the tool or computer program are not inspected on a lot-by-lot basis. Some characteristics are not entirely controlled by the tool or program. Thus, the qualification record should include a list of those piece part or assembly characteristics which will require lot-by-lot inspection.

PREPARATION OF WORK, INSPECTION INSTRUCTIONS, AND SHOP TRAVELERS

Production engineering should prepare the necessary work instructions and operation sheets as well as the raw material requisitions for each part/assembly as needed. Inspection/quality engineering should review these documents on a sample basis, and determine their adequacy and conformance to the inspection/quality and workmanship requirements of the contract and the company.

The operation sheet usually notes the first piece, in-process, and final inspection stations for each product. Shop travelers denote the route of material throughout the manufacturing operations. These travelers accompany each lot through the fabrication, assembly, and inspection.

Some shop travelers provide space for inspection results, thereby eliminating the need for a separate record.

The inspection/quality engineer should coordinate with production and production engineering personnel in periodic process reviews for changing conditions.

Inspection instructions are prepared by inspection/quality control engineering as described in Chapter 8.

INSPECTION OF THE WORK IN PROCESS

Stores personnel select the raw material specified on the piece part operation sheet and cut the required amount for fabrication of the manufactured lot. The material is submitted to the area fabrication or patrol inspector for code verification. This may be done by a simple chemical or physical inspection/test such as the application of a chemical reagent or a hardness check. The results should be noted on the production traveler.

When the issued raw material is not completely used during lot fabrication, the residual material should be submitted, by production, to the area inspector for code verification before being returned to the stores area.

The characteristics of the first piece of each fabricated part are inspected after each operation to assure that the setup is correct. See Chapter 9 for a description. The inspection results are recorded on the shop traveler. As noted, characteristics controlled by a qualified tool or computer program are inspected in accordance with the frequency established for the tool or program. The uncontrolled characteristics are included in the lot-by-lot inspection. When the in-process inspection is performed by production personnel, the procedure described in Chapter 9 should be followed.

SURVEILLANCE DURING MANUFACTURING OPERATIONS

The patrol inspector is in a strong position to quickly detect any chronic trouble spots in the production process. Prompt feedback can provide tremendous assistance toward the ongoing improvement of product quality. The patrol or roving inspector monitors the following elements of the manufacturing processes.

- Setup—to determine that the
  —latest drawing and manufacturing instructions were used
  —proper sequence of operations were done
  —tools and fixtures used were subject to prior qualification approval

- Part placement on the tool

- Cleanliness of the work and tool surfaces

- Materials—to insure the presence of the appropriately annotated move tags

- Any necessary corrective actions

Surveillance of the special process operations is described in Chapter 15.

FINAL PIECE PART INSPECTION, ACCEPTANCE, AND IN-HOUSE MOVEMENT

It must be emphasized that detail parts inspection does not guarantee that the completed product will function satisfactorily. Such things as adjustments and product tolerance may affect the ability of the parts to be properly assembled and function. Accordingly, operational testing of the end product is usually necessary to assure that the unit will perform satisfactorily. However, the results of the detail parts inspection can provide valuable data.

At the final piece parts inspection station, examinations and sampling plans are performed in accordance with the instructions prepared by the inspection/quality engineer as described in Chapter 8. When the traveler indicates the quantity of parts inspected during the in-process operation, that amount may be deducted from the final inspection sample.

Upon completion of the final parts inspection, the conforming lot is tagged with an acceptance ticket and the results recorded. See Chapter 17 for the description of the identification methods of the inspection status of parts throughout the manufacturing process.

Before movement of the production lot to the next manufacturing center, assembly, or stores area, the final inspector reviews the traveler to verify that all applicable manufacturing, rework, and reinspection operations have been completed. When the lot is found unacceptable, a discrepancy report is processed (see Figure 14-1). The final inspection record is noted with the report number, and a rejection tag is attached to the lot. The material is then moved to a holding area or to the materials review crib. See Chapter 16 for a description of the method of processing nonconforming material.

Accepted material is noted on the inspection record (see Figure 8-12), and an acceptance move ticket (see Figure 9-2) is attached to the lot. This ticket notes the date of inspection, the drawing number and its configuration level, the quantity accepted, and the material's next destination. The inspector's acceptance stamp is also applied to the tag. This tag remains with the material until the last item of the lot is disposed of at the next fabrication, assembly, or stores area.

When material is rejected, but can be reworked at the production area where the rejection occurred, the nature of the rejection and the quantity rejected is noted on the inspection record or production traveler. The material is tagged with a salvage tag (Figure 14-2) noting the same information, and the material moved to the manufacturing station for rework. The reworked characteristics are subsequently reinspected. The salvage tag is removed and retained with the lot inspection record. The inspection record or traveler is stamped, the move ticket is attached, and the lot forwarded to the next scheduled area. When the material is rejected during in-process inspection, it is routed with the balance of the lot.

The production supervisor should insure that the material is adequately protected from handling damage and adverse environmental conditions before movement to the next in-house area.

Upon receipt of the accepted lot from the previous manufacturing center, the receiving department's supervisor should review it for evidence of prior inspection, count, handling, and environmental damage. If found acceptable, the supervisor usually notes the acceptance on the move tag and processes the lot through the subsequent manufacturing, assembly, or stores operations. If a discrepancy is noted, the supervisor records that,

MATERIAL REVIEW/QUALITY CONTROL
DISCREPANCY REPORT

PART NO./REV.	VENDOR NAME/DEPT. NO.	VENDOR CODE	DISCREPANCY REPORT NO. **8219**
PART NAME	P.O./OPER. NO.	JOB NO.	

LOT QUANTITY	SAMPLE		INSPECTED BY:	DATE	INITATING DEPT.
	SIZE	DISCREPANT			

NO.	TYPE	CHARAC. (FROM DWG. SPEC. ETC.)	DISCREP. (LIST EXTENT OF NON-CONFORM.)	CODE	QTY

CODE

I —
P C O U P E. OTHER
D. PLANT 3 FAB ITEMS
C. PLANT 2 FAB ITEMS
B. PLANT 1 FAB ITEMS
A. PURCHASED MAT'LS/SERVICES

II =
P U O R P G
5. MATERIAL
4. DIMENTIONAL
3. DATA/CERTS. MISSING OR INCOMPLETE
2. DAMAGED AT ASSEMBLY OR IN TRANSIT
1. WRONG OR INCOMPLETE ITEM

6. FINISH
7. PROCESS
8. MARKING
9. TEST/FUNCTIONAL

"PMRB REVIEW"

ME/PC

	QTY	ENG	OC
☐ RETURN TO VENDOR D.M. # ____	☐	☐	☐
☐ REWORK INST. NO. ____	☐	☐	☐
☐ SCRAP (EST. COST) $ ____	☐	☐	☐
☐ REFER TO MRB	☐	☐	☐
☐ OTHER	☐	☐	☐
		APPROVAL	

MRB DISPOSITION

	QTY	ENG	OC
☐ USE AS IS	☐	☐	☐
☐ PROCESS RFD/RFW NO. ____	☐	☐	☐
☐ REPAIR INST NO. ____	☐	☐	☐
☐ OTHER	☐	☐	☐
		APPROVAL	

☐ REPAIR ☐ REWORK INSTRUCTIONS D.R.*

QTY.	INITIATED BY/TITLE	DATE

REWORK BY DEPT.	CHARGE TO DEPT	ESTIMATED COST OF REWORK/REPAIR $

METHOD OF REWORK/REPAIR:

DISPN.	INSPECTOR	DATE

ANALYSIS AND CORRECTIVE ACTION	PREVIOUS OCCURANCES:

SIGNATURE (ANALYSIS)	DATE	SIGNATURE (CORRECTIVE ACTION)	DATE

AUTHORIZED SIG./TITLE	CUSTOMER DISPOSITION	CONT. NO.
	RFD/RFW ☐ APPROVED ☐ DISAPPROVED	RFD/RFW ☐ APPROVED ☐ DISAPPROVED
	CUSTOMER ACTIVITY IDENT.	SIGNATURE DATE

QA FORM 114-011 11-91

FIGURE 14-1 Deficiency Report

```
                              SALVAGE
                               DO NOT USE

 Part No.                    Rev.     Part Name             Date

 Dept.        Shift          Operator        Quantity          Sequence
              1st ☐ 2nd ☐ 3rd ☐                          Responsible │ Rejected
 Discrepancy:


 Inspector:                        Foreman:

 White-Plant Mgr.; Yellow-Prod. Control; Pink-Q.A.; Manilla-Attached to Material    Form No. 114-013
```

FIGURE 14-2 Salvage Tag

refers the matter to the area inspector, and returns the lot to the preceding production supervisor. The area inspector should maintain a list of these discrepancies, and periodically gives it to the inspector at the responsible production department. A second copy of the list is given to the inspection/ quality engineer for subsequent analysis and corrective action, when warranted.

When the material requires submission to a customer's representative, the final piece parts inspector notifies the representative of its availability and obtains evidence of this acceptability on the inspection record and move tag.

After fabrication of the last item in the lot, the move ticket should be given to the area inspector who retains it with the lot inspection record.

RECORDS

All move and salvage tickets, records of inspection, surveillance, corrective action requests, and audits are maintained under the jurisdiction of the performing department's inspection personnel. A second copy of each record is provided to the inspection/quality engineer for subsequent analysis and report preparation. See Chapter 20.

CORRECTIVE ACTION

A copy of each discrepancy report should be forwarded to the responsible production supervisor for review and corrective action. A second copy should be provided to the area's inspection/quality personnel for coordination with the responsible production supervisor in the implementation of the corrective action.

When the discrepancy is of a serious or of a repetitive nature, the area quality/inspection engineer should process a corrective action request to the responsible production supervisor (see Figure 14-3). This usually requires a response within a specified time period. If the response is not received, or is considered unacceptable, a second corrective action request is usually sent to the production supervisor's supervisor. At the committed time of corrective action, the inspection/quality engineer should review the effectiveness of the action. See Chapter 22 for additional details of the corrective action program.

In addition to in-process inspection operations, a well-run inspection/quality organization can arrange for its program to extend into other manufacturing and support services, such as production control, material handling, and maintenance.[1] The inspection/quality engineer can advise the other groups of any operational problems.

EXAMPLES

One company experienced a high rejection rate due to rust on highly polished surfaces of several machined parts. Investigation noted that the machining area was adjacent to the plating baths which exuded acid fumes and caused the rust. Moving the plating baths to another area corrected the problem.

Parts awaiting manufacture were stacked adjacent to a machine. This was a hazard to the area employees, and sometimes resulted in damage to the parts by passing handling equipment. The production supervisor was advised of this condition and assigned the parts fabrication to a number of additional machines, thereby reducing the amount stacked at each machine.

At another company, an inspection/quality engineer, analyzing the high rejection rate at a subassembly area, noted that the surfaces of many anodized sheet metal cabinets were scratched. This was caused by improper handling during the anodizing operations. The problem was eliminated by exercising greater handling care, and by placing liners between each stacked sheet.

JUST-IN-TIME MANUFACTURE

Companies using just-in-time manufacture must insure that the products coming off the machines are of acceptable quality without the delay encountered in the subsequent inspection, and, as applicable, rejection and

```
┌─────────────────────────────────────────────────────────────────┐
│         PROCESS OF NOTIFICATION FOR CORRECTIVE ACTION            │
├─────────────────────────────────────────────────────────────────┤
│ TO:                          SUBJECT: REQUEST FOR CORRECTIVE     │
│                                        ACTION                    │
│                                                                  │
│                              FROM:              DEPT:            │
│                                                                  │
│                              DATE:                               │
│                                                                  │
│ ATTN:                        REF. P.O. NO.:                      │
├─────────────────────────────────────────────────────────────────┤
│ PART NAME:                             PART NO.:                 │
│ QUANTITY:            JOB NO.:           REQUEST NO.:             │
├─────────────────────────────────────────────────────────────────┤
│ DESCRIPTION OF DISCREPANCY:                                      │
│                                                                  │
│                                                                  │
│                                                                  │
│                                                                  │
│ (ENTER BELOW A REPORT AF YOUR FINDINGS AND CORRECTIVE ACTION)    │
├─────────────────────────────────────────────────────────────────┤
│ SUGGESTED CORRECTIVE ACTION:                                     │
│                                                                  │
│                                                                  │
│                                                                  │
├─────────────────────────────────────────────────────────────────┤
│ REPLY: (PLEASE RESPOND BY _____ ) DATE: _____  │
│                                                                  │
│                                                                  │
│ COPY NO. 1 – ORIGINATOR                                          │
│ COPY NO. 2 – RECEIVER                                            │
│ COPY NO. 3 – RETURN TO ORIGINATOR                               │
│ COPY NO. 4 – PURCHASE MATERIALS INSPECTION (BUY ITEM ONLY)      │
│                                                                  │
│ THIS IS COPY NO. 1 – 2 – 3              SIGNATURE:              │
│ F #1001 BREV12/87                                                │
└─────────────────────────────────────────────────────────────────┘
```

FIGURE 14-3 Corrective Action Request

rework operations. The use of statistical quality control can usually determine the process' capability to meet the required tolerances without the need for inspection. When control has been established and confirmed, audit inspection can be used to determine quality levels, while allowing the process to continue. Another method of determining product quality without holding up production, is accomplished through the use of continuous sampling plans. See Chapter 24 for a discussion of these plans.

REFERENCES

1. Stiles, Edward M. *Handbook for Total Quality Assurance*. Waterford, CT: Prentice Hall, 1969. pp. 33–36.

CHAPTER FIFTEEN

Special Processes Control

INTRODUCTION

In order to assure product quality, certain manufacturing operations require review and control of the process, in addition to the inspection/test of the product characteristics. Assuring quality products produced from special processes, rests upon the assumption that they are manufactured by qualified operators in qualified procedures which, through some destructive means, have demonstrated capability of producing acceptable products.

These processes include the following:

- Welding
- Applying organic finishes
- Plating
- Soldering
- Anodizing
- Heat treating
- Case hardening
- Casting and forging
- Molding

The common factor in all these processes is the fact that the inspection/testing of the product can only partially determine the quality of the product. The control of these processes include the following elements:

- Preparation of the special process specifications
- Preparation of work, inspection, and test instructions

- Qualification of the procedure and equipment
- Qualification and training of the operators and inspector/testers
- Process surveillance and product inspection/testing
- Corrective action and records

PREPARATION OF PROCESS SPECIFICATIONS

The special process specifications are generally prepared by the company's engineering department. They describe the necessary elements of the process, including the acceptability criteria, and the qualifications and tests. Frequently these specifications are obtained from the specifications and standards issued by applicable government or industry standards organizations.

PREPARATION OF WORK INSTRUCTIONS

It is customary for the production engineering department to elaborate on the specifications by providing clarifying and supplementary requirements which are pertinent to the individual company. These instructions are sometimes called Process Specification Notices (PSNs). See Figure 15-1 for an example. PSNs include the customer's and company's quality and workmanship requirements and the operation procedures.

To insure that the PSNs are correct, a qualification sample is fabricated. This may be the actual product, or a material representative of the product. The sample is subjected to process conditions to insure that the resulting part is representative of all the characteristics of the procedure. To demonstrate that the product can meet quality requirements, it is frequently necessary to perform destructive tests on the sample. Some special processes also require the preparation and use of workmanship specimens. These represent the minimum acceptable workmanship quality. When approved, the specimens are used to supplement the inspection instructions. When required, the sample and the procedure are submitted to the customer for approval prior to being used.

Any significant revisions to the PSN may require a requalification of the procedure, the preparation of a new sample, and a reinspection.

INSPECTION AND TEST INSTRUCTIONS

The inspection/quality engineer prepares instructions for the qualification, process surveillance, and product inspection/test. When possible, these

PROCESS SPECIFICATION NOTICE

1. **PURPOSE:**

   1.1 To provide a method for adhesive bonding of rubber products to aluminum surfaces.

2. **APPLICABLE SPECIFICATIONS and/or STANDARDS:**

   2.1 None.

3. **MATERIALS:**

   3.1 EC 847 Adhesive, Minnesota Mining & Mfg. Co., St. Paul, Minnesota. (Part No. 412-0028).

   3.2 *METHYL ETHYL KETONE*—Commercial grade.

   3.3 *ACETONE*—Commercial grade.

4. **PROCEDURE:**

   4.1 Aluminum surface to which adhesive is to be applied must be free of oil, grease, dust and other foreign substances. Clean with suitable degreasing solvent.

   4.2 Rubber product should be free of oil, dust, and grease. Talcum should be removed with acetone.

   4.3 Apply EC-847 by brush or flow gun to both the rubber surface and metal surface to be joined.

   4.4 Allow to dry until tacky, but no longer transfers to the finger when lightly touched.

   NOTE: Parts which cannot be conveniently assembled when tacky may be joined immediately after application of the adhesive.

   4.6 Equipment or excessive adhesive may be cleaned with *METHYL ETHYL KETONE* or *ACETONE.*

   4.7 For 90% of ultimate bond strength allow to dry, undisturbed, for a minimum of 48 hours.

   4.8 Coverage—approximately 200-250 sq. ft/gallon for medium brush coat of adhesive.

PREPARED BY	DATE	TITLE	**PSN**
APPROVED BY	DATE	APPLICATION FOR BONDING RUBBER PRODUCTS TO ALUMINUM	**56**

FIGURE 15-1   Process Specification Notice (PSN)

instructions are included in the PSNs. During the preparation of the qualification sample, these instructions are used to determine their adequacy in evaluating product characteristics.

QUALIFICATION OF PROCEDURE AND EQUIPMENT

After the PSN is drafted the production engineer performs the operation according to the procedure, to determine its adequacy. Several attempts may be needed. The inspection/quality engineer normally surveys these demonstrations, and performs, or monitors, the destructive and nondestructive tests on the qualification samples.

For some special processes, it may also be necessary to qualify the equipment used. This may be done by testing samples produced by the equipment and the process.

QUALIFICATION AND TRAINING OF OPERATORS AND INSPECTORS/TESTERS

The operators and inspectors/testers must demonstrate their ability to produce or inspect the product from these special processes. Special in-house training programs or those presented by schools or agencies may be used. Subsequent tests are administered to qualify the nondestructive tester to one of several grades of proficiency. See Chapter 24 for additional details concerning the training and qualification requirements of special process inspectors and testers.

PROCESS SURVEILLANCE

The area or patrol inspector generally maintains surveillance over the special process manufacturing operations. This includes reviewing the various operational steps to assure that the applicable procedure is being followed, and verifying that the operator and equipment, as applicable, have evidence of current qualification status.

Certain processes require the production of sample pieces at the beginning of each shift, and the successful performance of special tests on these samples, before production can start. Other processes require periodic test of solutions and baths. In most instances, checklists and audit forms are developed for use during each special process (see Figure 15-2).

INSPECTION/TEST

Each lot or, in the case of large equipment, each part, is submitted for in-process and final inspection. Special tests such as radiographic, ultrasonic,

Verificaton Area	Element	Verification Method	Reference
Paint Department	1. Mfg personnel shall perform the special process operations in accordance with the applicable process specifications and work instructions.	Check for presence of applicable P.S.N.'s for cleaning, pre-treatment and finishing in the respective areas performing these operations.	QAP 710 Para. 3.2
	2. Same as 1	Verify that cleaning and pre-treatment tanks are maintained at the required temperatures.	QAP 710 Para. 3.2 and applicable P.S.N.
	3. Appropriate records as specified in the operating procedures and instruction shall be maintained.	Check process records for indication that strength of chemicals is being maintained.	QAP 710 Para. 4.1 Applicable PSN
	4. Same as 1	Check material awaiting paint operations for evidence of cleaning/pre-treatment as applicable.	QAP 710 Para 3.2 Verify (thru review of inventory) that primers and paints are of the proper type (spec) as specified on the applicable P.S.N.
	5. Correct materials are being used.	Verify (thru review of inventory) that primers and paints are of the proper type (spec) as specified on the applicable P.S.N.	Applicable P.S.N.
Paint Department	6. Primer coating as specified.	Check application and thickness of primer coating.	Applicable P.S.N.
	7. Finish coating is as specified.	Check application and thickness of finish coating.	Applicable P.S.N.
Painted Material in Assembly Area	8. Finish coating is as specified.	Check to insure finish color is as specified.	Applicable P.S.N.
	9. Finish coat has adequate coverage.	Check for adequate coverage per acceptance criteria.	Q.C.I. 0700.5
	10. Excessive flaking or peeling.	Check painted surfaces for evidence of excessive flaking or peeling per acceptance criteria.	Q.C.I. 0700.5
	11. Evidence of Foreign debris.	Check painted surfaces for evidence of foriegn debris per acceptance standard.	Q.C.I 0700.5
	12. Excessive overspray or runs.	Check painted surfaces for evidence of excessive overspray or runs per acceptance criteria.	Q.C.I. 0700.5

FIGURE 15-2 Special Process Audit

QAP AUDIT EVALUATION RECORD SHEET

II NO._____ QAP NO._____ TITLE OF QAP_____

ISSUE DATE _____ EFF. DATE _____ _____

AUDITOR_____ _____ AUDIT DATE _____ NEXT AUDIT DATE _____

ELEMENT	1	2	3	4	5	6	7	8	9	10	11	12	13	14	15	16	17	18	19	20	TOTAL
OBSERVATIONS																					
DEFECTIVES																					

COMMENTS AND/OR DEFECTIVES	PROPOSED CORRECTIVE ACTION

FIGURE 15-2 Continued

dye-penetrant, and magnetic particle are performed using specialized equipment. See Chapter 25 for a description of these tests and the needed qualification of the inspectors/testers.

Rejected lots or parts are returned to the manufacturing area for rework. This may frequently require the preparation and approval of special procedures. See Figure 15-3 for an example. After the rework, the parts are reinspected.

CORRECTIVE ACTION

When a nonconforming product is found, a discrepancy report is prepared and given to the responsible production supervisor for review and corrective action implementation. One copy of the report is provided to the inspection/quality engineer for review. When the subsequent analysis reveals an out-of-control trend or condition, the inspection/quality engineer issues, to the responsible production supervisor, a Corrective Action Request, and the procedures noted in Chapter 22 are implemented. Corrective action may include, as appropriate, any of the following:

- Adjustment of solutions, equipment, or process

- Replacement of the solutions, equipment, or process

- Readjustment and recertification of the equipment or process

- Modification and requalification of the special process procedure

- Retraining and recertification of the operator

- Rejection of the product submitted, subject to evaluation

EXAMPLE

Here is how one company controlled its welding process.

Prior to the start of production, the weld engineer, a member of the production engineering department, prepared PSNs for all weldments to be used on the project. These procedures included a drawing for each major weldment. These drawings identified, at the applicable location, the PSN number for each weld joint. The engineer also prepared the special PSNs for the qualification of welds, equipment, operators, and testers.

Then the engineer prepared specimens of each weld joint using the applicable procedure. These samples were subjected to the destructive and nondestructive tests prescribed in the specification. A portion of the sample was also subjected, by the inspection/quality engineer, to the applicable nondestructive testing and visual inspections. The nondestructive tests consisted, as applicable, of magnetic particle, radiographic, dye-penetrant, or ultrasonic. In addition, destructive tests were performed on the weld samples. These tests included the root, side bend, and fillet weld soundness tests.

STANDARD WELDING PROCEDURE

THIS JOINT SHALL BE USED FOR   CLASS   TYPE(S)   AND IS APPLICABLE TO:
ALUMINUM CASTING REPAIR - CRACKS OR POROSITY

BASE METAL(S)
AL-356-T6 CSTG.

EDGE PREPARATION
REMOVE DEFECT - CHIP, GRIND, ROUTE OR MACHINE

CLEANING
WASH WITH ACETONE OR EQUAL - WIRE BRUSH USING S/S

PROCESS
M.I.G.

FLUX OR INERT GAS
ARGON

POWER SOURCE
CONSTANT VOLTAGE

CLASSIFICATION OF FILLER METAL AWS/ASTM
5356

POSITION OF WELD
FLAT OR HORIZONTAL

SPEED (IF AUTOMATIC)
N.A.

BACKING
N.A.

PREHEAT
ROOM TEMPERATURE

INTERPASS TEMPERATURE
N.A.

GOUGING (METHOD & LOCATION)
CHIP, GRIND OR ROUTE

REMARKS:

NON-DESTRUCTIVE INSPECTION SHALL BE PERFORMED IN ACCORDANCE WITH SPECIFICATION OF CLASS AND TYPE OF WELDING AS INDICATED ON APPLICABLE DRAWINGS.

REMOVE DEFECT - INSPECT USING A DIE PENETRATION METHOD. LEAVE NO SHARP CORNERS. IF CASTING IS CRACKED ALL THE WAY THROUGH A TAPERED HOLE SHOULD BE DRILLED AT EACH END AND IF POSSIBLE REMOVE AN EQUAL AMOUNT OF METAL FROM EACH SIDE TO EQUAL WELDING STRESS.

PASS NO.	FILLER METAL SIZE	TUNG. OR CARB. DIA.	AMPS	VOLTS	DC +/-
I	1/16"		240 290	27-29	

NUMBER OF PASSES - AS REQUIRED - STRINGER BEADS TO BE USED AS CONSISTANT WITH GOOD WELDING PRACTICE.

SKETCH OF WELD

DEFECT POROSITY   DEFECT CRACK

DEFECTS REMOVED & REWELDED

PREPARED BY:	REVISIONS			
	NOTICE	SYM	DATE	APPROVAL
DATE:				
APPROVED BY:				
DATE:				
APPROVED BY:				
DATE:				

PSN — 54-0114

CODE 93568	SHEET	OF

FORM 145

FIGURE 15-3 Repair Procedure

The failure of a weld specimen to pass any of the destructive or nondestructive tests due to the inadequacy of the weld procedure, required the weld engineer to revise the procedure and prepare new specimens with the revised characteristics. These specimens were then subjected to the tests.

After the welds proved to be sound and conformed to requirements, the PSNs were submitted to the customer, for approval, after which, they were issued to the production personnel.

Any procedure revisions, as noted in the PSNs, required new qualification samples and demonstrations. The revised PSNs, and the new qualification samples were submitted to the customer for approval.

RECORDS AND EVALUATION

All records of in-process and final inspections/tests, audits, and surveillances are maintained under the jurisdiction of the inspection agency performing the function. Copies are available to the inspection/quality engineer for review and analysis.

OPERATOR QUALIFICATION

Each weld operator was required to prepare specimens representative of the material and weld positions to be used during production. These specimens were subjected to the qualification tests prescribed in the PSNs, under the surveillance of the inspection/quality engineer. After passing these tests, the welder received a qualification card, certifying his or her ability to perform the applicable operations.

Failure to pass the tests required that the operator receive additional training in the deficient areas. During the training period, the operator was restricted to other area tasks, such as cleaning and preparing welds joints.

INSPECTOR/TESTER TRAINING AND QUALIFICATION

Each weld inspector was trained to perform all nondestructive tests required for the weldments in production. See Chapter 24 for a description of the special training programs used. The inspectors were also required to demonstrate proficiency in this testing by passing a written exam and by demonstrating the ability to detect nonconformances on specimens containing known deficiencies. Failure to demonstrate proficiency in these tests, required retraining.

The weld engineer then prepared test specimens representing the material and the weld joints under production. These specimens showed the minimum acceptable workmanship requirements. After the weld inspector reviewed the specimens and found them to be in accordance with the specifications and the visual weld quality requirements, they were retained as samples of the minimum acceptable production weld quality. These specimens were also used as referees in the event of disputes regarding the visual acceptability of production welds.

IN-PROCESS INSPECTION AND SURVEILLANCE

At the start of each day's production of specified critical welds, sample weldments were produced by each operator. These samples were subjected to specific destructive tests, such as notch-break tests. Continued weldment production could not proceed until the samples were found acceptable.

Each weldment was stamped with the welder's identification number. The inspection/quality engineer used this information to determine the quality level produced by each welder, and to establish any need for retraining and requalification. All major weldments were visually inspected. Small welded parts were inspected to a lot sampling plan in accordance with the instructions.

Each type of weld deficiency was identified by a special code. Defects in the weldment were identified on the part by this number, and listed on the weldment variance report. A copy of the report was transmitted to the production supervisor. Upon rework, the material was resubmitted to the weld inspector. The results of the inspection were recorded on a report which listed the number of weldments inspected, the number and nature of the observed deficiencies, and the identification of the weld operators. The weld inspection records were analyzed, on a periodic basis, by the inspection/quality engineer, and incorporated into a monthly management report.

SURVEILLANCE

On a daily basis, the inspector, at each weld area, performed a survey. On a monthly basis, the inspection/quality engineer performed an audit of the weld area. This included a review of the operations of the production welders as well as those of the weld inspectors. The results of these audits were noted on the monthly management report. See Chapter 21 for details of the audit programs.

NONDESTRUCTIVE TESTING

In the process of developing a nondestructive testing area, in particular, when radiographic testing was performed, great care was taken to insure employee safety. These precautions included the preparation of an enclosed, shielded area, and the provisions of fail-safe measures to insure that the testers were not subjected to harmful rays emanating from the equipment.

The nondestructive testing and procedures were initially qualified for their ability to perform the required tests completely and accurately. These qualifications were repeated when major changes were made in the test requirements or in the equipment used.

WELD EQUIPMENT

When weld machines were used in production, it was necessary to qualify their ability to consistently produce acceptable welds. Specimens were initially, and then on a daily basis, subjected to destructive tests to prove the adequacy of the machines.

These practices may be performed at different intervals, but must comply with the requirements of the PSNs, the applicable customer, and/or military specifications.

CHAPTER SIXTEEN

Nonconforming Supplies Control

INTRODUCTION

The following elements should be considered in the control of nonconforming supplies.

- Definitions
- Segregation and identification
- Material review area
- Material review board (MRB)
- Preliminary material review board (PMRB)
- Final MRB disposition
- Corrective action
- Variance reports
- Field returns
- Vendor control

DEFINITIONS

Nonconformance is defined as any material, part, or product in which one or more characteristics do not conform to the requirements specified in the contract, specification, drawing, or standard. A nonconformance is generally stated as a departure from a specific requirement. The definition of the nonconformance should not be left to the discretion or judgment of the inspector. An example of this condition is a test procedure which specifies a parameter without denoting its criterion of acceptability. This requires the tester to record the data and judge its acceptability, or submit it to the engineer for review and disposition of the product.

REQUEST FOR WAIVER (RFW): When approval is needed to use a nonconforming product, a Request for Waiver (RFW) is generally processed.[1]

REQUEST FOR DEVIATION (RFD): When it is contemplated that a product will be produced in the future with nonconforming characteristics, a Request for Deviation (RFD) is processed to obtain authorization.[1]

EXAMPLES

Inspection reveals a nonconforming preproduction sample of a raw casting. A change in the casting pattern to correct this condition will take a lot of time, thereby adversely affecting the company's production schedule. Accordingly, an estimate of the time needed for the pattern revision is obtained from the foundry, as well as the number of nonconforming castings to be produced pending correction. This quantity is then submitted to the MRB, with an RFD. They will determine the disposition of the still unproduced castings.

While the MRB is processing some nonconforming supplies, more are discovered in the process of production. These also have the same discrepancies. Both an RFW for produced nonconformance and an RFD for an anticipated nonconformance will need to be processed in order to use all the supplies.

In the case of unavailable raw material, and the engineer refusing to revise the drawings, an alternate material may be suggested. This request for approval is made by processing an RFD.

TYPE I NONCONFORMANCES: Those which may involve "health, safety, performance, effective use or operation, weight, appearance (when a factor), durability, reliability, or interchangeability of the item or its replacement parts."[1]

TYPE II NONCONFORMANCES: Those departures from "contractual or engineering requirements which do not affect the characteristics noted in Type I above."[1]

TYPE III NONCONFORMANCES: Those deviations from supplemental requirements which do not depart from contractual or engineering requirements; for example, a roughing dimension stipulated on a manufacturing engineering instruction which will not affect the dimension of the finished part.

Standard rework methods are defined as those which

1. Are permitted in the contract, drawing, specification, or standard.

2. Can be utilized to complete a missing operation.

3. Can be reworked to specified requirement by standard methods in the manufacturing area in which the nonconformance was detected.

Respective examples include

1. A casting peened to correct a porous condition.
2. Machining a part surface omitted during the production operation.
3. Redrilling an undersized hole.

Repair is defined as additional operations, other than standard rework methods, which will render nonconforming parts useable, but will not result in the parts being in complete conformance to the requirements. For example, an oversized hole is filled and the plug welded into place. Then the hole is drilled to the specified size.

SEGREGATION AND IDENTIFICATION

When nonconforming items are found, they are positively identified and diverted from normal material movement channels. This identification and segregation is necessary to insure that this material is not inadvertently incorporated with the normal production material and used. The identification may include a copy of an officially designated discrepancy report (DR) (Figure 14-1) or a salvage tag, as applicable. When the material can be reworked, it may be identified on the inspection record or assembly variance sheet, and returned to the production operation.

For example, a discrepancy during the assembly can be reworked by the assembler. This nonconformance may be the installation of an incorrect part or the failure to tighten a fastening device to the specified requirements. In those instances, the discrepancy is noted on the assembly variance sheet, one copy retained with the inspection record, and the other copy provided to the production supervisor. When the nonconformance is corrected, the production operator initials the variance sheet and returns it to the inspector. The reworked area is inspected and the examiner signs off of the variance sheet and the inspection record.

When a nonconformance is noted on a major weldment, the inspector marks the discrepancy code number, discussed in Chapter 15, on the variant area. The weldment variance sheet is annotated with the location and code. When the repair is completed, the production operator initials the appropriate weldment location and resubmits the part. The inspector examines the designated repair and initials acceptability on the weldment variance sheet.

Inspecting drawings for the proper formats is another way to correct nonconformances at the production location. The drawing inspector uses a transparent overlay which is identified with the number of the drawing being examined. Nonconformances are noted on the overlay at the applicable location. Both items are returned to the drawing room supervisor. After correction, the drafting personnel initial the overlay and return it with the drawing to the inspector. After reexamination, the inspector signs and dates the overlay and files it as a record of inspection.

When a discrepancy is detected by the production operator or tester, a salvage tag is attached to the item. The symptom is noted on the tag (such as "will not fit" or "does not work"), and the part placed at a specially designated location in the assembly or test area. Periodically, the items are reviewed by the inspector, who determines the actual nonconformance of the item from its drawing or specification requirements.

When the material cannot be reworked in the production area, the inspector completes a DR, and attaches its hard copy to the material, which is then moved to the designated review area. When the material is large, bulky, or too heavy to be moved, it may be located in a designated area within the production or assembly area. This area must be clearly identified as a nonconforming materials hold area. No other material can be placed in the area and the material cannot be removed except by authorization of the designated inspection/quality personnel.

While completing the DR, the inspector must assure that the nonconformances are noted on the report in terms of their exact departure from the specified requirements. When it is feasible, variables data should be cited on the report to describe the nonconformance. This will aid the subsequent reviewing personnel by denoting the extent of departure from the specified requirement.

MATERIALS REVIEW AREA

One or more materials review areas, as designated by the inspection/quality personnel, should be located at specified locations of the production or assembly areas. These are caged or otherwise enclosed, and are kept locked when the authorized personnel are not in attendance. Usually, a materials review clerk is assigned to work in this area. The responsibility of this clerk is to locate the nonconforming material, maintain records of its review, including final disposition, and present the material and supporting documents to the members of the MRB. The clerk is also responsible for arranging the movement of the material after final disposition by the MRB.

The inspector and materials review clerk distribute copies of the discrepancy report in accordance with company instructions. Generally an advance copy is transmitted, by the inspector, to the production control department immediately upon rejection of the product. A copy is also forwarded, by the inspector, to the project engineer, to provide notification that the material will be awaiting MRB review. The remaining DR copies are filed by the clerk in a suspense file, awaiting the MRB's final disposition of the nonconforming material. Once the final determination is received, the clerk completes the report distribution. The inspection/quality copy of the discrepancy report is held in the material review's suspense file until the disposition is finalized. It is then filed with the disposition documents (such as shipping orders, and evidence of reinspection of the rework).

MATERIAL REVIEW BOARD

In most organizations, one or more MRBs are utilized. Some organizations have separate MRBs for each project. The MRB consists of a member of the inspection/quality department, the project engineer, and, when required, the customer's representative. Other members of the company may be utilized, including representatives from the service department, when a field return is involved, and the safety engineer, when a safety-related item is under review.

PRELIMINARY MATERIAL REVIEW BOARD (PMRB)

The MRB may authorize other members of the company to make certain preliminary determinations. The members of the PMRB often include representatives from the production control, production engineering, purchasing, and inspection/quality departments. In making materials dispositions, they usually consider several conditions which will affect their decisions as well as those of the MRB. These considerations include: determining production control's needs as applicable to the nonconforming items; the economical feasibility of the repair or rework of the nonconformance; the ability of obtaining replacement purchased supplies expeditiously; the frequency of prior occurrences of the same or similar discrepancies; and the results of prior corrective actions for similar nonconformances.

Based on these considerations, the PMRB then classifies the nonconformance as Type I, II, or III, as defined earlier in this chapter. Then the PMRB may decide to rework the material, return it to the vendor or scrap it.

FINAL MRB DISPOSITION

The PMRB refers all matters except as noted above to the MRB, who determines the final disposition. This review considers the possible effect of the discrepancy upon the product's fitness for use, as well as upon the contractual or company's technical and workmanship standards. The number of prior occurrences of the same or similar nonconformance and the effectiveness of the prior corrective actions are also considered. The MRB may make any one of the following determinations.

Use as is

The materials review clerk processes the annotated DR, removes its hard copy from the material, attaches an acceptance inspection move tag, and forwards the material to its originally designated location.

Request customer approval

When this is required, an RFW or RFD is prepared (see Figure 16-1), and sent to the customer. Pending approval, the materials review clerk notes the RFW/RFD number on the DR and retains the material in the review area. After customer approval, copies of the authorization documents are attached to the inspection/quality copy of the DR and filed. The hard copy of the DR is removed, an inspection move ticket attached, and the material routed to the originally designated area.

Rework or repair

The repair method should be clearly defined on the discrepancy report, or a special rework instruction should be prepared. Whether the repaired item is submitted to the MRB or processed through normal inspection channels should be noted. The materials review clerk attaches a copy of the repair instructions to the material, and arranges for it to be moved to the designated production area for repair. After repair or rework and reinspection, the material is returned to the MRB, if required. All paperwork, including DR and repair instructions, are processed by the appropriate personnel.

Scrap

Many companies require approval from the program manager or the project engineer for this disposition. The material is forwarded to an area for destruction or for defacement so that it may not be utilized on production contracts. The materials review clerk removes the hard copy of the DR with the noted disposition, and files it.

Return to vendor

The purchasing copy of the DR, with the disposition noted, is sent to the purchasing department, who prepares a material return order (MRO), authorizing shipment to the supplier, and forwards a copy to the materials review clerk. The clerk arranges for the movement of the material to the shipping department. A copy of the shipping notice with the waybill number and date of shipment recorded, is provided to the materials review clerk, who files it with the DR.

DOD - STD - 480A

REQUEST FOR DEVIATION/WAIVER (SEE DOD - STD - 480 OR 481 FOR INSTRUCTIONS)	DATE PREPARED	PROCURING ACTIVITY NO.

I. ORIGINATOR NAME AND ADDRESS

2. ☐ DEVIATION ☐ WAIVER

3. ☐ MINOR ☐ MAJOR ☐ CRITICAL

4. DESIGNATION FOR DEVIATION/WAIVER				5. BASE LINE AFFECTED	6. OTHER SYSTEMS/CONFIGU-RATION ITEM AFFECTED
A. MODEL TYPE	B. MFR. CODE	C. SYS. DESIG.	D. DEV/WAIVED NO.	☐ FUNC-TIONAL ☐ ALLO-CATED ☐ PRO-DUCT	☐ YES ☐ NO

7. SPECIFICATIONS AFFECTED - TEST PLAN				8. DRAWINGS AFFECTED			
	MFR. CODE	SPEC./DOC. NO.	SCN	MFR. CODE	NUMBER	REV.	NOR. NO.
A. SYSTEM							
B. ITEM							
C. TEST PLAN							

9. TITLE OF DEVIATION/WAIVER	10. CONTRACT NO. & LINE ITEM

II. CONFIGURATION ITEM NOMENCLATURE	CLASSIFICATION OF DEFECT		
	12. CD NO	13. DEFECT NO.	4. DEFECT CLASSIFICATION ☐ MINOR ☐ MAJOR ☐ CRITICAL

15. NAME OF PART OR LOWEST ASSEMBLY AFFECTED	16. PART NO. OR TYPE DESIG.	17. LOT NO.	18. QTY	19. RECURRING DEVIATION/WAIVER ☐ YES ☐ NO

20. EFFECT ON COST/PRICE	21. EFFECT ON DELIVERY SCHEDULE

22. EFFECT ON INTEGRATED LOGISTIC SUPPORT, INTERFACE, ETC.

23. DESCRIPTION OF DEVIATION/WAIVER

24. NEED FOR DEVIATION/WAIVER

25. PRODUCT EFFECTIVITY BY SERIAL NUMBER

26. SUBMITTING ACTIVITY AUTHORIZING	TITLE

27. APPROVAL/DISAPPROVAL

A. ☐ APPROVAL RECOMMENDED	B. ☐ APPROVED ☐ DISAPPROVED
C. GOVERNMENT ACTIVITY	SIGNATURE DATE

DD FORM I SEC 60 **1694**

FIGURE 16-1 Request for Waiver/Deviation

All use-as-is and repair decisions require full concurrence of the MRB. Any material approved by the MRB, or after completion of the approved repair methods, is treated as normal material, unless otherwise specified by the MRB.

CORRECTIVE ACTION

In order to minimize, or eliminate, further nonconformances, the corrective action copies of each DR are forwarded, by the inspector, immediately after rejection of the material, to the supervisor of the responsible area. He or she reviews the DR and investigates the cause of the nonconformance. The supervisor writes a detailed statement of the anticipated corrective action on the DR, which is returned to the materials review clerk for file.

When the discrepancy is on a purchased part, the corrective action copy of the DR is forwarded by the inspector to the purchasing agent, who sends it to the applicable supplier. The vendor annotates the copy of the DR with the proposed corrective action, which is forwarded to the materials review clerk for file.

The materials review file is used by the PMRB and the MRB when considering the disposition of subsequent material with the same or similar nonconformances. The boards note the number of previous occurrences and when it exceeds a previously determined level, specific action should be taken relative to the disposition of the nonconforming lot. This may include a refusal to process the nonconforming material pending a review of the proposed corrective action.

At times, the engineering member of the MRB provides a series of use-as-is dispositions for the same nonconformance. Some companies designate a maximum number of such decisions permitted for any nonconformance. When this number is exceeded, the inspection/quality member of the MRB may refuse to accept the engineer's disposition until an agreement has been reached for the necessary drawing changes. The rationale for this action is the assumption that the original requirement is probably not needed since the frequent permission, by the engineer, to use nonconforming parts did not apparently affect the part's fitness for use.

The materials review file is utilized by the inspection/quality engineer for analysis of the defect trends and the effectiveness of corrective actions. Results of these analyses are included in the periodic management reports.

VARIANCE REPORTS

A variety of variance report forms are utilized by different companies to record and process nonconforming material. These reports may be of various configurations depending upon the size of the company, the nature of the product, and the area where the discrepancy is discovered. Some are described and illustrated below.

Deficiency report

This is used when a nonconformance is found by the inspector during lot-by-lot inspection. It is submitted for MRB action.

Salvage tag

This type of variance report is used for material waiting the inspector's determination as to the exact nature of the nonconformance. The tag is attached to the product, by production or test personnel, when a part cannot be installed, or fails to operate satisfactorily.

Assembly/test variance report

This is used to record deficiencies found during assembly/test operations.

Weldment variance report

This is used to report deficiencies found during the weldment inspection operations.

Information Required

This enables the affected departments to perform their assigned functions. All information identified with an * applies only to the Deficiency Report (DR).

Description of the nonconformance

This should be an exact description of the product or service's variance from specific requirements noted on the document used to perform the inspection/test. Whenever feasible, the use of quantitative data is preferred. This enables a precise definition of the extent of the nonconformance and hence aids in the determination, by the MRB, of the ability to rework or utilize the nonconforming product.

Quality inspected and found nonconforming

This information is needed to determine the quality level of the inspected lot. It also enables the MRB to determine the extent of this nonconformance.

*Record of the previous occurrences

This information is valuable to the MRB in deciding the effects of previous corrective actions and the frequency of this type of nonconformance.

Classification of discrepancy

Some companies provide a code for each type of discrepancy which is useful when data concerning nonconformances are incorporated in computer printouts, and used in subsequent analyses of the quantities and types of nonconformances encountered. More about this in Chapter 27.

*Disposition

Provisions are needed, on the report, to record the recommendations of each member of the PMRB and MRB.

*Deficiency analysis

Frequently, it is required that the engineering member of the MRB provide an analysis of the nonconformance, its possible effect on the product, and a justification for the recommended disposition.

*Corrective action

At times, the only corrective action cited is the rework of the discrepancy. This is not usually considered acceptable, since action *correcting the condition* causing the discrepancy is needed in order to avoid the recurrence of the discrepancy. More about this in Chapter 22.

*Estimated cost of rework or scrap

For companies having a quality cost program, this information is valuable in order to determine the cost of the nonconformance. When the precise cost is not easily available to those preparing the variance report, an estimate is often acceptable. See Chapter 28 for more information concerning a quality cost program.

*Signatures and dates

Space should be provided for the signatures of the applicable members of the PMRB and MRB and the dates signed.

*Responsible department

This is the department responsible for the nonconformance. It is important to fix responsibility to enable effective corrective action to be taken.

*Method of repair or rework

If sufficient space is available, the method of rework or repair is noted on the report. If this space is not available, a repair order or instruction is needed. When used, reference to the repair order or instruction number is made on the variance report.

Distribution

When the disposition of the nonconformance is to be determined by the MRB, a DR is prepared. This report often consists of as many as seven copies, so that distribution may be made to all personnel affected by the variance. The distribution is made in two sequences. Initially, after material inspection and rejection, the inspector transmits an advance copy of the DR to production control. This serves notice that the part is being held up, and provides an opportunity to arrange for replacement parts, should they be needed, prior to MRB disposition. The inspector also forwards an advance copy of the DR to the project engineer for review and subsequent material evaluation. For in-house rejections, the corrective action copy of the DR is forwarded by the inspector to the supervisor of the responsible area. For purchased part rejections, a copy of the DR is forwarded by the receiving inspector to the supplier, or to purchasing for transmission to the supplier. In either case, the inspector attaches the hard copy of the DR, acting as a rejection tag, to the nonconforming material. The other copies of the DR are transmitted, with the material, to the materials review clerk. He or she notes on the inspection/quality copy, the location of the material in the review crib, and places the other copies of the DR in a suspense file awaiting disposition instructions from the MRB.

If the MRB decides to return the material to the vendor, the purchasing department prepares an MRO. If the nonconforming material is to be reworked in house, purchasing negotiates that cost with the supplier.

After all actions and dispositions have been accomplished, the inspection/quality copy of the DR is filed, with all associated documents, in the materials review file, and one copy transmitted to inspection/quality engineering for use in their subsequent analyses. The balance of the DRs are transmitted to the applicable personnel of the other departments, such as production control, manufacturing, and controller.

FIELD RETURNS

When a field return is processed, authorization is prepared by field service. They issue a return order describing the customer's complaint. One copy is forwarded to the applicable inspection/quality personnel, who will coordinate the returned product's inspection. When possible, the inspection/test is performed using the same procedures that had been used on the product before shipment. If the material is a vendor-supplied item and special inspections/tests must be performed by the supplier, the inspector examines the item for identification and evidence of handling damage, prepares a DR, and provides a copy to purchasing, who issues an MRO. On in-house fabricated items, inspections results are recorded on the field return order, and a DR is prepared noting the departure from the applicable drawing or specification. The material is then routed to the MRB.

Field service personnel also determine the validity of the complaint, whether the item is still under warranty, and take the appropriate action with the customer. In all instances, if a part replacement is required, it should be provided as soon as possible. This is often done before responsibility is determined. Any costs to the customer are decided subsequent to the investigation, and negotiated with the customer after the replacement part has been shipped.

For companies having a configuration control program, a copy of all DRs which resulted in use as is or repair decisions are provided to the configuration manager for incorporation into the equipment log.

VENDOR CONTROL

Suppliers are encouraged to notify the company before shipping material, whenever they run into a problem meeting the quality and technical requirements of the purchase order. To encourage the implementation of this concept, some companies provide the means for their suppliers to request approval using RFDs or RFWs.

The supplier is required to specify the number of discrepant parts already produced as well as any additional quantities in the process of production. The cause for the discrepancy, and corrective actions being taken, and the anticipated date of effectivity of these actions are all noted on the vendor RFD/RFW.

The inspection/quality engineer then prepares a DR and processes it to the MRB. The results of the disposition are then forwarded by phone or mailed to the supplier.

If the material is to be shipped as is or repaired by nonstandard methods, the supplier is requested to reference the RFD/RFW number on the material and shipping documents. A copy of the executed DR is provided to the receiving inspection personnel, by the materials review clerk, for its use.

The inspection/quality engineer maintains a log of all vendor RFW/RFDs. This is utilized in the periodic rating of the vendor and the determination of subsequent use of MRB actions on the supplier's products.

When the product is of the supplier's design, or the supplier's organization has competent engineers who are familiar with the product and its application in the end item, consideration may be given to permit the supplier to utilize its own MRB.

The supplier's MRB, and its procedures for processing nonconforming supplies, must be approved by the company's MRB. The supplier's MRB may only process Type II nonconformances. These actions are subject to periodic reviews by the company's MRB personnel, and the company's customer.

Periodically, the company's MRB personnel will audit, at the supplier's facilities, its implementation of the nonconforming supplies procedures, as well as the effectiveness of the corrective actions previously promised by the supplier.

REFERENCES

1. *DOD-STD 480*. Configuration control, engineering changes, deviations and waivers. Washington, D.C.: U.S. Government Printing Office, Superintendent of Documents.

CHAPTER SEVENTEEN

Movement Control

INTRODUCTION

A company should establish and implement rigid controls over the identification of material, during its movement through production areas, and while in stores locations. This identification should not only denote the material by part number and revision level, but also indicate its inspection status.

Product identification is of primary importance to assure that material is not mixed in with material at various production stages and to insure that no production operations are omitted. It is important that the inspection status is specifically defined to prevent the inadvertent mixing of inspected items with those not yet inspected. Of particular importance is the identification of the status of nonconforming material.

POINTS OF CONTROL

The inspection status of production material is generally identified at the various stages of production and inspection. These stages may include the following:

- Before and after receiving inspection
- Between manufacturing centers
- Within manufacturing centers
- At various inspection points
- During assembly/test operations
- Before shipment
- In stores areas

METHODS OF IDENTIFICATION

There are many methods of identifying the material. The choice of the method will depend upon the nature of the product and process, the stage of production, the size and complexity of the product, the organizational structure of the company, and so on. Whichever method is utilized, it is important that all personnel involved with the product are fully aware of the methods. The following identification methods may be used.

- Move tickets
- Tags and labels
- Production control travelers
- Inspection or special process stamps
- Location at specific geographical areas

The application of the identification may be on, or attached to, the product or to its containers.

LOT CONTROL

Many companies utilize a lot control program. This is useful in tracking the material from the initial release of the raw material throughout the various phases of production, inspection, stores, and into the final end item of the shipped equipment.

MOVE TICKETS

Move tickets identify the status of the applicable lot. In some companies, move tickets of different colors are used to indicate the type of material in the lot. For example, a blue ticket may denote a finished part, a green one indicates a semifinished lot (requiring additional manufacturing operations), and a yellow ticket may designate raw material. This type of designation makes it easier for the material handlers to determine the next location for the material (such as finished stores, raw material stores, and production).

In the final assembly areas, the equipment is usually accompanied by an inspection folder made out for each end item. This contains the production and inspection instructions, the applicable drawings or specifications, a production traveler, and an assembly variance sheet. The completion of each production and inspection operation is noted on the traveler. All rejections, subsequent rework, and reinspection operations are noted on the variance sheet. As noted in Chapter 16, nonconforming components, when discovered in the assembly/test operations, at times, may be located in a specially designated area in the production, inspection, or test locations.

Many companies wish to maintain lot control without recourse to the detailed procedures just described. In addition, to overcome the problem presented by split lots during the production operation, the following procedure is used.

A quantity of piece parts is designated as a lot when it has reached an inspection location. At that point, the lot number is designated in accordance with the date of inspection. For example, a lot inspected on February 6, 1989, is designated, on the inspection tag and inspection record, as lot number 2-6-9. If two or more lots of the same part number are inspected on the same day, the lot designation is 2a-6-9, 2b-6-9, and so on.

The inspection tags remain with the lot until the last item is fabricated. At that time, the inspection tag is removed and replaced with a new inspection tag, denoting the new part number and the next manufacturing station or assembly area. When the finished or semifinished parts are moved to the stores area, the identification tag of the final operation is retained in that area, until the last item in the lot is disbursed. When part of a lot is issued from the stores area, the area inspector is summoned, and attaches a partial lot identification tag or label to the container. This label notes that the material was removed from an inspected lot and its number. The tag on the material remaining in the stores area is posted with the number of pieces removed and the number remaining. Periodic audits by the inspection/ quality personnel insure that all material in the production and stores areas are identified with the appropriate lot inspection tags.

A major benefit of this identification method is the ability to track any lot in the production or stores area to the applicable inspection record. This is of particular importance when material is shipped from one company plant to another. Any problem with material received from the sending plant could be traced to its inspection record and the appropriate actions, when applicable, taken. Thus, if a nonconforming part is found, during assembly or test, a review of the pertinent inspection record determines whether that characteristic had been inspected. This may result in revising, as needed, the instruction of the part.

MOVEMENT OF MATERIAL

To insure that material, during the production operations, is properly protected against handling damage, the production or packaging engineering department provides appropriate crates and boxes for each part configuration. The supervisors of each manufacturing center are given the responsibility of insuring that the material, while under their jurisdiction, is adequately protected. In some companies, the supervisors are also required to sign the move tickets indicating that the material has been inspected by them, had no evidence of damage, and is properly protected while in transit. In these companies, the supervisors in the production sections or stores areas receiving the lot, are required to sign the move tickets upon receipt, signifying that they have inspected the material and found that there is no evidence of any in-transit damage. When some damage is found by a receiving supervisor, the matter should be called to the attention of the area inspector, who should coordinate corrective actions with the inspector of the previous area.

STORES CONTROL

The storeroom supervisors are similarly responsible for examining the material upon receipt for damage and for the appropriate inspection move tags. The supervisors are also responsible for organizing the storeroom bins in such a fashion as to insure material disbursement on a first-in-first-out basis. With the exception of standard hardware items (nuts and bolts), no commingling of the received lots with the same material in the stores area should be permitted. In addition, separate locations should be maintained for surplus material, as well as for customer-owned material. Material which has shelf-life requirements should also be properly identified with the expiration date and located in a special area. Periodic reviews of these areas should be conducted by the store personnel who should remove, from current status, any material which has exceeded its shelf life.

Periodic audits should also be conducted by the inspection/quality personnel to assure that the applicable procedures are maintained. See Chapter 21 for additional information concerning the audit programs.

INSPECTION STAMPS

Figure 17-1 illustrates examples of inspection stamps customarily used in a manufacturing facility. Rigid control of the stamps issued to the inspection personnel is maintained by most companies. Each inspector/tester is responsible for the appropriate maintenance and use of the assigned stamps. Special stamp configurations are issued for the various inspection/test and audit functions.

The inspection supervisor usually maintains a record of the stamp recipients. Stamps should not be loaned to other personnel or used without authorization. When a stamp is reported lost, the use of the stamp, if found, should be restricted for a specific period of time. Similarly, stamps issued to personnel who leave the company or the department, should be withdrawn from issue for a period of time. Stamp imprints must be legible or should not be considered acceptable.

RUBBER STAMPS

ACCEPTANCE

STEEL STAMPS

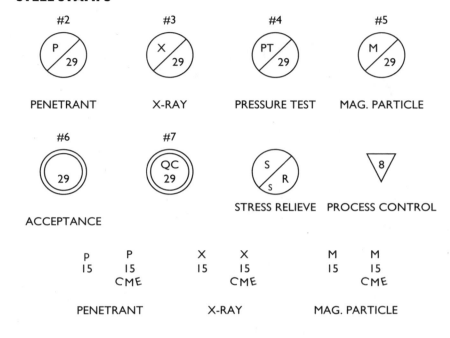

| PENETRANT | X-RAY | PRESSURE TEST | MAG. PARTICLE |

ACCEPTANCE

STRESS RELIEVE   PROCESS CONTROL

| PENETRANT | X-RAY | MAG. PARTICLE |

FIGURE 17-1   Inspection Stamps

NONCONFORMING MATERIAL IDENTIFICATION

As described in Chapter 16, special DR tags are attached to nonconforming materials which are referred for MRB action. Salvage tags are used for material in the assembly and test areas, rejected by production or test personnel, awaiting a decision as to its status.

CHAPTER EIGHTEEN

Final Assembly, Inspection, and Test

INTRODUCTION

This chapter discusses controls during the final assembly, inspection, and test operations of end items. The following control elements usually include:

- Preliminary planning
- Inspection/quality program establishment
- Inspection/surveillance of work in-process
- Final inspection/test
- Final acceptance and submission for customer approval
- Records, reports, and corrective actions
- Control and sampling tests

PRELIMINARY PLANNING OPERATIONS

The preliminary production and inspection planning operations described in Chapter 14 apply to the subassembly and assembly operations.

In most companies, test engineering develops the required test procedures for use at in-process and final test stations. These usually include the data sheets for the recording of the actual test results for each characteristic.

Equipment and facilities for the testing are developed, or existing facilities modified by test engineering, as necessary.

Special locations are usually provided for components and subassemblies which have been rejected by the production assemblers and testers.

The test procedures should be reviewed by the project inspection/quality personnel to assure that all the contractual and engineering specification performance characteristics are considered. The review should also include the need for any in-process testing to assure the adequacy of the subassemblies and assemblies to meet the end item test requirements.

INSPECTION/QUALITY PROGRAM ESTABLISHMENT

The project inspection/quality personnel should develop the inspection procedures and instructions, including inspection checklists (Figure 18-1) for use during the assembly operations. Flowcharts (Figure 18-2) are usually developed for each subassembly and assembly line. These denote each production, inspection, and test station, and, when applicable, points of submission, when required, for customer review.

Assembly variance sheets are used to record all rejections made during the assembly inspection/test operations. Equipment history folders are prepared for each end item. The production operations sheets, travelers, inspection check sheets, and variance sheets are incorporated in these folders, which accompany each end item of equipment throughout the assembly and test operations.

For companies having a configuration control program, inspection/quality procedures are generally developed for the verification of the as-built final equipment against the configuration control log.

Prior to the start of production, and during the preparation of the assembly flowchart, the project inspector should determine, with the customer, when applicable, at which point of assembly or test the customer representative wishes to be present. This position is usually noted on the flowchart. Based on this information, the assembly inspector has the responsibility of notifying the customer's representatives when the product is available for review.

INSPECTION/SURVEILLANCE OF WORK-IN-PROGRESS

During the assembly process, the area inspector generally maintains surveillance over the production operations. This usually includes the review of all special processes performed in the area, as well as various elements of the production assembly operations. Some of the reviews include the following:

- Assurance that the assembly tools, such as crimping tools and torque wrenches, bear current calibration status markings. See Chapter 25 for additional information concerning calibration systems.

Instruction: Inspect each assembly for all characteristics indicated. Record nonconformances on Variance Report Form 302-1.	
Top Carriage Serial No. _____	Elevating Gear Box (12009054) Serial No. _____
Clutch Assy (12008099) Ser. No. _____	Ring Gear (12008250)S/N_____
Reference: Drawing 12008100.	

Item No.	Characteristic	Inspector
1.	Assure prior acceptance of Top Carriage Weldment.	
2.	Verify proper installation of two (2) Bearings 12008188 and 128189. Assure Bearings are packed with grease (00428-0049) prior to installation, ref: section A-A.	
3.	Verify proper installation of four (4) Seals 12008186 and two (2) Seals 12008187. Assure seals are installed in the proper direction, ref: section A-A.	
4.	Inspector to verify proper installation of Trunnions. P/N 12008584 L/H side and 12008585 R/H side into Top Carriage and that seals have not been damaged, and also for presence of P/N 12008191 retainers and set screws.	
5.	Verify proper installation of two (2) Gaskets 12008192, two (2) Covers 12008190 and Retainer 12008191. Assure mounting hardware is torqued 20 IN LBS + 8 IN LBS. Section A-A.	

FIGURE 18-1   Inspection Check Sheet

- In process reviews for the application of required torques specified in the work instructions.
- Review of the parts and components in the assembly bins for properly identified inspection move tags.
- Review of all parts awaiting assembly to insure that they reflect the latest engineering changes at the specified points of effectivity. See Chapter 10.

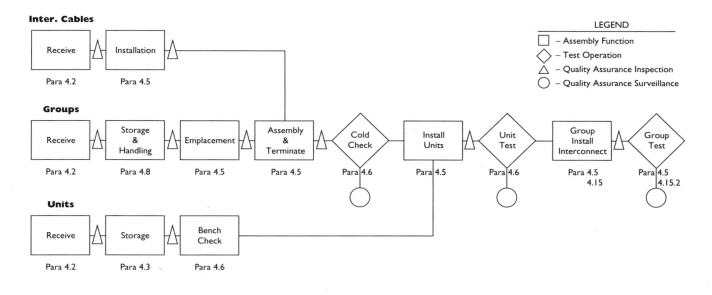

FIGURE 18-2 Inspection Flowchart

When an engineering change is to be effected within the next several units of equipment, the inspector reviews the material in the assembly bins and stores areas to ensure that all superseded parts, in excess of the amount needed for the several units prior to the point of effectivity, have been removed from the area.

In these companies, a key characteristic inspection list (Figure 10-4) may be included in the equipment folder for each applicable unit. This KCI is noted with the unit serial number for which the identified engineering change is to be effected. One KCI form is placed in this folder for the initial equipment to be changed, and in the folders of a number of subsequent units of equipment.

The KCI form may also be used when the inspection/quality engineer deems it necessary to review several final end items of equipment for the presence of any problems reported from the field. See Chapter 22 for a discussion of the use of the KCI as a measure of corrective action.

During the assembly operation, equipment inspection is conducted at each stage identified on the assembly flowchart. The inspector notes the results on the inspection check sheet. When a nonconforming characteristic is found, the check sheet is noted and a description of the discrepancy is recorded on the equipment variance sheet. This is then given to the production supervisor. The equipment is either retained at the original station, or moved to a position alongside the assembly line. After rework, the repair operator signs the variance sheet and returns it to the inspector. After reinspection, the examiner acceptance stamps the variance and the inspection check sheets. The equipment is returned to the assembly line and moved to the next assembly position.

When the variance cannot be corrected at the assembly location, the defective component is removed and placed in the designated nonconforming material location in the assembly area. A replacement component, when needed, is installed. Periodically, the area inspector and the project engineer inspect the material in this area for determination of its precise lack of conformance. A DR is then prepared, and the material processed in accordance with the program described in Chapter 16.

At the completion of the assembly operations, the inspector should review all the documents in the equipment folder for evidence of completion of all production, inspection, rework, and reinspection operations. At that point, for equipment under a configuration control program, the as-built configuration is verified against the equipment configuration control log, as described in Chapter 10. The equipment is then prepared for test and moved to the designated area.

FINAL INSPECTION/TEST

Final end item testing is generally performed by the members of the inspection/quality department. In some companies, it is performed by engineering test or production test personnel. These tests are then under the surveillance of the inspection/quality department. Some companies have developed a program, discussed in the earlier chapters, of performing surveillance, on a sample basis. In those instances, the inspection/quality auditor reviews, on a random basis, a retest of selected characteristics of the test procedure.

Prior to the start of the end item test, the assembly inspector should check the test equipment to insure that they bear current calibration tags. See Chapter 25. The test equipment is also reviewed to assure that it corresponds to the equipment specified in the test procedure. When required, the customer's representative is notified by the area inspector/tester.

The failure of the product to perform as specified, is noted on the test data sheet. Any nonconforming equipment characteristic or component is noted on the variance sheet. For testing done after rework, a new data sheet is attached to the test procedure, and the retested results are posted therein. The test then continues according to procedure.

Here too, when a component is responsible for the test failure, it is usually removed by the tester or rework operator, and placed in the nonconforming material location of the test area, pending determination from the component drawing or specification. A replacement component is installed. The nature of the rework is noted on the test variance sheet and signed by the rework operator. The rework is then examined by the area inspector, who records the results on the test variance sheet.

After rework and reinspection, the inspection/quality engineer, the project engineer, the test supervisor, and, when applicable, the customer's representative, usually determine the effect of the rework on those previously tested characteristics. The extent of retesting is then decided. Once completed, the test data sheet is signed and dated by the tester and the inspection/quality personnel who had witnessed the test.

Upon completion of these actions, the product is usually subjected to a "clean-up" operation. This consists of touching up any sections which have been marred during testing. For equipment which requires the incorporation of preservation fluid, the process is performed by the production personnel, under the surveillance of the inspection/quality personnel, who audit for proper lubricants use, as noted on the lubrication diagram, and for shelf life of the fluids.

FINAL ACCEPTANCE AND SUBMISSION FOR CUSTOMER APPROVAL

The end item equipment is then readied for shipment. Final shipping documents are prepared by the production control personnel. These documents refer to the method of shipment preparation, the destination, and list all accompanying material, such as spares and instruction and maintenance manuals. When applicable, the assembly inspector presents the shipping documents for review and technical approval by the customer's representative. If unavailable, an area inspector representing the customer signs or stamps the shipping documents. The material is then moved to the shipping area for the preparation as discussed in Chapter 19.

RECORDS, REPORTS, AND CORRECTIVE ACTIONS

The contents of the equipment history folders should be periodically reviewed by the inspection/quality engineer for analysis and preparation of periodic management reports. See Chapter 20 for details concerning these operations. Copies of the executed configuration control logs, when used, are forwarded, by the assembly inspector, to the configuration control manager.

Discrepancies noted during assembly and test are usually brought to the attention of the assembly supervisors. Components or detail parts which create difficulty in assembly or do not permit the equipment to perform in accordance with the test requirements are brought to the attention of the production supervisor and the responsible area inspection/quality personnel. The engineering department is advised of all test failures for its consideration of possible redesign efforts. Corrective actions are conducted in accordance with the procedures discussed in Chapter 22.

The assembly inspector/quality personnel, in some companies, are part of an interdepartmental corrective action quality improvement team, which meets at specified intervals, or when a significant problem occurs. Analysis of the problematic conditions are made and assignments given to the individual team members for their investigation and recommendations of any corrective actions.

Control Tests

During the production phase, it is not feasible to examine every characteristic on the end item which had been previously tested during the preproduction test. Many of these tests often require special equipment and are time consuming. Accordingly, various contracts or company engineering programs require preproduction tests of selected characteristics. The project engineer usually coordinates this effort with marketing and the customer, if applicable. The frequency of testing and a control test procedure is developed by the test engineer, in conjunction with the project inspection/quality personnel.

Generally, the control test procedure requires that the inspection/quality engineer, at specified intervals, select the units to be tested, and participate in the testing, or in its surveillance. Any failure to meet the control test is reviewed by the inspection/quality engineer, the project engineer, and the customer, as applicable. As a result of the review, nonconforming characteristics should require retesting in equipment already fabricated and tested, as well as the incorporation of any changes in design or inspection/quality procedures to be utilized for subsequent production units.

Sampling Tests

Some contracts require that, on a periodic basis (for example, once a month), or on a sampling basis (for example, one out of ten units), a completed unit is selected and subjected to control tests. The lot from which the sampling unit is selected is held in abeyance pending testing. When a failure is encountered, all units in the lot are subjected to the retest of the failed characteristic. A failure analysis is also conducted, by the inspection/quality and project engineers. Results of the analysis will decide the corrective action to be taken on all subsequent production units.

Burn-in testing on electronic equipment is treated in a similar fashion. This consists of operating the component or equipment for a protracted period of time to eliminate the infant mortality phase. The lot from which the burn-in samples are selected is held pending the completion of these tests.

CHAPTER NINETEEN

Preparation for Shipment Control and Field Service

SHIPMENT CONTROL

This chapter discusses the controls normally exercised during the preparation for shipment operations. These include the preservation, packaging, labeling, packing, and loading of material shipped to the customer's specified destinations, as well as those used for interplant shipments, and returns of rejected material to the supplier. The following elements of control are discussed.

- Procedures and instructions preparation
- Inspection/quality program preparation
- Preproduction inspection
- Shipping area surveillance and inspection
- Interplant shipments
- Shipment to suppliers
- Vendor control

PROCEDURES AND INSTRUCTIONS PREPARATION

Larger companies often include in their organizational structures a packaging engineering department who is responsible for developing procedures and instructions used by the shipping department in all phases of its operations. The packaging engineering department also designs boxes and develops methods of cleaning, preservation, packaging, crating, boxing, and labeling.

Companies which maintain a product liability prevention program provide special procedures for the appropriate packaging and labeling of the shipments. These procedures are designed to insure that the necessary warning and hazard labels are affixed to the equipment and packages of safety-related items. The company safety engineer prepares the necessary safety checklists and instructions for use by the packaging engineers and by shipping personnel.

Various government handbooks and standards, such as Handbook 37, MIL-P-116, and Mil-STD-130, are available for use by the packaging engineers, as guides to the selection of materials and the method for each phase of the preparation for shipment program. These documents are useful, not only on military contracts, but also as guidance for commercial use. The Interstate Commerce Commission also provides rules and regulations governing the methods of preparation for commercial shipments. The contracts department of the company usually transmits to the packaging engineering personnel and shipping supervision any customer-mandated requirements for the preparation of the shipment.

The packaging engineer usually provides to the shipping department supervisor, the applicable drawings, sketches, and special procedures defining the packaging, packing, and labeling requirements. In some companies, these drawings are issued as a part of the engineering drawing package, as discussed in Chapter 10. The packaging engineering department may also be responsible for the development of any special tote boxes and other material handling devices for use during the in-process transportation and storage of material during the manufacturing operation. Methods for processing interplant shipments and materials returned to suppliers are also provided by the packaging engineering department.

The shipping department supervisor generally prepares the necessary procedures and instructions for department use. For companies that do not have a packaging engineering department, the shipping department supervisor is assigned the responsibility for packing and box design. Information concerning the customer's shipping requirements are provided by the contracts department. See Figure 19-1 for an example of the type of instructions provided by this department.

When necessary, the shipping supervisor may contact the project or production engineer for assistance in the design of any special packages and boxes required for the project.

INSPECTION/QUALITY PROGRAM PREPARATION

The project inspection/quality engineers generally prepare their programs for the shipping operations for the project under their jurisdiction. Procedures include review of the packaging engineering instructions and surveillance and inspection of the preparation for shipment operations.

SHIPPING INSTRUCTIONS

RELEASE DATE: _____   SALES ORDER _____

CUSTOMER ORDER NUMBER _____   PART NUMBER _____

NSN _____   TOTAL QUANTITY _____

PART NAME _____   CODE _____

UNIT METHOD			INTER. QTY.		
CLEANING METHOD			CONTAINER		
UNIT QUANTITY			DOMESTIC		
PRESERVATIVE TYPE			OVERSEAS		
WRAP			EXTERIOR CONT.		
CUSHIONING			LEVEL		
DESSICANT					
BAG			CURE DATES		
CONTAINER					
BAG					
OVERWRAP			SPECIFICATION		
CONTAINER			IDENTIFICATION		
APPROPRIATION					

REMARKS:

FORM E-1925 REV. 12/83

FIGURE 19-1 Shipping Instructions

The inspection/quality engineer usually reviews packaging engineering drawings, sketches, and procedures to assure that they include the applicable contractual requirements and the company's workmanship standards. The engineer ascertains that the materials and processes reflect the latest provisions of the Interstate Commerce Commission relating to the preparation for shipment. Checklists for the material inspection, throughout the preparation for shipment process, are developed using such documents as MIL-P-116 and Handbook HB 37 as guides.

PREPRODUCTION INSPECTION

A pilot lot or major item of equipment is usually subjected to preproduction inspection and tests. These are designed to demonstrate the ability of the packaged or packed items to meet the engineering specifications. These tests include destructive ones such as the drop test and railroad humping test. They are witnessed by the project, packaging, and inspection/quality engineers, and the customer, when required.

SHIPPING AREA SURVEILLANCE AND INSPECTION

Upon arrival in the shipping area, and prior to the shipment operations, each major item of equipment or each lot of spares or maintenance parts, is reviewed by the inspector for the shipping notice, evidencing prior technical approval by the company and by the customer's representative, when applicable. Surveillance of special processes used in the shipping areas are performed by the inspection/quality personnel. Periodic checks of the solutions used are made under the jurisdiction of these personnel. These include checks of the petroleum solvents, preservative oils, and fingerprint neutralizer. In addition, samples from the heat seal machine are taken, on a daily basis, and subjected to pull and water submersion tests.

A sample from each lot of preserved parts is usually selected to determine the adequacy of the preservation methods and to check for conformance with the packaging engineer's requirements. Sample rejection may result in the represervation of all items in the lot, and corrective actions. A sample of each production lot of packaged parts is also selected by the shipping inspector and reviewed for proper item packaging and the incorporation of the specified labels.

Each boxed or crated lot or major item of equipment is inspected for proper boxing/crating operations, specified markings, and the incorporation of the applicable documents, handbooks, and supplementary material. Prior to authorizing the shipment for loading, the shipping documents are submitted to the customer's representative, when applicable, for approval. When the customer is not available, the shipping inspector indicates approval by stamping the shipping documents.

When the shipment comprises a complete truck or railroad carload, the inspector usually examines the loading of the material for proper bracing and attachments to prevent shifting during transportation. At times, the shipping inspector may examine the cargo, after it has been loaded on board a transport ship, to assure that the equipment or boxes have not been damaged, that they are stored at the specified ship location (above or below deck), and that they are properly braced to prevent shifting during transportation.

INTERPLANT SHIPMENTS

Interplant shipments are reviewed by the inspector for proper identification, count, and adequate protection from environmental and handling damage during transit. The inspector should insure that the final move ticket, properly certified as having been accepted at the sending plant, is attached to the material, and the shipping notice contains the acceptance stamp of the shipping inspector as well as the inspection lot number.

SHIPMENT TO SUPPLIERS AND VENDOR CONTROL

The packaging and identification of nonconforming material returned to the supplier for repair or replacement is inspected for proper protection against handling damage during transit. A copy of the debit memo (Figure 19-2) describing the nonconformances in the returned lot, is attached to the material being returned.

When packaging and packing of a shipment are to be performed by an outside subcontractor, the inspection/quality engineer should review the purchase order issued to the subcontractor, for the incorporation of the proper preservation, packaging, packing, and labeling instructions, for material identification, and for any applicable inspection/quality clauses.

Before a purchase order is placed with the packaging subcontractor, the inspection/quality engineer generally performs a vendor survey at the subcontractor's facilities to determine its capability to perform the shipping operations in accordance with the purchase order requirements.

FIELD SERVICE AND INSTALLATION

Some companies are required to set up the product, at the customer's facilities, and make the necessary equipment adjustments. This type of

DEBIT MEMORANDUM									D–24015	

DEBIT MEMORANDUM   D–24015

DATE	REFER CORRESPONDENCE TO:	REASON FOR DEBIT ⟶ ☐	OUR PURCHASE ORDER NUMBER

SHIP TO:	DEBIT TO:	REASON FOR DEBIT

REASON FOR DEBIT

1. PRICE DIFFERENCE BILLED AT CORRECT
2. DEFECTIVE MATERIAL
3. SHORT SHIPPED
4. OVER SHIPPED
5. SEE BELOW

AUTHORIZED BY

RETURNED VIA   ☐ PREPAID   ☐ COLLECT

PO ITEM	JOB	SUB JOB/ TASK	QUANTITY	PART NUMBER	REV LTR	DESCRIPTION	REJECT REPORT NO.	UNIT PRICE	U/M
								TOTAL VALUE	

CARRIER	WAY BILL NO.	NO CONF	GROSS WT	DATE SHIPPED	CHARGES

NOTE: ALL REJECTED MATERIAL MUST BE RETURNED TO COMPANY PREPAID IN ISSUING CREDIT PLEASE REFER TO OUR DM NO.

FORM 110 107 REV 8-84

FIGURE 19-2   Debit Memo

equipment is usually quite complex and requires the special skills of the company personnel to ready it for the customer's use. Equipment such as mainframe computers, radar installations, telecommunications equipment, complex machine tools and the like are examples of typical equipment requiring company setup.

Field equipment installation is usually done by the company's service department. They install the equipment at the specified locations, make the necessary adjustments, and perform the scheduled operations to demonstrate the adequacy of the equipment to fulfill its intended function. In some instances, this demonstration is also used as a means of training the customer's personnel in the use, operation, and maintenance of the equipment.

During the installation, it is not unusual to find that some nonconformances in various characteristics exist which may hinder the ability of the equipment to be properly installed or function as intended. This may require some rework or replacement of components by the service personnel.

Records of the difficulties encountered during the installation are provided by the service personnel in their reports to the engineering and inspection/quality departments, who review them and initiate the appropriate corrective action on subsequent production equipment (see Chapter 22).

In some companies, inspection/quality personnel accompany the service personnel, and participate in the installation and initial operation of the equipment. They also

- Inspect the equipment for any handling or environmental damage.

- Perform operational phases of the equipment, according to the instructions.

- Provide test results to the company's inspection/quality engineers for their review and analysis.

- Troubleshoot to determine the cause of any field failures.

- Perform any necessary replacements, rework, reinspection, or retests.

- Demonstrate maintainability requirements.

In some companies, the time needed for equipment installation and setup is determined. This value is used as a measure of the quality of the equipment as delivered. A decrease in this rate, over a period of time, is often an indication of the improving quality of the equipment.

PREPRODUCTION TESTING

For certain types of equipment, or on some contracts, preproduction tests are performed at the customer's site or testing area. These are done by, or under the jurisdiction of, the company's engineering personnel, with the customer providing surveillance. At times, personnel from the company's inspection/quality department are present to provide reinspection of any rework performed during the tests. They may also gather failure information and relay it to the inspection/quality engineers for their evaluation and for implementation of any corrective action on subsequent production equipment. After preproduction testing, the company project engineer usually prepares the test report and submits it to the customer's representatives for approval, when required. The inspection/quality engineering personnel review the test report for conformance to the equipment specifications. In some contracts, the fabrication of production equipment cannot initiate until the preproduction test has been successfully completed, and the test report approved by the customer.

FIELD PRODUCTION TESTS

Some contracts, generally those with the military, require that several units from initial production equipment which have been successfully tested at the company's facilities, be tested in the field, or at the customer's test sites. These tests are designed to demonstrate the capability of the equipment to successfully operate under the specified field conditions for the required period of time, or the number of miles of operation. They are, in a sense, a test of the durability and reliability of the equipment under actual field operational conditions.

These tests are usually performed by customer personnel, in accordance with a prescribed plan. After each phase of the tests, the equipment is examined to determine whether any of its characteristics had deteriorated during the test. Any discrepancies are immediately documented in an equipment performance report (see Figure 19-3). Copies of the performance report are sent to the applicable company personnel, including the inspection/quality engineering. Responses are generated by the company, noting the results of the deficiency analyses, the determination of the possible causes for these nonconformances, and the corrective actions implemented. The investigations and responses are usually coordinated by the company's inspection/quality engineering personnel. See Chapter 22 for a full description of corrective action programs.

During field tests, the company's service personnel provide customers with whatever assistance may be needed to rework discrepant areas and to obtain any needed replacement components. Often the official field performance reports may take some time to be prepared by the customer personnel and provided to the company. Therefore, the field service personnel, at the test site, provide advance reports of the problem areas. This enables the inspection/quality personnel to perform the analyses of the cited nonconformances, and to initiate speedy corrective actions on the equipment in production. In some companies, personnel from the company's inspection/quality department are also present at the test site to witness these tests and the customer's examinations of the equipment.

After all tests, the equipment is given a final examination and is completely disassembled for a detailed visual inspection of its components and detail parts. Subsequently, company inspection/quality personnel are invited to the test site to participate in the inspection of the disassembled equipment and to certify the validity of the customer's final equipment

EQUIPMENT PERFORMANCE REPORT

DATE: OCTOBER 3, 1980	OFFICE SYMBOL STEAP–MT–U

TO: COMMANDER
    WARNER–ROBINS AIR LOGISTICS CENTER
    ATTN: MM11CA (2)
    ROBINS AIR FORCE BASE, GA 31098
	FROM: COMMANDER
	    US ARMY ABERDEEN PROVING GROUND
	    ATTN: STEAP-MT-U
	    ABERDEEN PROVING GROUND, MD 21005

1. EPR NO.: K2-28	2. TECOM/AVSCOM PROJ NO.: 1-CO-210-000-003	3. TEST TITLE: TRUCK, TANK, 5000, A/S 32R-9

I MAJOR ITEM DATA

4. MODEL: A/S 32R-9	5. SERIAL NO.: 32R-9-1391
6. QUANTITY: ONE	7. LIFE PERIOD: 5190 MILES
8. MFR:	9. USA NO.: R-3

II PART DATA

10. NOMENCLATURE/DESCRIPTION: TUBE	12. MFR PART NO.: N/A
11. FSN: N/A	14. MFR.:
13.DRAWING NO.: N/A	16. NEXT ASSEMBLY: PUMPING STATION
15. QUANTITY: ONE	18. PART TEST LIFE: 4523 MILES
17. MAC FUNCTIONAL GRP: 18	

III INCIDENT DATA

19. DATE OF OCCURANCE: SEPTEMBER 30, 1980		20. TYPE OF REPORT:		21. ACTION TAKEN:	
22. MAINT. SP , ELM, CODE: RAM		X	A. INCIDENT	X	A. REPLACED
23. OBSERVED DURING	24. TEST ENVIRONMENT:		B. INFORMATION		B. REPAIRED
X A. OPERATION		25. INCIDENT CLASSIFICATION:			C. ADJUSTED
B. MAINTENANCE	80°F, DRY		A. CRITICAL		D. DISCONNECTED
C. INSPECTION			B. MAJOR		E. REMOVED
D. OTHER		X	C. MINOR		F. NONE

IV INCIDENT DESCRIPTION

26. DESCRIBE INCIDENT FULLY (INCLUDE IMPACT OF INCIDENT ON MAC CODE IDENTIFIED IN BLOCK 22):

THE 1/2 INCH TUBE CONNECTING THE BOTTOM OF THE FILTER BYPASS VALVE TO THE OVER-WING NOZZLE PRESSURE CONTROL VALVE CRACKED AT THE 90° BEND. THE INCIDENT WAS ATTRIBUTED TO CONNECTING A METAL TUBE BETWEEN A STATIONARY FILTER BYPASS VALVE AND THE UNSECURED PRESSURE CONTROL VALVE.

INCIDENT CLASSIFICATION IS SUBJECT TO RECLASSIFICATION

27. DEFECTIVE MATERIAL SENT TO:

28. NAME, TITLE & TEL EXT OF PREPARER:
    E. C. WONG
    TEST DIRECTOR
    AV 283-5151
	29. FOR THE COMMANDER:
	    EDWARD H. ROBERTS
	    C, AUTOMOTIVE & GENERAL EQUIP. DIV.
	    MATERIAL TESTING DIRECTORATE

VARCOV FORM 2134

FIGURE 19-3 Equipment Performance Report

reports. At that time, the company's prior responses to each field equipment report are presented to the customer's engineering and test personnel by the members of the inspection/quality engineering department and the company's project engineer.

Since tests are performed early in the production phase, the results and subsequent corrective actions often play very important parts in providing production equipment a high degree of quality and reliability. In addition, these tests demonstrate the capability of the product design to enable the equipment to perform its intended functions. Thus the corrective action program, if scrupulously followed, can provide equipment which has an ever increasingly high level of quality, performance, and reliability.

CHAPTER TWENTY

Evaluation

INTRODUCTION

This chapter and Chapter 21 present the elements used to evaluate the success of the inspection quality program and its implementation. Chapter 22 will present the corrective actions employed when the program and/or its implementation are not entirely successful.

In order to insure that products and services of world class quality are produced, it is necessary to constantly monitor the success of the inspection/ quality program.

BENCHMARKING

Some basis or comparison, or benchmark, is established in order to measure the progress of the improvement. Usually, benchmarks are the technical and quality levels of the leaders in the industry. By comparing its products to those of the leaders, it is possible for a company to measure its progress in meeting and eventually surpassing those levels. Of course, it must be understood that the competition will not be standing still, and that they will also strive to improve their products. Accordingly, the effort to provide products and services at world class quality levels becomes an ongoing operation, with the introduction of ever-increasing efficiencies, and the fabrication of products at continuously higher technical and quality levels.

Some industries may not be of sufficient size and scope to include many companies that provide the same or similar products. Thus other benchmarks must be developed. These may include attributes of company operations which can be compared to similar characteristics of leaders in other industries; for example, measurements of progressively improved cost effectiveness, and improvements in its internal quality goals, ease of manufacture, and employee turnover.

Some companies also establish internal benchmarks which are based upon a measurement of their improvement against some pre-established goals.

These are used to measure the improvement of each individual department relative to its own goals. The levels of comparison may include any of the following.

Engineering department

The benchmark may be the reduction in time from the date of design conception to the release of manufacturing drawings, or the decrease in the number of engineering changes subsequent to the initial drawing issue.

Manufacturing organization

The benchmark may be based upon the number of items produced without any rejection, or the increased efficiency of the operation.

Inspection/quality organization

The basis of comparison may be the number of shipments accepted by the customer without any defects, or the rapidity and effectiveness of its corrective action program.

Personnel department

The benchmark may be the speed at which replacement personnel requisitions are filled, or the number of training programs implemented, and their effectiveness in quality improvement.

SELECTION

It is important that the methods used to evaluate the inspection/quality programs, be unbiased and provide a true picture of the degree of quality and of its improvement. For example, when comparing the internal quality levels of the product, the base of comparison should be selected so that the change in the quality level of one product is not measured against that of another more complex product with a greater level of manufacturing difficulty, unless special provisions are made to compensate for these different complexity levels.

When applicable, the company and its inspection/quality organization should be aware of and make use of the large variety of statistical methods which apply to evaluation. Simpler techniques are recommended by Dr. Juran in the fourth edition of his *Quality Control Handbook*. They include the following:

- For summarizing data, use frequency distributions, histograms, and indices.

- For controlling process quality, use control charts (both attributes and variables).

- For evaluating quality to previously defined levels, use attributes and variables sampling plans.

See Chapter 24 for additional details about a number of statistical techniques.

By the same token, care must be taken not to employ highly sophisticated statistical techniques when a simpler method is equally effective. The more complex the techniques, the greater the difficulty in their implementation, and the greater the possibility of error in their results. Also, a more sophisticated technique will often present a greater degree of difficulty in explaining the results to management personnel, who may not be well versed in statistics. Similarly, the methods of measurement and data reporting should include language which is meaningful to those personnel to whom the reports are directed. For example, one of the most effective techniques of describing to management the quality levels and their subsequent improvements, is the presentation of improved product costs and increased company profits. More examples of nonstatistical techniques used in evaluating quality levels are discussed later in this chapter.

RECORDS

Records of the inspection/quality program must be developed and accumulated to reflect its activities. In some companies, however, inspection/quality records are developed and maintained merely as a matter of routine. Once the records have been prepared, they are filed and not looked at again, unless some special occasion arises, such as the customer requesting verification of some required examinations.

OBJECTIVES

In most other companies, there are usually four principal reasons for the preparation of inspection/quality records.

Contractual requirements

These stipulate that inspection/test, shipment, and customer acceptance records be maintained. For some customers, such as the government and large prime contractors, records are required to demonstrate the degree of implementation of a contractually specified inspection/quality program. These may include records of incoming, in-process, final piece parts, and end item inspection/tests. Also, records of management reports, corrective actions, and audits of the inspection/quality program are required.

Product liability prevention programs (PLP)

Those companies, who have developed product liability prevention programs maintain considerable records for use in the event of litigation due to product failure resulting in a death or injury. These records are kept to provide proof that the product had been adequately inspected and tested, and that no nonconforming supplies were shipped to the user. Also, as had been discussed in Chapter 10, records of the drawing controls and design reviews are needed.

Management action

One of the most important objectives for maintaining inspection/quality records is for their use by managers in production, engineering, and tool procurement. When the records are analyzed, the information enables managers to control and improve product and service quality, identify out-of-control situations, and determine the effects of any corrective actions.

Since current inspection/quality programs involve the contributions of all company departments, many types of records, which had not been used in the past, are now maintained. Examples of some of the applications of these records include the following:[1]

- Measuring service promptness against target goals
- Evaluating quality against top competitors
- Eliminating unnecessary changes in engineering drawings and other documents issued by departments such as purchasing and manufacturing engineering
- Identifying invoicing errors by cost of correction
- Pinpointing software quality by errors per lines of code
- Determining project status against company goals
- Assessing company-wide management achievements against strategic goals

Documentation for International Standards Organization (ISO) certification[2]

For those suppliers that wish to engage in business with European companies, it is becoming increasingly important to maintain records attesting to the supplier's ability to implement a total system of quality control as it complies with the applicable ISO 9000 standards. These suppliers must be registered and audited by the applicable agencies before being accredited.

The documentation necessary should include the policies, standard operational procedures, and quality control programs for the applicable processes and services provided by the supplier. Included are those records and instructions similar to the traditional total quality control specifications and standards.

It is recommended that the applicable ISO standard be reviewed to insure that the documentation of the company's inspection/quality program includes all other pertinent elements of the ISO standard. Chapter 34 of this text describes additional details about the ISO standards. Copies of the applicable standard can be obtained from the ASQC Technical Committee, P.O. Box 3005, Milwaukee, WI 53201–3005.

DESIGN OF INSPECTION/TEST RECORDS

Some companies have each department design the documents and record formats necessary for its individual needs. This, at times, results in the duplication of documents.

Other companies maintain a staff function for the development and implementation of a systems approach for preparing documents.[3] This eliminates duplication and provides standardized formats. In these companies, each department may prepare document drafts for its use in accordance with standards provided by the staff function. These, however, should be submitted to, and approved by, the system personnel before they are issued.

This approach provides for a systematic determination of the needs for, and the methods of, document control. The following elements are recommended in the implementation of such a program.

1. Identify information needed by the company, its customers, suppliers, regulating agencies, and all other potential record users.

2. Develop means for collection, reduction, retention, and retrieval of the inspection/quality data.

3. Provide traceability of data to physical products, when needed.

4. Design and provide the forms, with users' concurrence.

5. Create record files for retention and retrieval.

In designing the formats for the data, the following characteristics should be considered.

1. Determine the need for manual or electronic data processing. The choice is generally predicated on the volume of data, extent of multiple use, and company experience with the use of electronic systems.

2. Establish the characteristics of the form, including size; paper weight, grade, and color; ink color; heading and identification instructions; arrangement of formats, and the like. Consideration should be given to the ability of the format to be utilized by means of standard office machines, typewriters, and word processors. In addition, the ability to store and file the documents in existing facilities should be kept in mind.

3. Provide for flexibility in the system to incorporate future data needs.

4. Provide a means of receiving information from other than standard formats, such as by telephone or facsimile, and incorporating it into the standard format.

5. Provide for periodic reviews of all forms and reports to determine the need for their continued use or revision. This can be done by soliciting comments and recommendations from users.

Another method to determine whether certain reports are still needed, is to temporarily suspend their distribution at random intervals and wait for comments from the original recipients. It is surprising how many people will be unaware that they have ceased receiving these reports, indicating their lack of need for these documents.

Since a major objective of inspection/test records is to provide data for subsequent analyses, the record format should make it easy to perform these analyses. In addition, consideration should be given to the ease of completing the necessary record forms by the operating personnel. Attention should also be paid to their working climate. For example, inspectors whose work requires them to wear gloves, or whose work is dirty, would have to remove their gloves or clean their hands before filling out the inspection record. Requiring these personnel to prepare, on the spot, extensive written reports, is certainly not conducive to an efficient operation. In those cases, a record form which merely required the inspector to place a check mark at the appropriate location would suffice for the given need. Another method would be the use of a record format containing preprinted types of nonconformances, so that the inspector would merely be required to put tally marks on the form to denote the number and types of defectives. This format would also be easy to use for subsequent analysis. See Figure 20-1 for an example.

Some examples of inspection records are illustrated in Figure 8-12, Inspection Instruction and Quality Record Sheet; Figure 18-1, Inspection Check Sheet; and Figure 20-2, Purchased Material Inspection Record. Examples of other types of forms, such as those used for special processes, audits, corrective action, and drawing review are illustrated in the applicable sections of this text.

When designing the inspection/test records format, consideration should be given to the type of statistical techniques which may be used for subsequent analyses. For example, when the data is to be used to prepare standard X-bar and R control charts, provision should be made for recording the data in the form of a column of three to five values, so that the average and range can easily be calculated at the end of each group.

Many types of software are available that can be used to record information using computers at the inspection/test stations. This software not only records the data, but also calculates the statistical information required for the subsequent analysis, such as the average, range, standard deviation, control chart limits, and many others. See Chapter 26 for further details.

ANALYSIS OF ASSEMBLY VARIANCE SHEETS

JOB	MONTH	PREPARED BY:		NO. OF UNITS		

		IN PROCESS	FINAL	TOTAL	TEST
ASSEMBLIES	MISSING	II			
	DAMAGED				
	INCOMPLETE				
PARTS	MISSING	卌			
	LOOSE	卌 卌			
	INCORRECT	III			
	DAMAGED	II			
HARDWARE	MISSING	卌			
	LOOSE	卌 卌			
	INCORRECT	卌			
	DAMAGED	II			
WORKMANSHIP	BURRS	III			
	CLEANLINESS	I			
	WELD SPLATTER	I			
	ROUTING	I			
	ADJUSTMENTS	II			
	IMPROPER ASSEMBLY	III			
MISC.	PAINT	卌 II			
	WELD				
	MISSING OPERATION	I			
	IDENTIFICATION	卌			
FUNCTIONAL	MECHANICAL MALFUNCTION				
	ELECTRICAL MALFUNCTION				
	HYDRALIC MALFUNCTION				
	PROCEDURAL PROBLEMS				
	ADJUSTMENTS				
	DEFECTIVE COMPONENTS				
	CALIBRATION				
	MISC.				
	AIR SYSTEM MALFUNCTION				
LEAKS	FUEL				
	LUBRICANT				
	COOLANT				
	HYDRALIC				
	AIR				
	WATER				
	EXHAUST				
	TOTALS				
TOTAL DEFECTS PER UNIT		GRAND TOTAL			

FIGURE 20-1 Inspection Record—Tally Marks

QUALITY CONTROL DEPARTMENT INSPECTION RECORD

PART NO./REV.			ECN/NCR		QPL NO.		VENDOR/MFG. DEPT							JOB NO.			
NOMENCLATURE					P.O. NO.		P.O. NOTES		COMM. CARD NO.					I.I. ISSUE NO.			

LOT/ DATE	QTY. LOT SIZE	SAMP SIZE AQL %	NO. DEF.	SAMP SIZE AQL %	NO. DEF.	SAMP SIZE AQL %	NO. DEF.	SAMP SIZE AQL %	NO. DEF.	SAMP SIZE AQL %	NO. DEF	DISPOSITION				
												INSP.	ACC/ REJ.	D.R. NO.	REMARKS	CUST. I.D.

CD/ C FORM 0700.1.1S

FIGURE 20-2 Purchased Material Inspection Record

Depending upon the size of the company, and the complexity of the product, the results of the inspection/tests may be noted on a very simple form or a highly elaborate one. The record should be no more complex than absolutely necessary. The inspector/tester on the production floor should spend as little time as possible performing nonproductive work, such as recording results. This chore detracts from and, at times, adversely affects, the performance of the principal function of the inspector. At the start of the inspection/quality program's planning phase, a determination should be made of the record requirements for each inspection/test station.

RECORD RETENTION

During the planning period, the need to keep each type of record and its retention time should be considered.

Current Status

In general, inspection/test records are maintained, in a current status, at the location at which the operation is performed for a predetermined period of time, for example, three months. At that time, those records retained for a longer period of time, should be placed in containers and sent to long-term storage areas. The containers should be identified, by the area supervisor, with their contents, the department in which the contents have been prepared, and the retention period.

When, during the planning phase, it has been determined that there is no requirement for any long-range storage, these records may be destroyed, after review by the section supervisor and the department manager. It is desirable, however, that some notation of the destruction be made in the area's file. For example, "the in-process paint inspection records for the period 3/1/88 to 6/1/88 were destroyed on 6/15/88."

Long-Term Storage

A member of the top management staff, usually the contracts or legal department manager, should develop a list of the records utilized by each department, and the length of retention time for each. This listing should be reviewed and approved by each department head, issued in a company procedure, and distributed to the applicable personnel.

The retention period for the contractually required inspection/quality records is frequently specified by the customer. This period is generally noted as a number of years from the date of contract completion. For product liability prevention programs and for tax purposes, it is often necessary to retain some data for a longer period of time. The list of record retention periods should be reviewed and upgraded at regular intervals, and upon the receipt of each new contract.

RECORD RETENTION TRANSMITTAL & DESTRUCTION NOTICE				
ORIGINATING DEPARTMENT				
DEPT NO.	DEPARTMENT NAME		PREPARED BY	DATE
RECORD TITLE AND CONTENTS (SPECIFIC DETAILED DESCRIPTION IS REQUIRED)		DATE, SERIAL NUMBER ALPHABETICAL RANGE, ETC.		OFFICE SERV CONTAINER OR BOX NUMBER
		FROM	TO	
BOX 1				
BOX 2				
BOX 3				
BOX 4				
BOX 5				
DESTRUCTION DATE	JOB NO.	DEPT HEAD APPROVAL		DATE
OFFICE SERVICES				
DATE RECEIVED	RECEIVED BY	ROOM	AISLE	SECTION

NOTICE OF DESTRUCTION

THE ABOVE RECORDS ARE SCHEDULED FOR DESTRUCTION ON _____

SUBJECT TO DEPARTMENT HEAD AND LEGAL AUTHORIZATION.

☐ DESTROYED AS SCHEDULED. ☐ EXTEND DESTRUCTION PERIOD UNTIL _____

REASON: _____

_____ SIGNATURE _____ DATE _____

DESTRUCTION AUTHORIZATION			
DEPARTMENT HEAD	DATE	LEGAL DEPARTMENT	DATE

FORM NO.106-006 6/82   WHITE-DESTRUCTION NOTICE PINK-CONTROL YELLOW-DESTRUCTION AUTHORIZATION GOLD-RECEIPT

FIGURE 20-3   Record Retention/Destruction Form

When a file is to be prepared for long-term storage, the department clerk should process a record retention/destruction form (see Figure 20-3). This form should be signed by the department manager and forwarded, with the boxes of records, to the storage area.

When any material to be stored is not on the retention list, the supervisor should check with the applicable department for the appropriate retention period.

The clerk generally records the storage area location number on the boxes and on the file retention form and returns one copy to the originating department.

File Retrieval

When it is necessary to retrieve a file for reference purposes, the storage clerk is notified. The clerk provides access to the file and records, and notes on a reference log the name of the requesting party, the department, the date, the box number, and a description of any contents of the box which may have been removed.

Records Destruction

The contracts/legal department should notify the storage manager when a contract has been completed so that the retention cycle for the records can be determined. In addition, when any activity on a contract has been renewed, a new retention period for the documents should be assigned by the contracts/legal department.

The storage clerk should periodically review the destruction file. One month before a file destruction date, the storage clerk should send a copy of the destruction notice to the applicable department head and to the contracts/legal department for approval. Then the storage manager should arrange for the further retention, if applicable, or the destruction of the files, and verification of the destruction, by a person assigned by the contracts/legal departments. Records of the destruction should be noted on the destruction form and filed in the storage area.

As noted in Chapter 10, records retained for PLP purposes, are usually stored under the jurisdiction of the head of the engineering department. Due to the state of flux of the PLP laws in many states, it is often necessary to retain many of the PLP records for a considerable length of time, generally for the life of the product involved. The retention periods are usually determined by the legal and engineering departments and the PLP coordinator, who must also give authorization for the destruction of any material.

Frequently, there is insufficient storage space for the retention of all the records. Thus, many companies find it necessary to convert some records to microfilm or microfiche, or enter them on computer discs. Further, some companies find it advisable to make duplicate copies of certain records, particularly for PLP purposes, and file these records in a duplicate storage area. This is done to insure that the set of records is available in the event of a fire or other catastrophic event which could result in the destruction of the original copies.

Vendor Records

When it is necessary to retain certain records for a given period of time after the completion of the contract, the outside suppliers of the applicable products must be advised. It is often customary for the company to require that permission be granted by it, before the supplier destroys any of these records. To insure that the supplier retains the records for the appropriate length of time, periodic audits of the suppliers's facilities are performed.

When the company's customer requires that the records be retained for a certain period of time after the contract's completion, care must be taken in determining the retention requirement of the supplier's records. The amount of time should be based upon the completion date of the prime contract, rather than on the date of completion of the purchase orders. This is because purchase orders for subcontracted supplies are often completed prior to the project with the prime contractor.

INFORMATION REQUIRED

As applicable, the following information should be included in the inspection/test records.

- Department or supplier where the product was produced
- Name of inspectors/testers, or their stamp
- Date of inspection/test
- Identification of item inspected/tested, including part name, number, and configuration level
- Characteristics that were inspected/tested

For inspection sampling purposes, the characteristics are listed in groups by degree of importance and amount of inspection. This listing is usually identified by the classification (critical, major, minor) and the AQL number of the sampling plan used.

When sampling inspection is not used and the item is large, it is the custom for the characteristics to be listed in an orderly progression as they appear around the item.

All test characteristics are usually tested 100 percent. Thus they are generally not arranged in the order of importance, but in a sequence most suitable for test performance.

Number of items inspected

When sampling inspection is performed, the number of characteristics inspected for each group is usually specified by its sample size. The lot size is also specified.

Inspection/test results

The number of nonconforming items in the sample is noted at the appropriate section of the inspection record. The nature of each nonconformance is specified for each variant characteristic. For some records, such as assembly inspection records, the acceptance or rejection may be indicated by a check mark adjacent to the characteristic inspected in the column marked ACCEPT or REJECT.

When the nature of the nonconformance is not entered on the inspection record, it is customary to reference the number of the discrepancy or variance report. For test records, the departure from the test characteristic is usually spelled out at the appropriate location in the body of the test record. The actual variance which caused the test failure is noted on the attached variance sheet.

Some companies do not record the nonconformance of a test characteristic. They merely retest the nonconforming characteristic after repair and enter the results of the subsequent test. This is a poor practice, since it does not provide the information needed to determine the quality level of the test characteristics, and thus does not permit the implementation of applicable corrective actions to preclude recurrence of the deficiency.

Lot identification

As noted, in some companies this lot designation is established at the point of final piece part inspection. For assembly inspection and test, the serial number of the unit usually serves in lieu of the lot number.

Disposition of the sample

When a nonconformance is noted during the inspection, the part is identified and processed for rework at the production station, or for disposition decision by the MRB (see Chapter 16).

When the sample is found totally in conformance, it is usually returned to the lot. Some companies may keep the sample separate from the rest of the lot for re-examination, if needed. Other companies have the sample marked with an acceptance stamp, and returned to the lot.

Disposition of the lot

When the lot is accepted, it is usually identified with an inspection move tag and moved to the next production, assembly, or stores area. Any nonconforming parts in the sample of an accepted lot, are treated according to the description in the previous section.

When the lot is rejected in accordance with the provisions of the sampling plan used, it is processed using the procedure described in Chapter 16. When a decision has been made to screen the lot, it is 100 percent inspected for the nonconforming characteristic. The results are usually recorded on the discrepancy report, or on the inspection record.

The next section describes the analysis of the records and its subsequent incorporation into management reports.

DATA ANALYSIS/REPORTS

As noted, the principle objective of maintaining inspection/test records, is for their subsequent use in the analysis and the incorporation of the results into reports provided to various levels of management. Management reports are provided for informational purposes, as well as for the implementation of suitable corrective actions, when warranted. It is through the analysis of the data that a measure of the quality performance of the organization can be determined. The degree and nature of the analysis should be determined prior to designing the inspection/test record formats.

OBJECTIVE

As noted, before proceeding with data analysis, the inspection/quality engineer should establish the documental needs of the organization, the methods used to reduce the data to a meaningful format, and how the analyses will be used. These determinations will then help to establish the method of analysis. Some of the following considerations should be given.

Who will receive the results of the analysis? As applicable, any of the following:

- Corporate or division head
- Executive committee
- Upper and middle management
- Engineering, program and plant management
- Suppliers
- Purchasing department
- Controller
- Customers
- Regulatory agencies
- Inspection/quality supervision and management
- First tier production supervision

How will the report analyses be used? This may include any of the following:

- Corrective action of discrepant conditions
- Long-range corrective action of the system
- Selection of suppliers
- Qualification of suppliers
- Determination of personnel training needs
- Determination and correction of out-of-control quality trends
- Improvement of process capabilities

- Identification and certification of products and services
- Reports to regulatory bodies
- Determination of production equipment and processes capabilities
- Determination of engineering design and drawing effectiveness
- Determination of corrective actions effectiveness
- Marketing decisions
- Historical records for product liability actions

CATEGORIES OF REPORTS

As applicable for each program, reports may be issued for any of the following:

- Individual items or commodities
- Manufacturing operations and/or processes
- Suppliers or manufacturing departments
- Each plant or the whole company

METHODS OF ANALYSIS

When analyzing inspection/test data, it is important that an unbiased base, which is consistent from one reporting period to another, is used for proper comparison of the quality levels. Some companies use a base of dollars per direct labor (D/L) dollars, when the data is based upon the output of direct labor personnel. For example, the report for period A shows the cost of scrap and rework in a fabrication department to be $10 per $100 of direct labor. The report for period B shows a cost of scrap and rework as $9 per $100 of direct labor, reflecting a reduction from period A to period B of $1/$100 D/L.

Some companies use, as a base, the dollars of sales per period. This may present a problem, since the cost of scrap and rework produced in a reporting period may not be directly related to the sales dollars for that period unless some provision is made to accumulate those costs for each contract. To use this method, the equivalent sales dollars must be calculated as each portion of the contract is produced.

Another method used to measure the quality level of assemblies or parts is the percent of units rejected compared to the number of units inspected in any period of time. This is acceptable if the units from one period to another represent the same degrees of complexity. In some cases, this is not so. For example, when most electronic assemblies consist of solder joints, count the number of connections in each type of assembly, and report the rejection rate in numbers of defective solder connections per 10,000 inspected. This provides an unbiased basis of comparison from period to period and from manufacturing area to manufacturing area, notwithstanding the varying product mix from department to department. Similarly, the comparison of weld quality may be based on the number of inches of weld found nonconforming per 100 inches inspected.

At times, it is desirable to compare one production area with another, each manufacturing different products. For example, the quality levels of the various departments, such as machine shop, paint, assembly, welding, and drawings and technical documents preparation could be compared. Accordingly, the method used to calculate the quality level in each department is its normal base of measurement. The quality levels from one period to another are compared. The amount of change in each department is then compared to the degree of change in the other departments. A Pareto listing (see Chapter 24) can then be provided, which shows the relative degrees of improvement, and their significant contributors, in the quality levels of each department.

Some companies utilize a method of comparing the quality levels in the various areas against industry standards, when available. For example, at one time, a standard was utilized by the major electronic equipment manufacturers, for the expected number of 3.2 defective solder connections per 10,000 connections. This was acceptable provided the work consisted primarily of hand-soldered connections. However, when a large amount of work included other characteristics, such as the installation of mechanical fastening devices, or means other than solder connections, some other basis of comparison had to be utilized.

In developing a method for data analysis, the method of manufacture and the opportunities for operational error must be considered. For example, in the previous discussion, it is assumed that the production of each solder connection presents the same opportunity for error. This can only be considered when the soldering is performed by hand, and each solder connection provides its own individual opportunity for error. However, when the connections are produced by a wave soldering method, all connections are produced under the same operating conditions. Thus the process condition which causes a nonconformance to one solder connection would result in the same nonconformance to all the connections. Consequently, the number of defective solder connections should not be used as a basis of comparison. See Chapter 24 for discussions of several statistical techniques available for the evaluation of quality levels.

The objectives of data analyses are primarily directed to providing information, not only of the quality levels, but also for the purpose of corrective action implementation. It is important that quality reports identify the significant contributors to each type of nonconformance. For example, in reporting the quality levels of electronic assemblies, some companies find it desirable to provide a Pareto listing of the most significant categories of deficiencies, in the order of their degrees of contribution to the major nonconformances reported. Thus: insufficient solder, 50 percent of the total number of defects; loose hardware, 26 percent; missing hardware, 10 percent; and so on. Often this listing is presented in the form of a declining quality index, with number *1* assigned to the most significant contributor, number *2* the next highest contributor, and so on. This listing can then establish the priority for the investigation and implementation of corrective action. In the example, it would appear that the initial priority would be for the investigation of the contributing causes of insufficient solder; the next priority would find the causes for the loose hardware, and so on.

REPORTS

Data analyses are of little value, unless the results are reported to those personnel who can provide the appropriate corrective action.

HIERARCHY OF REPORTING

No more details should be provided in reports than is necessary for the accomplishment of corrective actions. Thus, the lower level of supervision should receive the complete details of the quality levels and their significant contributors. The plant managers should receive a summary analysis of the quality level of the plant as a whole, with a breakdown of the quality levels and most significant nonconformances in each department. Top management should receive an analysis of the total company's quality levels with a short description of the significant developments and quality levels for each major department and each plant in the company. The effect of the quality program on the profitability of the company could also be included in the report to top management. See Figure 20-4 for an example of the distribution of an inspection/quality report.

INFORMATION PROVIDED IN THE REPORTS

A typical management report should include the following information, as applicable.

- Current and previous quality levels
- Significant contributors to the major nonconformances, and the relative amount of each type

SECTION I — Quality report summary

This section provides a digest of the significant conditions and developments relative to the "quality program" activities of the company's Inspection/Quality departmental personnel.

A detailed analysis of the elements discussed in this section will be found in subsequent sections of the report.

Distribution of this section of the report will, in general, be made to the company's Executive Committee and Senior Staff personnel of the affected organizations.

SECTION 2 — Service and manufacturing areas

This section presents, in individual subsections, an analysis of the inspection results of materials processed through the various manufacturing and engineering laboratory areas. In each subsection, quality index charts reflecting a quantitative quality level and Pareto analyses, denoting the most significant contributors to the quality index, are presented. The results of corrective actions instituted for the most significant conditions of the previous reports are described in each subchapter.

The following subsections are incorporated in this section.

2.1 Purchased material inspection
2.2 Machine shop
2.3 Wired equipment
2.4 Final assembly and test
2.5 Micro-electronics laboratory
2.6 Engineering data
2.7 Technical data

Distribution of the subsections will, in general, be made to the appropriate supervisory personnel in each area.

SECTION 3 — Audits

This section presents an analysis of the results of the "quality program" audits performed by the Inspection/Quality personnel in the company's manufacturing and engineering areas. These audits are performed to determine the degree of conformance to the policies and procedures prescribed in the company's Quality Assurance Policies Manual.

The results of each audit report are distributed to the applicable section supervisory personnel as each audit is completed. Distribution of this section will, in general, be made to the manufacturing, engineering, and inspection/quality assurance supervisory personnel of the applicable areas.

SECTION 4 — Corrective action

This section presents an analysis of all Materials Review and subsequent corrective actions performed in the manufacturing and engineering areas during the reporting period.

Distribution, in general, will be made to the Materials Review members of the appropriate programs for their utilization in subsequent MRB actions.

SECTION 5 — Quality costs

The current quality-related cost program provides for the accumulation and definition of the quality related failure, prevention, and appraisal costs in each manufacturing and engineering area.

Distribution of this section, will, in general, be made to the appropriate personnel in the Controller's office as well as the supervisory personnel in those organizations reflected as significant contributors to the reported failure costs.

SECTION 6 — Special tasks

This section presents a summary of the results of the special tasks and miscellaneous assignments performed by the inspection/quality departmental personnel.

Currently, this section incorporates discussions of the quality assurance proposal and new contract review efforts, departmental training programs, development of the procedures and policies of the Quality Assurance Policies manual, development of the micro-electronic quality and inspection program.

Distribution of this section will, in general, be made to the supervisory and senior staff personnel of the applicable organizations.

FIGURE 20-4 Contents and Distribution Monthly Report

- Recommended corrective actions and relative departmental responsibilities

- Effectiveness of previous corrective actions

- Quality cost information, including explanations of variances from departmental budgets

- Relation to the established benchmarks for each area and for the company as a whole

- Customer relations, both internal and external

- Other information such as results of internal audits and procurement of new equipment

EXAMPLES

Here is how an automotive supply manufacturer utilized its quality reports for management action. This organization was a multi-plant company with a quality manager at each plant, reporting to the director of quality assurance.

On a monthly basis, the quality managers issued to the respective plant managers, quality reports for the plants under their jurisdiction. The report defined the current and previous quality levels and the targeted quality goals for the plant and for each production station in the plant. The report also pinpointed current and anticipated quality problems, the significant contributors to these problems, and the recommended corrective actions.

Each month, the plant quality and production managers met with the executive vice president and the director of quality assurance, and reviewed the reports for the plants under their jurisdiction. The significant contributors to the quality indices were discussed at length, as were the corrective actions and the effectiveness of previous actions. When the plant managers believed that correction of any condition cited in the report, was not within their areas of responsibility, they presented the problem to the executives and requested their assistance. For example, when a piece of equipment was adjudged responsible for a number of major nonconformances, and the plant manager believed it should be replaced or subjected to major overhaul, the budget director and the maintenance department head were invited to the meeting and were requested to provide assurance that action would be taken to investigate and/or rectify the matter.

On a quarterly basis, the director of quality assurance provided a quality trend analysis to the divisional chief executive officer and the members of the company's executive committee. These meeting attendees were expected to respond to all areas in the report which affected their operation and denote what corrective action, if any, would be taken. At the same time, the director of quality assurance was required to respond to any questions posed by the attendees. The information and commitments given at the meeting were incorporated into the minutes and the progress of promised actions was followed up at subsequent meetings.

Another company processed their quality reports differently.

The quality assurance department issued a quality-related cost report which provided a Pareto listing of the five most costly nonconforming conditions encountered during the reporting period. On a weekly basis, the managers of manufacturing, engineering, production engineering, purchasing, tool shop, inspection, and quality control met to discuss the current report. Brainstorming sessions were held to discuss the causes of rework and scrap of the items on the listing. When the attendees could not determine the causes during the meeting, they were assigned to investigate the conditions in their respective areas of responsibility and report, at the next meeting, on the progress of the investigation and subsequent corrective actions. At one time, a high and repetitious costly defect rate in the manufacture of a complex part was determined to be caused by an inadequate tool. The tool shop manager stated that the controller had refused to provide funds for the procurement of a replacement for the soft tooling which had been used since the start of production of this equipment. The controller's explanation was that the number of parts on order was, by his determination, too small to warrant the expense of hard tooling. The quality control manager subsequently calculated the quality failure costs anticipated in the following month due to the tool's inadequacies, and presented them to the controller. Upon comparing the anticipated scrap and rework costs for the item in question with the cost of the replacement tooling, it became obvious that the failure cost was far in excess of the replacement tooling cost. Thus the requisition for the tool was approved and the matter resolved.

By correcting the conditions of each high-cost item reported at the weekly meetings, the failure cost for this company was reduced from an initial $60/$100 D/L to $1.23/$100 D/L in 18 months. In addition, the rejection customer rate was reduced to near zero and the inspection costs lowered by 50 percent over the same period (see Figure 20-5).

One important observation must be made. It is highly important that before any report is issued affecting supervisory or management personnel, the reporter should first discuss the matter with the affected personnel. This provides the opportunity for those individuals to initiate corrective action before the issuance of the report, as well as to be prepared to respond to the next higher level of supervision about the problems discussed in the report. This action demonstrates to the company personnel that the inspection/quality function is one of service to the company and its personnel, and not one which merely points out errors.

REFERENCES

1. Juran, J. M. *Upper Management and Quality: Juran's Quality Control Handbook* (4th ed). New York: McGraw Hill, 1988, Chapter 8.

2. Ruzicka, Robert K. *Documentation-Configuration Management: Juran's Quality Control Handbook* (3rd ed). New York: McGraw Hill, 1951, Chapter 19.

QUALITY FAILURE COST 1972 THRU 1977
– MANUFACTURING ONLY –

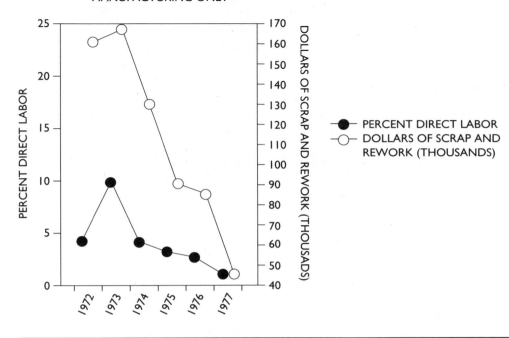

FIGURE 20-5 Quality Cost Graph

Quality Audits and Surveys

INTRODUCTION

A vital part of the inspection/quality program is the independent audit operation. To insure this independence, the audit should be conducted by personnel who are not responsible for the performance or supervision of the function being audited.

The audit is usually performed by selecting a predetermined number of samples from a product, procedure, process, or program, and evaluating their conformance to, or their degree of, implementation of applicable requirements. After the audit, the data are analyzed and the results incorporated into a report.

The result of a well-planned and implemented audit is the presentation of the item, procedure, or program at a point in time, without interfering with the production operation. By performing a series of these audits at periodic intervals, an inference can be made about the extent of implementation of the item, procedure, or program.

The beneficial result of the audit is the determination of any areas or elements which may require corrective action, improvements, or modifications. The audit may also reveal that there is an adequate compliance with the requirements, and no corrective action is needed. This area or element may then serve as an example of an A-1 condition to be emulated by other areas.

PURPOSE OF AUDITS

The purpose of some audits is to provide an independent assurance of the following conditions.[1]

- Plans for attaining quality are such that if the procedures are followed, they will result in the intended quality.

- Products are fit for use and safe for users.

- Working conditions are safe and not detrimental to the health of the employees or community.

- Laws and regulations are being followed.

- Procedures are adequate and are being implemented.

- Deficiencies are identified and corrective actions are being taken.

- Opportunities for improvement are identified and appropriate personnel are alerted.

- Management is making decisions, allocating resources, and improving morale with help from the audit results.

APPLICATION OF AUDITS

Inspection/quality audits are applied to a variety of operations such as the following:

- Policies and objectives, conducted by the highest levels of management

- Performance against company objectives, also conducted by upper management

- Degree of implementation of plans, systems, and procedures, conducted by special auditors

- Product compliance with specifications or fitness for use, conducted by inspection/quality engineers or special auditors

- Evaluation of the quality program for an individual contract, conducted by customer personnel

- Evaluation of the supplier's implementation of the purchase order's quality requirements, conducted by inspection/quality engineers or outside consultants

- Regulations to determine conformance to the procedural elements, conducted by the FDA, OSHA, EPA and similar agencies

CONTROLLING ELEMENTS

The following elements generally control the audit.

- Definitions

- Human relations
- Auditor's qualifications
- Characteristics and criteria establishment
- Frequency
- Performance
- Evaluation of the results
- Investigations and corrective action

Definitions

The following terms are customarily used during audits.

ELEMENT: This applies to a single item as detailed on the audit checklist. For example, "audit the degree of maintenance of inspection records at the receiving inspection areas."

CHARACTERISTIC: This applies to a distinct and definable feature required to implement the element. For example, "determine the use of the specified sampling plan as noted on the inspection record."

OBSERVATION: This applies to the verification of the implementation of one characteristic on a single sample audited. For example, "audit of the use of the proper sampling plan on a single inspection record."

Human Relations

Frequently, personnel whose operations are being audited are uncomfortable and concerned that any discrepancies revealed during the audit may reflect adversely upon them by providing results which supervisors could use to rate them unfavorably. There are also fears that the audits may result in biased, ambiguous, and erroneous evaluations. Accordingly, the auditor must be cognizant of these concerns and take appropriate precautions to allay them. It is vital that the findings are unbiased and based purely upon the facts as they are perceived by the auditor.

Prior to starting, the auditor should advise the affected personnel of the intent of the audit. It is important that they know that the audits are being performed at the request or concurrence of their managers and that there is no intention, when a noncompliance is detected, to attribute blame to any specific individual. Assurance should also be given that the purpose of the audit is to determine whether any areas require correction or improvement, and that the audits and the subsequent reports will be problem- not people-oriented.

In order to assure that there are no disagreements in the standards and criteria used, the auditor should review these with affected personnel. The methods used to conduct the audits, and the criteria of acceptability of each element being audited, should be established and agreed upon.

Auditor's Qualifications

Auditors should have received the basic education and training applicable to inspection/quality control personnel. They should be knowledgeable of the technical aspects of the operations being audited. In view of the human relations aspects of the audit process, it is also important that the potential auditor receive some special training in those disciplines.

While on-the-job training can be used to a certain extent, some prior formal training and education in these disciplines should be provided before the auditors are assigned to perform important evaluations on their own. Chapter 24 provides additional information about auditors' training.

There are a number of excellent courses given by schools and technical organizations on the subject of auditor proficiency. The American Society for Quality Control provides a certification for the auditor discipline after the candidate has been subjected to and passed a series of tests on the subject.

Characteristic and Criteria Establishment

Initially, a priority list of the elements to be audited should be established. This is often based on the product's fitness for use or on the contractual requirements.

For an audit to be performed properly, it is necessary that its elements, characteristics, and methods, as well as the quantity to be reviewed, are determined before the start of the audit. This insures that a proper random sample will be selected, which is not influenced by any stumble-on observations. For example, during an audit, a noncompliance may be detected before the sample has been selected. This variance should be corrected, but should not be included with the observations of the subsequently selected samples.

The elements and characteristics to be audited should be listed on a checklist developed for each product, area, or procedure (see Figure 21-1). The areas in which the element is to be verified should be noted on the checklist. For example, "Examine inspection records in each of the following areas: receiving, fabrication, electrical shop, welding, paint, nondestructive test, final equipment test, and shipping."

The applicable paragraph number of the procedure being audited should be noted on the checklist, for example, "Paragraph 3.2 of inspection/ quality procedure 1020."

And the method of verification of each characteristic should be noted on the checklist. For example, "Select at random, five records from each location, and verify that the recorded sampling plan is in accordance with the plan specified in the procedure."

QUALITY ASSURANCE POLICY (QAP) AUDIT CHECK LIST				
NO._____ QAP NO._____ QAP TITLE _____ ISSUE DATE _____				
ELEMENT NO.	ELEMENT	VERIFICATION AREA/FACILITY	QAP PARA NUMBER	VERIFICATION METHOD

FIGURE 21-1 Audit Checklist

FREQUENCY

To insure that a proper estimate of the degree of procedural implementation, over a period of time, is obtained, it is necessary that a series of audits be periodically performed. This should be established at the initiation of the audit program and noted on the checklist of the applicable procedure or product.

In some companies, the initial frequency of auditing inspection/quality manual procedures is set at a quarterly basis. When a series of audits reflects complete conformance, subsequent ones may be performed at less frequent intervals. Conversely, when the results reflect a significant number of noncompliances, audits should be performed more frequently.

Self-audits performed for regulatory bodies should be conducted, as a minimum, at the frequency established by the regulation. It is usually advisable to perform preliminary audits prior to the official regulatory ones. This is done to determine any weak areas and to develop the necessary corrective actions prior to the official audit.

Performance

There are a number of standards and guidelines for the performance of audits. One of the principal guides used for the audit of quality systems has been issued as ANSI/ASQC Q1–1986, "Generic Guidelines for Auditing Quality Systems."[2]

Prior to performance, the auditor should become thoroughly versed in the characteristics to be evaluated, the sampling plans to be used, and the criteria of acceptability for each characteristic.

The auditor should first meet with the responsible area supervisor to explain the audit methods, the characteristics to be evaluated, and the criteria of acceptability. When an audit program has just been initiated, it is important that all affected supervisors be assured, in advance, of the purposes of the audit. These are: to insure that personnel thoroughly understand the procedures involved and not to fault any individual for failure to implement the program; and to improve procedures, when necessary. The auditor should solicit the supervisor's comments regarding the procedure being audited, any problems with it, and any suggestions for its improvement.

It is important that the area supervisor, or some designee, accompany the auditor. This insures that the auditor is made aware of the locations of the elements and data being audited. It also insures that the supervisor is immediately made aware of any noncompliances and, when feasible, initiates on-the-spot corrective action.

To the maximum extent possible, the auditor should refrain from depending upon any verbal information from the operating or inspection personnel, since it is frequently nonproductive. The information is often biased and reflects the intentions of these personnel to provide information which, they believe, is expected by the auditor. So, any questions should be directed to the area supervisor, and generally for the objective of locating the applicable records or areas being audited. Usually the records should stand by themselves in demonstrating conformance to the procedure or program under audit.

If it should become necessary to question area personnel, the auditor should use good questioning techniques. Questions should require an explanation rather than a *yes* or *no* response. There should never be an appearance that the question is posed in order to trap the operator or inspector. When the explanation is lengthy, the auditor should summarize it to confirm that it is completely understood. When the area personnel volunteer an example to the auditor, additional samples should be selected, since the example may have been previously prepared for the audit. The auditor should maintain a show-me instead of a tell-me attitude.

In establishing the reliability of the audit data, it is important to remember that the auditor's observations are the most reliable, the records reviewed are second in importance, and the things that the auditor is told are the least reliable.

During the audit, small talk should be kept to a minimum, although it may be necessary to engage in some conversation so as to put personnel at ease. During breaks, or at lunch, conversation may continue about the audit. At these times, some informal information may be obtained which may be useful for the evaluation, but not part of the formal questions posed during the audit.

The auditor should select the specified number of samples, in a random manner, from each area noted on the checklist. Due to the statistical risks associated with sampling, caution should be exercised in making general inferences based on results of the findings from a sampling of elements without considering the effects of sampling errors.

The audit results should be entered on the record sheet (see Figure 21-2). When insufficient items are available in an area to meet the specified sample size, the auditor should perform a 100 percent evaluation of the characteristics or elements that are available. The number of observations taken and the number found in noncompliance should be entered in the appropriate location of the record sheet. The specific noncompliance should also be detailed, as well as any comments relative to the characteristic.

The area supervisor should be advised of any noncompliances. Comments indicating concurrence or disagreement with the auditor's findings should be solicited. In addition, any on-the-spot corrective actions which are taken should be noted. This information should be entered in the appropriate space on the audit record sheet. If the corrective action is to be taken at a later date, the anticipated date of completion should be noted.

Evaluation

After the evaluation, the auditor should tally the results and calculate the degree of compliance with the procedure or program. These results should then be evaluated against the criteria previously established. The results and the evaluation rating should be reported to the area supervisor expe-

QAP AUDIT EVALUATION RECORD SHEET

II NO._____ QAP NO._____ TITLE OF QAP_____

ISSUE DATE _____ EFF. DATE _____ _____

AUDITOR_____ AUDIT DATE _____ NEXT AUDIT DATE_____

ELEMENT	1	2	3	4	5	6	7	8	9	10	11	12	13	14	15	16	17	18	19	20	TOTAL
OBSERVATIONS																					
DEFECTIVES																					

COMMENTS AND/OR DEFECTIVES	PROPOSED CORRECTIVE ACTION

FIGURE 21-2   Audit Record Sheet

then be evaluated against the criteria previously established. The results and the evaluation rating should be reported to the area supervisor expeditiously. A copy of the audit results should also be provided to the inspection/quality engineer for reference in any subsequent inspection/quality management report.

Reports

The report should describe the details of the audit plan, including the names of the personnel conducting the audit, the areas and procedures audited, and the personnel contacted. In addition, the number of observations made and the number found in noncompliance should be noted. An appendix may be included which provides additional details of the audit, including any standards and reference documents used.

The report should contain a conclusion, recommendations for improvement, and follow-up for corrective actions. It should also highlight any significant noncompliances including backup information, which may require immediate action by management.

Copies of the report should be provided to the area supervisor and managers involved in the audit. The summary, conclusions, and recommendations for action should be provided to top management when the overall quality performances revealed by the audit reflect major areas of noncompliance affecting the safety of users and employees, and/or product fitness for use.

Investigation

When major problems are revealed by the audit, it is important that further investigations are conducted to determine the root causes and extent of these conditions. These investigations may be conducted by the auditors, when it is part of their mandate, or referred to management, by a separate report, for an expeditious follow-up. In the latter case, enough details of the audit and recommendations for the follow-up should be provided to insure that management has received sufficient information to perform an adequate review. In some companies, routine follow-up investigations and resultant corrective actions are conducted by line and operating supervision, monitored by the inspection/quality engineer.

Corrective Action

When, during the audit, any characteristics are found in noncompliance, they should be rechecked immediately after the promised date of completion of the corrective action. When the total number of noncompliances to the procedure or program exceed the established criteria, the entire procedure should be reviewed again immediately after completion of the corrective action.

During subsequent evaluations, if the noncomplying characteristics are still deficient, a corrective action request (see Chapter 22) should be forwarded to the area supervisor. This request should ask for a full investigation and implementation of corrective actions and an estimated completion date.

When the audits or subsequent investigations reveal that the procedure may require some revisions, the matter should be addressed to the applicable inspection/quality engineer for the necessary action.

PRODUCT AUDIT

Some companies conduct audits of their products to determine their quality levels upon delivery to their customers. These audits may be performed for any of these reasons.

- To determine the effectiveness of the entire inspection/quality operation
- To establish information which may be used for improving inspection effectiveness and product quality
- To fulfill the company's policy requirement for an independent audit
- To investigate customer reports of nonconforming product
- To completely evaluate some product characteristics which may not be tested during normal inspection
- To follow up on any problems with products currently in production

Points of Product Audit

These audits may be conducted at various points of operation.

After acceptance by inspection

This is usually performed to determine the quality of the inspection operation. At times critical characteristics of the audited product are examined by noninspection personnel using measuring equipment different from those normally employed.

After product movement to the stores areas

This audit evaluates the effectiveness of the sampling plan and of the inspection operation. It also determines the effectiveness of the drawing change control program.

After packaging and before shipment

This method determines the adequacy of the preparation for shipment operations. It requires the unpackaging and repackaging of a sample of the products.

After receipt by the user

This method is probably the one which best demonstrates the effectiveness of the complete production, shipping, and inspection/quality operations. This procedure is, of course, the most effective one but the most difficult to administer, and should be used only in those instances where a severe quality problem exists or is anticipated.

During proof testing

This procedure subjects the product to operating conditions and evaluates the adequacy of the engineering design and of the manufactured product. When the testing is performed at an external test site, the audit may commence prior to the unpackaging operation, so that the effectiveness of the shipping operations can also be evaluated.

PROCESS AUDITS

As discussed in Chapter 15, products whose quality cannot be completely determined by inspection or test alone, must include evaluations of their production processes. Accordingly, these processes are subjected to frequent audits to assure that the required procedures, materials, and equipment are utilized in accordance with the specified process instructions and procedures. Usually, checklists are developed for each special process procedure and utilized in the evaluations. The auditor should visit the areas in which the processes are performed and determine whether the implementation of the procedures is being carried out.

For example, when evaluating a weld process, the auditor should witness the preparation of the weld joint to determine whether the proper cleaning operations are being performed, the use of the specified weld rod, the application of the proper sequence of welding, and many other elements of the procedure. At other times, the auditor may determine whether the welder has evidence of prior qualification approval and has prepared, when required, the daily weld specimen. In addition, the auditor should review the method of storage of the weld rods and the application of the proper postweld cleaning operations. Since weld inspectors have generally been qualified, the audit of the weld process may be assigned to the weld inspector in lieu of a special auditor.

SURVEYS

There are many questions relative to the effective operation of a company which cannot be determined by the audit system. These areas of operation usually have recourse to the performance of surveys. Audits require established criteria of acceptability for measurement. They are designed to discover discrepancies in the elements of the system and provide alarm signals for the correction of problem areas. Surveys, generally, do not have any such criteria. They are used primarily to discover opportunities for the company or unexpected threats to the company's welfare.

Here are a number of elements which cannot be determined by audits and which require the performance of surveys for evaluation.

- Relative standing of the company in the marketplace
- Analysis of increased user satisfaction against cost, convenience, product life, and the like
- Opportunities for reducing the cost resulting from poor quality
- Proper equipment utilization
- Time studies substitute
- Examination of product design specifications for completeness, freedom from ambiguity, and fitness for use
- Review of customer complaints, effectiveness, and speed of corrective actions
- Personnel's understanding of the company's quality policies and objectives

There are many other items of the company's operations which can be evaluated through the performance of periodic independent surveys. Several principle surveys include those performed to identify Japanese companies that merit the Deming Quality Award. In this country, the surveys performed for the Malcolm Baldrige Quality Award are prime examples.

Third Party Surveys

In many industries, various agencies perform surveys and audits. For example, the Underwriters Laboratory determines the safety of electrical equipment; the Federal Aviation Association determines the air-worthiness of aircraft and its components; and the American Bureau of Shipping evaluates the sea-worthiness of ships and major components.

Some audits and surveys are conducted by independent consultant organizations and laboratories to verify various elements of their client's quality improvement programs and characteristics of their products. At times, outside consultants are used to perform surveys at a company's supplier facilities.

EXAMPLES OF SURVEYS

Occasionally, surveys are performed to obtain information relative to the use of equipment, or to the amount of time expended in the performance of specific inspection/quality functions.

The use of time studies of an inspection/quality operation is not generally considered desirable. The inference may be made that they mask a desire to speed up the inspection operation, which is usually not considered in a favorable light. The information, if required, which could be gained from the time studies, can be obtained by the means of a survey operation called work sampling.

This study consists of the auditor visiting the applicable areas of operation periodically during the day. The extent to which the pre-established activities are being carried out during each visit is observed.

EXAMPLES

A company had a receiving inspection department of approximately 250 personnel. The inspection manager was concerned with the length of time it took to process material through the area. He did not wish to clock the performance of the inspection personnel. Accordingly, he decided to have the area audited using the work sampling technique.

The auditor prepared a record sheet similar to the one shown in Figure 21-3. The various area functions were noted on the sheet. It also included a column listing various times of the day in hourly increments.

Prior to the start of the survey, the auditor discussed the nature of the review with the area supervisors. The auditor made it clear that the review was being performed to determine the types of nonproductive work being performed in the area, and was not to determine those inspectors who were not performing their duties in a timely manner. The supervisors were also assured that the audit would not reveal the names of the personnel being surveyed, but merely the ratio of the time spent by the whole group, in each activity, to the total day's activities.

The auditor visited the area at the approximate times noted on the record sheet. The times varied slightly from period to period, so that the personnel would not be aware of the precise time of survey, which would probably have an affect on their normal routines. As the auditor walked by each inspection position, he noted the instantaneous activity of the inspector and made a tally mark at the appropriate location of the record sheet. At the end of each day, the auditor recorded the number of available inspectors for the day (total inspectors for the area, less absentees and inspectors assigned to work temporarily in other areas). At the end of the audit period, all the tally marks were totaled for each column of activities, and the fraction of time spent by the group on each operation was calculated by dividing the total in each column by the number of available inspection hours. Approximately 400 observations were taken.

A Pareto analysis was conducted on the results of the audit, and the operations reflecting the greatest amount of time expended, were investigated. In the example cited, the results of the survey showed that 45 percent of the time was spent on the actual inspection of the product, 35 percent was spent on various noninspection activities, and 20 percent of the time was spent in preparation for the inspection and the documentation of the inspection results. Further review of the noninspection activities revealed that a considerable portion of that time was spent in obtaining gages and drawings from the central gage crib. Subsequent investigation revealed that all inspectors lined up at the crib at the beginning of each shift, awaiting the receipt of material. Thus, a significant part of each inspector's time was spent in waiting for the crib attendant to pull the necessary gages and drawings before the inspector could start working.

As a result, a revision to the operation was made to reduce this nonproductive time. This consisted of arranging for the area inspection clerk to

WORK SAMPLING RECORD																
DOCUMENTATION			SETUP			INSPECTION		NON-BENCH ACTIVITIES			CONSULT W/SUP	IDLE TIME				NO. OF AVAILABLE PMI
P/W	REC	DWG/ SPEC	SAMPLE	MATERIAL	SETUP	MECH	ELEC	MOVE	P/W SPEC ETC.	MSG EQUIP		AT BENCH	NOT			
													AT BENCH	IN AREA		
																9:00 MON 10:00 11:00 1:00 2:00 3:00
																9:30 TUES 10:30 11:30 1:30 2:30 3:30
																8:45 WED 9:45 10:45 1:45 2:45 3:00
																9:15 THU 10:15 11:15 1:15 2:15 3:15
																8:30 FRI 9:30 10:30 12:30 1:30 2:30
																TOTAL
																PCT.

FIGURE 21-3 Work Sampling Record

withdraw, before the start of each shift, the necessary gages and drawings needed to inspect the first two lots. As the inspection of each lot was completed, the clerk obtained the gages and drawings required for the inspection of the subsequent lots. This revised procedure resulted in a saving of 50 inspection hours per day at the cost of one inspection clerk, as well as accelerating the department's activities.

Another use of the work sampling operation is in the determination of the need for additional equipment. For example, a test supervisor requested an additional piece of equipment. The inspection manager did not believe that the equipment was needed. Accordingly, the inspection engineer was requested to perform a survey to establish the degree of utilization of the available equipment in question. By performing a work sampling study, the auditor reviewed the areas where the equipment was being used, and the types of equipment in use. After taking 200 observations on each of 33 pieces of the test equipment of the types requested, it was found that two units were in use 75 percent of the time, four others were in use 40 to 60 percent of the time, and the rest of the equipment was used less than 20 percent of the time. The analysis concluded that sufficient test equipment was available, and that the problem of insufficient availability was primarily due to poor scheduling and inadequate utilization. A subsequent review revealed that the test equipment was generally held at the test position while preliminary operations were being performed on the product. Accordingly, a rescheduling of the nontest functions was made and the test equipment was not requisitioned until all the nontest functions had been completed.

It is important to insure that a sufficient number of observations are made during the work sampling studies so that the results are statistically significant. This allows for the calculation of the standard deviation of the data, thus providing a statistically valid confidence range for the values calculated.

REFERENCES

1. Gryna, Frank M. "Quality Assurance," *Juran's Quality Control Handbook* (4th ed). New York: McGraw Hill, 1988, Chapter 9.

2. *ANSI/ASQC Q-1-1986*. Milwaukee, WI: ASQC, 1986.

CHAPTER TWENTY-TWO

Corrective Action

INTRODUCTION

Earlier chapters presented the first three phases of an inspection/quality program: planning, implementation, and evaluation. This chapter discusses the final phase of the program: corrective action. It is anticipated that, during the planning phase, the hazards of the production or service operations would have been anticipated, thereby avoiding most of the inspection/quality problems, and providing high quality products and services. However, one cannot predict all the problems of the operation. Consequently, the inspection/quality program must provide a means for the investigation and correction of nonconformances. Once a discrepancy is encountered, there should be little excuse for the same problem to arise in the future. A good inspection/quality program should provide the controls to enable rapid feedback of any problems and to correct the conditions that caused these nonconformances. The proper plan assures that these corrective actions are applied so as to have a long-range effect, thereby minimizing the problems associated with operating under crisis management conditions.

CONTROLLING ELEMENTS

The following elements describe the corrective action program of a typical company.

- Definitions
- Notification
- Follow-up
- Effectiveness evaluation

- Customer complaints
  - Internal
  - External
- Field reports
- Cross-functional teams
- Records and audits

Definitions

At times, there is a misconception about the term *corrective action*. Some companies assume it refers solely to the repair or rework of a nonconforming item. Actually, there are two types of corrective actions.

Incident

When a nonconformance is not of a critical or major significance and is a single random occurrence, it may be classified as an individual incident. Accordingly, investigation into the cause of this nonconformance is generally not pursued. Only the correction of the specific nonconformance is required. For example, lot inspection reveals that several piece parts have minor nonconformances and these variances do not reappear in subsequent lots.

Condition

When the nonconformance is of a major, critical, or continuing nature, it is classified as a nonconforming condition. After repair or rework of the specific nonconformance, an investigation should be conducted to determine the cause of this nonconformance. This should lead to the implementation of action to prevent its recurrence. An example of this condition is when an analysis of an inspection/quality record reveals that some part characteristics are found nonconforming in a number of lots of similar parts. Another example is the discovery, on a control chart, of a series of consecutive points approaching an out-of-control limit.

Notification

In many companies, when a nonconformance is first detected, a copy of the discrepancy or variance report is provided to the production operator, his or her supervisor, or to the part supplier. When the discrepancy is of a critical or major nature, or is reflected in a quality trend analysis, the responsible agency is usually notified of the problem by means of a Corrective Action Request (CAR) or Vendor Discrepancy Report (VDR). See Figures 12-6 and 14-3 for examples of these forms.

The inspection/quality engineer usually reviews the discrepancy to determine if the problem is of a chronic nature, or of major significance, requiring the attention of upper management to investigate and correct the system.

Before notification is made to the production personnel, consideration should be given to the nature of their responsibilities. When the production operator works in an atmosphere of self control, the information is provided directly to the operator. Self control is when the operator knows what to do, is able to determine the success of the operation, and can adjust the operation, if necessary, to meet the requirements. Notification of the nonconformance to the production personnel should be limited to those conditions which are operator controlled. In other instances, nonconformances should be referred to the appropriate levels of production supervision and/or management. When providing this information, remember that the production operation is rapid, leaving very little time for studying a lengthy listing of discrepancies. Accordingly, the information given by the inspection/quality personnel should be such that it can be read at a glance. Some companies utilize charts, signal lights, closed circuit television, and other similar means to provide this information. Summaries of the nonconformances should be presented in a Pareto chart highlighting the most frequent or critical nonconformances to enable the production operator or supervisor to focus attention on the vital few.

In providing information to production personnel, it must be understood that, while the inspector deals with measurements and their departure from specifications, the operator, in order to effect the necessary corrective action, must convert this information to the applicable process elements. Thus, it would be helpful that any recommendations relative to process changes are included in the nonconformance descriptions.

When notifying a supplier of any discrepant conditions, the inspection/quality engineer should first verify the validity of the complaint. The CAR or VDR should show a specific description of the nonconformances. Consideration should be given to the disposition of the nonconforming supplies, and the responsibility for screening the lot and/or the payment for the rework or repair of the variant supplies. At times, it may be desirable to notify the supplier by phone to speed up the corrective actions for future production.

When it is believed that the cause of the nonconformance is not the responsibility of the CAR or VDR recipient, a response should be made stating that fact and naming the responsible agency, if known. The complainant should then transmit the CAR or VDR to the designated person, department, or vendor.

When the CAR or VDR is the result of a quality analysis, the information given should be detailed enough to assist the recipient in the investigation and subsequent implementation of corrective actions. As an example, an analysis of a supplier's quality history reflected that, for the last ten shipments inspected during the reporting period, 30 percent of the lots were rejected. The VDR listed the significant contributors to the rejection rate, by part number, and by the types of nonconformances. It showed the part numbers of the five items which represented the highest rejection rate, and the most significant causes for these rejections, for example, dimensional 55 percent of the total rejections; workmanship, 30 percent; and incorrect parts, 10 percent.

When the CAR or VDR is initiated on the basis of a customer's complaint, sufficient time should be noted to enable the processing of a response to the customer within the required period.

Follow-Up

When the response to the CAR or VDR is received, the complainant should review the documents for completeness and adequacy of the proposed corrective actions. When a response is not received within the specified time period, or is deemed inadequate, the complainant may provide, to the next level of management of the responsible organization, a new CAR or VDR. The original recipient of the complaint should be advised that this action is being taken before the new CAR or VDR is issued.

Effectiveness Evaluation

Shortly after the proposed corrective action completion date, the complainant or inspection/quality engineer should review the applicable areas to determine the effectiveness of the corrective action. If the action is deemed unsatisfactory, a new CAR or VDR should be issued to the responsible department supervisor or vendor with a copy to the next level of management.

Customer Complaints

Internal

Complaints received from a customer's resident representative, are usually issued in some form of a quality deficiency report (QDR), and a written or verbal corrective action request (WCAR or VCAR). These complaints often result from a lack of company conformance to a procedural element of the contractually specified inspection/quality program.

The inspection/quality engineer, as a rule, performs a preliminary review to determine the validity of the complaint and the severity of the reported condition, as well as the departments responsible for the correction of the problem. Subsequently, copies of the complaints are usually transmitted by the inspection/quality engineer, by means of a CAR or VDR, to the responsible personnel in the company departments, or to the applicable supplier. In addition, the area inspection/quality engineer usually performs the necessary investigations and, when applicable, initiates the required corrective actions.

The inspection/quality engineer should then accumulate and analyze the responses from the other departments relative to their investigations and corrective actions, and issue a consolidated reply, when required, to the customer's resident representative.

Some companies have established a procedure for holding regularly scheduled meetings with customer's resident representatives. Here, all internal customer's complaints issued during the period are usually discussed, and the results of the corrective actions are evaluated.

External

A complaint from the customer or company service department relative to a problem encountered in the field, should be sent to the company's contract department. It transmits the information to the inspection/quality engineering department, and, as applicable, to the project engineer, manufacturing, purchasing, and field service personnel, and the safety engineer. This procedure should be followed whether the complaint is in the form of a formal or informal notification.

The inspection/quality engineer should perform a preliminary review and make the following determinations.

- Validity of the complaint
- Possible impact of the indicated requirements on the inspection/ quality program
- The extent of participation by company departments or subcontractors required for corrective action
- Time limits imposed for response

If the investigation and corrective action time is estimated to exceed the imposed time limit for response, the inspection/quality engineer should prepare an interim report outlining the action taken to date, and requesting an extension for the completion of the response. The request should be transmitted, through the contracts department, to the original complainant.

A log of all external complaints should be maintained by the inspection/ quality engineer. This log should include a record of the customer's identification of the complaint, the product investigation report number (Figure 22-1), the due date for response, and a brief description of the complaint.

The inspection/quality engineer and the personnel from the applicable departments should perform the following activities pertinent to their areas of responsibility.

- A review of the manufacturing processes, tooling, and inspection/ quality control procedures and instructions, for adequacy relative to

```
┌─────────────────────────────────────────────────────────────────────────────┐
│                                                                             │
│  QUALITY ASSURANCE PRODUCT INVESTIGATION REPORT        PIR NO. _____      │
│                                                                             │
│  UNIT SERIAL NO. _____ PART NO. _____        │
│  CUSTOMER IDENT NO. _____ NOMENCLATURE _____        │
│  REPORT NO. _____ DATE _____         │
│                                                                             │
│  DISCREPANCY: _____        │
│  _____         │
│  _____         │
│  _____         │
│  _____         │
│                                                                             │
│  ANALYSIS AND CORRECTIVE ACTION: _____        │
│  _____         │
│  _____         │
│  _____         │
│  _____         │
│                                                                             │
│                                                                             │
│  INVESTIGATION                                                              │
│                                                                             │
│                                                                             │
│      1.  Applicable manufacturing, quality control, inspection/test         │
│          procedures and instruction have been reviewed and:                 │
│          _____Found adequate                                               │
│          _____Have been corrected                                          │
│      2.  Similar items in stock and current production have been reviewed:   │
│          _____Cited condition not present                                  │
│          _____Discrepant material removed and/or corrected                 │
│          _____Stock depleted - item not applicable                         │
│      3.  Engineering change being processed.  Reference _____           │
│      4.  Based upon this investigation                                       │
│          _____Condition may exist on equipment in field                    │
│          _____Condition does not exist on equipment in field               │
│      5.  _____Field services will correct discrepancy in field.            │
│      6.  Purchase orders reviewed for adequacy of technical and quality      │
│          requirements.                                                       │
│          _____Found adequate                                               │
│          _____Have been corrected                                          │
│      7.  _____Sub-contractor has been advised of condition and requested   │
│              to take necessary corrective action.                           │
│                                                                             │
└─────────────────────────────────────────────────────────────────────────────┘
```

FIGURE 22-1   Processing of Notification for Corrective Action

the complaint. Corrections, when needed, should be made to these documents, processes, or to the tooling.

- A survey of the stores, assembly, and production areas. Any material, parts, or assemblies found nonconforming in the designated characteristics should be removed and forwarded to the materials review area for disposition. See Chapter 16.

- A review of purchase orders for the material in question. These must reflect the pertinent technical and quality requirements and must be corrected when found wanting.

- A determination for an engineering change relative to the complaint. If needed, the change should be made, and the applicable ECN number and the nature of the change noted on the report.

- A determination, in consultation with the project engineer, whether the cited condition may exist on equipment in the field. If so, a decision regarding appropriate corrective actions should be made.

- The preparation of a KCI (see Figure 10-4). This should note the condition reported by the customer and should prescribe the inspection interval (date, unit serial number, and shop order number) for the review and be processed as noted in earlier chapters.

The lots, or end items of equipment containing the applicable parts, should be inspected 100 percent for the characteristic(s) indicated on the KCI. The results should be recorded on the KCI and retained with the part or unit inspection records.

Upon receipt of the responses from the areas affected by the complaint, the inspection/quality engineer should review and analyze the data. This should be entered on a product investigation report (PIR) which describes the complaint, the analysis of the cause for the cited discrepancy, the results of the investigation, and the corrective actions taken to prevent a recurrence.

Based on this analysis, a draft response to the complainant should be submitted to the project engineer for concurrence, and then forwarded to the contracts department for transmission to the customer. Included in the response to the customer should be the final executed copy of the PIR. The date of the response to the customer should be recorded on the complaint log. All information generated by the complaint and its investigations should be retained by the inspection/quality engineer, and utilized for incorporation into subsequent management reports.

Field Reports

At times, first article or early production units are tested at customers' installations or proving grounds, for conformance to the performance, durability, and reliability requirements of the contract or company engineering specifications. These tests usually simulate the actual operating and environmental conditions which the equipment will experience.

Information received as a result of these tests are of considerable value to the supplying company, in verifying the current quality of the engineering design, and the manufacturing and inspection/quality operations as they relate to the equipment in production. The information and subsequent corrective actions, when utilized judiciously, should serve as means of insuring a continuous improvement in the quality of the manufacturing processes and engineering design. Accordingly, it is of extreme importance that a follow-up of the test results is conscientiously performed to obtain the maximum benefits.

Generally, members of the company's field service, project engineering, and/or inspection/quality control departments, as well as the customer's representatives, when applicable, are present during these tests. Usually, a visual inspection of the equipment is conducted upon its arrival at the test site. The results are reported on some form of an equipment performance report (EPR) (see Figure 19-3) or, in some companies, an unplanned event report (UER).

Each testing incident is reported on the EPR and classified according to its degree of severity. Copies of the EPRs are usually forwarded to the company's contracts and inspection/quality engineering departments. These reports are processed in the manner similar to that of other external customer complaints.

At the conclusion of all the tests, each unit is disassembled at the test site, and reviewed by the customer, when applicable, and the company personnel. Any additional nonconformances noted during the teardown inspection, are reported on a supplementary EPR and processed.

A final report is issued, by the customer or company's service department, to the company's inspection/quality engineering department, who prepares a final analysis, outlines the incidents by EPR number, and classifies each problem according to its degree of severity. In addition, a Pareto analysis is provided, by responsibility for the failure. See Figure 22-2 for an example of this analysis. An additional report is prepared by the inspection/quality engineer, describing the failures attributable to the company, and the corrective actions implemented for each type (see Figure 22-3).

A final meeting is held at the test site, where a review is made of all the EPRs generated during the test period, and the results of the investigations and corrective actions. At the conclusion, production approval for the equipment is granted, and the fabrication of the balance of the production units is permitted.

Cross-Functional Teams

Many companies have adopted programs using interdepartmental teams to investigate quality problem areas and recommend actions for their correction. The teams operate in a number of areas.

Design involvement teams

They review the design of new products for manufacturability, and consideration of customers' needs. The first article and early production units

Analysis of Customer Field Complaints

Following is an analysis of the Field Reports received from Rock Island and APG on Howitzer Carriges.

	First Article Tests	Initial Production Tests	Acceptance Tests	Total
Total EPRs	17	40	13	70
Total QDRs	6	0	8	14
Total				84
Total Occurrences	23	40	21	84

Defect Analysis by Occurrences

	First Article Tests	Initial Production Tests	Acceptance Tests	Total	% of Total
Design/Drawing	13.5	21	37	71.5	56.4%
Maintenance		5	26	31	24.4%
Information only		6		6	4.7%
Testing error		5		5	3.9%
Not company equipment	4	1		5	3.9%
Company responsibilities	4.5			4.5	3.5%
Investigation pending		1	1	2	1.6%
Not valid	1	1		2	1.6%
				127	100%
No. of carriages tested	2	3	9 - 59		

Total carriages shipped as of 1/1/91 62

Defect Analysis by Occurrences

	First Article Tests	Initial Production Tests	Acceptance Tests	Total
1. Improper heat treat of spring clip for lift clevis retention	1.0			1.0
2. Restricted lube tubes for axle	1.0			1.0
3. Obsolete type quick release pin	1.0			1.0
4. Equilibrator leak	1.0			1.0
5. Paint adhesion problems	0.5			0.5
Total	4.5			4.5

See Figure 22-3 for corrective action for the above

FIGURE 22-2 Analysis of Customer Field Complaints

```
BRIEF DESCRIPTION OF CORRECTIVE ACTION

Item 1

   a) All discrepant material removed from stores.
   b) Replacement parts provided to field.
   c) Key characteristic instruction initiated.

Item 2

   a) Drawing changed to add plugs to holes prior to shot blast.
   b) Flush unit prior to assembly.
   c) Units in field corrected.
   d) Key characteristic instruction initiated.

Item 3

   a) All discrepant material removed form stores.
   b) Replacement parts provided to field.
   c) Key characteristic instruction initiated.

Item 4

   a) Operation sheets/Manufacturing instruction revised.
   b) Random occurrence.
   c) Key characteristic instruction initiated.

Item 5

   a) Process audit conducted indicated conformance.
   b) Outside consultant reviewed process and concurred.
   c) Key characteristic instruction initiated.
   d) Engineering requested to review and revise drawings.
```

FIGURE 22-3   Corrective Action Description

are monitored, during fabrication and test, by these teams, for the presence of any problem areas. When a problem in the production, test, or operational areas occurs, the team members participate in the review of the nonconformances and implementation of applicable corrective actions in the design and drawing.

Production quality problem solving teams

They meet at scheduled intervals to review nonconformances encountered during production operations. They participate in the investigation for the underlying conditions causing the nonconformances, and recommend, as well as follow up on, the corrective actions.

Operational review teams

They investigate the quality complaints received from the customer or field service personnel. They analyze the cited problems, respond in a timely manner to the customer (when required) about the actions being taken, and provide to the production and engineering personnel the necessary information and the results of their investigations.

Companies that utilize cross-functional teams frequently include, in their organization, a quality steering committee, made up of upper level management personnel. This committee reviews the progress of the teams, and makes the necessary management decisions. These may include revisions to the company's production or inspection/quality systems, or the expenditure of funds needed to correct any major problems. This committee often sets management quality policies and benchmarks, and evaluates the company's achievements against these goals.

Records and Audits

Records of all nonconformances, quality analyses, CARs, VDRs, and follow-up actions are usually maintained by the inspection/quality engineering department. These documents are utilized for further analysis and incorporation into the regular management quality reports.

Periodically, the inspection/quality engineer, during the performance of the scheduled audits (see Chapter 21), includes a review of the effectiveness of prior actions for correcting the nonconforming conditions. Their effectiveness, as well as recommendations for further actions, when needed, are also included in the quality reports.

CHAPTER TWENTY-THREE

Personnel and the Inspection/Quality Function

INTRODUCTION

The selection, training, and evaluation of inspection/quality department personnel should be given the highest priority. This chapter discusses the various elements of this operation including the following:

- Job classification
- Types of personnel
- Selection
- Training
- Qualification for special needs
- Promotion/Transfer
- Compensation
- Evaluation
- Termination

Elements of compensation and the problems of inequitable wage scales between production and inspection/quality personnel are discussed. Also, the problem of dead-ended positions and some recommendations for its solution are presented.

JOB CLASSIFICATION

Introduction

Prior to selecting personnel, it is essential to determine the characteristics of the vacant positions and the personnel attributes needed to fill these positions.

In small companies, most managers have a general understanding of the qualifications desired for the inspectors. In many instances, the department manager or supervisor has an intuitive understanding of the characteristics required for the inspection function. Generally, a manager believes that the inspector only needs to have some understanding of the basic inspection methods and possibly some knowledge of the type of manufacturing operations at the plant.

In the early days of industrial operation, inspectors were usually transferred from production. At that time, these transfers were considered as promotions, with accompanying increases in pay and, in the eyes of the inspector's former associates, elevation to more prestigious positions.

As the manufacturing operation became more complex, and the products more precise, it became necessary to enhance the capabilities of the inspectors to meet more stringent needs. Accordingly, it was found that the knowledge obtained as former production operators, did not provide all the necessary skills to perform the inspection operation. Additional skills were needed to meet the increased accuracy requirements of inspection.

As the plants grew in size and the inspection operation more stringent, it was found necessary to increase the functions of the inspection/quality operation. As more inspectors were required to keep up with the production schedules, it became necessary to provide a chief inspector to supervise the efforts of the inspectors, as well as to train them in the techniques and in the use of the newly developed equipment. As the products increased in complexity, so did the measuring equipment. Thus inspectors needed even more knowledge. The chief inspector could no longer depend on verbal instructions to assure that the inspection/quality personnel had all the information needed to properly perform their function. Thus it became necessary to prepare and control written instructions and records. The inspection/quality department members needed to be capable of preparing the instructions and inspection record formats. They also were required to have the capability of reviewing and analyzing these records to determine the quality levels of the products, and to pinpoint problem areas which required corrective actions. Specialists were also needed to inspect and test the various attributes of the products produced through special processes. Testers were needed to perform the operational and performance examinations of the finished products. In short, as the plants grew in size and the products increased in complexity, a whole variety of inspection/quality disciplines were needed to meet these increased requirements.

Further, it became apparent that close coordination of the inspection/ quality and the other company personnel was necessary. Thus, the membership of the inspection/quality department had to include personnel who possessed the knowledge and skills necessary to effectively interact with other departments, such as engineering, production engineering, and production control.

As a result of the increasing numbers and skills of personnel needed in the inspection/quality department, it became apparent that using the intuitive approach to assess qualifications was no longer adequate. This eventually led to the establishment of job descriptions which defined the attributes and skills required for the various positions in the department.

Development

The use of job classifications became formalized in the early 1900s. At that time, an industrial engineer, Frederick Taylor, developed the concept of scientific job analysis and evaluation. His principle was based on the division of each job into small measurable increments, and assigning a time limit for the performance of each increment. This led to the breakdown of each job category, and eventually led to the conveyerized approach of production and assembly line operations.

The characteristics needed for each job were detailed in descriptions. Each job category was given an assessed time for its performance, which was subsequently tied to the pay commensurate with the ability of the operator to perform or exceed the specified time allowance. As a result of the predominance and strengthening of labor unions, it became necessary to negotiate with the union each job category and its pay scale. The results were included in the union contract, thus restricting the worker to perform only those functions defined in the skill category. The influence of union contracts did not immediately affect the inspection/quality department, since, in most companies, these personnel were considered under the general category of management, and thus were not incorporated into the union. However, the use of job classifications in the other departments of the company became strong motivation for the application of these concepts to the inspection/quality operation. Currently, the use of job classifications is predominant throughout all industries and for all job categories, including supervisory and management positions.

Uses of Job Classifications

While job classifications are primarily used for purposes of hiring the inspection/quality personnel, many other applications became evident as time progressed.

Use for promotion

Using the job classification of a higher position, enables a supervisor to determine the capabilities of superior employees to meet these other requirements, thus providing the supervisor with a greater degree of confidence as to the ability of the candidates to qualify for the new position. At times, some characteristics of the new job may not be within the capability of the inspection/quality personnel being promoted. The supervisor may still desire that the promotion take place, but, based on the job classification, can provide the needed training to the eligible employee.

Transfer

Similarly, the job classification is of value when there is a need to transfer the inspection/quality personnel to another position, either within or out of the inspection/quality department.

Evaluation

Before the use of job classifications, determining employee performance was purely dependent on the supervisor's judgment. This was at best arbitrary and subject to the momentary mood of the supervisor at the time of the evaluation. Frequently, no formal evaluation was conducted unless some special event occurred which made it necessary. Even when the evaluations were regularly performed, it was difficult for the supervisor to impartially consider an employee and insure that the standards used for one individual were equivalent to those used in the evaluation of another. This frequently led to hard feelings on the part of the employees when they compared their ratings with each other.

The availability of job classifications makes an impartial and equivalent evaluation for all personnel in the department possible. Performing an evaluation of the inspector's performance against each element of the job description eliminates comparisons between individuals and helps to determine any areas which need improvement.

Information Required

Job classifications are prepared in a variety of ways depending upon the type and size of the company. In some companies the descriptions contain a few elements of the job and its requirements. Others go to a great length in providing characteristics spanning a large area of requirements. Some of the prime considerations usually included in the job descriptions of the more progressive companies are discussed here.

General requirements

This section briefly describes the type of duties to be performed. For example, a job classification for the entry level inspector may state that the employee will be required to inspect minor mechanical or electronic components using simple measuring equipment, such as plug gages, micrometers, ammeters, calipers, thread gages and the like.

Special skills

This section discusses any special skills needed for the job. For example, a job classification for a higher grade of inspector may specify that the employee must possess the ability to apply trigonometric calculations to perform the inspection operations.

Special work conditions

This section presents any special or unusual conditions under which the inspector must operate. Thus a job description for a weld inspector may note that the inspector will work in a noisy and dirty area and may often be required to wear a protective mask.

Education

This section discusses any special education requirements. For example, a job description for an inspection/quality auditor may state that the employee has to have completed four years of high school or technical school, and has to have taken a course in human relations.

Training

This section stipulates that the employee must have had a certain number of years of experience in the inspection/quality operations of similar products. This section may also allow the substitution of several years of education for a number of years of prior training or experience.

Product Value

Some companies include, in the job description, the value of the product upon which the employee will be engaged. This element is usually included when the product is quite costly and an error in the processing may result in a high dollar value loss.

Miscellaneous

This space is reserved for any other characteristics to be included. For example, the section may include information relative to the position to which the employee reports or the next higher position to which the individual can be promoted. This section also includes the statement that the employee must be capable of performing the duties of lower classification inspection/quality personnel.

Job Categories or Labor Grade

Most companies include their job classifications within a number of labor grades or job categories. Thus, job classifications from several departments may be included in the same labor grade. For example, a senior inspector's job classification may be included in the same labor grade as that of a production engineer or model maker. These groups are developed for purposes of standardizing the company's wage structure. Each category is represented by a wage range within its grade. The determination of these wages and their ranges is often quite arbitrary, and frequently based upon the wages prevalent among similar companies in the geographical area. Some companies, in order to determine the wages in a labor grade, assign points to each characteristic in the job classification. The sum of the points provides the value of the job.

Companies may provide from seven to ten labor grades in which all the company's functions are included. In union shops, the labor grades for union personnel are negotiated with the union and are incorporated into its contract.

EXAMPLE

This company fabricates and tests a variety of automotive and electromechanical equipment and components. The inspectors perform their functions in the machine shop and the following areas: hydraulic, special processes (plating, welding, and painting), mechanical and electronic assembly, and testing.

The inspection/quality department classifies its personnel as Class A, Class B, Class C, and senior inspector, as well as inspection/quality engineer, tester, and auditor.

Class C is the lowest inspection grade, and used for entry level inspectors, who are engaged in routine inspections.

Class B inspectors are required to be proficient in any one area of the company operation. They are to be able to meet the inspection requirements, in their disciplines, at the highest levels encountered in the company.

Class A inspectors are required to be proficient in two or more disciplines encountered in the company. They are also required to be capable of training lower categories of inspectors in their areas of proficiency, and of developing the necessary inspection instructions for these personnel.

The senior inspector grade is for those who are competent in three or more disciplines of the company operations. Under certain conditions, they may act as group leaders, assigning work to various inspectors. They are responsible for keeping abreast of the latest measuring equipment and of performing research into the latest inspection techniques. They assist, when necessary, in the design of gages and inspection fixtures. They are also required to be capable of instructing lower level inspectors in these new techniques.

The tester classification is provided for personnel who test mechanical, hydraulic, electromechanical end items and their components.

The auditor classification is provided for personnel capable of developing audit check sheets and performing procedural and product audits. These are conducted both in-house and at suppliers' facilities.

The inspection/quality engineer classification is for personnel capable of developing sampling plans, performing capability studies on equipment and processes, and using statistical techniques in the analysis of inspection/test records. The engineers are also required to be able to initiate corrective actions and act as liaison with customer and supplier personnel, as well as with personnel from other company departments.

TYPES OF PERSONNEL

An inspection/quality department is made up of various types of personnel, depending upon the products provided and the size of the company. In large companies, many of the functions are performed by personnel who specialize in the applicable disciplines. The personnel of smaller companies usually combine the implementation of several functions.

To fulfill the functions described in Table 6-1 (page 49), the typical inspection/quality organization generally includes the following personnel. As previously noted, there are generally three or four inspector grades, with increasing degrees of skill.

Companies involved in the preparation of drawings and technical publications may include, in the inspection/quality department, inspectors of drawings and technical documents, such as handbooks, instruction, and maintenance documents. They examine document formats and conformance to company and customer workmanship requirements. In manufacturing companies, gage and tool inspectors are often included in the inspection/quality organization.

The average department usually contains several administrative personnel who perform the necessary clerical tasks. They may work as materials review clerks, as attendants in the tool and gage crib, and in similar positions.

Some small companies often assign to the inspection department a variety of functions which, in a large company, are performed by the quality control department. Personnel in these departments are frequently called inspection engineers or quality specialists. Their duties may include performing audits and vendor surveys; developing and controlling inspection instructions and records formats; acting as members of the materials review board; analyzing inspection/test records and preparing quality reports; developing, designing, and procuring special measuring equipment; providing the necessary statistical analyses; representing the inspection/quality department in interdepartmental committees; initiating necessary corrective actions; and following up on their effectiveness.

The inspection/quality department may contain several levels of supervisory and management personnel, including group leaders, supervisors, superintendents, chief inspectors, managers, and so on.

See Chapters see 36–39 for the types of inspection/quality personnel in the construction, service, food, and drug processing organizations.

SELECTION OF INSPECTION/QUALITY PERSONNEL

Introduction

Inspectors differ widely in their ability to find defects and interpret specifications.[1] Accordingly, it is important, before hiring any new inspectors, that a thorough review is made of their capabilities. Unless their potential performance can be determined through the interview and by a battery of tests, any lack of ability will be disclosed only after they are on the job. By placing the right person in the job initially, the headaches that the supervisors will save will be their own.

To determine the ability of candidates to meet pertinent job requirements, some companies include a special questionnaire with their employment applications. This questionnaire elicits information pertinent to the inspection/quality operation which will provide useful data for the selection decision. Other companies subject their applicants to a variety of tests designed to establish their capabilities.

The information obtained on the questionnaire and tests include such elements as vocational and outside interests, ability to make emotional adjustments, mechanical and inspection aptitudes, understanding of spatial and mechanical relations, and many others. Elements of the tests should pertain, as much as possible, to the particular job being filled. In addition, physical tests are given, including special evaluations of the applicant's visual acuity and color perception.

Currently, there is antidiscrimination legislation addressing the fairness of pre-employment tests relative to minority personnel, so care must be exercised in the development and application of these tests to insure that they do not include any biased elements.

It must also be understood that the results of these tests by themselves, do not provide completely valid answers about the competence of the applicants. Frequently, the same standardized tests are utilized by many companies. Thus, applicants, in all probability, have applied to a number of these companies, and been subjected to the same tests. This may have given them the opportunity to develop a proficiency in responding to the questions and enable them to better cope with the tests. Accordingly, the results must be carefully evaluated and utilized during interviews to probe deeper into the applicants' capabilities.

New inspection/quality personnel should be carefully monitored during their early assignments. Any failures to measure up to the department's standards must be quickly determined and acted upon. This close scrutiny will determine the extent of any potential training needed.

Some companies require a trial period of employment for several months before new inspectors are given tenure.

Job Requirements

As mentioned, most companies use job descriptions as a basis of applicant qualifications. When these descriptions do not exist, it is important that the inspection/quality supervisor, before processing a requisition for a vacant position, make a list of the attributes needed for the job. This information, or, when available, the specific job description, should be included with the requisition. In addition, any special requirements should also be listed.

Initial Interview

In most companies, before submitting a requisition for a new employee, the inspection/quality supervisor must receive approval from the department manager. Unless the hire is for replacement of personnel leaving the department, this approval is generally predicated upon the prior incorporation of the additional position into the approved budget. After approval, the requisition is forwarded by the supervisor to the personnel department who then recruits for the position. The candidates are required to fill out applications which provide information concerning their personal characteristics, including address, prior employers, education, and, at times, reasons for seeking the employment in the company. Often, a special questionnaire, requesting information concerning some attributes of the candidate relative to the functions of the position, is included with the application.

In the past, the application included questions about the age, sex, and ethnic or religious background of the applicants. Due to the antidiscrimination legislation, the request for this information can no longer be included.

After reviewing the applications and the questionnaires for a preliminary match of the qualifications with the requirements, the interview is initiated. This is conducted to evaluate, by personal observations, the qualifications noted on the applications as well as to obtain additional information about the candidates. A skilled interviewer can, by careful questioning, determine whether the applicants appear forthright and present an appearance of confidence and an ability to conduct themselves in an acceptable manner. The interviewer generally tries to put the applicants at ease before the start of the questioning period. At times, the candidate may request information about the company and the particulars of the job, including the salary structure and other personnel information. Information provided should be direct and in accordance with company practices.

If the applicant satisfactorily passes the preliminary review, arrangements are usually made for an interview to be conducted by the department supervisor. At other times, the results of the interview are documented and forwarded to the supervisor, with the completed application and questionnaire. If the contents of the documents appear satisfactory to the supervisor, a second interview is arranged, by the personnel department, between the applicant and the supervisor.

Final Selection

As the supervisor reviews the documents and comments by the personnel department, particular attention should be paid to the information pertinent to the specific job. A list should be made by the supervisor, of any apparent strong and weak points of the applicant, as revealed by these documents. This information should be reviewed, in depth, with the applicant during the interview.

Frequently, part of the interview may include a demonstration, of the candidate's ability to perform an inspection on sample products. While the candidate may be nervous and not perform with the usual or expected degree of proficiency, the supervisor can generally determine the candidate's familiarity with the gauging and test devices, as well as evaluate the ability to perform the functions in accordance with standard acceptable procedures.

While the supervisor is discussing the available job with the candidate, care must be exercised to limit the comments to the technical aspects of the job, and refer any discussions about pay scale, promotional opportunities, and any other administrative elements, to the members of the personnel department. The supervisor should never promise the candidates any wage increase within a subsequent period of employment unless these increases are in accordance with company policy.

Results of this interview are customarily relayed to the personnel department. The supervisor's recommendation, relative to the applicant, should be a significant element in the decision to hire the individual. When, for some reason, the personnel department decides to override the supervisor's recommendation, the matter should first be discussed with, and seriously evaluated by, the manager of the inspection/quality department. If the personnel department's decision appears justified, the manager should carefully explain their reasons to the inspection supervisor. However, since the supervisor is the person most knowledgeable of the work that the potential employee will be asked to perform, hiring a candidate over the supervisor's objection should rarely, if ever, be done.

During, and subsequent to, the interview, discussions are generally held about the past positions that the applicant held, and the reasons for leaving them. Usually the applicant's references are called; the information obtained may be of questionable value. In most instances, the references given are those who would be prone to give a good report, whether justified or not. When contacting past employers, the required information is rarely received in full. Fear of potential lawsuits by the employee arising from a poor reference, has caused many companies to refrain from providing opinions about past employees. In these companies, the previous supervisors of the applicable personnel are cautioned to refrain from providing any comments other than the fact the employee had indeed worked for the company at the specified position for the specified number of years. Other companies require that all inquiries about past employees be referred to the personnel department, who generally provide the same kind of information.

Initial Employment Period

After the candidates are hired, the first day of employment is usually spent in the personnel department's office. There they are provided with additional information concerning the administrative nature of the job, such as vacations, sick leave, merit and salary reviews, pensions and profit sharing plans, if they exist, expectations from management, and rules of conduct in the organization.

After reaching their department, the new employees are greeted by the supervisor who had interviewed them, and who introduces them to the department personnel. New employees may also be taken for a tour through the work area and acquainted with the specific areas in which they will be engaged. In many companies, a copy of the company procedures and the inspection/quality manual are given to them, and they are given time to review the pertinent sections of the documents. Shortly before the end of the first working day, the supervisor usually meets with them and answers any questions they may have relative to their position and the contents of the manuals. The supervisors must take care that they answer all questions in a direct manner, and not pass off some question in an offhand fashion. The supervisor should present a posture of directness and integrity, and not be afraid to refer to the appropriate company personnel, for any responses to questions which can not be fully and honestly answered. The supervisor should volunteer to assist new employees with any work-related problem.

Indoctrination or Trial Period

Some companies provide an introductory training program for newly hired inspection/quality personnel. This is designed to indoctrinate new employees with information concerning the products and components that they will encounter and the elements of the company's quality program.

During the first several months, it is desirable for new employees to work under the direct supervision of a senior inspector or group leader. The designated individual should arrange to provide all assistance necessary to familiarize the new employees with the duties and areas of operation, as well as provide introductions to the personnel from the inspection/quality and other departments with whom the employees will customarily be in contact.

Without giving the impression that the new employees are being particularly watched, the senior inspector or group leader should monitor their work to insure that no problems occur as a result of unfamiliarity with the place of operation or the company's procedures. This surveillance will provide an opportunity to determine whether the new employees require any additional training or indoctrination. During the trial period, the supervisor should make a special effort to visit the area at frequent intervals, and be available to answer any questions about the operation for which the new employees may require clarification. This will also demonstrate a continued interest in the workers' performance.

Sources of New Employees

When there is a surplus of potential inspection/quality applicants, most of the open positions are filled from the applicants walking in the door. Some may have applied in the past, and their previous applications should be on file with the personnel department. In some companies, where the reputation for good stable employment and the fair treatment of employees exist, a list of unsolicited potential candidates are usually on file with the personnel department. When there is a shortage of candidates, recourse is usually taken to one or all of the following methods.

In-house transfer

In many companies, open positions are posted to enable potential candidates in other departments to apply. These personnel should receive preference in consideration for the open jobs. At times, the inspection/quality supervisor may become aware of an employee in another department who had expressed interest in working for the inspection/quality department. At other times, a department may have need to reduce the manpower in its operation. Efforts are generally made to place laid-off personnel into other jobs within the company. At other times, an employee in one section of the inspection/quality department, or in other departments, may not be fully capable of meeting the requirements of the current position, but would be suitable for the open position in the inspection/quality department. In any case, when a transfer is contemplated, discussions should first be held with the supervisor of the candidate's current department. In addition, time must be given to finding a replacement for the employee's old job before the transfer to the new assignment.

Promotion

Initial recourse should be made to promote personnel within the company before attempting to obtain candidates from the outside. This practice is desirable since it motivates employees. Further, the external reputation of the company is enhanced when it becomes known that a promote-from-within policy exists.

To this end, it is the policy of some personnel departments to include, in all employees' records, references to their capabilities and interests relative to potential positions in other company departments. This list should be carefully reviewed when an opening occurs in any department, and potential candidates within the company are considered for the open position.

Employment agencies

When it is necessary to recruit personnel from the outside, advertising in the want ads or to employment agencies is customarily done. In the case of management positions, professional search agencies are sometimes used. Depending upon the labor market conditions, the agency or search organization's fee may be paid by the company or by the candidate.

Besides searching for potential candidates, a good employment or professional search agency saves the personnel department time by screening out unqualified candidates before recommending them. Some agencies subject the candidates to preliminary tests which are usually of psychological and in some cases, of technical nature.

Technical schools

Recruiting graduates from technical schools or community colleges or, for entry level positions, from high schools is another way to find new employees. At times, representatives from the personnel and inspection/quality departments visit these schools to discuss, with the graduating class, potential job opportunities at the company. This is often followed up by testing those students who express interest in employment.

Technical societies

The local chapters of technical associations such as the ASQC, ASME, IEEE, and other organizations frequently provide employment services to their membership. In addition, job opportunities can be posted on the bulletin boards at technical seminars.

In-house recommendations

Many companies have a program of granting awards to current employees for recommending candidates for open positions. Employees who are content with their jobs, can serve as creditable recruitment personnel for open jobs, testifying, by their own experience, the desirability of employment in the company.

At other times, the inspection/quality supervisor may request that job candidates from other departments, if found unacceptable for the position to which they applied, be interviewed for the open positions in the inspection/quality department.

Current Problems in Recruitment

It has become increasingly difficult in many companies to obtain qualified candidates. Semiliterate graduates, who have exceedingly low skills in the most elementary phases of reading comprehension and mathematics, make the selection of qualified applicants almost impossible. It may therefore be necessary to hire employees who do not fully qualify for the open positions, and depend upon in-house training to provide the missing skills.

This problem is intensified, when the pool of potential employees are high school dropouts. Thus, as is discussed in the next section, the company's training program should include courses in reading comprehension and elementary mathematics.

Some companies work in conjunction with the local technical schools or community colleges to develop work-study programs. Here, the curriculum is adjusted to allow selected students to work at the plant in jobs pertinent to their technical education, during designated free periods. At other times, students may be assigned, on a part-time basis, to participate in the company's management training program. In these programs, students are introduced to the different phases of the company's operation, so that, after graduation, they may be qualified for an entry-level supervisory or management position.

An ever-increasing number of progressive companies, aware of this problem, try a long-range approach to mitigate the situation. Some form a partnership with the local schools by providing equipment, material, and funds. Others provide employees to act as instructors to supplement the school faculty. Some companies adopt specific schools and act as supporters in the motivation of students. These companies often have students visit their premises to acquaint them with the environment that they will be facing upon leaving school. There are a number of companies who provide funds and scholarships to higher level schools, for students who have attained some measure of proficiency in their studies. These companies promise positions in their organizations, to those students who have successfully completed their studies.

In addition, federal, state, and private endowment organizations provide funds to enhance and improve the educational systems. Some of these funds are given to high schools with high dropout rates. These funds are used to pay for the coordinated efforts of the entire city system, including city administration, social agencies, businesses, and education. Through counseling and motivation, the goal is to keep the potential dropouts in school.

TRAINING

Introduction

Training is a shortcut method to learning from experience or from accumulated mistakes. Every employee, especially in the inspection/quality organization, should undergo some form of training upon entering the department. This is applicable even if the employee has considerable experience. Every organization is different, and performs its functions in a unique manner. Consequently, training needs to be given to all new employees even if it is merely to acquaint them with the procedures, operations, and products unique to the company.

Training programs should be tailored to the company and to the specific job. While there are a number of areas of the operation which differ only slightly from one company to another, the training program developer cannot assume that these areas reflect all the activities of inspection/quality personnel. Accordingly, the general elements of the operation and an individual's expertise relative to those elements should be determined. Then the training efforts can be focused on an individual's weak areas.

Training should be an ongoing effort. At one time, it was considered sufficient to provide a training program just once, and leave the on-the-job experience to take care of any new skill needs. However, most companies operate in a dynamic mode. It has been estimated that the average knowledge half-life of an employee is not more than ten years. After that time, the knowledge of the job, due to its obsolescence, will be reduced 50 percent. Recently, the electronic industry underwent the obsolescence of three major disciplines. Over a period of ten years, an inspector, whose principal area of discipline was vacuum tubes and their circuitry, found that there was little or no need for this discipline. It had been superseded by semiconductors. In a short period of time, semiconductors were reduced by the introduction of microminiaturized componentry. In addition, an inspector who had become expert in wound type servo components found that in the ten-year period, these components gave way to microcircuits. Examples of the obsolescence of techniques can be cited in every industry.

Further, there is a tremendous impact on employees when an entire industry becomes obsolete, or is driven from the scene by the competition from companies in the world market. The inspection/quality personnel who had been trained and employed by these companies over an extensive period of time, find that their specialized skills are less useful, and that it is necessary to learn techniques to process the new products. This often requires skills of several magnitudes higher than for the evaluation of the former products.

There is no question that the company benefits by assuring that its employees are trained in the latest techniques. The question, however, arises as to the extent of company responsibility to prepare its employees in meeting the demands of the new technologies. Some argue that, in order to survive the tremendous changes which affect their present field and to prepare for entrance into an entirely new field of endeavor, it should be the employees' responsibility to keep abreast of these latest techniques. There are several schools of thought, however, relative to the company's responsibility for training employees to enter a field other than one in which the company is currently involved. Most companies believe that this training is not within their areas of responsibility, and is certainly not cost effective. However, a few companies, emulating the programs utilized by Japanese industries, believe that their interests in employees' welfare extend beyond their individual areas of operation. Thus, in Japan, when it appears, for example, that there will be a decrease in the requirements from its automotive production areas, companies develop their employees' skills for production in the shipbuilding industry. The understanding is that it is more cost effective to utilize an employee who has taken a considerable period of time and effort to be indoctrinated into the work ethics and skills of the industry, than to train a new employee in the specific techniques needed for the new industry.

The answer to where the responsibility for the individual company lies is still being discussed. However, when it appears that the company may no longer have use for the present skills of some of its employees, it should, as a minimum, encourage and support employees' efforts to learn new skills. This is particularly true when the company's product changes, or advanced technology is introduced into its operations. On the other hand, employees owe it to themselves to be constantly alert to the new techniques available in their disciplines. Even if a particular company does not feel responsible to enhance its employees' skills beyond those of current use, for the country's industries to stay competitive, it should be the concern of whole industries; the federal, state and local governments; the professional societies; and the academic field.

EXAMPLE

Here is how one company avoided the loss of competent personnel due to skills obsolescence.

This company had been making electromechanical products for the dry-cleaning industry for many years. It had created a group of highly skilled personnel in all their areas of operation. When its market forecast indicated that the use of its type of products would probably be reduced by one-half in the next five years, all the department heads met and reviewed the choices available to them. After a number of brainstorming sessions, first by the department heads, and then by the members of the middle and lower management, they came up with the following possible alternatives.

1. Continue production of the current products and reduce staff as needed.

2. Merge with another company producing different products with a higher potential for sale than those currently being made.

3. Investigate the possibility of improving operations and skills to take a larger share of the market for the products currently being produced.

4. Investigate the possibility of supplementing the current product mix with items which have a higher potential for sale, using similar skills and capital equipment.

The decision finally made was the last one (number 4). Accordingly, a committee was formed of the top management personnel, who formed subcommittees of management and supervisory personnel from each department. These committees investigated the types of products which could most effectively utilize the capabilities of their company, its employees, and its equipment. They also determined the skill and training needs required for the production of these products, and their potential markets.

After six months of study, the results and recommendations were submitted to the company's executive board who then narrowed the recommendations down to two new products. One was the fabrication and assembly of components for an aircraft guidance system to be produced under subcontract for companies manufacturing these systems for the military. The other was the design, production, and assembly of electromechanical speakers for sale to drive-in fast food chains.

Once the decision was made, the various departments started to review their current equipment and manpower skills. One of the major efforts to be undertaken was the retraining of current employees in the fabrication and inspection of the new components and products. An experienced training director was hired, who took inventory of the current manpower skills and developed the educational programs needed to update employees' skills. The programs were reviewed by the applicable department supervisors and managers, and implementation schedules were established. Training programs for the inspection/quality department were managed by the chief inspector with the guidance of the training director.

Since the training programs were directed to current employees, there was no need to include courses for their familiarization with company procedures and the inspection/quality manual. Therefore, the program concentrated on the new inspection/quality skills needed for the new products. This included such courses as gear inspection, precision mechanical parts and assemblies inspection, clean room operations, nondestructive testing, gyroscopic assemblies testing, and others of similar nature.

The chief inspector decided to take advantage of this opportunity to introduce, into the department, training in the principles of data analysis, the preparation and use of control charts, application of statistical quality control to selected components, methods of troubleshooting and implementation of corrective actions. In addition training programs were utilized for the development and implementation of interdepartmental design review and corrective action teams.

The results of these programs were highly successful and enabled the company to enter into the new businesses with a high degree of success. In addition, the use of the new techniques helped to produce the current products in a more efficient manner and at a higher quality level. This led to the ability of the company to capture a higher share of the market for its former products.

Chapter 24 describes some of the training programs which are available for inspection/quality personnel.

Planning the Training Program[2]

Before a company develops a comprehensive training program for its inspection/quality department, it is advisable to consider a number of key factors, including the prime reasons for the program.

What are the inspection/quality challenges and problems facing the company? Today this is the extent of competition by foreign and domestic organizations, who have adopted the concept of providing products and services of world class quality.

What are the knowledge and skills needed to solve these problems? Companies that desire to compete successfully against world class organizations, must develop programs which utilize the efforts of all personnel to attain, or exceed, at an economic level, the quality of the competitive products and services. In addition, these companies must be prepared to constantly update their employees' skills and utilize interdepartmental committees to provide products at ever-improving quality levels.

In addition, companies that are located in areas with a shortage of available skilled workers, must develop training programs to overcome this handicap. In view of the unavailability of sufficient potential employees who have successfully received, from the area elementary and secondary schools, the basic educational needs, the company must be prepared to develop and implement training techniques in such basic areas as elementary mathematics and reading comprehension. This is particularly essential when the company fabricates products which require a relatively high level of technical knowledge.

The skills needed by the company should include an understanding of the various tools for problem solving as well as the ability of integrating quality concepts and considerations into the employees' jobs. These skills may be technological, statistical, and managerial.

An inventory should be taken of the knowledge and skills currently possessed by the company's personnel, as well as the availability of training facilities and capabilities currently utilized by the company. These may include on-the-job facilities, apprentice training programs, and the use of outside training courses, such as those provided by the local secondary, vocational, and community college extension courses.

A decision should be made as to what categories of employees are to be trained, as well as the subjects presented to them. Consideration should be given to the training materials required, as well as the cost of development and implementation of the programs. Once these are decided, priorities and schedules should be established for the development and implementation of the training program.

Program Development

When the company is contemplating the introduction of a full-scale training program, a broad-based task force should plan it. The task force should include representatives from the management of line departments, major service departments, the training department (if available), and inspection/ quality control. These personnel will be able to consider the total training needs for the company and provide the inference of full management support.

When the training program is only being developed for inspection/quality personnel, it may not be possible to obtain the cooperation of the managers from all the other company departments. If that is the case, the task force should consist of the managers, as well as a number of supervisors from all the sections of the inspection and quality departments and representatives from as many other departments as can be persuaded to join.

The task force should provide general recommendations for the various elements of the proposed inspection/quality training program. These recommendations should include a definition of the purpose of the program. This may mean making each level of management aware of its quality responsibilities, as well as preparing its employees in the skills and techniques needed to implement this recommendation.

Another recommended element may be the training of unskilled personnel in prerequisite requirements to enable them to perform the required inspection/quality functions.

Two other recommendations are identifying the agency responsible for the development and implementation of the training program, and setting the general criteria for each course of the program. Criteria may include the cost and length of the course, the flexibility of the program, and its intended students.

The Planning Agency

Based upon the recommendations of the task force, the first task is to determine which department or agency should be responsible for the development, implementation, and evaluation of the program. Many companies have found it advantageous to use one department, such as personnel. Thus, training programs for one department can mesh with the needs of the other departments. Some companies include, as part of their training program, several general courses relating to the entire company's operations, which are usually provided by a centralized agency. Those courses specific to the activities of the department are presented under the jurisdiction of the individual department. Whichever method is selected, it is important that a central body or individual has the responsibility of reviewing all the training programs prior to their implementation, to assure that there is no repetition of courses.

Some companies, at the start of program development, usually hire a consultant to advise them in setting up the program and monitoring the early phases of implementation. Other companies may hire a competent training director for this operation. Wherever the coordination responsibility lies, it is important that all department heads have the opportunity to provide input into the elements of the program, relative to their specific areas of operation. It is also important that an overall view of the company's needs is considered and that the training and indoctrination phases address all these needs.

Following the actions recommended by Dr. Deming, as implemented by the Japanese industries, some companies insure that basic inspection/quality techniques are presented to all the members of top management. Those companies who intend to utilize statistical quality control or statistical process control, should insure that the concepts and the use of these techniques are included in the courses given to management. In the past, the introduction of these techniques, which were barely understood by management, proved to be less than successful. Management support and its understanding of special inspection/quality techniques, are most important to the success of training programs and to the resultant effects on product quality.

This discussion is not meant to discourage the use of training programs for inspection/quality personnel even though upper management may not consider its personal involvement to be useful in improving the company's bottom line. As noted earlier, it would be advisable, under these circumstances, to apply several elements of the training program for a period of time, without the involvement of top management, and wait for the beneficial results to appear. Then, an approach to management may prove to be more successful, particularly when the benefits to the bottom line become apparent.

Unified Training Goals

Each company has its unique needs and its special methods for their attainment. Nevertheless, it is important that the program not be presented in a haphazard manner. The simplest method of training employees may be all that is necessary. However, to be truly effective, a goal should be established for the entire program plan. This goal should address every need and job in the organization. Once these goals are defined, it may be decided that, initially, various elements of the operation are not to be included in the program. Nevertheless, all the elements should be positively considered, and the lack of inclusion in the program of any element should be based upon a specific determination. It may be necessary to delay the introduction of many elements due to cost and time considerations. But a definite consideration should be applied to each and every need of the company. It is for that reason that a central authority should be designated to define all the elements, and to insure that those which are to be incorporated, are developed so as to meet the specified goals. It would also be highly desirable that a stated policy relative to the training program, is established and approved by top management.

Implementation Methods

Training programs may be implemented by any number of means. Some of the programs utilized by many companies include one or more of the following methods.

Formal Classroom Sessions

Instructors present the elements to be taught. The use of visual aids, films, lectures, slides, and the like can be applied, as desired. There are many films and slides prepared by consultants and experts which can be procured or leased. The Education and Training section of the American Society for Quality Control has a wide variety of training films available for use, by its membership, through their local sections. A number of universities provide films of actual classroom presentations on specific subjects, which can be used by applicable personnel, in obtaining degrees in the quality sciences.

It is advisable that the classroom discussions lead students to acquire skills which can be utilized when they return to work. Accordingly, many instructors find it beneficial to have each student present a problem from the workplace, relative to the subject under discussion, which can be resolved in class.

It is also important that the instruction is presented in the manner and language which is relatively familiar to the students and not in the jargon of the specialist. Since students usually come from a variety of experiences, backgrounds, and educational levels, it is also important that the instructor determines, at the outset of the course, the levels of subject matter expertise of each student. Programs fail in many cases either because the presentation of the subject matter is above the students' level in scope and prerequisite knowledge, or is so elementary that the students become bored and quickly lose interest.

At the start of the course, the instructor can request that students provide a brief description of their areas of employment, their past experience or training relative to the subject matter at hand, level of formal education, and the principal reason for attending the course. This information can also be included in the student's application for the course, so that the instructor

```
┌─────────────────────────────────────────────────────────────────┐
│                                                                   │
│  SEMINAR NO.                        DATE                          │
│                                                                   │
│  I.  Name _____  _____   │
│      Company _____  │
│      Title _____ Dept. _____   │
│                                                                   │
│  2.  Major Products/Services _____  │
│                                                                   │
│  3.  How many years experience have you had in the subject area   │
│      of this meeting _____                                 │
│      and in your present position_____?                    │
│                                                                   │
│  4.  Is this the first SAM seminar you have attended?             │
│      a.    ☐  Yes          b.    ☐  No                            │
│      If this is not your first SAM seminar, when did you last     │
│      attend SAM seminar?                                          │
│      Month _____ Year _____                       │
│                                                                   │
│  5.  Your level of education.                                    │
│                                                    Graduate      │
│      HS              College         Adv. Study    Degree        │
│                                                                   │
│      ☐                ☐                ☐              ☐           │
│                                                                   │
│  6.  How did you learn of this seminar?                          │
│      a.  ☐  SAM announcement addressed to you                    │
│      b.  ☐  SAM announcement addressed to                        │
│             (please indicate addressee) _____   │
│                                                                   │
│             _____    │
│                                                                   │
│      c.  ☐  Advertisement (Please specify) _____    │
│                                                                   │
│             _____    │
│                                                                   │
│      d.  ☐  Other (Please specify) _____    │
│                                                                   │
│             _____    │
│                                                                   │
└─────────────────────────────────────────────────────────────────┘
```

FIGURE 23-1 Profile of Background and Interests

can determine beforehand the desires and backgrounds of the students and slant the program accordingly. See Figure 23-1 for an example of this document. To insure that the course has satisfied students' needs, some instructors solicit students' comments at the end of each session. Critique

7. If someone recommended that you attend this seminar, please indicate below.
   a. ☐ Your immediate superior
   b. ☐ A prior participant at this meeting
   c. ☐ A fellow executive
   d. ☐ Personnel Department
   e. ☐ No one recommended—initiated own registration

8. Are you a member of:

   ☐ ASQC   ☐ ASME
   ☐ IEEE   ☐ Other (Please specify)
   ☐ ASA   _____

   Is *Quality Magazine* mailed directly to you?   ☐ Yes   ☐ No

9. What age group are you in?

   a. ☐ Under 25   f. ☐ 45–49
   b. ☐ 25–29   g. ☐ 50–54
   c. ☐ 30–34   h. ☐ 55–59
   d. ☐ 35–39   i. ☐ 60–64
   e. ☐ 40–44   j. ☐ 65 or over

10. Your objective in attending this seminar: _____
    _____
    _____

11. Your major problems in subject field: _____
    _____
    _____

12. Who is responsible for management development and/or training of personnel in your organization?
    Name_____
    Title_____
    Address_____

FIGURE 23-1   Continued

forms, such as Figure 23-2 can be used. At the end of the course, students are given a final form (Figure 23-3), and are requested to critique the entire course, its method of presentation, and its applicability to their individual needs. Usually, the student's identification on the form is optional.

NAME (Optional) _____ DATE _____ SEMINAR NO. _____

1. What was the most beneficial topic discussed today?

2. What was the least beneficial topic discussed today?

3. What recommendations would you make to improve today's session?

4. What recommendations would you make concerning tomorrow's session.
   (i.e., what would you like covered or changed?)

5. Please rate the course content on the scale below:

Excellent	Good	Fair	Poor
20 19 18 17 16	15 14 13 12 11	10 9 8 7 6	5 4 3 2 1

6. Please rate the course presentation on the scale below:

Excellent	Good	Fair	Poor
20 19 18 17 16	15 14 13 12 11	10 9 8 7 6	5 4 3 2 1

7. Additional comments:

FIGURE 23-2   Daily Appraisal Sheet

One company provided a series of courses which contained subjects across the entire spectrum of the company's operations. The instructors were, for the most part, managers, supervisors, and engineers of the company. These courses were given in the evening, after the regular work hours, and were provided in conjunction with the local schools. While attendance at these courses was purely voluntary, a record was noted in the employee's personnel file, indicating interest in improving his or her skills.

SEMINAR NAME _____ YOUR NAME _____

Date _____

A. WHAT ASPECT OF THE COURSE WAS MOST BENEFICIAL TO YOU? _____

_____

_____

B. WHAT ASPECT OF THE COURSE WAS LEAST BENEFICIAL TO YOU? _____

_____

_____

C. METHODS OF INSTRUCTION—Please check the box that best represents your reaction to the instructional methods used.

	very much	some extent	not at all	N/A
How well did the lectures hold your interest?	☐	☐	☐	☐
Were the lectures practical enough for your purpose?	☐	☐	☐	☐
Was there effective interaction within the group?	☐	☐	☐	☐
Were workshop sessions helpful?	☐	☐	☐	☐

D. REACTION TO THE MEETING AS A WHOLE

	very much	some extent	not at all
To what extent did the meeting live up to your expectations? If not, please explain:	☐	☐	☐

Would you recommend this meeting to others?   YES   MAYBE   NO

Please record your overall reaction to this meeting by placing an X in the scale below.

Excellent	Good	Fair	Poor

20 19 18 17 16 15 14 13 12 11 10 9 8 7 6 5 4 3 2 1

E. COMMENTS & SUGGESTIONS _____

_____

_____

_____

For additional comments, please use reverse side.

FIGURE 23-3   Program Appraisal Form

Workshops

Frequently, classroom programs include, as part of the curriculum, workshops which supplement the elements discussed by the instructors and provide individual participation in the learning process. In a typical workshop, students usually participate in the solution of problems presented in the classroom. They may also work with the other attendees, in solving problems that they brought from the workplace. For example, when studying data gathering and reduction, and the statistical control chart preparation, raw measurements data taken from a machine tool are brought in by a student. Using additional information provided in the classroom, the data are reduced into the form of a Pareto chart, or into a frequency histogram. Statistical attributes, such as averages and ranges, are determined, the statistical control limits calculated, and X-bar and R charts are prepared. From these, students determine whether the process has attained statistical control. Any out-of-control points or trends are examined, and students recommend areas for investigations and implementation of corrective action. The inspectors who brought in the data, upon return to their workplace, utilize the measures recommended by the class. After making the suitable process corrections, the inspector gathers a set of data, and, at the workshop, reviews it and determines, with other students, whether the process has been brought back into statistical control.

Other uses of the workshop can be made by each student presenting, at the end of a set of sessions, the particular problems encountered at work relating to the subject matter discussed in the class. The attendees then participate in offering possible remedies for these problems. Subsequently, students apply the recommendations at their workplace and report the results back to the class.

Case Studies and Role-Playing

The instructor presents a staged situation and assigns class members to act out specific roles. The class comments on the situation and offers solutions to the problems presented.

Simulation

Selected students are given a problem to solve. For example, they are supposed to develop a set of sampling plans which can reduce the cost of inspection for a particular situation. They are requested to simulate data and select the sampling plan which meets the objective. The rest of the class then critiques the plan and offers alternate plans, if required, or if the proposed plan does not meet the objective.

Use of Technical Schools

Many technical schools and community colleges offer evening courses applicable to the inspection/quality function. In addition, professional societies such as ASQC provide, at national and regional levels, courses in inspection/quality disciplines. Many companies encourage their employees' participation in these programs, paying tuition when students have attained a passing grade.

Home Study

To accommodate the inspectors who cannot attend evening classes, some companies arrange with training organizations to provide correspondence courses for employees to study at home. Here too, the fees are paid by the company upon the successful completion of the courses.

A number of home study courses are provided by professional societies such as ASQC, as well as by other organizations and consultants.

Self-Instruction

These methods use videocassettes and films, usually accompanied by workbooks. They are utilized by small groups of viewers who discuss the information presented, and consider potential workplace applications. There are many sources of cassettes and films, ranging from subjects of quality awareness to metrology and statistics.

The ASQC provides many training cassettes to its membership sections. In addition, consultants such as Drs. Juran, Deming, Crosby, and many others provide courses on audio and videocassettes for use by members of inspection/quality organizations. Issues of the ASQC periodical *Quality Progress* make reference to many of these courses.

On-the-Job Training

Some companies provide time during work hours for inspection/quality personnel to learn or update their skills. This is usually accomplished by working under the close supervision of a mentor, such as another experienced inspector, group leader, or supervisor. When instruction is performed on the job, the following steps are usually followed.

1. The task is explained and its importance to the job emphasized.

2. The details of the task are outlined.

3. The employees are requested to repeat the details, to insure that they fully understand them. Questions are encouraged. This enables the mentor to provide clarifications. From a subsequent analysis of the questions, the mentor utilizes this information to improve future presentations.

4. Students are then requested to perform the task, under the supervision of the mentor, who points out the need for any corrections.

5. Students continue performing the work without the presence of the mentor, who subsequently checks back to assure that the work is progressing in a satisfactory manner, and refers to any needed corrections.

6. If all the above have been satisfactorily performed, and it appears that students have a good grasp of the subject, the mentor leaves them to continue their task without interference.

7. After a period of time, the mentor returns to the students for a review of the work and to respond to any residual questions.

Varied Assignments

Some companies have adopted procedures whereby inspectors are temporarily assigned to other areas. There are at least three advantages with this practice. First, it gives inspectors an opportunity to become familiar with disciplines in other departments. For example, a fabrication inspector in the machine shop may be temporarily transferred to the electronic inspection area. At another time, the inspector may be assigned to the weld shop or the assembly areas. Second, this program enables the use of additional inspectors in areas with heavy work loads. And third, by working in these different areas, inspectors become aware of their peers' problems, and can develop their capabilities to better service these areas during normal operations.

Some companies utilize special classrooms for introducing new, revised, or special operations to the inspectors and production personnel.

Use of Professional Societies

Members of professional societies such as the ASQC, American Management Association (AMA), and others can take advantage of their programs on inspection/quality elements. These are often presented at monthly meetings of the local sections.

Use of Manuals or Technical Handbooks

New inspection/quality personnel are generally provided with the company operations and inspection/quality manuals. It is expected that they will become familiar with the contents of the documents applicable to their operation. Early on, they may frequently review various portions of the manuals as they perform their duties until they have become fully cognizant of the contents. In some companies, new employees are given tests on the applicable manual sections, to determine whether they have absorbed the essential elements. A number of companies provide some time, at the workplace, to review any new procedures or instructions, before their implementation, to assure that inspectors understand all the changes.

Determining Students' Eligibility

Courses are given by inspection/quality personnel for a variety of reasons. Often, they are presented because management has made a commitment to train all employees of a certain department in the techniques of a specific discipline. At other times, the courses are given because customers require it. Accordingly, the designated employees are enrolled in the program without any pre-determination of their aptitudes or interests in the subject matter. Some employees may not be completely prepared for the specific contents of the course.

Therefore, it is important, that the training director, or designee, develop a screening process to determine students' interests and aptitudes.

EXAMPLE

This example illustrates a typical problem which may be encountered.

A number of students, upon completion of a course in statistics were discussing the class events. Two of the students were arguing about whether the fraction $\frac{1}{3}$ was larger in value than the fraction $\frac{1}{5}$. One student said that it was obvious that $\frac{1}{5}$ was larger, since five was larger than three. This revealed that the student, who had been subjected to the study of statistics, requiring some basic knowledge of mathematics, had little or no understanding of elementary arithmetic. Thus, the course in statistics was evidently beyond the student's capability and as a consequence, wasted.

In order to satisfactorily screen for students' interests and abilities, it is suggested that a detailed description of the course contents and its prerequisites be made. Then a positive determination is made concerning the basic knowledge of potential students for learning the course material and assurance that students are neither under- or overqualified for the course. Some companies, as part of the training program, subject potential students to a preliminary examination to determine their knowledge of elementary mathematics and reading comprehension. This information is analyzed and qualified personnel are selected to take the course.

For students who lack the prerequisite knowledge, a special preliminary course in basic reading comprehension and elementary mathematics is given to them before enrolling them in the course as originally planned.

To insure that students are interested in the course a conference should be held with them before the start of the training program. At that time, the subject matter of the program should be presented, together with the uses to which the course material can be applied. Comments should be solicited, and questions answered relative to the potential benefits of the course. Those employees who feel that there will be no merit in their taking these courses should be excused from participation. Of course, the determination, by the employees, to take the course may not be entirely truthful, since students may be concerned that not taking the course would be adversely viewed by their supervisors. Therefore, it is important that potential students are assured that their participation, or lack of it, will have no adverse effect on their present jobs.

Evaluation of the Program

Periodically, the training director should evaluate the whole training program on a number of considerations.

- Attendees' comments
- End-of-course test results

- Any management reluctance to taking tests
- Course effects on students' work
- Program effect on overall quality improvement

For some managers who resist taking tests, some other method of course evaluation may be needed for them. Determining the course's effect on students' work may be difficult to evaluate completely. Discussions with the students' supervisor and the department manager may provide some insight.

The program's effect on overall quality improvement may be determined by evaluating the product or service over time. Of course, any improvement may not be entirely due to the training program. However, studying the elements which did improve may indicate the effectiveness of the training program. After evaluation, the training director should issue a report to top management, analyzing the results of the survey and making any necessary recommendations for program revisions.

Program Revisions

Program revisions may include adding new courses, dropping ineffective ones, and changing others to better meet students' needs. As new skills are developed, and when new products are introduced, new or revised courses should be developed and provided to applicable personnel. It is also advisable that overview or refresher courses be periodically given to former students to insure that they have retained the information learned.

Qualifications of Instructors

Instructors for in-house programs may be selected from employees or hired specifically for the task. Either way it is important that instructors demonstrate, as a minimum, the following qualifications.

- Thorough familiarity with the subject matter
- Interest in teaching
- Affinity with learners
- Patience
- Ability to exercise tact
- Sense of fairness and impartiality
- Knowledge of teaching procedures and devices
- Skills in understanding people and their learning difficulties
- Ability to lead not drive

- Cheerful disposition expressing confidence
- Systematic habits in organizing ideas

Why Training Programs Fail[2]

Training programs have not lived up to their expectations for a number of reasons.

Cultural resistance

Some line managers believe that employees are fully aware of their jobs and that any needed information should be learned on the floor. The suggested remedy for this attitude is to take time to provide reluctant managers with the factual data relating the advantages of the specific course to the improvement of productivity and quality in the department. The ideal method of overcoming resistance is to secure, at the outset, the support of top management, and start the training program at the upper and middle management levels. Failing that, the introduction in the program of case examples relative to the solution of problems in the department should help to alleviate the managers' resistance.

Lack of managerial participation

Many managers believe that the hours expended in the training programs are deducted from productive work. Since the line managers are quite aware of the effect of quality problems on the production operations, it would be advantageous to request input from them for the course contents. As mentioned, their participation in the program would be stimulated by having them included in the program development task force.

Lack of problem-oriented courses

Many courses are designed to merely present techniques. To resolve this problem it is advisable to obtain from line managers and students, a list of quality problems on the floor, and demonstrate how the techniques presented in the course can be used to solve real problems.

Instructor inadequacies

One of the major difficulties in developing adequate training programs is the unavailability of competent instructors. One remedy is to initiate the programs using outside consultants who teach potential company instructors. Another remedy is to take advantage of the many fine courses available by professional societies and consultants in instructor training. Some companies present in-house training programs for potential instructors.

Mixed levels of participants

It has been found that by including, in the same class, operating personnel and their supervisors, the classroom discussion is inhibited. It is recommended that, when possible, attempts should be made to restrict the attendees at a class to personnel at the same or similar levels.

Lack of job application

Ideally, courses should be designed so that students can use the knowledge gained during the classroom discussions on the job. This should be done so that the results of job applications can be presented for evaluation and discussion by the class.

Overly complex language

This problem is particularly applicable to courses in statistics. Too frequently, instructors are carried away with their knowledge of the subject matter and use terminology which is barely understood by students. They will often become bored and cease to follow the presentations. Instructors must be aware of students' limitations in understanding the profession's jargon. One way to remedy this situation is for the initial presentation to be made, as a pilot run, before a small group, for the purpose of critiquing the language used.

Operational deficiencies

At times, the classes are conducted in poorly equipped classrooms. They may be too small to accommodate the number of participants. They may also be located in noisy and poorly heated or ventilated areas. A major problem may exist when the instructor utilizes visual aids, the contents of which are too small to be read by students in the center and rear of the classroom. In addition, for courses which are given for a protracted period time, arrangements should be made for lunch and coffee breaks.

See Chapter 24 for examples of training programs utilized for various levels of employees.

QUALIFICATION

Introduction

Many inspection/quality personnel are subjected to special training programs in order to be able to perform certain inspections or tests. These training programs are performed either in-house or at technical schools and special agencies. Examples of these qualification programs are those utilized for nondestructive testing, special processes examination, nuclear construction, auditing, and others.

Nondestructive Testing Qualification

Nondestructive testing (NDT) operations include such examinations as radiographic, magnetic particle, dye-penetrant, ultrasonic testing, and others.

Courses are provided by special schools with skills in the science of NDT. The program consists of a specified number of hours of classroom instruction and hands-on experience, followed by aptitude tests. These usually consist of two parts, the first one containing a series of questions about the course material, and the second part a demonstration of the student's ability to detect and measure faults in prepared specimens. One example of NDT certifications is that provided by the American Society of Non Destructive Testing (ASNDT). This organization qualifies the testers in one of the following three classifications, depending upon their proven expertise.

NDT level I

This is for the individual who has had sufficient experience and training to properly perform the necessary tests. He or she is responsible to personnel at NDT levels II and III.

NDT level II

This is given to a tester qualified to direct and carry out the test in the manner certified. This tester should be able to set up and calibrate equipment (where applicable), read and interpret indications, and evaluate them with reference to the applicable codes and specifications. This tester shall also be able to organize and report NDT results.

NDT level III

This is given to a tester who is capable of establishing techniques, interpreting specifications and codes, and designating particular test methods and techniques to be used. The tester shall also be able to assist in establishing tests and acceptance criteria when none are available. This level of tester shall be responsible for conducting examinations for NDT level I and II personnel.

Maintenance of Qualifications

In some companies, the testing personnel are subjected to periodic re-evaluations relative to their skills. When they fail to meet the standards, they are required to go through additional instructions and submit to a requalification test.

Company Qualifications

Companies perform qualifications of their inspection/test personnel by a variety of methods. The most common one evaluates inspectors' performance while engaged, at a certain level of difficulty, in examination or testing operations. These personnel usually start at an initial level of expertise, working on the examination of products requiring a lower skill. Then they are permitted to move to the next higher order of expertise, working on products requiring a greater level of skill. This continues until the inspector/tester has reached the area which requires the highest examination skill utilized by the company. At that point, they are assigned, when needed, to train lower level personnel.

PROMOTION

In order to maintain proper morale within the organization, it is the responsibility of the inspection/quality department supervisors and managers to make all opportunities for advancement available to their employees. Hence, any potential openings should, whenever possible, be filled by personnel from within their departments. This should be done, even if the supervisors feel that the employees are too important in their present functions to be spared. But, as noted, the actions that a supervisor or manager takes, or does not take, are closely observed by others in the department, as well as those in associated activities. Supervisors and managers who have developed a reputation of always taking care of their employees become known as desirable supervisors. They will generally have little difficulty in finding replacements in their organizations. There are cases where certain department heads have long lists of potential candidates for their organizations as a result of their reputations for fairness and consideration of their employees.

TRANSFER

Frequently, inspection/quality works with other departments to coordinate employee training and educational needs. This enables the preparation of employees to qualify for openings throughout the company.

Inspection/quality department personnel, by virtue of their function, often provide employees to fill openings in other departments. It is not rare to find that manufacturing supervision, production control, product and production engineering, purchasing, and other departments are filling their openings from personnel in the inspection/quality department.

While this, at times, may become a problem to inspection/quality department supervisors through the loss of key personnel, it helps to provide motivation to the other department employees. It demonstrates to them that one of the prime benefits of working in the inspection/quality department is their exposure to personnel from other departments, and hence, subsequent access to higher paying jobs within the company. Further, the transfer of inspection/quality personnel to other departments often provides an understanding, by personnel in other departments, of the philosophy of the inspection/quality functions, as well as the concepts of insuring the manufacture or procurement of quality conforming products. In addition, this arrangement would also make possible the transfer of personnel from other departments to fill inspection/quality vacancies.

Inspection/quality department supervisors should not stand in the way of their employees' advancements. However, they must assure that any move is in fact an advancement, and not a lateral transfer. The inspection/quality supervisor should determine whether the transfer is permanent or not. For the supervisor to demonstrate concern for the employees in the department, it is desirable to review the new job requirements with the potential transferee, to ensure that he or she understands the new assignment and feels qualified to fill it. In addition, the inspection/quality supervisor should request sufficient time to find a replacement, before the transfer is effected.

While it is good practice to promote employees from within, care must be taken when inspectors are being considered for supervisory positions. Good inspectors may not necessarily become good supervisors. There are many aspects of the supervisory position which go beyond the ability of performing a good inspection operation. For one, the supervisors must be able to command respect from their personnel, and provide guidance and motivation in the performance of their duties, as well as cope with many administrative problems. A number of companies have created the job of group leaders within the inspection/quality organization. This position partially prepares the inspectors to take on many of the administrative and supervisory functions, and helps inspectors to develop the ability to meet these new requirements when they are promoted.

Similarly, the promotion of an inspection supervisor to the position of inspection or quality manager should also be carefully reviewed. Managerial candidates must be capable of developing programs of inspection or quality control. They must also be able to maintain liaison with other department managers. Matters of policy are frequently under the purview of the inspection/quality manager. In addition, he or she must be able to develop and submit budgets for the department, as well as insure that department operations are conducted so as to stay within the budget constraints.

Before a supervisor is to be promoted to a managerial position, some preliminary training in inspection/quality management techniques is desirable. There are a number of excellent courses provided during evening sessions of universities and community colleges. In addition, technical associates such as ASQC present courses. Some companies provide in-house training programs for potential inspection/quality supervisors and managers.

COMPENSATION

In many companies, the major problem with compensation is the discrepancy between inspectors' earnings and those of production operators. For example, production operators are paid for any required overtime. Since inspection/quality personnel are considered members of management, their compensation is based on an annual salary. Therefore, they are not usually paid any more for working overtime. Since production employees and inspectors are in frequent contact, they are constantly aware that their take-home pay is often lower than that enjoyed by production personnel.

Some companies attempt to provide some compensation for inspector's overtime work. When direct payment is not feasible, other means are utilized. When overtime work is frequently required, inspectors are sometimes given compensatory time off during slow periods. At other times, their wage classification provides more sick pay and personal leave with pay, than that for production personnel. In other companies, the inspection personnel are provided with bonuses, at the end of the year, based upon their extra time worked.

Inspection Versus Production Pay

Another problem is the relationship of inspectors' salary structure with that of production personnel. Many inspectors believe that, since they are evaluating the quality of production operators' work, they are entitled to receive a higher pay scale. These inspectors believe that the qualification requirements of their job and the value, to the company, of the work performed by them, are greater than that of production personnel. Some companies recognize the discrepancy between the pay scale of the production vis-à-vis the inspection personnel. Accordingly, their job classifications take this into consideration. The wage group of the inspectors in these companies is at a higher rate than for the equivalent production personnel.

Nonfinancial Advantages

When inspectors complain about pay discrepancies, their supervisor can point out the many advantages inspectors enjoy over production workers.

Inspectors have a wider range of contacts in their day-to-day operation. This may subsequently lead to higher paying jobs in other departments. These contacts also serve to make the job more interesting and widens the inspectors' horizon for future job enhancement.

Inspectors generally enjoy a higher social status in the company's structure. Since the inspectors' position includes the evaluation of the work of the production personnel, the inspection job is often compared with that of the production supervisor, who also evaluates the work of operators.

Inspectors have more opportunity to utilize judgment while performing their job, while production operators must perform their work exactly as defined in the work instructions and operation sheets.

Incentive Pay

While the use of incentive pay is generally not considered desirable, since it infers that inspectors may sacrifice quality of work in favor of quantity, some companies have endeavored to provide some means of compensating inspectors based upon their output, without affecting the accuracy of their work. This is fairly difficult to accomplish, since the inspectors' output must be studied over a period of time to develop a standard of comparison. Further, consideration must be given to the diversity of inspectors' work from lot to lot. One method is to establish standards using the average performance rate of the entire inspection group. This is possible when the types of inspection lots are fairly consistent over a period of time. The incentive then can be based upon the number of pieces inspected, or the average number of lots processed during a given period. The accuracy of inspectors' work can be determined by an audit.

Dead-End Jobs

As noted earlier in the discussion of job classifications, each one is associated with a salary range. Theoretically, the inspector starts at the lowest step of the range, and moves up to the highest range. When the top pay is reached, unless the scale for the total classification is increased, the inspector can not receive any further pay raises. This is often frustrating to inspectors, who have performed satisfactorily throughout the period of employment and may feel dead-ended in their job.

Companies have attempted various ways to overcome this problem. One way is to redline the pay scale. This is done by allowing pay increase beyond the highest wage of the job classification. This method is generally not considered satisfactory when it is practiced for a long time. Redlining a job pay, if used frequently, would tend to break down the salary structure, since the salary range would no longer have meaning. To overcome this condition, inspection supervisors should be encouraged to prepare for the eventuality of redlining the salary of most of their employees. Supervisors should develop measures, in advance, for the preparation of their inspectors to fill higher level categories within their departments.

In most companies, the inspection operation is broken down into a number of job classifications. To move from one grade to another, inspectors must usually show a proficiency in two or more disciplines. To provide opportunity for inspectors to develop additional proficiency, supervisors periodically assign inspectors to different areas. This enables them to develop experience in a number of additional disciplines, so that they can be promoted to higher job categories in the department.

In lieu of actual on-the-job experience in other inspection disciplines, one company utilized a set of training programs, provided by technical organizations or correspondence schools. This enabled inspectors to enhance their job knowledge.

In order to provide the advancement from the highest scale, senior inspectors can move to other areas within the department. This includes providing opportunities for inspectors to work periodically in supervisory or administrative positions. Training programs can also be offered to these inspectors so that they can be promoted to other positions in the department, such as auditor and quality/inspection engineer.

Salary Range Improvement

Companies should compare their salary scale with those of similar organizations in the geographical areas. Suitable adjustments should be made to the pay ranges so that they remain competitive.

Entry Level Training

Another problem related to equitable compensation of inspectors is the unavailability of competent job candidates in the company's locale. In order to recruit inspectors, it is often necessary to hire them at levels above the entering grade. This often results in veteran inspectors learning that new inspectors, who have not yet developed competence and experience, are making the same or even higher salaries than the veterans. This situation certainly does not help advance personnel morale. To overcome this problem, the company should minimize the hiring of personnel at higher than the entering grade by developing training programs for new hires with little or no prior inspection experience. With additional schooling, these new employees will be ready to fill entry level inspection positions.

EVALUATION

Job evaluation is the objective appraisal of an individual's job performance over a period of time. It should not be considered an exact science, but rather as a systematic and logical approach to the relationship between the position and the monetary rewards.

Uses of Job Classifications

When available, most companies use job classifications for employee appraisals. Performance is usually measured against criteria in the classifications. Usually, the personnel department initiates the process by sending appraisal forms to the department manager for each employee who is to be evaluated during the specified time period (for example, every six months or every year). The manager transmits the forms to the applicable area supervisors who rate the employees by comparing their performances to the applicable job descriptions. Some companies utilize a numerical score, from 1 to 10, for this evaluation. Others do not. Instead they depend upon supervisors to qualitatively evaluate employees' performance against each element of the job description. In either case, the rating is purely a subjective consideration and not based upon any scientific method of evaluation. Thus, supervisors must be careful to insure that the review is based upon a considered determination of the employee's performance and is not influenced by any momentary bias or prejudice against the employee. It is also important that the evaluation method, for each employee, is based upon the same considerations.

In many companies, the merit review is also used to determine whether a wage increase is warranted, and at times, the amount of the increase. In addition, the decision may be made as to whether the employee merits a promotion to the next higher department classification, or even whether the employee's performance is below standards which may require that termination procedures be initiated.

By providing regularly scheduled reviews, the need for inspectors to periodically request salary increases is minimized. These reviews also provide the rationale for supervisors to critique the work of their personnel at periodic intervals, a function which has often been neglected. Thus any momentary opinions, are offset by the supervisors' requirement to consider their inspectors' total performance over the entire rating period.

Use of Other Evaluation Criteria

When a company does not have defined job descriptions, some other method must be used for employee evaluation.[3] Some of the following criteria, as applicable, can be used to evaluate inspection personnel.

1. Knowledge and abilities
    — Inspection capabilities
    — Defect prevention and failure analysis capabilities
    — Data recording methods and techniques
    — Cost reductions
    — Statistical applications as applicable
    — Other job-related abilities

2. On-the-job interpersonal relations
    — Cooperation with peers
    — Cooperation with management and supervision
    — Cooperation with manufacturing, engineering, and other company personnel
    — Relationships with suppliers and customers

3. Training
   —Help and guidance to manufacturing and engineering personnel to improve product quality
   —Participation in volunteer committee action for product improvement
   —Assistance to fellow inspectors in lower job classifications

4. Professional development
   —Quality certifications and awards granted by professional societies
   —Participation in quality association activities
   —Enrollment in courses for other inspection/quality disciplines

Follow-up of Merit Reviews

All inspection/quality personnel should be advised of the results of their merit reviews. This is particularly necessary when a need for employee corrective actions is indicated. Often supervisors neglect this element since most are reluctant to discuss employee shortcomings. But, unless employees are made aware of how well they are doing, they cannot correct any problems, or refute any perceived unfair evaluations. In one case, an inspector resigned because he believed that, in the absence of any other intimation, his supervisor did not consider his work up to par. In fact, the inspector was highly regarded by his supervisor.

To overcome the tendency of supervisors to renege on discussing the reviews with their personnel, some companies require that the employees sign a copy of their merit review, signifying that they have discussed their supervisor's comments. In a number of companies, employees are requested to add their comments relative to their supervisor's findings. Of course, supervisors should point out areas requiring corrective action, and express their willingness to help employees improve their performance in these areas.

Where the merit review is an element of the salary review, supervisors should advise their employees that their salary increase may depend upon their ability to effect corrective action in problem areas. Supervisors may also note that the progress of employee improvement will be monitored during the period prior to the next review session.

Evaluation of Supervisors

Inspection supervisors are also periodically rated by their managers. Here too, when job descriptions are available, they should be used in the reviews. When no job classifications are utilized, recourse must be made to other job features. Figure 23-4 shows a list of some supervisory elements which could be used, as applicable, in these evaluations.

Technical Evaluation

(Can be expressed in units or percentages of the group activities)

1. Quantity and quality of output
2. Completion time or maintenance of work schedules
3. Costs of operation (degree of variation from approved budget)
4. Ability to retain personnel—inspector/quality personnel turnover
5. Number of reprimands or disciplinary actions issued by the supervisor
6. Amount of material incorrectly inspected by the group
7. Idle time—worker hours lost or wasted
8. Idle time—equipment hours lost
9. Safety hours lost due to accidents
10. Number of complaints or grievances made to superiors
11. Completeness and precision of reports
12. Degree of contribution by the group to the implementation of the corporate goals for product and process quality improvement.

Personal Traits on Which a Supervisor Can Be Rated

1. Relations with other supervisors
2. Knowledge of the characteristics and abilities of subordinates
3. Skill in training subordinates
4. Fairness and impartiality in dealing with subordinates
5. Character of discipline
6. Willingness to make difficult decisions
7. Success in making and carrying out work plans
8. Knowledge of work supervised
9. Resourcefulness in meeting difficulties
10. Skill in giving and following orders
11. Ability to learn new work
12. Initiative in own work
13. Control of temper
14. Loyalty to job and employer
15. Degree of involvement in interdepartmental activities for quality improvement
16. Cooperation with personnel from other departments, customers, and suppliers

FIGURE 23-4 Evaluation of Supervisors

Group evaluation

Currently, a number of quality experts do not consider individual employee evaluations as desirable or productive. Their rationale for this thinking is based upon one or both of the following:

1. Taking a lesson from the Japanese industries, some experts believe that employees should be encouraged to work as a group, and not as individuals. Accordingly, any evaluations should be directed to the results of the group's activities, and each individual's contributions to the group's total operation.

2. Providing a specific quantitative goal as an objective, the attainment of which is to be evaluated, some quality professionals believe, tends to limit the direction of inspection/quality personnel. These experts recommend that evaluations be made as to the degree of success of the efforts towards a continuing product quality improvement program.

TERMINATION

When it is necessary to terminate personnel from the inspection/quality organization, the supervisor or manager must be careful to precisely follow the company's standard practice, as well as those established by the personnel department. When dismissal results from employees' actions, advance notification of their shortcomings should have been provided to them so that they could have effected corrective action. If they failed to do so satisfactorily, the personnel department should be advised, in writing, of the problem employees, and its guidance should be solicited. A final discussion should be held with a member of the personnel department relative to the actions recommended or to be taken. It is important that the supervisor obtain the concurrence of the personnel department before final termination. At times, it may be possible to transfer the individuals to operations or departments more suitable to their capabilities. Great care must be taken to preserve an air of fairness and compassion in these difficult situations. It is important to remember that the rest of the organization is watching these actions and wondering whether the same considerations would be given to them should the situation arise.

When personnel must be released due to a staff reduction required by budget, action should be initiated to relocate the affected employees. Personnel in the inspection/quality organization are fortunate, since many of their skills are useful in other company activities. Furthermore, since they are exposed to members of other departments, it is easier to transfer to any of these departments with suitable openings. Failing that, many companies have a policy of searching outside the company for possible positions for laid-off personnel. Local chapters of ASQC frequently maintain a list of inspection/quality openings. If the approach to possible sources of employment is made well in advance of the layoff date, it is important that the names of the affected employees are not divulged until the very last minute. An example of an embarrassing occurrence which resulted from not taking this precaution is cited in the following paragraph.

EXAMPLE

During a period of staff reduction, the personnel department provided to a number of employment agencies, the names of the personnel to be terminated. It is not difficult to imagine the surprise and consternation of the affected employees when the agency contacted them. At this time they had been unaware that they were scheduled to be terminated.

The inspection/quality managers, as well as the personnel department, must be constantly aware that the company's reputation is at risk should it become known that firing and/or staff reduction is a constant operation and that there is a lack of consideration concerning employee welfare during these actions. This becomes strongly evidenced when recruitment, at a later date, is thwarted by the reluctance of potential employees to apply. This is particularly evidenced when there is a shortage of skilled personnel in the company's geographical area. Companies with good reputations relative to their employee relations, often have lists of potential employees, thereby providing a pool of qualified personnel just waiting to become employees.

Some companies have adopted a policy of providing severance pay in lieu of prior notification of dismissal. In these companies, terminated employees are not aware, until the end of the last day of employment, of their status. The rationale for this action is the avoidance of any unpleasant act by employees before the termination date. While the reasoning for this action appears to have some merit, it often leaves an unpleasant reaction by the terminated employees and a feeling of resentment long after the termination. This action is also viewed by the remaining employees as an unpleasant act. Some companies believe that it is more desirable to notify employees beforehand of the impending termination so that they may take actions to locate new jobs.

REFERENCES

1. Juran, J. M. *Manpower: Juran's Quality Control Handbook* (3rd. ed). New York: McGraw Hill, 1957, Chapter 17.

2. Gryna, Frank, M. *Training for Quality: Juran's Quality Control Handbook* (4th ed). New York: McGraw Hill, 1988, Chapter 11.

3. Carter, L. Jr., & Carter, G. M. *A Motivation Program for Inspectors*. 1983. Milwaukee, WI: ASQC, 1983, p. 525.

Skills and the Inspection/Quality Function

INTRODUCTION

This chapter discusses the skills normally required by inspection/quality personnel. It presents the methods of training personnel, and the programs used to upgrade their skills. In addition, several methods of moving these personnel from one skill category to another are outlined.

GENERAL REQUIREMENTS

Inspectors should be conscientious, thorough, and detail oriented. They should have the ability to carry out routine instructions and orders faithfully, and render their inspection decisions in a fair and equitable manner. They should have good eyesight and a high degree of color perception, and they should possess manual dexterity. They should be ethical in all their dealings with their peers and other company, customer, and supplier personnel.

ACADEMIC AND TECHNICAL REQUIREMENTS

Inspectors should, as a minimum, have some academic background, at least through four years of secondary school education. They should be proficient in shop mathematics, and have some knowledge of basic inspection techniques and the manufacturing equipment used in fabrication. Special process inspectors and testers should have some understanding of the processes involved, and should be proficient in their testing techniques. All inspection personnel should have the ability to record results in a clear and legible manner. For some assignments, such as soldering inspection and nondestructive testing, inspectors should be certified in specific techniques.

All inspectors should be knowledgeable of their operational procedures and should understand the function that their section plays within the inspection/quality organization, and with other company departments. In many companies, an understanding of the concept of variation and the use of basic statistical concepts are required for all inspection personnel.

The inspection/quality engineering personnel should, in addition to the above-mentioned qualifications, have some college or technical school background. The equivalent number of years of inspection or technical operational experience is also acceptable. They should have knowledge of more advanced statistical techniques and the basic concepts of inspection and quality control. For specialized assignments, such as auditing and interdepartmental group liaison, they should have the experience or training needed to perform these tasks.

Inspection/quality engineers should be able to perform the required analyses of inspection/test data and include the results in comprehensive management reports. They should also be able to determine the actions necessary to correct variant conditions. Inspection/quality engineers should possess the capability to prepare inspection/quality procedures and instructions and to develop inspection record formats.

The administrative personnel should possess a relatively high degree of reading comprehension and the ability to perform the assigned clerical functions. Those assigned to special positions, such as materials review clerks and tool and gage crib attendants, should have a thorough understanding of these functions and the procedures and concepts relating to them.

Supervisory personnel should have an understanding of human relations as they pertain to their phase of the inspection/quality operation. They should have a high degree of knowledge of the operations that they supervise and be able to train and motivate personnel under their jurisdiction. In addition, they should be able to command the respect of their employees. Supervisors should be able to maintain the respect of their employees. Supervisors should be able to maintain cooperative relationships with other members of the inspection and quality departments, as well as with members of other company departments. See Chapter 5 for additional details about the skill needs of the inspection/quality supervisor.

Group leaders may initially have been members of the higher grades of inspectors, and thus should be fully acquainted with the capabilities of the personnel in their group.

Inspection/quality superintendents or chief inspectors should be able to develop the department's operating budgets of the department; be capable of implementing the functions of their groups within the budget restraints; and should provide an accounting for any variances from the budget. They should be able to implement the policies of the department and set up programs for the motivation and training of their personnel, as well as the personnel in other departments, when required. Superintendents should be capable of coordinating with the personnel department in the establishment of job descriptions and wage scales, and of participating in the hiring, firing, and transfer of employees. Chief inspectors should have the ability to investigate, and determine the need for, the type of measuring equipment required for the inspection of the company's products, and to establish the inspection requirements for future products. They should also be able to make group assignments and to set up programs for the training and re-assignment of personnel, when needed.

Inspection/quality managers should be capable of setting policy for the department. They should be able to coordinate, with other department heads, the development of the company's quality policy and the necessary standard procedures for its implementation. Managers should be able to work with other department heads in setting and implementing quality improvement programs and establishing the measurement benchmarks. They should be able to participate in the activities of the top management quality steering committees, when they exist, to monitor the effectiveness of the quality improvement programs. These activities may include the recommendation for any necessary policy and company structure changes, and the application of the necessary funds for quality improvement efforts. Managers should be capable of representing their company in industrial and technical associations and professional societies to develop quality and technical standards for the products of their industry. They should be able to coordinate with the company's customers to establish quality and workmanship standards for the respective contracts, as well as to determine the needs for a product's fitness for use.

Figure 24-1 shows detailed lists of the knowledge and skills needed by the various levels of inspection/quality personnel.

SUPPORT PERSONNEL

- Company's inspection/quality organization and program
- Elementary statistical techniques
- Support functions' effects on quality of the product
- Interdepartmental corrective action committee operations
- Improvement methods for applicable support services

ELEMENTARY PREREQUISITES

This section describes a number of training programs which can be utilized to provide some of the skills listed in Figures 24-1 and 24-2.

Implementation of these techniques can only enhance a company's ability to provide world class quality products.

ENTRY-LEVEL INSPECTORS

Elementary shop mathematics
Basic communication skills
Bench work
Shop drawing reading
Specification interpretation
Basic measuring equipment
Inspection and quality control basic principles
Inspection report preparation
Basic statistical concepts
Inspection/quality organization

HIGH LEVEL INSPECTORS

Technical mathematics
Inspection standards
Geometric tolerancing and dimensioning
Advanced measuring equipment
Metrology principles
Material inspection, including destructive and
    nondestructive testing principles
Inspection/quality management
Advanced communication skills
Technical writing
Basic statistical concepts
Technical sciences
Quality awareness
Company quality improvement program
Interdepartmental group activities participation
Technical knowledge of processes, as applicable,
    e.g., heat treat and welding, manufacturing
    processes, electronic instrumentation, gage
    inspection, etc.

INSPECTION/QUALITY ENGINEERS

Technical writing
Advanced statistical concepts
Reliability, product safety, and product liability
    prevention concepts and practices
Tool and gage making and their inspection
Audits
Software control and computer application
Inspection/quality procedures and instructions
    preparation
Advanced inspection and quality principles
Quality costs
Quality information equipment
Human relations and motivation
Facilitor training
Total quality control concepts
Vendor selection and control
Inspection/quality planning
Data analysis and management report preparation
Problem investigation and corrective action
    implementation
Technical subjects related to company's products
    and processes
Design review

GROUP LEADERS AND SUPERVISORS

Company inspection/quality policies
    and procedures
Company quality product improvement programs
Basic statistical principles and applications
Advanced communication skills
Basic supervision
Inspection/quality management
Employee relation principles
Union shop operations when applicable
Budget preparation and implementation
Motivation and cost effectiveness
Industrial supervision
Skills referenced above for higher level inspectors

SUPERINTENDENTS AND CHIEF INSPECTORS

Total quality control principles
Development and implementation methods for company
    quality policies
Training program development
Human relations and coordination with personnel
    from other departments
Job descriptions and wage scale preparation
Employee relations, discipline, and motivation

MANAGERS AND DIRECTORS

Quality mission and its effect on sales and profit
Life cycle quality costs
Total quality control
Quality improvement programs
Statistical techniques
Benchmarking for quality improvement methods
Inspection/quality policies establishment
Motivation for quality
Training for quality
Interdepartmental relationships for quality improvement
Technical and professional societies roles in quality improvement
Management quality reports preparation and analysis
Effective corrective action implementation
Tracking company's quality improvement efforts status
Monitoring industry's quality improvement trends
Guru knowledge, i.e., Drs. Deming, Juran, Crosby,
    and others' teachings

TOP MANAGEMENT

Quality awareness
Inspection/quality control principles
Quality control's contribution to company's profit picture
Basic statistical techniques and possible effect of their use
    on company's competitive picture
Human relations and motivation programs
Establishing quality improvement goals and measuring their
    degree of attainment
Top management responsibilities for quality improvement
Japanese quality concepts understanding
Audit methods for quality improvement efforts
Quality improvement steering committee participation

FIGURE 24-1   Inspection Personnel Knowledge and Skills

FIRST LEVEL PRODUCTION SUPERVISORS

Company's policy for quality and quality improvement
Inspection/quality control basic concepts
Department's role in company's inspection/quality program
Basic statistical techniques concepts
Quality reports' purposes
Corrective action methods and implementation
Interdepartmental quality participation

OPERATORS

Company's quality goal
Individual's role in company's inspection/quality program and role of the operators in its implementation
Basic statistics
Individual's importance to company's competitive position
Product application in the field
Corrective action methods
Quality improvement committee activities

ENGINEERS

Company's inspection/quality organization and program
Advanced statistical techniques and their use for product design's improvement
Design review
Configuration control and product liability prevention program
Reliability and maintainability
Investigation and corrective action concepts
Materials review board activities

FIGURE 24-2 Noninspection Personnel Knowledge and Skills

As noted in earlier chapters, sufficient qualified personnel are frequently unavailable to work in inspection/quality departments. They lack basic oral and written communication skills, and they are not proficient in the basic elements of mathematics. Consequently, prerequisite courses should be given to those employees who have not acquired the basic knowledge needed for entry-level inspectors.

Reading comprehension

Courses are available to improve employees' comprehension level to the 12th grade. These courses include grammar, spelling and punctuation, and the relationship of verbs and subjects.

Basic mathematics

These courses include discussion of the primary operations of addition, subtraction, multiplication, and division. Also, training in the use of fractions and operations involving fractions and mixed numbers are included. The use of decimals and mixed decimals, and the principle of rounding off numbers are also presented in these courses.

BASIC COURSES

The following courses should be given to inspection/quality personnel at the applicable levels of operation. These are designed to provide some of the skills outlined in Figure 24-1.

Communications skills

These courses discuss the methods of oral and written communication. Preparation and presentation of concise and accurate technical reports are included.

Shop mathematics

This course describes methods of dealing with numbers with bases other than ten, and the use of square roots and the powers of numbers. Weights and measures and conversion methods are presented, as are the subjects of ratios, proportions, and percentages.

For the higher levels of inspectors, courses in simple trigonometric functions and some elementary algebraic concepts are available. In addition, metrics and calculation methods for dimensions of screw threads, tapers, and speed ratios of pulleys and gears are provided.

Technical mathematics

Elementary algebraic concepts, right angle trigonometry, basic vector concepts, systems of linear equations, factoring, and algebraic fractions are presented. For the more complex inspection/quality operations, information concerning quadratic equations, basic analytical equations, trigonometric identifications, and basic complex numbers are provided.

Bench work

Courses in the basic elements encountered in factory bench work operations are available. These courses include equipment such as vises and clamps; types and uses of hammers and chisels; characteristics of various types of files; adjustable and nonadjustable wrenches, drills, reamers, broaches, taps and dies, and contour machines; methods of soldering, brazing and wiping; principles of hand forging, gas welding, flame cutting, and arc and resistance welding; tolerances; and the three-wire method of checking screw threads.

Shop drawing reading

The fundamentals of engineering drawings, orthographic projection, sketching, dimensioning, tolerancing, sectional and auxiliary views, and true position tolerancing are included in the basic courses.

Specification interpretation

The use of specifications and the incorporation of their requirements to provide technical direction are presented. This includes discussions of the special methods for understanding the technical and quality elements of specifications, including the relationship of specification subparagraphs to the total requirements of the inspection/quality function.

INSPECTION/QUALITY COURSES

Mechanical inspection

The principles and use of the general mechanical measuring devices are presented including the following: fixed gages, micrometers and verniers, surface plates and accessories, screw thread gages, dial indicators, surface measurement equipment, angular measurement gages, hardness testers, depth and height gages, gage blocks, comparators, and sine bars.

For more sophisticated measurements, the use of the following devices are reviewed: optical flats, electronic gages, measuring machines, microscopes, coordinate measuring machines, application of electronic and pneumatic gages, and torque measurements.

Metrology

Courses are available providing the principles and applications of precision mechanical inspection equipment and their design. This course includes the discussion of both linear and angular measurements, as well as gage inspection and gage tolerances.

Material inspection

Courses are available presenting the various nondestructive test methods including dye penetrant, magnetic particle, eddy current, and ultrasonic testing. The applicable inspection standards, testing procedures, codes, and specifications, as well as qualification methods of the test devices and processes and the certification of nondestructive testers, are discussed. Methods are provided illustrating the required data preparation for these tests.

Electronic inspection

Courses are available in the methods of utilizing precision electrical and electronic measuring equipment, such as, electrical meters, including those used for resistance measurement; AC and DC voltage; current; power;

frequency; time; and wave shape. In addition, the applications of junction and zener diodes, transistors, power supply circuits, analog and digital circuits, linear amplifiers, digital integrated circuits, gates, flip-flops, and many others are included.

Electrical and electronic diagrams

Courses are available describing electronic drawing practices, tracing circuits, component identification, common connection points, and the use of schematics, blueprints, layouts, wiring diagrams, block diagrams, and functional diagrams. In addition, an understanding of the basic electronic components and use of schematic symbols, color codes and markings, and electronic standards are provided.

INSPECTION/QUALITY PRINCIPLES

Organization and management

The objectives and goals of inspection/quality management, and those of industrial management as they apply to effective economic control of quality assurance activities, are presented.

Inspection management

Courses are available describing the philosophies, concerns, and organization of the inspection/quality operation. Included are facilities, inspector selection and training, planning, procedures, records, process control, corrective action, and specifications.

Quality management

Instruction is provided in the philosophies, concerns, and implementation methods of quality management techniques and concepts, and the application of quality control to improve market share, profit, customer image, and reputation. In addition, the implementation of quality improvement programs, use of Dr. Deming's 14 points, and disciplines of other quality experts, such as Drs. Juran and Crosby, are presented. The elements of quality planning, communication of quality objectives, quality cost analysis, quality systems, Japanese quality revolution, quality circles, and other motivational techniques are also provided. Programs for product liability prevention, reliability, auditing, manufacturing, product safety, quality information systems, and human factors are also discussed in these management courses.

Quality assurance concepts

Courses are available which discuss various quality assurance programs, safety, application of measuring equipment, process testing methods, codes, specifications, qualification of personnel, sampling plans, audits, and surveys.

INSPECTION/QUALITY ENGINEERING

The following subjects are included in the courses provided for inspection/quality engineering.

Process control	Inspection and test support
Special process studies	Information systems
Nonconforming material control	Communication
Vendor quality assurance	Interdepartmental liaison
Quality specifications	Quality cost analysis
Defect analysis	Auditing
Corrective action	Motivation and human factors
Manufacturing planning for quality control	Customer relations
	New design control
Systems design	Special process studies

Technical writing

These courses present the following subjects: organizing ideas, constructing sentences, word usage, punctuation, avoiding cliches, active and passive voice, technical presentations, preparation of technical descriptions, proposals, progress reports, instructions, and evaluation reports.

Reliability

These courses deal with the following elements: application of reliability control techniques; types of failure rate curves; reliability as related to quality control; types of reliability, such as design, manufacture, and field; systems reliability; foundations of reliability; failure distribution models; hazard functions; estimation in product testing; failure analysis and prevention; estimation and prediction; and testing and demonstration.

STATISTICAL APPLICATIONS

Basic concepts

These courses present the basic elements of statistics, including the following subjects: operating characteristics, significance testing and sampling, frequency distributions, control charts, sampling, basic laws, probability distributions, central limit theorem, normal and bi-modal distributions, sampling procedures, concepts of variability and randomness, Shewhart control charts, confidence limits, and tests of hypothesis.

Advanced statistical concepts

This is a continuation of the basic statistics courses. It presents the following topics: correlation and regression; design of experiments; Taguchi method; design of sampling plans; capability studies; statistical process control; statistical quality control; application for reliability measurements; control chart and run analysis; attribute data analysis; process improvement methods; troubleshooting with attribute data; comparing averages; *t*, Chi square, and *F* distributions; queuing techniques; and linear programming.

TECHNICAL

The basic processes and equipment utilized in product fabrication are presented in these courses. A number of the special processes are also described, including the skills needed for the inspection/testing of the applicable processes and products.

Technical sciences

The following basic scientific concepts are described in these courses: measurement, motion, power and energy, impulse and momentum, vectors and vector analysis, rotational mechanics, and rotational motion.

Engineering instrumentation laboratory

Modern engineering instruments, such as those used for the measurement of temperature, pressure, mechanical and electrical power, and fluid properties are described in these courses.

Metallurgy

These courses provide the principal elements of metallurgy, including the following subjects: metal classification, identification, mechanical testing, grain structure, heat treat of ferrous metals, cast iron, welding, metal finishes, fatigue and crystallization, strength of metals, and thermal expansion and contraction.

Materials and industry processes

Metals and nonmetals application, characteristics and properties, and materials fabrication are reviewed in these courses.

Related machining practices

Presentation of the basic machining practices are provided in these courses, including the following elements: shop safety; measuring tools; and manufacturing tools such as lathes, milling machines, band and cutoff saws, and grinding and abrasive machining.

Manufacturing processes

Casting, forging, heat treatment, high production processes, and plastics and rubber processing are presented in these courses.

Heat treatment

These courses present the following elements of heat treatment:

Hot working of steels

Defects in ingots

Heating for rolling products

Tubing

Forging

Pressing

Decarbonizing

Finishing temperatures effect

Surface defects

Internal defects as result of heat treatment

Cold working of steel

Microstructure

Hardness from cold working process

Annealing

Furnaces

Fuels

Temperature measurement and control

Cooling media and controls

Welding inspection and testing

These courses describe the following operations encountered during the inspection/testing of welds:

Equipment

Welder tests

Weld preparation

Structural welds inspection

Tank work

Seam and spot welding

In-process inspection

Pipe work

Visual inspection

Tack and seam spacing

Gauging of fillets

Nondestructive tests

Testing with air, water, and oil

Magnetic and sonic testing

Destructive tests

Spot weld tests

Code requirements for fusion welds

Welding symbols

Protection of welder and weld inspectors

Mechanical power transmission

The subjects treated in these courses include gears and enclosed gear drives, electric motors, chain and chain drives, belt drives, and shaft misalignment.

Pressure measuring and control instruments

These courses review the uses and principles of the following instruments: manometers, draft gages, differential elements, dead weight testers, bourdon tubes, spiral and helical pressure meters, chemical pressure gages, pressure indicators, and recorders.

Gage making and inspection

These courses discuss the following subjects.

Classification	Indicators
Accuracy and tolerance	Ball gages
Materials	Gaging teeth of spur gages
Proportions	Sine-bar
Thread gages	Angles
End measuring gages	Templates
Making and inspecting caliper, limit, flat surface, angular, taper, contour, and pin gages	

Functional gaging

These courses supplement those in gage making and inspection. They include the following subjects: low cost functional gage design, datum selection, modifiers, and establishing company gage policy.

ADMINISTRATIVE COURSES

There are many courses available which provide training in the administrative aspects of the inspection/quality operations.

Computer-aided inspection/quality control

These courses include: methodology, procedures and administrative functions associated with software, types of software documentation, software used in inspection/quality control, configuration control, design reviews, and library controls.

Courses in computers in the inspection/quality control function discuss topics such as the following: data processing elements, hardware and software, data base management systems, design and use of computer-aided manufacturing and information systems, mini-computers, microprocessors, and application to industrial processes.

MANAGEMENT COURSES

Industrial supervision

Methods for inspiring cooperation, improving morale and discipline, training new employees, improving work methods, and problem solving are presented in a number of management courses.

Production management

Courses are available which describe management objectives and goals, organization and functions, and self-measurements of results against goals.

Total quality management

These courses describe the establishment of total quality programs, including continuous quality improvement programs. Statistics and how they relate to the company's profit picture are discussed. Other topics include the following: leadership in establishing quality goals, benchmarks and evaluating the results against the goals, participation in interdepartmental quality improvement, design and steering committee activities, role in preparation for future quality and technical needs, and application of resources for improved quality performance as revealed by results of the current quality efforts.

Modern supervision

These courses discuss the following elements: planning, organizing, and controlling techniques; planning the manager's time; delegating responsibility with authority; establishing quality standards; and measuring performance against goals methods.

Employee relationships

There are many courses which discuss the following elements: awareness of employees' desires; methods of conducting interviews, induction, job training, employee rating, job evaluation, counseling, transfers, and promotions; handling problems of physically handicapped, minority, and older employees; methods of program evaluation; relation to the company with the community; employee turnover, attendance, unrest, and productivity; and union relations, when applicable.

CHAPTER TWENTY-FIVE

Facilities, Equipment, and the Inspection/ Quality Function

INTRODUCTION

This chapter presents a discussion of the facilities and measuring equipment generally utilized in the inspection/quality operation. Consideration of the use of inspection equipment for future products is also discussed.

A program of equipment selection, maintenance, and calibration is described, including the possible use of some production equipment as media of inspection.

An integral part of inspection/quality planning is to determine the availability of adequate facilities and measuring equipment for the inspection, and process control of products and services.

At the outset, the newly assigned inspection/quality manager should determine the current availability of facilities and equipment, and their adequacy for efficient department operations. In many cases, some additional or modified equipment and facilities would be highly desirable, and attempts may be made to obtain this equipment. In all probability, management may be reluctant, at the time, to provide additional funds. This is particularly true when the existing departmental budget did not allow for the required funds. Accordingly, the manager will have to make do with what is available, while marking time until the next budget period arrives. Then, the opportunity to obtain funds for the desired improvements may be available. Many inspection managers and supervisors, when faced with this dilemma, do not attempt to obtain funds for the entire requirement at one time. They generally include some provisions, at each budget period, to slowly improve their facilities and equipment inventory. Unfortunately, it may take several years before the desired level has been reached.

At times, new or modified equipment can be obtained when a new product is fabricated, or when the company has received a new contract. Pending the availability of the funds, the inspection/quality supervisor should accumulate the information for the selection of this equipment and facilities.

FACILITIES

In many companies, little attention is generally paid to the facilities used by inspection personnel. Since inspectors spend a considerable part of the workday in the close scrutiny of the products, it is essential that their comfort and ease of operation are considered. Inspectors, working in a location which has been selected haphazardly, someplace in the middle of the manufacturing area, amidst noise and activity, cannot perform their duties effectively and accurately. The strain of operating in such an atmosphere can only have an adverse effect on morale. Further, inadequate inspection facilities demonstrate, not only to inspectors, but also to the rest of the organization, that management does not consider high product quality important. A well-lighted, clean, and properly located inspection area portrays a positive attitude and demonstrates concern for the quality effort. This also has a desirable effect upon any suppliers or customers who may visit the plant.

One company placed its highly developed and sophisticated standards laboratory near the entrance to the manufacturing facilities. The laboratory was housed in a glass-enclosed area which was well lit and fully temperature and humidity controlled. The visitors, before entering the laboratory, were escorted into a clean antechamber where they were subjected to a blast of air to remove any dust or lint from their clothes. Clean white laboratory coats and slippers were given to them before entry. All laboratory equipment was visible through the windows, as were the operations of the personnel, who were dressed in white laboratory coats.

While the laboratory was primarily utilized to calibrate inspection/quality measuring equipment, the appearance and location of the area was also utilized as a showplace. In addition, all inspection areas in the plant were located at clean, well-lit stations. Special lighting arrangements were made to distinguish the inspection from the production locations.

Inspection/quality supervisors rarely have a say about the facilities. This occasion only appears when an addition to the plant is being built, when a major revision of the manufacturing facilities is being planned, or when a new product is being developed. However, it is important that inspection/ quality supervisors are aware of the type of facilities which would provide the most effective and comfortable place for its employees.

Generally, the plant layout is developed under the jurisdiction of the plant or production engineering department. Therefore, it is important that inspection/quality supervisors maintain close contact with those departments so as to insure that they are notified when any changes are contemplated. Considerations should be given to the following elements when new inspection facilities are developed or when existing ones, modified.

- Planning
- Location
- Layout
- Personnel safety and comfort
- Flexibility
- Special areas
- Lighting

PLANNING

In planning an inspection area, the following elements should be considered: nature of the operations, size of the products, accuracy requirements of the operation, amount of products to be inspected during any given period, and timeliness of the operation. It may be necessary to coordinate with personnel in manufacturing, production engineering, and production control to obtain this information. It may also be necessary to review, with the plant engineer, the availability of the required space, electrical outlets, power, and compressed air sources. For example, a coordinate measuring machine in an inspection area should not be affected by the vibration of the passing material handling equipment or the neighboring machine tools. The machine should be placed on an insulated surface, near the appropriate electrical and compressed air sources. Since filtered air at a constant pressure is needed, a separate air compressor should be provided. Finally, a winch should be used to move heavy products on and off the machine.

LOCATION

The location of the inspection facilities within the manufacturing areas must be considered. The inspection crib should be as close as possible to the manufacturing areas without affecting the adequacy of the inspection operation.

The need for inspection results in a timely manner must also be considered. Thus, first piece inspection, the results of which are needed to continue production, should affect the location and availability of inspection facilities to a greater extent than the inspection of a lot sample which is moved to the stores area after inspection.

The flow of material into and out of the area must also be considered. For example, the inspection area for vendor-supplied material is usually located near the receiving area. This enables rapid material movement from its receipt to its inspection. Further, this location helps to reinforce the policy that all supplier materials are not to be moved into production or stores areas without having been inspected. Provision for the inspection of heavy or bulky material, at a location close to the stores area, should be made, so that the material is moved only once after receipt.

Frequently, it is necessary to locate inspection stations adjacent to the production machines. This is done to enable patrol inspectors to move easily and to provide rapid feedback to the production operator. This is usually done for first piece inspections, audits, and for material inspected on a conveyerized production or assembly line.

Products should also be protected from possible pilferage by personnel not involved in the inspection operation. Small expensive products, which can easily be moved, should be inspected in an area that is not easily available to passersby.

Further, consideration should be given to the necessity of communication with personnel at other locations. For example, samples submitted to the testing laboratory for analysis should be manufactured as close as possible to the laboratory.

LAYOUT

To determine the size and layout of the inspection area, an engineering study should be performed. If this is not feasible, the inspection supervisor and the plant engineer should determine the space requirements. To obtain a relatively true estimate, the inspection methods used and time required for each should be determined. Thus, inspection operations which require precise, careful, and time-consuming efforts would move slowly through the area. This would require more space for material awaiting inspection, or for additional inspectors.

The inspection area should provide space to enable personnel from other departments such as engineering, manufacturing, and production control to work with inspectors at the station, when required. Allowance should be based on the amount of space needed for each inspector to perform his or her work efficiently. Space should be provided for inspection records, instructions, and specifications (when not located in a special inspection crib), as well as the storage of frequently used small measuring instruments, any visual aids, and inspection samples. There should be space for inspectors to prepare records, and places to store personal belongings.

PERSONNEL SAFETY AND COMFORT

In determining the location of the inspection area, one of the prime considerations should be the safety and comfort of inspection personnel.

Requiring inspectors to perform precise operations near welding torch sparks, or directly below a moving overhead crane bearing heavy products, or adjacent to noxious fumes, is not conducive to accuracy or morale.

FLEXIBILITY

The possibility of future expansion and a space for the indoctrination of new inspectors should be considered in planning the inspection area layout. Consideration should also be given to the need for separate areas for material that is: awaiting inspection, completely inspected, rejected, and awaiting movement to the review area.

SPECIAL INSPECTION/TEST AREAS

Some inspection areas such as gage rooms, standards laboratories, and clean room operations require special attention. These areas, as applicable, must be temperature-, humidity-, and dust-controlled and must be free from external vibration, noise, and similar disruptions.

At times special test areas such as those for nondestructive examinations, which require special equipment, are required. In addition, certain operational tests may require enclosed soundproofed areas, if they are to be performed properly without affecting the safety and comfort of workers in adjacent areas.

LIGHTING[1]

One of the most significant factors that affects inspection operations is proper lighting. Some of the factors for consideration, as presented by the Society for Illumination Engineers, are described in the following sections.

Intensity

This is the amount of light falling on an object, expressed in footcandles (amount of light one foot away from the object provided by a standard candle). A 100-watt bulb, without reflection, gives an intensity level of about five footcandles at a distance of five feet. The recommended light intensity for inspection areas ranges from 100 to 500 footcandles, with the most difficult inspection recommended at a light intensity of 1000 footcandles.

See the referenced standard for a more detailed breakdown of light intensity requirements for the various industries and types of inspection.

Color

This characteristic of lighting is particularly important in the visual inspection of a product's aesthetic attributes. The color of lighting can influence the ability to judge the color of a product. For precise color matching, it is customary to check products under two different color lights. If they match, they will normally match under any color. For less critical matching, northern daylight is generally used. Storekeepers can disguise the true appearance of a product using colored lights. The familiar statement, "Put on the blue light, the customer wants to buy a blue suit," may be true. Meat and vegetable markets use colored lights. By providing a red tint, meat will appear red and fresh. By using a green-tinted light, vegetables will generally appear fresh. Many states have forbidden the use of colored lights to augment the appearance of food products.

Tarnish or stains show up better under one color light than another. The background color is important in determining color variation. Normally, a neutral light gray is used for close color match. For determining certain color defects, a contrasting background shade of the same luminosity is helpful.

Certain colors have a physical effect on inspectors. It is generally believed that a green light tends to have a calming effect on emotions. Accordingly, this color is chosen for wall paint in areas used for detecting different odors and taste, as well as for audio checking, where calm concentration is needed.

Diffusion

This refers to the softness or harshness of light in forming shadows. In detecting textural defects, such as cracks in porcelain, a hard light will cast a sharp shadow and enable defects to be observed more easily than in a diffuse light. At other extremes, tarnish spots or slight color variations in highly polished articles can be determined only under soft diffused light. At times, special boxes are built over fluorescent fixtures so that the light is further diffused through white cloth, and is reflected equally on the article from all sides.

Fluorescent fixtures are extensively used in inspection and production areas. The tendency is toward increased softness of shadows. But a harder light is frequently needed for the detection of many types of defects. In addition, variation of intensity through spotlighting is often desirable in areas requiring concentrated operator or inspector attention, provided that this is not carried beyond the limits of background contrast.

Where shape or texture is important, angle lighting is an advantage. The eye is rested by occasional changes from low to high intensities, monotony is reduced, and errors or accidents are prevented.

Direction

For determination of shape and texture, this is as important as light diffusion. Lighting direction should be such as to emphasize the defect or texture and make it easy to locate. Often, maximum defect detection can be obtained with lights headed almost toward inspectors, but with resultant glare and eye strain. Here, a compromise must be reached.

Light should be polarized, in some cases, to find shiny spots on normally dull surfaces. The use of automatic scanning methods to replace or supplement visual inspection should be considered.

Background Contrast

This is defined as the difference in both intensity and color between light on the object viewed and light on the background or surrounding area. The modern trend is to illuminate industrial and inspection areas with a uniform diffused light. A background contrast of the ratio of about 3 to 1 in intensity, and occasionally a variation in color, may make defects easier to detect, and reduce inspectors' fatigue and monotony. Special attention should be paid to this contrast requirement for inspections requiring concentrated and rapid detection such as for conveyerized operations. For detection of defects, a background light which will emphasize the contrast between the defective and the good is usually selected. Normally, this background light is at the opposite end of the spectrum from the defect color if it tends to be darker than the surrounding area. For example, a blue light will emphasize pink stains on a white or yellow background. A red light will emphasize pink on a gray background.

Special Situations

Flickering, particularly with a single fluorescent tube, is objectional even though it may not be consciously noticed. Lighting costs must be considered, as should the heat generated from lights, particularly in an air-conditioned area.

MEASURING EQUIPMENT

In order to accurately inspect products, the proper measuring equipment must be available. This equipment must be of a degree of accuracy which is based upon product tolerance. The rule of thumb generally utilized is an accuracy ten times the product's tolerance. Thus, when a product tolerance is in the thousandths, the measuring equipment must have an accuracy in the ten-thousandths. Consequently, one of the principal functions of inspection/quality supervisors is to select the appropriate measuring equipment of the accuracy needed for the products to be inspected.

SELECTION

In addition to equipment accuracy, inspection supervisors must consider the skills necessary to complete measurements. In general, measurements at the lower level of accuracy, for example, in the hundredths or thousandths, normally require no special skills. However, as the accuracy requirements become greater, inspectors' aptitudes become increasingly important. Therefore, the measuring equipment's ease of operation must be considered. For example, when feasible, the use of fixed gages in lieu of those with variable measurements is preferable. The need for a high degree of skill in gage use is replaced by the controlled characteristics of the fixed measuring device. Some companies provide fixed gages for all inspection measurements. At times, this creates a problem, especially when several inspectors need to use the same device at the same time. Therefore enough fixed gages must be provided or alternate inspection methods must be used. Computer-aided measuring devices also provide the needed accuracy without too much dependence upon inspectors' skills.

Nevertheless, it is often necessary to enhance inspectors' measuring skills to meet a product's accuracy requirements. Training programs are available.

Another important consideration in the selection of measuring equipment is the time needed to perform the measurement. Thus, when a large number of measurements must be taken in a short period of time, automated devices should be considered. The incorporation of measurement capabilities into production operations also provides an effective and timely method of measurement.

Finally, the cost of the equipment plays an important role in its selection. Frequently, supervisors must decide between the cost of sophisticated measuring equipment and the time needed to perform measurements using traditional devices. However, the accuracy of measurements must not be sacrificed in these trade-offs.

Before selecting sophisticated measuring equipment, a study should be made concerning its degree of use. Assuming that one piece of equipment is adequate for department needs, provision must be made for any downtime. This may result from equipment failure, as well as the need for its periodic recalibration and maintenance. An additional piece of the same equipment may be needed so that inspection operations are not unduly held up. Some distributors of the more sophisticated equipment provide users with a buffer stock of the frequently needed maintenance and replacement parts. Others provide rapid repair or maintenance service. In any case, some user training to troubleshoot, calibrate, and repair the equipment is needed. The costs of these activities should also be included in the trade-off analysis.

CALIBRATION

Some formal program is essential to insure the continued accuracy of measuring equipment throughout the inspection cycle. This method requires the periodic recall of each item of equipment, based upon some preestablished schedule.

Here too, the same accuracy criteria described for the measuring equipment must be applied to the standards used in calibration. When the original accuracy of the measuring equipment is extremely high, it may be difficult to provide a standard. Thus, a lower ratio of accuracy must be utilized. When this is done, there is a degree of uncertainty in the measurement results, and some caution must be exercised when using the calibration data. Frequently, a statement of this uncertainty limit is included in the calibration results.

TRACEABILITY

Since the products provided by one plant are generally utilized by other plants or companies, it is necessary that the same base of measurements is utilized by all organizations. This way the measurements of one can be equitably compared with the measurements of the other. Thus, a central organization provides the accredited physical standards for the country. In the United States, this organization is known as the National Institute of Standards and Technology (NIST), formerly the National Bureau of Standards (NBS). Each country has its own standards organization, which is correlated with the International Standards Association for uniformity of all prime standards used in measurements throughout all the industrial countries of the world.

The formal calibration program calls for the measurements of each company to be traceable to national or international standards. This traceability is performed through a hierarchy of standards (see Figure 25-1) of ever-increasing accuracy, utilized by each company. In most companies, the working gages and measurement instruments are periodically checked against the working standards maintained in the company's gage crib or calibration laboratory. These standards are, in turn, periodically checked against transfer standards of a still higher degree of accuracy. The transfer standards may be maintained in the company's standards laboratory, or by outside calibration service organizations. The transfer standards of the calibration service organizations are then transported, at specified intervals, to the national or international standards agencies. Thus, if the cycle is followed as required, the accuracy of all measuring devices used by every company in the industrial world are traceable to the same national or international standards.

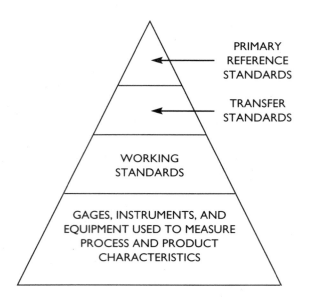

FIGURE 25-1 Hierarchy of Standards

ESTABLISHMENT OF INITIAL FREQUENCY

As part of the calibration program, each item of measuring equipment should be assigned a frequency for its recalibration so that its accuracy is maintained. See Table 25-1 for the initial frequencies established by a manufacturing organization. In many cases, the initial frequency is established purely on a good estimate of the time of accuracy retention, or at a frequency customarily utilized by the industry in question. At other times, the frequency may be established based upon a customer's requirements, technical associations's standards, or as specified by the measuring equipment manufacturer.

Adjustment of Frequency

Each item of measuring equipment should be inspected for accuracy through the use of designated working standards. Depending upon the inspection results over a period of time, the frequency of recalibration may be adjusted. Thus, if after a pre-established number of calibrations, no adjustment is found necessary to restore the accuracy of a group of measuring devices, the recalibration frequency of that group can be lengthened. Conversely, if during any calibration period, the measurement equipment is found to be outside of its tolerance, its subsequent recalibration cycle should be shortened.

MEASURING EQUIPMENT OR STANDARD	METHOD	CALIBRATION CYCLE
Precision Gage Blocks (Transfer)	Outside Lab	18 Months
Thread Measuring Wire	Outside Lab	18 Months
Rockwell Hardness Tester Brinell Hardness Tester	Test Block	Every Setup (notation not required on calibration record)
Micrometers, Inside, Outside Depth, and Thread Mikes	Gage Blocks	6 Months
Verniers, Calipers, Depth Height Gage, and Hite-icator	Gage Blocks	6 Months
Dial Bore Gage and Set Master	Gage Blocks	6 Months
Indicators	Gage Blocks	6 Months
Ames Wall Thickness Calipers	Gage Blocks	6 Months
Parallels	Indicator	12 Months
Sine Bars and Sine Plates	Outside Lab	12 Months
Square Blocks and Angle Plates Box Parallels	Cyl. Square	12 Months
Thread Ring Gages Up to $\frac{1}{2}$ Inch	Outside Lab	12 Months
Thread Ring Gages Over $\frac{1}{2}$ Inch	Outside Lab	24 Months
Thread Plug Gages	Outside Lab or Super-Mike	24 Months
Surface Plates	Outside Lab	24 Months
Torque Wrenches	Torque Analyzer or Outside Lab	4 Months
Cylinder Square	Outside Lab	12 Months
Plug Gages (Below 1")	Super-Mike	3 Months
Plug Gages (Above 1")	Super-Mike	6 Months
Pressure Gages	Dead Weight Tester	4 Months
Thermometers (Standard)	Outside Lab	12 Months

NOTE 1: Equipment which by design requires calibration at time of use, e.g. Hardness Test Equipment, Super Micrometer, etc. shall be cycled on a 12-month frequency for maintenance.

NOTE 2: Government-furnished gages, masters, and or standards shall be calibrated on a 24-month frequency unless otherwise specified. This 24-month frequency to be measured starting with the first month's full contract production quota.

TABLE 25-1   Initial calibration schedule

CALIBRATION INSTRUCTIONS

Following instructions generally insures that all calibrations are adequately performed. Usually, standard measuring devices are calibrated in accordance with simple instructions. For example, a micrometer would be examined over gage blocks. The perpendicularity of the gage faces would be measured, as would the amount of play in the movement of the screw. Fixed gages would be calibrated against fixed gage standards. For more complicated gages, the calibration would be performed using instructions provided by the equipment manufacturer. There are also standard calibration instructions provided by technical organizations and government agencies. When no instructions are available the company will need to prepare its own.

IDENTIFICATION

In order to comply with the calibration program, it is necessary to identify the measuring equipment by individual serial number marked on the instrument. When the gage is too small, the marking is often placed on a tag or on a container for the gage.

RECORDS

Generally, a calibration record card is made out for each item of measuring equipment. It shows the following information.

- Equipment serial number
- Description
- Storage location
- Usage location
- Calibration frequency, acceptance criteria, and instructions
- Inspection date
- Gage inspector's identification
- Date of next calibration
- Inspection results (preferably in variables data)
- Products inspected by the equipment, if it is nonstandard

The dates of the current and subsequent calibrations and the initials of the gage inspector are posted on a sticker or tag attached to the gage. For small gages, where there is insufficient space, or when it is not feasible to apply a sticker, some companies color code the gage, denoting the month or week of recalibration. Other companies do not place the information on the measuring equipment, but depend upon the gage clerk or laboratory technician to recall the equipment as needed.

RECALL

A short time before the measuring equipment is due for recalibration, a notification should be sent to the user personnel. When the gage has not been returned to the inspection crib by the specified date, the gage inspector usually visits the location and picks up the gage. Some companies perform the inspections at the product inspection/test locations. The gage inspectors or test equipment technicians are provided with carts which contain the necessary equipment and standards for the recalibrations.

AUDIT

Periodically, the inspection/quality engineer should perform an audit in the areas where the measuring equipment is used, stored, and calibrated. The audit determines the extent of conformance to the company's gage control procedure.

PERSONALLY OWNED MEASURING EQUIPMENT

Many companies require their production and inspection personnel to use their own standard inspection equipment, such as micrometers and verniers. These gages should be registered with the gage inspector, recalibrated, and controlled in accordance with the calibration procedures. Some companies do not maintain calibration control of personally owned gages. In those companies, the gages are not utilized for acceptance inspection purposes.

E X A M P L E

Here is an example of a typical gage control program. The following program elements are important.

- Designation of responsible organizations
- Selection of measuring equipment

- Receipt and utilization
- Calibration
- Records
- Recall
- Out-of-tolerance evaluation
- Storage and handling
- Subcontractor control

Responsible Organizations

The identification and responsibilities of the various organizations within the company relative to the identification, calibration, and maintenance of the records of measuring equipment and their standards, are defined.

Selection of Measuring Equipment

This requires the inspection/quality engineer to determine, at the start of each project, the special measuring equipment needs. This insures the availability of equipment with the degree of accuracy needed.

Receipt and Utilization

The measuring equipment is assigned a serial number upon receipt, and its calibration control record is prepared. All new, reworked, and externally calibrated measuring equipment are sent to the responsible organizations for their initial inspection, verification of vendor-supplied calibration records, and serial numbering. When the equipment is defective, inoperative, or is past its reinspection, the personnel using or storing it attach a rejection tag and return the equipment to the responsible organization.

Calibration

The responsible organizations establish, with the production and project engineers, the calibration schedule for all special measuring equipment under their jurisdiction. The initial calibration frequency should be established and adjusted on the basis of the following:

- Severity of the environment
- Severity and frequency of use
- Sensitivity of the measuring device
- Accuracy of the required measurements

- Importance of the characteristic to be measured
- Calibration history of the equipment
- Contract requirements, when applicable

The program permits the use of production tooling, such as drill jigs, templates, casting patterns, and computer programs, as inspection media. When so used, this tooling is to be initially inspected and assigned a frequency of reinspection. This frequency may be stated in time or in numbers of pieces produced. The frequency is established with production engineering personnel, who will determine the amount of tool usage. It is then processed in accordance with the calibration control procedures.

The program does not permit the use of personally owned gages for purposes of acceptance inspection.

Measuring equipment which cannot be adjusted to the required accuracy are identified with a rejection tag and held in the materials review area pending final disposition instructions by the MRB.

Records

The responsible organizations are required to prepare and maintain calibration control records for all measuring equipment under their jurisdiction. Measuring equipment is identified with a calibration label. Special tags are applied to identify any limitations of the equipment's use, or when the equipment requires no calibration. Thus, when a meter has a degree of accuracy at only one section of its scale, the tag should identify the section that can be used. This limitation is also noted on the calibration control card.

Recall

On a monthly basis, the gage inspection clerk or instrument technician reviews the calibration control records and determines which equipment will be due for recalibration. The clerk notifies the affected personnel, via memorandum or computer printout, to return the equipment to the gage crib or instrument laboratory for recalibration.

Upon completion of the recalibration, the gage inspector or instrument technician records the results on the inspection record and annotates the calibration card with the required data. A new calibration tag is applied to the measuring equipment.

When the company has a lot of measuring equipment, calibration may be quite costly and time consuming. Therefore, different methods for establishing the recalibration frequency are used. For example, a company with a lot of electronic test equipment, may install elapsed time meters on it. These meters record the number of hours that the equipment operates; thus, the calibration frequency is based on this data. Other companies put seals on their calibrated measuring equipment. After a predetermined time period, any equipment with its seal still intact requires no calibration. Still other companies, when a large quantity of gages are returned to the gage crib after use, have the gage crib attendant note the dates of issue and of return on the control card for each gage. When the date for recalibration has been reached, the crib attendant will note the actual period of time that the gage had been in use, as reflected by the dates of issue and return recorded by the clerk. If the number of months that the gage had been in use is less than the specified frequency period, the gage clerk advances the recalibration date by the additional months that it had not been used.

Out-of-Tolerance Evaluation

During recalibration, if special measuring equipment is found out of tolerance, the results are referred to the inspection/quality and project engineers to determine the possible effect on products. If adversely effected, all items inspected or tested by the equipment since the previous calibration, are recalled and reinspected. Products found nonconforming as a result of the reinspection, are then rejected.

Since product recalls due to out-of-tolerance measuring equipment conditions can become quite troublesome and can have a serious effect on production schedules, some companies utilize special precautionary measures to assure that this condition happens rarely, if at all. One such measure is to use the principle of narrow-limit-gaging in the inspection of the measuring equipment. This principle provides a set of dimensions within the equipment's tolerance band. Thus, when inspection reveals that the characteristic is beyond this dimension, but still within the required limits of the gage, the equipment is adjusted or otherwise repaired as if it had exceeded the original limit. While this reduces the original tolerance band of the measuring equipment, it eliminates the need for product recalls.

Storage and Handling

The program mandates that all personnel storing, transporting, or using the measuring equipment must insure that it is protected against handling or environmental damage while under their jurisdiction. If the equipment has been damaged or appears inoperative, a hold tag is applied, and the equipment is returned to the appropriate inspection area for recalibration.

Subcontractor Control

When company-owned measuring equipment is provided to its subcontractors, the purchase order should include the requirement that the equipment iş to be maintained, calibrated, and controlled in accordance with procedures equivalent to the company's program. Similarly, products on order requiring inspection by the supplier's measuring equipment must also be suitably controlled.

When a company's working or transfer standards are shipped to an outside laboratory, the purchase order should specify that the calibration is to be performed in accordance with controlled procedures. The purchase order must also include the requirement that documentation of the specific calibration results is to be provided to the company. This must reflect traceability of the laboratory's standards to the NIST standards, as well as reference the environmental conditions under which the calibration had been performed, the results of the recalibration, any out-of-tolerance conditions noted prior to recalibration, and the certificate number of the standards used.

REFERENCES

1. *IES Lighting Handbook* (5th ed). New York: The Illuminating Engineering Society, 1972.

CHAPTER TWENTY-SIX

Computers and the Inspection/ Quality Function

INTRODUCTION

The proliferation of computers in every phase of production and quality makes it essential that quality professionals and production managers become totally versed in their use and application. This section discusses the following:

1. The use of computer-aided manufacturing (CAM) equipment and the quality control of its output

2. The availability and use of computer-aided inspection equipment

3. Several methods used to determine the accuracy of the computer-aided inspection equipment

4. The availability of computer software for use in inspection/quality data analysis

5. Considerations before procuring inspection/quality software

TYPES OF COMPUTERS[1]

Computers are generally categorized by their power, word size, and extent of their memory. The capabilities of the computer are designated by the form of its word size. The word size is a fixed number of bits (binary digits, 1s or 0s) which serve as the basic logical unit of information. Normally called a byte, a machine's word size defines the amount of information handled and the number of memory cells available to store data. Examples of the types of computers are 250K, RAM (Random Access Memory), $5\frac{1}{4}''$ versus $3\frac{1}{2}''$ discs, and hard versus diskette drives.

Mainframe Computers

These include large scale, general purpose computer systems. They are designed around a 32-bit and larger word size which allows rapid access to an extremely large memory space. They contain a significant amount of on-line storage, and are readily accessible by smaller computers through human intervention. Due to the sensitivity of its operational features, this equipment requires housing under special environmental conditions. This makes it mandatory for the equipment to be based in specially constructed facilities.

Minicomputers

A minicomputer is a general purpose computer similar to the mainframe, but is usually smaller and less expensive and has less memory space. It is designed around the 16-bit word size, which distinguishes it from the larger machines.

Microcomputers

A microcomputer may be incorporated into a wide variety of equipment including 8-bit and 16-bit structures, with wide-ranging power capabilities. Personal and home computers are included in this category. Due to the relatively low cost and limited capacity of most microcomputers, they are often developed for a single user or application. However, they can be processed to handle a wide variety of applications, such as numerical analysis, data bases, graphics, word processing, data acquisition and similar tasks.

Microcomputers can also function as the primary user interface into a computer network. They can use off-line computing power while retaining ability to connect into more powerful minicomputers and mainframes. Personal computers or microprocessors are increasingly used in quality operations.

COMPUTER-AIDED MANUFACTURING EQUIPMENT (CAM)

Planning for Computer Projects

A plan to introduce the use of computer-aided manufacturing equipment (CAM) into production operations should be developed. The plan should be prepared and implemented under the guidance of the managers of the departments contemplating the use of this equipment, as well as the members of the supporting agencies who will be dependent upon the results. This plan should include the following elements:

- Current and future equipment uses ranked in order of importance

- Consistency with engineering, manufacturing, and inspection/quality department's function objectives

- Specific projects to meet each department's needs. These projects should contain a definition of their scope, the nature of the tasks, the skills required and available, the estimated cost, and a schedule of implementation

- Follow-up of each project's progress through completion, and its budget

The successful implementation of a computer project, at times, runs into a number of snags. Some of the problems are listed in Figure 26-1.

Precautions in Using CAM Equipment

Several major problems are encountered by first-time users of CAM equipment. It can only perform those functions which have been put into the computer data bank. For example, when an operation is manually controlled, the operator will raise the tool piece as it approaches the section of the fixture or holding device which lies in the path of the tool. The computer- or tape-controlled tool, will often hit the fixture unless specific provisions are incorporated into the instructions.

In addition, CAM equipment, such as numerically controlled machines (NC), do not automatically account for the position of the part on its fixture. This necessitates that the part be locked into a position by the fixture. A special fixture, unique to the part, must be created.

Quality Control of CAM Equipment

To accept the results of CAM equipment, there must be a method of establishing the validity of the programming input. This entails flowcharting the program and punching a card deck or tape, which is run through a computer providing an initial printout to check for mechanical errors. The deck is then transferred to magnetic tape or to the computer's memory. Trial testing of the computer program for actual use can be performed by: (1) building a self-test program; (2) in-cycle gaging; or (3) using faulty items and running trial checks. This is a long process since all variables must be taken into consideration.

Self-test program

This speedier method entails making trial runs on both programs until either breaks down. The reasons for the breakdown are then examined to determine whether it is in the main or in the self-test program. The two are then rerun. This process is continued until satisfactory results are attained.

Disorganized indexing systems
Troublesome data maintenance
Insufficient interrelationship with design reviews and engineering changes
Misunderstanding of equipment's operational procedures
Unrealistic expectations, beyond the equipment's designed capabilities
Improper programs
Improper and unreliable equipment

FIGURE 26-1   Problems in Implementation of Computer Programs

---

To verify the continued accuracy of the machine, known defectives are periodically inserted. The material produced between these periodic verifications are segregated, until confidence has been established about the accuracy of the program.

In-cycle gaging

Software is available for use with NC equipment that can compensate for machine thermal movement, setup tolerances, and tool wear. Software is also available which can predict when the failure of a rotating machine tool or part is imminent or when the cutting tool is worn.

Qualification

For NC equipment, the tape is usually qualified before use. This is done by checking the tape against the engineering design specifications, followed by the measurement of the trial or first piece of the machined part against its engineering drawing. Once the tape has been qualified, it is not necessary to check each lot. Care must be taken, however, that only those characteristics controlled by the tape are so treated. In addition, some control features of the fabricated item should be checked to insure its proper positioning on the tool. After qualification of the tape, a frequency of recalibration should be established and the tape is controlled in accordance with the provisions discussed in Chapter 25, "Control of Measuring Equipment."

Automated Inspection

Automatic inspection on the production equipment is usually performed by coupling a transducer to a computer. The transducer can take the form of dimensional indicators which are transferred to the computer.

The characteristics of the piece part are measured and automatically recorded by the computers, or the recording can be performed by hand-held instruments attached to a data collecting bank. The most common types of automated inspection equipment are either computerized, tape driven, or mechanical.

COMPUTERIZED EQUIPMENT

Computers may be analog or digital. Digital computers are almost exclusively used in automatic testing applications. It is possible to have printouts made simultaneously with inspection. The printouts may provide actual readings of the characteristics or indicate that the individual characteristic is satisfactory. The computer may also be programmed to merely indicate that the test is satisfactory or denote that portion which is not in accordance with requirements. It may be used for permanent storage of test results, thus replacing manual data records. When needed, printouts can be provided to off-line stations.

The program is the key element in the proper functioning of the computer. The characteristics that are to be inspected, the parameters to which they are to be inspected, and the sequence of the inspection operations must all be created by means of the program. It is the communication link between the operator and the computer. At times, the program may also call for the memory storage of bits of information relative to the selected characteristics. This information is used to determine its relationship to, and acceptance of, subsequently inspected characteristics.

TAPE-DRIVEN EQUIPMENT

Tape-driven equipment requires the use of a perforated tape which calls for the equipment to test, in a certain sequence, individual characteristics. It then provides a readout, or other indication, of whether the product tested is satisfactory. The tape that drives the NC machine, is an outgrowth of the perforated music rolls which drove the player pianos of old. The adequacy of the tape used to drive the test equipment is extremely important, since the equipment can do no more than what the tape directs it to do.

MECHANICAL EQUIPMENT

This may take various forms. It may involve an automated gaging operation which, in addition to measuring a particular dimension, will identify those parts which are out of tolerance. Mechanical equipment may also involve an arrangement whereby the machine, through the use of plungers or other apparatus, determines if a particular component of an assembly has been installed or not. The machine can reject those items not containing the component.

OTHER COMPUTER APPLICATIONS

The use of computers has many other applications within the inspection/quality organization besides testing. Some are listed below:

- Calculation of quality cost data, new product design, and reliability data
- Process regulation and feedback
- Calibration
- Field performance feedback
- Quality improvement analysis
- Training
- Configuration control and inspection reports
- Corrective action and index of deficiency codes
- Management reports
- Statistical analysis

COORDINATE MEASURING MACHINE (CMM)

A CMM consists of a series of interconnected linkages. The following factors may affect the accuracy and precision of the equipment.[2]

- Geometric
- Thermal distortion
- Kinematic errors
- Static and dynamic errors
- Work piece errors
- Probe/tool work piece interaction

Geometric Errors

There are six parameters associated with the six degrees of freedom of the equipment. Measurements are made to determine the accuracy of each of these parameters as they relate to each other.

Thermal Errors

Any change in the machine's thermal stability or in its control system will affect its performance. A localized heat source near the center of a machine component will cause a temperature gradient. Thermal lag due to dynamic change in ambient temperature affects dimensional accuracy. For example, if a work piece and machine table are at a stable ambient temperature, and that increases with time at a constant rate, the temperature of the work piece will lag due to the time needed to absorb the heat change. The temperature of the table will lag still further because of its larger mass, thus creating a temperature differential between the work piece and the table.

Kinematic Errors

This involves the relative motion errors of the different machine elements thus affecting its performance.

Static and Dynamic Error

Each element of the machine vibrates measurably under dynamic operation. The interaction between a CMM probe and the measured work piece may have a considerable effect. These vibrations can affect its accuracy and repeatability by relative movement between the probe and the work piece. Vibrations are caused by any of the following:

- Outside sources through the foundations
- Unbalancing external forces in the surrounding areas
- Bearing defects
- The machine itself, during one or several natural frequencies
- Air disturbance when using bearings or hydraulic systems
- Probe movement from one measuring location to another
- Probe speed as it approaches the measuring location

Foundation, unbalancing, or bearing errors cause problems with machine geometry such as flatness and straightness.

Work Piece Errors

The method of manufacture of the piece part may cause error. Induced stresses in the work piece degrades the accuracy of the subsequent measurements. The machinability characteristics of the work piece, such as hardness and roughness, may also lead to measurement errors.

CMM PERFORMANCE TESTING

A uniform methodology has been developed by the American Society of Mechanical Engineers, (B89.1.12) Committee on CMM. This provides standardized methods for specifying and testing the performance of CMMs with three linear axes perpendicular to each other. Testing for repeatability, linear displacement accuracy, and streamlined artifact testing with a socketed ball bar are discussed in the standard.

Repeatability Testing

This is a test of how well the equipment can indicate the same value for the same measured part under similar conditions. The part is measured using a precision ball mounted on the machine table near the center of the work zone. The probe is repeatedly (ten times) located in the center of the ball and its *X, Y,* and *Z* coordinates.

Linear Displacement Accuracy

This is the difference between the true displacement of the probe along the machine axis and that recorded by the measuring system. It is measured by using a step gage or a laser interferometer system.

Socketed Ball Bar Test

This method uses a gage consisting of two precision tooling balls. It partially simulates a real measurement. A socketed ball bar is used. The fixed socket is mounted on the machine table and the free socket is mounted in the probe holder. One end of the ball bar is inserted in the fixed socket and the free socket is engaged with the movable ball. The ball bar is rotated and the position of the free ball (*X, Y,* and *Z* coordinates) is measured at eight points equally spaced in a circular path. The procedure is repeated at different locations on the machine for different bar lengths.

An alternate method, not in the standard, is used. The length of each ball bar used is accurately measured on another measuring machine.

Most manufacturers of CMM equipment provide, at a price, a master checking plate for use in the periodic calibration of the CMM.

COMPUTER SOFTWARE

Machine Language[1]

The only language that a computer can understand is its own. All other languages must be translated into this machine language by programs, often referred to as compilers or interpreters.

Each machine language consists of binary strings of 1s and 0s, and is unique to its manufacturer. Usually, it cannot be transferred between manufacturers, or various models of the same manufacturer. Currently, equipment is available which can make the machine language of one type compatible with that of another.

Software Applications

Software packages are available for a wide variety of applications. They can be procured in any size and price range. A number of software packages available for inspection/quality functions include the following:

- Calibration
- Capability studies
- Data acquisition and evaluation
- Inspection/Quality management
- Sampling
- Statistical methods
- Supplier quality assurance
- Training

The ASQC publication *Quality Progress* annually lists, in the March issue, the types and sources of the latest software packages. Many are available through national and regional ASQC sections for loan to its membership.

Software Quality[3]

The software quality control element evaluates and measures compliance with requirements and goals established by the software engineer. This is usually performed through a series of in-process and final inspections at the place of manufacture. The final software product is usually evaluated by checking its metrics. These deal with certain attributes of the product, such as its performance and traceability against defined criteria.

Sets of metrics have been developed by the Rome Air Development Center. A list of metrics has also been adopted by the Institute of Electronics and issued as its Quality Metrics Standard P1061. Table 26-1 shows the quality software factors and criteria of evaluation.

As is evident from Table 26-1, the complexity of software requires the use of several complementary methods. Both software products and processes must be examined. Metrics can be evaluated by the producer and user to determine whether the product has the properties which will enable it to meet the performance and traceability requirements established by the user's specifications.

In the past,[4] software quality was basically a manual review of paper products, which included specifications, source codes, and test results.[5] Most of the products included documents, data flow diagrams, structured

FACTOR	CRITERIA
Correctness: The extent to which a program satisfies its specifications, and fulfills the user's objectives	Traceability Completeness Consistency
Reliability: The extent that the software can be expected to perform its intended function with the required precision	Consistency Accuracy Simplicity Error tolerance
Efficiency: The amount of computing resources and codes required by the program to perform a function	Execution efficiency Storage efficiency
Integrity: The extent to which access to the software or the data by unauthorized persons can be controlled	Access control Access audit
Usability: The effort required to learn, operate, prepare input, and interpret the output of the program	Training Communicativeness Operability
Maintainability: The effort required to locate and fix an error in the operational program	Consistency Simplicity Conciseness Modularity Self-descriptiveness
Testability: The effort required to test the program to ensure that it performs its intended function	Modularity Simplicity Self-descriptiveness Instrumentation
Flexibility: The effort required to modify the operational program	Modularity Generality Expendability Self descriptiveness
Portability: The effort required to transfer a program of one hardware configuration and/or software environment to another	Modularity Self-descriptiveness Machine independence
Reusability: The extent to which a program can be used in other applications. Related to the packaging and scope of the functions that programs perform	Generality Software system independence Machine independence Self-descriptiveness
Interoperability: The effort required to couple one system with anther	Modularity Data commonality Communications commonality

TABLE 26-1 Quality software factors and evaluation criteria

charts, program design language, source codes, test cases, and test results. Most of this data were in computer files. The current availability of computers to quality personnel provides access to these files. There are, however, few tools on the market for specific software analysis and quality control. Code analyzers are the most prevalent tools available. Also, general office automation tools will help maintain software QA records and reports. Other tools can be developed inside the organization. These may include collection and analysis of software metrics data, evaluation and review of software products and processes, and collection and analysis of corrective action data.

Due to the complexity of the software and the expense of complete evaluations, companies usually select, for review, only those elements and criteria levels pertinent to their applications.

There are a number of methods currently available for product measurement. The most common method is based upon a ratio of compliances to inspections.

There is also a problem of setting acceptable passing scores. The best measure of acceptance levels seems to be one in which pass/fail criteria are determined after each set of measurements is made. In this case, each element is assigned one of two criticality numbers depending upon the result of noncompliance. For example, one for errors that are fatal to the system and zero for all others, can be used. A good or passing score would thus be the one resulting from no open discrepancies against fatal system failure elements (criticality number 1).

In most instances it is economically unfeasible to perform a complete evaluation of all software parameters. Some software production organizations and users will often take recourse to statistical sampling of the applicable factors and criteria. The results of these evaluations generally lead to a warranty, from the producer, of the accuracy or adequacy of the software within a specified range of conformance. For example, a software package for standard deviation calculation may specify that, for 90 percent of the output, the determination is correct to three significant figures. To verify the accuracy of the statement, the user would set the confidence level, determine the sample size, run the test of the number of outputs right and the number wrong, perform the calculation of the statistical model, and verify the producer's degree of software confidence.

Figure 26-2[5] shows the method used by a government agency to evaluate a number of software packages for conformance against their specified criteria of acceptability. Figure 26-3 lists some of the considerations for procuring software for inspection/quality functions. Figure 26-4 lists some of the common problems associated with software applications.

I. *Configuration Management Plan*
   A. Software identification, numbering, and marking of baseline items and its subsequent revisions
   B. Operation of engineering release system
   C. Operation of configuration control board including change evaluation and preparation of engineering change proposals
   D. Systems to be used for configuration accounting
   E. Planned quality assurance measures applied to configuration management, including provisions for configuration audits and maintenance of audit records
   F. Delineation of personnel authorized to place material under control, remove controlled items, and direct changes in configured items
   G. Procedures for precluding the use of control facilities as a depository for untested, unapproved, obsolete, or uncontrolled computer programs and supporting documentation

---

FIGURE 26-2   Software Evaluation Methods

II. *Technical specification*
   A. Flowcharts depicting sequence of operations, branch and decision points, and allocation of functions to individual routines
   B. Timing and sequencing of individual routines with requirements for operations such as data transfers, in and out memory, and interrupt operations
   C. Storage allocations between programs and individual routines
   D. Data base characteristics including content and location of files and tables
   E. Individual routine characteristics
   F. Format and content of input data and output data
   G. Quality assurance provisions including test/verification requirements, methods of verification, test facility requirements, and test plans and procedures
   H. Completeness with respect to contractually imposed performance requirements

III. *Test plans*
   A. Concepts and philosophy
   B. Performance requirements including limits and methods to determine conformance to technical specifications
   C. Qualification test implementation, as applicable
   D. Identification of simulation and/or data generation vehicles
   E. Procedures for test conduct and delineation of responsibilities for test direction, operation, and observations
   F. Requirements for equipment and computer simulation other than software under test

IV. *Control and reporting procedures*
   A. Subprogram testing, program testing, acceptance testing, and system integration testing, including parameters to be checked, tolerances, and method to be used to determine compliance (i.e., analysis of recorded data, examination of displays, hard copy outputs, equipment response)
   B. Description of input/output data format and method used for validation of input data
   C. Requirements of equipment necessary to support testing, proof testing of equipment, customer approval, if required, and control of equipment changes
   D. Identification and verification of computer programs used in data reduction

V. *Test and evaluation reports*
   A. Identification of program errors detected and corrective action taken
   B. Identification of problems encountered and proposed, or actual solutions
   C. Discussion of logic modifications considered necessary, along with supporting flowcharts

VI. *Input/output test data*
   A. Conclusion
   B. Recommendations
   C. Proposals

VII. *Library controls*
   A. Different computer software versions are accurately identified and documented
   B. No unauthorized modifications are made to these items
   C. Approved changes are incorporated
   D. Computer software submitted for test are the correct version
   E. Availability of a computer software library to be used for control purposes
   F. Controls over changing software
   G. Controls to ensure physical security of software against unauthorized cases

FIGURE 26-2   continued

VIII. *Work tasking*
    A. Identification, documentation, and issuance of work instructions related to software development
    B. Tools, techniques, and methodologies employed to perform work which will support the quality objective

IX. *Subcontractor controls*
    A. Flow down of contract requirements to subcontractors, as applicable
    B. Methods used in verification or certification of purchased items, including tapes, cards, and complete computer programs

X. *Product verification by inspection*
    A. Witnessing and monitoring end item tests
    B. Witnessing and monitoring of intermediate testing, such as subroutines, when necessary
    C. Verification of software media and format (e.g., cards, tapes, or discs) for compliance with applicable specifications

---

FIGURE 26-2   continued

---

1. List present and future requirements in detail.

2. Survey all packages available for that application.

3. Examine package documentation and user manuals.

5. Check if package has sufficient application parameters.

6. Check for availability of adequate maintenance aids.

7. Draw up list of suitable packages available for application.

8. Try out each package with corporate data, if available and applicable.

9. Determine whether package can link into corporate data base plans, if applicable.

10. Conduct benchmarks (comparison trials) if performance is critical.

11. Allow end users to implement benchmarks on a temporary basis, if end user interface is critical.

12. Negotiate and write an appropriate contract.

FIGURE 26-3   Preparation for Software Procurement[1]

1. Packages do not fully adapt to changes in requirements.

2. Packages require modification when installed, and subsequent maintenance becomes as expensive as current in-house application.

3. Maintenance becomes expensive, at a later date, when hardware, operation system, terminals, network, or user requirements change.

4. Packages are hard to maintain due to poor documents, no provision for user-created codes, poor structure, absence of source code, excessive complexity, low-level language, and poor quality coding.

5. They are difficult to maintain due to in-house modifications that are ill-documented and difficult for others to understand.

6. Packages do not fit with corporate data base implementations and strategy.

7. Software supplier ceases operation.

FIGURE 26-4   Software Application Problems

REFERENCES

1. Orkin, F. I. "Computer and Quality," *Juran's Quality Control Handbook* (4th ed). New York: McGraw Hill, 1988, Chapter 27.

2. Cohen, P. H., & Sikennany, M. R. "Evaluation Program of the C.M.M." *Quality Progress.* Milwaukee, WI: ASQC, January 1988, p. 59.

3. Daughtry, Taze. *The Search for Software Quality.* Milwaukee, WI: Quality Progress, ASQC, November 1988, p. 29.

4. Espiella, G. *Selecting SQC/SPC Software.* Milwaukee, WI: Quality Progress, ASQC, March 1987, p. 28.

5. *Defense Supply Agency Manual (DSAM 8200, Sec. IX), Quality Assurance for Computer Software,* April 1985. Cameron Station, Alexandria, VA.

CHAPTER TWENTY-SEVEN

Quality Level Measurements

INTRODUCTION

This chapter presents an overview of the design and use of inspection/test and process data for the evaluation of product quality levels. A number of statistical techniques are illustrated. The concept of statistical process control is discussed and examples of its use are cited. A discussion of the more common sampling plans is also presented.

While there are a large variety of statistical methods available to determine product and process quality, it is not always necessary to use them. Frequently, simple methods of analysis, provide suitable measurements. Chapter 20 described a number of these methods and their uses.

This chapter will present a number of statistical techniques in current use. The literature provides references to many sources of these and other techniques for use in a variety of conditions. As suggested in Chapter 20, the simplest techniques that will do the job should be used. More complex statistical methods, while valuable for specific functions, when used for simple process and product evaluations may often lead to misinterpretations. These often fail to provide the desired results, that is, communicate the evaluation results to the proper level of management who can initiate the appropriate corrective actions.

To obtain adequate management reaction, it is important that they are aware of the concepts utilized and their terminology. Some companies provide introductory courses in statistics to management personnel. These courses are designed to provide an overview of the statistical techniques utilized by the organization. It is not necessary, however to provide many details of the techniques, including their derivations or the mathematics involved in their development. When formal courses in statistics are not provided to management personnel, it is important that inspection/quality engineers who prepare reports provide sufficient information which thoroughly explains the basis and limitations of the evaluation results. The language of the reports should be keyed to the recipients' level of understanding. The use of jargon should be avoided. When performing measurements and statistical analyses, it is important to remember the corporate goals relative to inspection/quality control and product quality improvement. Once the company's goals are defined, each department should prepare individual goals, which if properly attained, will contribute to the realization of the corporate goal. All goals should specify the period of time for their accomplishment and the methods to be used for their measurement.

For example, the goal for the manufacturing department could require that the quality level of its products are to improve from a process average of 5.0 percent to that of 2.5 percent within a 12-month period. Evaluations of the process average should be made in, perhaps, quarterly increments to determine whether the goals are being attained. When the results of these evaluations show that they may not be reached, a review of the process should be done to identify impediments. Corrective action should then be initiated. When investigation reveals that the action taken will not significantly correct the condition, it may be necessary to revise the goal to a more attainable measure.

A company who wishes to provide products and services of world class quality may find that its goals should be based on the quality levels attained by leaders in the field, and predicate its goals on bettering the world leaders' quality levels. To attain world class quality levels, it is important that the product improvement program is management driven. In addition, each employee of the company should become part of the total effort for product improvement.

APPLICATION OF STATISTICAL TECHNIQUES

This section discusses some common statistical techniques utilized by many companies in measuring their product and process quality levels. Details about these techniques and other statistical methods are available in the literature. The object of this chapter is to merely point out some of the available techniques and their uses.

Concept of Variation

All products and processes are subject to variation. This concept is prevalent in all of nature as well. No two snowflakes are exactly alike. Each section of the human body differs from its corresponding section. Each individual exhibits differences in physical, mental, and social attributes.

Variations can be divided into two types. Random or common variations are those built into the process. Changes in these variations, generally require a revision to the basic elements of the process. However, more recent thinking questions whether this concept is entirely correct. Some professionals believe that a number of the common causes may be resolved by operational personnel.

Nonrandom variations are not natural and not inherent to the process. These are caused by unpredictable or erratic conditions and are usually referred to as assignable or special causes. They can be recognized and are generally correctable by the operational elements of the organization.

Variations may exist within the part itself, among parts produced during the same period, and among parts produced at different periods. Many factors contribute to these variations, for example, machine vibration, faulty tools, loose bearings, careless operators, and weather conditions.

It is important that the distinction be made between the two types of variations, in order to correct those conditions which are considered assignable or special, and designate for management action those which are random and common.

Definitions

Here are a number of terms customarily used during the application of statistical techniques.

SAMPLE: A limited number of measurements taken from a larger source, such as the population.

CENTRAL TENDENCY: The arithmetic mean used for symmetrical distributions or for distributions which lack a dominant single peak; used as measure in quality. The mean may be calculated by adding the values of all the observations and dividing the result by the number of observations. In the control chart, this is called the X-bar. It may also be calculated by multiplying the frequency of the readings within a cell by the values in the cell, adding the results and dividing by the number of observations.

THE MEDIAN: The middle value when the values are arranged according to size. It is used for reducing the effect of extreme data values which can be ranked but are not economically measurable, such as shades of color, visual appearance, and odors. The median is the horizontal scale value of the percentile graph where the curve reaches the height of 50 percent.

MODE: The value which occurs the most often in data. It is used for severely skewed distributions, describing an irregular situation where two peaks are found or for eliminating effects of extreme values.

MEASURES OF DISPERSION: The data scattered around the central tendency, or mean value. The extent of the scatter is called the dispersion or variation. It is the second most fundamental measure in statistical analysis.

RANGE: The difference between the maximum and minimum value in the data. For a series of observations the range can be used to determine the estimate of the standard deviation. It is the simplest statistic to calculate.

STANDARD DEVIATION (SIGMA): The most important measure of variation. It is the root mean square deviation from the average, of a series of values, divided by the number of values. It can also be calculated by adding the frequencies of each cell, multiplying the sum by the square root of the values for each cell, dividing this value by the number of values, subtracting the result from the average squared, then taking the square root of the result.

COVARIANCE: The expected value of the product of the deviations of two random variables from their respective means. Used to give information on the relationship of observations of characteristics X and Y.

STATISTICAL QUALITY CONTROL (SQC): Statistical quality control, as discussed in this chapter, deals with the collection, tabulation, and evaluation of data utilized in operational activities. The evaluation is performed using statistical control charts. When a state of control has been established, any elements in the control chart which appear outside the limits can be analyzed by operational and inspection/quality personnel or by corrective action committees. They can also examine a series of runs of consecutive points on the same side of the average value. These analyses will determine whether the correction of out-of-control points are within the jurisdiction of these organizations, or must be referred to the appropriate management team.

STATISTICAL PROCESS CONTROL (SPC): Statistical process control, as discussed in this chapter, is the review of the processes and products which require management investigation and correction to meet customers' or engineering requirements. The techniques of SQC are usually applied to improve the quality of the process or product to meet the competitive world market standards.

PROBABILITY: The ratio of the number of outcomes in an exhaustive set of equally likely outcomes that produce a given event to the total number of possible outcomes. The chance that a given event will occur. It is important to understand the laws of probability since the development of sampling plans and control charts are governed by them.

INDEPENDENCE: The outcome of each event has no effect on the outcome of any other event.

PERMUTATIONS: The number of ways to arrange a set of objects. For example, three books can be arranged in six different permutations.

COMBINATIONS: The number of ways a set of objects can be arranged without regard to the order. The three books in the previous definition can be arranged in only one combination.

Probability Laws

Addition law

This is used when the event can occur in different ways. The probability that an event will occur is calculated by adding the probabilities of occurrence of the possible ways. For example, in a game of dice, the probability of winning on the first toss is calculated by adding the probability of tossing either a seven ($\frac{1}{6}$ or 0.167) or an eleven ($\frac{1}{18}$ or 0.056), which equals the sum of both probabilities ($0.167 + 0.056 = 0.223$).

Multiplication law

This is the probability that events will occur simultaneously or in succession. It is the product of the probabilities of the several events. For example, a box contains 10 balls; four are black and 6 are white. If a person selects two balls from the box at random, the probability of selecting a black ball is $\frac{4}{10}$. If this happens, there will only be nine balls left in the box. Thus, in accordance with this law, the probability of selecting a white ball after the black is $\frac{4}{10} \times \frac{6}{9} = \frac{24}{90}$.

Types of Data

Discrete data varies in steps. For example, the number of defects on a painted surface, or the number of personnel absent during a shift. *Continuous* data can take any potential value within a given range. Owing to the limitations of measurements, this data are often reflected in steps but have the potentiality of narrowing the elements until they become a continuous line. The intervals between the values depend upon the accuracy of the measuring system. For example, when measured with a gage, the length of a shaft may result in a value of 1.250. When measured with a gage of a higher degree of accuracy, the shaft length may result in a value of 1.2496. This difference in the values is due to the accuracy of the measuring equipment and not to the data itself.

STATISTICAL QUALITY CONTROL

Process and product data are available in the organization in great quantities. In order to utilize it for statistical evaluation, it is necessary that it is collected and classified in a reasonable and measurable manner. Statistical techniques provide a number of methods for grouping this data so that it can be visually reviewed and analyzed.

Planning

Before data collection, it is advisable to determine the type of data needed and the method of collection. Some of the considerations are as follows:

- Use of variables or attributes (go-no-go) data. Variables data is more useful than attributes, but more expensive to collect

- Definition of requirements for preserving the order of measurements

- Determination of the requirements for collecting data in groups

- Definition of the methods for data analysis and assumptions needed

- Determination of the suitability for the application of computer programs, when available

Data Collection

- Data should be selected in a random manner.

- Data and all conditions present should be recorded.

- Sample data should be examined to assure that the process shows sufficient testability to make predictions valid for the future.

Some companies have developed computer systems for data collection using bar codes, inputting all levels of the manufacturing process, from receiving inspection to final end item assembly inspection and unit test. All defects are recorded on a computerized information system by operators and inspectors using bar code wands. Data are reviewed daily, weekly, or monthly and fed back to corrective action and quality improvement teams.

Data Tabulation

Various methods of data tabulation are used. These include the use of tally sheets, and grouped tabulations. This data may then be incorporated into various frequency distribution charts, such as bar and line frequency histograms and frequency polygons; Pareto charts; indices; graphs; and distribution curves, such as probability, hypergeometric, binomial, poisson, and normal.

Frequency histograms

Scanning the raw data will usually not give any meaningful information. But grouping the measurements by like dimensions, and recording the frequency of these observations in each group or cell, results in a frequency distribution. This can be converted into a frequency distribution curve. These are grouped frequencies of a set of observations. They are arrangements showing the frequency of occurrences of the value in ordered class. The interval along the scale of measurement is termed a *cell*. The *frequency* for any cell is the number of observations in that cell. The *relative frequency* for any cell is the frequency of that cell divided by the total number of observations. The rough working rule is to aim for 15 to 20 cells. Cell boundaries should be halfway between two possible observations, and the intervals should be equal.

Frequency distributions

The data may be plotted with the frequency of occurrences posted on the vertical axis and a quality characteristic such as inches, feet, or volts plotted on the horizontal scale.

Cumulative frequency distributions

At times, it is advantageous to tabulate the frequencies of values less or greater than the respective cell boundaries. This may be presented graphically. Plotting the curve on a probability scale tends to smooth the curve to something like a straight line.

Hypergeometric distributions

This distribution is required whenever a sample is drawn from a finite lot. This is based on the consideration of the ratio of the sample n to the population size N. When the problem involves the partial exhaustion of the lot so that the samples, once drawn, are not returned to the lot, resulting in the probability of the event not being constant, recourse must be made to the hypergeometric probability law. There are tables of the hypergeometrical function called the cumulative distribution table, from which these values can be obtained without needing to go through a maze of calculations.

An example of the use of this distribution is the calculation of the probability of the number of rejects in a sample of 5, assuming that the average fractional defective is 0.06. The problem can be solved by using the multiplication and addition theorems of the probability law. These values can also be determined through the use of the binomial theorem, if it can be assumed that the exhaustion of the lot has small effect on the $p = 0.06$ reject rate. These calculations are often burdensome, but hypergeometric and binomial tables are available.

Fortunately, there is little change in probability from one draw to the next due to partial exhaustion of the lot when it is large compared to the sample size. Thus in most calculations, it can be assumed that the sample is taken from an infinite population and a simpler form of calculation known as the binomial distribution can be used.

Binomial Distribution

This is used when the probability of occurrences of an event can be assumed to be constant. The rule is that one can assume the probability of an infinite lot when the sample size is less than one-tenth the lot size.

The binomial distribution is used to calculate the percent or the number of defectives that can be expected. The solution of these problems involves the use of the laws of probability as depicted in the binomial distribution. When there are many values to be calculated, a large number of mathematical calculations may be needed. Since the binomial is a frequency distribution, it has an average and standard deviation. Calculations result from the fact that the average of the binomial distribution is p bar, and the standard deviation is equal to the square root of p bar times $(1 - p$ bar)/ sample size. Thus, if a sample of 5 were drawn from a lot with 6 percent defective, we can calculate that the average of the frequency distribution is 0.06 and the standard deviation is the square root of 0.06 times $(1 - 0.06)$ divided by 5.

The binomial probability distribution is used for the development of sampling plans for attributes inspection. For small lots, the hypergeometric distribution is used. See the "sampling" section later in this chapter. When tables or curves of the hypergeometric and binomial distributions are available, it is simple to solve these problems. When they are not available, the difficulty in their use depends upon the number of terms to be calculated.

Poisson distribution

Calculations involving hypergeometric and binomial distributions, are often burdensome, particularly if many terms are involved, and n is large. However, another frequency distribution is available which provides these calculations and can approximate any term of the binomial. This approximation is called the Poisson law of distribution. The larger the value of n (sample size), and the smaller the value of p (fraction defective), the closer is the value of the Poisson to the binomial distribution. The Molina graph provides summations of the individual Poisson terms.

The Poisson may be used in its own right when there is a small probability of occurrences, with each unit having many opportunities of occurring but being extremely unlikely to occur at any given opportunity. Examples of the Poisson is the number of calls from a group of telephones or the number of imperfections in a large painted surface. The use of the Molina table is a great time-saver by providing approximate answers rapidly, which is good enough in normal industrial practices. The larger the n, and the smaller the p, the closer the approximation to the true probability.

In the use of the binomial distribution, a sample of a definite size is taken and the number of defective items determined. In the Poisson, the number of defects in a unit is determined. There is no sample size.

NORMAL CURVE

The normal curve is the approximation of the binomial and the Poisson distributions. Most of the calculations revolve around a type of frequency distribution termed a normal, bell, or Gaussian curve. When the standard deviation (sigma) is computed for a normal curve, approximately 68 percent of all the readings in the distribution will occur between plus and minus one standard deviation from the mean, 95 percent between plus and minus two standard deviations, and 99.73 percent of the values between plus and minus three standard deviations from the mean. This concept enables the prediction of the percentage of values between two different values. One may also use an existing table of the areas under the curve.

Pareto Charts

This chart is used to determine priorities and sort out the vital few from the trivial many. The focus is to identify significant areas for improvement or problem resolution. This chart is based on the concept that the greatest number of actions and events are the results of a relatively small number of causes.

STATISTICAL QUALITY CONTROL

Many useful actions are related to future production rather than completed lots. Frequency distributions and control charts reveal the patterns of variation of the production process from which the samples were taken. To draw conclusions about an unknown universe, it is necessary to rely upon the numerical values derived from samples drawn from the universe. These values generally include the sample mean and variance. Thus, if a variable has some quality characteristic such as a dimension, the universe may be thought of as a potentially unlimited output of the manufacturing process in question, or the universe may be considered as a particular lot of manufactured products from which samples have been taken.

Normal Curves

The graphs for X-bar and R, with limits calculated to predict areas under the normal curve, can be developed.

The process may be described by two characteristics, its central line or mean, and its dispersion or spread around the mean. After the control limit displays a condition of statistical control, the average of the population can be estimated by calculating the average of several samples. The spread of the population may be estimated from some measure of the ranges from the samples.

The averages of a series of samples form a distribution which is smaller in spread than the distributions of individual values. This distribution is approximately normal even when the distribution of the entire population is not normal. Thus a process can be monitored by graphing the average and the variation of samples over a period of time, as reflected by the X-bar and R chart. The control limits of both charts can be estimated by calculating the average of the X-bars and the average range. Methods are provided to determine the control limits for individual values to determine the relation of the controlled process to the specification tolerance limits.

Control Charts

The control chart (Figure 27-1) is a method of monitoring and analyzing the quality of the output of a process through sample measurements of selected characteristics. A control chart is a chronological graphical comparison of actual product characteristics with limits, which reflect the ability to produce characteristics as shown by past experience. It is used to identify and separate the usual from the special or unusual variations. Control charts tell when to leave the process alone, or when to take some kind of action. They assess the process to determine if it is statistically stable, and if it is capable of meeting specification requirements. The stability of the process must first be established in order to determine its capability.

Many problems can be corrected by operational personnel. A number of the problems, however, can only be solved by management. These are described as system flaws in which the system encompasses all the sources of variations including those caused by machines, measurements, environment, and/or operational elements.

Random or common causes are discussed in a later section entitled "Statistical Process Control."

Since any method of measurement will have its own inherent variability, information given by control charts is always influenced by variations in measurement. It is also important that notes are made about any unusual occurrences during production which might provide help in the investigation of assignable causes of variation.

Planning for Use

Before the control charts are initiated, a decision should be made about which production or inspection stations, and which quality characteristics are to be considered. In addition, a determination should be made about the selection of the subgroups, the control charts' limits, and the type of charts (that is, variables or attributes).

Use of Variables Control Charts (X-Bar, R)

This type of control chart can be used when the actual values of the characteristics are measured. This chart generally requires the plotting of many characteristics, as opposed to merely one for each item on the attributes charts. It is thus necessary to decide which characteristics and operations should be under control chart study and why. In addition, the following elements should be determined.

- Sample size

- Frequency of sample selection and inspection

- Personnel who should measure and report results (for example, operator or inspector)

AVERAGES

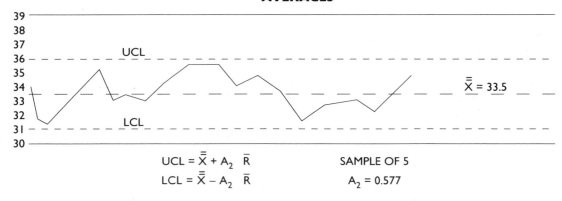

$$UCL = \bar{\bar{X}} + A_2 \bar{R}$$
$$LCL = \bar{\bar{X}} - A_2 \bar{R}$$

SAMPLE OF 5

$A_2 = 0.577$

RANGES

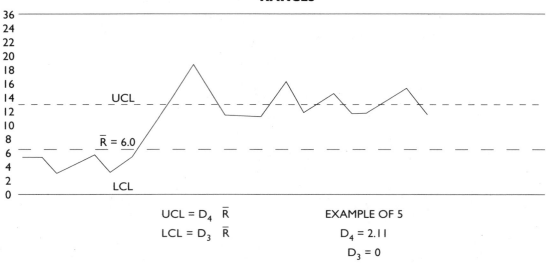

$$UCL = D_4 \bar{R}$$
$$LCL = D_3 \bar{R}$$

EXAMPLE OF 5

$D_4 = 2.11$

$D_3 = 0$

FIGURE 27-1   Control Charts

- Method of measurement
- Number of samples taken before the control chart is analyzed and interpreted and any action taken

Establishing subgroups is important. It is usually done in the order of production. At times, however, this may not be an adequate basis for subgrouping. For example, charts of two machines will not determine the differences in their outputs. Thus different subgroups may be needed, such as the output by machines, by spindles, cavities in a mold, operators, inspectors, and shifts. The breakdown is a matter of judgment based upon the difficulty to meet tolerances, known assignable causes of variation, and the ability to investigate and correct in an economical manner.

Starting the control charts

The following steps are completed.

1. Raw data are recorded on tally sheets or frequency histograms.
2. Subgroup characteristics are calculated.
3. Average value of the statistics (average and range) are calculated.
4. Trial control limits for the average and range are calculated.
5. Points and control limits are plotted on the charts.

These initial control limits are appropriate for the analysis of past data. They may need modification before being utilized for subsequent production. Points of current production for 16 to 25 subgroups or more are first plotted. Any points outside of the trial control limits on both charts are removed and the X-bar and R averages and their control limits are recalculated.

Continuing the control chart

Then, the following steps are done.

1. Revised standard values of the control chart are selected.
2. Points are plotted on the charts.
3. New control limits are calculated.
4. Any evidence of lack of control is determined.
5. Conditions responsible for any out-of-control points are investigated and corrected, when under the jurisdiction of the operational personnel.
6. After correction of the above conditions, standard values (X-bar and R) are reviewed and revised as necessary, and new control limits are calculated.

Reports and action based on the control charts

1. Action is taken to bring the process into control at satisfactory levels.
2. Specifications are reviewed in relation to an adequate control of the production processes and capabilities, and information is provided to management regarding quality levels.

Choice of variables inspection control charts

The process must be something which can be quantitatively measured. If, however, acceptance is on a sampling basis and characteristics can be tested as a variable, the charts can be used to reduce inspection costs. A variables control chart for measurements based on five test results per sample is as powerful as an attribute chart based on 50 test results.

Attributes Charts

X-bar and R charts may be applied to any quality characteristic that is measurable. When this condition does not exist, recourse must be made to the use of any of the following charts for attributes.

P charts

P charts, for fraction defectives, may be applied to the results of any inspection that accepts or rejects individual items. The p charts as applied to lot-by-lot or 100 percent inspection are generally used to discover the following:

1. Average proportion of nonconforming articles.

2. Out-of-control low spots that indicate relaxed or inadequate inspection standards, or erratic causes for quality improvement which may be converted to constant improvement.

3. Out-of-control high spots for attention and corrective action.

4. Suggested places for X-bar and R charts, when 100 percent inspection is not being performed.

5. Whether successive lots may be considered representative of the process. This may influence the severity of inspection.

When it is appropriate to count the total number of nonconformities in each article or group of articles, it may be useful to use a control chart technique based on the Poisson. This is the c or u chart.

C charts

C charts, for number of defectives in single units, have more restrictions. The subgroups size must be constant in the sense that the different subgroups have equal opportunities for nonconformances to occur.

The c chart can be used for the approximation of control limits involving binomial calculations. Tables for the Poisson distribution are available which provide ease of calculations and which can be used for quick determinations. C charts are often used for analysis of clerical errors and industrial accidents.

The c chart is the same as the chart for u. It is useful when the number of nonconformities possible on a unit is large but the percentage of a single nonconformity is small. For example, the number of surface irregularities on a painted sheet.

U charts

U charts, for nonconformances per unit, are used when the opportunity for occasional change from subgroup to subgroup exists. These charts may also be used when several nonconformities occur in a single unit.

NP charts

The np chart applies to the number of rejected items in subgroups of constant size. This is a direct count of the number of nonconforming items in a subgroup.

INTERPRETATION OF CONTROL CHARTS

Most quality experts agree that about 85 percent of all problems in business are due to common causes and can be corrected only by management action. The other 15 percent are due to special causes and may be corrected by the personnel immediately involved in the process, such as the operator, production supervisor, or setup personnel. Control charts can help provide a clue to the possible causes of the problem, such as the pattern of the distribution, its trend, shift in process average, repetitive cycle, and changes in population.

The use of control charts enables a judgment as to whether or not a constant system exists in the process, or if chance causes are present. If a chance cause does exist, a hunt for assignable causes is initiated. At times, it may be economically justifiable to leave the process alone. The use of the control charts and follow-up actions should be mandated by the needs of the process to meet specification requirements and the economical justification for investigation.

Normal Charts

When quality characteristics and processes are under statistical control, it can be inferred, unless the process has changed, that within the designated confidence limits, future production will result in these characteristics remaining within the indicated values. By finding the area under the normal curve, the percentage of product with the indicated values and within the control limits can be determined.

This statement of statistical control makes no inference about the ability of the process to meet the product tolerance, unless the specification tolerance limits are within the statistical control limits.

It has also been shown that, even when the process does not operate as a normal distribution, control charts of averages of groups of measurements will also act as if they came from a normal population, and hence the same inferences can be made.

When the control chart reflects that the process is under statistical control, it represents the capabilities of the operation. Thus, as long as the process exhibits control, the operator can do no better than to continue producing parts with the amount of variation contained within the statistical control limits. This understanding, if properly applied, will reduce the frequency of adjustments to the process which, in the past, had been performed when the operator incorrectly believed that the process was going to produce nonconformances. However, conditions such as tool wear may in time affect the distribution's central line, or the spread of the measurement values may be affected by conditions of the tool.

Sample Size and Frequency Distribution

The larger the sample size, the less spread among averages and standard deviations, even when drawn from the same lot. Calculating the average and standard deviation from the total population provides what is called the *true average* and standard deviation.

The standard deviation of the sample equals the true standard deviation divided by the square root of two times the sample size. Therefore, when a frequency distribution is truly normal, that for the spread of averages is also normal. The distribution of the standard deviations of the averages is not normal, but approaches normalcy as the sample size becomes larger. Use in industry of sample sizes of 50 to 100 will provide good approximations of standard deviations.

The control limits define the amount of variation due solely to chance. If the process is operating within these limits, it is considered stable and predictable. Also these limits represent the best that the process can do. If this is not satisfactory, a change to the basic system may be required. For example, the type of machine, tool, or the part design may have to be changed.

The control limits are calculated from the process data and have no relation to the product specification. Once statistical control has been established, the capability of the process to meet specifications can be evaluated.

Assignable causes are usually indicated by points outside the control charts limits. These limits are generally set at three sigma points. At times, to insure stricter control, limits may be set at less than the three sigma points. Whatever the decision, which is generally based on the economics of the situation, assignable causes are indicated by any points falling outside of these control limits. *Out of control* means that assignable causes of variation are present. Even when all points are within the limits, lack of control may be indicated by the rule of extreme runs. For example, 7 consecutive points on one side of the central line, 10 out of 11 consecutive points, 12 out of 14, 14 out of 17, 16 out of 20, and so on, indicate the presence of assignable causes.

In some manufacturing processes, even occasional out-of-control points indicate that assignable causes may not be the basis for action. These conditions lead to the assignment of special rules governing the basis for action. A rule, for example, may be set that consideration for investigation and corrective actions is made when more than one point out of 35, or two points out of 100, are outside the limits.

INVESTIGATION OF OUT-OF-CONTROL POINTS

When points on the control chart indicate the presence of assignable causes and the decision has been made to investigate these conditions, corrective actions are taken by the designated operational personnel. When assigned, an adjustment or replacement of the tool may be made by the operator or setup personnel. More frequently, the matter is assigned to an interdepartmental corrective action committee for review. Possible causes for the out-of-control conditions are discussed. Assignments may then be given to the appropriate committee members for further investigation and corrective actions. After implementation, the committee maintains a close review of the applicable control charts to determine whether the condition has been corrected during the processing of subsequent production quantities.

When the actions taken do not correct the condition, the matter is generally referred to a higher level of management for review. Similarly, when the control chart denotes the product's failure to meet the required specifications and the process cannot be adjusted, the matter is also referred to the next level of management for consideration. Management actions are described in the section entitled "Statistical Process Control."

It must be noted that lack of control may occur because universes may differ by average only dispersion only or both average and dispersion.

Shifts in Averages

Shifts in the universe average may be sustained over a period of time. They may be frequent or irregular, gradual or systematic. In these cases, the chart is of great value to the machine setter. Unless the changes in the universe average takes place within the subgroup, the R chart will show control.

Sustained shifts occurring after the control limits have been established, may result in all out-of-control points falling outside one control limit and all suspicious runs upon the same side of the curve. But if shifts occur during the establishment of the limits, the evidence of lack of control shifts from one side of the line to the other, at the time of shift of the process average. In this case, no R charts are necessary.

Shifts in Dispersion

The importance of the R chart depends upon the type of production process. Many tend to have a relatively uniform dispersion even though the process centering changes from time to time. In such processes, lack of statistical control will be detected in the X-bar chart, and the R chart adds relatively little useful information. In general, variability of the dispersion shown on an R chart is particularly evident when the operator's skill is involved.

Usually, the first step in improving the process is to try to bring the dispersion under statistical control. On an automatic machine, the process is usually uniform at least for a short time. Correction for tool wear and setter's adjustment can be controlled easily, but not the basic variability of the machine.

In a hand-operated job, the condition is different. While an X-bar chart is useful in controlling the setter's operation, the main source of error is likely to be the operator. These errors are usually of random nature, reflecting odd erratic performance of all kinds due to the lack of concentration or lack of skill. Such errors will result in an increase in the variability of the process and will be detected by the large ranges of the samples taken during the period of poor workmanship. Thus the range chart should be regarded as the operator's personal chart.

Shifts in Both Average and Dispersion

Changes in both averages and dispersion will be reflected in both X-bar and R charts.

Failures in Process Control

There are many reasons for past failures in the implementation of process control.

1. Lack of management commitment, understanding, and participation

2. Tendency to use the charts by themselves and not follow up on the out-of-control points for corrective action

3. Lack of participation by all functions of the organization

4. Inadequate training and understanding before starting process control

Precontrol

Precontrol gives the operator direct control of the process. The tolerance band is divided into three zones, a target zone and two cautionary zones close to each specification limit. The worker measures a pair of individual values periodically. If both fall into the cautionary zones or either falls outside the tolerance, the operator adjusts the process immediately. Otherwise, the process is left alone. The subgroups of the two do not attempt to estimate the distribution parameters, but only sense whether the distribution is safely within the tolerance, or has either moved toward a tolerance limit or grown wider than the tolerance limits. This rapid warning allows the operator to make adjustments before nonconforming work is produced. Precontrol requires no calculations or charting.

Software for SQC

Mini and personal computers are available for the statistical analysis of all kinds of data, including those used for control chart preparation. The software can provide calculations of the sample parameters and control limits. Most software can also provide summaries and analyses of raw data, out-of-specification values, histograms, checks for runs within control limits, tests for normality, process capability calculations, Pareto analyses, trend analyses, and the like.

See Chapter 26 for additional information about the use of computers in inspection/quality control operations.

STATISTICAL PROCESS CONTROL

Introduction

SPC techniques are implemented when management action is needed to correct or improve the product or process. These techniques are utilized when

1. The problem is referred by the operational corrective action committee for evaluation and correction of out-of-control conditions as indicated on the statistical control charts, which cannot be resolved by the committee.

2. The process does not exhibit the ability to meet customer or engineering requirements, and cannot be adjusted by operational elements.

3. It is intended to improve the quality of the process and/or product over its existing capabilities.

The investigation of these conditions is conducted by upper level management operating as a function of the company management's quality steering committee.

Committee Review

When the matter has been referred by the operational committee, or when it has been decided to improve the quality of the product or process, the quality steering committee meets to discuss the problem. It decides whether to continue to review the condition, based upon the need for action and the possible economical impact of the resulting decision. At the initial discussion of the problem, a preliminary determination is made concerning the possible changes needed in tooling, process improvements, personnel, organizational structure, and the like.

When the decision is rendered to undertake the investigation, a proposed program budget is prepared. This program includes an estimate of the steps for the investigation and the anticipated costs for their implementation, in addition to the anticipated costs for the correction of the problem.

After receipt of the preliminary cost approval from the company's executive committee, any subsequent significant cost changes should be approved before further action is taken.

Method of Review and Investigation

The committee should review all available data provided by the operational corrective action committee. These usually include copies of the statistical control charts of the applicable process or product, the results of any investigations performed by the corrective action committees, and their recommendations and suggestions.

A flowchart of the process is prepared, depicting all operations and functions performed, starting with the marketing and contract operations, and continuing through the engineering, manufacturing, inspection/quality control, field service and any other elements pertinent to the problem. Details of each process should be presented in the chart including all the possible inputs and outputs of each station.

At times, it may be desirable to develop a cause-and-effect or fish-bone diagram. This presents the categories of all possible contributing factors, such as materials, methods, machines, and personnel, and their effects on the process.

After studying the statistical control and process flowcharts, and the cause-and-effect diagram, a brainstorming session is usually held and each element presented is discussed, recorded, and reviewed by the participants. In many organizations, a Pareto chart is prepared to help establish priorities for the investigation.

STATISTICAL TECHNIQUES

Many techniques described in the literature can be used to investigate the elements of the process. Short descriptions of a number of these techniques are provided in the following sections.

Statistical Inference

The significance of the data resulting must be determined. Whether the values could have occurred by chance alone, or due to some specific reason must be decided. To make this meaningful, the statistician attaches a probability factor that an outcome will occur due to chance. This concept is called the *significance of the value,* at the specified level of probability. For example, the control chart techniques establish that any points outside of the six standard control limits will occur, by chance, less than 0.3 percent of the time. Thus, it may be inferred that any outside points have occurred due to some assignable cause at the 99.7 percent confidence level.

Errors of Two Kinds

This statistical hypothesis tests the validity of the assertion, and is carried out by the analysis of a data sample. It is important to realize that the values reached may have one of two kinds of errors: (1) The hypothesis can be rejected when it is true, at the specified level of significance. This is called the type I error, and usually denoted by the symbol α; (2) The hypothesis may be accepted when it is false, called the type II error, and denoted by the symbol β.

In statistical experiments, the Null Hypothesis H_0 is used. This concept asserts that the observed results are due to chance or coincidence and that the results of the analysis prove nothing. The experiment is performed to produce evidence that is so strong as to refute H_0.

Probability tables are used in significance testing that are usually computed at 5 percent and 1 percent levels. Significance levels are not used by themselves to make decisions. They merely serve to act as measures of the strength of the evidence and must be used with other information, such as the cost of making an error, or the cost of obtaining additional data.

Process Capability

In order to improve it, the calculation of the capability of the current process to produce products at specified levels of quality must be determined. When the process is in statistical control, the process capability C_p is six times the standard deviation. When statistical control is not evident, it is necessary to calculate the capability ratio C_{pk}. This is the tolerance width over the process capability ratio. Thus an acceptable process capability is one which is of the order of two-thirds to three-fourths of the tolerance or less.

Process Capability Measurement

Process capability refers to the variation in a process about some target value. This can be calculated using two types of techniques: (1) Those that measure the present process performance; what the process is doing; and (2) those that estimate the inherent process capability; what the process can do under certain conditions.

If the process is under statistical control, the measure of the process performance results in determining its capability. This measurement is made through the use of frequency distributions, probability paper, histograms, plots of individual measurements, or attribute data analysis.

A quick measurement of process capability is to take ten measurements and calculate the range. The process capability is then defined as six times the standard deviation and calculated as twice the range of the sample.

In many applications, the results of a process capability study are used to determine which process or machine is to be used to produce products within specific tolerance limits. The production engineering department prepares and retains a list of the capabilities of each process and tool used in the company. It is used to assign tools to manufacturing operations. Those processes or tools with lower capability indices are retained for the production of less accurate products or are scheduled for repair or replacement, as necessary. In addition, there are many other uses for the capability index. Some of those include the following:

- Choice among alternate processes or tooling

- Evaluation of machine setup

- Establishment of control limits

- Selection of workers

- Determination of the economic capabilities of the process for testing data significance

- Determination of the desirability of process and product improvement efforts

Test for Significance

There are various statistical techniques which can be used for testing the significance of data. Some of these techniques are described in the following sections.

Student's *T* Test

This method is used to test whether an observed mean differs significantly from some assumed value, or to test whether two observed means differ significantly from each other.

Student worked on the assumption of a normal population with mean μ and variance σ^2. When a sample of n measurements is taken, its mean is calculated as $\overline{X}$ and the sample standard deviation as s. The fraction $\frac{\overline{X} - \sigma^2}{s}$ is denoted by t. The test is called the t test. With a standard value of μ and an observed mean of $\overline{X}$, based on a sample of observations, it may be determined whether the difference of $\overline{X} - \mu$ might be due to change (say at the 5 percent level), or whether it should be regarded as evidence that the population mean is different from the standard value. This test may also be used in testing the difference between two means. Thus, for example, to test the differences in the average values of some product characteristics procured from one supplier with those procured from another, the $\overline{X}$s for each product can be calculated. If the two products are equal, the expected value of $\overline{X}_1 - \overline{X}_2$ is zero. If, on the other hand, the product characteristics from one supplier are different from those of the other, the average of the one would be greater than that of the other. These differences can be tested for significance, using the student's t test. If it turns out that the difference is significant, the null hypothesis that the products are alike at the stated level of significance can be rejected.

Chi² Test

This test is useful when the data is in the form of actual counts, such as number of defects or number of accidents. Thus the Chi² test tells whether the counts actually observed differ significantly from those expected.

This test may be used when a proposed new method is compared with the standard method, and discrete data are provided. For example, the difference in the number of porous areas on the surface of castings produced by two different heat treatment methods can be determined. The Chi² test may require elaborate calculations. However, charts are available which, for different degrees of significance, can provide the appropriate determination.

F Tests

The F test is used in the analysis of variance technique and is the basis of the design of experiments described in the next section. This test is used in a manner similar to the t test when the number of factors is more than two. Under the previous method of experimentation, separate experiments were needed for each pair of factors. This often required a large number of experiments. The F test can be conducted by comparing the ratios of the estimates of variances from each pair of factors. When the factors are similar, the estimates of the variances from each would be the same thus the ratio of the one variance with the other would be close to one. When the ratio is large, it is expected that the null hypothesis (that there is no difference) would be rejected. Comparing the ratios in an F table will establish the degree of significance for the different factors.

Design of Experiments (DOE)

This method is a way of efficiently planning an investigatory testing program. DOE can be used to optimize the design or process so that the desired results will be attained in production. DOE can also be used to investigate the basic factors or relationships within a design or process. DOE uses a number of methods, including the analysis of variance technique. This method applies the use of the F tests. In addition, the technique also determines the effect of the interactions of the various factors with each other and the degree of significance of these interactions. This method is especially valuable when the effect of each variable is not known or even the types of variables known.

In planning an experiment using the statistical DOE techniques, the following process should be used.

1. Provide a statement of the problem.

2. Choose the factors and levels.

3. Choose the experimental design (full or fractional factorial, block designs, and so on).

4. Perform the experiment.

5. Analyze the data.

6. Prepare the conclusions and recommendations.

The following different types of statistical experimental designs are available:

- Block designs (One factor analyzes main effects)
- Analysis of covariance
- Factorial designs
- Process optimization designs (process control and optimization)

Within each of these designs, there are a number of subdesigns which can be used. For example, the group of factorial designs contains full and fractional factorials, in addition to some other factorials.

Analysis of Variance (ANOVA)

This method is used to break up the total variations observed in an experiment into fractions that can be tied to specific variables. The F test is used as the criterion for significance. It tells whether the contribution to the total variance made by a variable had a significant effect on the results and thus introduced extra variation. This technique identifies the variation in a designed experiment. It names the significant sources of variation, calculates the amount of variability attributable to the source, and measures the effect of the source on the product output, as well as the degree of interaction among two or more factors.

Taguchi Method

This is an adaptation of the ANOVA method based on the assignment of a quality loss function to a product. There is some dispute by a number of statisticians concerning the accuracy of this method, some saying that too little attention is paid to the interaction effect of the factors.

Correlation

This method describes the extent to which one variable can be inferred when another is known. The statistic is called the correlation coefficient r. It can be positive or negative and is always between -1 and $+1$. When $r = 0$, there is no relation between X and Y. Tables are available showing how large r has to be before the null hypothesis can be dismissed. This statistic is usually determined by referring to a simple formula or graph which shows the relationship of one quantity to another. For example, if the information given is that today's price for apples is 45 cents per pound, then the positive relationship existing between cost of apples and quantity can be determined.

Linear Regression

This is another name for curve fitting and is an application of the method of least squares (MLS). The t test can be used to determine whether the slope of the line differs significantly from zero, or an F test used to determine whether adding a quadratic term to an equation leads to a significant reduction in the error variance. This technique starts with a simple estimate of the problem. For example, suppose two concentration measurements of the same salt solution are 7.06 percent and 8.1 percent. It is assumed that the discrepancy only reflects sampling and experimental error. What percent should be reported? MLS provides a better measure than averaging the two test results. It can be shown that if the error of measurements is normally distributed, the most precise estimate is obtained when the factor is chosen so that the sum of the squares for each value is as small as possible.

Linear Programming

This is a method of operations research—a branch of management science which seeks methods for making good choices. Linear programming is often called the simplex or transportation method, because it is useful in transportation problems. However, it may be used in the solution of many other problems such as inventory control, warehousing, and the determination of the optimum mixes of a distillation operation. To operate in a linear programming method, all of the following factors must apply:

1. Several numbers such as w, x, y, and so on, must be selected, so that no number is negative and the sum of all the numbers satisfies some given inequality. For example, the sum of w, x, and y does not exceed T (a total number).

2. There must be one or more additional constraints on various combinations of w, x, and y. For example $(w + x)$ equals or is less than 100, $(2x + y)$ is less than 5, or $(x^2 + 2xy + y^2)$ is less than w.

3. There must be a payoff function. For example, $P = (a_i w + a_2 x + a_3 y + \ldots)$. The object of linear programming is to find w, x, and y so

that they satisfy all the inequalities, and at the same time make P as large as possible. This technique may also be used to determine a second or third best alternative.

This iterative approach of calculation starts with any acceptable solution, arrived at by guessing, solves the inequalities, and then repeats a number of adjusting routines. This eventually leads to the optimum solution. These techniques are not difficult to calculate, but can take a considerable amount of time; however, the factors can be programmed into a computer for solution.

An example of the linear programming technique is in the solution of a transportation problem. Suppose there are three factories at different locations and with specific production capabilities. Material must be delivered to four different stores with varying amounts of the product for each store. The shipping cost from each factory to each store is given. The object is to fulfill all the constraints of cost, factory capabilities, and store requirements in combination so that the cost of shipment is minimized.

Queuing

This is often referred to as the waiting line technique. The typical problem relates to a facility service channel such as a bank teller's window, a telephone switchboard exchange, a toll booth, an airport landing field, or an inspection tool crib. The facilities may have more than one channel and may be adjusted to changes in traffic but generally cannot exceed some fixed value. Customers may arrive at the facility at more or less irregular intervals, enter a service channel, and eventually get served and depart. Customers may depart before getting served. In all queuing problems there is an assumption that one does not want their customers to get too impatient, or have too long a wait.

Game Theory—Monte Carlo Techniques

These are simulation techniques. A computer model is developed, and each component is defined in terms of its distribution and numerical parameters. The relationship between the components and the final result is then expressed in a model equation.

The Monte Carlo technique uses a random number generator to draw values at random intervals from each component distribution and combines them, using the model equation, to obtain a simulated value of the overall result. This process is repeated many times and represents a simulation of what would happen if, for example, many assemblies were randomly made from components having the characteristics described in the model. The simulated assembly dimensions can then be summarized in a histogram or similar form and used to set assembly tolerances or to evaluate previously defined ones.

Introduction

In the past, the use of 100 percent inspection was ineffective when used for most acceptance operations. This concept was based on the fact that 100 percent inspection often provided less than 100 percent accuracy due to inspector fatigue which generally occurred when considerable quantities were examined over a long period of time.

It has been estimated that the inspection accuracy did not usually go beyond 85 percent. In addition, some products, like gunpowder, fuses, and electric light bulbs could not be inspected 100 percent, since the products would be destroyed as a result.

Thus, a more effective method was needed. Initially, some attempts were made to introduce a form of sampling for inspection of products which would be destroyed. These plans were usually employed arbitrarily. For example, one plan called for testing 10 percent of the product without regard to the sample size. Subsequent knowledge about the statistical validity of sampling plans revealed that this type of plan was without any scientific basis, since the plan's effectiveness was based purely on the actual sample size and the acceptance number.

Subsequently, a more scientific basis for sampling was developed and is currently used. This method uses the probability functions as applied by the binomial and Poisson distributions and, on the occasions when the lot being sampled is of finite quantity, the hypergeometric distribution.

In lot-by-lot acceptance sampling, the question is not necessarily the estimation of the lot quality, but what to do with the lot presented for inspection. Dr. Juran describes the two types of sampling plans: (1) sampling to accept or reject a lot, and (2) sampling to determine if the process, which produced the product, was within acceptable limits.[1]

Sampling Plans Risks

Sampling plans are guided by laws of chance. All lot-by-lot plans are certain to pass some defective product, if it exists. The selection of sampling plans requires an economic decision of the risks the user is willing to face, with all things being equal. As mentioned earlier, it is important that the types of risks involved are understood.

The α risk of rejecting a product when it is acceptable by the established criterion, and the β risk of accepting the lot when it is rejectable, are the two types of risks involved when sampling inspection is used. These risks have been scientifically determined and quantified so that they are known when the sampling plans are selected. Plans can be classified in accordance with the risks and the application of them.

The β risk is specified quality level for each lot, in terms of fraction defective or defects per unit. The level has a selected probability of being accepted by the consumer. This level, generally set at 10 percent probability, is known as the *Lot Percent Defective* (p_2) and labeled as the consumer's risk or β.

A specified quality level for each lot such that the sampling plan will accept a stated percentage of submitted lots having this quality level (AQL) is called p_1. This probability, generally set at 0.05 percent, is referred to as the producer's risk or α. The risk of accepting a lot of p_1 quality is $(100 - 0.05)$ or 0.95 percent.

Operating Characteristic Curves (OC)

When selecting a sampling plan, recourse is generally made to the OC curves. These depict, for each sampling plan, the probability of the acceptance of lots which contain the specified quality levels (fraction defectives or defects per unit). As a rule, the user of the plan concentrates attention on one or two points of the curve such as the 95 percent and 10 percent probability lines rather than on the whole curve.

OC Curve of an Ideal Plan

This is represented as a vertical line at the desired p, and would require 100 percent inspection. For example, if the consumer can take a chance of some lots having an unacceptable quality level, say, 2.5 percent defective, 100 percent inspection would be required, and the OC curve would be shown as a vertical line at the 2.5 percent quality level.

The acceptance number c need not be zero, although zero acceptance numbers have some psychological advantage. OC curves of plans with the acceptance number c greater than zero are superior to those with comparable plans with $c = 0$. For desired protection against lots containing some stated percentage of defects, large acceptance numbers involve large sample sizes, with greater ability to discriminate against satisfactory and unsatisfactory lots.

In an example of two OC curves with $n = 100$ and $c = 0$, or $n = 240$ and $c = 2$, all give equal protection to the consumer, but the plan with $c = 0$ gives the producer less protection against the rejection of acceptable lots. Generally speaking, the larger the sample size, the steeper the slope of the OC curve. The degree of discrimination of any sampling plan depends entirely upon the sample size and the acceptance number of the plan.

Randomness

Probability calculations require that the samples are drawn randomly, that is, each item is assumed to have an equal chance of being selected. When it is impracticable to mix the lot, the best that can be done is to select the samples by avoiding any type of bias. For example, if the units are packed in layers, samples are drawn from each layer.

Random digits can be generated rapidly by modern computers. In addition, there are many tables of random numbers available, usually in the appendices of statistical texts.

Stratified Sampling

In many lots, random sampling may be difficult, so stratified sampling is used. The difference between these plans is exhibited in the OC curves. The Statistical Research Group makes the following suggestions when using stratified sampling.

1. When possible, inspection lots should be divided on the basis of factors that are likely to lead to quality variations.

2. Samples should be drawn
    a. in proportion to the size of the sublot.
    b. from all parts of the sublot.
    c. blind.

Sampling Plan Uses

Sampling plans are developed to satisfy different degrees of significance. In most instances, at the time of sampling, the inspector is unaware of the lot's quality level as received. Thus, sampling inspection cannot determine the quality level of each inspected lot. Instead, for each sampling plan used, the inspector can only determine the probability of accepting a lot from a source at the quality levels represented between the 95 percent and 10 percent level of significance of the applicable OC curve. In the long run, however, products inspected from stable, controlled processes, with little or no rejected lots, will be accepted at the designated AQL.

Inspection by Attributes and by Variables

In attributes lot-by-lot inspection, each lot is considered separately. Acceptance or rejection is based on the evidence of one or more samples drawn randomly. A systematic lot-by-lot sampling plan requires two numbers: n (sample size) and c (acceptance number). For some plans such as the military standard MIL-STD-105, the lot size N is also used in the selection of the sampling plan.

For example, the plan may state, "Take a random sample of 13 from a lot of 100. If the sample contains more than zero defects, reject the lot; otherwise accept it."

In variables sampling plans, a measurement is made of specified quality characteristics of each unit of the sample. These measurements are then summarized into a simple statistic (average), and the result compared with an allowable value defined in the plan. A decision is then made whether to accept or reject the lot.

One advantage of using variables plans over attributes sampling plans with the same degree of protection, is the requirement of smaller sample sizes. The more information there is about the product, the greater the risk that can be taken.

The disadvantage of using variables sampling plans is the need for inspectors to record the actual measurement of each characteristic of the sample. In addition, some calculations relative to determine the average of the measured values and their dispersions are required. Variables plans are available based on known distributions with known or unknown standard deviation (sigma).

When there is no basis for estimating the standard deviation, the inspector must begin by using the unknown sigma plans. When many lots are expected from the same production source, it is a good idea to start collecting data to provide a basis for calculating the standard deviation. This usually calls for a control chart for R. If this chart shows statistical control in the dispersion, one can switch to a known sigma plan, which requires smaller sample sizes for the same degree of protection. When a known sigma plan is used it is advisable to maintain control charts for R or sigma to check the assumption that the sigma remains in statistical control.

SAMPLING PLAN IMPLEMENTATION

Single Sampling Plans

Commonly, each product lot is considered separately. Acceptance or rejection is based on the evidence of one or more samples randomly drawn from the lot.

Double Sampling Plans

A smaller sample is taken from the lot, and if it meets some specified requirements, the lot is accepted or rejected. If it meets some other specified requirements, a second sample is taken and acceptance or rejection of the lot is based on the number of defects in both samples.

Multiple Sampling Plans

The implementation is the same as for double sampling only more than two samples are taken.

Choice between Single and Multiple Sampling Plans

This choice depends on the history of the product. If lots have been frequently accepted or rejected in the past, it is cheaper to use double or multiple plans, since the decisions can be made at the first sample, which is smaller than the sample for the equivalent single plan.

The disadvantages of using multiple plans are the administration aspects, since they require keeping more detailed records. Also the problem of random selection of the additional samples is increased.

Average Outgoing Quality Level (AOQL) Plans

AOQL plans provide assurance that the average of accepted quality will be no worse than the indexed AOQL value. These plans are based upon the 100 percent lot inspection after rejection. Often, this is impracticable or inconvenient, as when the producer chooses not to do the screening, or when the customer returns the entire rejected lot, forcing the producer to improve the quality.

Chain Sampling

These plans utilize information over a series of lots. The effectiveness of the plans depends upon the following:

1. Steady production
2. Lot submittal in order of production
3. The use of attribute sampling
4. Confidence that the lots are at the same quality level

These plans, developed by Harold F. Dodge, are called CSP-1. They utilize single sampling by attributes inspection with a small n and $c = 0$. They are useful when inspection is costly, and sample sizes relatively small. Under certain conditions they may also be useful with large samples. The prime disadvantage of chain sampling is that moderate changes in quality are not easily detected.

Continuous Plan

When it is not possible to segregate individual lots for sampling inspection, as in conveyerized inspection, the Dodge continuous sampling plans are available. Based on the AOQL concept, the plan starts with 100 percent inspection until some consecutive number of defect-free units are found. Then, inspection on a sampling basis is done. If a defect is found when on sampling, 100 percent inspection is resumed until a specified number of consecutive good pieces are found, at which time sampling inspection is resumed. Continuous sampling plans were developed by Harold F. Dodge and modifications issued by Dodge and Torrey. MIL-STD-1235 provides a tabulation of these plans. The prerequisites for single level continuous plans are as follows:

- Inspection must involve moving product.
- Rapid 100 percent inspection must be feasible.
- Inspection must be relatively easy.
- Product must be homogeneous.

CSP-I Plans

This continuous sampling plan provides a series of graphs which can be used to select the applicable plans based on the AOQL desired. For example, consider a plan with initial sample size $i = 35$ and fraction sampled $f = 1/10$. One hundred percent inspection is used until 35 successive defect-free units are found. Sampling at the rate of $1/10$ is then instituted. If a defective is found, 100 percent inspection is reinstated.

CSP-2 Plans

These plans allow sampling to continue even if a single defective is found. One hundred percent inspection is performed until i successive, defect-free units are found. Then sampling is in effect at rate f until a defective is found. One hundred percent inspection is reinstituted only if a second defective is found in the next i or fewer units.

All continuous plans are based on the AOQL, thus requiring 100 percent inspection during which time only conforming products are accepted. This controls the average fraction defective of accepted products at some predetermined level.

Multilevel Continuous Sampling Plans

These plans provide for reducing the sampling rate each time i successive units are found free of defects. For example, if 100 percent of the units in order of production are inspected, and if i consecutive defect-free units are found, inspection is shifted to level f_1, where, $f_1 = 1/2$. If a defective is found, 100 percent inspection is resumed. If no defectives are found at level f_1, inspection is shifted to level f_2, where $f_2 = 1/4$. If no defectives are found, inspection is shifted to level f_3, where $f_3 = 1/8$. If a defective is found at level f_2 or f_3, inspection is shifted to the previous level. See Military Hand Book H-107-single level continuous sampling plans[2] and Military Hand Book H-106-multilevel continuous sampling plans for more information.[3]

Skip Lot Plans

Skip lot inspection depends on a continuous process with reasonably stable quality. These plans are also based on the AOQL concept. OC curves can be developed for these plans, known as the Dodge SkSP$_2$. Here is an example of the use of a Dodge plan with $i = 15$, $f = \frac{1}{3}$ and $c = 0$.

Ten units from each lot submitted are inspected until 15 consecutive lots are acceptable. Then $\frac{1}{3}$ of the lots are sampled at random. Inspection is continued at that rate if no defectives are found. When a nonconformance is found, all lots are inspected until 15 consecutive lots are found acceptable. AOQL values given are based on the assumption that rejected lots are all inspected 100 percent. May use MIL-STD-105 for skip lot sampling by substituting the number of lots for the number of pieces as the sample size.

A major advantage of using skip lot inspection is the reduction of total inspection time, in addition to the reduction of the number of items inspected. This includes the time taken to prepare for the inspection, such as the selection of the samples, obtaining and setting up the gages, preparation of the inspection report, and other inspection activities.

Cum Sum Sampling Plans

These plans provide for the continuous inspection approach and are particularly useful when inspection/testing is destructive. Product acceptance is based upon the accumulation of the observed number of defectives. This procedure establishes two zones of acceptance and rejection. The product is accepted or rejected according to the cumulative sum of defectives observed.

For example, a sample of five per day is taken for seven days. The total number of defectives is recorded. If fewer than two defectives, the seven days of production is accepted. Otherwise, it is rejected. A similar plan is used in reliability testing.

Demerit Sampling Plans

This plan is based upon the classification of defects (C/D) of the inspection instruction. Each class is weighted in the order of importance of the characteristics, and a comparison of the accumulated demerits is made with a standard. If a statistical distribution for this index can be established, it is then possible to set acceptance criteria for lot inspection.

Lot Tolerance Percent Defective (LTPD) Plans

The LTPD is the worst product quality that customers are willing to accept. Plans can be developed to provide a specified limiting quality protection customers. These may be used for isolated batches (one-time or intermittent production) where no control over the process can be had. An example of a LTPD is when a customer expresses willingness to accept a maximum of 6.5 percent defective no more than 5 percent of the time. Thus, the consumer's risk is 5 percent.

Sequential Sampling

This type of sampling plan involves a unit-by-unit inspection with the sample units selected one at a time. After each unit is examined, the decision is made to accept, reject, or inspect another unit. Sampling terminates when the cumulative inspection results determine that lot acceptance or rejection can be made. The sample size is not fixed in advance, but depends on the inspection results.

It is possible to continue sampling until all the units of the lot are inspected. However, this is not generally practical. Thus these plans are usually truncated, which means that they require that an acceptance or rejection decision be made after a specified number of units have been inspected.

For a large majority of lots, the total sample size under this plan will be smaller than that under single or double sampling.

Lot Plot Plans

This variables inspection plan was developed by Dorian Shainin. It employs a histogram and rough estimates of the distribution extremes to determine lot acceptance or rejection. It uses a standard sample size of 50. See Grant and Leavenworth *Statistical Quality Control* for additional details.[4]

Grand Lot Schemes

A given sample size can be jointly applied to several lots if they are homogenous. Introduced by L.E. Simon, this plan reduces the economic impact of a necessarily large sample size by as much as 80 percent.

Bulk Sampling

The product may be of gaseous, liquid, or solid form. It is usually sampled by taking increments of the material, blending them into a single composite sample and then, if necessary, reducing the gross sample to a size suitable for laboratory testing. The samples are selected across the width of the product flow. The objective is to determine the average quality level.

PREPARATION FOR SAMPLING

Before sampling inspection is initiated, instructions are prepared as described in Chapter 8. The characteristics to be inspected are listed in the instructions and classified by their orders of importance, or degrees of seriousness.

A separate sampling plan is used for each seriousness class, for example, large sample sizes for major defects, and small sample sizes for minor defects. A common sampling plan for each class is generally used, but the allowable number of defects varies from class to class, for example, no critical defects are allowed, but some major and minor defects may be permitted. The sampling plan is indicated by the corresponding AQL.

The criteria may also be based on demerits per unit, that is, all defects are converted to a scale of demerits based on the classification system. Selection of sampling plans are generally based on the following criteria.

- Seriousness of the defect on the product's use

- Average number of parts to be inspected

- Cost of administration

- Prior lot quality information

- Acceptability of plan to the producers

SAMPLING SCHEMES AND SYSTEMS

While sampling plans are often used solely in the inspection of individual lots, sampling schemes are generally used in acceptance control, when the applications involve a steady flow of product from the producer. For example, the requirement $N = 134$ and $c = 3$ is a sampling plan. The requirement Code J, 1.0 percent AQL is a sampling scheme, and MIL-STD-105-D and its civilian version ANSI/ASQC Z-1.4 are sampling systems.

AVAILABILITY OF SAMPLING PLANS

The literature contains references to many varied sampling plans, schemes, and systems developed by quality professionals and statisticians. These can be selected by the inspection agency without the need of a statistician. However, the agency personnel should have some understanding of the concepts and limitations of the plans.

Between producers and customers, it is generally best to use published procedures and standards. Unique plans specifically generated for a given application may be used internally.

Single attributes sampling plans, indexed by AQL, give high assurance of lot acceptance when process quality is equal to or better than the AQL. These plans are developed for producers' protection. Consumers' risks are controlled under switching rules discussed later in this chapter. MIL-STD-105 and ANSI/ASQC 7.1.4 are the best sources.

Lot percent defective plans are available in MIL-STD-105 identified as LQ plans. The Dodge-Romig plans, indexed by LTPD, are also available and more frequently used.

AOQL plans, indexed by AOQL, are available as Dodge sampling plans.

Variables sampling plans are available by Bowker and Goode and by the military standard MIL-STD-414.

Continuous sampling plans are available by Dodge, the military standard MIL-STD-1235, and military handbooks H-106 and H-107.

MILITARY STANDARD SAMPLING PLANS

The most popular sampling plans in use today are those developed for government procurement use. The MIL-STD-105 scheme for inspection by attributes provides plans which are designed to control the producer's process using its switching rules. The sampling plans are identified by their AQL and the sample size code letter.[5]

Definitions

ACCEPTANCE QUALITY LEVEL (AQL): This is the maximum percent defective (or number of defects per unit) that, for the purpose of sampling inspection, can be considered satisfactory for a process average.

OPERATING CHARACTERISTIC CURVES (OC)S: Shown for each sampling plan in the standard, these indicate the percentage of lots or batches which may be expected to be accepted under the various sampling plans for a given process quality.

AVERAGE OUTGOING QUALITY (AOQ): The average quality of outgoing product, including all accepted lots or batches plus all rejected lots or batches after the rejected lots or batches have been 100 percent inspected and all defectives replaced by non-defectives.

AVERAGE OUTGOING QUALITY LIMIT (AOQL): The maximum of the AOQs for all possible incoming qualities of an acceptance sampling plan.

Sample Size Determination

The standard provides a table of sample size code letters (see Table 27-1). It contains, for each group of lot size numbers, the equivalent sample size

SAMPLE SIZE CODE LETTERS

LOT OR BATCH SIZE			SPECIAL INSPECTION LEVELS				GENERAL INSPECTION LEVELS		
			S-1	S-2	S-3	S-4	I	II	III
2	TO	8	A	A	A	A	A	A	B
9	TO	15	A	A	A	A	A	B	C
16	TO	25	A	A	B	B	B	C	D
26	TO	50	A	B	B	C	C	D	E
51	TO	90	B	B	C	C	C	E	F
91	TO	150	B	B	C	D	D	F	G
151	TO	280	B	C	D	E	E	G	H
281	TO	500	B	C	D	E	F	H	J
501	TO	1200	C	C	E	F	G	J	K
1201	TO	3200	C	D	E	G	H	K	L
3201	TO	10000	C	D	F	G	J	L	M
10001	TO	35000	C	D	F	H	K	M	N
35001	TO	150000	D	E	G	J	L	N	P
150001	TO	500000	D	E	G	J	M	P	Q
500001	AND	OVER	D	E	H	K	N	Q	R

TABLE 27-1 Sample Size Code Letters

code letters for three general inspection levels and four special inspection levels. Once the inspection level, usually general level II, has been decided, the sample code letter is selected based on the lot size. The applicable sample size is determined from the master table (see Figure 27-2) for the specified AQL.

Before using these sampling plans, the characteristics to be inspected are arranged, on the instructions, in order of importance and classified as critical, major, and minor (sometimes minor A and minor B), as defined in the standard.

Each lot is submitted to inspection, and the specified number of sample pieces is selected for each classification in accordance with the designated AQL. When inspection reveals the number of defectives equal to or less than the number specified in the sample table as *ac*, the lot is accepted. The lot is rejected when the number of defectives in the sample equals to or exceeds the *re* (one more than the acceptance number).

The samples are randomly selected. The lot is arranged so that each item in the lot has an equal opportunity for selection. If the products have been thoroughly mixed before selection, it may be assumed that the samples are random. Once the decision is made to accept the lot, it is identified and moved to the next production or assembly station, or to the stores or shipping areas.

When a lot is rejected as a result of sampling inspection, it is generally moved to the materials review area for disposition determination. When it

ACCEPTABLE QUALITY LEVELS (NORMAL INSPECTION)

Sample Size Code Letter	Sample Size	0.010	0.015	0.025	0.040	0.065	0.10	0.15	0.25	0.40	0.65	1.0	1.5	2.5	4.0	6.5	10	15	25	40	65	100	150	250	400	650	1000
A	2	↓	↓	↓	↓	↓	↓	↓	↓	↓	↓	↓	↓	↓	↓	↓	↓	0 1	1 2	2 3	3 4	5 6	7 8	10 11	14 15	21 22	30 31
B	3	↓	↓	↓	↓	↓	↓	↓	↓	↓	↓	↓	↓	↓	↓	↓	0 1	1 2	2 3	3 4	5 6	7 8	10 11	14 15	21 22	30 31	44 45
C	5	↓	↓	↓	↓	↓	↓	↓	↓	↓	↓	↓	↓	↓	↓	0 1	1 2	2 3	3 4	5 6	7 8	10 11	14 15	21 22	30 31	44 45	↑
D	8	↓	↓	↓	↓	↓	↓	↓	↓	↓	↓	↓	↓	↓	0 1	1 2	2 3	3 4	5 6	7 8	10 11	14 15	21 22	30 31	44 45	↑	↑
E	13	↓	↓	↓	↓	↓	↓	↓	↓	↓	↓	↓	↓	0 1	1 2	2 3	3 4	5 6	7 8	10 11	14 15	21 22	30 31	44 45	↑	↑	↑
F	20	↓	↓	↓	↓	↓	↓	↓	↓	↓	↓	↓	0 1	1 2	2 3	3 4	5 6	7 8	10 11	14 15	21 22	30 31	44 45	↑	↑	↑	↑
G	32	↓	↓	↓	↓	↓	↓	↓	↓	↓	↓	0 1	1 2	2 3	3 4	5 6	7 8	10 11	14 15	21 22	30 31	44 45	↑	↑	↑	↑	↑
H	50	↓	↓	↓	↓	↓	↓	↓	↓	↓	0 1	1 2	2 3	3 4	5 6	7 8	10 11	14 15	21 22	30 31	44 45	↑	↑	↑	↑	↑	↑
J	80	↓	↓	↓	↓	↓	↓	↓	↓	0 1	1 2	2 3	3 4	5 6	7 8	10 11	14 15	21 22	30 31	44 45	↑	↑	↑	↑	↑	↑	↑
K	125	↓	↓	↓	↓	↓	↓	↓	0 1	1 2	2 3	3 4	5 6	7 8	10 11	14 15	21 22	30 31	44 45	↑	↑	↑	↑	↑	↑	↑	↑
L	200	↓	↓	↓	↓	↓	↓	0 1	1 2	2 3	3 4	5 6	7 8	10 11	14 15	21 22	30 31	44 45	↑	↑	↑	↑	↑	↑	↑	↑	↑
M	315	↓	↓	↓	↓	↓	0 1	1 2	2 3	3 4	5 6	7 8	10 11	14 15	21 22	30 31	44 45	↑	↑	↑	↑	↑	↑	↑	↑	↑	↑
N	500	↓	↓	↓	↓	0 1	1 2	2 3	3 4	5 6	7 8	10 11	14 15	21 22	30 31	44 45	↑	↑	↑	↑	↑	↑	↑	↑	↑	↑	↑
P	800	↓	↓	↓	0 1	1 2	2 3	3 4	5 6	7 8	10 11	14 15	21 22	30 31	44 45	↑	↑	↑	↑	↑	↑	↑	↑	↑	↑	↑	↑
Q	1250	↓	↓	0 1	1 2	2 3	3 4	5 6	7 8	10 11	14 15	21 22	30 31	44 45	↑	↑	↑	↑	↑	↑	↑	↑	↑	↑	↑	↑	↑
R	2000	↓	0 1	1 2	2 3	3 4	5 6	7 8	10 11	14 15	21 22	30 31	44 45	↑	↑	↑	↑	↑	↑	↑	↑	↑	↑	↑	↑	↑	↑

(Each AQL column is given as Ac Re. ↓ = Use first sampling plan below arrow. ↑ = Use first sampling plan above arrow. Ac = Acceptance number; Re = Rejection number.)

FIGURE 27-2 MIL-STD-105 Master Table

has been decided to screen the lot for acceptable pieces, the lot must be reinspected 100 percent for the presence of the characteristics, or group of characteristics, found non-conforming during sampling inspection. After removing the non-conforming pieces, the balance of the lot is transported to the designated production, assembly, or stores areas. The non-conforming pieces are moved to the materials review area for disposition determination.

The military sampling plans are based on protecting the producer against the rejection of acceptable lots. They depart somewhat from the true statistical concepts by considering the lot size in the determination of the sample sizes. Table 27-2 is an exhibit of a document generally used by companies in the selection of the sample sizes according to MIL-STD-105.

Switching Rules

Normal inspection is used when there is no evidence that the product quality is better or poorer than the specified quality level. It is usually used at the start of inspection and is continued as long as there is evidence that the product quality remains consistent with specified requirements.

When normal inspection is in effect, if any two out of five consecutive lots have been rejected for a specific class of defects, tightened inspection is used for that class of defects.

Tightened inspection uses the same quality level sample size as at normal inspection, but decreases the number of defectives permitted in the sample.

LOT SIZE	SAMPLE SIZE	AQL ACC	1.0% REJ	SAMPLE SIZE	AQL ACC	2.5% REJ	SAMPLE SIZE	AQL ACC	4.0% REJ	SAMPLE SIZE	AQL ACC	6.5% REJ
2–8	100%	0	1	5	0	1	3	0	1	2	0	1
9–15	13	0	1	5	0	1	3	0	1	2	0	1
16–25	13	0	1	5	0	1	3	0	1	8	1	2
26–50	13	0	1	5	0	1	13	1	2	8	1	2
51–90	13	0	1	20	1	2	13	1	2	13	2	3
91–150	13	0	1	20	1	2	20	2	3	20	3	4
151–280	50	1	2	32	2	3	32	3	4	32	5	6
281–500	50	1	2	50	3	4	50	5	6	50	7	8
501–1200	80	2	3	80	5	6	80	7	8	80	10	11
1201–3200	125	3	4	125	7	8	125	10	11	125	14	15
3201–10000	200	5	6	200	10	11	200	14	15	200	21	22
10001–35000	315	7	8	315	14	15	315	21	22	200	21	22
35001–150000	500	10	11	500	21	22	315	21	22	200	21	22
150001–500000	800	14	15	500	21	22	315	21	22	200	21	22
500000-Up	1250	20	21	500	21	22	315	21	22	200	21	22

TABLE 27-2 Single Sampling Plans for Normal Inspection—Company Plan

When five consecutive lots are accepted while on tightened inspection, sampling is returned to normal inspection.

Reduced inspection uses the same quality level as for normal inspection, but requires a smaller sample. Switching from normal to reduced inspection occurs when

- The preceding ten lots have been on normal inspection and no lot has been rejected at initial inspection.

- The total number of defectives from the preceding lots is less than or equal to the applicable limiting number in table VIII of the standard.

- Production is at a steady rate.

- Reduced inspection is found desirable by the responsible authority.

Normal inspection may be instituted when a lot is rejected while on reduced inspection, or other conditions noted in the standard prevail.

Discontinuation of Inspection

When ten consecutive lots are on tightened inspection, inspection may be discontinued pending action to improve the process quality. If the supplier has had an otherwise excellent record for similar products, the specified AQL may be investigated for possible changes.

Process Control

At times, sampling inspection may be supplemented by other factors of the production process.

When a process has been under statistical control, the use of control charts may supplement product sampling inspection. In those instances, it may be necessary to periodically inspect small lot samples while depending almost entirely on the application of the control charts for product acceptance.

Using information provided by tool and process capability studies, as well as the receipt of material from qualified suppliers and production operators, can reduce the levels of product inspection.

Knowledge of an engineering characteristic pertinent to the process may also reduce inspection. For example, products from a punching operation may, after the qualification of the die, only need the inspection of the first and last piece of the lot, since the stability of the tool will assure that the products in between are also conforming.

At times, products which require destructive inspection cannot be examined in sufficient quantity to provide confidence. In those cases, maintaining audit control over the process may be desired. This audit may be supplemented by the destructive inspection of a small product sample. In other situations, a load short of destruction can be applied to a suitable product sample.

Currently, less recourse is needed for product inspection. The use of CAM equipment provides capabilities for 100 percent automatic inspection. However, it is advisable that some small sampling inspection is conducted at periodic frequencies to insure that the process continues under control.

REFERENCES

1. Juran, J. *Upper Management and Quality, Juran's Quality Control Handbook* (4th ed.). New York: McGraw Hill, 1988, Chapter 8.

2. *Handbook-H-107, Single Level Continuous Sampling Procedures and Tables for Inspection by Attributes.* Washington, DC: Sup. of Documents, April 1959.

3. *Handbook-H-106, Multi-Level Continuous Sampling Procedures and Tables for Inspection by Attributes.* Washington, DC: Sup. of Documents, October 1958.

4. Grant, Eugene, & Leavenworth, Richard S. *Statistical Quality Control* (5th ed.). New York: McGraw Hill, 1980.

5. *MIL-STD-105, Sampling Procedures and Tables for Inspection by Attributes.* Washington, DC: Government Printing Office, April 1963.

CHAPTER TWENTY-EIGHT

Budgets and Quality Costs[1,2]

INTRODUCTION

The economics of the inspection/quality operation are discussed, and the methods of establishing departmental budgets described. The preparation of the budget and its submission for approval are illustrated, including the justification for each line item. Periodic reviews with management, including the analysis and justifications of budget variances, are also illustrated.

This chapter presents a program of measurement and evaluation of quality-related costs. The forms and techniques used to improve product quality levels, reduce inspection/test costs, and minimize scrap and rework costs are identified. An example of the successful application of this program is provided.

INTRODUCTION TO BUDGETS

Budgets are important because they show the inspection/quality department's financial goals, provide a means to periodically review these goals, measure the degree of implementation of the goals, and help make necessary adjustments within the department.

In order to develop a proper budget, inspection/quality supervisors and managers must do some preliminary planning. This provides the rationale to review the various aspects of the department's operation and helps to identify opportunities for improvement.

Budget processing is a measure of converting departmental activities into terms of dollars. Thus, any improvements needed in the operation, can be presented in terms of money—a terminology which is more readily appreciated and recognized by top management.

Since the inspection/quality department's budget is but one of various departmental budgets in the company, it should be prepared with a common format and in a language common to the whole company.

The budget elements should encompass only those functions under the control of the applicable supervisor or manager. Some companies include elements, such as depreciation of facilities, taxes, and cost of utilities, over which departmental supervisors have no control. This policy detracts from the basic concept of holding the individuals responsible only for those areas over which they have control. When these other elements are included, supervisors should list them separately from those items which they do control.

To be effective, the budget should be clearly understood by the lowest level of supervision that will be held accountable for its implementation. Everyone should agree with the budget's financial restraints. This requires that all levels of supervision and management participate in budget development.

DISAGREEMENT WITH BUDGETS

There are occasions when some inspection/quality supervisors are not in full accord with all budget elements as they affect their operation. The department head should then carefully review their objections, and try to justify those areas which cannot be amended to the supervisors' satisfaction.

At times, even the department head may not be in full agreement with some elements of the budget as directed by upper management. Here too, it is important that top management carefully evaluate these objections and make every effort to explain the reasons for the mandates. Since department managers are totally responsible for budget implementation, full consideration should be given to their objections. Occasionally, however, corporate decisions are made which are beyond the control, and sometimes comprehension, of the various levels of management. However, these decisions must be enforced. It is the department managers' responsibility to implement these elements to the best of their abilities and motivate the lower levels of supervision to do the same.

These occasions provide excellent opportunities for inspection/quality supervisors to carefully review their operations to determine the possibility of improvement, so as to meet the objectionable budget features.

For example, upper management, department managers, and section supervisors frequently disagree with the requirement to reduce the work force beyond recommended and traditional levels. This often occurs when top management deems it necessary to retrench the company's work force because of low profits or decreased business. Reviewing the inspection/quality departments may identify more efficient methods of operations, such as the use of increased sampling, if it will not affect outgoing product quality, or the substitution of inspection techniques which will reduce the number of personnel needed.

Nevertheless, the proposed elements of the originally submitted budget, which had to be eliminated, should not be forgotten, if they really have merit. The inspection/quality managers should keep these improvements in abeyance pending some change in the economic and/or political atmosphere of the company and reintroduce them at a later date.

Supervisors/managers at times play games with their budget submissions. They are aware that, in most instances, any unused funds in an approved budget are automatically canceled at the end of the fiscal period. This encourages the rapid expenditure of these funds even if there is no longer a need for them.

In addition, it is the policy of many financial officers to relate the budget submitted for the current year to the amount approved and spent during the preceding year. Thus, some managers inflate the budget request for the current period beyond what is actually needed. Then any variances from the approved budget can be decreased due to the inflated earlier budget. But a knowledgeable finance director can usually see through the ploy and take suitable measures to rectify the condition. In addition, these games cannot help to make a department more efficient.

TYPES OF BUDGETS

Capital budget

This type of budget usually applies to expenses which are normally depreciated over several years, such as buildings, major tools, and major measuring equipment such as x-ray, coordinate measuring machines and computers. The company controller sets precise rules as to what can be considered a capital expense.

Direct budget

This budget is one which controls the costs of all labor, services, and supplies that are directly associated with a special product or project.

Overhead or indirect budget

This budget includes the costs for labor, services, and supplies which are used to support the product or project's direct charges. It is not applied to any specific product, but used for all products. An overhead rate, including all indirect costs, is applied as a percentage to the direct budgeted or project's costs. Overhead functions include support services, such as production control, purchasing, clerical, supervisory, and executive costs, as well as sundry supplies, such as paint, small tools, and gages.

			OVERHEAD BUDGET PROJECTION												
DEPT. NO.					FISCAL YEAR				NAME						
EXP. CODE	V F	DESCRIPTION	AUG	SEPT	OCT	NOV	DEC	JAN	FEB	MAR	APR	MAY	JUNE	JULY	TOTAL
01	F	SALARIES	21072	24670	33007	27837	27684	26437	27828	28278	33445	29025	27096	34945	341324
04	F	OVERTIME EXP.	6	5											11
06	F	FREIGHT IN	25												25
10	F	APPL. ENG. BUR.	737												737
13	F	VENDOR REWORK			95										95
18	F	MAT (M&E)	44		63	100	100	100	100	100	100	100	100	100	1007
31	F	PERISH TOOLS		162	296	225	225	225	225	225	225	225	225	225	2483
34	F	SUPPLIES—OFF.			541	100	100	100	100	100	100	100	100	100	1441
35	F	SUPPLIES—OTHER			561	100	100	100	100	100	100	100	100	100	1466
37	F	OUTSIDE SERV.	18	10	5942	2160	2400	2280	2400	2400	2880	2400	2280	2880	28050
49	F	SUBS. DUE		19	35	50	50	50	50	50	50	50	50	50	504
52	F	TRAVEL	639	662	624	1250	1250	1250	1250	1250	1250	1250	1250	1250	13175
90	F	TRAINING			17	50	1200	50	50	50	50	50	50	50	1617
90	F	CORP., INC.		9											9
		TOTAL	22541	25537	41186	31872	33109	30592	32103	32553	38200	33300	31251	39700	391944

FIGURE 28-1 Overhead Budget Projection

Many companies consider their inspection/quality functions as overhead costs, not assignable to any specific product (see Figure 28-1). Others include these costs in the direct budget. Nevertheless, it is advisable for department supervisors to compute their anticipated costs as if they were considered direct costs, so that tighter control of expenditures can be maintained.

Personnel budget

Some companies require, in addition to the total departmental budget, a listing of the number and types of personnel anticipated for the new fiscal period. This information is useful to the company's personnel department so that they can plan for any additional recruitment. See Figure 28-2.

INDIRECT MANPOWER PROJECTION										
BASIS: $1,500,000 D/L FISCAL YEAR: 1981 DEPT: 114 NAME: QUALITY ASSURANCE										
FUNCTION OR TITLE	PRESENT STAFF	CHANGES ONLY + OR − INDICATED MONTH				NO. REQ'D AT % OF BASIS				
		1ST QUARTER	2ND QUARTER	3RD QUARTER	4TH QUARTER	80%	90%	100%	110%	120%
DIRECTOR QA	1					1	1	1	1	1
MANAGER	1					1	1	1	1	1
QTY. SPECIALIST	5					5	5	5	5	5
(INCLUDES ONE DUE JULY)										
CLERK TYPIST	1					1	1	1	1	1
INSPECTORS	13	+3	+2							
(INCLUDES 2 OPEN REQS)						14	15	17	18	19
EQUIV. INSP. IN O/T	5	−3	−2							
SAFETY ENGINEER	0	1				1	1	1	1	1
TOTAL MANPOWER	26	27	27	27	27	26	27	28	29	30
TOTAL SALARIES REQUIRED @ 11 1/2 MONTHS										

FIGURE 28-2 Indirect Manpower Projection

PREPARATION

Since money matters are usually within the province of financial or accounting departments, it is advisable that inspection/quality supervisors utilize the expertise of these personnel to prepare budgets. The department head should solicit, from each section manager and supervisor of the inspection/quality department, a budget forecast. All anticipated equipment, capital expenditures, supplies, and personnel should be included. This information is then accumulated for the entire inspection/quality department and submitted to the budget director, or other members of the financial department, depending upon the company organization.

COST CENTERS

These are logical subdivisions of a department activity chosen to fix budget responsibilities to the applicable supervisor, and to provide a basis for collecting actual cost data. To simplify the assignment of responsibilities, these centers usually follow organizational boundaries.

In most companies, budgets are also prepared for each project. Thus, it is possible that some expenditures may cross cost centers. Thus, it may be necessary to define the specific portions of the project budget under the responsibility of the applicable inspection/quality supervisors. For example, the project's inspection hours may include those expended in receiving, process, final inspection, and test, each of which may be under the jurisdiction of different area supervisors.

INDICES

The budget director and inspection/quality department head generally prepare the indices used to develop each budget line item. These indices may vary with activity, such as direct manufacturing labor hours, sales dollars, number of lots to be inspected, number of piece parts, and special costs for each project. For special operations, such functions as configuration control or special documentation may need to be considered. At times, it may be necessary to develop, for each cost center, an activity index that expresses the relationship between the degree of activity and the budgeted costs.

BASES

With overhead or indirect expenditures not assignable to a specific project, it may be necessary to establish a base of measurement for inspection/quality labor requirements. Thus, if the number of inspection hours, instead of the number of production hours, are considered as a base of measurement, the actual percentage applied will have to be decided. The base of measurement may be established by several methods.

Historical Base

This may be obtained from data gathered during previous years. Thus a record of the ratio of inspection to direct labor hours, may provide the base for the oncoming period.

At times, it may be necessary to develop different ratios, depending upon the type of activity involved. For example, in-process electronic equipment inspection may require a higher inspector/direct labor ratio than that for simple machined parts inspection. Further, when the production operation is largely controlled by proven stable machine tools and computer-aided manufacturing devices, instead of operators, a smaller ratio may be used.

At other times, it may be necessary to develop a different base when the project is one for products which require more sophisticated production and inspection operations. The ratio may need to be based on the results of special engineering studies of the more significant inspection/test operations, and not on past operations.

Market Standards

Some recourse may be made to ratios which are traditionally used by the other companies producing the same or similar products. This method should be used with extreme caution, since every company operates differently, even when producing the same products. Some companies may use more stable machine tools, or more sophisticated manufacturing operational programs.

Engineering Studies

These studies, often needed for complicated inspections and tests, are done by observing the tests and determining the time they take. The tests are usually lengthy, time consuming, and repetitive. The time study results include information needed to troubleshoot for a failed characteristic and its subsequent rework and retest. Production engineering time studies are similar to those for production operations. These studies are important when direct costs are included in the project budget.

Actual Time Spent

In new jobs it is often necessary to provide a tentative budget until precise determination of inspection/quality time can be obtained. Then the actual time spent in inspection/test of the product in early stages of production should be measured. It is then extrapolated into an expected time for the balance of the project, and used as part of the budget forecast. A factor based on the learning curve of the operation is usually applied. This factor considers that the initial operations usually take longer until some experience has been developed.

RATIO

After determining the bases, they are incorporated into suitable ratios which may vary for the degree of activity. For example, when lots of different sizes are inspected, the time spent per piece will be smaller, since sampling, when used, will reduce the actual number of pieces examined.

Different production cycle periods may require different amounts of inspection for each lot. Thus, the inspection time at the project's beginning will often be high, because of first piece qualifications. Similarly, at the project's end, small lots are submitted for inspection. They represent replacement parts for those items scrapped during production.

Since rejected lots require more time to process than accepted ones, this additional time should be considered. The percentages used in estimating the inspection costs may be provided as a percent of direct labor cost, as a ratio of inspectors to production personnel, as lots inspected per day, as inspection costs per dollars of sales, and many others. Each ratio has its problems which should be considered.

CONTRACT REVIEW

When a proposal for a new contract is processed, it is necessary to price out the anticipated costs for inspection/test and quality operations. These determinations are based on the practices of the company as described in the previous sections. After the contract is granted, these costs may be used in the budget preparation. Figure 28-3, Quality Control Estimate Sheet, shows one way to determine inspection/quality costs.

MARKET FORECAST

Frequently, new contracts are received after the budget's submission and approval for the fiscal period. These new contracts will, of course, impact upon these budgets. To make this event less disruptive, some companies include in the budget forecast an estimate based on the probability of receiving new contracts during the applicable fiscal period. Their marketing/sales department develops at times a factor of probability which is provided in the sales forecast. The inspection/quality budget considers the same probability factor.

Thus, if during the proposal review, it was expected that 10 additional inspectors were to be needed for new contracts, and the sales forecast assigned a factor of 50 percent as the probability of receiving this contract, then the inspection/quality budget would include 10×0.50 or 5 additional inspectors with the fiscal year's budget forecast. Of course, upon receipt of the contract, an adjustment would be necessary and included in a supplementary budget.

FUNCTION		D.L.	IND. L.	D.L.	IND. L.	D.L.	IND. L.	D.L.	IND. L.	D.L.	IND. L.	REMARKS

The full form:

PRODUCT			FILE NO.
CUSTOMER			DEL. SCHED.
REFERENCE			
SOURCE OF DATA			

PRELIMINARY DATA		NO. OF DWGS.
COMPONENTS		DET.
GEARS		
CAST/PLATE		ASSY.
MISC.		

FUNCTION		D.L.	IND. L.	D.L.	IND. L.	D.L.	IND. L.	D.L.	IND. L.	D.L.	IND. L.	REMARKS
ANALYSIS	CUST. SPEC.											
ANALYSIS	COMP. SPEC											
ANALYSIS	TEST SPEC.											
ANALYSIS	DWG. REV.											
ANALYSIS	P.O. REQ.											
LIAS.	CUSTOMER											
LIAS.	VENDOR											
LIAS.	P.M.I.											
INST.	P.M.I.											
INST.	INPROC											
EQUIP.	P.M.I.											
EQUIP.	INPROC.											
EQUIP.	TEST											
Q.C. ENGAG.												
Q.C. TOTAL												
INPROC. INSP.												
TEST												
RELIABILITY												
P.M.I.	COMP. (M)											
P.M.I.	COMP (E)											
P.M.I.	PL/CAST											
P.M.I.	GEARS											
P.M.I.	MISC											

TEST AND INSPECTION EQUIPMENT

REMARKS	
SUBMITTED	APPROVED
DATE	DATE

FIGURE 28-3   Quality Control Estimate Sheet

ACCOUNTABILITY

Companies use different methods to evaluate supervisors' accountability in budget implementation. A recommended method is outlined here.

Initially, the budget director provides a computer printout of the previous year's budget, and the line-by-line variances in its implementation. The department head justifies the new budget against the previous one and explains any differences.

All budgets must be approved by the budget director and the head of the company. At times, it may be necessary for the department manager to appear before the company head to justify some, or all, budget elements.

After approval, a computer printout, listing each line item by account code number and the budgeted allowance, is given to the department heads. In turn, they extract those elements applicable to each departmental cost center, and provide copies to the applicable inspection/quality supervisors.

The department heads are usually held accountable for the implementation of each item. In turn, the appropriate inspection/quality department's section supervisors should be delegated, by their department head, the responsibility for the implementation of their portions of the budget.

MEASUREMENT OF ACTUAL COSTS

The establishment of cost centers, activity indices, standards, and bases provides a measure of what the costs should be. To determine what the costs actually are requires additional tools.

A timekeeping system which provides inspection/quality personnel with account codes, requisition forms for ordering supplies and services, and time cards for charging their time to the proper accounts is needed. See Figure 28-4 for an example of a set of account codes.

Data processing systems (manual or otherwise) are needed to process the basic time and expense data into prompt summaries and reports for cost centers and programs.

A budget office is needed to coordinate the budgeting and reporting of expenses. There must also be a program of reviewing budget variances and of implementing any necessary adjustments.

It must be understood that notwithstanding budget approval, actual expenditures must also be approved prior to issuance of the requisitions. Some companies provide expenditure limits for each department head for budget-approved elements without requiring prior authorization. For example, the department head may be permitted to purchase budget-approved supplies up to $500 without prior approval. Usually, personnel requisitions must be approved by the human relations department prior to having them issued. Other expenditures must be approved by the next higher executive before implementation.

A record of all expenditures is usually kept by the department head or, as designated, by lower level supervision. The ways that labor expenditures

01—Salaries

The pay for all exempt and nonexempt personnel. Both straight time and premium of overtime pay are included in this account.

18—Material for repair and maintenance of machinery and equipment.

This account is used for normal repair and maintenance of machinery and equipment, including that of inspection and testing measuring equipment.

25—Tuition

This includes cost for inspection/quality personnel training, both in-house and at outside facilities. This includes the cost of tuition and travel to and from the point of instruction, if external training facilities are used.

31—Perishable tools

This includes cost of procurement of small tools and gages, and their calibration by outside facilities.

34—Supplies—Office

This includes the cost of paper, pens, pencils, and other items used in clerical work by departmental personnel.

35—Supplies—Other

This includes cost of material used up during manufacturing inspection. Examples are dye penetrant, magnaflux, and radiographic supplies.

37—Outside services

This includes labor and services incurred by temporary help and job shoppers as well as the cost of certain functions performed by this help outside of the plant.

49—Subscriptions and dues

Magazines, technical journal subscriptions, and dues to management or technical associations, when company paid, are included in this account.

52—Travel

All expenses incurred by employees traveling on behalf of the company, including mileage for personal auto, rail or air transportation, taxi, car rental, meals, and other travel-related costs.

FIGURE 28-4 Overhead Expense Codes

---

are accumulated depend upon whether they are considered as direct or indirect. Usually direct labor charges are entered using time clock or are posted on a record for the appropriate project. All expenditures are usually denoted by a specific code such as "Inspection supplies chargeable to a project code number 35-V," or "Indirect labor, code 101F."

Capital expenditures are tracked by the department head and budget director. This includes the verification of the implementation of the expenditures, as noted in the capital budget. This review may include verifying the date of requisition issuance, the date of equipment receipt, and the date of initial use. When the justification for the capital expenditure will result in a cost savings, this information is also accumulated by the department head. See Figure 28-5 for a report of the capital appropriation's implementation. For major capital expenditures, the financial department

LINE	DESCRIPTION OF PROJECT ($000)	ACCOUNT CLASS		DEPT./PROGRAM		REMARKS (SHOW AR NUMBER IF ISSUED)	CLASSIFICATION THIS PAGE
		COST	%	PAY OUT	*		
1	LAYOUT TABLE, VERNIER SCALES AND SPARE PARTS	CAPITAL $12	100%	114 YRS.		PROVIDE CAPABILITY FOR RAPID LAYOUT OF CASTINGS AND FORGINGS	❏ APPROVED PRIOR YEAR
2	INDEXING HEAD	CAPITAL $ 6	100%	114 YRS.		ENABLE MORE RAPID INSPECTION OF PRECISION MACHINE PARTS	❏ COST REDUCTION
3	SUPER MICROMETER ELECTRONIC HEAD	CAPITAL $15	100%	114 YRS.		ENABLE CALIBRATION OF STANDARD INSPECTION GAGES	❏ NORMAL REPLACEMENT
4	GAGING FIXTURES	CAPITAL $15	100%	114 YRS.		ENABLE MORE EFFICIENT SETUP AND INSPECTION OF PRODUCTION QUANTITIES	☒ IMPROVEMENTS
5	STANDARD INSPECTION EQUIPMENT (PARALLEL BARS, VERNIERS, INDICATORS, ETC.)	CAPITAL $10	%	114 YRS.		REPLACE AND IMPROVE EXISTING STANDARD INSPECTION EQUIPMENT	❏ EXPANSION CURR. PRODUCTS
6	INSPECTION WORK BENCH, CABINETS, ETC.	CAPITAL $ 5	%	114 YRS.		REPLACE EXISTING WORN AND USED EQUIPMENT	❏ EXPANSION NEW PRODUCTS

LINE	COST X	AUG.	SEPT.	OCT.	NOV.	DEC.	JAN.	FEB.	MAR.	APR.	MAY	JUNE	JULY	1ST	2ND	3RD	4TH	1983	1984	1985
														FISCAL YEAR 1981 ⟶ 1982						
1				B/C		D		12												
2				B/C	D		6													
3			B/C	D		15														
4			A	B	C	D			15											
5		A		B/C		D	10													
6				B/C		D	5													

STATUS: A-START ANALYSIS B-SUBMIT AR C-PLACE ORDER D-INSTALLED

FIGURE 28-5 Capital Appropriation Implementation

may conduct an audit to assure that the implementation schedule, as noted on the capital budget, is accomplished.

All expenditures are accumulated by the finance department or the budget director. Monthly computer printouts are usually provided to the department head. These lists depict the amount charged to the department by the account code number, the budgeted amount for the item, and any variances.

VARIANCE ANALYSIS

Usually, the department head is required to provide a written explanation for all variances, positive or negative, exceeding a stipulated dollar amount (for example, $100), or percentage (for example, 10 percent) (see Figure 28-6). Prior to issuing the variance report, each section head is required to provide justification, to the department head, of the variances attributable to their activities.

To fine-tune expenditures, some companies have adopted a practice in which, every month, the department head provides the anticipated expen-

BUDGET VARIANCE ANALYSIS

MONTH OF   DECEMBER 1979   DEPT. NO.: 114   NAME: QUALITY ASSURANCE

ACCT. NO.	DESCRIPTION	PROJECTED			ACTUAL		EXP. OF MAJ. VAR. VS. PROJECTION
		EXPENSES	BUDGET	VARIANCE	EXPENSES	VAR. VS. PROJ.	
01F	SALARIES	27,684	30,649	2,965	26,422	1,242	01F ABLE TO MEET REQMNT.
	*JOB SHOPPER BUDGETED AGAINST 01F NOW BEING CHARGED TO 37F						WITH REDUCED O.T.
18F	MAT. (M&E)	50	100	50	–	50	
31F	PERISHABLE TOOLS	150	225	75	1	149	31F CALIBRATION SRVICES
							EXPENDED NOT BILLED
34F	SUPPLIES, OFFICE	50	1000	950	–	50	
	*CURTAILED DEVELOPMENT OF WORKMANSHIP STANDARD MANUAL						
35F	SUPPLIES, OTHER	50	100	50	–	50	
37F	OUTSIDE SERVICES	2,400	100	(2,300)	1775	625	37F (1) WEEK JOB SHOPPER
	*SEE EXPLANATION OF 01F ABOVE						$$$ NOT BIL'D THIS MONTH
49F	SUBS., DUES	50	50	–	12	38	
52F	TRAVEL	1,000	1,250	250	622	250	52F VEND. TRAVEL CURTAILED
	*VENDOR TRAVEL CURTAILED DUE TO UNAVAILABLE QUALITY ENG. PERSONNEL						DUE TO HIGHER PRIORITY WK.
80F	TRAINING	150	200	50	–	150	80F CERTIFICATION COSTS
							INCURRED NOT BILLED THIS
							MONTH
	TOTALS	31,584	33,674	2,090	28,832	2,752	

FIGURE 28-6 Budget Projection—Variance Analysis

ditures for each budget element for the subsequent period, and an explanation of any anticipated variances.

In some companies, the department head and budget director periodically meet with the company head to discuss budget implementation and to account for any significant variances. This meeting emphasizes the importance that top management pays to the budget. At times, this meeting is held concurrent with the periodic quality program meetings.

E X A M P L E

The budgeting process of an inspection/quality department for one company is outlined in the following sections.

This company utilized a combination of historical data and engineering studies to estimate expenditures. The budgeted inspection/quality time was calculated as a percent of direct production hours. The incorporation of costs from anticipated new contracts was predicated upon the estimates included in the prior proposal, using the probability factor provided by the sales/marketing department. Each line item of the budget was calculated using the following methods.

Based on the direct labor forecast for each manufacturing department, the inspection hours were estimated as a percentage of direct labor hours. An estimate was also made of the number of hours needed to reinspect rejected items. This estimate was obtained from a record of past rejection rates for similar equipment.

The estimate of inspection/quality work force costs was broken down by months (including allowances for vacations, sick days, holidays, merit increases, and the like), as well as an estimate for supervisory and management costs.

Special inspection/quality costs were calculated for operations above the normal lot-by-lot inspections. These included the following:

- Qualification of parts and assemblies for initially submitted lots on the new contract. This was determined by estimating the inspection time for each part and assembly in the program. For purposes of calculation, the drawings were divided into those for simple and complex machined parts, assemblies, major weldments, and final end items of equipment. An estimated time was established for each category.

- First article testing, provided by engineering.

- Time required for review and analysis of contract and specifications, participation in postaward conference, engineering change, and configuration control.

- Special inspections such as optical and nondestructive testing.

- Measuring equipment calibration.

- Liaison with suppliers, in-house departments, and customer personnel.

- Participation in MRB and configuration control board activities.

- Performance of vendor surveys. These were calculated by the anticipated number of trips to each major supplier.

- Clerical and administrative costs.

- Development of special workmanship standards, inspection and quality procedures, and program quality plan.

- Performance of project quality audits.

- Maintenance of inspection/test equipment and facilities.

- Cost of perishable tools, gages, and supplies (office and sundries).

- Cost of technical society dues, subscriptions, travel, and training.

A separate budget was submitted for capital expenditures, including costs for any special test equipment and facilities for first article and production tests, to be procured or fabricated for the program.

VARIANCE ANALYSIS

The inspection/quality manager reviewed the various elements of the budget with the department's section supervisors and discussed the variances for each section. Justifications for variances exceeding $100 were developed and needed adjustments were determined. Many variances were due to the delay in receipt of the vouchers for the supplies and services ordered during the month.

At the end of the month, the inspection/quality department head, the controller, and the production and quality managers of each plant met with the president of the company to review the budget variance reports and the plant quality reports. As a result of that meeting, adjustments, as needed, were made to budget estimates for the subsequent months.

QUALITY-RELATED COSTS

This section presents a program of quality improvement through cost optimization. It identifies and utilizes those quality-related costs which assist management to minimize expenditures and optimize

- Quality of design/engineering actions.
- Quality of manufactured products.
- Inspection/quality improvement efforts.
- Selection and control of suppliers.

It should be noted that the quality-related costs discussed in this program, do not represent the quality department costs per se. While many of these are included, the quality-related costs include those expended by many company departments and its suppliers.

To focus on it as a tool for continuous improvement, it is necessary to recognize that a quality-related cost system is not an accounting system which tracks actual business expenditures. It is also not a financial system, in the traditional sense of the term, but it is important that the inspection/quality department attempt to utilize and present its case in accounting terminology. Dollars can be meaningfully added across departments and/or products and compared to other dollar measures to gain an understanding of the financial significance of poor quality. Thus, it is a program whereby the quality-related costs are defined in a language that management can understand, that is, dollars.

Quality-related cost information helps management identify quality problems and opportunities that might otherwise pass unnoticed because they have become institutionalized in budgets and standards. Using dollars helps managers evaluate the relative importance of quality problems and provides guides as to which to tackle first. Quality-related cost information, in dollars, can be used to help demonstrate the worth of quality improvement programs, to aid in the capital budgeting of these projects, and to evaluate the organization's financial success in achieving quality objectives.

OBJECTIVES

The most important aspect of a quality-related cost system is its use as a tool to achieve continuous product and service improvement. This approach has three phases.

1. The cost of poor quality is estimated as a one-shot study and the findings utilized to identify specific quality projects for improvement. The size of true quality problems is quantified in a language that would have an impact on upper management. Major opportunities for cost improvement are identified by denoting the vital few. Opportunities for reducing customer dissatisfaction and associated threats to product salability are identified.

2. The accounting system is expanded to quantify quality costs with the results published as a continuing scoreboard. It is expected that this publication would stimulate managers to take action to reduce costs.

    Many companies have not established financial controls of such costs as scrap, rework, and field failures, since the controls are across departmental lines. The objective of this evaluation is to expand budgetary and cost controls to cover the nondepartmental costs of poor quality.

    Publication of quality-related costs do not, in themselves, stimulate improvement. However, scoreboards, if properly designed, can be a healthy stimulus to competition among departments, plants, and divisions.

3. A quality-related cost system provides an opportunity to improve profitability, through quality improvement. The system serves as a tool to manage continuous quality improvement. It tracks trends, identifies improvement opportunities, communicates the effects of these activities, and generally indicates how a company manages the quality aspects of its business.

Definitions

Quality-related costs are incurred by many departments, and, for the purpose of this program, are broken down into the following categories:

PREVENTION COSTS: These are incurred to prevent nonconformances and to keep failure and appraisal costs to a minimum.

Prevention costs may include the following:

- Test and inspection planning
- Quality planning
- Qualification tests
- Preparation of planning procedures
- New product reviews
- Process planning including capability studies
- Process control
- Quality audits
- Supplier quality evaluation
- Training
- Local and corporate quality control engineering

APPRAISAL COSTS: These are incurred in the formal evaluation of product quality for conformance to specified requirements.

Appraisal costs may include the following:

- Incoming inspection and source inspection/test
- In-process inspection and test
- Final inspection and test
- Product quality audits
- Calibration
- Inspection/test materials and services
- Evaluation of stock including product testing in field storage or in stock to evaluate possible degradation
- Spot check inspection
- Production operator checking
- Dispositioning of inspected lots
- Quality report/charting

FAILURE COSTS: These are incurred by the failure of the product to meet specified requirements. They are divided into internal and external costs.

Internal failure costs may include the following:

- Scrap including labor and material
- Rework
- Failure analysis

- Supplier scrap and rework
- Screening and/or 100 percent inspection of rejected lots
- Reinspection/Retest of rework
- Avoidable process losses
- Downgrading, that is, the difference between normal selling price and reduced prices
- Defective stock
- Actual yield less than process capability target
- Shipments less than scheduled
- Direct labor variance, that is, extra workers
- Corrective action team activity
- Administrative action on nonconforming products
- Premiums on raw material for emergency shipments
- Special freight charges

External failure costs may include:

- Defects found after product is shipped to the customer
- Warranty charges
- Complaint adjustment
- Returned material, that is, concessions made to customers due to substandard products accepted as is, or to conforming product that does not meet fitness for use
- Consumer adjustment
- Downgrading products
- Customer ill will
- Customer policy adjustment

Some companies include in the exterior failure costs, expenditures at customers' facilities due to suppliers' nonconforming products. Analysis of their manufacturing costs, supplemented by market research into costs of poor quality, can identify the vital few areas of these high costs. This information can lead to problem identification at the suppliers' facilities.

Many customers are employing life-cycle costing approaches. The users' cost is not merely the acquisition cost but also the total cost of the product over its useful life. Thus, the cost of current and potential product failure is factored into the original acquisition cost. In economic terms, the purchase price is penalized for its previous failures. In addition, customer quality failure costs are those incurred because of real or perceived product failures. They become evident to suppliers when charge backs are agreed upon, and the bill is presented by the customer. Sometimes the cost is paid to keep customers happy whether the claim is justified or not. Whether or not customers are aggressive in collecting these costs, they are just as real to customers. Therefore, these costs cannot normally be estimated by manufacturers. They often include the following:

- Equipment repair costs after warranty
- Additional equipment to make up production
- Travel costs and time spent to return defective merchandise
- Loss of productivity while equipment is idle
- Cost of backup or surplus equipment

It would be desirable if an automatic notification is provided, by customers, to suppliers of significant product failures which may occur after warranty.

Customer Dissatisfaction Costs

These are due to lost sales as a result of external failures. Customers who have switched to other manufacturers or products can no longer provide the contributable cost information. This requires knowledge of the number or frequency of defects and volume of sales lost due to customer dissatifaction.

Loss of Reputation Costs

This is the most nebulous of all, since a detailed understanding of the market environment is needed. The number of complaints received may be a small percentage of the total number of dissatisfied customers who are spreading word of the manufacturer's poor quality. The dissatisfaction may result from the following:

- Lack of product availability. Customers expect that the product is usable upon receipt. If defective on arrival, customers tend to be quite vocal in their complaints.

- Product price. A defective product which is seen as having a premium price will likely generate more complaints than one which has been discounted.

- Product safety. A hazardous product elicits a sense of personal affront. Customers feel that manufacturers do not care about them. Customers will complain a lot about this type of defect.

- Competition in a weak industry. If customers assume that there is no alternative, then they will be unlikely to complain. However, at the first op portunity customers may bolt and try a new entrant into the market.

Hidden Costs

Some costs have, in the past, been routinely accepted as normal and inevitable, but are, in fact, costs of poor quality. They can accumulate. Some report that they may be as large as three to five times the reported failure cost. Examples of hidden costs include the following:

- Redesigning the product due to deficiencies in its fitness for use
- Changing the manufacturing process due to its inability to meet product specifications
- Potential lost sales
- Software changes for quality reasons
- Costs included in standards because history shows that a certain level of defects is inevitable and allowances should be made
- Extra material purchased to allow for anticipated scrap
- Time standard allowances to cover manufacturing scrap and rework
- Extra, unanticipated manufacturing costs such as for additional space, inventory charges, and overtime
- Scrap not reported—hidden due to fear of reprisals or included in other accounts
- Excess process costs for acceptable products. Here, a process is set for filling the product to a higher level than needed, because the process variability is large and will not assure minimum requirements
- Errors in support operations such as order filing, production control, and purchasing
- Poor supplier quality, usually included by the vendor as the cost of the procurement

Controversial Costs

These may be many and varied and include the costs of overhead on top of direct labor and material included in the cost of scrap and rework. One approach is to use variable overhead but exclude the fixed overhead. Another controversial cost is unavoidable manufacturing waste; for example, the trim removed from the beginning of a coil or wire or the excess material surrounding plastic parts. These are usually not considered as defects but part of the normal process.

Other controversial costs may be

- Profit loss on scrapped product
- Product liability costs
- Depreciation of measuring equipment
- Preventive maintenance
- Tool maintenance
- Production delays due to high scrap rates
- Loss in morale
- Loss in sales and good will

It is important that all cost categories be reviewed and approved by management. However, if there is a problem, it may be wise to separate the objectional costs from the others. It is important to note that the cost of poor quality is now being applied to all areas of the company, for example, the cost that occurs when a customer receives a wrong shipment.

ESTABLISHING THE PROGRAM

The personnel responsible for the development and implementation of the quality-related cost (QRC) program should establish a listing of potentially problematic elements for each category of costs. In practice, the program usually initiates with the measurement of appraisal and failure costs. It is advisable to start with the cost of scrap and rework to get management's attention. Reports generally define these cost categories in dollars, as a percent of sales, or as a percent of manufacturing added costs (defined as labor and overhead). The definitions of the categories should be tailor-made for each organization and based upon local needs. Agreements should be reached on all categories before any data is collected.

MAKING THE INITIAL STUDY

Often accountants will not wish to make a study which will add to cost categories normally tracked in financial reports. In that case, the preparing agency should perform an individual study. Either way, it is advisable to present to management, data that is already available, particularly if it is couched in dollars, in order to show that the quality problem is large.

Once management has accepted the need for a quality-related cost program, it should chair a task force to establish cost elements. This committee should include personnel from the accounting and major line functions. Initially, it should prepare a list of elements for each quality-related cost category, finalize the definitions of each category and element, and assign responsibilities and schedules for data collection.

OBTAINING THE INITIAL FIGURES

The best approach, at the outset of the study, may be to get an estimate of these costs. This approach needs only a modest amount of effort. Within a few days or weeks, enough quality-related costs will be found to tell whether there is a major cost reduction opportunity or not, and where that opportunity should be concentrated.

A more elaborate approach is to enlarge the accounting system. This requires efforts from various departments and takes a long time, perhaps months, to gather the needed information. In the initial stages, however, estimates are good enough, since there are many opportunities for finding the gold-in-the-mine areas.

PRESENTATION TO MANAGEMENT

The grand total of the quality-related costs found should be presented to management. Costs may be so large as to be not believed. This problem can be circumvented if management had agreed to the cost categories, and if the accounting department helped to accumulate the data.

The best presentation is the relation of total quality-related costs to business measures such as the following:

- A percent of sales
- Profit—sometimes costs are larger than profit
- Current problems such as lack of floor space, increase in production time, need for more production personnel, or the use of overtime
- Per share of common stock outstanding
- A percent of goods sold
- A percent of total manufacturing costs
- Effects on break-even point

GETTING PROGRAM APPROVAL

The following steps are recommended.

1. Establish that the costs are large enough to justify action.

2. Use successful case history, if available.

3. Show opportunity, by a reasonable goal, for cost reduction, for example, failure costs reduced by half in five years.

4. Compare return on investment from the reduction of failure costs with returns from added sales.

5. Demonstrate effect of quality improvement on sales income.

OBJECTIVES AND USER INVOLVEMENT IN QRC SYSTEM

The QRC system should satisfy the requirements of many functions of the company, including top management, operations, engineering, accounting, and marketing. An accounting system for failure costs will only be effective if it meets managerial information needs. The system must be specific in what it measures. It must be monitored to ensure that the operations are under control and that QRC targets are met.

Managers who use the system should be active participants in its design. They should be fully informed as to the potential decision-making and operations-monitoring functions of the system.

Responsibilities

A good QRC system is not one delegated solely to the quality or accounting department, but one which requires input from all areas to effect quality improvements, including manufacturing, engineering, quality, and support areas such as purchasing and production control. Each of these groups provides opportunities, through formal quality improvement projects, to realize continuous improvement in products and services provided.

Guidelines

There is no right way to calculate QRC; however, it is best to adhere to ASQC guidelines (see *Principles of Quality Costs, 1990,* by the ASQC Quality Cost Committee).

QRC is a business analysis tool, but it may not always be the best one to use in every instance. In day-to-day project decisions, QRC analysis must be performed by the affected work group.

It is important not to get mired in gathering too much detail or making the QRC data base too accurate. That level of sophistication is appropriate for individual projects. Then traditional financial tools can be applied. Definitions or procedures should only be changed when it is truly significant and necessary to meet new business objectives.

QRC tends to increase during the first few years due to everyone getting better at recognizing its elements. Management should be prepared for this condition. An official document of definitions and forms should be set up and used to clarify questions that rise during the program as well as to train new employees. Management should be assisted in defending QRC reports against assigned or allocated QRC tasks from a corporate financial office.

Collection of Data

Data may be collected from any of the following sources.

Existing accounts

These include inspection costs and warranty expenses.

Account analyses

Review the contents of established accounts such as customer returns which report cost of all goods returned. Review initial return documents for those due to poor quality.

Basic accounting documents

Some inspection may be done by production. Getting the names of these employees from payroll studies can determine the amount of inspection time.

Estimates

Some production workers spend time reworking defective material. Arrange for temporary rework records to evaluate this repair time.

Work sampling

Randomly observe repair activities and the percent of time spent doing rework.

Allocation

Some engineers may spend time in product failure analysis. Estimate the time spent.

Standard cost data

Scrap, rework, and replacement of field samples may be useful data; however, some of it may be obsolete.

Accumulation of Cost Data

For a successful program, the finance department's current methods should be used as much as possible. Some methods, however, may require modifications or additions. These should be kept to a minimum. If the normal financial report does not provide a specific record of manufacturing rework or scrap costs, broken down into useful categories, the QRC team may need to provide the necessary data, in lieu of the financial department revising its data collection program.

For example, initially, the QRC committee may need to price out the cost of an item scrapped during inspection. This can be done by the inspector recording on the deficiency report the number of direct labor hours which went into the rejected product. This time can be extracted from the production operation sheet. The cost of the raw material included in the scrapped item could be obtained from purchasing or manufacturing engineering. In the same way, the cost of rework could be estimated, with the assistance of the manufacturing engineering department. Another method for accumulating the rework cost is to use a rework card on which all such operation hours are recorded. This data can be included in a computer runoff, if one exists, and can subsequently be reported at regularly scheduled intervals.

Inspection/test and production labor costs are usually maintained by the financial department. In addition, the other appraisal costs can be accumulated by establishing code identifications for each category and recording the number of hours used for these functions. Thus, the cost of measuring equipment maintenance and the cost of any material used to perform these evaluations can be readily available.

At the outset of the program, a list of the elements should be prepared and reviewed with the financial organization. In addition, for each element, the base of measurement of the characteristic and the means of collecting and analyzing the data should be developed.

Too many QRC elements should not be introduced at one time. Potentially successful programs failed because they were too ambitious at the outset. The ideal program should start with the type of data available, without too much change. As the program proves effective, it will then be easier to add additional elements and fine-tune the QRC program.

Analysis

Whenever possible, it would be helpful if normal financial reports included data relative to QRC elements. When this is not possible, the QRC team should supplement the regular reports.

For example, it may be desired to price out the rework costs of rejected products, and to classify these costs by product, nonconforming characteristic(s), reason for the rejection, and the production department or personnel responsible for the defective items. The financial report generally provides information concerning the total rework costs by department; however, it may be necessary to manually review each rework ticket to cull out the other information. Using this data, a quality failure cost analysis can be periodically prepared. This can be presented in a Pareto analysis, by amount of cost, which will provide the priority for the investigation of the most significant defective material costs. After implementing the appropriate corrective action, the rework costs can often be greatly reduced. The initial program success provides the ammunition needed to have the financial reports modified.

Reports

QRC analyses results can be presented in graphs, tables, and/or as narratives. Reports can be provided to upper management monthly and quarterly, and to middle and lower management more frequently. Improvement reports can be issued quarterly, because these results are slow to attain. Report publication should be a joint operation between the quality and accounting departments.

A quarterly quality failure report (see Figure 28-7) denotes the dollar value of scrap and rework generated by plant, department, and product. The most significant contributors to these costs, by part number, responsible department, or supplier, are also included. These reports should be distributed to the responsible personnel in the engineering, procurement, manufacturing, manufacturing engineering, and inspection/quality departments.

On an annual basis, or sooner, the QRC team should present a company-wide report to the members of the executive and quality steering committees. This report should highlight the quality-related costs for the whole company, the highest failure cost, their most significant contributors, by plant and department, the total quality-related costs for the previous period(s), and the recommendations for corrective actions.

Many companies do not wish to reveal to outsiders, such as the government and auditors, the actual extent of their quality-related costs. Since the purpose of the QRC program is as a management tool to reduce nonconformances and to provide continuous improvement, it is only necessary to demonstrate that the program's objectives are being implemented. Accordingly, some companies have applied coded designations to reflect these various costs. For example, a company may publish its failure costs as so many B units. A B unit could represent the number of dollars of failure costs per $100 direct labor, or per $1000 of sales. The actual value of the B unit would be confidential, only available to the company personnel who are participating in the QRC program. The use of these coded designations is acceptable as long as the ratios they represent remain constant over the reporting periods. Results, reflecting a continuing reduction in B units from period to period, indicate that the program is working.

Using Data and Corrective Actions

Responsible departments should review the areas under their jurisdiction for conditions which led to significant failure costs. Engineering should review pertinent drawings and designs in an effort to possibly relax applicable characteristic tolerances, and to make the necessary adjustments, when possible. Manufacturing and manufacturing engineering personnel should investigate the processes and controls for those areas and products

JULY 1987

INDEX	DEPARTMENT NO.	NAME	REWORK $	SCRAP $	TOTAL $	TOTAL/ 100 D/L $
I	20	WELDING	274.45	–	274.45	2.27
2	50	MACHINING	155.34	108.57	263.91	1.54
3	10	SHEET METAL	–	196.62	196.62	3.15
4	40	ELECT/HYD	153.18	3.32	156.50	1.28
5	132	ENGINEERING	92.80	–	92.80	–
6	141	MFG. MGMT.	53.46	–	53.46	–
7	70	ASSEMBLY	–	–	–	–
8	30	PAINT	–	–	–	–
9	60	PROD. TEST	–	–	–	–
			729.23	308.51	1037.74	1.31

JUNE 1987

INDEX	DEPARTMENT NO.	NAME	REWORK $	SCRAP $	TOTAL $	TOTAL/ 100 D/L $
3	20	WELDING	333.19	5.25	338.44	1.72
2	50	MACHINING	183.14	205.45	388.59	1.54
–	10	SHEET METAL	–	–	–	–
4	40	ELECT/HYD	108.79	–	108.79	0.67
I	132	ENGINEERING	1282.06	–	1282.06	–
5	141	MFG. MGMT.	95.12	11.01	106.13	–
6	70	ASSEMBLY	88.48	–	88.48	0.67
7	30	PAINT	49.49	4.50	53.89	0.81
8	60	PROD. TEST	22.94	–	22.94	2.65
			2163.11	266.21	2429.32	2.11

FIGURE 28-7 Quality Failure Report

reflected in the significant failure costs. Purchasing should utilize the reports to apply corrective measures for those suppliers noted as contributors to significant failure costs. Quality engineering and inspection should adjust the preventive and appraisal costs for those items, products, and suppliers contributing to significant failure costs.

Each periodic failure report should be scrutinized by the implementing department for recurrent areas of significant failure costs. A thorough review should be conducted by a plant corrective action committee to determine the causes for these deficiencies and implement appropriate actions. When correction is found to be outside the jurisdiction of the committee, the matter should be referred to the executive quality steering committee for resolution.

EXAMPLE

This company was a multiplant organization producing heavy equipment (trucks, bridges, self-powered generators, and the like) for various governmental and commercial applications.

The responsibility for the development and implementation of the QRC program was given to the quality assurance department. The director of quality assurance appointed a member of the quality engineering section to develop the program.

Initially, the quality engineer met with each department head and discussed the program elements. After a brainstorming session, it was decided to start the program with only those cost elements which were currently tracked by the controller's department. It was also decided that for the trial period, only the quality failure costs would be tracked. After a period of six months, the progress of the program would be reviewed by department heads and a determination would be made as to whether the program should continue, be expanded, or be dropped.

Since the company was working on government contracts, it was necessary to develop a QRC program which, as a minimum, would meet the basic elements of the military specification Mil-Q-9858A. Paragraph 3.6 states:

> Costs related to quality: The contractor shall maintain and use quality cost data as a management element of the quality program. These data shall serve the purpose of identifying the cost of the prevention and correction of nonconforming supplies e.g., labor and material involved in material spoilage caused by defective work, correction of defective work, and for quality control to be exercised by the contractor at subcontractor's or vendor's facilities. The specific quality cost data to be maintained and used will be determined by the contractor. These data shall, on request, be identified and made available for "on-site" review by the Government Representative.

Program Development

The quality engineer listed the minimum elements which were necessary in order to meet the basic requirements of an effective QRC program. These elements were divided up into the prime categories of Appraisal, Prevention, and Failure (internal and external). These elements are shown in Figure 28-8.

PREVENTION

Costs of preparation of in-process inspection instructions
Costs of preparation of in-process test procedures
Supplier pre-award and post-award surveys
In-plant audits
Contract and specification analysis
Preparation of manufacturing operation sheets
Cost of in-process inspection (not for acceptance)

APPRAISAL

Costs of final inspection and test
Costs of measuring equipment used for final product inspection and test
Cost of maintenance and calibration of measuring equipment
Cost of purchased parts inspection

FAILURE COSTS (INTERNAL)

Cost of rework and scrap of nonconforming products
Cost of reinspection of replaced and reworked parts
Cost of processing rejected material (MRB)
Investigation and corrective action rejection

FAILURE COSTS (EXTERNAL)

Warranty costs
Replacement of field failure parts
Investigation of field rejections and corrective actions

FIGURE 28-8   QRC Program Elements

Data Collection

After meeting with the various department heads, the methods of cost collection were determined. All costs of labor, supplies, and equipment were identified by special codes designated for each type of expenditure. These costs were included in the controller's weekly computer runs and identified separately by the assigned codes.

Rework charges were noted, on special rework cards, by the operators. These cards were marked, at the time of preparation, with the code designation of the department responsible for the deficiency. Thus, when a nonconformance was determined as resulting from an improper manufacturing operation sheet, the rework cost was charged to the manufacturing engineering department. When it was due to an error in the engineering drawing, it was charged to the engineering department. When due to a vendor-supplied item or service, it was charged to the responsible vendor.

And when due to a production department, it was charged to the responsible manufacturing section. Costs for reinspection of rework or replacements were also charged to the responsible department or supplier.

The rework costs were included in special computer runs, which listed them by the responsible department or supplier.

Scrapped material was priced out by inspection personnel and recorded on deficiency reports. The labor cost was taken from the operation sheets and the material cost was provided by the purchasing department.

Base of Measurement

All costs were reported in dollars per $100 of direct production labor.

Analysis and Reports

Weekly computer runoffs were provided by the controller to the quality engineering department who performed a Pareto analysis. This consisted of arranging the failure costs in a declining quality index, based upon the highest cost. Monthly, these costs were included in a QRC report to management.

Because the rejected parts were not identified by number or defective characteristic, the quality engineer had to manually review each rework card for this detailed information.

Monthly QRC reports were prepared by the quality engineer for each plant, department, and program (see Figure 28-9). They showed, by declining index, the cost of scrap and rework for the reporting month as compared with the index for the previous month. A monthly supplementary scrap and rework cost report (see Figure 28-10) was provided to each plant manager, noting in a declining quality index, the manufacturing department, its rework cost, scrap cost, and their significant contributors. A quarterly, company-wide quality-related report showed, in order of cost, the department, its scrap and rework costs for the past quarter, and a comparison with that of the preceding quarter.

Corrective Action

After reviewing the monthly reports, each plant production and quality control manager met with the applicable engineering, manufacturing engineering, and purchasing personnel. These costs were reviewed and tasks were assigned to investigate and implement appropriate actions to correct the most costly nonconformance causes. Since the responsible personnel had previously received copies of the deficiency reports, most of the investigations and corrective actions should have already been initiated.

When the subsequent monthly quality failure cost reports reflected the same conditions as previously reported, the matter was referred to the plant corrective action committee who then performed a more thorough investigation. This often included the application of statistical process control

	FISCAL 1980—FIRST QUARTER (AUGUST–OCTOBER 1979)				FISCAL 1979—FOURTH QUARTER (MAY–JUNE 1979)			
FUNCTION	REWORK $	SCRAP $	TOTAL $	TOTAL PER 100 D/L $	REWORK $	SCRAP $	TOTAL $	TOTAL PER 100 D/L $
A. INTERNAL COST								
1). PLANT A	5094	3307	8401	2.75	7651	2572	10223	3.12
2). PLANT B	866	936	1802	1.31	1946	1083	3029	1.62
3). PLANT C	N/A	N/A			N/A	N/A		
TOTAL MFG.	5960	4243	10203	2.00	9597	3655	13252	2.23
B. PURCHASED PARTS								
1). 110-13 CHARGE								
2).								
3).	2310	370	2680	0.53	1800	1397	3197	0.54
4).								
TOTAL PURCHASING	2310	370	2680	0.53	1800	1397	3197	0.54
C. ENGINEERING								
1). MFG. ENG.		406	406					
		23	23			295	295	
TOTAL ENGINEERING		429	429	0.08		295	295	0.05
D. EXTERNAL COSTS								
1). 126-82 WARRANTY	N/A				N/A			
2). QC INVESTIGATION			2500				2500	
TOTAL EXTERNAL			2500				2500	
GRAND TOTAL	8270	5042	15812	3.10	11397	5343	19244	3.23

FIGURE 28-9 Quality Related Analysis for All Plants: Failure Cost

techniques. When the problem could not be resolved at the plant level, the matter was referred to the executive quality steering committee for action.

Follow-up Action

At the expiration of the six-month trial period, a meeting was held with the company's department heads, and the progress of the QRC program was reviewed. It was decided that the program should be continued on a permanent basis.

It was also decided that additional elements could be added to the program, particularly rejected part information. Accordingly, the DR was revised to eliminate the manual review of rework cards by the quality engineer, and the information was entered into the computer. It was also decided that the prevention and appraisal costs should be measured.

MONTHLY REWORK/SCRAP ANALYSIS

INDEX	DEPT.	REWORK COST $	SCRAP COST $	TOTAL COST $	PART NUMBER	CONDITION
1	20	50.05	–	50.05	70-4347-0101	WELD REWORK
		189.07	–	189.00	NOT AVAILABLE	NOT AVAILABLE
		21.12	–	21.12	2288-0749-02	WELD REWORK
2	50	–	108.57	108.57	2288-0706	MACHINE DEFECTS
		109.76	–	109.76	NOT AVAILABLE	NOT AVAILABLE
		16.82	–	16.82	2288-0206	DIMENSIONAL
3	10	–	44.62	44.62	65A81-B637	PUNCHING
		–	152.00	152.00	2288-0181	DIMENSIONAL
4	40	153.18	–	153.18	NOT AVAILABLE	NOT AVAILABLE
		–	3.32	3.32	MS35059-26	DAMAGED
5	132	92.80	0.00	92.80	NOT AVAILABLE	NOT AVAILABLE
6	141	53.46	–	53.46	NOT AVAILABLE	NOT AVAILABLE

FIGURE 28-10 Monthly Rework/Scrap Analysis

Finally, a quality cost improvement program would be developed. Its goal was to reduce by 50 percent the quality failure costs within the next 18 months.

Results

As a result of the actions taken by the plant corrective action and executive quality steering committees, the significant causes of poor quality were eliminated, one by one, with new areas appearing on the quality index, but at much lower cost figures. Figure 20-5 on page 253 is a quality cost graph reflecting the degree of improvement in failure costs over a five-year period. It shows a reduction in failure costs from $25 per $100 direct labor to $1.23 per $100 direct labor. In addition, the cost of appraisal was reduced 50 percent and the outgoing quality level increased by 25 percent.

REFERENCES

1. O'Neill, Ann, R. *Quality Costs, Continuous Improvement* (43rd Annual Quality Conference). Milwaukee, WI: ASQC, 1988, p. 164.

2. Ulach, Kenneth, & Slahetka, R. *Cost of Quality as a Business Tool: ASQC*. Milwaukee, WI: ASQC, 1989, p. 306.

CHAPTER TWENTY-NINE

Quality Program Effectiveness

INTRODUCTION

One of the most important measurements is the one which determines quality program effectiveness over time. Periodic evaluations by management are essential to measure progress and to initiate corrective actions of any conditions or trends which preclude the attainment of the company's quality goals.

In addition, corporate management needs to be informed of any opportunities or threats, perceived by the members of the organization, to effect the well-being of the corporate structure vis-à-vis the competitive levels of quality and its improvement.

ESTABLISHMENT OF CORPORATE GOALS

Corporate quality goals are established by a written quality policy issued by the head of the company, and supplemented by a set of departmental goals needed to implement this policy.

An example of a statement of corporate policy specifies that "the desire of the company is to provide products and services in an economical manner which will meet the full satisfaction of its customers." An additional quality policy may stipulate that the company shall implement a program of continuous quality improvement in order to meet or exceed the competitive market quality for its current and future customers in the world market.

The criteria for the selection of the company's departmental objectives should be those which would best represent the measurable results of a function or process which is basic to customers' or users' satisfaction and company profitability. Thus, each department should convert the company objectives to terms applicable to its own operation methods, and establish suitable benchmarks which can be evaluated against its degree of implementation. At the end of a reporting period, the department head should prepare a report providing the pertinent data and the results of its individual analyses. In addition, the department's perception of the opportunities and threats to quality improvement should be reported.

Each company should select those objectives which are applicable to its specific operations and needs. Figure 29-1 lists suggested examples of company quality objectives.

STANDARDIZATION

For each objective, a quantitative goal and time period for its evaluation should be defined. Both short- and long-range values are provided for each objective.

It would be desirable if some single quantitative value could be used to describe the evaluation results. Unfortunately this is not possible for many elements evaluated by most companies. Thus they rely on a number of different standards of comparison which can be based on a number of elements. For example, product loss can be described by defects per unit; parts per million; material and labor cost for scrap or rework; historical standards, such as previous performance; comparisons with stated goals or benchmarks; competitive market quality; and customers' perception. Some examples of the standards which can be used as a basis of comparison are listed in Figure 29-2.

For each objective, a set of measurements should be prescribed. For example, the cost of scrap should be determined by the monthly accumulation of the rejection reports from all production and field sources. The production time hours expended on the scrapped item are taken from the process operation sheets and added to the cost of the raw or purchased item scrapped. The total rework charges for each department due to nonconforming drawings can be obtained by accumulating all the rework orders against that item at each stage of manufacture.

The MTBF for all new products should be determined during the prototype and production reliability testing.

The customer satisfaction index should be determined by market surveys, conducted by independent agencies.

Since the evaluation data are developed by many company departments, it is important that the terminology used for these analyses are standardized, so that they can be readily combined into a single program report. For companies which have computer facilities used to prepare these reports, it is important that all data codification is standardized, so that each bit can be converted to computer language using a common code.

Before developing the reporting program, each department's responsibilities for providing applicable data and analyses should be identified, as well as the reporting period. This is necessary to insure that all data received are for the same time period and are available when needed.

- Reducing production quality failure costs e.g., scrap, rework, and field failures

- Improving product and service reliability and life-cycle costs

- Reducing cycle time in design, development, and production

- Enhancing employees, customers, and suppliers' quality of life

- Operating so that products and services are best in class in the world market

- Utilizing the full cooperative endeavors of employees, suppliers, and customers to attain excellent products and services

- Reducing the number of field complaints and warranty claims

- Reducing, to a minimum, the response time to customers' complaints

- Improving nonproduct operations' effectiveness and quality (e.g., billing, office services, and payroll)

- Developing and maintaining human resources to the fullest extent

- Encouraging and rewarding departments and individuals in quality improvement programs

- Reducing, to a minimum, the number of engineering changes after design release to production

- Meeting customers' delivery dates per contract schedules

- Increasing attendance at company-supplied training programs on quality improvement

- Keeping, to a minimum, errors in order processing and billing

- Increasing the company's profitability

- Encouraging participative management by all departments and employees (i.e., all employees would have a voice in department operations)

- Maintaining the highest degree of ethics in dealing with employees, suppliers, customers, and the community

- Increasing the process capabilities for current and anticipated products

- Reducing inventory costs using just-in-time and similar methods

- Encouraging employee participation in professional and technical organizations

FIGURE 29-1   Company Quality Objectives

FORMAT

The organization responsible to prepare the total quality report to top management should incorporate the data for presentation. This report should be designed, whenever practicable, to be read at a glance. Top management cannot expend a lot of time going through stacks of statistical data at each reporting period. All significant information should be summarized in the first page of the report. Any supplementary information could be appended. Graphs or tables are preferred, so that the executive can readily evaluate the pertinent data.

Generally, the evaluation of each element should be provided with its previous performance report and the present variance from the previous

- Cost of scrap and rework to be reduced by 10 percent in two years and by 50 percent in five years.

- The mean time before failure (MTBF) for new products, designed in the next two years, to be increased 15 percent over the average MTBF of existing products, and increased 30 percent for products designed in the next five years.

- The competitive customer satisfaction index to be increased to number two in one year and to number one in five years.

- Production process efficiency to be increased 30 percent within two years and 50 percent within five years.

- The number of employees participating in the company's education programs to be increased twofold in one year and expanded to all employees in five years.

- The employee satisfaction index to be improved 25 percent in one year and 50 percent in five years.

- The number of engineering changes, after release to production, to be reduced 25 percent in one year and 60 percent in five years.

- The defect rate of suppliers' products to be reduced 20 percent in one year and 50 percent in five years.

- Top management participation in community and public affairs to be increased by 20 percent in one year and 50 percent in five years.

FIGURE 29-2 Comparison Standards

evaluation. Some reports identify the significant variances by some sort of mark such as an asterisk. A brief description of the significant conditions and their effect on variances can be provided. Reference can be made to the recommended corrective actions, and a report on the effectiveness of previous corrective actions can be included.

A typical report starts out with a brief statement of the general progress of the quality improvement operations, followed by comments concerning the potential improvements to the operation and any perceived threats to the success of the company's total quality program. This is followed by the tabular or graphical presentation of quality achievements, and is supplemented by an appendix containing interpretation methods and any information needed to explain evaluation methods.

AUDITS

Some companies include an audit by top management of the pertinent elements of the total quality program as part of its evaluation report. This audit is particularly used by Japanese industries where the President's Audit is annually conducted by the top executive and his or her staff in each facility of the company. The significant advantage of the President's Audit is in the impression portrayed to the company's employees of top management's intense interest in the quality improvement program.

These audits generally embrace each element of the company's quality goals and prime objectives. Currently a number of companies in this country are involved in developing quality improvement programs structured on the Malcolm-Baldrige Quality Award program.[1] For these companies, the executive audit embraces the following seven elements of the award's evaluation criteria.

- Leadership
- Information and analysis
- Strategic quality planning
- Human resource development and management
- Management of process quality
- Quality and operational results
- Customer focus and satisfaction

PRESENTATIONS

Many companies have the executive quality program report assembled into a comprehensive package which is provided at regular intervals (monthly, semi-annually, or annually) to the executive committee. These reports have usually attained the status of authoritative sources of essential information on the company's quality improvement program.

In order to retain this status, the presenting organization should insure that all reports are prepared in an acceptable format, with careful attention to the executives' needs. The reports must display objectivity, distinguish between important and nonimportant details, avoid portraying an atmosphere of blame, and should not create any false alarms, such as crying wolf.

Some companies have department managers regularly provide their phases of the total quality program report. These department heads present their analyses to the executive committee and briefly discuss the significant elements of the reports.

At times, the department managers have selected employees discuss areas of the report for which they had responsibility. This provides motivation to the participants in the pursuit of their quality improvement tasks when they realize the interest of the executives.

Other companies set aside special periods for individual employees engaged in participative action committees to present their results. These presentations are often conducted off-site and awards are given to exemplary employees and departments for their quality improvement efforts.

FOLLOW-UP ACTION

The executive staff usually evaluates the corrective actions discussed in the reports which may require management action. Any threats to the company's success noted in the reports are reviewed and investigated with the responsible personnel.

REFERENCES

1. Malcolm Baldrige National Quality Award. U.S. National Institute of Standards and Technology, Gathersburg, MD, 1992.

CHAPTER THIRTY

Competitive
Quality Levels

INTRODUCTION

This chapter describes a program of evaluating the company's standing in relation to competitive market quality levels. A description of the review methods of competing products' quality levels is provided. This chapter also discusses the review, by the inspection/quality department, of company sales and promotional literature, and product pamphlets, for assurance that they represent products within the company's manufacturing capabilities.

BASIS OF COMPARATIVE STANDARDS

The major purpose of the evaluation is to determine customers' expectations and how well the company's products and services serve their needs. Before an organization can set up the methods to determine these values, it must first establish the bases of measurement against which the results will be evaluated.

Companies have found that there are many characteristics relative to customer expectancies which go beyond product or service quality levels. Each contact with customers presents an opportunity for displaying the excellence or failure of the company's efforts. For example, an occasion where the customer is cut off while on hold during a telephone call, or receives an offhand, surly, or incorrect response to an inquiry, can go a long way in adversely affecting the company's relationship with its customers and their perception about the professionalism of its employees.

Therefore, it is important that evaluative measurements other than product or service quality are included. Also, since customers are in contact with personnel from many company departments, from the president to the switchboard operator, it is necessary that all employees are trained and indoctrinated in the concept of full-hearted quality assurance. Some considerations which should be evaluated may include employees' manner of behavior during customer contacts; frank and honest answers to customers' questions and inquiries; and assurance that any commitments made to customers, whether stated officially in contracts, or during subsequent conversations, are forthright and honest.

When a commitment cannot be fulfilled, the customer must be notified expeditiously, and a revised commitment made. Thus, when a delivery schedule cannot be met, a full investigation into the cause of the delay should be made by a responsible member of the company's management and immediate action taken to rectify the condition so that it is not repeated. The customer should be advised of the actions taken to expedite the product's delivery, including the measures taken to preclude the delay from happening again. The customer may forgive the initial delay, but would certainly lose all regards for the company's credibility if the delay occurred a second time, especially for the same reason.

This applies even more emphatically when a product does not fully meet the customer's quality requirements. Here too, it is important that any problem be immediately brought to the customer's attention. A company that knowingly ships a nonconforming product with the expectation that the customer will be unaware of the nonconformance can hardly be considered as a responsible and reliable supplier. In notifying the customer of the nonconformance, the information provided should reflect the results of a thorough investigation, the correction of the responsible conditions, and assurance that this nonconformance will not recur.

EXAMPLE

See Chapter 13 for an example.

STANDARDS OF EVALUATION

It would be helpful if the customers' perceptions of quality could be evaluated by a single measurement. Unfortunately, there are too many characteristics to enable the use of a single standard. Thus, it is necessary to develop a list of characteristics against which this perception could be measured. Figure 30-1 shows some characteristics used by many companies.

Each company can select those attributes which serve best its goals. Each goal should have a measurement and time period associated with it so that it can be used to determine subsequent improvement or decline of the company's market position. In order to attain the company's goals of competitive market quality, each department must establish its own internal goals and benchmarks relative to their processes and efforts toward the company's goals.

On-time shipments

Product performance against that of its principal competitors

Product and service reliability (MTBF)

Life-cycle costs

Deviations and waivers requested of customers

Timeliness of responses to customers' complaints

Effectiveness and timeliness of corrective action resulting from customer or field complaints

Number of engineering changes subsequent to drawing release to production

Warranty costs

Number of field returns

Involvement of top management in quality improvement activities

Software quality

Billing defects

Mean time to repair

Customer-supplied training programs

Lost sales due to quality

Company's percent of market share

Company's support at customers' sites

Replacement parts availability

Response to changing market conditions

Results of customer audits and their follow-up

FIGURE 30-1   Standards of Evaluation

MEASUREMENTS

As noted in Chapter 29, in order to properly evaluate the measurements, the terminology and any computer codes should be standardized. For example, delivery against contract schedule can be exhibited in a graph over time showing how many shipments were made: more than 20 days early, 10–20 days early, on time, 10–20 days late, and more than 20 days late.

Product performance versus that of other companies can be expressed in a table which lists customers' ratings of the company for a number of product characteristics such as equipment reliability, software quality, documentation, and life-cycle costs.

Product reliability improvement could be shown by the increase of MTBF for products designed in the current year against the average MTBFs for products designed in previous years.

Life-cycle costs, in maintenance dollars spent by customers, could be accumulated for each type of product with current designs, and compared with the average of these costs for products with designs of previous years.

The number of deviations and waivers requested from customers could be compared to the number of such requests for previous products. The timeliness of responses to customer complaints could be shown as the average number of elapsed days per incident from receipt of a complaint to its resolution. The current year's performance could be compared to that of previous years.

Effectiveness of corrective actions taken on customer complaints could be shown as the decrease in the number of complaints for similar conditions reported during subsequent years. Warranty claims in parts per million per dollar of sales, could be accumulated for each product over the years.

DATA COLLECTION METHODS

Figure 30-2 lists some ways to collect data relative to the customers' perceptions of quality.

AUDITS

Some measures of customer perception can be obtained by the evaluation of audit results. Pre- and postaward audits are generally performed by customers. Pre-award audits are done to determine the company's capability to fulfill contract requirements. Postaward audits are periodically conducted after the contract is granted to determine the degree of implementation of the company's quality programs. These audits are done in accordance with customers' developed checklists or, for government work, for compliance to such military specifications as Mil-I-45208 or Mil-Q-9858.

Some companies have their field service personnel conduct reviews of product applications at customers' sites. During these audits, the field service personnel can determine the users' perceptions of product or service quality. Field service personnel may also resolve any customer misconceptions about the function and operation of the product.

To insure that this important contact is properly utilized, auditing field personnel must be thoroughly informed about the equipment's operation and the relative company responsibilities.

For example, a company provided equipment which included some customer-supplied components. The customer's operating personnel were unaware of this fact. Accordingly, any deficiencies they encountered in these components were considered supplier failures. Company field service personnel who were knowledgeable of this information were able to correct the misunderstanding and thus maintain acceptable customer perceptions.

Some companies implement a program whereby members of their top management periodically visit major customers' sites. These show customers the high regard that management has about its product's quality and its customers' perceptions. These visits also make it possible for management

INTERNAL EVALUATIONS

- On-time shipping data versus shipping schedule
- Warranty and replacement costs
- Analysis of returned goods and field replacement
- Number of customer field complaints per product
- Analysis of reports from the service departments
- Repair costs per product
- Analysis of spare parts for significant conditions
- Billing defects per 1000 orders
- Costs of poor quality for each product and each process

CUSTOMER EVALUATIONS

- Responses to company-issued questionnaires
- Warranty card information—limited to product quality as initially received
- Vendor rating summary reports—while the names of the competing suppliers are not divulged, the order of quality of the individual company against that of the other suppliers is shown
- Management and field service visits to customer sites
- Test results at customer sites

INDEPENDENT MARKET RESEARCH DATA

- Responses to blind questionnaires requesting the ranking of each competing company on selected characteristics such as service, technical support, and product quality
- Quality rankings on the basis of 1 to 10 for reliability, documentation, training, and customer service
- Comparison of the perception by several manufacturers of the same type of project; a cumulative performance rating of the top companies included in these annual studies, can be listed in descending order of rating

OTHER EVALUATIONS

- These may be from trade associations, consumer group publications, government regulatory agencies, or similar organizations
- Quantity of equipment ordered
- Dollar volume of equipment ordered
- User sample product evaluations—usually performed for rating purposes
- Data obtained by company personnel performing tests and analysis of competing products
- Data obtained by independent laboratory testing of company and competitors' products

FIGURE 30-2 Data Collection Methods

to become aware, firsthand, of any problems customers experience. Additionally, any misunderstandings between customers and the company can be cleared up during these visits.

PRESENTATIONS

The results of competitive market reviews are usually incorporated into the total quality program reports described in Chapter 29. These reports are reviewed by middle and upper management and indicate the company's competitive quality level in the marketplace. Analyses of each element of the report provide executives with information which enables them to determine the threats and opportunities available to the company.

CORRECTIVE ACTION

Competitive quality analyses are of little value unless some positive action is taken as a result of their findings. The conditions affecting each element should be thoroughly investigated and the necessary actions taken to correct them. This may range from correction of obsolete procedures to revision of the company's entire marketing or production structure. The success or failure of these actions can be determined by data subsequently gathered for the applicable element(s). Thus, a company can become a world class quality organization.

REVIEW OF MARKETING PROMOTIONAL DATA

Some companies find it advisable to have some department independent of the sales/marketing organization review their promotional literature and product and service catalogs. This is done to insure that no commitments are made to potential customers which are beyond the company's capabilities. The following procedure is recommended.

1. A set of checklists should be prepared for each product or service brochure.

2. After approval, these should be distributed to the sales/marketing personnel, sales representatives, dealers, distributors, and sales agents of the company.

3. The checklists should include information relative to the capabilities of the company to provide the applicable equipment or services. See Figure 30-3 for an example of this checklist.

Review for the presence of and conformance to the following:

1. Applicable safety codes and standards

2. Applicable government regulations

3. Product limitations

4. Inherent safety hazards

5. Required safety precautions during use, maintenance, servicing, and operation

6. Complaint procedures and reporting requirements

7. Scope of the warranty—be specific

8. Product performance

9. Assurance that the product and its use are correctly specified

10. Absence of unrealistic comments or elaboration of the product or its performance

11. Product information currentness

12. Requirements for the use of only approved replacement parts or components

13. No inference that the product complies to a specification, code, or standard which is not applicable

14. Requirement that the product is to be maintained or disassembled in accordance with the company's approved procedures

15. No overstatement about the intended use or purpose of the product

16. No permission to alter or change the product in any way which fits a use for which the product was not intended

17. No description of the product which is in conflict with the company's manufacturing capabilities

FIGURE 30-3 Sales/Marketing Literature Checklist

4. A copy of the checklists should be provided to the company organization responsible for monitoring promotional literature.

5. This organization should develop an inspection checklist to be used for their evaluation of the sales literature. See Figure 30-4 for an example.

6. The preparing agency should review the material against the checklists and submit it to the company's contracts, legal, and monitoring agencies for approval.

7. The sales literature should be released and distributed.

8. The preparing agency should ensure that all the sales literature and product brochures are periodically reviewed for conformance to the latest configuration of the products.

Review the literature for the following characteristics.

1. Product and use correctly stated and implied

2. Pictorial presentations not in conflict with other data

3. Technical data (e.g., sheets, safety statements, specification reliability, performance, etc.) approved by the company's engineering and safety personnel

4. Statements relative to guarantees, warranties, suitability for use approved by the company's engineering, contracts, and legal departments

5. Absence of exaggerated statements (expressed or implied) as to the equipment's capabilities

6. Information presented so as to be easily understood by customers and users

7. Consideration given to translation of the information into the language and technical competence of customers users

8. Translation of information correct

Reviewed by _____ Date _____

Follow-up action needed and effected

Signed by _____ Date _____

FIGURE 30-4   Sales Promotional Literature Inspection Checklist

CHAPTER THIRTY-ONE

Inspection Function Improvement

INTRODUCTION

This chapter provides some techniques to use to measure and improve inspection output and accuracy and to remedy variant conditions.

In addition, a program is described for the evaluation of measuring equipment accuracy. Suggested methods for the compensation of problems of inaccurate equipment are discussed.

DEFECT PREVENTION TECHNIQUES

The most effective method to improve inspection output is in the prevention of defects through a quality improvement program. The methods described in this book, when successfully employed, can reduce the need for product inspection, since there is confidence that there are no deficiencies.

As discussed, methods used to correct chronic defective conditions are different from those used for the investigation and correction of sporadic and chance defective conditions. The application of Pareto analysis establishes an order of priority in the investigation and correction of the most significant discrepancies.

The use of statistical techniques are essential in determining the conditions responsible for these deficiencies. The most useful one is the statistical process control chart. This establishes whether a process is in statistical control and enables the differentiation of chance from chronic conditions.

INSPECTION OUTPUT MEASUREMENT

In order to develop a program to increase inspection output, the current output must be determined. This is usually done by each inspector posting in a log information concerning each lot inspected. This method has the additional advantage of providing quality level data for each inspection station, which can be subsequently analyzed. When inspection time is applied directly to the project or to the output of the department, this time can also be posted.

Inspection time applied as a direct charge can be input using a time clock or a computer. These methods are also useful in the implementation of a QRC program.

Since the amount of time spent inspecting different products and different-sized lots varies, a more detailed analysis of output to determine the average time is required. Some companies separate the time for each type of inspection. By breaking down these times, the method of data collection and analysis is simplified.

INSPECTION OUTPUT IMPROVEMENT

Once the average time for each type of inspection operation has been established, several methods may be used to increase the output.

Industrial Engineering Studies

Traditional engineering studies used in production operations are generally not applicable to the inspection function. The use of time studies is not considered suitable, since they often infer a desire by management to speed up the inspection function, and hence reduce the attention paid to ferreting out deficiencies. Thus, other methods are used.

One is to review the operations by a senior inspector or group leader during the examination of complex items. The other inspectors are then trained to examine these or similar items using the same techniques employed by the senior inspector. While no attempt is usually made to time study these operations, it is assumed that the inspection by a highly qualified person is a more efficient and accurate method than one performed by a less qualified individual. This method has the advantage, not only of reducing inspection time, but also of insuring that the operation is performed accurately.

At times, while observing the senior inspector, the engineer determines a simpler and less time-consuming method of inspection. For example, for a large, complex assembly, the engineer determined that a more efficient sequence of operations could be used. In that case, the inspection instruction was revised to include the sequence.

Another method of study is to break the inspection function of a complex item into its individual elements. These are then noted on a flowchart, and the job is discussed with the inspectors for their ideas. A new, more effective, method is often established as a result of these studies.

Engineering studies can be accomplished through the use of work sampling studies. These were discussed in Chapter 27. For example, one study revealed that a large percentage of time spent in a receiving department of 200 inspectors was used to stamp inspected parts. When the request to eliminate this operation was turned down, the stamping was performed by a clerk instead of the inspectors.

Another method to consider is the utilization of fixed gages or inspection fixtures instead of variables types of equipment. This is especially helpful for large quantities. In addition, the application of computer-aided measuring equipment often provides for speedier inspection operations. For example, the introduction of coordinate measuring equipment in one company reduced the inspection time of complex parts by 75 percent and enabled the use of lower skilled inspectors.

Engineering studies of the workplace often lead to improvement of the work conditions which may have caused inspection fatigue and monotony. Changes in these conditions frequently result in a more efficient operation and in more highly motivated personnel.

Some additional changes in the inspection process also result in more efficient operations. For example, the point-to-point wiring inspection of a large item of electronic equipment had previously been performed by two people, one calling out the wiring points from the drawing, and another verifying its actual location. Only one inspector was needed after the wiring point locations on the drawings were recorded on an audio tape. Another example was the reduction of test time for hydraulic refueler equipment. Initially, the test, which consisted of filling the tank and measuring the rate of defueling, was performed on each tanker individually. Since it took a long time to refuel each tanker, the tester experienced a considerable amount of idle time. By testing two tankers at a time, the refueling operation of one tank was performed while the defueling rate was measured on the other tanker. This reduced the length of each test to almost one half.

INSPECTION REDUCTION

As previously discussed, the more information available about the production process, the greater the confidence in the resultant product's quality level. Thus, when a supplier or manufacturing process has consistently demonstrated high quality levels for products from their facilities, the amount of inspection can be drastically reduced.

Use of Inspection Data

The use of suppliers's data and their performance records can sharply reduce the amount of inspection. At times, after a supplier had been qualified as consistently producing acceptable product, acceptance upon receipt can be based merely upon inspection of the shipment for identification, handling or environmental damage, and availability of supplier's data. Subsequent audits of incoming lots for selected characteristics can be made to insure that the quality level is maintained. In addition, these audits can confirm that the suppliers' data are representative of the quality of the products received.

This concept is similar to the Japanese approach, wherein they perform a high degree of inspection on the initial shipments while assuring that the supplier maintains the process under control at its facilities. This subsequently reduces or altogether eliminates receiving inspection.

This approach can be applied to in-house operations. In fact, the manufacturing process is more readily adaptable to this type of control. A positive evaluation of a manufacturing department or operator can establish the confidence in the quality of its product, leading to reduced inspection. The products and processes can be periodically audited to insure that the quality level is maintained.

Reduced inspection can also be accomplished using any one of the following plans detailed in Chapter 27.

- Qualification
- Process capability studies
- Use of production equipment
- Sampling inspection
- Zero acceptance plans
- Double and multiple sampling plans
- Skip lot inspection
- Continuous sampling plans
- Sampling by variables

INSPECTION ACCURACY

Inspection accuracy is the degree to which the inspector correctly makes decisions about product quality, that is, accepts conforming products or rejects nonconforming products. Inspectors are as susceptible to the concept of self-control as production operators. Three basic principles govern the inspection operation.

Inspectors must know what they are supposed to do

Inspectors must have a clear definition of the criterion of acceptability. For example, if this criterion consists of several pages of specifications which are overly descriptive, then the product is difficult to accept or reject. The specification must be clear and unambiguous. It should, for efficiency, be reduced to the basic elements of acceptance or rejection, so that a decision can be made without recourse to the inspector's judgment. The characteristics of the specification or drawing should, to the maximum extent, be expressed in quantitative terms with a specific tolerance. Statements such as "the product shall meet the highest quality pertinent to the industry" are hardly sufficient for the inspector to determine the acceptability of products.

When it is not possible to convert the criteria to quantitative terms, some other means should be established to reduce the degree of uncertainty. For example, the surface of a rough casting should be inspected against samples with established acceptable surfaces. Wire dress should be illustrated by actual glass-case models of correct and incorrect dress. Acceptable and unacceptable solder joints should be illustrated by pictures. Acceptable weld surfaces should be determined by comparison with samples of welds depicting the minimum acceptable surfaces.

Inspectors should know how they are doing

Inspectors should be provided with information that describes their ability to make correct decisions. There are many methods which can be used to advise inspectors about the accuracy of their decisions. One way is to have some other inspector or quality engineer reinspect an individual's samples. In some companies, the reinspection results are accumulated over a specified time for each inspector and a final score relative to the accuracy of the inspector's decisions is provided.

Inspectors must have a way of regulating their performance

It is important that inspectors are advised of specific errors in accuracy as soon as they are discovered. This way inspectors can verify the error and make the necessary operational adjustments. At times errors may be due to faulty or inaccurate measuring equipment rather than to the inspector.

In addition to these principles of self-control, inspectors must also be able to make correct decisions, and be able to use the knowledge of their performance to regulate future operations. When this is absent, management should take measures to provide adequate motivation to inspectors by stressing the importance of the job and the effect of errors on outgoing product quality and hence on the company's competitiveness.

Inspection Errors

There are three categories of inspection errors: technique, inadvertent, and willful.

Technique errors

These may be due to a number of factors such as a lack of capacity for the job, color blindness, insufficient education and training, lack of natural aptitudes, and ignorance of what the job requires.

Inadvertent errors

These errors are ones of which the inspector was unaware. Errors may be made in spite of inspectors' best intentions. Errors may be due to fatigue, inaccurate measuring equipment, or incorrect or indefinite specifications or criteria of acceptance. For example, an instructor at the start of a study period passed around a sheet of paper containing a paragraph of technical information. He requested the attendees to count the number of Gs on the page and record it on the sheet which was returned to the instructor. Upon analyzing the results, it was found that over 80 percent of the attendees had incorrectly counted the number of Gs. The reasons for these inadvertent errors cannot be truly determined, but methods are available which can compensate for them. These will be discussed later in this chapter.

Another type of inadvertent error is also procedural. These are errors due to the results of loose or imprecise procedures. An example of this condition is the inadvertent shipment of uninspected or rejected material to assembly and stores areas due to the result of poor movement procedures.

Willful errors—inspector initiated

Inspectors, at the time of making these errors, were aware of them and intended to continue. Inspectors are subject to many pressures from production operators, supervisors, and customers' representatives. At times, this may lead to collusion, or, at the other extreme, a desire to get back at the personnel who had been harassing them. Several examples of willful errors are cited.

In a foundry, an inspector was to check the hardness of specimens taken from each pour. The results were posted on a log which was periodically given to a quality engineer for analysis and determination of the acceptability of the pour for its tensile strength. The results of several weeks' recordings showed that the spread of hardness readings was less than would be anticipated for the type of metal poured. On investigation, it was found that the inspector was tired of the constant testing, and in lieu of performing these examinations, arbitrarily assigned a hardness number for each specimen at the end of the day, keeping the values close to the norm.

EXAMPLE

Here is a more serious example of a willful error. A company was in the process of welding large sheets of aluminum for use in vessels to transport liquid natural gas. These welds were subsequently x-rayed and reviewed by the company's radiographer for defects in accordance with specifications.

The location of each inch of weld was indicated on the x-ray by placing lead markers on the plate. Upon review of the x-rays, the radiographer noted on an inspection record the deficiencies for each location as defined on the x-ray. When a section was found out-of-specification tolerance, a copy of the inspection sheet was provided to the production supervisor who then made the necessary weld corrections. The inspection sheet, with the corrections noted, was returned to the radiographer who x-rayed the appropriate sections, identified the repair x-ray, and attached it to the end of the roll for the applicable plate. Once completed, the radiographer submitted the roll of x-rays to the customer's representative for review and approval. At times, however, the customer's representative took exception to the radiographer's interpretations and refused to accept the plate until the disputed areas were corrected. The radiographer, on reviewing the customer's comments, would often find no justification for them, and after a considerable discussion, frequently had his interpretation accepted. At times, however, the customer's representative would be adamant about the rejection, and not accept these findings. Thus, the radiographer had to resubmit the disputed area to the production supervisor requesting that it be re-welded. Here too, the radiographer was subjected to considerable arguments before the plate was reworked.

An employee of the company, who had been fired for dereliction of duties, accused the company of falsifying welded plates x-rays and hence shipping plates with defective weldments to customers. These accusations, if true, would have been of a serious nature, since the integrity of the welds was essential for safety. When advised of the accusations, the company president immediately requested an investigation of the alleged condition by the company's director of quality assurance. After reviewing all the x-rays taken to date for the full program, the director found that, in fact, some falsifications had been made, although a reexamination of the areas in question did not reveal any area which was in violation of the specifications. Further investigation revealed the following:

1. The radiographer had become thoroughly demoralized by the constant need to justify his interpretations with the customer. Knowing that the x-rays which were disputed were fully acceptable, he took the following action:

2. Finding an area of the x-ray which *could* be disputed, the radiographer x-rayed another section of the plate—one which had no imperfections—identified it as a repair x-ray, and attached it to the end of the roll.

3. This action resulted in the reduction of disputes between the radiographer and the customer's representative. The radiographer knew that the product was acceptable but wished to reduce the areas of unjustifiable disagreements.

4. As a result of the investigation, the responsible radiographer was fired and all other radiographers were instructed that, in the future,

submission of the completed x-rays to the customer would be made only by the inspection supervisor. Also, a control was included in the inspection process for an additional review, by the quality engineer, of all x-rays before presentation to the customer's representative. This assured that no falsification had occurred.

Inspection shortcuts

These are unauthorized operational omissions which the inspector believes are of dubious value.

Flinching

Tendency for the inspector to falsify results of borderline products. Sometimes this occurs when the reports are modified to conform to results which the inspector expects. An example of this type of error is the rounding out of points in a laboratory graph to reflect a smooth curve.

Rounding off

This disposes of unneeded accuracy. The inspector rounds off to the next scale division. Rounding off is sometimes desirable, but when precision readings are needed, it should not be practiced.

Willful errors—management initiated

Conformance to quality standards is sometimes subordinated by management to other priorities such as quantity, cost, and delivery. This frequently gives the inspector multiple standards to meet. Management's failure to act on nonconformances and defect causes indicates to inspectors that it is not that concerned about quality. The inspectors judge management's real interest by their deeds and not their propaganda. An example is the continuing acceptance of the same discrepancies by the MRB. Inspection, after a while, will stop rejecting the item. Similarly, if management makes no firm response to inspectors' suggestions of quality or clarification of vague instructions, then they conclude that the real concern is elsewhere.

Management fraud

Some major notorious quality errors are traceable to decisions by management or engineers rather than to inspectors. Sometimes a manager attempts to deceive the customer through fictitious quality records. This usually requires a confederate. If inspectors knowingly participate, they share in the responsibility. At times, they may be reluctant accomplices. Examples of the most notorious cases include the falsification of the following: semiconductor qualification records, strength records of special bolts used in aircraft construction, and x-rays used on the Alaska pipeline.

REMEDIES FOR INSPECTION ERRORS

Checking for Errors

Inspectors' dignity should be preserved when reviewing the accuracy of their work. The inspectors should be advised of any problems in a location apart from other personnel. The results of these reviews should not be divulged to peers or production.

Conventional methods are the checking of inspection results, assignment of weights, and the use of components of errors as indices of accuracy. The use of a demerit method with acceptability expressed as demerits found for lots checked is often advantageous. The disadvantage of most plans is that inspection accuracy depends on the quality of work submitted, a factor which inspectors cannot control.

To remedy this condition, the use of the Juran-Melsheimer[1] method is applicable. This method is independent of incoming quality. Also responsibility must be clear. The inspector should not be held responsible for acceptance of defects under orders or through incorrect measuring equipment.

Technique Errors

Correction of these types of errors requires providing additional inspector training for the missing skills. Check inspection (accept and reject decisions) are usually used to determine technique errors. This is performed by repeat inspections (same inspector, no knowledge of prior inspection) or round robin (same product, independent examination by multiple inspectors).

Other methods include using standard array samples, sometimes called job samples. A sample of a prefabricated mixture of various defects is presented to the inspector being evaluated. All samples were previously graded by teams of experts and numbered for ready analysis. The inspector's score and pattern point to any need of further training.

Job descriptions must precisely define the inspection duties required and the physical aptitudes needed to implement them. At the time of hire or transfer of duties, inspectors are usually given a physical examination to determine their aptitudes. Included is an acuity check.

Inspectors' performance data are studied as part of the evaluation. A review is then made of inspectors' work methods to discover the difference between superior and inferior work. These studies often discover the secret know-how knack for superior performance or the secret ignorance in poor performance. If technique errors are due to lack of job capability, retraining will frequently not work. To correct this condition, there is a need to foolproof the inspection methods, introduce redundance in the design, or use various fail-safe or similar methods.

Another method is to eliminate inadvertent errors by using automated inspection devices. Once the setup is correct and stable no inadvertent errors can occur.

Additional methods utilize sense multipliers such as, optical magnifiers, sound amplifiers, and other devices to magnify unaided human senses. The optimum level of magnification must be determined by experimentation. For example, a magnifying glass is used to discover surface defects. Then determination is made as to whether they are visible with the unaided eye. This is used when the specification denotes that visual (by the naked eye) defects are rejectable.

Physical standards, such as colored plastic chips, textile swatches, forging specification photos, templates which line up holes, and inspection units in pairs, are also available to eliminate technique errors.

Block off scales of measuring equipment which are beyond specification tolerances block out inspectors' views of characteristics for which they are not responsible.

Reorganization of work to reduce inspection fatigue helps eliminate errors. Operations can be broken up into periods of rest, rotation to other inspection duties, job enlargement, and so on. Inspectors' work areas should be studied for adequacy of lighting, space, and other attributes.

Procedural Errors

To correct inspection errors due to poor or inadequate procedures, they must be studied and changed. It is important to know whether the problem is management or operator controllable. For example, to correct an inadequate procedure which allowed uninspected material to be moved to assembly or stores areas, the following corrections were made.

An acceptance tag was prepared and stamped at the last fabrication inspection point. Assembly and stores personnel were responsible for accepting only material bearing stamped tags. Uninspected material was held in special identified areas and did not bear a stamped tag. Rejected material had a deficiency tag attached and was transported to the materials review area.

Willful Errors—Inspector Originated

This type of error is readily determined and correction requires a change in inspector attitude. Motivation programs should place special emphasis on job importance, measurements of performance, incentives, and the like.

The remedy for flinching is an atmosphere of respect for the facts. The principle influences are the examples set by inspection supervisors and management.

Willful inspection errors can be minimized by:

- Filling jobs only with personnel of proved integrity.

- Restricting the inspector to the job of fact finding, while the line inspection supervisor negotiates with production supervisors and customers.

- Conducting regular inspection checks and independent audits to detect errors.

- Taking prompt action when these errors are discovered.

If these approaches are not successful, it may be necessary to retrain, or transfer inspectors to less critical operations. In the worst cases, it may be necessary to replace them.

Willful errors—Management Originated

There are few remedies for this condition. The only recourse is to indoctrinate management in the need for ethical behavior and a strong commitment to the quality improvement program.

What recourse do inspectors have to contend with this type of problem, especially when management fraud is involved? They are caught on the horns of dilemma. Refusal to participate may be cause for dismissal. The only action that inspectors can take, short of resigning, is to refer the matter to their supervisor or manager. The manager will have the same problem in reacting to this condition. However, it is, at times, helpful for the inspection/quality supervisor to point out to the fellow manager, the danger in pursuing fraudulent operations.

One case was resolved in the following manner. The company head wished to use some material which had been rejected by the inspection department upon receipt. The inspection supervisor discussed the matter with the company head and pointed out the potential danger of using this discrepant material. She noted that even if the material did not have a deleterious effect on the function of the end item, the records would show that rejected material had been used. In the current climate of product liability claims, should a failure occur during use of the final equipment which incorporated the company's product, an investigation would reveal the use of nonconforming material, even if it was not responsible for the failure. Furthermore, even if the material's inspection records were no longer available, testimony, under oath, of company personnel who were aware of the problem would no doubt reveal the use of this rejected material. Upon reflection, and with the realization of a greater potential danger to the company, the company head rescinded his request for the material. Of course, it would probably not have been wise to have pointed out, at the time, management's responsibility to maintain an ethical posture in dealing with product quality.

MEASUREMENT ERRORS[2]

The measurement process is essentially a comparison of a characteristic's value with that of the applicable standard. Because the standard bears some relationship to the absolute unit of the parameter being measured, the observed value can be related or stated in terms of the absolute or true value.

Errors in Measurement

Errors of measurement have a direct bearing on inspectors' ability to judge conformance. The discussion of measurement errors is of a complex nature, often difficult to fully understand. The measurement error is generally made up of two components: the error of accuracy and the error of precision (see Figure 31-1).

The error of *accuracy* is a measure of the displacement of the observed value from the true value. It is a fixed and constant error. It is the extent to which the average of duplicate measurements of one single unit of a product agrees with the true value. The difference between the average and the true value is called the error (also called systematic error, bias, or inaccuracy), and is the extent to which the instrument is out of calibration. Accuracy is the ability to hit the bull's-eye. However, if the magnitude of this difference is known, it may be expressed in terms of the true value or in terms of the assigned value of the equipment being measured. The error can be positive or negative. The correction needed to put the instrument into calibration is of the same magnitude as the error but of the opposite sign. The measuring equipment is still considered accurate if the error is less than the total or maximum error allowable for the equipment.

The error of *precision* is a measure of the closeness of a series of measurements of the same characteristic and the same product. It is a random error and establishes the degree of reproducability of the measurement process.

Irrespective of the accuracy of calibration, an instrument will not give identical, repeated readings, even on a single unit of product. Instead the measurements scatter about the average. The ability of the instrument to reproduce its own measurement is called precision, and this varies inversely with the dispersion of multiple measurements. The inherent precision of an instrument parallels the inherent process capability of a machine tool. Quantification of the precision in terms of the standard deviation of the replicated measurements is expressed by σ, the statistical symbol for standard deviation. Recalibration, normally, cannot improve the precision of the instrument. This may not be as easy. However, the degree of imprecision is measurable and reproducible and, therefore, predictable.

If the precision error is within specified tolerances, it may be acceptable. If not, quantifying the error in terms of the standard deviation, could enable the utilization of the data by compensating for the error in the final determination of product acceptability.

Errors in accuracy and precision are quantified as a difference between the average of multiple, replicated measurements and the true value. Each term is surrounded by a fringe of doubt or limit of uncertainty. The expression for accuracy, therefore, must show the extent of these doubts, if the full meaning of the number is to be conveyed. The two errors result

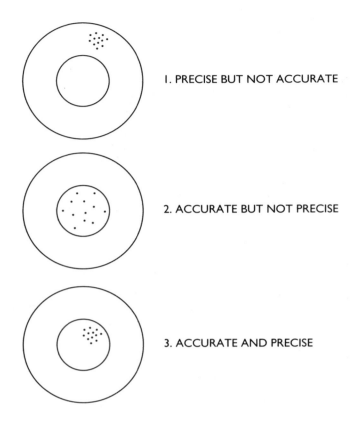

FIGURE 31-1 Accuracy and Precision

from the inadequacies of equipment, material, personnel, or techniques used during the performance of these measurements.

There are other sources of error which may affect, to a considerable degree, the true determination of the characteristic's value. One such error results from the lack of recognition of the principle of significant figures. For example, the value 105 with three significant figures denotes that the value under consideration is between 104.6 and 105.4. Yet the number on the drawing or specification is 105.0, which appears to be the same number, but actually provides different information. This number indicates that the value lies between 104.96 and 105.04. Therefore, it denotes an accuracy to the fourth significant figure.

A measurement should never be recorded to more significant figures than can be readily established by the observer. In this regard, the observer must be able to read to one figure beyond the recorded value. Therefore, the inspector should use measuring equipment which is equal in accuracy to one significant figure beyond that specified on the drawing. On the other hand, the measuring equipment used need not be greater in accuracy than one significant figure beyond that specified.

Sources of Error

Errors of inaccuracy and imprecision have their origins in several components of measurement.

Within operator variation

The same operator, inspector, or technician, even with the same measuring system and the same unit of product, will come up with a dispersion of readings.

Between operator variation

This is the variation between two operators using the same measuring equipment on the same product. This can be exhibited as both systematic error and difference in dispersion.

Materials variation

One cannot always conduct repeated tests on the same unit of product since it can be changed or destroyed by the test. In other cases, the standard is consumable, so that material variation affects the standard as well. The problem of perishable material may require the use of calibration which relates time to degradation suffered.

Test equipment variation

Measuring equipment is subject to numerous sources of error, both within a single instrument and between instructions; for example, nonlinearity; hysterisis, such as gear backlash; drift due to temperature rise; and sensitivity to exterior noise, such as magnetic, thermal, and electrical fields. These instrument troubles are multiplied by fixturing problems, that is, connecting measuring instruments into larger equipment units, and then conducting the tests. Fixturing problems include making proper electrical connections, fastening mechanical linkages, and locating probes.

Test procedure variation

Where more than one test procedure is available to conduct measurements, it is essential to determine their relative variations, since there should be just one criterion for judging the adequacy of the procedure.

Interlaboratory variation

Major problems exist within and between companies performing examinations on the same product. Often standard procedures have been evolved for the purpose of resolving this problem.

Composite Errors

The observed measurements is the result of contributing variables. σ^2 observed $= \sigma^2 w + \sigma^2 m + \sigma^2 e + \sigma^2 p \ldots$, where σ observed is the standard deviation of the observed measurements and the others are standard deviations which affect the precision. Note that the effect of some component source of variation can often be quantified through a simple design of experiments.

Defining an Uncertainty

The limits of possible error in connection with any measurement can be defined, and whether it is possible to perform the measurement within such limits of accuracy can be determined. In the process, the factors contributing to the overall error of measurement can be identified and, if practical, they can be eliminated. If this is not practical, the observer can express the measurement as a magnitude within defined limits of uncertainty. In publishing results, it is necessary to make clear the extent of error to allow a proper evaluation of the measurements.

Effect of Referenced Standards

Accuracy of an instrument is the difference between T true value and $\overline{X}_m$, the average of the repeated measurements. The reference standard is assumed to be the true value. A small difference can make a close approximation. If the true value is needed, however, published measurements can be referred to "as maintained by the NIST (formerly NBS)."

When this error is large enough, the appropriate explanation consists of a statement appended to the data stating, for example, "this value is accurate within $+/- b$ units or within $+/- y$ percent." If it is necessary, test conditions such as temperature and range can be mentioned. It is a mistake to show the value as $+/- b$ without an explanation, since it is not clear whether b is a measure of systematic error or an explanation of standard deviation of repeated measurements. For the appropriate explanations, see NBS Handbook 91.

Effect of Imprecision

Quantification of results is made through expression of standard error (standard deviation). In publishing data, a statement should be appended to the standard error which clears up any possible confusions in interpretations. Unless otherwise stated, it should be the practice to relate the published standard error to the published average, citing the number of observations in the average.

If uncertainty is expressed as a multiple of the standard error, the statement should specify the number of multiples used. An appropriate form is "____ with an overall uncertainty of 3.0 ft./sec."

When systematic errors and imprecision are combined, the published results must make clear that both types of errors are present and significant. A recommended statement is: "____ with an overall uncertainty of + /− 1.5 percent based on a standard error of 0.5 percent and an allowance of + /− 1.0 percent for systematic error."

Negligible Errors

Results may be published in such a way that the significant figures themselves reflect the extent of uncertainty. For example, "the length is 1065.1 inches, correct to five significant figures." The conventional meaning is that the true value lies between the stated value and + /− 0.5 inches.

Programs to Reduce Error

Each major variation is a component of multiple subvariations. Reducing the overall error usually involves two related programs.

1. Quantifying the composition of error which are not equally important. The determination may follow the Pareto principle. Through statistical design of experiments it is possible to quantify the main component contributing to the error and determine its degree of influence on the measurement in question.

2. Finding ways to reduce the major variations through improved techniques or new technology. The cause may not be due so much to operator techniques as to the lack of adequate engineering or technology.

3. Another way to reduce measurement error is to take a second measurement of a critical characteristic using a different piece of equipment or a different method.

Interlaboratory Test Programs

Major problems result from interlaboratory errors. It may be necessary to develop an interlaboratory test program coincidental with test method development. The program generally centers on round robin tests. It requires a great deal of preparation, including the following:

■   Use of technical committee

■   Participation in planning with the laboratories

- Use of modern statistical design of experiments
- Multiple regressions

Due to the importance of this problem, standards have been developed for materials and interlaboratory test methods (see *Special Technical Publication 335* by the American Society of Testing Material).

REFERENCES

1. Zeccardi, Joseph J. *Inspection and Test: Juran's Quality Control Handbook* (4th ed.). New York: McGraw Hill, 1988.

2. Suntag, Charles, & Silverman, Sam. *Making Meaningful Measurements*. Philadelphia: Electronic Industries, February and March, 1965, p. 90.

CHAPTER THIRTY-TWO

Dealing with Customers

INTRODUCTION

This chapter discusses the general methods used by many companies relative to inspection/quality assurance features of customer/contractor relationships. This chapter covers the various elements of maintaining liaison with customers both internally and externally, as well as understanding of customers' requirements. The various elements of contract and specification review and analysis and using these reviews when dealing with customers' representatives are presented.

The inability of many organizations to determine their current and potential customers needs is often a serious impediment to quality improvement efforts. The market must be studied by one or a combination of several techniques. These include sending questionnaires to potential customers, face-to-face contact, obtaining information from sales representatives, visiting customers and product users at their place of operation, studying what the competitors in the field are providing, and using the services of third party research organizations who are familiar with the products and services of the applicable markets.

It is important that when a study is made of customers' wants, the right questions are asked. Often, unless the questions are appropriately worded, the answers will not fully provide the needed information. Frequently, customers' perceptions about the company and its products is not too closely related to the requirements spelled out in customers' specifications.

LIAISON—EXTERNAL

It is definitely poor policy to wait until a problem rises, resulting in customer complaints, before correcting it. Many times, rather than registering a complaint, customers just cease doing business with the company. At other times, customers may not be aware that their suppliers can help them reduce the costs of poor quality. For example, when a product, after its warranty period has expired, fails to operate properly, customers often accept the costs of poor quality without complaining to suppliers. If suppliers know about the problems, customer assistance could be provided to mitigate the expense caused by the product's poor quality. Suppliers, being aware of these problems, could take the appropriate corrective actions. This would improve product quality while keeping the business which would otherwise have been lost.

Some companies have their senior executives periodically visit their customers' facilities to view, firsthand, the application of their products. These face-to-face discussions serve two purposes. First, they demonstrate management's interest in customers' wants and needs. And second, they enable open discussion between customers and company representatives about the positive and negative features of their products as perceived by customers.

It is also important that when suppliers contemplate some product design change, they meet with their customers to obtain their comments about this proposed change. At that time, some additional changes pertinent to perceived customers' needs may be found desirable.

Some companies include top members of the inspection/quality department in their customer visits. They discuss current and anticipated product problems with the applicable personnel from the customers' inspection/quality department. The discussions should be frank and open, and customers' recommendations should be solicited. These face-to-face contacts will also enable suppliers to review customers' methods of inspection and testing. At times, it may be discovered that these examinations are not similar to those conducted by suppliers. At other times, it may be discovered that customers are attempting to utilize the product in a manner which is beyond its capabilities. Discussing these elements can provide a better understanding on both parties about the product, its applications, and methods of examination. In addition, the contacts among the inspection/quality personnel lead to a better relationship in the event of future problems.

The results of these discussions should be analyzed and reviewed with the applicable company personnel. Any actions necessary to rectify negative findings should be implemented as soon as possible. These actions may require some changes to the product design, process of manufacture, or the inspection/quality program. Some of these actions may need to be delayed until the product is redesigned. At any rate, customers should be advised of any suppliers' actions relative to their complaints, and the time frame for their accomplishment.

These face-to-face meetings should be repeated at periodic intervals. It may, however, be impracticable to visit the facilities of all customers. Holding periodic meetings and workshops with groups of customers would partially perform the desired functions. At such time, tours through the plant, administrative, and engineering areas are often desirable. Naturally, any customers' recommendations for product or process improvements should be encouraged and considered.

LIAISON—INTERNAL

The customers' resident representatives' confidence in the integrity of contractors' inspection/quality personnel must be established early in relationships. To better control customers' exposure to contractor personnel, it is customary for specific inspection/quality department members to maintain liaison with these representatives. They are specially trained in the company's inspection/quality policy and procedures and the applicable contractual requirements, and have the ability to maintain good relationships. They must be completely honest and above board in all their dealings. This does not infer that all the company's problems are discussed with customers. However, any quality deficiencies in customers' products should be first discussed with them before shipment. The contractors' personnel should on no occasion knowingly allow a situation to exist which will cause embarrassment to the customers' representatives. It must be understood that once the representatives have lost confidence in contractors' inspection/quality personnel, their value is diminished insofar as customer relations is concerned.

When advised by customers of a specific problem, the designated company personnel should review the situation with them and promise to have an immediate investigation performed. A specific time table for reporting results and, when required, corrective action, should be given and met. When the promised date cannot be met, the contractor's personnel should immediately advise customers, provide an interim report, and set a new completion time.

The customers' representatives may sometimes be incorrect about the validity of the complaint. Nevertheless, it should be reviewed. If investigation reveals the lack of validity, it should be pointed out as diplomatically as possible. The reason for the contractor's position should then be validated. There may be times when customers' complaints are based on judgment. This generally occurs when the complaint is about the implementation of a contractually mandated inspection/quality program, or an interpretation of the customer's specification or other contractual document. While discussing the possible misunderstanding, additional clarifications of the applicable company's procedure should be provided so that the misunderstanding does not recur. At times, the matter cannot be thoroughly resolved and it may be necessary to refer the problem to the customer's supervisor or some other member of the organization, such as the procurement or engineering department. Referring the matter should never be done without the knowledge or presence of the customer's representative; going over his or her head is usually nonproductive, since the battle may be won, but the war will probably be lost.

To minimize the necessity of referring problems to customers' upper management, periodic meetings with the representatives and the contractor's inspection/quality personnel should be held. Here, all unresolved issues should be discussed and corrective measures recommended. Written minutes of the meeting should be maintained. Other company members may attend, when the discussions involve their activities. It may be advantageous to sometimes invite the representative's supervisor to attend these meetings. This is particularly important when there are frequent contract misinterpretations by the resident representative.

Some customers' representatives may not have received sufficient training in the inspection/quality aspects of the contract. To minimize the effects of this problem, some companies invite the representatives to participate in the training programs provided for contractor personnel. At other times it may be advisable to recommend additional training in a special discipline.

Periodically one company conducted training programs for its inspection/quality personnel relating to customers' quality programs as well as its own procedures and manual. The customers' inspection/quality personnel were invited to attend. This program helped immeasurably to familiarize everyone with one another's policies and procedures. Questions and recommendations from all parties were encouraged, discussed, and acted on. Thus, a better understanding of all customer and contractor inspection/quality requirements was enjoyed by all.

One important element of the interrelationship between customer and company personnel is to restrict dealings on quality matters to designated members of the inspection/quality department. An example of the importance of this policy is discussed in the next section.

EXAMPLE

A company had considerable trouble with the activities of the resident customer's representative. At times the effect of these problems resulted in substantial delays in product acceptance and shipment. Most of the time, the customer's actions were justified. At other times they were not. Every time such an occasion resulted in shipping delays, it had been the policy of the company's contract personnel to refer the matter to the customer's procurement department, who then contacted the representative and presented the complaint to him. As a result, the representative, in an attempt to defend himself, often denied the accusations, and pointed out the company's failure to comply. His defense often resulted in recriminations about the company's overall program implementation which transcended the original complaint. Subsequently, the customer's procurement personnel referred the additional complaints to the company's contract personnel, who, in trying to refute these new allegations, provided additional recriminations. As a result, the relationship between the representative and the company steadily deteriorated. Thus, the representative became even more rigid and, at times, arbitrarily reviewed and rejected the company's program and products.

When a new director of quality assurance was hired, he requested that any future problems be referred to him or to the inspection/quality department manager for resolution. After some delay, this request was granted and implemented. As a result, all quality-related problems were handled by the company's designated inspection/quality personnel and the resolutions were processed orderly and factually.

To maintain positive relationships with customers' representatives, all their requests should be processed by the designated inspection/quality personnel. This insures that there is no undue interference with production activities, schedules, or incentives, as applicable. This also insures the most suitable and timely resolution to any problems, real or perceived.

The implementation of this program is important for several reasons, as follows:

1. Results in proper and timely actions by customers and contractors.

2. Establishes only valid complaints, thus reducing unnecessary re-work.

3. Results in high confidence, cooperation, and trust between customers and contractors.

LIAISON—FIELD COMPLAINTS

Customer confidence should continue after the product is shipped. Suppliers should not wait until complaints are received from the field, but should establish contact with users before problems arise. One company had their inspection/quality manager contact the customer's facility just before initial shipment to request that the recipient notify him of the equipment's condition upon receipt and of any subsequent problems. He also stated that any problem, no matter how slight, should be brought to his attention so that he could rectify it and prevent its recurrence. These actions demonstrate to customers and users the company's continued interest in product quality and its desire to address any problem occurring in the field.

Some companies provide users with stamped, self-addressed follow-up cards. These request information about product quality while in use. Other companies contact users a short period after delivery, to determine their satisfaction or to obtain suggestions about any product features. Users should be given a telephone number (preferably an 800 number) to call with any questions concerning the product's operation or related services.

It is equally important that once information is received about some adverse condition, the company initiate an immediate investigation and correction actions, if needed. The complainant should be notified of the actions taken. When none is deemed necessary, the complainant should be advised of the reasons for that decision.

At times, complaints are addressed from users to resident customers' representatives. They should be encouraged to discuss the complaint with the designated company's inspection/quality personnel. If possible, a copy of these field complaints should be issued directly to those personnel. Here, too, immediate investigation and applicable action should be taken and the resident representative should be advised accordingly.

ANALYSIS OF INSPECTION/QUALITY REQUIREMENTS

Important to customer relationships is the contractors' complete understanding of the contractual requirements, so that the inspection/quality program can address and implement all technical and quality elements. Some companies have taken the position that any failure to understand each and every element of customers' requirements would be brought to their attention by the customer before any damage had occurred and before the product was fabricated. This is a fallacious assumption, since the product's failure to meet all contract requirements is often discovered at a time in the production cycle which could cause significant costs and delays. This results from the company's lack of knowledge, and its failure to implement contract requirements during planning and production. These omissions may not be noted until some time after the product has been delivered. This not only results in increased expenditures to correct field discrepancies, but also causes customers to lose confidence in the company's ability to produce acceptable products. This translates into lost business.

Also important to customer relationships, is the ability to refute any customer requests which are not contractually required. Some companies will often comply with these noncontractual requests. This decision, however, should be based upon costs and production schedules. Frequently, however, the request to provide a product in excess of the contract requirement is made by customer personnel who are not entirely familiar with the contract requirements. This can occur when resident representatives request incorporation of elements based purely on their expectation to have the company comply with some procedure that was utilized at another facility. Accordingly, it is important that the designated inspection/quality personnel have a thorough knowledge of all technical and quality contract requirements.

The designated inspection/quality personnel must develop proficiency in understanding and interpreting customers' requirements. Most product and performance specifications incorporate, by reference, a complete hierarchy of secondary specifications which, in turn, make use of many tertiary specifications. All these must be fully understood. Since these specifications often include a considerable number of documents, it is highly improbable that the designated engineers will have them available at the time of contract review.

A company dealing with specific categories of customers and products should maintain a library of the common specifications customarily invoked. It is important that these specifications are kept up to date. There are services available which, for a price, will provide the company with up-to-date specifications. In government contracts, an index of current specifications used by various agencies is available at a nominal cost. The government also has a service which will, for a nominal cost, provide all revised or new specifications for each commodity ordered. An efficient inspection/quality department will utilize this library and become familiar with the applicable specifications as they are released or updated. Some companies have a practice whereby each new and revised specification, upon receipt, is analyzed by a knowledgeable individual, and a copy of the major elements or changes is attached to the specification. This negates the need for a complete specification review at the time of contract review and inspection/quality program preparation.

SPECIFICATION REVIEW AND INTERPRETATION

When analyzing contract specifications, inspection/quality personnel must determine all the referenced specifications and other documents applicable to the technical and quality requirements. In many instances the full specification is not invoked by the contract. Therefore, the extent of the referenced specifications should be understood, and only those elements which have been spelled out in the contract should be considered. Often the contract itself references technical and inspection/quality requirements which are supported by various referenced specifications.

Contracts may include sections entitled "Scope," "Applicable Specifications," "Referenced Documents," "Delivery Requirements," "Preparation for Shipping," "Marking," "General Provisions," and "Lists of Drawings." Each of these sections discusses specific technical and inspection/quality requirements. Therefore, it is important to determine the order of precedence, in case of conflict, of the various sections. Care should be taken to review the entire contract and all the specified documents, instead of relying on the nomenclature of the section. Thus a section entitled "Quality/Inspection Requirements" would normally incorporate the elements of interest to the inspection/quality personnel; however, for example, the section entitled "Shipping and Marking" will often reference the inspection/quality specifications pertinent to those functions. The contract's general provisions will also reference a number of technical and inspection/quality requirements, such as the order of precedence of various referenced documents and the processing of engineering changes.

It is also necessary to be aware of the applicable dates of issue of the referenced documents. Some contracts will specify the required dates. Others may provide a statement to the effect that the issue in effect at the receipt of the contract or the implementation of the proposal is to be used.

When reviewing the referenced specification, several rules of interpretation should be applied. Most specifications list the product construction and performance features in individual paragraphs. The methods of test for the conformance of these features are usually referenced in a separate section, entitled "Quality Assurance" or "Test Requirements." For example, the performance requirements may state that the equipment "shall operate on a level highway at a speed of 50 miles an hour when tested in accordance with Para. 4.3." Paragraph 4.3 may state that the speed of the vehicle shall be tested on a level highway after the vehicle has reached the speed of 50 miles an hour and the speed measured for a distance of five miles by use of an accelerometer attached to the vehicle.

Sometimes the test method conflicts with the performance requirements. For the previously mentioned performance requirement, the test specification may state that the vehicle shall be tested on a slope of 15° at a speed of

15 miles per hour, after testing for speed on a level highway. In this instance, the slope testing is at variance with the lack of a performance requirement, and hence should not be considered applicable. This discrepancy should be discussed and resolved at the postaward meeting.

The primary, as well as the secondary and tertiary specifications, usually contain statements at the start of the paragraph which list the applicable requirements such as, "the specifications listed below shall be of the issue in effect at the date of the invitation for bid or proposals. They are applicable to the extent referenced therein." Thus, when a paragraph in the specification notes, for example, that the brake fluid in the vehicle shall have the viscosity specified in SAE "Supplement L4," it means that only that part of the referenced SAE document which discusses the viscosity of the fluid applies. All other elements of the document are not applicable.

Many specifications do not address the examination methods for all construction and performance requirements. The extent of conformance demonstration is usually left to contractors. Unfortunately, this concept is not always shared by customers or their representatives. In this case, contractors should describe, in the inspection/quality program, the manner and extent to which each specification element will be examined. Thus, when the program plan is submitted to the customer for concurrence or approval, the matter is brought to attention, and approval of the plan infers approval of the methods.

Frequently, customers' specifications do not detail product workmanship requirements, or they are general statements such as "acceptable workmanship" or "best commercial practices." Such vague statements are difficult, if not impossible, to implement. Further, interpretations vary between customers and suppliers and from one customer's representative to another. In the absence of specific contractual workmanship standards, a set should be developed by the company for all applicable product characteristics. These standards should be incorporated into the company's inspection/quality manual or project program, and presented to customers at the outset of contracts, preferably at the postaward meeting. Agreement with the standards should be obtained and, if possible, included as part of the contractual terms.

EXAMPLE

This company produced automotive vehicles for commercial and government applications. Product specifications stated that all painted surfaces were to be smooth and exhibit complete coverage, with no weeps, runs, sags, or other imperfections. Accordingly, all vehicles with any signs of these imperfections were rejected by the customer's representative and returned to the contractor for repair and resubmission. The repair, which consisted of touching up the imperfection, often resulted in a spotted appearance, which was highly unsatisfactory. Since the specification provided no quantitative criteria for acceptance, only a vehicle which had no signs of imperfections, no matter how slight, was considered acceptable. This caused considerable expense and delay. Consequently, the contractor's quality engineer prepared, with the customer's representative, a paint ap-

Scope: This instruction is to be incorporated in the visual inspection of painted surfaces.

1.   *Controlling Elements*
       1.1   This instruction shall be implemented through the control of the following elements:
                (a)   Definitions
                (b)   Criteria of Acceptability

2.   *Definitions*
       2.1   The following definitions are used for the classification of painted surfaces.
                (a)   *Type I*—Major external and major internal surfaces visible during normal operating conditions.
                (b)   *Type II*—Surfaces other than Type I requiring paint finishes per specifications.

3.   *Criteria of Acceptability*
       3.1   The following chart indicates cause for rejection of the applicable types of painted surfaces.

| | | Applicability | |
Item no.	Characteristics	Type I	Type II
101	Color of film not as specified	X	X
102	Lack of adhesion (flaking, peeling)	X	X
103	Minor scratches, cuts, abrasions	X	
104	Minor gouge marks, checks, pits, runs, overspray, foreign debris	X	
105	Scratches, cuts, abrasions with exposure of bare metal	X	X
106	Gouge marks, checks, pits with exposure of bare metal	X	X
107	Foreign debris whose removal would expose bare metal	X	X
108	Finish not to specified thickness	X	X

FIGURE 32-1   Paint Appearance Standard

pearance standard (see Figure 32-1). This was then submitted and accepted by the customer's procurement and quality personnel and was used as the basis of acceptance by all customer's representatives. This simple standard resulted in significant improvement in the appearance and acceptance of vehicles and reduced processing delays, while not deteriorating product quality and usability.

Generally, the engineering drawings show many characteristics which are included for the ease of manufacture and do not have any effect on product usability. In most instances, the drawings, which are part of the contractual requirements, make no provision for the extent of examination required. As a result, customers' representatives may require that all characteristics on the drawing be checked 100 percent. At other times, contractual documents may provide a general statement that, except for the 100 percent performance testing of end items, sampling inspection may be permitted. Sometimes a sampling system such as MIL-STD-105 is specified. To avoid any problems with those characteristics on the drawing, the inspection/

3.1 The method of classifying defects for the purpose of applying AQLs shall be as follows:

(a)   Critical Defect—A defect which is likely to result in hazardous or unsafe conditions or likely to prevent performance of the tactical function of a major end item.

(b)   Major Defect—A defect other than critical which is likely to result in failure or to reduce materially the usability of the unit of product for its intended purpose.

(c)   Minor A Defect—A defect which is not likely to reduce materially the usability of the unit of product for its intended purpose.

(d)   Minor B Defect—A defect which is a departure from established standards having no bearing on the effective use or operation of the unit of product.

Note: Concurrence in classification of defects shall be indicated on Inspection Instructions by the applicable Quality Control Manager or assigned Quality Engineering personnel.

FIGURE 32-2   Defect Classification

quality program should provide a classification for the selection of characteristics to be assigned to specific sampling plans or AQLs (see Figure 32-2).

In considering the extent of examination, some problems may arise. For example, when a drawing note states that "the component shall be able to operate for a period of 2500 hours under specified environmental conditions," it is obvious that this characteristic cannot be examined on a lot-by-lot basis. The inspection/quality plan should provide some means of assuring that the characteristic in question meets requirements without recourse to lot-by-lot inspection. This can be done with a provision that such characteristics shall be demonstrated during the end item pre-production test, thereby demonstrating that the design of the part in question is adequate. This provision could also note that any significant change should require a requalification of the item or a demonstration, by engineering analysis, that the change will not affect the part's ability to meet specified requirements. It is important that these provisions are developed well in advance of the start of production, preferably while planning the program.

CHAPTER THIRTY-THREE

Dealing With the U.S. Government

GUIDE TO FEDERAL ACQUISITION REQUIREMENTS[1]

Doing business with the government is different from selling to commercial customers. The government contractor must abide by certain rules, specifications, and drawings. If it does not, it may find itself in difficulty. The principal document for government procurement is a set of regulations called the Federal Acquisition Regulations (FAR), replacing, for military procurement, the Defense Acquisitions Regulations (DAR) and Armed Service Procurement Regulations (ASPR). Some of the major differences between commercial and government procurement practices are as follows:

1. The government conducts business through certain authorized agents. Procurement Contracting Officers (PCOs) usually place the contract and authorize major changes and payments, and Administrative Contracting Officers (ACOs) supervise contract performance.

2. The government has the unilateral right to revise its contracts. Contractor's entitlement to equitable adjustments in price and delivery is spelled out in the contract, but performance of the contract as changed must continue pending negotiations.

3. The government contract contains extensive audit and work surveillance rights. The contractor is obligated to maintain and retain certain records and submit these to audit on demand. If these audits reveal a failure to conform to requirements, the contractor may be subject to penalties or price adjustments.

4. Under certain types of contracts, there are limitations of costs the contractor may recover.

5. Participation in government contracts will require varying degrees of cooperation and compliance with other governmental goals and objectives, such as equal opportunity and buy American.

6. The government has an absolute right to terminate all or any part of the contract at any time. The termination may be made for either the convenience of the government, whenever the need dictates, or for default if the performance is unsatisfactory. Termination for convenience of the government is subject to equitable compensation to the contractor according to the provisions of the termination clauses of the contract.

7. Most government contracts require that specific quality systems are in place that could be monitored and evaluated. They base these requirements upon the supposition that the government-support organizations, like the Defense Logistic Agency (DLA) and the Defense Contract Administration Service (DCAS), are resident or have complete access to contractor's facilities to assure that it complies with each requirement. Supplies usually cannot be shipped without government inspection and acceptance at suppliers' facilities. The Quality Deficiency Report (QDR) is the primary method used by the government of notifying contractors of need for corrective action. If the condition is severe, no product will be accepted until appropriate corrective action can be positively demonstrated. Some recent contracts utilize newer corrective action methods under their In-Plant Quality Evaluation System (IQUE).

PARTS OF THE CONTRACT

Schedule

This is tailored to each transaction and represents the substance of the deal. It includes a statement of work to be done or the supplies to be furnished, the price, specifications, the delivery schedule, and any special conditions.

The list of supplies and services is followed by the specifications or other descriptions to which the work must conform. Many of the specifications refer to other documents, for which the contractor is responsible to the extent referenced in the primary documents.

The delivery section specifies the time, place, and method of delivery for supplies or place of performance for services. Large items are usually inspected and accepted at the contractor's plant and shipped on Government Bills of Lading (GBL).

In addition, the schedule contains many special provisions applicable to the specific contract, for example, use of government-owned property, options for additional quantities of supplies, and special test procedures.

General Provisions

This is the boilerplate of the government contract and consists mainly of clauses required by state or federal regulation. Some of the provisions are discussed in their major categories.

Performance

This may include government inspection and acceptance requirements, use of government property, provisions for resolving disputes, and many others.

Inspection and acceptance

This describes the contractor's responsibility for delivering products or performing services on schedule and for assuring that they conform to contract requirements. The Contract Administration Office is responsible for assuring the fulfillment of the contract requirements. The government may conduct inspections and tests to determine if the goods are in conformity. The type and extent of inspection and testing depend largely on what is being procured. The contract will designate the place of inspection.

There are various types of inspection clauses. The standard clause provides that items are subject to inspection and tests by the government before acceptance. The government has the right to reject nonconforming items, have the defects corrected at the contractor's expense, or accept the nonconforming products at a reduced price. Acceptance is final, except with regards to hidden defects or fraud. The contractor must provide facilities and assistance to the government inspectors at its own expense. The contractor must maintain an acceptable inspection system and provide appropriate quality assurance controls and records.

Additional provisions

- Subcontracts
- Use of government property
- Patents, technical data, and copyrights
- Bonds, insurance, and taxes
- Disputes
- Payments
- Contract cost principles
- Contract changes
- Terminations
- Public policies

Quality Assurance Requirements

Depending on the nature and complexity of the product, the following quality assurance clauses may be invoked on government contracts.

No specific requirements

The government does not perform any product inspection at the source, but instead relies on the contractor's internal quality controls.

Contractor's responsibility provisions

The contractor is responsible for product inspection and test before delivery. The degree of inspection and test and the responsibility for their performance are as defined in: (1) Section 4 of the product specification, (2) federal drawings, and (3) the standard inspection clause of the contract.

Standard inspection requirements

The contractor shall establish and maintain an inspection system acceptable to the government. This requirement is included in the standard inspection clause and is not further defined by any specification. This clause is invoked when, for reasons of practicability (for example, purchase of a commercial item), or because of the nature of the supplies (that is, the item serves a function that is not materially or consequently related to military operations), it is not necessary to further describe what constitutes an acceptable inspection system.

Inspection system requirements—Mil-I-45208

This is in addition to the standard inspection clause. It requires that the contractor establish an inspection system in accordance with specification Mil-I-45208. This specification is addressed primarily to the inspection function. It is usually invoked when conformance to the quality requirements of the contract can be determined by inspection and test alone. This clause is referenced in contracts when technical requirements are such as to require quality control by in-process, as well as final end item inspection. Included here are control of such elements as measuring and test equipment, drawings and changes, inspection, documentation, and records.

Quality program requirements—Mil-Q-9858

This, in addition to the standard inspection clause, requires that the contractor shall establish and maintain a quality program in accordance with the specification MIL-Q-9858. This is required when the technical requirements of the contract requires control of work operations, in-process controls, and other factors, such as organization, planning, work instructions, documentation, and advanced metrology.

Copies of or additional information about these clauses or about selling to the government can be obtained from the Superintendent of Documents, U.S. Printing Office, Washington, D.C. 20402.

CONTRACT AND SPECIFICATION INTERPRETATIONS[2]

The underlying factor which creates much difficulty in interpretation, is the need for the PCO to utilize definitive specifications before they are available. Detailed specifications are needed from the technical personnel at an early date. Thus, specifications, or substitutes used as models, are generated before sufficient engineering efforts have been accomplished. If detailed specifications are not available, hybrid ones, containing some detailed requirements and numerous performance requirements, are written. In both of these cases, the result is often a contract where the rights of the parties are open to question.

The following are some examples of contract and specifications interpretations which had been presented at a course in government contracts at George Washington University.

Some of the most difficult problems encountered by contractors dealing with government contracts are the general catch-all specifications, such as, best design practices, good workmanship, high polish, and the like. What constitutes compliance with this type of specification?

For example, suppose a contract specifies that the racks to be provided must be square at the corners. While this seems simple enough, does this mean that the corners must be joined exactly at a 90° angle? Suppose a contractor decides to take a sheet of metal and bend it to a 90° angle. Would that be grounds for rejection?

Most of these problems are resolved using common sense. Some, however, cannot be and the reason is cost. A contractor who has a fixed price contract, in a highly competitive bid, naturally wants to furnish the government with the minimum required. On the other hand, the government wants the maximum that can be read into the contract. What is the government entitled to? Is strict compliance with the specification necessary? Or is substantial performance sufficient?

To compensate for this condition, it is incumbent upon the contractor to try to have the government modify the specification so that it is specific in its requirements.

The government should not require any more than is actually needed. Requiring gold-plated products will eventually bring the price of the product up and perhaps limit the potential bidders to those who are qualified to provide this gold-plated product even when it is not needed.

The contractor should attempt to have the specification clarified so that there will be no ambiguity about any of its characteristics. It is better to have the clarification made at the time of proposal or early in the contract, when the contracting customer personnel are available, than to keep silent and hope that the government's inspectors will take the same position as the contractor. Thus the requirement for square corners should be amplified to provide a tolerance of the squareness such as 90° plus or minus 1°.

When there can be no specific requirements imposed, such as that for good workmanship, the contractor should provide a company standard which details the elements of good workmanship and have the specification or contract appropriately modified and approved.

Doctrine of Strict and Substantial Compliance

The courts have held that the government may insist upon strict compliance with specifications. At times, the contractor will contend that the articles offered are as good as or even superior to those called for in the contract. The courts have ruled, however, that the contract must be followed in strict compliance.

While the doctrine of *strict compliance* is a well-accepted standard of performance in government contracts, it does not appear to be suitable for catch-all specifications. An examination of the facts in past government contracts will show that strict compliance is usually applied to specifications which are subject to precise measurements in size, weight, speed, and numbers, and not to specifications which are naturally general and unspecific. For these, the courts have adopted a different standard of performance, one of *substantial compliance*.

EXAMPLE

A contractor was required to fabricate approximately 200 radio sets in a best and workmanlike manner. Government inspectors found three types of deficiencies in the installation: (1) too much solder, (2) improper wire lacing and dressing, and (3) split pairs of wires. No other specification had been provided about the method of soldering or wiring. The review board looked into all facets of the contract and held that the contractor had, in fact, met its obligations. The fact that the alleged deficiencies affected appearance and convenience rather than operation, led the board to rule that the contractor had substantially complied with the contract.

To decide whether the standard of performance had been met, the contract review board will usually rely upon expert testimony presented at the trial. The type of contract (production or research), the use of the equipment, the custom and usage of the trade, the state of the art, and discussions of the parties prior to and after the execution of the contract all enter into the deliberations.

Ambiguous, Defective, and Conflicting Specifications

The focal point of any contractual relationship is the statement of work. This usually consists of specifications, drawings, models, and other descriptive material. It is not unusual for this material to contain ambiguities, defective requirements, and conflicting provisions.

Which party to a contract is responsible for these ambiguities? What is the effect of defective specifications? How are conflicting contract requirements resolved? The rules which are followed are those applicable to commercial transactions, as well as government contracts.

Interwoven in this problem is the issue of impossibility of performance. A contract with these problems generates conditions which make it impossible for the contractor to meet all the requirements.

Ambiguous provisions

This is a problem of contract interpretation. The standard of interpretation is the contract's meaning that a reasonably intelligent person acquainted with all the operative usages, and knowing all the facts and circumstances prior to, and contemporary with, the contract, would infer.

Rules for Interpretation

Primary rules

1. Technical words and works of art are given their technical meaning unless the applicable context or usage indicates a different meaning.

2. A writing is interpreted as a whole and all writings forming part of the same contract are interpreted together. It is improper to interpret a single word, phrase, or sentence out of context.

3. All circumstances accompanying the transaction may be taken into consideration with the exception of oral statements made by the parties of their intentions. The circumstances under which a contract was made may always be shown as the objective. The meaning of the writing at the time and place when the contract was made, and all the surrounding circumstances at that time, necessarily throw light on the contract's meaning.

Secondary rules

1. A reasonable and effective interpretation meaning is preferred to one that is unreasonable or of no effect.

2. The principal purpose of the contract is given great weight in determining the meaning of the contract or any part of it.

3. Where there is an inconsistency between general and specific provisions, the specific ones ordinarily qualify the meaning of the general ones.

4. Where words bear more than one reasonable meaning, an interpretation is preferred that operates more strongly against the party who drafted the language.

Additional interpretations that apply only to government contracts

1. If a drawing or specification is capable of more than one interpretation, and the contractor follows an interpretation that is reasonable, that will prevail over one advanced by the government, even though the government's interpretation may be more reasonable.

2. Even though the government may admit that a provision is ambiguous, the contractor is not necessarily safe in relying on its interpretation of the ambiguous language. When the intended meaning is not clear and the ambiguity is so patent that a prudent bidder would be aware of it, the prospective bidder cannot enter into a contract without asking for clarification. Afterward, it may be too late to request or expect adjustment.

3. Thus when it has been established that a contract provision is ambiguous, it is equally important to establish that this entitles a contractor to some remedy.

Defective Specifications

It has been held that the government, by implication, warrants that items manufactured by a contractor in strict accordance with the government's specifications will be accepted. However, if the specification permits the contractor to manipulate various factors to achieve a particular characteristic, there is no implied warranty. If the contractor knows, or should have known, that in following the specification the item produced will not meet the purpose intended, then the government incurs no liability for payment of any contractor-incurred costs.

But if the specification is defective and the implied warranty rule is applied, the contractor is entitled to a change within the meaning of the standard contract article.

Conflicting Specifications

Many contracts have conflicting specifications, and some contain a provision such as the following: "Anything mentioned in the specification and not shown on the drawings, or shown on the drawings and not mentioned in the specifications, shall be of like effect as if shown in both. In case of difference between the drawings and specifications, the specification shall govern." When the configuration baseline has been approved, the product drawings reflect the applicable specification requirements. Thus, the drawings are not in conflict with the specification.

Other specifications usually list a number of subordinate and general specifications with a note such as, "the specification of issue on the date of the proposal shall be in effect to the extent as noted below," for example, "the final coating shall be applied in accordance with the applicable sections of paint specification—MIL-STD-192." This statement brings into effect only those elements of the paint specification that deal with the final coat, and the balance of the specification does not apply. In other instances, the general provisions of the contract may establish an order of precedence, if documents conflict with one another. For example, the statement may note that "in case of conflict, the following order of precedence shall apply: the contract schedule, the contract's general provisions, the equipment specification, the referenced specifications, the drawings, and the specifications listed on the drawings."

An example: A frequent problem with the contract is when the work to be done is shown on the drawings and not mentioned in the specification. In a case where the specification failed to mention using special hardware in the equipment specifications, yet were shown on the drawings, the contractor was held liable to perform by incorporating this hardware in the equipment, the board holding that silence on the part of the specification when the drawing specifically called for the hardware did not excuse the contractor from installing the hardware in the equipment.

Another problem arises when the proposal states that the contract item must be interchangeable with a government-furnished model with respect to all parts with certain exceptions. The model was available for examination prior to the submission of bids and was given to the winning bidder. What takes precedence in case of conflict when there is no language in the contract? In one case, the contractor contemplated furnishing Class A transformers which were cheaper than Class C. After the award of the contract, the government stated that Class C was required. Since the model had Class C transformers, the contractor was ordered to use Class C.

In another case, the government-supplied model did not meet the specification. The contract stated that in case of conflict, the specifications govern. Prior to bid, the contractor was advised by government representatives that there was no material difference between the model and the specifications except as noted in the proposal. When the contractor built a preproduction model, it failed the environmental tests. The government's model also failed these tests. The contractor then had to redesign the equipment to meet the environmental specifications. The board ruled that: (1) the contract did not contemplate any redesign by the contractor; (2) the contractor had no way of knowing, beforehand, that the model did not meet the environmental specifications; (3) the model was a part of the contract specifications; and (4) there was an implied warranty that a product made in conformity with the model would meet the performance of the specification. Thus, since the government-furnished property (GFP) was not suitable for its intended purpose, the contractor was entitled to an equitable adjustment under the terms of the contract's GFP clause.

Another situation may exist when the contract specifies that the equipment to be produced shall be identical to the model. This at times is impossible to implement, since between the time of model construction and the production contract, many changes could have been made in the model's replacement parts. In fact, some parts may no longer be available. Thus, it is important that the bidder notify the government that it would be desirable if the language were changed to specify that the product would be *interchangeable* with, rather than *identical* to, the parts in the model.

Another problem arises when the government provides a set of manufacturing drawings and a specification. The contractor must produce in accordance with the drawings and also meet the specification. Frequently, it happens that fabrication to the drawings will not result in a product meeting the specification. Unless the contract specifies an order of precedence, the contractor may have a problem in receiving payment for the work performed. Even if the product is subsequently accepted with the performance discrepancies, the contractor may lose due to the delay in having a verdict granted. This has led some bidders to incorporate, in the contract price, the cost of time needed to review the drawings to assure that the equipment can be fabricated accordingly. Some later contracts, especially for the U.S. Army, have included a Preproduction Evaluation Clause, which makes it the contractor's responsibility, as part of its price, to review the drawings before production. This could assure that there are no errors or no-fit conditions which would preclude the production of equipment in accordance with the specifications. This clause provides rapid methods for submission and approval of revisions to the discrepant drawings.

Note

It should be noted that these interpretations were in effect at the time of this book's preparation. Before using these interpretations for specific contractual purposes, readers should determine whether any of them have been revised.

GOVERNMENT QUALITY ASSURANCE SPECIFICATIONS

This section consists of abstracts of the customary quality specifications used by the government in its procurement of supplies and services.

Mil-Q-9858A: Quality Program Requirements[3]

The contractor shall develop and maintain an effective and economical quality program, planned and developed in consonance with the contractor's other administrative and technical programs. Design of the program shall be based upon consideration of the technical and manufacturing aspects of production and related engineering design and materials. The program shall assure adequate quality throughout all areas of contract performance, for example, design, development, fabrication, processing, assembly, test, maintenance, packaging, shipping, storage and site installation.

All supplies and services under the contract, whether manufactured or performed in the contractor's plant or at any other location, shall be controlled at all points necessary to assure conformance to contractual requirements. The program shall provide for the prevention and ready detection of discrepancies for timely and positive corrective action. The contractor shall make available, to the government representative, objective evidence of quality conformance. Instructions and records for quality shall be controlled.

Authority and responsibility of those in charge of design, production, testing, and inspection of quality shall be clearly stated. The program shall facilitate determination of the effects of quality deficiencies and quality costs on price. Drawings, engineering changes, measuring equipment, and the like shall be effectively managed for the creation of required quality. Effective control of purchased materials, subcontracted work, manufacturing, fabrication, and assembly work conducted within the contractor's plant shall be controlled completely. The program shall include effective execution of responsibilities shared jointly with the government or related to government functions such as the control of government property and government source inspection.

The quality program, including procedures, processes and product shall be documented and subject to review by the government representative. The program shall be subject to the disapproval of the government representative whenever the contractor's procedures do not accomplish their objectives.

MILITARY HANDBOOK H-50: EVALUATION OF THE CONTRACTOR'S QUALITY PROGRAM[4]

This section consists of an outline of the elements in Handbook H-50 used by government representatives to monitor the contractor's implementation of specification Mil-Q-9858.

Quality program management

This includes identifying the functions and activities that directly affect quality and assigning specific authority and responsibility for these functions.

Initial quality planning

This shall be performed in conjunction with all other functions. Planning shall be timely and shall provide operational review to assure compatibility between quality requirements and affected manufacturing operations, processes, and techniques.

Work instructions

These are to be used to explain how a job will be done, the order in which actions are accomplished, set-up information, speeds, feeds, associated drawings, specifications, and the like. Work instructions shall be kept current and complete. Standards for work operations are to be prepared. Compatibility of instructions with associated inspection and testing shall be evaluated. They shall be reviewed on a systematic basis for accuracy, completeness, and compliance.

Records

Records shall be maintained for all essential activities and be made available to the government when required. Effective means shall be utilized for assuring currency, completeness, and accuracy. Inspection records shall include the number and kind of defectives and other essential data. Records shall show the cause of error, how corrected, and action to prevent recurrence. Management action shall reflect record use analysis and use.

Corrective action

The quality program shall insure prompt detection and correction of assignable causes. Adequate action shall be taken to correct the cause of defects in products, facilities, and functions (design, purchasing, testing, and so on). Corrective action to arrest unfavorable trends shall be taken before deficiencies occur. Corrective action shall be assured at the supplier's facilities. Data analysis and product examination shall be conducted on scrap and rework to determine extent and cause of defect. Effectiveness of corrections shall be reviewed and monitored later.

Costs related to quality

The specific quality cost data needed shall be determined. Cost data shall be collected and identified, including the cost of prevention and correction of defects. Cost data shall be used in managing quality, and shall be available to the government representative.

Facilities and standards

Procedures shall be available for assuring engineering adequacy of drawings, currentness and completeness of drawings, and availability and control of supplementary documentation needed to produce articles in conformance with design. The procedures shall insure compliance with contract requirements for proposing, approving, and implementing engineering changes.

Measuring and testing equipment

Measuring equipment necessary to assure that products meet technical requirements shall be available and used, properly maintained, and inspected on a regular basis for required accuracy. Controls shall be available to prevent equipment use when they are inaccurate, and to correct, repair, or replace them when needed. The program shall comply with MIL-STD-

45662, Calibration System Requirements. Measurement standards shall be required, available, and used. Certification of standards shall be traceable to national standards. Suppliers shall be required to have a calibration system per MIL-STD-45662 to the extent applicable.

Production tooling use as media of inspection

These tools shall be checked for accuracy prior to use and reinspected at intervals to assure continued accuracy.

Control of purchases

The program shall assure that products and services furnished by suppliers meet contract requirements. The program shall provide for the selection of suppliers on the basis of their ability to perform satisfactorily as well as evidence of their capability to produce quality products. The supplier's quality efforts shall be reviewed at intervals consistent with their product's complexity and quality. The program shall provide sufficient receiving inspection of all supplies and services furnished to contractor. There shall be adequate procedures for source selection.

Purchasing data

This data shall require suppliers to have effective control of product quality. Purchasing documents shall refer to the item's specific design, manufacturing and testing requirements, quality systems, direct shipment, and all other applicable routine and special requirements (for example, routine manufacturing, inspecting, testing, and packaging requirements). Purchasing documents shall provide for prime contractor and/or government source inspection when appropriate.

Manufacturing control

Inspection of supplier's material shall be performed to the extent necessary upon receipt. The amount of receiving inspection shall be adjusted on the basis of objective data. Effective control shall be maintained for preventing the use of nonconforming raw material.

Production processing and fabrication

Production processes shall be accomplished under controlled conditions, including documented work instructions, adequate production equipment, and appropriate working environments. Work instructions shall provide criteria for determining whether production, processing, and fabrication work is acceptable or unacceptable. Approval and rejection criteria shall be provided for all inspection and monitoring actions. Approved and rejected products shall be properly controlled. For highly specialized and complex processes, more detailed work instructions shall be prepared.

Completed item inspection and test

Completed items shall be given a final inspection and test which indicates overall quality. Final testing shall adequately simulate performance in use. Inspection and test problems or deficiencies shall be promptly reported to designers. Reinspection and retest of all items which were reworked, repaired, or modified after initial end product testing shall be performed.

Handling, storage, and delivery

Adequate work and inspection instructions for the handling, storage, and delivery of material shall be prepared, implemented, and monitored.

Nonconforming material

The program shall include an effective system for controlling nonconforming material. It shall be properly identified, segregated, and disposed. Procedures for repair and rework of nonconforming material shall be documented and acceptable to the government. Scrap and rework cost and loss data shall be maintained and available to the government for review. Repair and rework activities shall comply with documented procedures. Holding areas for retention and storage of nonconforming material shall be adequate.

Statistical quality control and analysis

Contractor-designed sampling plans shall be available for review by the government representative, and shall provide valid confidence and quality levels. The contractor shall be aware of the degree of protection afforded by his or her sampling plan and shall enforce all the conditions required for its valid use.

Indication of inspection status

There shall be available an effective system for identifying the inspection status of products that is different from that of the government.

Coordinated Government/ Contractor Actions

Government inspection at subcontractor or vendor facilities

The contractor's purchasing documents shall require government source inspection of supplies only when the government so requests. Clauses in Paragraph 7.1 of MIL-Q-9858A shall be included in purchasing documents when source inspection is required. Copies of applicable purchasing documents shall be provided to the government representative at the supplier's plant.

Government property (GP)

Procedures shall make provision for the examination of GP upon receipt, consistent with the practicality, to detect damage in transit, verification of quantity, and inspection for complete and proper type. These procedures shall include the requirements for periodic inspection and precautions to assure adequate storage conditions and to guard against damage from handling and deterioration during storage. Procedures shall also require functional testing, either prior to or after installation, or both, as required by the contract, to determine satisfactory operation, identification, and protection from improper use or disposition.

Damaged government-furnished material

Examination of GFM upon receipt to detect any shipping damage shall be performed by the contractor. This is usually limited to visual inspection. In most cases, disassembly or testing is neither required nor desirable. Inspection shall be performed to make certain that GFM is of correct type and is complete. Periodic inspection during storage shall be conducted to detect any signs of deterioration, to assure compliance with reinspection requirements and limitations on storage time, to assure maintenance of proper conditions, and to determine current status of the GFM. Functional tests shall be performed before or after installation, or both, as required by the contract and applicable specifications. Only qualified personnel may perform such tests. Appropriate identification and safeguarding of GFM shall be taken to prevent any unwarranted use of improper disposal. Examination shall be performed to verify quantity received.

Bailed property

This refers primarily to equipment provided to the contractor for a special purpose and not for incorporation into deliverable products. Initial inspection shall be performed immediately upon receipt to detect any shipping or other damage, and to determine that the equipment is complete and of the proper type. Suitable records of initial and periodic inspections shall be maintained. Adequate storage facilities and protection measures shall be provided including maintenance of property in good repair and condition.

MIL-I-45208: INSPECTION SYSTEM REQUIREMENTS [5]

Note

This program is used for products whose quality can be determined by inspection or test alone. This specification addresses itself only to the inspection elements of the program, as contrasted to Mil-Q-9858, which addresses itself to all contractor functions which are involved with contract implementation. Here is a summary of the specification requirements:

The contractor shall provide and maintain an inspection system which will assure that all supplies and services, whether manufactured or processed by the contractor or procured from subcontractors or vendors, which are to be submitted to the government for acceptance, conform to contract requirements. The contractor shall perform or have performed the inspections and tests required to substantiate product conformance to drawing, specification and contract requirements, and shall also perform or have performed all inspections and tests otherwise required by the contract. The contractor's inspection system shall be documented and shall be available for review by the government representative prior to the initiation of production and throughout the life of the contract. The government may, at its option, furnish written notice of acceptability or unacceptability of the inspection system. The contractor shall notify the government, in writing, of any change to the inspection system. The inspection system shall be subject to disapproval if changes thereto would result in a nonconforming product.

HANDBOOK H-51: EVALUATION OF A CONTRACTOR'S INSPECTION SYSTEM[6]

The following is a summary of the elements of H-51 which are used by the government representative in evaluating the contractor's implementation of military specification Mil-I-45208.

Documentation, Records, and Corrective Action

Inspection instructions

Instructions shall be clear, complete, and up to date. Required instructions shall be available and current, including those for the examination and testing of raw materials, work in process, and completed items, as required by the item specification and other contract requirements. Instructions shall provide criteria for product approval or rejection.

Records

The contractor shall maintain adequate records of all examinations and tests. Records shall indicate the number of items that passed and the number that failed inspection. Records shall indicate the number and types of deficiencies found, and the corrective actions taken.

Corrective action

This shall be taken promptly to correct all conditions which caused defects in products to be submitted for government acceptance. Corrective actions shall be directed at deficiencies in meeting specification requirements, contract requirements, and all other inspection and testing requirements necessary to substantiate product quality.

Drawings and changes

The contractor's inspection system shall provide procedures which assure that only the latest applicable drawings, specifications, and instructions, including all approved changes, are used for fabrication, examination, and testing. The latest revised drawings shall be used in all manufacturing areas and test and examination points.

Measuring and test equipment (M&TE)

Gauges, testing, and measuring equipment which are necessary to assure that products meet technical requirements shall be available and procedures established for their use. MT&E shall be properly maintained and calibrated on a regular basis to assure that they are of the required accuracy. Continuous control of these devices shall be maintained to prevent their use if they become inaccurate, and to correct, repair, or replace them as needed. Required certified measurement standards shall be available, used, and traceable to national standards. Tooling used as inspection equipment shall be proved for accuracy prior to use. Such tooling shall be reinspected at intervals established in a manner which assures its adjustment, replacement, or repair before it becomes inaccurate. Procedures shall comply with MIL-STD-45662. Inspection equipment and facilities shall be made available to the government representative for verification of the contractor's results, when required. The contractor shall provide personnel to perform this inspection, if warranted.

Process controls

A review shall be made for any contract or specification requirements for control of specific manufacturing processes or operations. Such control procedures shall be an integral part of the inspection system.

Indication of inspection status

The contractor shall have an effective system for identifying the inspection status of products, which shall be distinctly different from that of the government.

Government-Furnished Material

This section is identical to the section noted GFM discussed under H-50.

Nonconforming material

An effective system for controlling nonconforming material shall be available. Adequate, documented procedures shall be used to properly identify, segregate, and dispose of nonconforming material. Documented procedures shall be used for repair and rework of nonconforming material. Repair and rework activities shall comply with these procedures which shall be acceptable to the government. Holding areas for the segregation and temporary storage of nonconforming material shall be available and adequate.

Qualified products list (QPL)

Provisions shall be available for a complete and effective inspection of all products on the QPL.

Sampling inspection

Required sampling procedures shall conform to applicable specifications or other procurement documents. Contractor-designed sampling plans shall be available for review and approval by the government.

Inspection provisions

The government representative shall determine whether the contractor has elected to use any inspection equipment or procedures other than those specified or referenced in the contract. The contractor shall submit written proposals to the government for each alternate inspection procedure or piece of equipment he or she desires to use and demonstrate the effectiveness of each to the government representative. Alternative procedures and equipment shall, at least, be equal to those specified in the contract. The contractor shall continue to use originally required procedures and equipment until receiving approval to use alternatives.

Government's inspection at subcontractor's or vendor's facilities

Purchasing documents shall include the requirement for government source inspection of supplies only when the government so requests. Clauses in paragraph 3.12 of MIL-I-45208A shall be used in purchasing documents when government procurement quality assurance procedures (PQAP) at source are required. Documents and reference data for purchases applying to the government contract shall be made available to the government representative for review. When required, copies shall be furnished to the representative in accordance with his or her instructions.

Receiving inspection

All incoming material shall be inspected as necessary to assure conformance with contractual requirements. Government representatives shall be notified of all defects found in material subject to government PQAP at source. The contractor shall require each supplier responsible for defective material to coordinate corrective actions with the supplier's own government representative.

Government evaluation

The government representative shall evaluate the contractor's inspection system and the supplies it generates. The representative will also make all the necessary verifications and evaluations to determine the inspection system's effectiveness in supporting the quality requirements of the detailed specifications, drawings, and contract.

MIL-STD-45662: CALIBRATION SYSTEM REQUIREMENTS[7]

The contractor shall establish and maintain a system for the calibration of all measuring and test equipment used in the fulfillment of his contractual requirements. The calibration system shall be coordinated with his inspection or quality control system and shall be designed to provide adequate accuracy in the use of measuring and test equipment. All measuring and test equipment applicable to the contractor, whether used in the contractor's plant or at another source, shall be subjected to such control as is necessary to assure conformance of supplies and services to contractual requirements. The calibration shall provide for the prevention of inaccuracy by ready detection of deficiencies and timely positive action for their correction. The contractor shall make objective evidence of accuracy conformance available to the government representative.

All operations performed by the contractor in compliance with this standard will be subject to the government verification at unscheduled intervals. Verification will include but not be limited to the following: (1) surveillance of calibration operation for conformance to the established system and (2) review of calibration results as necessary to assure accuracy of the system. The contractor's gages, measuring, and testing devices shall be made available for use by the government when required to determine conformance with contract requirements. If conditions warrant, the contractor's personnel shall be made available for operation of such devices and for verification of their accuracy and condition.

HANDBOOK H-52A: EVALUATION OF CONTRACTOR'S CALIBRATION SYSTEM[8]

This section is a summary of the elements of H-52A which are used by the government's representative to evaluate the contractor's implementation of military standard 45662.

Calibration System Description

The written description shall include the following and shall be coordinated with the contractor's inspection system.

- Standards listing with nomenclature and identification number, and environmental conditions required to be maintained, including prescribed calibration intervals and sources of M&TE.

- Forms, labels, and decals to be used.

- Description of the calibration program and its implementing procedures. The reports of calibration shall be available to the government.

- Adequacy of standards with respect to accuracy, stability, range, and resolution shall be determined.

- Environmental controls shall be developed to the extent necessary, based on factors that may affect accuracy, including temperature, humidity, vibration, cleanliness, and others.

- Compensating corrections shall be utilized.

- Housekeeping/cleanliness of applicable areas shall be maintained.

Intervals of Calibration

M&TE shall be calibrated at established intervals based on stability, purpose, and degree of usage. Intervals shall be adjusted based on results of previous calibrations. A recall system shall be mandatory and used in compliance with intervals. Historical records of calibrations results shall be maintained. Calibration due notices shall be issued. MT&E shall be promptly released for calibration, when notified. Overdue notices shall be provided, when required.

Calibration Procedures

Written procedures for calibration of MT&E and standards shall be available and incorporate the following:

- Method of calibration
- Specification of the degree of measurement accuracy
- Specification of either the measurement standard to be used or its required accuracy
- Statement that calibration shall be performed by comparison with higher accuracy level standards

Out-of-Tolerance Evaluators

A procedure shall provide for using out of tolerance data to:

- Adjust the calibration interval.
- Determine M&TE adequacy.
- Determine adequacy of calibration, measuring, and test procedures.

- Identify and prevent the use of M&TE which does not perform satisfactorily.

- Define significant out-of-tolerance conditions.

- Identify reporting channels.

CALIBRATION SOURCES (DOMESTIC AND FOREIGN)

M&TE shall be calibrated using standards traceable to national standards.

Standards shall be calibrated by commercial facilities capable of performing the service, a government laboratory, the NIST, or a foreign national laboratory whose standards are comparable to international or U.S. standards.

Standards calibration reports shall be supported by certificates, reports, or data sheets attesting to date, accuracy, and environmental conditions. Subordinate standards shall be supported by the same data when essential to achieving the accuracy control of MIL-STD-45662.

Certificates from laboratories other than government ones or the NIST shall indicate the standards used and shall have indicated comparison at planned intervals with national standards. Contractor sources other than government laboratories or the NIST shall be capable of performing the service to the satisfaction of MIL-STD-45662.

Application and Records

Records shall support all requirements of MIL-STD-45662. Schedules and procedures shall be followed.

Records shall include identification of item, recalibration interval, date of last calibration, and results of out-of-tolerance conditions.

If accuracy must be noted on the calibration report or certificate, records shall cite its number or a copy of it shall be provided.

Calibration Status

Labels or other means shall be provided to monitor adherence to calibration schedule. The system shall indicate date of last calibration, responsible personnel, and date when next calibration is due. Items not calibrated to their full capability or requiring functional checking only shall be labeled to indicate condition.

Control of Subcontractor

Delegation shall be provided to suppliers through purchasing documents which shall stipulate requirements for implementation of MIL-STD-45662 to the degree necessary. The contractor shall assure subcontractor compliance.

Storage and Handling

- Shall not adversely affect M&TE calibration.
- Shall be packaged properly when required.
- Shall be maintained under adequate storage conditions.
- Shall be reported if improper.

Note

Handbooks H-50, H-51, and H-52A, previously described, and DSAM 8200.1, discussed in the next section, are noncontractual documents used purely to guide government representatives through the evaluation of the contractor's inspection and quality assurance program. A knowledge of the elements included therein is of value to contractors' inspection/quality personnel.

DEFENSE SUPPLY AGENCY MANUAL (DSAM) 8200.1: PROCUREMENT QUALITY ASSURANCE[9]

This manual covers the government representative's actions relating to the implementation of the PQAP. The object of these procedures is to insure that the contractor complies with the contractual requirements.

Authority

The government representative cannot require the contractor to do more than is required by the terms of the contract.

Procedures review

The contractor shall be given wide latitude in the development of a written quality program. No specific format shall be prescribed by the government. The quality program need not be incorporated in one publication.

The government may notify the contractor of inadequate procedures but should not tell him or her how to do the job.

The government representative's planning of the PQAP program must be done in an early period.

The procedures evaluation shall be performed by the government at a specified frequency, and with the use of checklists.

Product verification inspection

This includes initial product inspection (IPI), and it shall be accomplished by the government, by establishing, with the contractor, the locations in the plant where the physical characteristics are evaluated. IPI is normally conducted by the government at the same location as the contractor's inspection/test operations. Higher assembly examinations may be performed in lieu of detailed parts inspections.

Continuing product inspection, by the government, shall be based on results of IPI and may be performed at reduced or intensified levels based on a schedule listed in manual.

Corrective action

See note about the use of the IQUE methods. The government's representative shall require the contractor to implement, as applicable, one of the following corrective actions:

Method A

This is used when on-the-spot corrective action for minor defects can be taken, and follow-up is not considered necessary.

Method B

This is used when on-the-spot action cannot be taken or an initial procedural review reveals an inadequacy. The government representative uses form DD1715 (QDR) to request corrective action within a specified time period.

Note

This is one of the most troublesome corrective action methods. Frequently, the government representative is unable to distinguish between the need for Method A or B. Also, responses by the contractor to Method B are generally not considered adequate by the government representative, based on a lack of full understanding of the problem by either the contractor or the representative. Intercontractor/government meetings is one way of dealing with this problem.

Method C

For serious quality problems, the government representative sends a letter to the contractor's top management requesting immediate action to correct the observed discrepancies and their causes. The letter may be signed by the ACO to denote the seriousness of the problem. Examples of when this method should be used include excessive number of DD1715s issued; repetitive deficiencies; contractor's negligence in preparing, following, or correcting required procedures; and evidence of deterioration in the contractor's quality system.

Method D

When the contractor does not take satisfactory actions, the government's quality assurance representative (QAR) may request the ACO to inform the contractor that all procurement quality assurance (PQA) actions will be suspended.

Method E

This is used when a subcontractor is involved and the problem's magnitude is equivalent to a Method C or D. This requests the prime contractor to take immediate action with the subcontractor.

SUBCONTRACTOR'S FACILITY PQA

This section discusses the requirement for the review of purchase orders by the prime contractor's government representative. Government PQAP action at the subcontractor's facility is required when there is a direct shipment by the supplier to the government's facilities.

Some evaluations shall be conducted by the subcontractor's government representative when they cannot be performed at the contractor's facilities. These evaluations are limited to PCO-ordered inspections and to selected procedures, processes, and characteristics. They are applicable when MIL-I-45208 or MIL-Q-9858 are imposed on the supplier.

This requirement is based upon the results of the government representative's review of the prime contractor's controls over supplier compliance. The QAR may request selected verification of portions of the subcontractor's program to assure that it is being implemented in accordance with the specification.

Subcontractor's Statement of Quality

This describes the appropriate certifications provided by the subcontractor for product elements for which actual inspection/test data are not provided by the supplier. The certifications should summarize the supplier's objective quality evidence (OQE) or reference the availability of OQE at the supplier's facility.

First Article Approvals

When requested by the PCO, the QAR will witness the tests to insure that they are performed according to procedures and that the data recorded are that which were observed.

Note

The QAR normally does not approve or disapprove the test report. This is done by the PCO or technical agency, but the QAR may provide comments on the contractor's first article report.

Engineering Changes

The QAR must process engineering changes, which are categorized as Class 1 and Class 2. Usually, the QAR reviews Class 2 changes for verification of the category, and the contractor may act on these changes without further approvals. Class 1 changes are reviewed by the QAR for proper information and approved or disapproved by the PCO before contractor implementation.

Nonconforming Supplies

Unless withheld by the PCO, approval of requests for accepting Type II (minor) nonconforming supplies is delegated to the QAR. Approval for use of Type I (major or critical) nonconformances is held by the PCO. This section discusses using the MRB and the methods of processing these requests using the referenced specifications such as MIL-STD-480 and 481.

Quality Data Evaluation

This section discusses the QAR's use of contractor data in performing PQA evaluations. This review will serve to determine the extent of the QAR's activities needed. The request for copies of the data may not be necessary. The QAR may use contractor's copies for the evaluation.

Authorization of Shipment of Supplies

This discusses the preparation and issuance of the government's acceptance and shipping document, DD250, and the use of certificates of conformance as a basis of acceptance by the QAR, when permitted in the contract.

Inspection and Acceptance of Technical Data

Data to be supplied to the government is usually noted in a list in the contract. The list will specify where the data inspection and acceptance will be performed. Usually contractor-supplied technical data, manuals, and drawings are approved by the technical agency, at destination. QAR action, when required, may determine the degree of implementation, by the contractor, of any mandated quality control procedures for this material and may inspect them for completeness before shipment.

Preservation Packaging, Packing, and Marking Requirements

This describes the extent of product and process evaluation of these functions by the QAR.

Processes

This section describes the evaluation of the contractor's degree of implementation of special processes according to specifications. These processes include nondestructive testing, welding, painting, and the like. Many of these require qualification or certification of equipment, processes, and/or personnel. The QAR may require the specialists' services in the ACO's office for assistance in these evaluations. The QAR and applicable specialists may need special training in the processes, especially for any innovations.

Qualified Products List (QPL)

When it is technically and economically feasible, suppliers may submit product samples for qualification testing even if they have no current contracts to produce these items. This program provides an opportunity of being placed on a special qualified products lists (QPL). Government contractors using these items must procure them from suppliers on a QPL. The qualification tests may be performed at a supplier's facility or government laboratory.

Note

One problem with the QPL program is the contractors' misunderstanding that QPL items meet specifications. This is not necessarily so. All this qualification states is that, at the time of the test, the product samples met the applicable requirements. It is still the contractor's responsibility to insure that subsequent supplies conform to the entire specification.

Usually, the contractor's purchasing department maintains copies of the latest QPLs and consults them when ordering. The contractor then gets the product and verifies that it had been fabricated at the location noted on the QPL.

QPLs are occasionally revised, requiring the contractor to maintain up-to-date lists. Suppliers may be added or removed from the lists for cause. In addition, as noted above, the contractor must insure that the supplier has performed all the other inspection/tests included in the specification and has current data attesting to this.

Reliability and Maintainability

Usually when a quantitative reliability and maintainability requirement is specified on the contract, there is also a provision that the contractor provide a written program for the implementation of these requirements in accordance with such specifications as MIL-STD-785 or MIL-STD-470. Sometimes, the requirement for a reliability program is not specified; however, a program should be implemented which includes procedures for design analysis, including the estimate of product reliability or maintainability and data collection and analysis. Corrective actions should be based on product qualification and acceptance tests, product evaluation and improvement programs, and field operations. Corrective actions should be included in the product design analysis.

Demonstration requirements using military standards or a complete method are required. Methods include sample size, test procedure, test plan, confidence levels, test hours of operations, and number and definition of allowable failures.

The QAR is usually required to witness the tests, review the documentation, failure descriptions, and analyses for accuracy and completeness, and verify that the required number of test hours have been performed.

Note

At times, the witnessing QAR may attempt to accept or reject the product relative to its reliability and maintainability requirements. This function is rarely given to the QAR or to his or her technical specialist. Acceptance of the product and report is usually a function of the government's procurement and technical office.

Automated Inspection

In the past, due to the equipment's complexity, the government had been reluctant to accept its results, particularly when it only provided an accept and reject decision. However, as more methods have evolved to demonstrate the equipment's accuracy, these methods have been gradually approved. The method for proving the equipment's accuracy includes verification of the program's accuracy. This may be done by flowcharting the program and running the tape or punched card through the machine for an initial printout to check for mechanical errors. The printout is checked for typing errors. The data are then transferred to the computer's memory, and the program is trial tested before actual use.

The QAR is required to evaluate the completeness and adequacy of the contractor's procedures and their implementation. In addition, the QAR is required to witness the self-tests of the contractor's automated equipment accuracy. It may be necessary for a product to be manually rechecked to verify the automated equipment's accuracy.

Test Procedures and Reports

This section discusses the special tests such as preproduction and model, not the normal production tests.

The QAR is usually required to witness or monitor the tests after the procedures have been approved by the responsible government agency. All witnessed measurements are noted on the original data sheets with the QAR initials or stamp adjacent to the date. The QAR and technical support personnel are required to review the test report for completeness and accuracy, and for the contractor's analyses and corrective actions. The report is sent to the PCO with the QAR's comments about general workmanship, adequacy of test equipment and methods, verification that tests were performed in accordance with the approved procedures, any problems, and concurrence or nonconcurrence with the contractor's recommendations.

Note

Here, too, the QAR is not authorized to accept or reject the report. He or she only verifies the findings and comments on them.

Visual Acuity and Color Blindness

QARs involved in the inspection of supplies for which the contract requires visual acuity and color vision, must be able to meet the same requirements as the contractor.

Single Standard Quality Control

If a contractor is producing the same type of product for commercial and government requirements, and wishes to maintain the same standard of quality for both, it is not necessary to separate the government and commercial parts and material. The contractor, however, must notify, in writing, the QA chief of the ACO agency. The following commitments must be made.

- The standard of quality of the commercial product will be the same as that required by the government contract.

- All commercial product material not conforming to the government standards will be handled according to contractually authorized nonconforming material procedures, and that disposition established in these procedures will be final and applicable to the entire lot under consideration.

- All procedures and operations will be subject to QAR disapproval.

Configuration Management

The QAR's planning should provide for sufficient coverage of the contractor's configuration management plan, when available, and ensure quality control of technical data.

The QAR must review contract work statements and administration assignments to determine the requirements for configuration management and controls. The QAR must obtain clarifications for vague instructions in the contract.

Where the contract requires approval of the configuration management plan by the PCO, the QAR and technical specialist must review the plan for conformance. If it contains deviations from the prescribed contract requirements, the QAR must advise the PCO of such shortcomings at the time the plan is furnished to the government for approval. In accordance with these instructions, the QAR cannot reject or refuse to release the plan for submission to the PCO, but can merely add his or her comments.

After PCO approval, the QAR is required to develop evaluation checklists for the purpose of assuring that the contractor effectively adheres to the approved plan. The QAR is required to monitor the prescribed examinations and corrective actions, as applicable. This involves the formal examination of the as-built unit configuration of the Contract Item (CI) against its technical documentation. This establishes the CI's initial product configuration identification. The physical configuration audit (PCA) is conducted under the direction of the PCO or systems/program manager. The extent of QAR participation is defined in the contract or in special instructions from the procuring agency. The QAR is required to review and process engineering change proposals, waivers, and deviations as described in the applicable sections of the manual.

Procurement Quality Assurance for Computer Software

The QAR is normally required to review and evaluate conformance to quality procedures, and to view and provide comments to the contractor's configuration management plan, technical specifications, test plans, and evaluation reports. The QAR must also perform product inspections, including the following:

- Witnessing and monitoring end item tests.

- Witnessing and monitoring intermediate testing, such as subroutines, where necessary.

- Verifying software media and formats for compliance and applicable specifications.

REFERENCES

1. *Principles of Government Contract Law.* Washington, DC: Office of Management and Budgets, Office of Federal Procurement Policy, September 1979.

2. *Interpretation of Specifications and Contracts* (Government Contract Seminar), George Washington University, May 3, 1962.

3. *Mil-Q-9858: Quality Program Requirements.* Washington, DC: Superintendent of Documents, December 16, 1963.

4. *Military Handbook H50: Evaluation of Contractor's Quality Program.* Washington, DC: Superintendent of Documents, October 31, 1960.

5. *Mil-I-45208: Inspection System Requirements.* Washington, DC: Superintendent of Documents, December 16, 1963.

6. *Military Handbook H-51: Evaluation of Contractor's Inspection Program.* Washington, DC: Superintendent of Documents, January 3, 1963.

7. *MIL-STD-45662: Calibration System Requirements.* Washington, DC: Superintendent of Documents, June 10, 1980.

8. *Military Handbook H52A: Evaluation of Contractor's Calibration System.* Washington, DC, August 17, 1984.

9. *Defense Supply Agency Manual DSAM 8200.1.* Cameron Station, Alexandria, VA, August 1976.

Dealing with International Companies

QUALITY ASSURANCE SPECIFICATIONS

International trade requires that there be complete understanding of how each item is measured; its acceptance criteria; how sampling is performed, including the degree of accuracy expected; and the terminology used in inspection and quality assurance activities.

In dealing with the North Atlantic Treaty Organization (NATO), this problem was alleviated. The allied quality assurance procedures (AQAPs) were issued. These are equivalent to the applicable U.S. government quality assurance specifications. Table 34-1 shows these AQAPs and their related U. S. specifications.[1]

INTERNATIONAL STANDARDS

Technical specifications may not, by themselves, guarantee that[2] a customer's requirements will be consistently met. Consequently, quality system standards and guidelines that complement relevant product or service requirements were developed. The series of standards, ANSI/ASQC Q90–Q94, embody a rationalization of the many and various national approaches to this sphere and is technically equivalent to the International Standards ISO 9000–9004.

The five standards in the ISO series were developed by the technical committee 176 of the International Standards Organization.[3] The American National Standards Institute (ANSI) and the ASQC adopted the ISO

AQAP NUMBER	QAP DESCRIPTION	U.S. EQUIVALENT
1	NATO Quality Control System Requirements for Industry	MIL-Q-9858A
2	Guide for the evaluation of a contractor's quality control system for compliance with AQAP-1	DOD Handbook H-50
3	List of sampling schemes used in NATO countries	No specific
4	NATO inspection system requirements for industry	MIL-I-45208A
5	Guide for the evaluation of a contractor's system for compliance with AQAP-4	DOD Handbook H-51
6	NATO calibration system requirements for industry	MIL-STD-45662
7	Guide for the evaluation of a contractor's calibration system for compliance with AQAP-6	DOD Handbook H-52A
8	Guide for the preparation of specifications for the procurement of defense material	No specific
9	NATO basic inspection requirements for industry	ASPR 7–103.5, now called FAR 7–103.5

TABLE 34-1 NATO Applied Quality Assurance Publications

series for use in the United States, resulting in the Q90 series. The technical content of both series is identical.

Information about any of these standards may be obtained from ASQC Technical Service Department, 611 East Wisconsin Avenue, Milwaukee, Wisconsin 53201–3005. Table 34-2 shows the relationship between the ANSI/ASQC Q90–Q94[4] series with the ISO 9000–9004. As an example, Figure 34-1 shows the ANSI/ASQC 094 elements.

The ISO 9000 series has been adopted by British companies as a tool for evaluating their suppliers. It requires that suppliers be audited and registered (if they pass the audit) as ISO 9000 suppliers. All other companies will accept this registration with little or no further auditing.

Starting in 1992, companies in the integrated European Community will require their suppliers to be audited and registered under the EN 29000 series which is technically identical to the Q90 and ISO 9000 series.

Courses on international standards are given by the British Standards Institute (BSI), the American Association of Laboratories Accreditation (AALA), the University of Georgia, Rochester Institute of Technology, and others. There are also many courses on registration in the United States.

There are a number of organizations involved in some form of registration procedure, including the ASQC, Chemical Manufacturers Association, and the Underwriters Lab (UL). ASQC has established a subsidiary corporation called the Registration Accreditation Board (RAB), to accredit companies that will register suppliers under the appropriate Q90/ISO 9000 standards.

The BSI issued a letter of understanding, stating that any registration performed by Underwriters Lab in the United States would be recognized

ANSV ASQC NUMBER	ISO EQUIVALENT NUMBER	ISO TITLE
Q90	9000	*Quality Management and Quality Assurance Standards: Guidelines for Selection and Use*
Q91	9001	*Quality Assurance in Design/Development, Production, Installation, and Service*
Q92	9002	*Quality Assurance in Production and Installation*
Q93	9003	*Quality Assurance in Final Inspection and Test*
Q94	9004	*Quality Management and Quality System Elements: Guidelines*

TABLE 34-2 ANSI/ASQC Q90–94 and ISO 9000–9004

as valid. For a fee, any company registered by UL can also be registered by BSI and listed in its directory.

After 1992, many U.S. companies will be required, as a result of doing business with the European Community, to be audited and registered under an applicable Q90/ISO 9000/EN 29000 standard. As this practice becomes more prevalent, other U.S. companies will honor the registration and reduce their supplier surveillance programs.

Actions are also being taken by the U.S. Department of Defense and NATO to revise their procurement procedures to make explicit use of the ISO 9000 series.

In the short term, quality strategies for doing business in Europe and worldwide will require the development of quality systems and certifications based on ISO 9000 standards. In the long term, the use of ISO 9000 series will be seen as a foundation for total quality improvement.

Currently, member states of the European Community are Belgium, Denmark, France, Germany, Greece, Ireland, Italy, Luxembourg, the Netherlands, Portugal, Spain, and the United Kingdom.

Two additional resources about European standards activity are maintained by the Commerce Department's NIST.[5]

The new directory, *European Regional Standards-Related Organization*, published by NIST, is designed to help federal agencies, standards writers, manufacturers, exporters, and others concerned with the standards-related activities in the European Community, and the European Free Trade Association.

The directory identifies more than 150 European regional organizations, both governmental and private, that engage in the standards development, certifications, laboratory accreditation, and other related activities.

Entries include address, telex, telephone, cable and fax numbers; acronyms; national affiliations of members; scope of interest; activities in standardization; laboratory accreditation and related fields; and the availability of standards in English.

INTRODUCTION

Organizational Goals
Meeting Company/Customer Needs
Risks
Costs and Benefits

SCOPE AND FIELD OF APPLICATION

DEFINITIONS

Organization
Company
Requirements of Society
Customer

MANAGEMENT RESPONSIBILITY

Quality Policy
Quality Objectives
Quality System

QUALITY SYSTEMS PRINCIPLES

Quality Loop
Structure of the Quality System (Quality Responsibility and Authority)
Organizational Structure (Resources and Personnel, Operational Procedures)
Documentation of the System (Quality Policies and Procedures, Quality Manual, Quality Plans, Quality Records)
Auditing the Quality System (General, Audit Plan, Carrying Out the Audit)
Review and Evaluation of the Quality Management System

ECONOMICS

Quality-Related Cost Considerations
Selecting Appropriate Elements
Types of Quality-Related Costs (Operating Quality Costs, External Assurance Quality Costs)
Management Visibility

QUALITY IN MARKETING

Marketing Requirements
Product Brief
Customer's Feedback Information

QUALITY IN SPECIFICATIONS AND DESIGN

Contribution of Specifications and Design to Quality
Design Planning and Objectives (Defining the Project)

FIGURE 34-1 ANSI/ASQC 094 Elements

Product Testing and Measurement
Design Qualification and Validation
Design Review (Elements of Design Review, Design Verifications)
Design Baseline and Production Release
Market Readiness Review
Design Change Control (Configuration Management)
Design Requalification

QUALITY IN PROCUREMENT

Requirements for Specifications, Drawings, and Purchase Orders
Selection of Qualified Suppliers
Agreement on Quality Assurance
Agreement on Verification Methods
Provisions for Settlement of Quality Disputes
Receiving Inspection Planning and Control
Receiving Quality Records

QUALITY IN PRODUCTION

Planning for Controlled Production
Process Capability
Supplies, Utilities, and Environment

CONTROL OF PRODUCTION

Material Control and Traceability
Equipment Control and Maintenance
Special Processes
Documentation
Process Change Control
Control of Verification Status
Control of Nonconforming Materials

PRODUCT VERIFICATION

Incoming Materials and Parts
In-Process Inspections
Completed Product Verification

CONTROL OF MEASURING AND TEST EQUIPMENT

Measurement Control
Elements of Control
Supplier Measurement Control
Corrective Action
Outside Testing

NONCONFORMITY

Identification
Segregation

FIGURE 34-1   Continued

Reviews
Disposition
Documentation
Prevention of Recurrence

CORRECTIVE ACTION

Assignment of Responsibility
Evaluation of Importance
Investigation of Possible Causes
Analysis of Problem
Preventive Action
Process Controls
Disposition of Nonconforming Items
Permanent Changes

HANDLING AND POSTPRODUCTION FUNCTIONS

Handling
Storage
Identification
Packaging
Installation
Delivery
After-Sales Servicing
Marketing Reporting and Product Supervision

QUALITY DOCUMENTATION AND RECORDS

PERSONNEL

Training: Executive and Management Personnel, Technical Personnel,
Production Supervisors and Workers
Qualification
Motivation: Application, Quality Awareness, Measuring Quality

PRODUCT SAFETY AND LIABILITY

USE OF STATISTICAL METHODS

Applications
Statistical Techniques

APPENDIX A: Sampling and Other Statistical Methods

This was not included in ISO 9004, but is used as a guideline.

Sampling Inspection

Uses of Sampling Inspection
Advantages of Sampling

FIGURE 34-1   Continued

Types of Sampling
Attributes Sampling
Variables Sampling for Percent Nonconforming

Basic Statistical Methods

Process Control Charts: P-Charts: X-bar–R Charts Combination
Acceptance Sampling, Lot-by-Lot Sampling, Continuous Sampling

Other Statistical Methods

Sampling Risk

Effective Use of Statistical Methods

APPENDIX B: Product Liability and User Safety

This is not part of ISO 9004, but is used as a guideline.

Company Policy Statement on Product Safety

Scope
Safety Standards
Legislation
Product Safety Council
Use of Third Parties

Design and Design Reviews Related to Product Safety

Documentation of Test Results

Safety Review of User's Manuals and Promotional Material

Field Performance Reporting System

Hazard Warnings

Retention of Records

Product Liability Information

Product Identification, Systems for Traceability During Recall

Product Liability Insurance

FIGURE 34-1 Continued

Copies of the directory are available for a small sum from the Superintendent of Documents, U.S. Government Printing Office, Washington, D.C. 20402.

A hot line has also been established and is maintained by NIST. It reports on proposed laws developed by the European Community and its two major standards development organizations in Brussels: the European Committee on Standardization and the European Committee for Electrotechnical Standardization. The hot line features recorded messages of draft laws and standards that might create technical trade barriers.

Proposed standards are also reported from the European Telecommunications Standards Institute which is working to unify the European telecommunications system. The hot line, (301) 921–4164, is updated weekly.

REFERENCES

1. "Inspection Clauses," *NATO Applied Quality Assurance Publications,* Philadelphia, PA, NATO Naval Publications and Forms Center.

2. Burr, John. "The Future ASQC Necessity," *Quality Progress,* Milwaukee, WI, June, 1990.

3. Mundel, August B. *International Commerce: ISO/TC-69 Contributor* (AQC). Milwaukee, WI: ASQC, 1989, p. 190.

4. American Society for Quality Control. *ANSI/ASQC.* Milwaukee, WI: ASQC, 1987.

5. American Society for Quality Control. "International Standards," *Quality Progress,* Milwaukee, WI: ASQC, December, 1990, p. 12.

CHAPTER THIRTY-FIVE

Miscellaneous Nonmanufacturing Industries

Chapters 35–39 are devoted to abstracts of applicable literature providing brief discussions of a number of nonmanufacturing services and industries. Although they have many quality attributes and techniques of the manufacturing industries, there are many different elements unique to the specific industry. Chapter 35 identifies those quality program elements and their related traditional operations. It also discusses support and administrative services.

ADMINISTRATIVE AND SUPPORT SERVICES

In all industries there are many support services needed to fulfill an organization's overall operation. These include such services as administration, personnel recruitment and evaluation, finance, maintenance, legal, sales and marketing, security, computer services, traffic, shipping, and receiving.

Quality failures in nonmanufacturing areas often go unnoticed. They are usually considered as part of the process. Some of these failures are: inaccurate market forecasts, wrong material received due to incorrect purchase orders, incorrect customer order entries, late shipments, missing accounts payable deductions, lack of courtesy during telephone calls, improperly performed maintenance work, poor quality hiring and personnel evaluation, accounting reports errors, incorrect billing, and many others.

These failures can, and often do, have a serious effect on customers' perceptions of the organization. Further, the ability of the company to efficiently produce and deliver a quality item is greatly influenced by the quality of work of the supporting and administrative departments.

Like the manufacturing operations, in order for the organization to attain world class quality status, it is important that each support and administrative operation develop and implement a quality control and improvement program.

The functions of the administrative and support departments are, in most companies, considered indirect functions. Thus, a breakdown of the costs, including those that are quality related, are rarely, if ever, included in the departmental financial statements. Accordingly, little information is provided to determine the effects of poor quality in the department as well as the whole organization. However, the quality of most outputs can and does have a considerable effect on the quality of the organization as perceived by customers.

Most of the operations performed by administrative and support services consist of a variety of clerical functions.[1] Thus it is important that adequate controls are exercised. Traditionally, very little, if any, attention has been paid to the quality of the clerical operations, except for the use of rudimentary methods such as proofreading typed or written documents.

ORGANIZATION

The operations of the support and administrative departments are usually performed under the direction of department heads. Subelements of the operation are delegated to various sections under the jurisdiction of managers or supervisors. Any determination of the operation's effectiveness is usually performed under the auspices of these departments. These functions rarely have an operation primarily dedicated to the planning, implementation, and evaluation of the service quality. Most likely, these elements are incorporated into others such as overall productivity and budget conformance.

PLANNING

It is essential that each group within the company considers the specific effect of its services on its customers, both internal and external. Each administrative and support department should develop and implement quality controls within its area of operation. In order to conduct its review in a scientific and orderly manner, each group should prepare a matrix listing all its functions, its suppliers, and its customers. This may also be achieved by preparing flowcharts of the operations, and defining the inputs and outputs at each station. This should enable the department heads to identify the following elements of their operations:

- Functions and tasks
- Interfaces (inputs and outputs)

- Interface requirements
- Measurements needed to verify and track activities' quality
- Corrective methods
- Continuous quality improvement plan

It may be desirable to draw upon the knowledge and experience of workers at all levels to obtain an understanding of the material and process characteristics needed for fitness-for-use requirements.

SPECIFICATIONS

Once the customers' requirements are defined, it is necessary to transmit them into internal specifications and instructions. This function, while followed through on product manufacture, is rarely applied to the support and administrative elements. However, it is equally important that employees understand job requirements, criteria of acceptability, method of measurement for conformance, and actions taken to correct nonconformances.

These procedures should be designed to give the same detailed instructions to the administrative and support personnel as the drawings and specifications provide for manufacturing operators. Unfortunately, in the support and administrative operations, these instructions are often nonexistent or poorly prepared. Few procedures, when used, are up to date. Others detail only what is to be done if things go right. Thus, when things go wrong, operators try to do what they think is right. Often, they guess wrong.

By understanding this lack of positive definition, the need for measurements, and the requirements to look at these processes in the long run, it is possible to adapt to the support and administrative functions most of the methodology of the manufacturing operations.

IMPLEMENTATION

While many quality problems similar to those encountered in the manufacturing operation are found in the support and administrative operations, there are a number of unique problems. Examples of some are detailed in the following sections.

Order processing

These may be internal requisitions prepared by many departments, and sent to the storeroom to be filled. The prompt and correct filling of these orders is important to the efficiency and quality of the manufactured products. Order errors include improper labeling, inadequate stock rotation, and lack of identification of shelf-life terms.

Usually, the order forms are checked by the storeroom clerk or the receiving department upon receipt of the material. In some companies, the quality department performs periodic audits of the stores areas.

Computation

Control of calculation is usually done by the operator. Sometimes, the supervisor may perform periodic checks. In some companies, special auditors periodically review the calculations on sample documents. With the use of computers, there are some means of fool proofing the computations so that gross errors can be detected.

Material protection and handling

Some companies have a packaging engineering department, which reviews each item on the product bill of materials to determine any special handling equipment needs. When required, this department designs and reviews the construction of the suitable equipment, tote bins, pallets, and containers. It is generally responsible for properly maintaining the equipment and repairing or replacing any nonfunctioning or damaged equipment. In one company, the quality control department performs periodic surveys to assure that the handling equipment is utilized on the product for which it was designed and that the equipment is properly maintained in accordance with specified requirements. When necessary, material ordered from outside sources are required to be transported in a manner established by the packaging engineering department.

Shipped material is usually packaged, labeled, and packed in accordance with customers' specifications. When these requirements are absent, the packaging engineering personnel design the method of preparation for shipment so that it is adequate to meet the Interstate Commerce Commission's handling requirements and those of the carrier. This department also provides methods for transportation of products returned to suppliers for replacement or repair.

EVALUATION

To properly assess conformance to the requirements, it is necessary that measurements are devised for each element in quantitative terms. To provide the proper appraisal of any nonmanufacturing operation, it is necessary to know and understand the importance of the operation to customers and the measurements necessary to evaluate it. Some appraisal methods used in support and administrative operations include the following:

- Accounting: Number of days reports are overdue and number of error-related reissues

- Maintenance: Number of reworks per 100 jobs

- Engineering: Cost variance from budgeted amounts

- Purchasing: Number of incorrect purchase orders

Evaluation of support and administrative performance is similar to that of manufacturing, but precautions must be taken because of human errors which are more prevalent in support operations. Typical errors and their remedies are noted here.

Misinterpretations of requirements

Remedies include providing precise definitions, checklists, and typical examples.

Inadvertent errors

Remedies include aptitude testing, reorganization of work to reduce fatigue and monotony, fail-safe designs, automation, and robotics.

Lack of adequate techniques

Remedies include discovery of successful worker's knack, training of other workers to use this technique, and engineering studies of the operators and provision of suitable facilities and equipment to properly evaluate the function.

Conscious errors such as coloration or bias

Remedies include design reviews of data collection plans, removal of atmosphere of blame (depersonalization of accountability), action on discrepancy reports, providing an explanation for lack of action, establishment of accountability, provision for balanced emphasis on goals, performance of quality audits, creation of compensation and incentives, and reassignment of work.

Evaluation is customarily performed through extensive use of measures of performance most responsive to cost and productivity. Control of documentation can be accomplished by one or more of the following:

- Simple reliance on well-designed forms and personnel's competence

- Proofreading by personnel other than those preparing documents

- Sample checking of the work done by preparers and analysis of the results to discover error patterns and to make corrections

- Fool proofing the operation

Evaluation of Clerical Operations

When checking clerical operations, there are four areas of concern: (1) the ability of the checker to fully comprehend what is to be done, (2) the ability of the checker to find all errors, (3) the feedback mechanism to give the clerks information on how to perform their jobs correctly, and (4) a record of the inspection results that can be used for analysis and continuous improvement. In none of these areas are the checkers entirely reliable.

Usually, most checkers in the administrative and support clerical operations are trained by fellow departmental workers. As a result, it is not surprising that the checkers' understanding of their job often differs from that of management. For example, when the checkers in one bank were asked what the value of the transactions were to be verified, they replied those over $10,000. Management thought that transactions over $5,000 were checked.

As a rule, the checkers find only a portion of the errors. Some managers attempt to use multiple checkers, each examining the same item. This provides deceptive results. Checkers know that the others exist, therefore they assume that any errors missed by the first checker would be found by subsequent ones.

The results in finding errors committed due to poor training are almost never used to help workers. In fact, checkers frequently make their own corrections of nonconforming characteristics, without feeding back to the original operators the type and quantity of errors found. Thus, it is important that checkers are instructed to document, in an inspection record, all errors found. This can then be used to implement suitable corrective actions.

In one company, the supervisor of the unit looks at the operators' work as it is being done. The leader selects recently completed items and determines if they were correctly processed. A record of these examinations helps to develop process control data. In special cases, the inspection process is based on a random sampling plan where the lot consists of sampling units of operator/time segments. Using random numbers, it is determined if a recent piece of work is to be inspected.

MANAGEMENT REPORTS

As in manufactured product quality, management quality reports should be prepared for support services. These may include the current quality levels of the operation or some subcomponent, their previous quality levels, the most significant contributors to out-of-control areas, the recommended corrective actions, and the results of previous corrective actions. These reports can be provided for most administrative and support functions, including shipping backlogs, costs per standard hour, maintenance emergency hours and their labor costs, errors in documentation, and many others.

CORRECTIVE ACTION

If they exist at all, there are many weaknesses in the traditional implementation and correction of quality control activities in administrative and support functions.

Lack of coordination

Support organizations rarely participate in the broad planning of quality. They usually conduct the planning of their own affairs with quality failures being considered only when a crisis develops. A proper organizational approach should include identification of work aspects which significantly affect product or operation quality. This can properly be done by a study team consisting of members of the support department and those of the quality control department, using a well-defined table of delegation.

Inadequate attention to quality improvement

Support departments generally do not consider chronic quality problems priorities for resolution. Instead, they are primarily concerned with the traditional priorities of their overall operations. To correct this condition, quality-related data should be incorporated in the management report to implement corrective actions, as needed. See Chapter 20 for additional information about this program.

Inadequate provisions for diagnosis

Support departments lack specialists in problem analysis. Hence, it must be performed by supervisors or outside specialists. A progressive step is to provide specialists or train selected members of the department in problem analysis.

Inadequate measures of quality operations

The measures that administrative and support departments use are those applicable to their primary concerns, costs, and productivity. A team study of their activities can identify the needed measures of quality performance and set up appropriate scoreboards. In order to obtain the support of management, it would be helpful to point out that advances in quality improvement can also have a positive effect on costs and productivity.

QUALITY IMPROVEMENT

In order to satisfy the department's goal of customer satisfaction, the process as well as the output should be improved by decreasing operational mistakes. For this, the display of leadership is most important. Management should persuade subordinates to seek common goals. This can be done through motivation, guidance, and encouragement. A frank, informal discussion should be held when the results of abnormalities are presented.

After quality is improved, indicators should be established to check whether output continues to be acceptable, improving, and satisfactory for customers. Indicators are also needed to monitor the continuing control of the intermediate processes. A cause-and-effect relationship should exist between the process indicator (cause) and the quality indicator (effect). With appropriate process indicators, prompt action can be taken when out-of-control conditions are revealed.

EXAMPLES

Several examples of quality improvement in support and administrative operations are detailed here.

Steel sheets were openly stored. Although they were treated with a preventative, some rusting occurred because material handlers had no way of applying the first-in–first-out procedure. Instead of providing additional storage space, as originally recommended, the quality improvement project suggested that periodically changing the color of the rust preservative would enable material handlers to identify and rotate the stock.

Poor customer service was caused by product identification tags lost in transit. They had been wired to pans. This was corrected by using tags with self-adhesive plastic envelopes.

Improve Operator's Knowledge

Worker training in the service industry is rather sketchy. Much training is on the job; one worker trains the next. Even when formal classes are held in such areas as bank teller functions, customer service, or data entry, clerks are repeatedly assigned to other clerks to learn the ropes. Little by little, the original instruction changes. Standardized formal training with frequent leader follow-up are essential to achieve clerical quality.

Tools

Clerical workers are in as much need of proper tools as manufacturing operators. These tools are pencils, forms, word processors, data, timely reports, diagnoses, x-rays, and the like. At times, workers do not have adequate tools. For instance, an office copier that works poorly can ultimately be coaxed to give some result but at the excessive cost of lost productivity and low worker morale. It is the leader's job to see that workers have adequate tools.

Pride of Workmanship

If workers are not able to perform the assigned task because of problems such as poor tools, inadequate training, and poor leadership, they are discouraged. This results in poor quality and low productivity. Workers are often blamed by poor managers for their own lack of leadership. Management should be constantly aware of these conditions and take appropriate corrective measures.

The benefit of improving quality in the nonmanufacturing areas goes beyond the financial gain.[1] It reduces stress and encourages better internal customer/supplier relationships, while increasing external customer satisfaction. To accomplish these desirable effects, an error-friendly environment must be established.

Historically, it has been human nature to equate error with failure. Consequently, there is a tendency to cover up or excuse errors because one does not want to be perceived as failing. An error-friendly environment is one which encourages open discussion of errors, because they are viewed as opportunities for improving quality and profitability. Employees are applauded for constructively pointing out problems, seeking to identify the root causes, and continuously pursuing permanent solutions. Managers need to help create an error-friendly environment by commending people who are willing to reveal problems, especially recurring ones. Through root cause definition, attention needs to be focused on the true solutions, rather than on looking for a person to blame.

CUSTOMER PERCEPTION—INTERNAL AND EXTERNAL

The support and administrative departments must continually monitor the quality of their products and services as perceived by customers. Popular methods are to send customers a questionnaire after the completion of each job, or at planned intervals.

An easy-to-complete form should be developed. Quantitative scales of zero to ten can be used to evaluate responses. The group can then summarize the responses and monitor these ratings. The questionnaire should address the following:

Quality of design

The questions should relate to the effectiveness of meeting customers' specifications and the appropriateness of products and service.

Quality of delivery

The questions should relate to the availability, responsiveness, professional rapport, and packaging of the product.

Recommendations for improvement

In reviewing customers' needs, it is important to understand that the stated needs are often different from the real ones. For example, a personnel office perceives the need to train the work force in some specialty. However, the line managers do not think that this would help their department in meeting its goals.

Customers' needs often go beyond products and services. At times, they include job security, self-respect, and continuing habits and other cultural conditions. An example of these needs is a department's reluctance to release some function, since the threat to ownership of an operation is seen as a threat to department status.

COMPARISON WITH THE COMPETITION

It is vital to be aware of the services developed by other support organizations, whether within the company or outside of it. A group may not have, at the time, any competition for its services. This does not preclude the possibility that other services are being developed in the home office. In addition, there is always a chance of duplication of efforts within the company. As a result, duplications may be revealed and eliminated. Knowing the competition can help the organization determine its advantages and shortcomings. This exercise helps to fine-tune the quality and cost of support services.

Another way to get information about the competition is to ask customers. In this quality survey, customers are asked about alternative sources they considered, the relative advantages and disadvantages of each source, and why the particular organization was chosen. Cost should be addressed. A worksheet can be developed showing how to benchmark the services. This should list the services and products provided, the percent of time provided for each item, the allocated costs for research and development for each item, and marketing efforts in each area.

Getting close to customers and understanding their expectations are essential to ensuring that services truly meet their needs. This can be done by answering the following questions:

- Specifically, what is the product?

- What are customers' expectations?

- How can performance be measured?

- How can routine feedback of product or service quality be obtained?

SUPPLIER INVOLVEMENT

It is also important to know suppliers and to involve them in the quality process. Suppliers can provide information, material, and services which affect the quality of the receiving department's services. The basic points are: to know who the suppliers are (internal or external), to establish their expectations, to build a relationship, and to communicate regularly.

EDUCATION

There has typically been a dearth of quality education in administrative and support departments. To properly apply quality methods, an education plan should be developed and implemented. Several areas should be considered.

- Quality awareness and importance, such as fitness for use and price of nonconformance
- Fundamental concepts, such as variation, process control, and supplier/customer relationships
- Tools, such as Pareto analysis, time sequence plotting, and checklists
- Problem solving methods

EMPLOYEE INVOLVEMENT

Employees can provide viable contributions in all aspects of departmental activities, as they affect quality planning, control, and improvement. The individual worker knows better than anyone else what makes his or her job effective.

STATISTICAL TECHNIQUES

The techniques available for manufacturing product quality improvement are also applicable to the administrative and support functions.

Frequency Analysis and Pareto Charts

These techniques establish the effect of variables, such as personnel, shifts, supervision, and equipment, on productivity. By using the Pareto principle, the analysis can detect the vital few customers who receive most of the impact of the department's service. This analysis can then be used to discover the needs of customers who are dissatisfied with services.

Regression Analysis

For example, the relation of document errors to cost of preparation or correction can be determined using this procedure.

Sampling

Traditional sampling or specially designed plans can be used to audit support operations.

Cause-and-Effect Diagram

This technique establishes a relationship between an effect and all its possible causes. In one order entry department, it was observed that 50 percent of incoming orders had to be corrected before they could be processed. The members of the quality improvement committee listed all possible causes under the four Ps: people, procedures, policies and plant (equipment). This group came up with dozens of possible causes.

- Plant (equipment)
  - Inadequate catalog
  - No catalog (unavailable information)
  - Computer deficiency

- People
  - Interruptions
  - Lack of accountability
  - Poor penmanship
  - Lack of training
  - Incomplete sales information (volume affecting time)
  - Bad assumptions
  - Poor performance because job is too complicated

- Policies
  - Job descriptions (responsibilities)
  - Nonstock special order items
  - Lack of minimum standards

- Procedures
  - Too complicated (customers lack of order details)
  - Price/Discount variation
  - Out of stock (poor product numbering system)
  - Discrepancies between order and quote

After brainstorming, a cause-and-effect chart was created. The group identified the most likely causes, and through a subsequent vote determined which areas to tackle first.

Problem solving should be results-oriented, not procedure-oriented.[2] For example, comparisons of actual data with targets, control limits, specifications, past data, and the results of similar processes may reveal some deviation. The causes of the major deviations should be clarified.

REFERENCES

1. Nader, Gary J. *Applying Quality Methods, Nonmanufacturing Areas*. Milwaukee, WI: Annual Quality Conference (AQC), ASQC, 1989, p. 14.

2. Kundo, Yushdolo. *Quality Control Activities in Administrative Departments*. Milwaukee, WI: AQC, ASQC, 1990, p. 6.

CHAPTER THIRTY-SIX

Commercial and Nuclear Construction

COMMERCIAL CONSTRUCTION[1]

In general, labor represents 66 percent of construction costs. Construction is highly technical and design problems are well understood. Drawings are checked, and industry standards, building codes, zoning restrictions, and engineering designs are available, but there are very few formal quality assurance requirements.

ORGANIZATION[2]

Responsibility for quality control is assigned to individual departments. The functional and support relationships for each element of the quality system are defined in a responsibility matrix attached to the company's quality policy.

The quality assurance department is generally quite small. It concurs on quality-related procedures, reviews quality control requirements in specifications, plans quality control, and audits quality systems. The contracting organizations' functions are related to each other through the company's standard policy as expressed by its processes and functions.

Thus, the project is directed by a manager, but each separate operation has its own supervision. This includes construction engineering, construction, all support services, and quality assurance.

PLANNING

Quality requirements are derived from engineering specifications, workmanship standards, and process/industry standards. When quality problems appear, each department or discipline reviews the contractor's performance to determine where the problems lie and their probable causes.

Quality systems, when they exist, vary from the requirements of such military quality specifications as MIL-I-45208 and MIL-Q-9858 and the Code of Federal Regulations, 10 CFR 50. These variances may include the following:

In the construction industry, the product of the specification refers to the design documents, engineering operations, procurement, construction, and project management services. The quality program is written in terms of these products, but the principle of conformance to specification requirements and fitness for use are the same.

The scope of the specification and its subdivisions usually relate to inspection functions only. The quality program includes the full scope of the operation, including design work control.

The responsibility assignment of the specification prescribes accountability for quality to the producing departments rather than to a centralized quality group. Within the production operation, this establishes the feeling of responsibility for the quality of its work.

PROGRAM IMPLEMENTATION

In the construction industry, prime attention is given to the selection and control of subcontractors.

Each functional manager has a set of standard procedures gathered, by reference to interfacing procedures, into a basic procurement manual. This is reviewed and approved by all functional managers, including quality assurance, to assure that there is an integrated system for a standard project. The project manager converts standards into project procedures. Any changes he or she makes usually require approval from the cognizant functional managers. Quality control activities are geared to the nature of the project. These activities emphasize control and efficiency rather than strict adherence to standard procedures in a nonstandard situation.

The project quality assurance engineers perform their reviews, functions, and audits at the project level. Deficiencies and corrective actions are also handled at the project level. The quality assurance manager of the prime contractor receives a copy of the audit results.

Subcontractor Selection

The selection team is made up of the buyer's contract specialist and engineering and quality engineering personnel, who visit the proposed subcontractor. They interview the supplier's management and their typical approaches, as they are imparted to the selection team. The prime contractor's quality plan and typical requirements are explained, and the written plan is given to potential subcontractors for further study. The shop and laboratories facility are toured and written opinions of the subcontractor's capabilities are prepared. A qualified bidders list is subsequently developed. All subcontractors' submissions to the prime are surveyed and qualified in some manner by the prime contractor.

Statement of Work (SOW)

A detailed SOW is developed and includes purpose, definitions, special conditions, quality training and material requirements, scope, specifications, schedule, drawings, process qualifications, and other applicable documents.

The SOW should be reviewed by the prime contractor with the subcontractors to identify actual or potential problems and to establish a definite understanding of the work. All resultant changes by subcontractors must be approved by the applicable functional management of the prime contractor. The final document results in a package offered for bid processing.

On contract initiation, the package may have inspection plans applied thereto. The official copy, with the inspection plans completed, becomes the historical record of the project.

SOW Quality Review

The quality engineers participate in the review. They identify special support, calibration, and process requirements. They determine if an item can be inspected and when a process is at the critical review points. They estimate the need for nondestructive testing requirements, and their points of application.

Engineering tolerances must be compatible with inspection. Critical inspection points are identified. All problems in the documents must be resolved prior to the start of work, or management is briefed on the risks involved.

Control Changes to SOW

The system requires that all changes are to be in writing and documented in the official copy.

Quality Improvement Programs

Traditional quality improvement programs are not usually developed for the construction industries. Any improvements are directed to the engineering designs and construction methods. In addition, there is no attempt to isolate quality-related costs and to initiate corrections due to excess costs. Traditional statistical quality control methods and techniques are usually nonexistent in the commercial construction industries.

NUCLEAR CONSTRUCTION

Nuclear plant construction is the most complex and demanding of all projects, requiring greater attention to detail than any other type of construction. It must comply with the requirements of the Code of Federal Regulations for Nuclear Operation (10 CFR 50).

Some nuclear power companies have worked closely with the Japanese on reactor design and fabrication improvements.[3] These constructions use innovative techniques from excavations to solid state control systems. Some techniques include load-indicating washers, postweld treatment with quartz lamps, drive rivets instead of bolts, large scale subassemblies, and aluminum cable trays.

ORGANIZATION

Appendix B of 10 CFR 50, put into law in June 1970, provides the quality assurance criteria for nuclear power plants. This code has 18 criteria and requirements. These are based on (1) the requirement for a utility to have a quality assurance organization, and (2) the utility having a workable quality assurance program of all activities, from the inception of a nuclear station and throughout every year of operation. This program must be under the purview of the quality assurance function. Audits are to be conducted to assure that there is agreement between standards and actual practice.

Public law places responsibility for all quality assurance activities directly on the applicant for a license to operate a nuclear power station. The criteria of design, procurement, and documentation encompasses most of manufacture as well as design engineering work.

The first 18 criteria of 10 CFR 50, Appendix B concerns the quality organization.[4] The code specifies that the responsibility and authority for quality-related activities are to be defined. Some handling and erection sequences for congested areas must accommodate safe rigging of late-arrived equipment.

Another planning innovation identifies assemblies that could be fabricated by suppliers in on-site shops, or adjacent to the structure, rather than built in place. This saves time and also reduces the number of deficiencies due to improved working conditions.

Appendix B of 10 CFR 50 provides for quality assurance requirements in the design, construction, and operation of these structures, systems, and components.[4] Satisfactory performance is required to prevent or mitigate the consequences of accidents that could cause undue risk to the health and safety of the public.

Criteria 11 of the Appendix B states that management of other organizations participating in the quality assurance program shall regularly review the status and adequacy of that part of the program which they are executing. Criteria 11 also specifies the need for written policies, procedures, and instructions, and personnel training.

This criteria also cover the provisions for selecting and reviewing specifications, drawings, and instructions for suitability of application of parts, equipment, and processes that are safety-related functions. This is to be performed by individuals or groups other than those who created the original design.

IMPLEMENTATION

Due to the safety requirements of nuclear construction, there is a greater need for quality assurance than for customary applications. Construction of nuclear-powered electrical generating stations involves many things: interpretation of a large amount of rules and regulations in drawings, specifications, codes, standards requirements, and their inclusion in the construction plans. In addition to 10 CFR 50, Appendix B, other applicable requirements and regulations are contained in national standards which specify the existence of an independent quality function with sufficient organizational freedom.

Criteria 1 states that the applicant may delegate to others, such as contractors, agents, or consultants, the work of establishing and executing the quality assurance program, or any part thereof, but shall still retain the responsibility.

In an engineering sense, as applied to nuclear power plants, the definition of quality relates to the safety of operations, that is, undue risk to the health and safety of users and the public.

PLANNING

Although the utility's vendor-supplied nuclear steam supply system (NSSS) has already been designed and purchased, the remaining responsibility for the design, installation, and operation extends to the utility's operator into the third and fourth level of the process. Also, the utility company remains responsible for components 40 years after they had been originally packaged and shipped.

The plan requires an organizational development where the utility company and the subcontractor's project teams are mirror images of each other.

The most critical factor is the utility company's intensive involvement in all phases of the architect/engineer's work scope. The utility contractually retains the right of approval of the final designs and the builder lists for major suppliers. In addition, the utility maintains approval rights over the subcontractor's controlling procedures.

Detailed construction planning is focused on the sequence of activities and the performance of tasks in parallel, whenever possible. A complete scale model of the generating station is, at times, developed from the actual design drawings. Hundreds of potential physical interferences and operational hinderences may be detected and corrected before construction using this technique. The model may be used later for orientation and training of operating personnel and for developing plant modification packages. Additional smaller models may be used to develop material published by such agencies as the American Concrete Institute, American Society of Mechanical Engineers, International Electric and Electronic Engineering, American National Standards Institute, and many others.

These agencies are also interested in the regulations. For instance, for the piping construction requirements of the CFR, several of the 18 criteria are of concern to an organization engaged in the use of welded pipe erection. This is discussed in four of the 18 criteria.

REGULATION IX—CONTROL OF SPECIAL PROCESSES

Heat treatment of welds and nondestructive examination must be performed under a qualified process and by qualified personnel. Maintenance records of the qualification of welders and test procedures are to be kept current through use of requalifications.

Criteria X establishes activities affecting quality, which verify conformance with the documented instructions, procedures, and drawings. These inspections are to be performed by individuals other than operators.

Requirement X—inspection

The examinations, measurements, and tests of material or products are to be performed for each work operation when necessary to assure quality. All steps in the process must be inspected, documented, and verified for compliance with specifications.

Requirement XIV—inspection, test, and operating stations

This requires identification of stations of individual items of the nuclear power plant.

Welding pipe erection

In addition to the marking system, a method of listing the status of inspection on welds can be developed.

Documentation of the identification of materials and of their inspections must be maintained for all these requirements.

Documentation

Criteria 11 deals with the concept of documented policies and instructions. Approximately 65,000 individual welds are, on the average, incorporated into nuclear primary and auxiliary systems of a pressurized water nuclear energy system. Associated with each weld are approximately 15 separate examinations or pieces of information which are to be recorded and accessible for the life of the plant.

Criteria V calls for the need to assure that all instructions, procedures, and drawings, including changes, are reviewed for adequacy and approved for release by authorized personnel.

Data Collection and Processing System

Piping traceability data system

This must be in place to develop codes for appropriate heat numbers and their associated products. As part of the welding inspection requirement, the heat number of the pipe or fitting between two welds must be recorded. The heat number codes are determined for each location. A computer program can be developed to compare these codes with the approved codes and flag any that are incorrect.

Similarly, the computer system can be used to record the location of each heat of filler material and compare that heat number with a list of approved numbers.

Welder qualification system

Approximately 78 different weld procedures, including position and thickness range combinations, are available for a single plant at each nuclear station. Normally, tens of thousands of separate qualifications must be conducted, listed, and reviewed. The code requires that welders use processes for which they are requalified at least once every 90 days. A computer system can provide a printout which may be in alphabetic order, by welder name, or in numeric order by weld number. It shows the processes for which each welder is qualified, and whether they were used within the required time interval.

Weld inspection data system

There are approximately one million separate pieces of data for a single reactor system. Each weld in a system is identified by a unique number. This number, plus the type of material, diameter and wall thickness, can be prepunched in a computer card. In addition, an inspection code, which represents the type of nondestructive test requirement, is prepunched on the cards, or entered in the computer tape.

After inspection, weld data are matched to the welder's number and the code for the inspection is punched in the card, or processed on the computer tape. A printout verifies erection and inspection performance. A computer program can also develop a printout of welders and all welds made between any set of dates. This can be used to schedule required random checks and to record performance. A table of the number of accepted and rejected welds may be included.

PROCUREMENT

Criteria IV, Procurement Document Control, specifies that procurement documents shall require contractors and subcontractors to provide a quality assurance program in their facilities consistent with the pertinent provisions of Appendix B.

Criteria VII calls for measures to assure that purchased materials, equipment, and supplies conform to the requirements on the procurement documents. The effectiveness of quality control by contractors and subcontractors shall be assessed by the utility, or designee, at intervals consistent with the importance, complexity, and quantity of the products and services.

Criteria VIII covers the identification and control of parts, materials, and components to prevent the use of incorrect or defective materials.

AUDITS

Criteria XVIII provides for a comprehensive system of planned and periodic audits to verify all aspects of the quality assurance programs and to determine their effectiveness. Audit results are to be documented and reviewed by the management having responsibility for the audited area.

SAFETY REPORTS

Appendix B specifies the inclusion, in the preliminary safety analysis reports, of a description of the quality assurance program to be applied to the design, fabrication, and testing of structures, systems, and components.

CORRECTIVE ACTION

Criteria XVI requires that conditions adverse to quality are to be promptly identified and corrected. Significant conditions are to be documented and reported to the appropriate management levels. When defects are discovered, they must not only be corrected, but also the underlying causes determined and corrected so that recurrence is prevented.

After final sign-off of the construction, it is necessary to determine the ability of the plant to meet the functional design basis. This must be determined before plant start-up. The code requires specific pre-operational tests of systems classified as safety related and some selected support systems, prior to the granting of an operating license. To strengthen this approach the following elements should be implemented:

1. Independent quality assurance approval of test procedures is required, for their capability to demonstrate system conformance and adherence to all applicable codes, industry standards, and specification requirements. Test engineers may, at times, be brought in from other industries to assist the quality assurance staff in this effort.

2. Test performance and data recording must be witnessed. This includes verification of valve positions, equipment starts, temperature, pressure, and flow rates.

3. Final data for conformance to the test requirements must be evaluated.

4. Resolution of test deficiencies and waivers must be reviewed and accepted.

The traditional construction quality control program provides for the inspection of the completed work and the rejection of any portion which does not meet the requirements. The subsequent rework is often detrimental to quality. In the modern project, an extensive in-process inspection program, including hold points, is implemented to assure that quality is maintained every step of the way. Problems can then be identified while they are easily correctable in the construction process. Many deficiencies can thus be prevented, resulting in a low rejection rate.

MANAGEMENT ATTITUDES TO QUALITY[5]

A survey was conducted of middle- to top-level managers in the nuclear industry concerning their attitudes toward quality control. The managers were from architectural and engineering organizations, nuclear reactor suppliers, and subcontractors.

Differences were found between managers who work in nuclear system supplier companies and those who work in architectural and engineering firms. The supplier managers were significantly less positive than the architects and engineers.

Factors which demonstrated positive attitudes toward quality assurance were the noninterference of the inspection function on work of the other organizations. It was also revealed that a formal quality assurance training program has little impact on attitude.

REFERENCES

1. Marshall, C. *Construction, Non-Nuclear* (AQC). Milwaukee, WI: ASQC, 1979, p. 460.

2. Dow, Thomas D. *Engineering Construction Quality, Non-Nuclear* (AQC). Milwaukee, WI: ASQC, 1979, p. 468.

3. Giardino, A. E. *Hope Creek Met The Challenge* (AQC). Milwaukee, WI: ASQC, 1988, p. 89.

4. Marash, S. A. *The Relationship Between Quality Improvement and Nuclear Regulation* (AQC). Milwaukee, WI: ASQC, 1988, p. 572.

5. Kirshenman, H. J. *Managerial Attitudes Towards Quality Assurance* (AQC). Milwaukee, WI: ASQC, 1983, p. 20.

CHAPTER THIRTY-SEVEN

Hospital Services[1]

INTRODUCTION

In the past, most hospitals collected information for the establishment of comparative norms on quality care characteristics. The information gathered included data concerning the average length of stays, the number of consultations, and appropriateness of days spent in special care units. Outcome measures provided data of such elements as the rate of hospital-acquired infections, and the total number of patients with unplanned re-admissions to the hospital within a short time after discharge. This consistent collection of their comparative information formed the original basis of hospital assessment of patient care.

Until the mid-1970s there was little attempt to introduce and implement a comprehensive quality assurance program in hospitals. Subsequently, several volunteer professional associations and regulatory agencies developed procedures and standards for the establishment of suitable quality programs capable of providing high quality patient care at an economical level. Initially, these programs were primarily directed to reduce the cost of patient care and of its administration. Recently, programs were established to encourage hospitals to develop quality assurance procedures for the control and improvement of quality patient care.

ORGANIZATION

Starting with the patient, the first area (or level) of provider is the physician. The second level includes the nurse, laboratory, pharmacy, anesthesiology, urology, radiology, patient education, and any other medical care function. The third level includes dietary, patient transportation, medical records, environmental control, material management, safety, social work, and housekeeping. The fourth area includes billing and accounting, academic, volunteer groups, pastoral care, reception, appointments, secretarial staff, and other support services.

EXAMPLE

An example of how one hospital is organized to meet Joint Commission on Accreditation (JCAH) standards is described here:[2]

Every committee, department, and function within the hospital was involved with quality improvement. Quality assurance (QA) authority is vested in the hospital's quality assessment committee. Representatives from the medical staff, the QA department, and hospital administration (including the president of the hospital), make up the governing board for hospital quality. The board's goal is to ensure the effectiveness of the QA programs. Its directives are carried out through the medical executive committee and the utilization review/quality assessment committee. Utilization review assesses the appropriateness and medical necessity for hospital admission, length of stay, and quality of care. This committee, in turn, supervises the efforts of the hospital QA committee and the medical staff, which regulate the hospital's function and departments.

The hospital's quality assessment committee (the top managers of the hospital, including the QA manager), reviews quality levels from each of its primary functional areas every month. The quality levels, reported by the hospital's QA department, describe how well or how poorly each of the functional areas is complying with JCAH guidelines. Other reports track how well the QA department and the quality program are functioning, as well as the results of the hospital's utilization review.

PLANNING

The Joint Commission on Accreditation of Hospitals (JCAH), a regulatory body governing the effectiveness of all hospital programs in providing quality patient care, was formed in 1951 by the major organizations involved in hospital-based care. This organization required medical facilities to provide an effective program for the review and evaluation of patient management. The regulations initially addressed the facilities, equipment, organization, and other structural elements needed for high quality care. Accreditation by the JCAH was voluntary.

On April 7, 1979, the JCAH approved a new quality assurance standard for hospitals. This required that every hospital or medical facility must have a comprehensive quality assurance program. All committees, functions, and activities concerned with quality assurance were to be integrated and coordinated in order to eliminate duplication and provide data useful to all activities in the facility.

The JCAH audited hospital performance using standards and procedures that are, frequently, more thorough than the FDA's GMP for medical producers and pharmaceutical companies. Failure to comply with the JCAH standards could result in loss of Medicare funding.

The JCAH accredits about five-sixths of the nation's community hospitals. Its stamp of approval allows hospitals to be reimbursed by Medicare without undergoing a separate government certification. This group evaluates the outcome of care when it gives its seal of approval, and hopes to have new standards in effect within several years. However, the vagueness of today's standards complicate the task of measuring how, or if, quality in the hospitals is changing.

Third Party Payers

The problem of health care became more complicated when third party payers got involved. These parties included private insurers, group health plans, and the government.

The federal government became closely involved through the Medicare and Medicaid health programs for the elderly and low-income families.[3] Thus, the government became involved with the quality aspects of the hospital's service. Government regulations relating to these programs resulted in the creation of the Professional Standards Review Organizations (PSROs). These groups were led by practicing physicians. They operated in various geographical areas, as designated by the government. Peer review was the basis of their evaluations, which had a dual basis: utilization review and quality assurance. The groups developed norms, criteria, and standards that were to aid both their objectives. The organizations reviewed individual instances of service and provided penalties for noncompliance.

While some success in the operations of these organizations was reported, there was criticism that the PSROs were not controlling cost or quality. As a result, new legislation was enacted and a new organization was initiated, the Peer Review Organization (PRO). The PRO contracts with the government agency to review services or items furnished to Medicare recipients. It is made up of licensed doctors of medicine, or has access to their services. The PRO looks at the completeness, adequacy, quality, and appropriateness of patient care, admissions, and discharges, and the validity of diagnostic and procedural information supplied by the provider.

A major shift in policy by the federal government in paying for Medicare is responsible, in large part, for the new quality consciousness in the hospitals.[4] On October 1, 1983, Medicare began phasing in a prospective system using fees set in advance for different procedures. Thus, diagnosis related groups (DRGs) came into being. Hospitals that provided care at lower cost than was set by the DRG would profit. Those that charged more would lose money. At the same time, the business community increasingly pressured doctors and hospitals to keep costs down by using intermediaries, such as health maintenance organizations (HMOs) and utilization review consultants to manage care and to reduce the cost of employee health insurance.

This seemed to work, as shown by the decrease in hospital inpatient days. However, the outpatient visits increased drastically for the same period. No one can say for sure whether the changes came from efficiency or from just cutting corners, or what its effect was on the quality of patient care.

IMPLEMENTATION

To provide optimum care for the management of patients' medical needs, there must be an organized plan addressing both direct and indirect influences on care. In approaching this analysis, it is necessary to delineate areas of providers, both medical and nonmedical.[5] Depending on whether the person is an inpatient or outpatient, certain areas in each level may be more or less important. For example, the outpatient may be more concerned with reception, appointments, pharmacy, billing and accounting, and service accessibility. The inpatient is more concerned with nursing, medical technicians, housekeeping, diet, and transportion. A total quality system defines all areas of patient interaction and management and controls the optimal care in each of these areas.

The quality assurance functions of the PRO system focus on patient outcomes and on system impact under the prospective payment system.[3] Each PRO contract contains specific outcome-oriented measurable objectives. These objectives may change over time and for each PRO.

In addition to objectives aimed on reducing hospital admissions and cost, the PROs are assigned five quality objectives:

1. Reduce unnecessary readmissions resulting from substandard care provided during the prior admission.

2. Assure that the provision of medical service (primarily pharmaceuticals) which, when not performed, have significant potential for causing severe patient complications.

3. Reduce avoidable deaths through improved emergency procedures.

4. Reduce unnecessary surgery or other invasive procedures.

5. Reduce avoidable postoperative or other complications.

New legislation is continually being enacted which has an effect on the quality assurance aspects of health care. Thus, although most of these regulations are designed for the prime purpose of reducing costs, many of them make it mandatory for hospitals to develop and implement comprehensive quality systems and improvement program.

The quality program of one hospital in an attempt to meet JCAH standards includes a written plan that clearly defines the program's organization, scope, accountability, and management. Employees are actively involved with quality assurance personnel through departmental monitors that specify performance criteria. These monitors are screened by the hospital QA department and then reviewed by the interdepartmental QA committee representing the hospital's patient care services.

The elements of the QA plan include the following:

- Integration and coordination of all activities
- Annual reassessment of the program's effectiveness
- Goals and objectives for patient care
- Effective and timely corrective action
- Full and active support of the president and medical chief of staff
- Intense effort to ensure patient satisfaction

At every step of the hospital process, patients have the opportunity to respond to the care they receive. This program involves a thorough analysis of all elements affecting patient care. Feedback from patients leads to constant process improvement.

MEDICATION[3]

Problems with medication outside the hospital include the following:

1. Physicians' failure to determine what other medications a patient is taking
2. Physicians' lack of discussion to determine any possible side effects of the medication
3. Overmedication, when a patient receives multiple prescriptions from different doctors
4. Lack of follow-up to prescribed medications

In the hospital, the following steps are usually taken.

1. The physician writes out an order for a medication program for the patient.
2. The nurse transcribes this order into a form.
3. A copy of the orders goes to the pharmacist.
4. The pharmacist dispenses the drugs, which are then delivered to the nurse's station.
5. The nurse administers the medication to the patient.

In a large hospital, the resulting network becomes formidable. The nurse becomes numerous people in many departments, including nursing supervisors, floor clerks, nursing assistants, and so on. The drug is not necessarily a simple pill, which the patient can take unaided, but often involves specialized techniques for dilutions, measurement, and intravenous administration. The need to keep adequate histories and fix responsibility creates added paperwork. Eventually, the system becomes so complex, that it becomes part of the problem.

EVALUATION

The patient is the main source of information regarding care. The medical staff and the employees are the next source. A feedback system must be initiated to aid in the control and acceptability of care. Patients and employees should be solicited for their perceptions of care, their opinions for ways of improvement, and both negative and positive observations. Patients should be free to voice complaints and compliments to selected employees in each service. These remarks should be documented. These can then be correlated with service activity and manpower. Employees should also be solicited for their perceptions of the system. Being inside the system, they can offer observations that have often been overlooked. As long as the employees observe that management is visibly supportive of their cooperation, they will actively assist in the achievement of maximum efficiency of the system.

Again, because of the impact of overall perception of care, it is essential, when establishing the quality assurance system, that the most significant provider in patient management, the physician, is not overlooked. In the past, administration or the QA coordinator had often decided what the physician should do to improve patient care. Therefore, the physician was usually overlooked in any consideration, for example, of the consolidation of medical records or the expansion of forms. Nor was the physician consulted about patient care or the kind of monitoring that should be utilized.

Once the levels of care are defined, and members of each of these areas identified for liaison with the QA committee, initial problem-solving strategies and education can begin. Once the significant few problems are determined and resolved, the emphasis can then be turned to problem prevention. Since all persons in the facility should be involved in the quality of patient care, they should have input into its evaluation and improvement. The structure of information flow should follow a pyramid design. The base represents all employees in the facility, and at the peak, the QA committee.

The initial quality activities should quantify existing problems in the patient care system. Consequently, problem-solving techniques will satisfy the immediate need. The customary method of viewing problem solving is by the following elements:

1. Realization that there is a problem

2. Identification of the problem

3. Identification of the cause(s)

4. Identification of the solution

5. Implementation of the solution

IMPROVEMENT

Use of Computer Programs[6]

This section describes three computer programs designed to improve the quality function in hospital laboratories. These include the following: (1) controlling serum verification and testing, (2) developing and updating local patient reference values (patient normals), and (3) scheduling routine maintenance of laboratory equipment.

In a hospital laboratory, quality control is a surveillance process in which the actions of people and the performance of equipment and material are observed in some systematic, periodic way. This provides a record of consistency of performance and actions taken when it does not conform to established standards. In order to provide prompt feedback and to readily implement corrective actions, the use of a microprocessor or larger computer system is suggested.

The aims of the program are consistent with the quality assurance standards adopted by the JCAH. These emphasize the hospital's quality evaluation activities rather than rigid numerical quotas and audit methodology. Under these standards, hospitals must be able to identify problem areas and other areas for investigation.

Serum Verifications

There is an extensive lag between the time observations are first recorded and the time statistical analysis results are received from outside diagnostic laboratories. This period can approach two months. If data result from some problem with the instrument, two months of faulty data could have accumulated. The computer program makes it possible to obtain an instantaneous, updated statistical analysis after each sample is analyzed. When an out-of-control point is reached, messages indicate this fact. Control charts are plotted above and below the mean. Data are compared against cumulative values and those from a moving data set.

Patient Reference Values

The physician relies on a range of acceptable (normal) readings to make an accurate diagnosis. A relatively large data base (500 or more patients) is necessary to develop patient normals. Furthermore, it is important that these normals be updated as frequently as possible. The computer program allows laboratory technicians to enter patient data immediately after it is obtained and receive an updated normal value which includes the data from the sample just entered. The normals represent a mean and plus or minus two standard deviations. Histograms are plotted for each test.

Maintenance Scheduling and Reporting

The hospital of today contains very sophisticated electromechanical equipment. To perform the desired function, the equipment must operate within specified levels of temperature, pressure, resolutions per minute, and similar characteristics. Regulations require that this equipment be monitored for safe and efficient operating levels. A computer program schedules the nondaily maintenance automatically. A log of maintenance activators is printed each day. Results are then entered. Daily and monthly maintenance reports are generated. The daily report lists actions which were not completed, messages for the laboratory manager, numerical values recorded by equipment name, a statistical summary of unfinished tasks, and a printout of the previous day's percentage of tasks completed. Equipment and descriptions may be added, deleted, or changed.

Organizational Activities

Many organizations involved in the health care service industry have taken steps to support and provide standards for the improvement of hospital patient care. In addition to the regulations and standards placed by agencies such as the JCAH and the federal PRO, organizations such as the Commission on Professional and Hospital Activities (CPHA) and the American Medical Association (AMA) have taken the lead in advocating quality improvement programs for patient care both in and out of hospitals.

CPHA Activities

The CPHA is a nonprofit organization founded in 1955 that provides the most comprehensive national health information in U.S. hospitals and other health care facilities.[1] This organization provides to its member hospitals comparative data bases to assure that their operations comply with JCAH regulations and to improve their health care delivery.

Medical record data collected by CPHA have traditionally been used for analysis within individual hospitals. The CPHA data base also contains some industrywide comparative data which can help answer questions among related health care facilities. This data base provides access to discharge/encounter level data and to CPHA's collection of comparative norms.

In the future, it is anticipated the CPHA will act as a national resource for defining and measuring patterns of medical care. These events must begin with the consistent definition and collection of clinical information reflecting norms and patterns of medical care. Comparing actual patterns with norms will provide a benchmark for assessing differences in quality and resource utilization patterns among hospitals.

The AMA

The AMA council on medical service proposed the following guidelines for voluntary peer review:[7]

1. The criteria utilized to assess the degree of essential quality elements should be developed and concurred by professionals whose performance will be reviewed.

2. Such criteria can be derived from any one of the three basic variables of care: structure, process, and outcome. Emphasis in the review process should be on statistically verifying linkages between specific elements of structures and process, and favorable outcomes, rather than on isolated outcomes.

   Structure is defined as the facilities, equipment, services, and labor available for care and the credentials and qualifications of the health professional involved.

   Process refers to the content of care, that is, how the patient was moved into, through, and out of the health care system, and the services that were provided during the care episode.

   Outcome refers to the results of the care and can encompass biologic changes in the disease; comfort; ability for self-care; physical function and mobility; emotional and intellectual performance; patient satisfaction; self-perception of health; knowledge and compliance with medical care; and variability of family, job, and social role functioning.

3. The evaluation of intermediate rather than final outcomes is an acceptable technique in quality assessment.

4. Blanket review of all medical care provided is neither practical nor needed to assure high quality.

5. Review can be conducted on a targeted basis, a sampling basis, or a combination of both.

6. Both explicit and implicit criteria are useful to the quality of care. Explicit criteria are highly structured, specific, and written; for example, specific laboratory and diagnostic tests. Implicit criteria tend to have little or no formal written structure and tend to be based more on the expectations and judgment of an expert practitioner acting as an evaluator.

7. Prior consultation as appropriate, concurrent peer review, and retrospective peer review are all valid aspects of quality assessment.

8. The quality assessment program should be linked with a quality assurance system, whereby assessment results are used to improve performance. The assessment results should be systematically conveyed to the practitioners reviewed, and such professionals should be assisted in improving their knowledge and in modifying their practice behaviors where indicated.

9. The quality assessment process itself should be subject to continued evaluation and modification as needed.

A Health Policy Agenda for the American People (HPA)[8]

In 1982, the HPA was initiated by the AMA to develop a long-term comprehensive plan for addressing major health care issues in the United States.[8] In Phase I of the project, 41 issues were identified as critical for the future of health care in this country. Phase II policy proposals are being developed to respond to these areas. The issues were divided into 6 work groups, who attacked the 41 issues. These issues are shown in Figure 37-1.

Phase I ended in May, 1984, resulting in the steering committee's approval of 159 principles, which were printed in a *Journal of American Medical Association* (*JAMA*) article.[9] These provided broad value statements of what should exist in a health care system.

RECOMMENDED HOSPITAL TRUSTEE ACTIONS FOR QUALITY IMPROVEMENT

As advocates for the community serviced by the hospital, board members should ensure that the care delivered by their organizations will be the best possible.[10]

To influence the hospital staff, it is necessary to demonstrate, at the board level, that the commitment to quality is an important part of the organization's mission. This must be communicated throughout the hospital. Another method is to see that resources are allocated to dealing with quality issues. A third way is to make clear that quality will be monitored and acted upon, and that the medical staff and management will be held accountable.

The two most meaningful reflections of a board's commitment to quality are time and money. The portion of the hospital budget devoted to QA and related activities is a practical measure of its commitment to quality care. Similarly, the amount of agenda time that a board devotes to quality issues is a measure of its commitment, as is its direction of the hospital's QA program.

To discuss levels of quality care, hospital board members should receive summary information, presented in graphics where possible, that compares

MEDICAL SCIENCE ISSUES

Availability of funding for biomedical research
Availability of human resources for biomedical research
Evaluation of health care technology
Technology transfer
Communication between the public and the health care community

EDUCATION ISSUES

Educating competent and caring practitioners in the health profession
Maintenance of professional competence of practitioners

HEALTH RESOURCES ISSUES

Health manpower: Graduates of foreign health professional schools; boundaries of practice; distribution of health professionals
Health care facilities: Definition and licensure
Health care technology: Supply and distribution; role of cost in availability; moral and ethical issues in its application

DELIVERY OF MECHANISMS AND PROCESS ISSUES

Planning and development of the health care delivery system
Resource allocation and access to health care
Health services research and evaluation

EVALUATION ASSESSMENT AND CONTROL

How peer review can be used to ensure high quality care
Kind of coordination among professionals regarding peer review

CERTIFICATION

Purpose of certification process
How cost and quality of care are affected by certifications

PROFESSIONAL LIABILITY

How and under what circumstances should patients be compensated
Who should bear the cost

PROFESSIONAL JUDGMENT

Degree to which judgment should be influenced by limited resources, cost containment concerns, and increasing patient expectations

ETHICAL CONSIDERATIONS

How society ensures a coherent framework for ethical considerations
Dealing with separate issues and individual cases on an ad hoc basis

EVALUATION

How it can ensure high quality health care

PAYMENT FOR SERVICE

Design for cost effective payment system
Role of government

FIGURE 37-1   HPA Phase I Issues

quality over time. This could contain, for example, information on mortality, infection, and patient complaint trends for the past quarter compared with those rates over the past several years.

In addition, the board may also want to pay attention to such indicators of patient service as waiting times, ease of understanding hospital bills, perception of quality of care, accessibility of parking, and overall patient satisfaction scores. The board should know if patients are willing to come back for future health care service, and if they would recommend the hospital to friends.

In one hospital, the board called for indicators such as benchmarks. The process began by developing quality indicators based on the hospital's organizational quality statement. Then each hospital department developed a matrix of processes important to its customers and under their control of the department.

Once the departments knew the definition of quality, the hospital-wide indicators important to customers, and their relationship to these indicators, they were equipped to improve quality.

In another hospital, departmental and interdepartmental teams were created to study and improve specific processes related to patient care. Using the team approach, this hospital involved departments and individual inputs into the process. Thus, responsibilities for implementation, ownership of solutions, and recognition for involvement were easily identified and maintained.

REFERENCES

1. Graves, Forest. "Measuring the Quality of Health Care for Decision Making." *QP*. Milwaukee, WI: ASQC, May 1987, p. 37.

2. Smith, Martin C. "Competition Leads to Quality Care." *QP*. Milwaukee, WI: ASQC, April 1990, p. 28.

3. Ryan, John. "Health Care Quality Assurance Regulation." *QP*. Milwaukee, WI: ASQC, May 1987, p. 27.

4. Millenson, Michael. "A Prescription for Change." *QP*. Milwaukee, WI: ASQC, May 1987, p. 16.

5. Gruska, Denise, & Gruska, Gregory. "A Total Quality System for Medical Facilities." *37th AQC*. Milwaukee, WI: ASQC, 1983, p. 560.

6. Keats, Bert J., & Goodin, Jim. "Interactive Computer Programs for Hospital Quality Control." *37th AQC*. Milwaukee, WI: ASQC, 1983, p. 565.

7. AMA's Council on Medical Services. "Quality of Care: A Report by the AMA's Council on Medical Service." *QP*. Milwaukee, WI: ASQC, May 1987, p. 22.

8. Balfe, Bruce E., Boyle, Joseph, et al. "A Health Policy for the American People." *QP*. Milwaukee, WI: ASQC, May 1989, p. 48.

9. Balfe, B. E., & Boyle, J. F. "Phase I: The Principles," *JAMA* 254: 2440, 2441.

10. Larsen, Karen. "Hospital Trustees Lead to Quality Efforts." *QP*. Milwaukee, WI: ASQC, April 1990, p. 31.

CHAPTER THIRTY-EIGHT

Banking Services[1]

INTRODUCTION[2]

Bank products or services include such items as checking accounts, personal savings, money transfers, loans, letters of credit, IRAs, CDs, and many others. The bank quality needs are dictated by a host of governmental regulations, by customers' expectations, and by the mechanization of vast numbers of banking transactions. Recently, a growing number of banks have recognized the increased need for quality and have adopted modern control procedures to match the advances made by computerization of bank services.

ORGANIZATION OF THE QUALITY DEPARTMENT

In a particular bank, the start-up of a quality control department was initiated by hiring a quality professional who developed an organization of approximately 25 personnel. Two-thirds of the staff were recruited from the outside and the balance transferred from within the bank. This mix was successful by providing the technology change between quality and banking.

PLANNING

In banking, attention has been given to design and production quality. Design quality is the level of service specified to meet customers' requirements, specified or implicit, for fitness for use. Examples include speed of service at tellers' windows and freedom from errors in monthly statements.

Production quality is the property of the work as it is produced; such as errors in calculations, checks charged to the wrong account, or excessive handling time.

Each banking process has an input and an output. In between are the processing steps. These generally take the form of manual or automated computer transactions. Errors frequently occur, such as dollar amounts which are transposed, dropped, or added; dates which are incorrectly recorded; cost requirements which are incorrectly formatted; and computer programs which have errors. In most cases, manual or automated intervention is necessary to correct the work.

A considerable amount of bank servicing operations include processing checks.[2] Thus, major efforts must be made to define and control this operation. A number of the mechanized processes lend themselves to the use of quality methods similar to those used in manufacturing. For example, depositing magnetic ink recognition symbols (MICR) are used to process checks and internal documents. These are usually preprinted and encoded by the bank of the first deposit. Normally, the MICR are applied when the check is originally manufactured. The magnetic characters are required to conform to ANSI specifications for magnetic strength, placement, and formation.

Quality control of each process must take into consideration the contribution of personnel involved with each function. They include the check originator; its recipient; the teller or clerk accepting the check for cash or deposit; and the clerks who inscribe, reconcile, process, repair, and do exception work.

Generally, most errors are caught and corrected before getting to customers. Any that get out usually result in a complaint with the resultant investigation tracing back to the date or source of the original transaction. Investigations are costly and time consuming.

IMPLEMENTATION

In order to provide an adequate quality program, it is necessary to establish norms and goals of performance measurement for each product and service, both internal and external. The current quality levels should be determined and the trends monitored. These are then compared with established standards. Proper measurement and reporting can then provide methods for quality control and improvement.

While nearly all methods of quality management are applicable, there are special controls applicable to banking operations. Process control is accomplished by collecting data, analyzing it to determine the system's capability, and using information on deviations from process capability to signal the need for corrective actions. Statistical process control systems are useful, particularly in check processing and microfilming.

Analytical studies are conducted to solve specific problems. Teller queuing, testing of new equipment for reliability, and sampling data files or operating information are a few samples.

Acceptance sampling involves the drawing of a sample of materials used in the performance of bank functions, testing the sample, and maintaining records of the quality level of the material tested.

Operator Errors

Quality control can only succeed when the people involved in each process know what constitutes an acceptable method to handle, write, or bundle banking documents.[2] These personnel must be trained to realize the importance and backbone of the system that permits a simple piece of paper to become the transfer agent for large sums of money.

The daily volume of transactions makes it mandatory that the quality of human operations are maintained at a high level. Even with automation, the amount of work performed by humans, such as verification and document signing, is tremendous. Mistakes and delays do occur.

One bank practiced a new approach called the Quality Improvement Program (QUIP). It involved supervisor participation, separate measurements of error rates, determination of achievable process capability, and problem solving help given in a supportive way to individuals who were not reaching desirable quality levels.

In one department, the basic operation consisted of receiving fund transfer instructions, which were edited and checked for balance adequacy. If approved, the necessary paperwork was sent for signature, and released to the next processing operation. During automation, the essential flow remained the same. In the QUIP approach, the first step consisted of determining what makes each operation correct. That became the definition of each job step. To assemble this information, the verifiers were asked to list what they were checking on each document. This list was compared with what management thought they were checking. Important differences or omissions were noted and reconciled. The result was a work list which, for the first time, told the operators what was expected of them. This list was useful in training both clerks and verifiers. The next step was for the supervisor to spend 1.5 hours per day, in 10-minute segments, going from clerk to clerk, to examine the last piece of work completed. The results, both good and bad, were individually recorded. Weekly records were summarized and processed for applicable corrective actions. Errors found fell into three categories:

- Improper training; the supervisor coached the clerk in the proper way.

- Systems problem; for example, the typewriter did not always function or the carbon paper in the form did not fully extend, causing lost dollar data. The supervisor moved the operator to properly working equipment or instituted steps to correct the equipment.

- Operator failure; the operator had made a mistake.

MICR Data

One of the basic problems in analyzing rejects is the incidence of wrong data in the MICR code line. Many orders start out with incorrect data provided to the bank stationer. Accordingly, this is an area which needs attention from the quality control department. It is important to understand the necessary controls to insure that the account number, routing-transit, and transaction control data required for each document ordered are correct. The real problem is that an incorrect check number is not only a single reject, but every item printed has the potential of becoming a reject.

The cost of correcting each rejected check ranges from $0.35 to $1.00. An average-sized bank, processing 500,000 checks a day, spends $400,000 per year for each 1 percent of rejects. Since the national average for rejects, as reported by the Bank Administration Institute, is between 2 and 4 percent, the average bank spends about $1 million per year on such rejects. This does not include lost business from dissatisfied customers. While not all the cost is avoidable, substantial savings are possible with MICR quality control.

A major source of MICR rejects is the original check printer. Those who specialize in MICR printing have defect rates of from 0.24 to 0.5 percent. Other printers contribute greatly to the reject rate. Not only is there a cost for the reconcilement, but the check user stands a risk that the rejected check will be classed as not being a cash item by the Federal Reserve System. The check then becomes a collection item and is subject to a fee.

To avoid check problems many banks have established test centers. Printers send a specified sample of checks to these centers before shipping the lot. If the checks meet specifications, the lot is shipped and used. Otherwise, the lot is reprinted. This is called predelivery sampling (PDS).

In practice, most commercial bank checks are ordered by users directly from the printer. The buying firm has no way of judging the quality of the magnetic ink characters.

Check Printing

Consideration should be given to the type and quality of paper stock used and its compliance to the bank's standards, the supplier's recommended document transport equipment, and the industry's standards. A determination should also be made of the quality of the magnetic ink being used, relative to its ability to provide an adequate signal for reliable reading.

All associated handling, during printing, collating, binding, packaging, and so on, can affect the system. Consideration should be made to the number of orders received which were not deliverable; and shipments made to the wrong party, or the right address with the wrong name, but not returned to the bank. These problems should be caught by the check manufacturer's quality control and monitored by the bank.

Customers' Forms

It is important that customers understand the nature and use of check and deposit tickets, and how to insure that they are accurate. Customers should be instructed in corrective actions when errors are spotted. In addition, customers should be able to properly identify each item deposited. Many daily problems involve settling differences because documents were not properly identified. Reduction of these problems can be obtained by innovative educational brochures and imaginative quality considerations.

Personnel Training

The branch office personnel must be motivated and properly trained to process deposits, validate transactions, prepare cash tickets, and complete other tasks. This training should also include the proper installation and placement of documents in tellers' machines. The bank personnel should be made thoroughly aware of the impact resulting from the flagrant use of rubber bands, paper clips, staples, and similar items. Controls should be installed and maintained to insure proper precautions during these processes.

Other Bank Operations

Controls should also be established for couriers, such as promptness of delivery and condition of the work as it arrives at the mail room. Using different containers and improving work and handling conditions should also be considered. Document preparation, such as removing staples and attachments by the proof operator, can reduce jams later. Too much encoding can bring about rejects. Misaligned ribbon is a problem. Erasures or stickers over encoding errors that cover other MICR data can be worse than the original errors.

Improperly placed block preparation can cause errors. So can worn-out ticket separators, which have been run too many times, thereby increasing rejects due to latent buildup of static electricity which creates MICR-read errors. All documents should meet ANSI specifications, which call for bond paper made from chemical wood pulp, and no use of recycled materials due to their lack of strength.

The automated equipment through which these items are processed determines the success or failure of quality programs. The reject, jam, and misread rates are the measures that are customarily utilized. High-speed sorters must be kept clean, and the input properly aligned. For good quality control, it is imperative that good records be kept and that errors or rejects are properly analyzed and positive feedback initiated. Any minor deviation from the norm can result in a major problem.

EVALUATION

The quality personnel should initially examine the work flow, the bottle-necks, and possible reject origins. Records must be meaningful, accurate, and properly used. Rejects for all changes that have occurred over time should be classified. For example, it may be noted that printing-caused errors and logical errors have increased, while paper-caused and unknown (other) errors have diminished.

The line manager must focus on a multitude of performance measures; the integrated impact on productivity, costs, and timeliness parameters; and the operation's quality level. A change in one parameter usually impacts on one or more others. The following performance measures should be considered collectively:

- Volume processed
- Unit processing costs
- Product profitability
- Outgoing quality level provided to customers
- Timeliness of product or service delivery
- Processes consistency with timeliness standards

Some of the analytical techniques which can be utilized in measurements and evaluations include the following:

Control charts and graphs

These present current performance levels as well as trends over time. Information provided in a chronological sequence shows changes over time. Graphical presentations provide added and meaningful visibility of data patterns. Types of graphs used include line graphs, bar graphs, histograms, pie charts, and frequency distributions.

Pareto diagrams

These present data arranged in order of magnitude. These identify which problem should be attacked and solved first. This technique is useful for establishing performance improvement strategies, plans, and priorities.

Cause-and-effect diagram

Also called fishbone and Ishkawa diagram. These techniques can be used to identify and relate the most common generic causes such as material, machines, methods, manpower, and measurement.

Brainstorming

Recently used in quality circles, it can supplement the cause-and-effect diagrams in determining the most significant relationships to investigate and correct.

CORRECTIVE ACTION

It is necessary to understand why the rejects occur. For example, the number of rejects due to paper folds and presence of foreign material may have changed. The reason may be due to unfolding these items before entry, or the reason may be the use of different equipment.

The most predominant reason for printing rejects is embossing. Analysis may show that this was due to the new generation printing equipment with a single hammer print mechanism as opposed to the old equipment which used multihammer mechanisms with different pressures for each character. Proper analysis must be submitted to management so that appropriate corrective measures can be implemented. This requires education of all the people involved to know not only that rejects occur, but also why they occur and what can be done to control them. For example, it is advisable to teach supervisors, operators, and repair personnel what constitutes embossed character problems by illustrating them.

A written specification for the quality of office supplies, ribbons, stickers, and other items should be developed for use in receiving inspection.

Automated reject and repair equipment can help get work qualified to move it out of the shop to meet transit deadlines. Damage often occurs to large business checks which are often intermingled with personal checks. To reduce this problem, several banks have couriers use locking trays that have a spring mechanism to keep the documents together rather than using rubber bands and bags. Other banks use a plastic bag that has a wide belt to bind the documents. They have proven successful in reducing jams on sorter equipment.

Usually, little can be done about items which belong to other banks. However, if it has been determined that another bank has an inscriber problem, it would be advisable to notify them. Some banks also notify other banks of wrong data in the MICR code line. Wrong check digits in wrong formats and similar problems can be detected on transit items and can be referred to the originating bank.

QUALITY COST

Detailed records of poor quality have not been kept by a majority of banks; a number of them have worked at definitions and instructions in banking terminology for collecting data on the four categories of quality-related costs. One bank, which had compiled such data, found that the total quality-related costs came to 37 percent of the total operating cost; 59 percent of these costs were for appraisal, 20 percent for external loss, 13 percent for internal loss, and 8 percent for prevention costs.

MOTIVATION

In a labor-intensive environment, the achieved level of quality is highly dependent upon performance. Employee training and motivation are essential to effective quality programs. Typical phases of management motivational programs include individual personnel development and training, labor planning and career development, and employee involvement and participation.

QUALITY IMPROVEMENT

One bank reported good results with more than one hundred quality circles. Organized departmental steering committees, composed of managers, planned the circles and established policies and procedures. Part-time facilitators were appointed and trained to assist and coordinate the quality circles. Membership was on a volunteer basis. Those who became circle members were given training in quality techniques, with examples from bank operations. Techniques included Pareto and cause-and-effect analyses. The bank operated professional, clerical, management, and facilitators' circles. Each worked at different types of problems, selected to fit their varying skills and experiences.

Most of the standards established by ANSI committees, other than basic print and location of the E 13 B characters, have not been widely adopted because they are voluntary. Pending the utilization of ANSI standards by all banks, each should establish education, monitoring, and feedback systems to create a more effective check processing system.

The recent failures of many U.S. banks due to ill-advised and improperly secured loans, make it essential for future quality programs to evaluate loan policies and their implementation.

There are also moves in government regulations to permit the banks to provide additional services, such as stock and bond transactions, to the public. This will necessitate that quality personnel in the banking industry become knowledgeable of these types of transactions.

REFERENCES

1. Langevin, Roger G. *Quality Control in Bank Operations* (AQC). Milwaukee, WI: ASQC, 1983, p. 131.

2. Vandenburgh, Roy N. *Quality Control of Check Processing* (AQC). Milwaukee, WI: ASQC, 1983, p. 126.

CHAPTER THIRTY-NINE

Hotel Services

INTRODUCTION[1]

Hotels and motels are not just one service, but generally include a whole package, including restaurants, bars, convention centers, and similar facilities. Some may be contracted out, such as ticket brokers, retail shops, or even restaurants, and others are inherently cost, instead of profit, centers, such as telephone departments and room service. Then, too, there are many different markets in the business sectors. At one end of the spectrum are the little mom-and-pop motels and chains which cater to budget travelers, and at the other end are the exclusive luxury resort or center city hotels modeled after the grand European tradition.

ORGANIZATION

In the chain hotels, quality is monitored daily by each hotel's manager and the head housekeeper.[2] There are generally two types of inspectors, regular and accounting. The regular inspectors provide an in-depth look at the overall operations. The accounting inspectors focus almost exclusively on the hotel's financial operations. The district director monitors customers' reports. In addition, many chains utilize separately contracted inspectors. Their job is to conduct unannounced inspections during overnight stays.

PLANNING

Company Quality Policy

Progressive hotel chains provide to their management and supervisory personnel a statement of quality policy. A example of such a policy is one provided by a budget motel chain:[2]

- Provide the best possible value for the lowest possible price. Never compromise on quality.

- Have the same regard to your associates in every level that you expect for yourself.

- Be honest in your dealings, both inside and outside the company.

- Give your people freedom. Let them be creative and let them make an occasional mistake.

- Do not be afraid of change.

- Never pinch pennies. But always watch them closely.

- Pay attention to details. They are what the customer notices.

Design Functions

The design functions for hotels include the feasibility study, the physical design, operating systems and procedures, and image or concept development.

Feasibility study

Because of the importance of location, new hotel projects begin with a feasibility study. This provides an analysis of the size and quantitative characteristics of the market. From this, the number of rooms and expected room rate are determined. After this analysis, the researcher determines what ancillary services the market will require, such as restaurants and convention and recreation facilities. Finally, an estimate of income and expenses is prepared for the number of guest rooms recommended, the projected room rate, and the recommended mix of services.

Physical design

If the calculation shows that the proposed hotel would be profitable over its expected life, then the next step is the hotel design. At the physical planning and construction stage, a number of other quality elements are set permanently. Mistakes at this stage can be very costly over the life of the property, both operationally and in terms of guest satisfaction.

Design standards exist in hotel construction, but in the case of large center city properties, the combined requirements of small sites, local zoning restrictions, and the particular market needs make each project unique. When it comes to highway locations where land costs are much lower and sites are larger, one is more apt to find standard designs, especially when the large chains are involved.

Operating procedures

The next planning phase element is the development of the operating procedures. This includes all aspects of running the property, from taking reservations and rooming the guests to taking out the garbage. The service is seen as a complex system, much like an assembly line, with each step in the process defined. Equally important is the need to establish service standards and identify potential sources of errors and guest dissatisfaction.

Image development

A major component of this is housekeeping and maintenance. Operating standards and procedures are also part of creating and maintaining image.

IMPLEMENTATION

Standards are points against which the operations will be measured. There are two types: internal, which measures how efficiently the organization is operating, and external, which are those factors with which guests are concerned. A common internal standard is labor productivity per occupied room per maid. A factor of major importance to guests is the number of walks—guests without reservations that the hotel could not accommodate and who roomed elsewhere. This is a crucial measure in evaluating the efficiency of operations. It tells how well the management is doing in fine-tuning its room sales when the house is full. It requires balancing reservations with no-shows, walk-ins, and stay-overs, in order to sell every available room, yet avoid walks.

EVALUATION

Most motel chains evaluate the quality of their service through four separate inspection processes: guest complaints and customer comment cards, company inspectors, secret shoppers, and audits by individual managers or district directors.

To get some indication of the quality of the service transaction itself, it is necessary to go to the parties involved in it. The first indicator is unsolicited guest complaints and compliments, in the form of letters, phone calls, or on-the-spot contacts. In some operations, the quality effort goes no further than trying to satisfy or mollify complaining customers. The more progressive companies do take a second step and make some evaluation or view of their customers' complaints in order to identify problem areas and trends.

The second approach is to solicit customer feedback through comment cards left in each room. These are often in the form of a postcard pread-dressed to the company's regional or corporate offices. This is to prevent negative responses from being concealed by local managers. Response cards do provide customers with a way of expressing themselves, which many customers find less threatening than complaining in person. This, however, presents a familiar problem in customer surveys, that of response bias. Generally, the only people who respond this way are the very pleased and very displeased customers. The generally satisfied and the indifferent customers won't bother to respond. There is also a potential misuse of these cards of which service executives must be aware. Unit managers have also been known to send in their own fictitious cards. Another drawback to the comment cards is that they usually are quite limited in the type of information they solicit, and provide little more than a hint of where there may be a problem. But longer questionnaires tend to discourage users.

One company got around customers' reluctance to respond to comment cards by giving away a new color television set each month. To enter the contest, all customers had to do was to fill out and send in the comment cards. Since guests included their name and address to receive the television, the hotel management had an opportunity to establish communication with them to discuss comments and any corrective actions taken to noted shortcomings.

In order to get around these problems, some companies use customer surveys. These permit more information to be solicited and are designed to provide representative population samples. The major drawback is cost. There are questionnaire design and distribution costs and tabulation expenses, and usually some incentive is given to encourage customers to respond.

Usually inspectors spend several days auditing the hotel. They generally work from a comprehensive checklist, which assigns points to each characteristic. These visits are unannounced, and rooms are selected at random. The physical premises are gone over with a fine-tooth comb. Operating records are checked for accuracy and completeness, on-going activities are observed, and key employees are interviewed. The greatest concentration given in the audit is to the condition of the hotel rooms and bathrooms. The accounting inspector reviews the internal controls, security, and cash-handling practices.

After the visits, a report is prepared, including an overall score. The report is given to the operation's manager and the regional or district directors who follow up on the items found wanting. The district directors periodically perform their own surveys, using the same checklists as the regular inspectors.

Another approach is to employ an outside inspection service. A firm is hired to send in people to test the operation's performance. Frequently, these inspectors only audit certain aspects, particularly security and cash-handling practice. They may, however, be asked to report on the entire operation and on other transactions in progress during their visit. The personnel sent to shop an operation must be trained to observe and evaluate the service according to company standards, but if these same individuals are sent too often, they may become known to the local staff, which greatly reduces the audits' effectiveness.

Quality Program

The statistical measures used to evaluate performance in hotels are quite simple. Most of them deal with costs as a percentage of related revenue. Others may be related to sales units, such as linen cost per occupied room. While productivity statistics may be compared to set standards, most of the data are compared to the results of prior periods or to budgeted figures. One motel chain evaluates the profit for the period against payroll guidelines which are based on a per occupied room formula.

One thing that is not present in the hospitality system is the notion of tolerances. It is expected that all procedures will be followed as they are written. There is no acceptable range. Acceptable means 100 percent performance. The hotel guest is buying one hotel visit, and management only gets one chance to score. On the other hand, there are almost an infinite number of factors to consider, and it is recognized that it is not always possible to adhere 100 percent to the standard.

IMPROVEMENT

The techniques of quality control in the hotel industry appear quite crude and unscientific. But there are many operations that have been doing well in this mode. The present status of the controls lie in the feasibility studies, that is, location evaluation where there is a well-developed methodology. In the area of concept and image development, hotels have made little progress. Most of the skills are intuitive. In the area of systems and procedures there has been a lot of progress in computerizing hotel rooms management and reservations functions, as well as back office accounting.

In the area of conformance measurement, companies produce a lot of statistics relating to efficiency of operations. Conformance to technical standards must be inferred based on evidence such as property inspection. The ultimate evaluation of any service transaction can only be made by customers, because they are the only ones who have both a firsthand knowledge of performance and a standard for evaluating it. The real frontier is determining customers' reactions to service.

Customers place a high value on the quality of interpersonal contacts. This is a quality characteristic which the hotel industry has barely begun to recognize. The service quality control systems are still product oriented, not service or customer oriented. However, techniques for meeting people and evaluating the quality of that contact do exist and can be taught. The industry must establish standards, and develop and train personnel in delivery methods for every aspect of service which consumers seek, in order to have any meaningful quality controls.

MOTIVATION[2]

In one company, quarterly bonuses are provided to the hotel's managers and supervisors by way of a three-step operation. The first item established is a unit's gross operating profit, based on a flexible budget with no specific goals, to be reached based on previous years' performance, or a similar benchmark. Second, the bonus is computed so that the motel managers cannot be responsible for local economy changes or other factors beyond their control. By staying within 3 percent of defined guidelines, managers are still eligible for 100 percent of their bonus. Motels missing their payroll guidelines by more than 7 percent are not eligible for a bonus. Third, a motel's quality inspection score determines the final bonus. The motel with the top quality score becomes every other motel's standard. Those that come within three percentage points earn 100 percent of the bonus. The company subtracts 10 percent of the bonus for each percentage point that a motel misses from the top quality goal.

TRAINING

Inspectors are trained on how to properly inspect a hotel. In one chain, a training program is given to all individual motel managers. This program includes the following:

1. The managers' training facility is included inside one of the motel facilities. This allows a real-life example of everything discussed during training.

2. Folders are given to new managers which provide a description of the corporation and an analysis of how a good manager operates. The program includes the following elements:
   a. Awareness of all company policies, procedures, and quality standards.
   b. Alertness to what is happening on the property. This includes walking around the premises, paying attention to details, noting deficiencies, and observing staff performance.
   c. Emphasis to take personal action, such as handling customer complaints, calling vendors to repair equipment, and working with the staff members to improve their performance.

3. Six quizzes, one after each subject is completed, and three tests, including a final comprehensive one.

4. Lectures which include an introduction to the motel's microcomputer system. Other items include landscaping, preventive maintenance, housekeeping, insurance and safety, purchasing and ac-

counts payable, front desk operation, sales and marketing, and payroll.

5. Classroom lectures are complemented by training videos produced by the American Hotels and Motel Associates and other sources. The videos emphasize such key controls as privacy, security, handling guest's complaints, and sexual harassment.

6. Interpersonnel skills training including a 16-module role playing simulation. This is designed to teach managers how to communicate with employees, including: addressing their self-esteem, increasing their understanding of given situations, stressing the need for two-way communication, getting them involved in problem solving, and establishing follow-up procedures to ensure that action is taken. The interpersonnel skills taught build on the idea that the manager should be a resource, not an authority figure.

REFERENCES

1. King, Carol A. *Quality Control in Hospitality Service Operations* (AQC). Milwaukee, WI: ASQC, 1983, p. 412.

2. Stratton, Brad. *Low Cost of Quality Lodging* (QP). Milwaukee, WI: ASQC, June 1988, p. 49.

BIBLIOGRAPHY

Those documents noted with the asterisk(*), can be obtained from the American Society for Quality Control, Customer Service Department, P. O. Box 3066, Milwaukee, Wisconsin 53201-3066, Tel. 800-248-1946 or Fax 414-272-1734. To request a complimentary catalog of publications call 800-248-1946.

Administrative and Support Organizations

Young, Barbara A. "Managing Quality in Staff Areas, Part 2." *QP* (December 1989): 29.

Analysis, Data

*Volume 1: *How to Analyze Data with Simple Plots:* 1979: Item T3501.

*Cox, Neil D. Volume 11: *How to Perform Statistical Tolerance Analysis.* Item T3511, 1986.

Analysis, Laboratory

*Bennett, C. A., & Friedman, N. C. *Statistical Analysis in Chemical and Chemical Industry.* New York: John Wiley & Sons, 1958.

Audits

ANSI/ASQC Q1–1986: Generic Guidelines for Auditing of Quality Systems. Item T26.

*ASQC Quality Audit Technical Committee. *How to Plan an Audit.* Item T801, 1987.

Ishikawa, Kaoru. "The Quality Control Audit." *QP* (January 1987): 39.

*Mills, Charles A. *The Quality Audit—A Management Evaluation Tool.* Order H0568, 1989.

Shimoyamada, Kaoru. "The President's Audit: QC Audits at Komatsu." *QP* (January 1987): 44–49.

Banking Services

Langevin, Roger G. "Quality Control in Bank Operations." *AQC* (1983): 131.

Vandenburgh, Roy N. "Quality Control in Check Processing." *AQC* (1983): 126.

Blueprint Reading

Carver & Helsel. *Blueprint Reading*. New York: McGraw Hill.

Coover & Helsel. *Programmed Blueprint Reading* (2d ed.). New York: McGraw Hill.

Day, Donald E. *Geometric Dimensioning and Tolerancing*. Canandaigua, NY: Daytec, 1987.

*Foster, Lowell W. *Modern Geometric Dimensioning and Tolerancing* (2d ed.). Item P319, 1982.

Ihne & Streeter. *Machine Trades Blue Print Reading*. New York: Amer. Tech. Society.

Westinghouse Learning Press. *Basic Blueprint Reading*. Palo Alto, CA: College Publications.

Communication

Smith, Alfred G. *Communication and Culture*. New York: Holt, Rinehart, & Winston, 1966.

Computers

Holmes, H. "Computer Assisted Inspection." *The Quality Engineer* 38:9, September 1974, pp. 211–213.

Keene, John. *Computers and Quality* (ASQC Congress Transactions). Milwaukee, WI: ASQC, 1981, pp. 625–631.

Construction Quality

*ASQC Energy Division. *Matrix of Nuclear Quality Assurance Program Requirements* (3d ed.). Item T71, 1982.

Kirschenmann, Harley J. *Managerial Attitude toward Quality Assurance*. AQC, 1983, p. 20.

*Mickelson, Elliot S. *Construction Quality Program Handbook*. Item H0529, 1986.

Costs, Quality

*ASQC Quality Costs Committee, Jack Campanella (Ed.) *Principles of Quality Costs* (2d ed.). Item H0593, 1990.

*ASQC Quality Costs Committee. *Quality Costs: Ideas and Applications* (Vol. 2). Item H0569, 1989.

*Harrington, H. James. *Poor-Quality Cost*. Item H0534, 1987.

Customer Satisfaction

Goodman, John. "The Nature of Customer Satisfaction." *QP*, February 1989: p. 37.

Malcolm Baldrige National Quality Award Guidelines (Administered by Malcolm Baldrige National Quality Award Consortium). ASQC, 1992.

Reimann, Curt W. "The Baldrige Award: Leading the Way in Quality Initiatives." *QP*, July 1989, p. 35.

Walden, James C. "Integrating Customer Satisfaction into Daily Work." *The Juran Reporter.* No. 8 1987, pp. 30–34.

Government Regulations and Specifications

All documents below can be obtained from the Superintendent of Documents, Government Printing Office, Washington, DC 20402.

Calibration System Requirements-MIL-STD-45662

Evaluation of Contractor's Quality System-H-50

Evaluation of Contractor's Inspection System-H-51

Evaluation of Contractor's Calibration System-H-52A

Guide For Sampling Inspection-H-53

Inspection System Requirements-MIL-I-45208A

Multiple Level Continuous Sampling Plans-DOD Handbook H-106

Quality Program Requirements-MIL-Q-9858A

Sampling Procedures and Tables for Inspection by Attributes-MIL-STD-105D

Sampling Procedures and Tables for Inspection by Variables-DOD Standard 414

Sampling Procedures and Tables for Determining Validity of Supplier's Attributes of Inspection-MIL-STD-109

Single Level Continuous Sampling Plans-DOD Handbook H-107

Hospitality Services

Fitzsimmons, James A., & Sullivan, Robert S. *Service Operations Management.* New York: McGraw Hill, 1982.

Hostage, G. M. "Quality Control in a Service Business." *Harvard Business Review* July-August 1975.

King, Carol A. "Quality Controls in Hospitality Service Operations." *35th AQC* 1983, pp. 412–417.

Stratton, Brad. "The Low Cost of Quality Lodging." *QP*, June 1988, p. 49.

Thorner, Marvin, & Manning, Peter B. *Quality Control in Food Service.* Westport, CT: Avi Publishing, 1976.

Hospital Services

Graves, Forest W. "Measuring the Quality of Health Care for Decision Support." *QP*, May 1987, p. 37.

Gruska, Denise A., & Gruska, Gregory F. "A Total Quality System for Medical Facilities." *AQC*, 1983, p. 560.

JCAH: Accreditation Manual for Hospitals (1980 edition). Chicago: JCAH, 1979.

Laffel, Glenn. "Implementing Quality Management in Health Care: The Challenges Ahead." *QP*, November 1990, p. 29.

Millenson, Michael L. "A Prescription for Care." *QP*, May 1987, p. 16.

Shaw, Roland A. "A Quality Cost Model for Hospitals." *QP*, May 1987, p. 41.

Spivock, Robert E. "The FDA Prescribes QA for Medical Device Manufacturers and Their Suppliers." *QP*, December 1985, p. 72.

Human Relations

McGregor, D. *Human Side of Enterprise*. New York: McGraw Hill, 1960.

Harris, D. H., & Chanby, F. B. *Human Factors in Quality Assurance*. New York: John Wiley & Sons, 1969

Davis, K. *Human Relations in Business*. New York: McGraw Hill, 1983.

*Barry, Thomas J. *Quality Circles: Proceed with Caution*. Item T191, 1988.

*ASQC Human Resources Division. *Human Resources Management*. Item H0540, 1987.

Inspection Improvement

Chemical Division Supplement: Interlaboratory Testing Techniques. Milwaukee, WI: ASQC, 1978.

*Camp, Robert C. *Benchmarking*. Item H0575, 1989.

Carter, C. L., & Carter, G. M. "A Motivation Program for Inspectors." *AQC*, 1983, pp. 525–528.

Czaja, S. J., & Drury, C. G. "Training Program for Inspectors." *Human Factors* 23, 4, July-August 1981, pp. 473–484.

Eisenhart, C. "Expression of the Uncertainties of the Final Result." *Science*, June 14, 1968, pp. 1201–1204.

*Gitlow, Howard, et al. *Tools and Methods for the Improvement of Quality*. Item H0582, 1989.

Goldbeck, J. M. "Measuring Inspector's Productivity." *35th AQC*, 1981, pp. 343–347.

Juran, J. M. "Inspector's Error in Quality Control." *Mechanical Engineering* 59, 10 October 1935, pp. 643–644.

Konz, S., Peterson, G., & Joshi, A. "Reducing Inspection Errors." *QP* 14, 7, July 1981, pp. 24–26.

McMaster, R. C. *Nondestructive Testing Handbook*. New York: Ronald Press, 1959.

Measurements and Calibrations (Technical Note 252). Washington, DC: U.S. Government Printing Office, p. 4.

Schumaker, R. B. F. "Systematic Measurement Errors." *Journal of Quality Technology* 13, 1, January 1981, pp. 10–24.

Thomas, J. H. "Productivity in the Quality Control Department." *ASQC Inspection Division Newsletter,* 7, 3, 1977, pp. 2–3.

Trobery, D. "Metrology = Calibration." *AQC,* 1979, pp. 513–520.

Turner, R. E. "Today and Tomorrow for NDT." *Quality Management and Engineering* (December 1974), pp. 36–41.

Weaver, L. A. "Inspection Accuracy Sampling Plan." *AQC,* 1975, pp. 34–39.

Woods, D. G., & Zeiss, C. "Coordinate Measuring and Finite Metrology." *QP,* March 1978, pp. 20–21.

Laboratory

Interlaboratory Test Techniques. Order RO 401, 1978.

Laboratory, Engineering Instrument

Stout. *Basic Electrical Measurement*. Englewood Cliffs, NJ: Prentice Hall, 1952.

Turner, R. D. *Basic Electronic Test Procedures*. New York: Rinehart & Winston, 1962.

Management, Production/Inspection

Alford, L. P., & Bangs, J. R. *Production Handbook*. New York: Ronald Press, 1946.

March, J. G., & Simon, H. A. *Organization*. New York: John Wiley & Sons, 1945.

Ott, Ellis. *Process Quality Control*. New York: McGraw Hill, 1975.

Peters, Tom, & Austin, Nancy. *A Passion for Excellence: The Leadership Difference*. New York: Warner Books, 1985.

White, John A. (Ed.) *Production Handbook* (4th ed.). New York: Ronald Press, 1987.

Management, Inspection/Quality

Guide to Inspection Planning: ANSI/ASQC E2–1984. Milwaukee, WI: ASQC, Item T23.

Thompson, J. *Inspection Organization and Methods.* New York: McGraw Hill, 1950.

Management, Top Quality

Crosby, Philip B. *The Eternally Successful Organization.* New York: McGraw Hill, 1988.

*Deming, W. Edwards. *Out of the Crisis.* Item P369, 1986.

*Juran, J. M. *Juran and Leadership for Quality.* Item H0581, 1989.

Mizuno, Shigeru. *Management for Quality Improvement.* Productivity Press, 1988.

Management, Total Quality

*Caplan, Frank. *The Quality System: A Sourcebook for Managers and Engineers* (2d ed.). Item H0523, 1990.

Carter, C. L. *The Control and Assurance of Quality, Reliability, and Safety.* 1986.

*Crosby, Philip B. *Running Things: The Art of Making Things Happen.* Item H0524, 1986.

*Crosby, Philip B. *Quality Without Tears—The Art of Hassle Free Management.* Item H0512, 1984.

*Feigenbaum, A. V. *Total Quality Control* (3d ed., revised 1990). Item P441.

*Ishikawa, Kaoru. *What Is Total Quality Control? The Japanese Way.* Item H0504, 1985.

*Juran, J. M. *Juran on Planning for Quality.* Item P387, 1988.

*Juran, J. M., & Gryna, Frank, M., Jr. *Quality Planning and Analysis* (2d ed.). Item P109, 1980.

*Juran, J. M. *Managerial Breakthrough.* Item P297, 1964.

*Walton, M. *The Deming Management Method.* Item H0541, 1986.

Material and Process in Industry

Boston, D. M. *Metal Processing.* New York: John Wiley & Sons, 1951.

Methods, Inspection

Carter, C. L. *Quality Assurance, Quality Control, and Inspection Handbook* (4th ed.). 1984.

*National Tooling and Machining Association. *Measuring and Gaging in the Machine Shop.* Item P320, 1981.

Metrology, Tools of

Busch, T. *Fundamentals of Dimensional Metrology*. Albany, NY: Delmar.

Farago F. T. *Handbook of Dimensional Measurement* (2d ed.). New York: Industrial Press, 1982.

Nonmanufacturing Industries

Nader, Gary J. "Applying Quality Methods: Nonmanufacturing Areas." *AQC* 1989, pp. 14–21.

Procedures and Forms

*Carlsen, Robert D. et al. *Manual of Quality Assurance Procedures and Forms* (rev. ed.). Item H0745, 1992.

Procurement

Procurement Quality Control, Fourth Edition (ASQC Customer Supplier Technical Committee), Item H0501.

Monden, Yasuhiro. *Applying Just in Time: The American/Japanese Experience*. 1986.

Product Liability Prevention

Suntag, C. "Product Liability Prevention Program." *AQC* 1983, p. 396.

Weinstein, A. S. et al. *Products Liability and the Reasonably Safe Product*. New York: John Wiley & Sons, 1978.

Quality Control, Introduction to

ANSI/ASQC Std.C-1: Specification for General Requirements for a Quality Program.

Banks, Jerry. *Principles of Quality Control*. 1989.

*Grifith, Gary K. *Quality Technicians Handbook* (2d ed.). Item H0747, 1992.

Quality Control Training Manual: State University of Iowa Section. Milwaukee, WI: ASQC.

Reference Handbooks

*Besterfield, Dale H. *Quality Control* (3d ed.). Item P278, 1990.

*Ishikawa, Kaoru. *Guide to Quality Control*. Item P104, 1976.

*Juran, J. M. *Juran's Quality Control Handbook* (4th ed.). Item H0511, 1988.

*Juran, J. M., & Gryna, Frank M., Jr. *Quality Planning and Analysis* (2d ed.). Item P109, 1980.

Peach, Dr. Paul. *Quality Control for Management*. Englewood Cliffs, NJ: Prentice Hall, 1964.

Stiles, Edward M. *Handbook for Total Quality Assurance: Volume 26*. Waterford, CT: National Sales Dev. Institute.

Reliability Technology

Bazowsky, Igor. *Reliability: Principles and Practices*. Englewood Cliffs, NJ: Prentice Hall.

*Ireson, W. Grant, & Coombs, Clyde F. *Handbook of Reliability Engineering and Management*. Item P398, 1988.

*O'Conner, Patrick D. T. *Practical Reliability Engineering* (3d ed.). Item P99, 1991.

Sampling

Cochran, William G. *Sampling Techniques* (3d ed.). New York: John Wiley and Sons, 1977.

Dodge, Harold F., & Romig, Harry G. *Sampling Inspection and Tables: Single and Double* (2d ed.). New York: John Wiley and Sons, 1959.

*Stephens, Kenneth S. *How to Perform Continuous Sampling (CSP), Vol. 2*. Order R 3502. Milwaukee, WI: ASQC, 1979.

*Schilling, Edward G. *Acceptance Sampling in Quality Control*. Item H0545, 1982.

Service Quality

Butterfield, Ronald W. "A Quality Strategy for Service Organizations." *QP*, December 1987, p. 40.

*Latzko, William J. *Quality and Productivity for Bankers and Financial Managers*. Item H0528, 1986.

Lawton, Robin L. "Creating a Customer-Centered Culture for Service Quality." *QP*, May 1989, p. 34.

*Rosander, A. C. *Applications of Quality Control in the Service Industries*. Item H0505, 1985.

*Rosander, A. C. *The Quest for Quality in Service*. Item H0555, 1989.

Software, Computer

Anderson, R. T., & Marton, T. L. *Guidebook for Management of Software*. Lockport, IL: Reliability Technology Associates, 1982.

Dunn, Robert, & Ullman, Richard. *Quality Assurance for Computer Software*. New York: McGraw Hill, 1982.

Glaushenner, A. *How-To-Buy Software*. New York: St. Martins Press, 1984.

Leveson, Nancy G. "Software Safety in Computer Systems." *Computer IEEE* 17, 2 February 1980, p. 53.

"1991 QA/QC Software Directory." *QP*, March 1991, p. 27.

Statistical Process Control

*Burr, John T. *SPC Tools for Operators*. Item H0561, 1989.

*Griffith, Gary K. *Statistical Process Control Methods for Long and Short Runs*. Item H0567, 1989.

*Berger, R. W., & Hart, T. H. *Statistical Process Control*. Item T150.

*Pyzdek, Thomas. *An SPC Primer*. Item H0657.

Statistics, Elementary

*ASQC Statistics Division. *Glossary and Tables for Statistical Quality Control* (2d ed.). Item H0518, 1983.

Bowker A., & Goode. *Sample Inspection by Variables*. New York: McGraw Hill, 1952.

*Braverman, Jerome D. *Fundamentals of Statistical Quality Control*. Item P275, 1981.

*Burr, Irving W. *Elementary Statistical Quality Control*. Item H0522, 1979.

Dixon, W. L., & Massey, F. J. *Introduction to Statistical Analysis* (4th ed.). New York: McGraw Hill, 1983.

*Duncan, Acheson J. *Quality Control and Industrial Statistics* (5th ed.). Order P 48, 1986.

*Grant, Eugene L., & Leavenworth, Richard S. *Statistical Quality Control* (6th ed.). Item P80.

Hicks, C. R. *Design of Experiments*. New York: Holt, Rinehart & Winston, 1982.

Ott, Ellis R. *Process Quality Control: Trouble Shooting and Interpretation of Data*. New York: McGraw Hill, 1975.

*Montgomery, Douglas C. *Introduction to Statistical Quality Control* (2d ed.). Item H0625, 1991.

*Shewhart, Walter A. *Economic Control of Quality of Manufactured Product*. Item H0509, 1980.

Statistics, Advanced

*Box, G. E., Hunter, W. G., & Hunter, S. J. *Statistics For Engineers*. Item P19, 1978.

Draper, Norman R., & Smith, Harry. *Applied Regression Analysis* (2d ed.). New York: John Wiley and Sons, 1981.

Hicks, Charles R. *Fundamental Concepts in the Design of Experiment*. New York: Rinehart and Wilson, 1982.

Wadsworth, H. M., et al. *Modern Methods for Quality Control and Improvement*. New York: John Wiley and Sons, 1986.

Standards, Domestic

ANSI/ASQC A2–1987: Terms, Symbols, and Definitions for Acceptance Sampling. Item T4.

ANSI/ASQC A3–1987: Quality Systems Terminology. Order T6.

ANSI/ASQC B1–1985: Guide for Quality Control Charts. Order T11.

ANSI/ASQC C1–1985: Specifications of General Requirements for a Quality Program. Item T16.

ANSI/ASQC E2–1984: Guide to Inspection Planning. Item T23.

ANSI/ASQC M1–1987: American National Standard for Calibration Systems. Item T35.

ANSI/ASQC Q 90–1987 Set: Quality Management and Quality Assurance Standards. Item T30.

ANSI/ASQC Q1–1986: Generic Guidelines for Auditing of Quality Systems. Item T26.

ANSI/ASQC Q3–1988: Sampling Procedures and Tables for Inspection of Isolated Lots by Attributes. Item T36.

ANSI/ASQC S1–1987: An Attribute Skip-Lot Sampling Program. Item T28.

ANSI/ASQC Z1.4–1981: Sampling Procedures and Tables for Inspection by Attributes. Item T18.

ANSI/ASQC Z1.9–1980: Sampling Procedures and Tables for Inspection by Variables for Percent Nonconforming. Item T24.

Martin Marietta Corp. *Quality Engineering Workmanship Standards Manual.* 1981.

Standards, International

Boehling, Walter H. "Europe 1992: Its Effect on International Standards." *QP*, June 1990, p. 29.

Lofgren, George. "Quality System Registration." *QP*, May 1991, p. 35.

Marquardt, Donald, et al. "Vision 2000: The Strategy for the ISO 9000 Series Standards in the 90's." *QP*, May 1991, p. 25.

Van Nuland, Yves. "The New Common Language for 12 Countries." *QP*, June 1990, p. 40.

Supervision, Industrial/Inspection

Given, Wm. B., Jr. *How to Manage People*. Englewood Cliffs, NJ: Prentice Hall, 1964.

Testing, Nondestructive

Hayward, G. P. *Introduction to NDT*. 1978.

Training

Hooper, Jeffrey H. "Making Statistical Training Effective" *QP*, February 1989, p. 24.

Writing, Technical

Dyer, F. C. *Executive's Guide to Effective Speaking and Writing*. Englewood Cliffs, NJ: Prentice Hall, 1962.

INDEX